WRITING *Sixth Edition*
ANALYTICALLY

David Rosenwasser
Muhlenberg College

Jill Stephen
Muhlenberg College

WADSWORTH
CENGAGE Learning™

Australia • Brazil • Japan • Korea • Mexico • Singapore • Spain • United Kingdom • United States

WADSWORTH
CENGAGE Learning

Writing Analytically, Sixth Edition
David Rosenwasser, Jill Stephen

Senior Publisher: Lyn Uhl

Executive Editor: Monica Eckman

Acquisitions Editor: Margaret
Leslie

Senior Development Editor:
Leslie Taggart

Development Editor: Mary Beth
Walden

Assistant Editor: Amy Haines

Editorial Assistant: Danielle F.
Warchol

Media Editor: Janine Tangney

Executive Marketing Manager:
Stacey Purviance

Marketing Director: Jason Sakos

Marketing Manager: Melissa Holt

Marketing Coordinator:
Brittany Blais

Marketing Communications
Manager: Courtney Morris

Senior Content Project
Manager:
Michael Lepera

Art Director: Jill Ort

Print Buyer: Susan Spencer

Senior Rights Acquisition
Specialist, Image: Jennifer
Meyer Dare

Rights Acquisition Specialist, Text:
Shalice Shah-Caldwell

Production Service:
Integra-Chicago

Text Designer: Jay Purcell, Pier
Design Co.

Cover Designer: Hanh Luu

Cover Image: photoresearchers.com

Compositor: Integra-India

For product information and
technology assistance, contact us at **Cengage Learning
Customer & Sales Support, 1-800-354-9706**

For permission to use material from this text or product,
submit all requests online at **www.cengage.com/permissions**.
Further permissions questions can be emailed to
permissionrequest@cengage.com.

Library of Congress Control Number: 2011921845

ISBN-13: 978-0-495-91008-4

ISBN-10: 0-495-91008-2

Wadsworth
20 Channel Center Street
Boston, MA 02210
USA

Cengage Learning is a leading provider of customized learning solutions with office locations around the globe, including Singapore, the United Kingdom, Australia, Mexico, Brazil, and Japan. Locate your local office at: **international.cengage.com/region**

Cengage Learning products are represented in Canada by Nelson Education, Ltd.

For your course and learning solutions, visit
www.cengage.com.

Purchase any of our products at your local college store or at our preferred online store **www.cengagebrain.com**.

Printed in the United States of America
3 4 5 6 7 15 14 13 12

Brief Contents

UNIT I THE ANALYTICAL FRAME OF MIND: INTRODUCTION TO ANALYTICAL METHODS 1

CHAPTER 1   Introduction: Fourteen Short Takes on Writing and the Writing Process 5

CHAPTER 2   Toolkit of Analytical Methods I: Seeing Better, Seeing More 23

CHAPTER 3   Analysis: What It Is and What It Does 53

CHAPTER 4   Toolkit of Analytical Methods II: Going Deeper 85

CHAPTER 5   Writing about Reading: More Moves to Make with Written Texts 105

CHAPTER 6   Making Interpretations Plausible 133

CHAPTER 7   Making Common Topics More Analytical 151

UNIT II WRITING ANALYTICAL PAPERS: HOW TO USE EVIDENCE, EVOLVE CLAIMS, AND CONVERSE WITH SOURCES 163

CHAPTER 8   Reasoning From Evidence To Claims 165

CHAPTER 9   Analyzing Arguments 191

CHAPTER 10   Using Evidence to Build a Paper: 10 on 1 207

CHAPTER 11   Making A Thesis Evolve 227

CHAPTER 12   Recognizing and Fixing Weak Thesis Statements 255

CHAPTER 13   Using Sources Analytically: The Conversation Model   267

CHAPTER 14   Finding, Citing, and Integrating Sources   283

UNIT III   MATTERS OF FORM: THE SHAPES THAT THOUGHT TAKES   315

CHAPTER 15   Forms and Formats Across the Curriculum   317

CHAPTER 16   Introductions and Conclusions Across the Curriculum   349

CHAPTER 17   Revising for Style: Word Choice   375

CHAPTER 18   Revising for Style: The Rhetoric of the Sentence   391

CHAPTER 19   Revising for Correctness: Grammar and Punctuation   417

CHAPTER 19 Appendix   446

Index   I-1

Contents

Preface xxiii

UNIT I THE ANALYTICAL FRAME OF MIND: INTRODUCTION TO ANALYTICAL METHODS 1

Finding Your Way in This Book: A Note to Readers 3

CHAPTER 1 Introduction: Fourteen Short Takes on Writing and the Writing Process 5

Order of the Short Takes 5

Thinking About Writing as a Tool of Thought 6

Analysis: A Quick Definition 6

Analysis Defined 6

What Do Faculty Want from Student Writing? 7

Breaking Out of 5-Paragraph Form 7

On Writing Traditional Essays in the Digital Age 8

What's Different About Writing Arguments in College? 9

Rhetoric: What It Is and Why You Need It 10

Two Key Terms 11

Writing About Reading: Beyond "Banking" 12

The Banking Model of Education—and Beyond 12

Freewriting: How and Why to Do It 13

Some Useful Techniques for Freewriting 14

Process and Product: Some Ways of Thinking About the Writing Process 14

Tips for Managing the Writing Process 15

How to Think About Grammar and Style (Beyond Error-Catching) 16

A Quick Word on Style Guides 16

How to Think About Writing in the Disciplines 18

Academic vs. Nonacademic Writing: How Different Are They? 19

Assignments 20

CHAPTER 2   Toolkit of Analytical Methods I: Seeing Better, Seeing More   23

Focus on the Details   23

A. The Heuristics   23

1. Notice and Focus + Ranking   24

Troubleshooting Notice and Focus   25

A Quick Note on 10 on 1   25

Try This 2.1: Doing Notice and Focus with a Room   26

Try This 2.2: Notice and Focus Fieldwork   26

2. The Method: Work with Patterns of Repetition and Contrast   26

Two Examples of The Method Generating Ideas   28

Doing The Method on a Poem   29

Doing the Method on a Poem: Our Analysis   30

Why Do The Method?   31

Try This 2.3: Experiment in a Group Setting with The Method—
Use a Visual Image by Adrian Tomine   32

Try This 2.4: Apply The Method to Arts & Letters Daily   32

3. Asking "So What?"   33

Asking So What?: An Example   34

Try This 2.5: Track the "So What?" Question   35

4. Paraphrase × (times) 3   36

How Paraphrase × 3 Unlocks Implications: An Example   37

Try This 2.6: Experiment with Paraphrase × 3   38

Try This 2.7: Paraphrase and Implication   39

5. Identifying the "Go To" Sentence   39

Some Examples of "Go To" Sentences   40

Try This 2.8: Identify the Features of "Go To" Sentences   41

Try This 2.9: Find One of Your Own "Go To" Sentences   42

B. Counterproductive Habits of Mind   42

Reacting Is Not Thinking   43

1. Premature Leaps   43

Make It Strange   43

Get Comfortable with Uncertainty   44

2. The Judgment Reflex   44

Three Cures for the Judgment Reflex   45

Try This 2.10: Distinguishing Evaluative from Nonevaluative Words   45

Try This 2.11: Experiment with Adjectives and Adverbs   45

3. Generalizing   46

Take My Word for It?   46

Antidotes to Habitual Generalizing   46

Try This 2.12: Locating Words on the Abstraction Ladder   47

Try This 2.13: Distinguishing Abstract from Concrete Words   47

4. Naturalizing Our Assumptions (Overpersonalizing)   47

Try This 2.14: Fieldwork: Looking for Naturalized Assumptions   47

"I Didn't Know You Wanted My Opinion"   48

Opinions: Are They Counterproductive Habits of Mind?   49

Habits of Mind in Psychology: A Psychologist Speaks   49

Voices From Across the Curriculum   49

Opinions—A Democratic Disease? A Political Science Professor Speaks   49

Voices From Across the Curriculum   50

Assignments   50

CHAPTER 3   Analysis: What It Is and What It Does   53

A. Five Analytical Moves   53

What Faculty Seek in Student Writing   54

Metacognition   54

Move 1: Suspend Judgment   54

Move 2: Define Significant Parts and How They're Related   55

Try This 3.1: Description as a Form of Analysis   56

Description as a Form of Analysis: Some Academic Examples   56

Move 3: Look for Patterns of Repetition and Contrast and for Anomalies (aka The Method)   59

Looking for Patterns: An Example   60

Move 4: Make the Implicit Explicit   62

Try This 3.2: Making Inferences   63

Implications versus Hidden Meanings   63

Try This 3.3: Inferring Implications from Observations   64

Move 5: Keep Reformulating Questions and Explanations   65

Science as a Process of Argument: A Biologist Speaks   66

Voices From Across the Curriculum   66

"2:30": An Example of the Five Analytical Moves in Action   67

Try This 3.4: Apply the Five Analytical Moves to a Speech   70

What It Means to Have an Idea   70

B. Distinguishing Analysis from Argument, Summary, and Expressive Writing   72

Analysis and Argument   73

Analysis versus Debate-Style Argument   73

Ethos and Analysis   74

Analysis versus Summary: The Example of *Whistler's Mother*   75

Summary Is a Focused Description   76

Analysis Makes an Interpretive Leap   76

Analysis and Personal Associations   78

Rhetorical Analysis of an Advertisement: An Example   79

References   82

Guidelines   82

Assignments   83

CHAPTER 4   Toolkit of Analytical Methods II: Going Deeper   85

1. Passage-Based Focused Freewriting   86

Passage-based Focused Freewriting: An Example   88

Passage-based Focused Freewriting: Another Example   89

Try This 4.1: Do a Passage-based Focused Freewrite   90

2. Uncovering Assumptions   91

Uncovering Assumptions: An Example   92

Uncovering Assumptions: Another Quick Example   92

Try This 4.2: Uncover Assumptions in Reviews   93

Uncovering Assumptions: An Economist Speaks   93

Voices From Across the Curriculum   94

Try This 4.3: Uncovering Assumptions: Fieldwork   94

3. Reformulating Binaries   94

Reformulating Binaries: An Example   96

Collapsing the Binary: A Brief Example   96

Reformulating Binaries: Two More Examples   97

Try This 4.4: Reformulating Binaries in a Familiar Expression   98

Try This 4.5: Reformulating Binaries: More Practice   98

Try This 4.6: Reformulating Binaries: Fieldwork   99

4. Difference within Similarity   99

Looking for Difference Within Similarity: An Example   100

Try This 4.7: Looking for Significant Difference or Unexpected Similarity   101

5. Seems to Be About X But Could Also Be (Is "Really") About Y   101

Seems to Be About X . . .: An Example   102

Try This 4.8: Apply the Formula "Seems to Be About X, But Could Also Be (Is "Really") About Y"   103

Assignments   104

CHAPTER 5   Writing About Reading: More Moves to Make with Written Texts   105

The Three Lives of a Reading   105

How to Read: Words Matter   106

Become Conversant Instead of Reading for the Gist   107

Owning the Reading   107

Focus on Individual Sentences   108

Pointing   109

Passage-Based Focused Freewriting (PBFF)   109

Paraphrasing   110

Keep a Commonplace Book   110

Try This 5.1: Writing & Reading with Others: A Sequence of Activities   111

Situate the Reading Rhetorically: Find the Pitch, the Complaint, and the Moment   111

The Pitch, the Complaint, and the Moment: Two Brief Examples   112

Audience Analysis: A Brief Example   113

Try This 5.2: Locating the Pitch and the Complaint   113

Seek to Understand the Reading Fairly on Its Own Terms   114

Entering the Thinking in a Reading: Uncovering Assumptions and Reformulating Binaries (A Reprise)   114

Tracking the Thinking Through Complication and Qualification: An Example   115

The Problem of Critique   116

What Do We Mean by Critical Reading? A Music Professor Speaks   117

Voices From Across the Curriculum   117

Reading Against the Grain   117

Use a Reading as a Model   118

Apply a Reading as a Lens   118
   Using a Reading as a Lens: "Self-Deprecation on Late Night Television"   119

Guidelines   129

Assignments   129

CHAPTER 6   Making Interpretations Plausible   133

Moving from Description to Interpretation   133

Making Interpretations Plausible Across the Curriculum   134

Plausible versus Implausible Interpretations: The Social Context   135

Interpretive Contexts and Multiple Meanings   136
   Specifying an Interpretive Context: A Brief Example   136
   The Role of Context in Interpreting Numerical Data   137

Intention as an Interpretive Context   138

What Is and Isn't "Meant" to Be Analyzed   140
   Meaning and Social Contexts   140

The Fortune Cookie School of Interpretation   141

The Anything Goes School of Interpretation   141

Making an Interpretation: The Example of a *New Yorker* Cover   142
   Using the Method to Identify Patterns of Repetition and Contrast   144
   Pushing Observations to Conclusions: Selecting an Interpretive Context   145
   Making the Interpretation Plausible   146
   Arriving At an Interpretive Conclusion: Making Choices   146

Guidelines   147

Assignments   148

CHAPTER 7   Making Common Topics More Analytical   151

Summary   152
   Strategies for Making Summaries More Analytical   152

Personal Response: The Reaction Paper   153
   Strategies for Making Personal Responses More Analytical   154

Agree/Disagree   156

Comparison/Contrast   156

Strategies for Making Comparison/Contrast More Analytical   156

Definition   158

Strategies for Making Definition More Analytical   158

Guidelines   159

Assignments   160

UNIT II   WRITING ANALYTICAL PAPERS: HOW TO USE EVIDENCE, EVOLVE CLAIMS, AND CONVERSE WITH SOURCES   163

CHAPTER 8   Reasoning from Evidence to Claims   165

A. Linking Evidence and Claims   166

The Function of Evidence   167

"Because I Say So": Unsubstantiated Claims   168

Distinguishing Evidence from Claims   169

Try This 8.1: Distinguishing Evidence from Claims   170

Giving Evidence a Point: Making Details Speak   170

How to Make Details Speak: A Brief Example   171

B. Kinds of Evidence: What Counts?   172

Questions of Relevance and Methodology: A Political Science Professor Speaks   173

Voices From Across the Curriculum   173

More Than Just the Facts   174

Statistical Evidence   175

Interpreting the Numbers: A Psychology Professor Speaks   176

Voices From Across the Curriculum   176

Experimental Evidence   177

Using Authorities as Evidence   178

Anecdotal Evidence   180

Try This 8.2: Finding Kinds of Evidence   182

Case Studies: Two Examples   182

Textual Evidence   187

Try This 8.3: Using Textual Evidence   188

What Do the Facts Really Tell Us?   188

Guidelines   189

Assignments   189

CHAPTER 9   Analyzing Arguments   191

The Rules of Argument: Syllogism and Enthymeme   192

Toulmin's Alternative Model of the Syllogism   193

Rogerian Argument and Practical Reasoning   195

Two Ways to Improve an Argument: Check for Unstated Assumptions and Qualify Claims   196

Figurative Logic: Reasoning with Metaphors   198

Everyday Thinking   199

A Brief Glossary of Common Logical Fallacies   201

Guidelines   205

Assignments   205

CHAPTER 10   Using Evidence to Build a Paper: 10 on 1   207

Developing a Thesis Is More Than Repeating an Idea   207

When and How to Use 1 on 10   208

Stuck in 1 on 10: The Problem of Five-Paragraph Form   209

Analyzing Evidence in Depth: "10 on 1"   211

Demonstrating the Representativeness of Your Example   212

10 on 1 and Disciplinary Conventions   213

Pan, Track, and Zoom: Using 10 on 1 to Build a Paper   213

Doing 10 on 1: A Brief Example (Tiananmen Square)   214

Try This 10.1: Doing 10 on 1 with Newspaper Visuals   215

Try This 10.2: Doing 10 on 1 with a Reading   216

Converting 1 on 10 into 10 on 1: A Student Paper (Flood Stories)   216

Revising the Draft Using 10 on 1 and Difference Within Similarity   218

Try This 10.3: Describing Evidence   220

Doing 10 on 1: A Student Paper (*Good Bye Lenin!*)   221

Try This 10.4: Marking Claims, Evidence, and Complications in a Draft   222

A Template for Organizing Papers Using 10 on 1: an Alternative to Five-Paragraph Form   223

Guidelines   224

Assignment   225

CHAPTER 11   Making a Thesis Evolve   227

Moving from Idea to Thesis Statement: What a Good Thesis Looks Like   228

Arriving at Thesis Statements: When and Where   228

Strong vs. Weak Thesis Statements   229

Finding the Tension in Good Thesis Statements   229

Try This 11.1: Spotting the Tension in Good Thesis Statements   230

A Note on the Syntax of Good Thesis Statements   231

The Reciprocal Relationship between Thesis and Evidence: The Thesis as Lens   232

Making a Thesis Evolve: A Brief Example   233

Try This 11.2: Qualifying Overstated Claims   234

The Evolving Thesis as Hypothesis and Conclusion in the Natural and Social Sciences   234

The Hypothesis in the Natural and Social Sciences: Four Professors Speak   235

Voices From Across the Curriculum   235

Six Steps for Making a Thesis Evolve   236

Evolving a Thesis in an Exploratory Draft: The Example of *Las Meninas*   237

Description to Analysis: The Exploratory Draft   240

Starting a Revision by Looking Again at the Details: The Method   240

Applying the Six Steps to *Las Meninas*   241

Knowing When to Stop: How Much Revising Is Enough?   244

Evolving a Thesis in a Later-Stage Draft: The Example of *Educating Rita*   245

Try This 11.3: Tracking a Thesis   247

The Evolving Thesis in Outline Form: Superman   248

Locating the Evolving Thesis in the Final Draft   249

Recognizing and Relocating Your Thesis: A History Professor Speaks   250

Voices From Across the Curriculum   250

Try This 11.4: Moving from Observations to a Thesis: Mall Cuisine   251

Mall Cuisine Goes International   251

Guidelines   253

Assignment   254

CHAPTER 12   Recognizing and Fixing Weak Thesis Statements   255

Five Kinds of Weak Thesis Statements and How to Fix Them   256

Weak Thesis Type 1: The Thesis Makes No Claim   256

Weak Thesis Type 2: The Thesis Is Obviously True or Is a Statement of Fact   256

Weak Thesis Type 3: The Thesis Restates Conventional Wisdom   257

Weak Thesis Type 4: The Thesis Bases Its Claim on Personal Conviction   258

Weak Thesis Type 5: The Thesis Makes an Overly Broad Claim   259

Getting Beyond the All-Purpose Thesis: A Dance Professor Speaks   260

Voices From Across the Curriculum   260

Try This 12.1: Revising Weak Thesis Statements   261

How to Rephrase Thesis Statements: Specify and Subordinate   261

Is it Okay to Phrase a Thesis as a Question?   263

Try This 12.2: Determining What the Thesis Requires You to Do Next   263

Guidelines   264

Assignment   264

CHAPTER 13   Using Sources Analytically: The Conversation Model   267

"Source Anxiety" and What to Do About It   268

The Conversation Analogy   269

Conversing with a Source: a Brief Example   270

Ways to Use a Source as a Point of Departure   270

Six Strategies for Analyzing Sources   271

Strategy 1: Make Your Sources Speak   271

Strategy 2: Attend Carefully to the Language of Your Sources by Quoting or Paraphrasing Them   273

Strategy 3: Supply Ongoing Analysis of Sources (Don't Wait Until the End)   273

Bringing Sources Together: A Psychology Professor Speaks   274

Voices From Across the Curriculum   274

Strategy 4: Use Your Sources to Ask Questions, Not Just to Provide Answers   274

Strategy 5: Put Your Sources into Conversation with One Another   276

Strategy 6: Find Your Own Role in the Conversation   278

Evaluating Sources in the Sciences: A Biology Professor Speaks   279

Voices From Across the Curriculum   279

Using Sources Analytically: An Example   279

Guidelines   280

Assignments   281

CHAPTER 14   Finding, Citing, and Integrating Sources   283

A. A Guided Tour of Research Methods
        by Reference Librarian Kelly Cannon   **283**

Three Rules of Thumb for Getting Started   **283**

Start with Indexes, Specialized Dictionaries, Abstracts, and Bibliographies   284

Indexes of Scholarly Journals   285

Finding Your Sources: Articles and Books   285

Finding Quality Sources: Two Professors Speak   286

Voices From Across the Curriculum   286

Finding Quality on the Web   **287**

Understanding Domain Names   287

Print Corollaries   288

Web-Published Gems   288

Wikipedia, Google, and Blogs   289

Asking the Right Questions   290

Subscriber-Only Databases   290

Try This 14.1: Tuning in to Your Research Environment: Four Exercises   291

Eight Tips for Locating and Evaluating Electronic Sources   292

Four Steps Toward Productive Research Across the Disciplines   293

B. Plagiarism and The Logic of Citation   **296**

Why Does Plagiarism Matter?   **296**

Frequently Asked Questions (FAQS) about Plagiarism   **297**

C. CITING SOURCES: Four Documentation Styles
        by Reference Librarian Kelly Cannon   **299**

The Four Documentation Styles: Similarities and Differences   **299**

1. APA Style   **300**

2. Chicago Style   **302**

3a. CSE Style Employing Name-Year (Author-Date) System   **303**

3b. CSE Style Employing Citation Sequence System   **305**

4. MLA Style   **306**

D. Integrating Quotations into Your Paper   **307**

E. Preparing an Abstract   **309**

Guidelines   **311**

Assignments: A Research Sequence   **312**

**UNIT III   MATTERS OF FORM: THE SHAPES THAT THOUGHT
               TAKES   315**

CHAPTER 15   Forms and Formats Across the Curriculum   317

A. Disciplinary Forms and Formats   317

The Two Functions of Disciplinary Formats   318

Using Formats Heuristically: An Example   318

Forms and Formats Across the Curriculum: Some Common Elements   319

Science Format (IMRAD) Compared with Other Academic Formats   319

Writing in the Sciences: A Biochemistry Professor Speaks   320

Voices From Across the Curriculum   321

How to Write—and Read—Scientific Formats: Three Professors Speak   322

Voices From Across the Curriculum   322

B. The Shaping Force of Common Thought Patterns   323

Deduction and Induction   323

Deduction   325

Induction   325

The Overlap   325

Thesis Slots   326

The Shaping Force of Thesis Statements   326

Try This 15.1: Predicting Essay Shapes from Thesis Shapes   327

The Shaping Force of Transitions   327

Try This 15.2: Tracking Transitions   328

C. The Rhetoric of Form   328

The Classical Oration Format   329

Three Common Organizing Strategies   330

Climactic Order: Saving the Best for Last   330

Comparisons/Contrasts: Two Formats   331

Concessions and Refutations: Giving and Taking Away   331

Try This 15.3: Locating Concessions and Refutations   332

D. The Idea of The Paragraph   333

How a Paragraph Says   333

How Long? Paragraphs, Readers, and Writers   334

Paragraphs Across the Curriculum: Some Common Patterns   335

Linking the Sentences in Paragraphs: Minding the Gaps   336

What a Paragraph Does: The Paragraph as Movement of Mind   337

Paragraph Structure #1: Topic Sentence, Restriction, Illustration   337

Try This 15.4: Label the Function of the Sentences in a Paragraph   338

Paragraph Structure #2: Observation -> Implication -> Conclusion   339

Paragraph Structure #3: Coordinate and Subordinate Paragraphs   340

Try This 15.5: Arrange Coordinate and Subordinate Sequences   342

Try This 15.6: Identify the Structure of Paragraphs   342

Finding the Skeleton of an Essay: An Example   344

Guidelines   346

Assignments   347

CHAPTER 16   Introductions and Conclusions Across the Curriculum   349

Introductions and Conclusions as Social Sites   349

How Much to Say Upfront   350

What Introductions Do: "Why What I'm Saying Matters"   350

Putting an Issue or Question in Context   352

Providing an Introductory Context: A Political Science Professor Speaks   352

Voices From Across the Curriculum   352

Introductions and Abstracts in the Sciences   353

Introductions in the Sciences: Three Professors Speak   353

Voices From Across the Curriculum   353

Integration of Citations in a Literature Review: A Brief Example   354

Introductions in Scientific Papers: A Brief Example   355

Framing Research Questions and Hypotheses: A Political Science Professor Speaks   355

Voices From Across the Curriculum   356

Introductions in the Humanities   356

How Much to Introduce Upfront: Typical Problems   357

Digression   358

Incoherence   358

Prejudgment: 358

Avoiding Strong Claims in the Introduction: An Economics Professor Speaks   359

Voices From Across the Curriculum   359

Using Procedural Openings   359

Using Procedural Openings: A Political Science Professor Speaks   360

Voices From Across the Curriculum   360

Good Ways to Begin   360

Challenge a Commonly Held View   360

Begin with a Definition   360

Lead with Your Second-Best Example   361

Exemplify the Topic with a Narrative   361

What Conclusions Do: The Final "So What?"   361

Beyond Restatement: Two Professors Speak   362

Voices From Across the Curriculum   362

Conclusions in the Sciences: The Discussion Section   363

Writing Conclusions in the Sciences: Two Professors Speak   363

Voices From Across the Curriculum   363

Conclusions in Scientific Papers: A Brief Example   364

Solving Typical Problems in Conclusions   364

Redundancy   364

Raising a Totally New Point   365

Overstatement   365

Anticlimax   365

Try This 16.1: Analyze Paired Introductions and
    Conclusions   366

Guidelines   371

Assignments   372

CHAPTER 17   Revising for Style: Word Choice   375

Style is Meaning   375

Style: A Matter of Choices   376

How Style Shapes Thought: A Brief Example   377

"Right" and "Wrong" Words: Shades of Meaning   377

Word Histories and the *OED*   378

Try This 17.1: Tracing Word Histories   379

What's Bad about "Good" and "Bad"   379

Concrete and Abstract Diction   380

Try This 17.2: Two Experiments with Abstract and Concrete Diction   381

Latinate Diction   381

Choosing Words: Some Rhetorical Considerations   382

Tone   382

Try This 17.3: Analyzing Tone-Deaf Prose   383

Formal and Colloquial Styles: Who's Writing to Whom, and Why Does It Matter?   384

Try This 17.4: Analyzing Effective Tone   385

First Person, Second Person or Third Person?   385

"I": Pro and Con   386

Using the First-Person "I": Three Professors Speak   386

Voices From Across the Curriculum   386

"You": Pro and Con   387

Jargon   387

The Politics of Language   388

Guidelines   389

Assignment   390

CHAPTER 18   Revising for Style: The Rhetoric of the Sentence   391

Operating Assumptions   391

The Primary Comma Rule: Identifying the Main Clause   392

How to Recognize the Four Basic Sentence Types & What They Do   393

The Simple Sentence: One Statement at a Time   394

The Compound Sentence: Two Items of Equal Weight   394

The Complex Sentence: Ranking the Value of Ideas or Information   395

The Compound-Complex Sentence: Using Syntax to Convey Complexity   396

Try This 18.1: Compose the Four Sentence Types   397

Try This 18.2: Identify the Four Sentence Types in Sentences You Like   397

Using Coordination and Subordination to Emphasize Meanings   398

Using Coordination to Balance This with That   398

Emphasis Rests at the End of Coordinate Clauses   399

Try This 18.3: Rearrange Coordinate Clauses for Emphasis   399

Using Subordination to Adjust Emphasis   399

How the End Affects Emphasis When Using Subordinate Clauses   400

Try This 18.4: Experiment with Coordination, Subordination, and the Order of Clauses   401

Parallel Structure: Put Parallel Information into Parallel Form   401

Try This 18.5: Find Examples of Parallelism   402

Try This 18.6: Correct Errors in Parallelism   402

Two Powerful Forms of Parallelism: Antithesis and Chiasmus   403

Periodic and Cumulative Sentences: Two Effective Sentence Shapes   403

The Periodic Sentence: Delay Closure to Achieve Emphasis   403

The Cumulative Sentence: Start Fast to Build Momentum   405

Try This 18.7: Write Periodic and Cumulative Sentences   406

Cut Extra Words to Achieve Greater Directness   407

Beginning With "It Is" or "There Is": Advantages and Disadvantages   407

Static versus Active Verbs: "To Be" Or "Not To Be"   408

Try This 18.8: Finding the Active Verb   409

Active and Passive Voice: Emphasizing the Doer or the Action   410

Try This 18.9: Converting Passive to Active   411

Sentence Style in Science Writing: A Biochemistry Professor Speaks   412

Voices From Across the Curriculum   412

About Prescriptive Style Manuals: A Word of Warning   412

Experiment!   413

Guidelines   413

Assignments   414

CHAPTER 19   Revising for Correctness: Grammar and Punctuation   417

The Concept of Basic Writing Errors (BWEs)   418

Why Grammar Errors Make Some People So Angry   418

Usage: How Language Customs Change   419

Usage: Some Examples of Right & Wrong versus Etiquette   419

When Usage Begins to Change Grammar   420

Usage as Cultural Marker   421

Try This 19.1: Discover the Rationale for Usage Choices   422

What Punctuation Marks Say: A Quick-Hit Guide   422

Nine Basic Writing Errors and How to Fix Them   424

Some Advice on Proofreading   424

BWE 1: Sentence Fragments   424

Noun Clause (No Predicate) as a Fragment   424

Verbal as a Fragment   425

Subordinate Clause as a Fragment   425

Test Yourself 19.1: Fragments   426

Using Dashes and Colons to Correct Fragments   426

BWE 2: Comma Splices and Fused (or Run-On) Sentences   427

Comma Splice   427

Comma Splice   427

Cures for the Perpetual Comma Splicer   427

Fused Sentence   428

Comma Splices with Conjunctive Adverbs   428

Test Yourself 19.2: Comma Splices   428

BWE 3: Errors in Subject–Verb Agreement   429

Agreement Problem: plural subject, singular verb   429

Agreement Problem: singular subject, plural verb   430

Agreement Problem: "each" must take singular verb   430

Test Yourself 19.3: Subject-Verb Agreement   430

A Note on Dialects and Standard Written English   431

BWE 4: Shifts in Sentence Structure (Faulty Predication)   431

Faulty Predication   432

Test Yourself 19.4: Faulty Predication   432

BWE 5: Errors in Pronoun Reference   432

Pronoun-Antecedent Agreement   432

Test Yourself 19.5: Pronoun-Antecedent Agreement   433

Ambiguous Reference   433

Test Yourself 19.6: Ambiguous Reference   433

Broad Reference   433

Test Yourself 19.7: Broad Reference   434

A Note on Sexism and Pronoun Usage   434

BWE 6: Misplaced Modifiers and Dangling Participles   435

Misplaced Modifier: modifier appears to modify wrong word   435

Misplaced Modifier: modifier appears to modify wrong word   435

Dangling Participle: subject that participle modifies does not appear in the sentence   436

Test Yourself 19.8: Modification Errors   436

BWE 7: Errors in Using Possessive Apostrophes   436

Apostrophe Error   436

Test Yourself 19.9: Possessive Apostrophes   437

BWE 8: Comma Errors   437

Comma Error: comma missing after introductory phrase   437

Comma Error: comma missing after introductory phrase   437

Comma Error: two commas needed around parenthetical element   438

A Note on Restrictive versus Nonrestrictive Elements   438

Comma Error: two commas needed around parenthetical element   438

Comma Error: restrictive elements should not be enclosed within commas   438

Comma Error: no comma setting off restrictive clause   439

Test Yourself 19.10: Comma Errors   439

BWE 9: Spelling/Diction Errors That Interfere with Meaning   439

Spelling/Diction Error: "It's" versus "Its"   440

Spelling/Diction Error: "Their" versus "There" versus "They're"   440

Spelling/Diction Error: "Then" versus "Than"   440

Spelling/Diction Error: "Effect" versus "Affect"   441

Test Yourself 19.11: Spelling/Diction Errors   441

Glossary of Grammatical Terms   441

Assignments   445

CHAPTER 19 Appendix   446

Index   I-1

Preface

When we first contemplated writing this book two decades ago, we wanted to produce a short monograph that would provide some kind of lingua franca for faculty teaching in cross-curricular writing programs. The first several writing pedagogy seminars we offered to faculty at our college taught us that the language we had learned in graduate school for talking about writing didn't work well with our colleagues from other departments. This turned out to be, in fact, an understatement.

So we read what our faculty had to say about what they'd learned in our writing seminars and what they wanted from student writing and used this information to develop a book that might sustain a faculty writing cohort on campus, allowing its members to talk to each other about writing across disciplinary lines. Six editions later, we are still working on that goal and learning about what college students need in order to succeed at academic writing both in first-year composition courses and in the various discourse communities they migrate among during their undergraduate careers.

The clearest consensus we've found among faculty is on the kind of writing that they say they want from their students: not issue-based argument, not personal reflection (the "reaction" paper), not passive summary, but analysis, with its patient and methodical inquiry into the meaning of information. And yet, most books of writing instruction devote only a chapter, if that, to analysis.

Among the reader reports that we pondered for this edition, we found faculty reporting that students are coming to them prepared to do five-paragraph themes and arguments but radically unprepared in thinking analytically. This edition of *Writing Analytically* remains committed to the goal of giving students the tools they need in order to engage in the analytical habits of mind that will be expected of them in their courses and in the world they encounter after graduation. Students who learn to analyze information and who know how to use writing in order to discover and develop ideas will continue to be in demand in the workplace, regardless of the form that writing takes or the medium in which it appears.

As the book demonstrates, the analytical process is surprisingly formulaic. It consists of a fairly limited set of basic moves. People who think well have these moves at their disposal, whether they are aware of using them or not. Analysis, the book argues, is a frame of mind, a set of habits for observing and making sense of the world.

Entering this analytical frame of mind requires specific tasks that will reduce students' anxiety for instant answers, impede the reflex move to judgments, and encourage a more hands-on engagement with materials. *Writing Analytically* supplies these tasks for each phase of the writing and idea-generating process: making observations, inferring implications, and making the leap to possible conclusions.

The root issue here is the writer's attitude towards evidence. The book argues that the ability of writers to discover ideas and improve on them in revision depends largely on their ability to use evidence as a means of testing and developing ideas rather than just supporting them.

Writing Analytically's employment of verbal prompts like "So what?" and its recommendation of step-by-step procedures, such as the procedure for making a thesis evolve, should not be confused with prescriptive slot-filler formulae for writing. Our book does not prescribe a fill-in-the-blank grid for producing papers. Instead it offers schematic descriptions of what good thinkers do—as acts of mind—when they are confronted with data.

We continue to believe that the book's way of describing the analytical thought process will make students more confident thinkers, better able to contend with complexity and to move beyond the simplistic agree/disagree response and passive assembling of information. We have faith in the book's various formulae and verbal prompts for their ability to spur more thoughtful writing but also for the role they can play in making the classroom a more collaborative space. When students and teachers can share the means of idea production, class discussion and writing become better connected, and students can more easily learn to see that good ideas don't just happen—they're made.

HOW TO USE THIS BOOK

Writing Analytically is designed to be used in first-year writing courses or seminars, as well as in more advanced writing-intensive courses in a variety of subject areas. Though the book's chapters form a logical sequence, each can also stand alone and be used in different sequences.

We assume that most professors will want to supply their own subject matter for students to write about. The book does, however, contain writing exercises throughout that can be applied to a wide range of materials—print and visual, text-based (reading) and experiential (writing from direct observation). In the text itself we suggest using newspapers, magazines, films, primary texts (both fiction and nonfiction), academic articles, textbooks, television, historical documents, places, advertising, photographs, political campaigns, and so on.

There is, by the way, an edition of this book that contains readings—*Writing Analytically with Readings*. It includes writing assignments that call on students to apply the skills in the original book to writing about the readings and to using the readings as lenses for analyzing other material.

The writing exercises in *Writing Analytically* take two forms: end-of-chapter assignments that could produce papers, and informal writing exercises called "Try This" that are embedded inside the chapters near the particular skills being discussed. Many of the "Try This" exercises can generate papers, but usually they are more limited in scope, asking readers to experiment with various kinds of data-gathering and analysis.

Interspersed throughout the text are brief commentaries on writing called Voices from Across the Curriculum. These were written for the book by professors at our college from disciplines other than English, Rhetoric, and Composition. The Voices speak directly to students on stylistic, rhetorical, and epistemological differences across the curriculum, including disciplinary protocols, such as the one governing the lab report in the natural and social sciences.

No single text or first-year writing course can prepare students for all of the kinds of writing they will be asked to do in college and in their professional lives. But writing texts like this one can school students in the attitudes and skills they'll need to adapt quickly to writing in the disciplines. Our book also foregrounds the many values and expectations that the disciplines share about writing.

WHAT'S NEW IN THIS EDITION

In general, we have responded to reader requests for more examples of writing using the book's heuristics, more bullet lists, more concise rationales, better contextualizing of the Voices from Across the Curriculum, and improved navigability to make the book more browseable and easier to use. We decided that the book's step-by-step "how-to" instructions for key heuristics, such as 10 on 1, uncovering assumptions, and "The Method" (looking for patterns of repetition and contrast) needed to be clearer and less embedded in text. We also wished to have an opening chapter that would better frame and preview the book (and the field of Rhetoric and Composition) without trying to cover everything in one chapter.

We have aimed for shorter paragraphs, more heads, and more directive heads. We have sought to make individual chapters browseable by including in the opening paragraphs of each a PowerPoint-like "slide" that lists the key writing procedures in the chapter.

Throughout chapters, our headings also seek to offer browseable advice rather than just stating topics. Readers repeatedly tell us that they like chapters such as Recognizing and Fixing Weak Thesis Statements, Using Sources Analytically, and Introductions and Conclusions, because the heads offer a kind of outline of the chapter's advice.

We are excited about the new first chapter and its modular format. Reviewers over the years have asked us to move a number of things forward in the book, such as our critique of five-paragraph form. If we were to comply with all of these requests, the whole book would be in chapter one! So we evolved a new first chapter, which takes the form of a series of short takes—previews of key topics in writing and writing instruction that are particularly useful to discuss early in a writing course. Because the chapter's organization is modular, students and faculty can take from it what they need when they need it. Cumulatively, the short takes tell a story about making the transition to college writing. Among the chapter's topics are writing in the disciplines, academic vs. non-academic writing, writing about reading, rhetoric, argument, analysis, freewriting, and the place of the traditional essay in the digital age.

The book now has two toolkit chapters instead of one (Chapters 2 and 4), making the book's central heuristics more prominent, more accessible, and more clearly arranged in a hierarchy of increasingly sophisticated skills. The second toolkit pulls uncovering assumptions, reformulating binaries, passage-based focused freewriting, difference within similarity, and "seems to be about X" out of chapters in which they have been buried and uses them to set up the Writing About Reading chapter, which follows.

The book's discussion of counterproductive habits of mind (much shorter and less like a jeremiad) now appears at the end of the first toolkit (Chapter 2), so that the chapter leads with concrete activities and positive advice before we supply rationale and admonitions.

Writing About Reading is now better foregrounded in the book and its importance is made explicit in the Writing About Reading short take in chapter 1. All of the book's heuristics are designed to deepen and particularize students' engagement with written texts. To clarify this fact, we have given our Writing About Reading chapter a new subtitle—"More Moves to Make with Written Texts," and we have relocated that chapter to Unit I, The Analytical Frame of Mind: Introduction to Analytical Methods from its place in the previous edition next to Conversing with Sources, which was near the end of the book.

The book's treatment of discipline-specific writing, especially writing in the natural and social sciences, is now more fully described and theorized, and it is supported by many new examples of student and professional writing in disciplines outside the humanities. Much new material has been integrated into the first two chapters of Unit III: Matters of Form: The Shapes that Thought Takes. New and revised Voices from Across the Curriculum are now integrated into the text and into the Contents by topic and discipline. Discussion of writing in the disciplines appears as one of the short takes in our new first chapter. We continue to believe in the importance of helping students see common values and habits of mind in writing across the curriculum as well as differences.

We have added new short and extended examples of student and professional writing that use the book's heuristics. In addition to the book's primary extended examples—*Whistler's Mother, Las Meninas, Educating Rita*—you'll find (in Chapter 5, Writing About Reading) a student essay applying readings from sociolinguistics to the conversation of male guests on late-night talk shows. Chapter 3 on the five analytical moves now includes a student's analysis of dentist jokes, which was delivered as a commencement address at Harvard dental school.

Chapter 9, Analyzing Arguments has been rewritten and includes new sections on Rogerian argument and practical reasoning as well as figurative logic. The brief glossary of common logical errors has also been significantly expanded with many new examples. The book is aligned with the thinking of Carl Rogers and others on the goal of making argument less combative, less inflected by a vocabulary of military strategizing that discourages negotiation among competing points of view and the evolution of new ideas from the pressure of one idea against another.

The discussion in Chapter 14, Finding, Citing, and Integrating Sources, now features a much expanded treatment of the four documentation styles—APA, Chicago, CSE, and MLA—compiled by reference librarian Kelly Cannon.

ACKNOWLEDGMENTS

First and foremost, thanks to our students who test drive and troubleshoot the book's writing advice. Thanks especially to our wonderful cadre of writing tutors who have developed workshops for students and faculty based on our book.

We continue to be grateful for the support of our publishers over the years. In particular, let us single out our developmental editor, Mary Beth Walden, for her sound advice, patience, and good cheer. Thanks too to Margaret Leslie, Leslie Taggart and to a host of others, past and present: Karl Yambert, Michael Rosenberg, Dickson Musslewhite, John Meyers, Michell Phifer, Karen R. Smith, Julie McBurney, Ellen Shraim, Kevin Loane, and Dan Silverberg (go Sox).

We are very grateful to our faculty colleagues at Muhlenberg who created workshops for our writing tutors on writing in their disciplines and then contributed expanded versions of these materials for the book: Keri Colabroy, Christopher Borick, and Mark Sciutto. Boundless thanks as well to Kelly Cannon, reference librarian extraordinaire, for his expanded contributions on how to think and act like a researcher.

The cross-curricular dimension of this book would be sadly impoverished without the interest and support of an enviable range of colleagues who participate in the writing cohort at our college. They have shared with us examples of good student and professional writing in their fields, writing assignments from their writing-intensive classes, and examples of their own writing: George Benjamin, Linda Bips, Susan Clemens, Ted Conner, Amy Corbin, William "Chip" Gruen, Brian Mello, Marcia Morgan, Jefferson Pooley, Pearl Rosenberg, and Jeremy Teissere. We are also grateful to Katherine Kibblinger Gottschalk of Cornell University for permission to quote her unpublished 4 C's paper on the correspondence of E.B. White.

Thanks to Kate Christein, Assistant Director of the Writing Center, for keeping everything up and running while we were stuck in front of our computer screens producing this revision. And thanks also to our colleague Linda Bips, with whom we co-direct the Writing Program. We and it would be much less sane without her. Grace Gardella has looked out for us in the English department. And we are grateful for the support provided by the folks at Pistachios—Colleen Hauck, Sidney Stecher, and Eric Serrano.

Deep thanks are due to Eddie Singleton, Scott DeWitt, Wendy Hesford, and their graduate students at the Ohio State University: our annual visits there have nourished our thinking about writing in countless ways. Christine Farris at Indiana University has been a friend of the book from its earliest days, and we cannot imagine sitting down to revise without the trenchant advice she offers us. Thanks too to her colleague, the unsinkable John Schilb and to Ted Leahey, teacher of teachers. And for the many conversations about teaching and writing that have sustained us we thank Richard Louth, Dean Ward, Kenny Marotta, Alec Marsh, Matthew Johnson, Matthew Hollrah, and Miles McCrimmon.

A number of past and present students have also graciously allowed us to use their materials in this edition: Bob Tarby and Anna Whiston for their major contributions, along with Emily Petchler Herstoff, Michelle Bielko, Molly Harper, Melissa Bressler, Sean Heron, Lauren Artiles, Elissa Davidowitz, and Christa Carlstrand.

Finally, for their understanding: our spouses, Mark and Debby, our children, Lesley, Sarah, and Lizzie—and the dogs.

We would also like to thank the many colleagues who reviewed the book; we are grateful for their insight:

Diann Ainsworth, *Weatherford College*
Jeanette Adkins, *Tarrant County College*
Derede Arthur, *University of California, Santa Cruz*
Joan Anderson, *California State University–San Marcos*
Candace Barrington, *Central Connecticut State University*
Maria Bates, *Pierce College*
Karin Becker, *Fort Lewis College*
Laura Behling, *Gustavus Adolphus College*
Stephanie Bennett, *Monmouth University*
Tom Bowie, *Regis University*
Roland Eric Boys, *Oxnard College*
David Brantley, *College of Southern Maryland*
Jessica Brown, *City College of San Francisco*
Christine Bryant Cohen, *University of Illinois–Urbana-Champaign*
Alexandria Casey, *Graceland University*
Anthony Cavaluzzi, *Adirondack Community College*
Johnson Cheu, *Michigan State University*
Jeff Cofer, *Bellevue Community College*
Helen Connell, *Barry University*
Kristi Costello, *Binghampton University – SUNY*
Cara Crandall, *Emerson College*
Rose Day, *Central New Mexico Community College*
Christopher Diller, *Berry College*
Susan de Ghize, *University of Denver*
Virginia Dumont-Poston, *Lander University*
David Eggebrecht, *Concordia University*
Karen Feldman, *University of California*
Dan Ferguson, *Amarillo College*
Gina Franco, *Knox College*
Sue Frankson, *College of DuPage*
Anne Friedman, *Borough of Manhattan Community College*
Tessa Garcia, *University of Texas–Pan American*
Susan Garrett, *Goucher College*
Edward Geisweidt, *University of Alabama*
Nate Gordon, *Kishwaukee College*
Katherine Hagopian, *North Carolina State University*
Devon Holmes, *University of San Francisco*
Glenn Hutchinson, *University of North Carolina–Charlotte*
Habiba Ibrahim, *University of Washington*
Joseph Janangelo, *Loyola University–Chicago*

Charlene Keeler, *California State University–Fullerton*
Douglas King, *Gannon University*
Constance Koepfinger, *Duquesne University*
Anne Langendorfer, *The Ohio State University*
Kim Long, *Shippensburg University*
Laine Lubar, *Broome Community College*
Phoenix Lundstrom, *Kapi`olani Community College*
Cynthia Martin, *James Madison University*
Lisa Maruca, *Wayne State University*
Andrea Mason, *Pacific Lutheran University*
Darin Merrill, *Brigham Young University–Idaho*
Sarah Newlands, *Portland State University*
Emmanuel Ngwang, *Mississippi Valley State University*
Leslie Norris, *Rappahannock Community College*
Ludwig Otto, *Tarrant County College*
Adrienne Peek, *Modesto Junior College*
Adrienne Redding, *Andrews University*
Julie Rivera, *California State University–Long Beach*
Jenica Roberts, *University of Illinois–Urbana Champaign*
John Robinson, *Diablo Valley College*
Pam Rooney, *Western Michigan University*
Linda Rosekrans, *The State University of New York–Cortland*
Becky Rudd, *Citrus College*
Arthur Saltzman, *Missouri Southern State University*
Deborah Scaggs, *Texas A & M International University*
Vicki Schwab, *Manatee Community College*
John Sullivan, *Muhlenberg College*
Eleanor Swanson, *Regis University*
Kimberly Thompson, *Wittenberg University*
Kathleen Walton, *Southwestern Oregon Community College*
James Ray Watkins, *The Art Institute of Pittsburgh, Online; Colorado Technical University, Online; and The Center for Talented Youth, Johns Hopkins University*
Lisa Weihman, *West Virginia University*
Robert Williams, *Radford University*
Nancy Wright, *Syracuse University*
Robbin Zeff, *George Washington University*

UNIT I

THE ANALYTICAL FRAME OF MIND: INTRODUCTION TO ANALYTICAL METHODS

Finding Your Way in This Book: A Note to Readers

WRITING ANALYTICALLY'S CHAPTERS can stand alone and can be used in any order, but there are organizing principles that determine the sequence of chapters.

The book's overall method is **recursive**. In addition to moving to increasingly complex writing tasks, the book assumes you will keep using the tools from Unit I as habitual practices in the writing you are invited to do in later chapters.

- Unit I (Chapters 1–7), The Analytical Frame of Mind: Introduction to Analytical Methods, concentrates on ways of training yourself to be more observant and to push observations to implications and conclusions.

- Unit II (Chapters 8–14), Writing Analytical Papers: How to Use Evidence, Evolve Claims, and Converse with Sources, incorporates the essential methods of Unit I into strategies for writing various kinds of analytical papers, including papers that require you to synthesize secondary sources and orchestrate a conversation among them. Thesis and evidence are key terms of Unit II.

- Unit III (Chapters 15–19), Matters of Form: The Shapes That Thought Takes, addresses such topics as organization, disciplinary formats, introductions and conclusions, and grammar and style. The emphasis throughout is rhetorical, focusing on the relationship between forms and the thinking these forms enable.

The book provides a view of writing in different academic disciplines and how they vary in their expectations of student writing. Interspersed throughout the text are sections labeled Voices from Across the Curriculum—discussions of disciplinary practices solicited from our colleagues in a variety of disciplines. Although the book respects stylistic difference, we argue that there is an underlying purpose and thought structure that the disciplines share.

Chapter 1

Introduction: Fourteen Short Takes on Writing and the Writing Process

THIS IS A "HOW TO THINK ABOUT ..." and "Where to Look for ..." chapter, consisting of a sequence of short takes on topics that are especially helpful to understand at the beginning of a writing course. Although you will find more extended discussions of most of these topics later in the book, we think you will find it useful to have them assembled here in compact, browseable form. Learning to be a better writer is not just a matter of acquiring skills. To a significant extent it involves learning new ways of thinking about what writing is and what it does.

Because the organization of the chapter is modular, you can easily skip around in it to sample what it has to offer. There is, however, a logic to the order of the short takes, which is why the chapter is not arranged alphabetically. Typically, each short take triggers the next. Cumulatively, the short takes tell a story about making the transition to college writing. Some of the entries will be more pertinent for you now than others. Return to the chapter from time to time and browse for concepts and key terms you have come to need.

ORDER OF THE SHORT TAKES

- Thinking About Writing as a Tool of Thought
- Analysis: A Quick Definition
- What Do Faculty Want from Student Writing?
- Breaking Out of 5-Paragraph Form
- Writing Traditional Papers in the Digital Age
- What's Different About Writing Arguments in College?
- Rhetoric: What It Is and Why You Need It
- Writing about Reading: Beyond "Banking"
- Freewriting: How and Why to Do It
- Process and Product: Some Ways of Thinking About the Writing Process

- How to Think About Grammar and Style (Beyond Error-Catching)
- A Quick Word on Style Guides
- How to Think About Writing in the Disciplines
- Academic vs. Nonacademic Writing: How Different Are They?

THINKING ABOUT WRITING AS A TOOL OF THOUGHT

Learning to write well means more than learning to organize information in appropriate forms and construct clear and grammatically correct sentences. Learning to write well means learning ways of using writing in order to think well.

The achievement of good writing does, of course, require attention to form, but writing is not just a thing, a container for displaying already completed acts of thinking—it is also a mental activity. Through writing, we figure out what things mean, which is this book's definition of analysis.

The book will make you much more aware of your own acts of thinking and will show you how to experiment more deliberately with ways of having ideas—for example, by sampling kinds of informal and exploratory writing that will enhance your ability to learn.

As the next few chapters will show, the analytical process is surprisingly formulaic. It consists of a fairly limited set of basic moves. People who think well have these moves at their disposal, whether they are aware of using them or not. Analysis, the book argues, is a frame of mind, a set of habits for observing and making sense of the world.

ANALYSIS: A QUICK DEFINITION

Just about all of the reading and writing you will do in college is analytical. Such writing is concerned with accurate description and with thinking collaboratively (rather than combatively) with readers about ways of understanding what things might mean. The problem is that much of what we hear on television or read online seems to be primarily devoted to bludgeoning other people into submission with argumentative claims. The book's analytical methods provide a set of moves that derail more unproductive responses, such as agree/disagree, like/dislike, and other forms of gladiatorial opinion-swapping.

Chapter 2 offers the first set of methods, along with discussion of the counterproductive habits of mind they are designed to deflect. Chapter 3 defines analysis in detail (in what we call the five analytical moves) and shows you how it operates differently from other forms of thinking and writing. For now, we offer the following list on the goals of analysis and its identifying traits:

Analysis Defined

1. Analysis seeks to discover what something means. An analytical argument makes claims for how something might be best understood and in what context.
2. Analysis deliberately delays evaluation and judgment.

3. Analysis begins in and values uncertainty rather than starting from settled convictions.

4. Analytical arguments are usually pluralistic; they tend to try on more than one way of thinking about how something might be best understood.

WHAT DO FACULTY WANT FROM STUDENT WRITING?

Here is a list of faculty expectations based on what faculty across the curriculum say at our seminars on writing:

- Analysis rather than passive summary, personal reaction and opinions
- Analysis before argument, understanding in depth before taking a stand
- Alternatives to agree-disagree & like-dislike responses
- Tolerance of uncertainty
- Respect for complexity
- Ability to apply theories from reading, using them as lenses
- Acquiring and understanding the purpose of disciplinary conventions
- Ability to use secondary sources in ways other than plugging them in as "answers"

Overall, what faculty across the curriculum want is for students to learn to do things with course material beyond merely reporting it on the one hand, and just reacting to it with personal response on the other. This is the crux of the issue that *Writing Analytically* addresses: how to locate a middle ground between passive summary and personal response. We call that middle ground analysis.

To these expectations, we would add that the ability to cultivate interest and curiosity is a great desideratum of faculty across the curriculum. They want students to understand that interest need not precede writing; interest is more often a product of writing.

BREAKING OUT OF 5-PARAGRAPH FORM

The shift from high school to college writing is not just a difference in degree but a difference in kind. The changes it requires in matters of form and style are inevitably also changes in thinking. In order to make these changes in thinking, you may need to "unlearn" some practices you've previously been taught. At the top of the unlearning list for many entering college students is 5-paragraph form—the rigid, one-size-fits-all organizational scheme that is still taught in many high schools.

If you have come to rely on this form, giving it up can be anxiety-producing. This is especially so when you are asked to abandon an all-purpose form and replace it with a set of different forms for different situations. But it's essential to let go of this particular security blanket.

So, what's wrong with 5-paragraph form? Its rigid, arbitrary and mechanical organizational scheme values structure over just about everything else, especially in-depth thinking.

The formula's defenders say that essays need to be organized and that the simple three-part thesis and three-body paragraphs (one reason and/or example for each) and repetitive conclusion meets that need. They also say that 5-paragraph form is useful for helping writers to get started. The problem with treating 5-paragraph form as a relatively benign aid to clarity is that like any habit it is very hard to break.

Students who can't break the habit remain handicapped because 5-paragraph form runs counter to virtually all of the values and attitudes that they need in order to grow as writers and thinkers—such as respect for complexity, tolerance of uncertainty, and the willingness to test and complicate rather than just assert ideas.

The form actually discourages thinking by conditioning writers to be afraid of looking closely at evidence. If they look too closely, they might find something that doesn't fit, at which point the prefabricated organizational scheme falls apart. But it is precisely the something-that-doesn't-seem-to-fit, the thing writers call a "complication," that triggers good ideas.

Finally, what about the perception that students need to master 5-paragraph form in order to do well on SAT exams and other forms of standardized testing? Standardized tests in writing usually don't encourage writers to take the kinds of risks in both form and content that good writers must learn to take. But it is a myth that SAT evaluators reward 5-paragraph form. In fact, the two criteria that most often earn high scores from graders are length (yes, length) and vocabulary (Michael Winerip, "SAT Essay Test Rewards Length and Ignores Errors," the *New York Times*, May 4, 2005, On Education). Readers of writing-based college entrance exams give high marks not to writing that has a tidy structure but to writing that avoids clichés and overstated claims and that employs sentence and essay structures capable of accommodating complex ideas. (*See Chapter 10 for alternatives to 5-paragrah form that can accommodate complexity. See especially the Template for Using 10 on 1.*)

ON WRITING TRADITIONAL ESSAYS IN THE DIGITAL AGE

You might be wondering why it is that colleges and universities continue to ask students to write traditional essays in an age when so much communication is dominated by the short and often multi-modal forms of the Internet. Does the arrival of the Internet with its blogs and web pages and YouTube clips mean that the traditional essay is rapidly becoming extinct? Why shouldn't college students spend their time learning to write exclusively in these new forms rather than learning to do a kind of writing they might not use after college?

There are several answers to these questions. First and most importantly, learning to write the traditional essay is the only way to develop the skills and habits of mind necessary for engaging in acts of sustained, in-depth reflection. Nor does it matter if you never write essays or lab reports or academic articles after college. It is not the presentation that matters—the forms of college writing—so much as what the forms allow you to do as a thinker.

In this chapter's short take on the writing process (*See Process and Product: Some Ways of Thinking About the Writing Process*), we point out that the form of a finished piece of writing does not disclose the process that would allow a writer to produce it. The necessarily concise lists of PowerPoints and of some kinds of writing on the Web don't just spring into being in that form. The careful compression in such forms is typically the product of writing as a tool of thought.

Finally, we are advising that traditional forms and formats are only a part of what you need to learn in order to grow as a writer and thinker. The first unit of this book, for example, although its assignments can lead to traditional essays, focuses primarily on ways of using writing in order to improve your ability to observe. This kind of writing—exploratory writing, writing to help you discover ideas—can fuel various formats, including multi-modal ones.

WHAT'S DIFFERENT ABOUT WRITING ARGUMENTS IN COLLEGE?

Insofar as you will be asked to write arguments in college, they will differ in significant ways from what you hear on crossfire-style talk shows and "news" programs. In made-for-TV arguments, people set out to defeat other people's positions and thus "win." Arguments in college are more *exploratory*—aimed at locating new ways of understanding something or at finding a tentative solution to a problem. Such arguments lead with analysis rather than position-taking. The claims you arrive at in an analysis are, in fact, arguments—analytical arguments.

Here are some of the differences between argument as it is too often conducted in the media and argument of the type cultivated by college writing:

- has more than two sides
- moves from much more carefully defined and smaller (less global) claims
- seeks out common ground between competing points of view rather than solely emphasizing difference
- uses potentially contradictory evidence to test and qualify claims rather than ignoring such evidence or housing it solely as concessions ("okay, I'll give you that point, but …") and refutations ("here is why you are wrong!")
- adopts a civil and nonadversarial **ethos** (self-presentation) and **rhetorical stance** (relationship with the audience) (*see Chapter 3*)
- avoids stating positions as though they were obviously and self-evidently true
- avoids cheap tricks such as straw man—misrepresenting or trivializing another's position so that it is easy to knock down and blow away—and name calling and other of the logical fallacies (*see Chapter 9*)
- includes much more evidence and careful analysis of that evidence

Targeting the Opinionated and the Argumentative We can cap this brief discussion of modes of argument in college by targeting two words that are sometimes misunderstood—**opinionated** and **argumentative**. These are not neutral terms. Saying that someone is opinionated is not the same as saying that he or she has opinions, nor is an argumentative person simply one who offers arguments. The opinionated person has too many opinions—a firmly held view on virtually everything, and the argumentative person is one for whom argument is a form of interpersonal warfare and for whom relationships tend to be competitive and adversarial. Both terms are associated with being close-minded and uncivil.

Although members of the academic world frequently disagree with each other and call attention to those disagreements, they do not lead with conflict and criticism. For knowledge to grow in the academic world, people have to continue to talk with each other and hear what each other has to say. *(See* Naturalizing Our Assumptions and "I Didn't Know You Wanted My Opinion" *in Chapter 2.)*

RHETORIC: WHAT IT IS AND WHY YOU NEED IT

Long before there were courses on writing, people studied a subject called rhetoric—as they still do. Rhetoric is a way of thinking about thinking. It offers ways of generating and evaluating arguments as well as ways of arranging them for maximum effect in particular situations. This book is a rhetoric in the sense that it offers methods for observing all manner of data and arriving at ideas. The division of rhetoric devoted to the generation of ideas is called "invention." *Writing Analytically* is an invention-oriented rhetoric.

In ancient Greece, where rhetoric was first developed as a systematic body of knowledge, emphasis was on public speaking. When Aristotle trained his students in rhetoric, he was preparing them to make arguments in the *agora*, the central assembly place in Athens where social, political, and religious issues of the day were decided. A person well-trained in rhetoric was adept at finding available arguments on the spot. Rhetorical training provided its practitioners with particular habits of mind.

Today, training in rhetoric continues to be especially helpful for all people who wish to enter public discourse and contribute to civil debate on key issues. In one of the best current textbooks on classical rhetoric, *Ancient Rhetorics for Contemporary Students* (Pearson/Longman 2004), authors Sharon Crowley and Debra Hawhee say about rhetoric that "its use allows people to make important choices without resorting to less palatable means of persuasion—coercion or violence" (2).

Unfortunately, the word "rhetoric" has suffered a serious decline in popular perception. To some people, rhetoric has come to mean something like empty, willfully deceitful, and sometimes just plain dishonest uses of language. People who think of rhetoric in this way will say things like "It was all just rhetoric," that is, all talk and no substance.

In order to make use of all that a rhetorical orientation toward writing and thinking can offer, you will first need to understand rhetoric as something other than a way of dressing up lies and making poor decisions sound respectable. We offer the following two ways of thinking about rhetoric—not just the rhetorics of the ancient Greeks, but the various kinds of rhetorics that have been invented since:

1. a rhetoric is a systematic body of techniques for coming to understand and find things to say about a subject (invention), and

2. rhetoric is also the term used to describe a speaker's or writer's way of using language to appeal to a particular audience.

It is from the second definition—rhetoric as a means of arranging language in order to persuade—that the negative definition of rhetoric has come. But finding a way of saying something so that others might hear and consider it does not necessarily mean that people skilled at rhetoric are puffed up tricksters.

The various academic disciplines you will study have rhetorics, which is a very helpful way to understand them. The struggles we all have with writing are to a significant extent rhetorical, because writers are concerned not just with what they want to say but with how to say it so as to be best understood by their target audiences.

It follows that stylistic decisions are always also rhetorical decisions. This is why writers cannot rely on a single set of style prescriptions for all occasions. Different styles have different rhetorical implications and effects. *(See the short take on Style Guides.)*

Two Key Terms

Here are two key terms from classical rhetoric that you will encounter in this book:

Heuristic: Although this word has other meanings in disciplines such as engineering, in classical rhetoric a heuristic was an aid to discovery. It comes from the Greek word *heuriskein*, which means "to find out" or "discover." *Heuriskein* is the Greek equivalent of the Latin word, *invenire*, which means "to find" or "to come upon" (Crowley 20). This book's analytical methods, such as the ones you will find in the two Toolkits (Chapters 2 and 4), are heuristics.

Commonplace: Rhetorical training provided rhetors—those who were skilled at public speaking—with pre-determined arguments called places that might fit any number of situations. The Greek word for "place"—*topoi*—gives us our word topic. Our word "commonplace" is descended from the way classical rhetoric treats commonplaces: as commonly held beliefs.

Here is a 20th-century definition of the term commonplace from an essay by David Bartholomae called "Inventing the University." Bartholomae argues that college writing—especially writing in the academic disciplines—requires students to learn not just forms and styles, but disciplinary commonplaces, the commonly held ways of thinking in the various academic communities that make up the university:

A 'commonplace,' then, is a culturally or institutionally authorized concept or statement that carries with it its own necessary elaboration. We all use commonplaces to orient ourselves in the world; they provide a point of reference and a set of 'prearticulated' explanations that are readily available to organize and interpret experience" (24).

This is a useful way of understanding what you are being asked to acquire in a college or graduate school education, the commonly held concepts that each discipline accepts as givens.

A rhetorical orientation is especially prominent in the following places in *Writing Analytically*:

- short take on Writing in the Disciplines in this chapter, which explains why you should think about disciplinary formats rhetorically
- Chapter 3, where analysis is defined rhetorically
- Chapters 15 and 16, where paper organization and types of introductory and concluding paragraphs are explained rhetorically
- Chapters 17 and 18, where word choice and sentence structure are treated rhetorically

WRITING ABOUT READING: BEYOND "BANKING"

Both the amount of reading and what you are expected to do with it will undergo significant upgrades in college. It is fairly common for those new to college writing to expect to write about reading in one of three ways: by handing it back on tests, by agreeing or disagreeing with it, or by registering a more elemental personal response, which is a common student misunderstanding triggered by the so-called "reaction paper." Much of the writing about reading you will be asked to do in college will move you beyond these three responses.

The Banking Model of Education—and Beyond

You will of course be responsible for retaining what you have read and "handing it back" on examinations. This is known as the **banking** model of education. The learner (in the banking model) is mostly a passive conduit taking things in and spitting them back out. Educational theorist Paolo Freire mounted a famous attack on this model, arguing that an education consisting entirely of "banking"—information in/information out—does not teach thinking. Being able to recite the ideas of others does not automatically render a person capable of thinking about these ideas or producing them.

Banking is not limited to quizzes and exams. It also occurs when teachers, through the best of intentions, do too much of the thinking for you. When there is discussion of the reading in class, for example, it often moves from a teacher's questions. If you write about the reading, this often takes place after the teacher has presented his or her explanations in lectures, maybe even with PowerPoints that foreground the teacher's selection of important points. In these ways, you are "protected" from the task of treating the reading as raw material, so to speak.

At some point, however, you have to figure out how to "process" complex course information for yourself. It is hard to learn to do a cartwheel solely by watching someone else do one. And the best way to learn is to write about the reading, not after the teacher has banked it for you but before.

Why write about reading? It will teach you how to do the things with readings that your teachers know how to do—how to find the questions rather than just the answers, how to make connections between one reading and another, how to bring together key passages from readings and put these into conversation with each other, and how to apply an idea or methodology in a reading to understanding something else.

Virtually all of the methods and procedures in this book can help you to write analytically about reading. See especially:

- Chapters 2 and 4, the two Toolkits of Analytical Methods, offer heuristics that are essential for analyzing reading
- Chapter 5, Writing About Reading: More Moves to Make with Written Texts, shows you how to use a reading as a lens
- Chapter 13, Using Sources Analytically: The Conversation Model, shows you how to put readings into conversation with each other and how to find your own voice in the conversation
- Chapter 7, Making Common Topics More Analytical, helps you with traditional assignments that involve writing about reading such as summary, comparison/ contrast, and the so-called "reaction" paper

FREEWRITING: HOW AND WHY TO DO IT

Freewriting is a method of arriving at ideas by writing continuously about a subject for a limited period of time without pausing to edit or revise. The rationale behind this activity can be understood through a well-known remark by the novelist E.M. Forster (in regard to the "tyranny" of prearranging everything): "How do I know what I think until I see what I say?" Freewriting gives you the chance to see what you'll say.

Author Anne Lamott writes eloquently (in *Bird by Bird*) about the censors we all hear as nasty voices in our heads that keep us from writing. These are the internalized voices of past critics whose comments have become magnified to suggest that we will never get it right. Freewriting allows us to tune out these voices long enough to discover what we might think.

There aren't many rules to freewriting—just that you have to keep your pen (or fingers on the keyboard) moving. Don't reread as you go. Don't pause to correct things. Don't cross things out. Don't quit when you think you have run out of things to say. Just keep writing.

There are various forms of freewriting. For academic and other analytical projects, we recommend **passage-based focused freewriting**. In passage-based focused freewriting (*see Chapters 4 and 5*), class members embark from and attempt to stay grounded in some short passage or single sentence (usually their choice) from the day's reading. In this way, they learn to choose and develop starting points for discussion, rather than rely on a teacher's questions.

The practice of freewriting has long been advocated by writer, teacher, and writing theorist Peter Elbow who argues that poor writing occurs when writers try to draft and edit at the same time. There are sound psychological and cognitive reasons for trying not to get too bogged down in "fixing" things in the early drafting stages. First, it is hard to keep your larger purpose in sight if you constantly worry about making mistakes or being wrong. You need to keep moving, even when you know parts of what you have written are not yet good enough. Second, it is hard to discover where to go next if you keep looking back. Some people keep reading what they've just written, hoping to find the next move. But when you instead try to write fast—to forge ahead without looking back—you are more likely to discover a new leaping-off point, some connection to another and possibly better idea. Freewriting lets this process happen. Give it the chance to surprise you.

Here are some of the things that regular freewriting accomplishes:

- develops fluency
- deters writer's block
- encourages experimentation
- requires you to find your own starting points for writing and run with them
- provides a nurturing alternative to rigidly format-driven writing
- allows you to observe your characteristic ways of moving as a thinker, your habits of mind

Some Useful Techniques for Freewriting

Here are some analytical methods from later in the book that work especially well to generate freewrites:

- Paraphrase × 3, Notice and Focus, and So What? from Chapter 2
- Making the Implicit Explicit from Chapter 3
- Uncovering Assumptions, Reformulating Binaries, Seems to Be About X, and Difference within Similarity from Chapter 4
- 10 on 1 in Chapter 10

PROCESS AND PRODUCT: SOME WAYS OF THINKING ABOUT THE WRITING PROCESS

Process and **product** are the usual terms for thinking about the relation between exploratory writing (such as freewriting) and the more finished kinds of assignments to which it may lead. The **process** includes everything you needed to do in order to get to the finished draft, which is known as the **product**. In classical rhetoric, the terms are **invention** and **arrangement** *(See the short take on*

Rhetoric). In the invention stage, you follow prescribed methods for coming up with things to say, material which can then be arranged into the most effective form (presentation).

Writing is a recursive, not a linear process. Generation and presentation require different kinds of writing and thinking activities, though in practice these phases overlap. Writers do not simply finish a rough draft, then revise it, and then edit it in the tidy three-stage process commonly taught in school. They might, for example, make several different starts at the same writing task, then revise it, then learn from these revisions that they need to do more drafting, and so on.

Your goal is to generate enough material to locate your best options. Even in disciplines that do not encourage forms of exploratory writing (such as psychology and the natural sciences), because they concentrate instead on the forms of finished products, you can make use of your own informal writing, dwelling longer in the process, so as to learn how to arrive at more thoughtful products.

To a significant extent, the final draft re-creates for the reader the writer's experience of arriving at his or her key ideas. Good analytical writing, at whatever stage, has an exploratory feel. It shares its discovery process with the reader. This is true, by the way, even in such tightly predetermined forms as that of the scientific lab report. The report format actually requires the writer to recreate the steps that took him or her to conclusions.

Tips for Managing the Writing Process

Start anywhere that gets you going. The writing process is nonlinear. Very few writers simply begin at the beginning and write straight through to the end. Sometimes your best bet is to write individual paragraphs and then arrange them later.

Allow yourself to write a crummy first draft if that is how you work best. Get something on paper before worrying about what others might think of it. A writer's assumptions about his or her audience can help to generate writing but can also create writer's block. When you get stuck or frustrated, don't worry—just keep writing.

If you draft on a computer, try not to hit delete prematurely. Instead, rename each of your drafts. Hang on to false starts; they may help you later.

Postpone anxiety about grammar and spelling and style. You can revise and correct your draft once you have given yourself the opportunity to discover what you want to say.

Know that what works for one writer might not work for another. There is no one right way to conduct the writing process. Some writers need to outline; other writers need to write first and then might use outlining later to figure out what is going on in their drafts. Some writers absolutely must write an introduction before they can move forward. Others need to jump in elsewhere and write the introduction last. Experiment! Devote some time to finding out what works for you.

Put your unconscious on the job. You can't always write through an act of will. Sometimes, when the words aren't coming, it helps to go do something else—take a shower, go for a walk. Often you will find that a part of your brain has remained on the job. We call this resource in the writing process **the back-burner**—the place where things keep quietly stewing while you are thinking about something else. If you are really stuck, take some notes right before bedtime and write as soon as you wake in the morning.

HOW TO THINK ABOUT GRAMMAR AND STYLE (BEYOND ERROR-CATCHING)

A mantra of the book is that a sentence is the shape that thought takes. The goal of the book's treatment of grammar and style is to get you to refocus your attention from anxiety about error-detection to particular interest in the structures of sentences.

Many people are unduly anxious about grammar—so much so that they have trouble writing. Error-avoidance is important in the final stages of drafting, but it is also a very limited and limiting perspective on sentences. Instead, look at sentences in terms of logic and rhetoric. Ask yourself, "So what that the sentence is constructed in the way that it is? How does this shape relate to the way of thinking that the sentence contains?"

You need at least a minimal amount of grammatical terminology for understanding the shapes of sentences. Try to acquire this vocabulary as early in a writing course as you can. You need to be able to recognize and construct the following: **dependent clause, independent clause, simple sentence, compound sentence, complex sentence, compound-complex sentence, cumulative sentence, periodic sentence.** (*See Chapter 18.*)

Because punctuation makes sentence shapes visible, you should also know the basics of punctuation. In particular, learn the primary rules governing commas. (No, the fact that you pause is not a reliable indicator.) *See the short guide to punctuation early in Chapter 19.*

Once you orient yourself toward thinking about the shapes of sentences, you will be able to use sentences that clarify for readers the way you organize your ideas and place emphasis. You will maximize your choices and increase your persuasive power. When analyzing the sentences of others, this knowledge will give you insight into the writer's thinking: how the ideas are ranked and connected.

As for error-catching, you can revise and correct your draft once you've given yourself the opportunity to discover what you want to say. And, as we have been suggesting here, instead of dwelling on errors, try to cultivate an interest in the shapes of good sentences. *See "go-to" sentence in Chapter 2,* which will tell you how to use the grammar and style unit to start recognizing the connections between the characteristic shapes of a writer's sentences and the way he or she thinks.

A QUICK WORD ON STYLE GUIDES

Style guides are fine, provided they don't acquire the status of law, which is to say that you shouldn't take them as offering the last word. Some style guides have acquired almost cult status—Strunk and White's *Elements of Style*, for example. Among E.B.

White's letters, now collected at Cornell University, are many in which White is clearly responding with discomfort to letter writers appealing to him as the ultimate authority on style.

In one letter, he writes, "There are no rules of writing (who could possibly invent them?); there are only guidelines, and the guidelines can, and should be, chucked out the window whenever they get in your way or in your hair. I have never paid the slightest attention to 'The Elements of Style' when I was busy writing. [...] If the book inhibits you or constrains you, you should build a bonfire and throw the book into the flames" (qtd. in "The Phenomenon of the Little Book: Letters to E.B. White on *The Elements of Style*," an unpublished talk by Katherine K. Gottschalk, given at the 2010 Conference on College Composition and Communication, pp. 5–6).

In an entertaining article by Catherine Prendergast, we also learn that *Elements of Style* was found among other do-it-yourself manuals on the bookshelf of Theodore Kaczynski, the Unabomber ("The Fighting Style: Reading the Unabomber's Strunk and White," *College English*, Volume 72, Number 1, September 2009).

The problem with subscribing to one set of style "rules" is that this practice ignores rhetoric and context. There simply is no one set of rules that is appropriate for all occasions. In his essay, "Style and Good Style," philosophy professor Monroe Beardsley takes this point one step further. He writes: "Many charming, clever, and memorable things have been said about style—most of which turn out to be highly misleading when subjected to analysis"(4). Changes in style, says Beardsley, always produce changes in meaning: "If the teacher advises a change of words, or of word order, he is recommending a different meaning" (13).

Here is one of the examples Beardsley offers in his measured attack on the rules in Strunk and White's *Elements of Style*. Strunk and White, offering the common stylistic advice that writers should seek to replace forms of "to be" with active verbs, suggest that the sentence "There were a great number of dead leaves lying on the ground" should be replaced with "Dead leaves covered the ground." Of this suggested change, Beardsley observes, "But isn't that a difference in meaning? For one thing, there are more leaves in the second sentence. The second one says that the ground was covered; the first one only speaks of a great number. Stylistic advice is a rather odd sort of thing if it consists in telling students to pile up the leaves in their descriptions" (6).

Similarly, the usual advice that writers should avoid the "not-un" formation produces not just a change in style but a change in meaning. Saying "I am not unhappy" is not the same thing as saying "I am happy"—which is the kind of bolder, more decisive statement that *Elements of Style* recommends.

So, style guides are useful provided you recognize that style guidelines always carry with them an unstated preference for a certain kind of approach to the world—a certain kind of speaking persona, which may or may not be suited to what you wish to say. Richard Lanham's very useful "paramedic method," which we discuss in Chapter 18, puts a lot of emphasis on active verbs, the active voice, and on reducing "Latinate" diction. This emphasis produces a vigorous style but one that is not consistent, for example, with the stylistic conventions of science writing.

HOW TO THINK ABOUT WRITING IN THE DISCIPLINES

There will be days when you feel that each classroom you walk into is asking you to learn a different language. To some extent you're right. To navigate your way across the curriculum successfully, you will need to recognize that matters of form are also matters of epistemology, which is to say that they are indicative of each discipline's ways of knowing. Embedded in a discipline's ways of writing—its key terms and stylistic conventions—are its primary assumptions about thinking, how it should be done and toward what end.

No single book or course can equip you with all that you will need to write like a scientist or a psychologist or an art historian. What this book can do is teach you how to think about discipline-specific writing practices and how to analyze them for their logic and rhetoric. Once you acquire these skills, you will find it easier to adapt to the different kinds of writing you will encounter in college. You will also learn to see the common ways of thinking that underlie stylistic differences. For now, let's focus briefly on some interesting differences.

Here are three brief examples of significant stylistic differences. Think about what makes each difference more than simply superficial. Contemplate what these rules reveal about the particular discipline's values. And how do these rules implicitly define the relationship of the writer to his or her subject matter and assumed audience?

A. In psychology and some other social and natural sciences, writers paraphrase and cite other writers but do not include the language being paraphrased. In English, religion, and other disciplines in the humanities, writers also paraphrase, but they quote the language being paraphrased.

B. It is still largely true that in the sciences, particularly the natural sciences, writers use the passive rather than the active voice. So, the scientist would write: "The air was pumped out of the chamber" (passive voice, which leaves out the person performing the action, leading with the action instead) rather than "We pumped the air out of the chamber" (active voice, which includes the person performing the action).

C. In the sciences, writers typically do not criticize other scientists' work, although in the opening section of lab reports they survey other relevant studies and use these to explain the need for their current research. By contrast, writers in the humanities and some social sciences commonly build a piece of writing and research upon the discovery of a problem—that will be stated explicitly—in someone else's writing and research.

At the end of the chapter, we suggest that you interview a professor (perhaps from your major) to collect brief examples of what he or she considers good writing in his or her academic discipline. Some disciplines accept a wider variety of suitable forms and styles than others. There are lots of acceptable ways to write a history, English, or economics paper but only one way to write an acceptable lab report in biology. Your best bet is to study examples of what different disciplines think of as good writing, especially in disciplines where there is no rulebook for matters of form.

For the book's specific advice on writing in the disciplines plus discussion of common denominators, see the following:

- Chapters 15 and 16, the opening chapters of Unit III, entitled Matters of Form: The Shapes That Thought Takes
- Voices from Across the Curriculum (interspersed throughout the text), written by professors in various disciplines who offer their perspective on such matters as introductions and determining what counts as evidence

ACADEMIC VS. NONACADEMIC WRITING: HOW DIFFERENT ARE THEY?

We conclude this chapter with some final reflections on what it means to call writing "academic." Not all writing that has proved central to academic disciplines—such as works by philosophers, novelists, or world leaders—was written by academic writers. And not all writing by academics is meant only for other academics. This is especially the case when academics are engaged in problem solving outside the university—in public policy or government, for example—or when they write for popular audiences. Scientists, such as Steven Pinker and Simon Baron-Cohen, for example, publish in both scientific journals and in more popular publications.

Nonetheless, academic writers are typically cautious about trying to translate their work into forms suitable for consumption by nonacademics. This is not just in-group behavior but a product of the nature of academic research and writing.

Scientists, for example, typically focus on very small, narrowly defined questions, such as the function of a single receptor in the brain or a single kind of cellular reaction. Also, much scientific research goes on for a long time. Public radio recently interviewed a scientist who is involved in a 40-year-long study of a particular small mammal, looking for changes in size and breeding habits in response to such factors as global warming. In science in particular and in academic fields more generally, the results don't come quickly or easily and are often necessarily uncertain.

Translating these carefully contextualized, narrowly focused, and often long-term studies in a way that would make them interesting and available to a general audience is difficult. This is so not only because nonscientists have trouble with scientific language but because nonacademic readers often distort or overextend the science writing they take in.

The single biggest difference between academic and nonacademic writing is the size of the claims. General audiences often expect bigger and more definitive claims than carefully qualified academic writing is willing to make. The desire for overly authoritative claims and immediate answers that characterizes mainstream media produces an appropriate wariness among scientists and other academics.

In any case, learning to write in one or more of the academic disciplines will change the way you think. The analytical habits of mind you will have acquired inside of your chosen disciplines will grant you confidence and independence as a learner. They will cause you to see more in whatever you read, to arrive at more carefully limited claims about it, and to have more patience with yourself and others as thinkers.

Assignments

1. **Write a Literacy Narrative.** Write a short autobiographical piece that presents a chapter in your history as a writer. Describe what you now take to be an especially formative experience in how you came to be the writer you are today. What practices and ideas has this experience or set of related experiences led to? You might begin by freewriting a draft for 15 minutes in class. This narrative offers a good way to begin exploring your ways of thinking about writing and about yourself as a writer. The early lessons we take in about writing—sometimes accidentally—affect many of us more than we recognize.

2. **Collect Samples of Good Writing.** Begin collecting examples of good writing in a discipline of your choice from a professor of your choice. You might, for example, begin a collection of introductory and concluding paragraphs because these are critical sites in all writing and are especially useful in understanding the ways different disciplines frame and present information.

3. **Experiment with the Five-Finger Exercise.** The primary shift in thinking that the book promotes is from the general and global to the particular and local—to a focus on words and sentences and details, rather than on the large (general) picture. In order to introduce this re-orientation, we offer a writing activity taken from a famous fiction writer, Ernest Hemingway. He called it his "five-finger exercise," probably by analogy with the exercises that piano players do in order to make certain ways of moving their fingers more automatic.

   Read the passage below, wherein Hemingway (calling himself "Your Correspondent") offers advice to a young writer (referred to as "Mice") who has come to him for advice. Then start practicing Hemingway's recommended exercise of *tracing impressions back to the details that caused them.*

   Everything we have to say in the book relates in one way or another to Hemingway's advice, which is relevant to writing of all kinds, not just fiction. To become more aware—which is key to becoming a better writer—we have to train ourselves to notice more: both our impressions of things and how these are formed. Becoming more aware of our own responses is step one. Step two is tracing these impressions back to the particular details of experience that caused them.

   Mice: How can a writer train himself?

   Your Correspondent: Watch what happens today. If we get into a fish see exactly what it is that everyone does. If you get a kick out of it while he is jumping, remember back until you see exactly what the action was that gave you the emotion. Whether it was the rising of the line from the water and the way it tightened like a fiddle string until drops started from it, or the way he smashed and threw water when he jumped. Remember what the noises were and what was said. Find what gave you the emotion; what the action was that gave you the excitement. Then write it down, making it clear so the reader will see it too and have the same feeling you had. That's a five finger exercise.

Mice: All right. [....]

Your Correspondent: Listen now. When people talk, listen completely. Don't be thinking what you're going to say. Most people never listen. Nor do they observe. You should be able to go into a room and when you come out know everything that you saw there and not only that. If that room gave you any feeling, you should know exactly what it was that gave you that feeling. Try that for practice. When you're in town stand outside the theater and see how the people differ in the way they get out of taxis and motor cars. There are a thousand ways to practice. And always think of other people. (Ernest Hemingway, "Monologue to the Maestro: A High Seas Letter," *Esquire*: October 1935 rpt. in *ByLine*)

Start practicing by doing the exercise aloud with others. Write down the three details you think contributed most to your response to a particular setting, such as a classroom or other place on campus. Then share these with the class or in a small group. Next, use the exercise to produce a short piece of descriptive writing about some location of your choice or that the class might visit as a group. Take time to just observe the scene, register your responses to it and write down details. Then recast your writing into a descriptive paragraph. Keep revising your description until you have a rendering of your "data"—the details—that will cause your readers to think and feel about the scene as you do. Try to limit the number of evaluative adjectives you use—words like *ugly, beautiful, depressing*, and so on. Let the details do most of the work.

Chapter 2

Toolkit of Analytical Methods I: Seeing Better, Seeing More

"Reserving judgments is a matter of infinite hope." Fitzgerald, *The Great Gatsby*

"See better, Lear." Shakespeare, *King Lear*

FOCUS ON THE DETAILS

This chapter offers a set of tools for training your ways of seeing and making sense of things—the world, images, and especially written texts. Rhetoricians call these tools *heuristics*, from the Greek word for discovery. Heuristic has the same root as Eureka— "I've found it!" All of the heuristics in this chapter seek to help you to discover things to say about whatever you are studying. The final third of the chapter surveys the counterproductive habits of mind that these activities seek to replace.

NOTICING

- Noticing significant detail is a skill that can be improved through practice.
- The ability to notice is blocked by common habits of mind: judging and generalizing and leaping prematurely to conclusions.
- One solution: experiment with eliminating the words *like, dislike, agree,* and *disagree* from your vocabulary, at least for a while.
- Another solution: slow down. Dwell longer in the open-ended, exploratory, information-gathering stage.

A. The Heuristics

There are two broad categories of heuristics in this chapter—observation strategies and interpretive prompts. Both seek to retrain the way you focus your attention from the global (general) to the local. Here is a list of the chapter's heuristics, each with a very brief summary of what it involves. We will then go on to explain each in more detail.

HEURISTICS

1. Notice and Focus + Ranking
   (select a few details as most important: What do you find
   most "Interesting" or "Strange"?)

2. The Method: Looking for Patterns of Repetition and Contrast
   (organize details into groupings based on similarity or opposition)

3. Asking So What?
   (make the leap from observing X to querying what X means)

4. Paraphrase × (times) 3
   (recast the key words in new language to question what they mean)

5. Identifying a "Go To" Sentence
   (locate the sentence shape a writer habitually uses; then ponder
   how that shape reveals the writer's habitual ways of seeing)

Note: these heuristics are not formulae for organizing papers. They are "thinking moves" designed to produce higher quality material that will eventually go into an essay or argument or report. The heuristics lend themselves to group work, to collaborative thinking, as well as individual work. The best way to get good at these observation and thinking skills is to try them out repeatedly with other writers. In Unit II, you'll be invited to put them to work in writing papers and other kinds of assignments.

1. NOTICE AND FOCUS + RANKING

RULES OF NOTICE & HABITS OF MIND:
SLOW DOWN

Not "What do you think?" &
Not "What do you like or dislike?"

> but

> "What do you notice?"

A few prompts:

> What do you find most INTERESTING?
> What do you find most STRANGE?
> What do you find most REVEALING?

The activity called Notice and Focus guides you to dwell longer with the data before feeling compelled to decide what the data mean. Repeatedly returning to the question, "What do you notice?" is one of the best ways to counteract the tendency to generalize too rapidly. "What do you notice?" redirects attention to the subject matter itself and delays the pressure to come up with answers.

Start by noticing as much as you can about whatever it is you are studying. Next, narrow your scope to a representative portion of your evidence, and then dwell with the data. Record what you see. Don't move to generalization, or worse, to judgment.

What this procedure will begin to demonstrate is how useful description is as a tool for arriving at ideas. If you stay at the description stage longer, deliberately delaying leaps to conclusions, you are more likely to arrive at better ideas. Training yourself to notice will improve your memory and your ability to think.

Step 1: Cast a wide net by continuing to **list details** you notice. Go longer than you normally would before stopping—often the tenth or eleventh detail is the one that will eventually lead to your best idea.

Step 2: Focus inside what you've noticed. **Rank** the various features of your subject you have noticed. Answer the question "What details (specific features of the subject matter) are most interesting (or significant or revealing or strange)?" The purpose of relying on *interesting* or one of the other suggested words is that these will help to deactivate the like/dislike switch of the judgment reflex and replace it with a more analytical perspective.

Step 3: Say why three things you selected struck you as the most interesting (or revealing or significant or strange). Saying why will trigger interpretive leaps to the possible meaning of whatever you find most interesting in your observations.

Discussion Let's pause a moment to ponder the key words in step 2: interesting, revealing, strange. What does it mean to find something *interesting*? Often, we are interested by things that have captured our attention without our clearly knowing why. Interest and curiosity are near cousins. To say that something is interesting is not the end but the beginning of analysis: then you figure out what is interesting about this feature of your subject and why.

The word *strange* is a useful prompt because it gives us permission to notice oddities and things that initially seem not to fit. Strange, in this context, is not a judgmental term but one denoting features of a subject or situation that aren't readily explainable. Where you locate something strange, you have isolated something to interpret—to figure out what makes it strange and why.

Along similar lines, the words *revealing* and *significant* work by requiring you to make choices that can lead to interpretive leaps. If something strikes you as revealing or significant, even if you're not yet sure why, you will eventually begin producing some explanation. What is revealed, and why is it revealing?

Troubleshooting Notice and Focus

In the Noticing phase of Notice and Focus, you will be tempted to begin having ideas and making claims about your subject. Resist this temptation. Many of those first stabs at ideas will be overly general, fairly obvious, and they will block further noticing.

A Quick Note on 10 on 1

In later chapters (4 & 10), you will encounter a key heuristic that is the cousin of Notice and Focus. It is called "10 on 1"—based on the notion that it is productive to say more about less, to make ten points or observations about a single example rather than making the same overly general or obvious point about ten related examples. Like Notice and Focus, 10 on 1 depends on extended observation but it reduces scope to a single representative piece of evidence.

Try This 2.1: Doing Notice and Focus with a Room

Practice this activity as a class or in small groups with the room you're in. List a number of details about it, then rank the three most important ones. Use as a focusing question any of the four words suggested above—*interesting, significant, revealing,* or *strange.* Or come up with your own focus for the ranking, such as the three aspects of the room that seem most to affect the way you feel and behave in the space. Then you might go home and repeat the exercise alone in the room of your choice. Start out not with "what do I think?" but with "what do I notice?" And remember to keep the process going longer than might feel comfortable: "what else do I notice?"

Try This 2.2: Notice and Focus Fieldwork

Try this exercise with a range of subjects: an editorial, the front page of a news-paper, a website, a key paragraph from something you are reading, the style of a favorite writer, conversations overheard around campus, looking at people's shoes, political speeches, a photograph, a cartoon, and so forth. (The speech bank at americanrhetoric.com is an excellent source.) Remember to include all three steps: notice, rank, and say why.

---

2. THE METHOD: WORK WITH PATTERNS OF REPETITION AND CONTRAST

THE METHOD

What repeats?

What goes with what? (strands)

What is opposed to what? (binaries)

     (for all of these questions) ---> *SO WHAT?*

What doesn't fit? (anomalies) So what?

"The Method" is our shorthand for a systematic procedure for analyzing evidence by looking for patterns of repetition and contrast. It offers a way to get the big picture without overgeneralizing—it is insistently empirical. It also has an uncanny ability to help you figure out what is most important in anything you read.

Using The Method induces you to get physical with the data—literally, for you will find yourself circling, underlining, and listing. Although you will thus descend from the heights of abstraction to the realm of concrete detail, the point of tallying repetitions and strands and binaries and then selecting the most important and interesting ones is to trigger ideas. The discipline required to notice patterns in the language will produce more specific, more carefully grounded conclusions than you otherwise might have made.

Like Notice and Focus, The Method orients you toward significant detail; but whereas Notice and Focus is a deliberately unstructured activity, The Method applies a matrix or grid of observational moves to a subject.

Step 1: List exact **repetitions** and the number of each (words, details). For example, if forms of the word *seems* repeat three times, write "seems × 3." With images, the repeated appearance of high foreheads would constitute an exact repetition.

Concentrate on substantive (meaning-carrying) words. Only in rare cases will words like "and" or "the" merit attention as a significant repetition. At the most literal level, whatever repeats is what the thing is about.

Step 2: List repetitions of the same or similar kind of detail or word—which we call **strands** (for example, *polite, courteous, decorous*). Be able to explain the strand's connecting logic with a label: manners.

Step 3: List details or words that form or suggest **binary oppositions**—pairs of words or details that are opposites—and select from these the most important ones, which function as **organizing contrasts** (for example, *open/closed, ugly/beautiful, global/local*). Binaries help you locate what is at stake in the subject—the tensions and issues it is trying to resolve.

Step 4: Choose ONE repetition or strand or binary as most important or interesting and explain in one healthy paragraph why you think it's important. (This ranking, as in Notice and Focus, prompts an interpretive leap.)

Step 5: Locate **anomalies:** exceptions to the pattern, things that seem not to fit. Anomalies become evident only after you have discerned a pattern, so it is best to locate repetitions, strands, and organizing contrasts—things that fit together in some way—before looking for things that seem not to fit. Once you see an anomaly, you will often find that it is part of a strand you had not detected (and perhaps one side of a previously unseen binary).

Discussion The method of looking for patterns works through a series of steps. Hold yourself initially to doing the steps one at a time and in order. Later, you will be able to record your answers under each of the three steps simultaneously. Although the steps of The Method are discrete and modular, they are also consecutive. They proceed by a kind of narrative logic. Each step leads logically to the next, and then to various kinds of regrouping, which is actually rethinking.

Tip: Expect ideas to suggest themselves to you as you move through the steps of The Method. Strands often begin to suggest other strands that are in opposition to them. Words you first took to be parts of one strand may migrate to different strands. This process of noticing and then relocating words and details into different patterns is one aspect of doing The Method that can push your analysis to interpretation.

The Method can be applied to virtually anything you wish to analyze—an essay, a political campaign, a work of visual or verbal art, a dense passage from some secondary source you feel is important but can't quite figure out, and—last but not least—your own writing.

It may be helpful to think of this method of analysis as a form of mental doodling. Rather than worrying about what you are going to say, or about whether or not you understand, you instead get out a pencil and start tallying up what you see. Engaged in this process, you'll soon find yourself gaining entry to the logic of your subject matter. To some extent, doing The Method is archaeological. It digs into the language or the material details of whatever you are analyzing in order to unearth its thinking. This is most evident in the discovery of organizing contrasts.

Binary oppositions often indicate places where there is struggle among various points of view. And there is usually no single "right" answer about which of a number of binaries is *the* primary organizing contrast. One of the best ways to develop your analyses is to try on different possible oppositions as the primary one. A related technique is to repeatedly recast the key terms in the binaries. *(For more on this technique, see "reformulating binaries" in Chapter 4: Toolkit of Analytical Methods II.)*

Two Examples of The Method Generating Ideas

Try noticing repetitions and contrasts in your own writing. This will help you to recognize and develop your ideas. In the paragraph below, you can see how the writer's noticing strands and binaries directs his thinking.

> The most striking aspect of the spots is how different they are from typical fashion advertising. If you look at men's fashion magazines, for example, at the advertisements for the suits of Ralph Lauren or Valentino or Hugo Boss, they almost always consist of a beautiful man, with something interesting done to his hair, wearing a gorgeous outfit. At the most, the man may be gesturing discreetly, or smiling in the demure way that a man like that might smile after, say, telling the supermodel at the next table no thanks he has to catch an early-morning flight to Milan. But that's all. The beautiful face and the clothes tell the whole story. The Dockers ads, though, are almost exactly the opposite. There's no face. The camera is jumping around so much that it's tough to concentrate on the clothes. And instead of stark simplicity, the fashion image is overlaid with a constant, confusing patter. It's almost as if the Dockers ads weren't primarily concerned with clothes at all—and in fact that's exactly what Levi's intended. What the company had discovered,

in its research, was that baby-boomer men felt that the chief thing missing from their lives was male friendship. Caught between the demands of the families that many of them had started in the eighties and career considerations that had grown more onerous, they felt they had lost touch with other men. The purpose of the ads—the chatter, the lounging around, the quick cuts—was simply to conjure up a place where men could put on one-hundred-percent-cotton khakis and reconnect with one another. In the original advertising brief, that imaginary place was dubbed Dockers World.

—Malcolm Gladwell, "Listening to Khakis"

First, Gladwell notes the differences in two kinds of fashion ads aimed at men. There are the high fashion ads and the Dockers ads. In the first of these, the word "beautiful" repeats twice as part of a strand (including "gorgeous," "interesting," "supermodel," "demure"). The writer then poses traits of the Dockers ads as an opposing strand. Instead of beautiful face there is no face, instead of "gorgeous outfit," "it's tough to concentrate on the clothes." These oppositions cause the writer to make his interpretive leap, that the Dockers ads "weren't primarily concerned with clothes at all" and that this was intentional.

In the student essay below, Lesley Stephen develops a key contrast between two thinkers, Sigmund Freud and Michel Foucault, by noticing the different meanings that each attaches to some of the same key words. The Method helps to locate the key terms and to define them by seeing what other words they suggest (strands).

Freud defines civilization as serving two main purposes. The first is to protect men against nature, and the second is to adjust their mutual relations. Freud seems to offer returning to nature as a possible solution for men's sexual freedom. I think Freud might believe that returning to nature by rejecting civilization could bring about sexual freedom, but that sexual freedom does not necessarily equal happiness.

Foucault completely defies Freud's idea that sexuality is natural and that repression exists as anti-sexuality. He believes that everything is created from discourse; nothing is natural. And because nothing is natural, nothing is repressed. There is no such thing as a natural desire; if the desire exists, it is because it is already part of the discourse.

By focusing on repetitions of the words "nature" and "natural" and then seeing what goes with what, the writer creates a succinct and revealing comparison.

Doing The Method on a Poem

Here is an example of how one might do The Method on a piece of text—in this case, a student poem. We use a poem because it is compact and so allows us to illustrate efficiently how The Method works. See also the use of The Method on a visual image in Chapter 6, Making Interpretations Plausible.

Brooklyn Heights, 4:00 A.M.
Dana Ferrelli

sipping a warm forty oz.

Coors Light on a stoop in

Brooklyn Heights. I look

across the street, in the open window;

Blonde bobbing heads, the

smack of a jump rope, laughter

of my friends breaking

beer bottles. Putting out their

burning filters on the #5 of

a hopscotch court.

We reminisce of days when we were

Fat, pimple faced—

look how far we've come. But tomorrow

a little blonde girl will

pick up a Marlboro Light filter, just to play.

And I'll buy another forty, because

that's how I play now.

Reminiscing about how far I've come

Doing the Method on a Poem: Our Analysis

1. *Words that repeat exactly*: forty × 2, blonde × 2, how far we've (I've) come × 2, light × 2, reminisce, reminiscing × 2, filter, filters × 2, Brooklyn Heights × 2

2. *Strands*: jump rope, laughter, play, hopscotch (connecting logic: childhood games representing the carefree worldview of childhood) Coors Light, Marlboro Light filters, beer bottles (connecting logic: drugs, adult "games," escapism?)

   Smack, burning, breaking (violent actions and powerful emotion: burning)

3. *Binary oppositions*: how far we've come/how far I've come (a move from plural to singular, from a sense of group identity to isolation, from group values to a more individual consideration)

   Blonde bobbing heads/little blonde girl

   Burning/putting out

Coors Light, Marlboro Lights/jump rope, hopscotch

How far I've come (two meanings of *far?*, one positive, one not)

Heights/stoop

Present/past

4. *Ranked repetitions, strands and binaries plus paragraph explaining the choice of one of these as central to understanding.*

Most important repetitions: forty, how far we've/I've come

Most important strands: jump rope, laughter, play, hopscotch, Coors Light, Marlboro Light filters, beer bottles

Most important binaries: jump rope, laugher, play, hopscotch versus Coors Light, Marlboro Light filters, beer bottles; burning/putting out

Analysis (Healthy Paragraphs) The repetition of *forty* (forty ounce beer) is interesting. It signals a certain weariness—perhaps with a kind of pun on forty to suggest middle age and thus the speaker's concern about moving toward being older in a way that seems stale and flat. The beer, after all, is warm—which is not the best state for a beer to be in, once opened, if it is to retain its taste and character. Forty ounces of beer might also suggest excess—"supersizing."

The most important (or at least most interesting) binary opposition is *burning versus putting out.* This binary seems to be part of a more intense strand in the poem, one that runs counter to the weary prospect of moving on toward a perhaps lonely ("how far *I've* come") middle-aged feeling. Burning goes with breaking and the smack of the jump rope, and even putting out (a strand), if we visualize putting out not just as fire extinguished but in terms of putting a cigarette out by pushing the burning end of it into something (the number 5 on the Hopscotch court). The poem's language has a violent and passionate edge to it, even though the violent words are not always in a violent context (for example, the smack of the jump rope).

This is a rather melancholy poem in which, perhaps, the speaker is mourning the passing, the "putting out" of the passion of youth ("burning"). In the poem's more obvious binary—the opposition of childhood games to more "adult" ones—the same melancholy plays itself out, making the poem's refrain-like repetition of "how far I've come" ring with unhappy irony. The little blonde girl is an image of the speaker's own past self (since the poem talks about reminiscing), and the speaker mourns that little girl's (her own) passing into a more uncertain and less carefree state. It is 4:00 A.M. in Brooklyn Heights—just about the end of night, the darkest point perhaps before the beginning of morning. But windows are open, suggesting possibility, so things are not all bad. The friends make noise together, break bottles together, revisit hopscotch square 5 together, and contemplate moving on.

Why Do The Method?

It does take some getting used to, working with The Method. It fragments everything; it can appear as if you are ignoring the usual cues by which you make sense of things, such as reading consecutively, from a to b to c, rather than looking for and tabulating all of the a's, all of the b's and so forth. And why read for pattern in the first place? Two answers are:

- The Method can help you to control in condensed form a wealth of information. The organizational grids will bring out the features of the subject that are most important, what the reading or image is most concerned with (which repeats), and what it is concerned or worried about (what is opposed to what).

- The Method can spur you to discover things to say about whatever you are analyzing. In the normal process of observing, and especially of reading, we are often not attending to what repeats or contrasts. We're just taking in the information—not *doing* anything with it. But when you do things with information, that promotes thinking; it makes you an active learner.

Try This 2.3: Experiment in a Group Setting with The Method—Use a Visual Image by Adrian Tomine

Often, it will seem strange at first to read or analyze in the somewhat mechanical form that The Method prescribes, so it makes sense to work collaboratively at first, in small groups or with everyone in the class, to collect the data. Appoint one group member as scribe. Keep each other on task—do each step discretely. As with Notice and Focus, prolong the observation phase and refrain from judgments and big claims, at least until you begin writing about what is important (step 4).

Try an image by Adrian Tomine—a frequent contributor to *The New Yorker* magazine and a graphic novelist. Just use Google Images for "New Yorker covers + Tomine" to obtain a range of possibilities. We suggest his August 24, 2009 cover, "Double Feature"—an image of a crowd at dusk beneath the Brooklyn Bridge. Then, for homework, repeat the exercise alone, using a second Tomine cover—we suggest the November 8, 2004 cover, "Missed Connection," featuring a man and a woman looking at each other from passing subway cars.

Try This 2.4: Apply The Method to Arts & Letters Daily

Select any article from our favorite website, Arts & Letters Daily (aldaily.com), and do The Method on it. You can actually apply The Method to anything you are reading, especially a piece you wish to understand better. You can use the front page of the newspaper, a speech from the American Rhetoric website, perhaps a series of editorials on the same subject, an essay, one or more poems by the same author (because The Method is useful for reading across texts for common denominators), and so on. You can work with as little as a few paragraphs or as much as an entire article or chapter or book. The key is to practice the procedure so that it becomes familiar: so that you will begin to look for repetitions and contrasts almost naturally.

3. ASKING "SO WHAT?"

PUSHING OBSERVATIONS TO CONCLUSIONS: ASKING SO WHAT?

(shorthand for)
What does the observation imply?
Why does this observation matter?
Where does this observation get us?
How can we begin to theorize the significance of the observation?

Asking So what? is a universal prompt for spurring the move from observation to implication and ultimately interpretation. Asking So what?—or its milder cousin, And so?—is a calling to account, a way of pressing yourself to confront that essential question, "Why does this matter?" It is thus a challenge to make meaning through a creative leap—to move beyond the patterns and emphases you've been observing in the data to tentative conclusions about what these observations suggest. In step 4 of The Method, when you select a single repetition, strand, or contrast and write about why it's important, you are essentially asking So what? and answering that question.

Step 1: describe significant evidence, paraphrasing key language and looking for interesting patterns of repetition and contrast.

Step 2: begin to query your own observations by making what is implicit explicit.

Step 3: push your observations and statements of implications to interpretive conclusions by again asking So what?

Discussion First, a note on implication—crucial to step 2, and a subject treated at length in the next chapter. For now, it is enough to know that implications are suggested meanings. We look at the evidence and draw a conclusion that is not directly stated but that follows from what we see.

For example, a recent article in *Foreign Policy* entitled "Bury the Graveyard" demonstrates that the reputation of Afghanistan as "the graveyard of empires" is a "bogus history," or myth. So what? The *implication*, unstated but palpable, is that the makers of U.S. foreign policy should seek out another version of the history of military intervention in Afghanistan—one that might put current military efforts there in a better light. When you ask So what? you are looking to make overt (direct, clear) what is at present indirect.

The tone of So what? can sound rude or at least brusque, but that directness can be liberating. Often, writers will go to great lengths to avoid stating what they take something to mean. After all, that leaves them open to attack, they fear, if they get it wrong. But asking So what? is a way of forcing yourself to take the plunge without too much hoopla. And when you are tempted to stop thinking too soon, asking So what? will press you onward.

For example, let's say you make a number of observations about the nature of e-mail communication—it's cheap, informal, often grammatically incorrect, full of abbreviations ("IMHO"), and ephemeral (impermanent). You rank these and decide that its ephemerality is most interesting. So what? Well, that's why so many people use it, you speculate, because it doesn't last. So what that its popularity follows from its ephemerality? Well, apparently we like being released from the hard-and-fast rules of formal communication; e-mail frees us. So what? Well, . . .

The repeated asking of this question causes people to push on from and pursue the implications of their first responses; it prompts people to reason in a chain, rather than settling prematurely for a single link, as the next example illustrates.

MOVING FORWARD

Observation --> So what? --> Implications

Implications --> So what? --> Conclusions

Asking So What?: An Example

The following is the opening paragraph of a talk given by a professor of Political Science at our college, Dr. Jack Gambino, on the occasion of a gallery opening featuring the work of two contemporary photographers of urban and industrial landscapes. We have located in brackets our annotations of his turns of thought, as these pivot on "strange" and "So what?" (Note: images referred to in the example are available from Google Images—type in Camilo Vergara Fern Street 1988, also Edward Burtynsky.)

If you look closely at Camilo Vergara's photo of Fern Street, Camden, 1988, you'll notice a sign on the side of a dilapidated building:

Danger: Men Working
W. Hargrove Demolition

Perhaps that warning captures the ominous atmosphere of these very different kinds of photographic documents by Camilo Vergara and Edward Burtynsky: "Danger: Men Working." Watch out—human beings are at work! But the work that is presented is not so much a building-up as it is a tearing-down—the work of demolition. *[strange: tearing down is unexpected; writer asks So what? and answers:]* Of course, demolition is often necessary in order to construct anew: old buildings are leveled for new projects, whether you are building a highway or bridge in an American city or a dam in the Chinese countryside. You might call modernity itself, as so many have, a process of creative destruction, a term used variously to describe modern art, capitalism, and technological innovation. The photographs in this exhibit, however, force us to pay attention to the "destructive" side of this modern equation. *[strange: photos emphasize destruction and not creation; writer asks So what? and answers]* What both Burtynsky and Vergara do in their respective ways is to put up a warning sign—they question whether the reworking of our natural and social environment leads to a sustainable human future. And they wonder whether the process of creative destruction may not have spun recklessly out of control, producing places that are neither habitable nor sustainable. In fact, a common element connecting the two photographic versions is the near absence of people in the landscape. *[writer points to supporting feature of evidence, which he will further theorize]* While we see the evidence of the transforming power of human production on the physical and social environment, neither Vergara's urban ruins nor Burtynsky's industrial sites actually show us "men working." *[writer continues to move by noticing strange absence of people in photographs of sites where men work]* Isolated figures peer suspiciously out back doors or pick through the rubble, but they appear out of place. *[writer asks a final So what? and arrives at a conclusion:]* It is this sense of displacement—of human beings alienated from the environments they themselves have created—that provides the most haunting aspect of the work of these two photographers.

The Gambino paragraph is a good example of how asking So what? generates forward momentum for the analysis. Notice the pattern by which the paragraph moves: the observation of something strange, about which the writer asks and answers So what? several times until arriving at a final So what?—the point at which he decides what his observations ultimately mean. We call the final So what? in this chain of thinking **"the ultimate So what?"** because it moves from implications to the writer's culminating point.

Try This 2.5: Track the "So What?" Question

The aim of this exercise is to sensitize you to the various moves a writer makes when he or she presents and analyzes information. Locate any piece of analytical prose—an article from Arts & Letters Daily online, a passage from a textbook, a paper you or a friend has written. Focus on how it proceeds more than on what it says. That is, look for places where the writer moves from presenting evidence (step 1) to formulating that evidence into patterns of connection or contrast (step 2) and then asking So what? about it (step 3). Identify these moves in the margin as we have done inside brackets in the Gambino example.

4. PARAPHRASE × (TIMES) 3

PARAPHRASE × 3: HOW TO DO IT

Locate a short key passage.

Assume you <u>don't</u> understand it completely.

Substitute other concrete language for ALL of the key words.

Repeat the paraphrasing several (3) times.

Ponder the differences in implication among the versions. Return to the original passage and interpret its meanings: what do the words imply?

Paraphrasing is one of the simplest and most overlooked ways of discovering ideas and stimulating interpretation. Once you begin paraphrasing regularly, you will swiftly understand why: paraphrasing inevitably discloses that what is being paraphrased is more complicated than it first appeared. And so it will get you to start questioning what important passages and key details mean rather than assuming you understand them.

The word *paraphrase* means to put one phrase next to ("para") another phrase. When you recast a sentence or two—finding the best synonyms you can think of for the original language, translating it into a parallel statement—you are thinking about what the original words mean. (Paraphrasing stays much closer to the actual words than summarizing.) The use of "× 3" (times 3) in our label is a reminder to paraphrase key words more than once, not settling too soon for a best synonym.

Note: You should also be aware that different academic disciplines treat paraphrase somewhat differently. In the humanities, it is essential first to quote an important passage and then to paraphrase it. In the social sciences, however, especially in psychology, you paraphrase but never quote another's language.

Step 1: Select a short passage (as little as a single sentence or even a phrase) from whatever you are studying that you think is interesting, perhaps puzzling, and especially useful for understanding the material. Assume you *don't* understand it completely, even if you think you do.

Step 2: Find synonyms for all of the key terms. Don't just go for the gist, a loose approximation of what was said. Substitute language virtually word-for-word to produce a parallel version of the original statement.

Step 3: Repeat this entire rephrasing several times (we suggest three). This will produce a range of possible implications that the original passage may possess.

Step 4: Contemplate the various versions you have produced. Which seem most plausible as restatements of what the original piece intends to communicate? Where can you not determine which of two restatements might win out as most accurate?

Step 5: Return to the original passage and reflect: what do you now recognize about the passage on the basis of your repeated restatements? What does it appear to mean? What else might it mean?

Discussion Like the other heuristics in this chapter, Paraphrase × 3 seeks to locate you in the local, the particular, and the concrete rather than the global, the overly general and the abstract. Rather than make a broad claim about what a sentence or passage says, a paraphrase stays much closer to the actual words. Most students think of paraphrase in the context of avoiding plagiarism ("putting it in your own words") and demonstrating their understanding of assigned reading. In more advanced writing, paraphrase serves the purpose of producing the literature review—survey of relevant research—that forms the introduction to reports in the sciences. Paraphrase as an act of analytical translation, however, goes further.

Why is paraphrasing useful? When you paraphrase language, whether your own or language you encounter in your reading, you are not just defining terms but opening out the wide range of implications those words inevitably possess. When we read, it is easy to skip quickly over the words, assuming we know what they mean. Yet when people start talking about what particular words mean—the difference, for example, between *assertive* and *aggressive* or the meaning of ordinary words such as *polite* or *realistic* or *gentlemanly*—they usually find less agreement than expected.

Here's a theory that underlies paraphrase as an interpretive tool. What we see as reality is shaped by the words we use. What we say is inescapably a product of how we say it. This idea is known as the constitutive theory of language. It is opposed to the so-called "transparent" theory of language—that we can see through words to some meaning that exists beyond and is independent of them. The transparent theory of language, which assumes that the meanings of words are obvious and self-evident, is rejected by linguists and other language specialists. They know that to change a word is inevitably to change meaning. So, to make paraphrase work for you:

- don't assume you know the meanings of words you encounter
- assume instead that words may have more than one clear meaning, depending on context.

How Paraphrase × 3 Unlocks Implications: An Example

Like the "So what?" question, paraphrasing is an effective way of bringing out implications, meanings that are there in the original but not overt. And especially if you paraphrase the same passage repeatedly, you will discover which of the words are most "slippery"—elusive, hard to define simply and unambiguously.

Let's look at a brief example of Paraphrase × 3. The sentence comes from a book entitled *The Literature Workshop* by Sheridan Blau.

> "A conviction of certainty is one of the most certain signs of ignorance and may be the best operational definition of stupidity" (213).

1. Absence of doubt is a clear indication of cluelessness and is perhaps the top way of understanding the lack of intelligence.

2. A feeling of being right is one of the most reliable indexes of lack of knowledge and may show in action the meaning of mental incapacity.

3. Being confident that you are correct is a foolproof warning that you don't know what's going on, and this kind of confidence may be an embodiment of foolishness.

Having arrived at these three paraphrases, we can use them to explore what they suggest—i.e., their implications. Here is a short list. Once you start paraphrasing, you discover that there's a lot going on in this sentence.

- One implication of the sentence is that as people come to know more and more, they feel less confident about what they know.

- Another is that ignorance and stupidity are probably not the same thing though they are often equated.

- Another is that there's a difference between feeling certain about something and being aware of this certainty as a conviction.

- Another implication is that stupidity is hard to define—perhaps it can only be defined in practice, "operationally," and not as an abstract concept.

As we paraphrased, we were struck by the repetition of "certainty" in "certain," which led us to wonder about the tone of the passage. Tone may be understood as the implicit point of view, the unspoken attitude of the statement towards itself and its readers. The piece overtly attacks "a conviction of certainty" as "a sign of ignorance" and perhaps ("may be") "a definition of stupidity." So by implication, being less sure you are right would be a sign of wisdom. But the statement itself seems extremely sure of itself, brimming with confidence: it asserts "a certain sign."

One implication of this apparent contradiction is that we are meant to take the statement with a grain of salt; read it as poking fun at itself (ironically)—demonstrating the very attitude it advises us to avoid.

Try This 2.6: Experiment with Paraphrase × 3

Recast the substantive language of the following statements using Paraphrase × 3:

- *"I am entitled to my opinion."*
- *"We hold these truths to be self-evident."*
- *"That's just common sense."*

What do you come to understand about these remarks as a result of paraphrasing? Which words, for example, are most slippery (that is difficult to define and thus rephrase), and why?

It is interesting to note, by the way, that Thomas Jefferson originally wrote the words "sacred and undeniable" in his draft of the Declaration of Independence, instead of "self-evident." So what?

Try This 2.7: Paraphrase and Implication

Two recent books on Abraham Lincoln offer a fascinating conflict in their accounts of the president's death. Use paraphrase to discuss the difference between these two accounts.

a. "Now he belongs to the ages"—Edwin Stanton, Lincoln's Secretary of War, as Lincoln expired, according to Doris Kearns Goodwin in *Team of Rivals*.

versus

b. "Now he belongs to the angels"—Edwin Stanton, Lincoln's Secretary of War, as Lincoln expired, according to James L. Swanson in *Manhunt*.

You might also consider for a moment an assignment a student of ours, Sean Heron, gave to a class of high school students he was student-teaching during a unit on the Civil War. He asked students to paraphrase three times the following sentence: "The South left the country." His goal, he reported, was to get them to see that "because language is open to interpretation, and history is conveyed through language, history must also be open to interpretation." Use paraphrase × 3 to figure out how Sean's sentence slants history.

5. IDENTIFYING THE "GO TO" SENTENCE

Every writer has a "go to" sentence, a characteristic way of putting things. With a little practice, you can learn to spot writers' "go to" sentences. These can reveal a lot about how the writer thinks and the ways he or she approaches the world.

Once you've acquired some of the specialized vocabulary of grammar and style, you will be able to see the shapes of sentences more easily and to understand what those shapes tell you about both the writer and his or her point of view on the subject at hand. But you don't need a lot of specialized vocabulary to begin; this exercise is based on careful description. (To acquire the terms and concepts you need, see Chapter 18, The Rhetoric of the Sentence and The Glossary of Grammatical Terms at the end of Chapter 19.)

Step 1: Select a single characteristic sentence from your own writing or from a reading—a sentence shape that repeats frequently or at certain habitual spots (such as the beginnings or ends of paragraphs).

Step 2: Describe the structure of the sentence: its basic shape. Identify what you think are the sentence's most distinctive features.

Step 3: Decide how this particular sentence shape reveals tendencies of the way the writer thinks. Consider sentence structure, word order, kinds of words, etc.

Discussion All of us have "go to" sentences that we fall back on in daily life—in speaking as well as writing. It is illuminating (and fun) to try to become aware of these. Our choice of sentence shapes is influenced by how we tend to think, but the shape we go to also varies according to the subjects we are writing and talking about and the rhetorical situation in which we are doing so.

A sentence is the shape thought takes. That is a mantra already offered in the discussions of grammar and style in Chapter 1, and it bears repeating. The particular ways of ordering words that each of us habitually goes to are actually features of who we are; our "go to" sentences embody how we characteristically respond to the world.

Some Examples of "Go To" Sentences

For example, if a person's "go to" sentence takes the form "Not only x, but y," he or she is inclined to define things thoroughly by contrasting what something is with what it is not. A person who says "I am not unhappy" is a person who wishes to avoid blunt claims and prefers subtler descriptions of mental states. A person who is not unhappy differs from a person who is happy and willing to say so. Note, by the way, how little technical vocabulary you actually need to talk about the shape and effect of these sentences.

Here's another example: "Although x, the fact is that y,"

> Although the President raised the number of troops in Afghanistan, the fact is that he presented a timetable for complete troop withdrawal.

> Although the show Cupcake Wars on the Food Network decadently panders to pop culture, the fact is that I cannot watch it without wanting to bake cupcakes.

With this sentence type, some technical vocabulary would help. The sentence begins with what is known as a subordinate or dependent clause. Subordination usually indicates a desire to qualify (put limits on) one's claims. The use of the phrase "the fact is" in the second half of the sentence, the independent clause, indicates a less qualified and more certain way of thinking. This is an interesting tension between the two halves of the sentence and thus the two different ways of thinking they suggest.

Here's one more example, taken from a student's memoir, of how sentence shape matches subject matter:

> I wish I could tell you more about that night, but it's kind of blurry. What do I remember? My father's voice, "Mommy passed away." I know I cried, but for how long I don't remember. My boyfriend was there; he only heard my end of the conversation. He drove me home from college. I guess that took a couple of hours. There was a box of tissues on my lap, but I didn't use any. He smoked a cigarette at one point, and opened up a window. The black air rushed in and settled on me like a heavy cloak.

Notice how flat and largely unembellished these statements are: "He drove me home from college"; "He smoked a cigarette at one point, and opened the window." Here again it is useful if you have a little technical vocabulary, but you don't need much.

It will help if you know the difference between *coordinate* sentences, in which everything is treated at one level of importance, and *subordinate* sentences in which some things depend upon and are set up as less important than other things. This writer and her sentences are shell-shocked by an unexpected tragedy that renders everything that happens the same, basically meaningless. The passage contains virtually no subordination and instead a number of short declarative sentences.

Try This 2.8: Identify the Features of "Go To" Sentences

Below are examples of "go to" sentences contributed by colleagues at our institution, taken from their own professional writing. What features do you see as distinguishing the shapes of these sentences, and so what? That is, (1) describe the shape of each sentence, and (2) suggest what the shapes "say" about the kind of thinker each writer is, and why you think so.

a. Earlier steel studies compared work, family, and community in ethnically defined neighborhoods surrounding the mills—in the case of Bethlehem within the "shadow of the steel stacks—until the lure of suburbia disrupted working class living patterns, changed neighborhood ethnic composition, and dispersed extended families, thereby complicating the very nature and definition of a steel community." (Susan Clemens, Professor of History)

b1. But there is another burden which, although also strongly related to the external political and historical events of the time, is internal to the text itself.

b2. But it is evident that, after the arguments that Adorno presents against Kierkegaard have been examined, Adorno's claims have less to do with Kierkegaard than with a desire to read something else into and against Kierkegaard. (Marcia Morgan, Professor of Philosophy)

c1. BCM 441 is a course concerned with the content, presentation, and evaluation of modern biochemistry.

c2. It is through metabolism that stored nutrients, ingested foods, and the energy of light are converted to complex biomolecules and the energy to drive cellular processes.

c3. As part of the project, Joe and his lab partner performed a pull down assay to detect stable protein-protein interactions, a chemical cross linking assay to detect transient interactions, and then prepared target protein bands for analysis by mass spectrometry. (Keri Colabroy, Professor of Biochemistry)

Try This 2.9: Find One of Your Own "Go To" Sentences

Locate a sentence in something you have written. Reading for repetition will help you find a characteristic sentence shape. You might try looking for key connecting words, such as "and" or "but" or "however" or "because" or for characteristic ways that your sentences begin and end. Remember that you are not looking for bad examples or to criticize your own writing. You're looking to identify and understand the sentence shapes you rely on. This exercise is useful to do in small groups. When time allows, we like having students present their "go to" sentence and analysis to the class.

B. Counterproductive Habits of Mind

Analysis, we have been suggesting, is a frame of mind, a set of habits for observing and making sense of the world. There is also, it is fair to say, an anti-analytical frame of mind with its own set of habits. These shut down perception and arrest potential ideas at the cliché stage.

So far, you have been working through the solutions. For the rest of the chapter, we will spell out in more detail the problems. Here's a quick review of the solutions.

***

SOLUTIONS THE CHAPTER HAS OFFERED:

Slow down: describe what you are studying; give yourself more chances to see what you think.

Start your thinking with the local rather than the global; trace impressions back to causes; apply the heuristics

Recognize and reject the reflex move to generalization and judgment

Assume you don't completely understand what you are studying; look for questions rather than answers; invite rather than flee uncertainty

THE PROBLEM

                                    leaps to

data (words, images, other detail) ---------> broad generalization

                leaps to

data ----------> evaluative claims (like/dislike; agree/disagree)

* * *

REACTING IS NOT THINKING

A lot of what passes for thinking is merely reacting. Ask someone for a description of a place, a movie, a new CD, and see what you get: good/bad, loved it/hated it, couldn't relate to it, boring. Responses like these are habits, reflexes of the mind. And they are surprisingly tough habits to break. All of the tools in the toolkit seek to slow down unthinking (reflex) reactions.

We live in a culture of inattention and cliché. It is a world in which we are perpetually assaulted with mind-numbing claims (Arby's offers "a baked potato so good you'll never want anyone else's"), flip opinions ("The Republicans/Democrats are idiots") and easy answers ("Be yourself"; "Provide job training for the unemployed, and we can do away with homelessness"). We're awash in such stuff.

On this note, we turn to a closer examination of four of the most stubbornly counterproductive habits of mind: (1) premature leaps, (2) the judgment reflex, (3) generalizing, and (4) naturalizing assumptions (overpersonalizing).

1. PREMATURE LEAPS

In a way, the premature leap is the most fundamental bad habit. The others—reflex judgments, generalizing, and overpersonalizing—are all versions of leaping too quickly to conclusions.

A classic example of the premature leap is the one that inexperienced writers make to arrive at a thesis statement before they have observed enough and reflected enough to find one worth using. These writers end up clinging to the first idea that they think might serve as a thesis, with the result that they stop looking at anything in their evidence except what they want and expect to see. Typically, they find themselves proving the obvious—some too general and superficial idea. Worse, they miss opportunities for the better paper lurking in the more complicated evidence screened out by the desire to make the thesis "work."

You'll know you are becoming a more accomplished analytical writer when the meaning of your evidence starts to seem less rather than more clear to you, perhaps even strange—and you don't panic. Then you will begin to see details you hadn't seen before and a range of competing meanings where you had thought there was only one.

Make It Strange

Making it strange rather than trying to normalize what you see and read is a productive habit of mind. It opposes our more usual habit to quickly render things familiar by locating them in comfortable and habitual categories. One purpose of writing, as the writer David Lodge suggests, "is to overcome the deadening effects of habit by representing familiar things in unfamiliar ways." *Defamiliarization* is a term used by artists, philosophers and psychologists to talk about the need to fight against the deadening effects of habit. The man who coined the term defamiliarization, Victor Shklovsky, wrote, "Habitualization devours works, clothes, furniture, one's wife, and the fear of war. . . . And art exists that one may recover the sensation of life" (David Lodge, *The Art of Fiction*. New York: Penguin, 1992, p.53).

The following quotation from an article entitled "The Transition to College Reading" remarks on the need for defamiliarizing in its account of students' misunderstandings of readings:

> "I find that [students] are most inclined to substitute what they generally think a text should be saying for what it actually says [. . . .] They want to read every text as saying something extremely familiar that they might agree with".
> Robert Scholes, "The Transition to College Reading,"
> *Pedagogy*, volume 2, number 2, Duke UP, 2002, page165.

What is interesting here is the idea that people actually substitute something they already think, their habitual frames of reference, for what is actually on the page.

Get Comfortable with Uncertainty

To short-circuit premature leaps and see though the veil of familiarity, you'll need to find ways of becoming more comfortable with uncertainty. In fact, it's a healthy practice to assume you're missing something, always. Prepare to be surprised at how difficult this can be. Why? Most of us learn early in life to pretend that we understand things even when we don't. Rather than ask questions and risk looking foolish, we nod our heads. Soon, we even come to believe that we understand things when really we don't, or not nearly as well as we think we do.

The nineteenth-century American poet Emily Dickinson, writes about this problem in her poem that begins "Perception of an object/Costs precise the object's loss." The point of the Dickinson poem is a paradox: when we think we understand something, we in a sense cease to see it. Our idea of the thing has replaced the thing itself, producing a form of mental blindness—loss of the object.

By training yourself to be more comfortable with not knowing, you give yourself license to start working with your material, the data, *before* you try to decide what you think it means. Only then will you be able to *see the questions,* which are usually much more interesting than the temporary stopping points you have elected as answers.

2. THE JUDGMENT REFLEX

In its most primitive form—most automatic and least thoughtful—judging is like an on/off switch. When the switch gets thrown in one direction or the other—good/bad, right/wrong, positive/negative—the resulting judgment predetermines and over-directs any subsequent thinking we might do. Rather than thinking about what X is or how X operates, we lock ourselves prematurely into proving that we were right to think that X should be banned or supported.

It would be impossible to overstate the mind-numbing effect that the judgment reflex has on thinking. The psychologist Carl Rogers has written at length on the problem of the judgment reflex. He claims that our habitual tendency as humans—virtually a programmed response—is to evaluate everything and to do so very quickly.

Walking out of a movie, for example, most people will immediately voice their approval or disapproval, usually in either/or terms: I liked it *or* didn't like it; it was right/wrong, good/bad, interesting/boring. The other people in the conversation will then offer their own evaluation plus their judgment of the others' judgments: I think it was a good movie and you are wrong to think it was bad. And so on. Like the knee jerking in response to the physician's hammer, such reflex judgments are made without conscious thought (the source of the pejorative term "knee-jerk thinking").

This is not to say that all judging should be avoided. Obviously, we all need to make decisions: whether we should or shouldn't vote for a particular candidate, for instance. Analytical thinking does need to arrive at a point of view—which is a form of judgment—but analytical conclusions are usually not phrased in terms of like/dislike or good/bad. They disclose what a person has come to understand about X rather than how he or she rules on the worth of X.

Three Cures for the Judgment Reflex

- Neither agree nor disagree with another person's position until you can repeat that position in a way the other person would accept as fair and accurate. Carl Rogers recommends this strategy to negotiators in industry and government.
- Try eliminating the word "should" from your vocabulary for a while. Judgments often take the form of *should* statements.
- Try eliminating evaluative adjectives—those that offer judgments with no data. "Jagged" is a descriptive, concrete adjective. It offers something we can experience. "Beautiful" is an evaluative adjective. It offers only judgment. Sometimes the concrete-abstract divide is complicated. Consider for example the word "green," a literal color with figurative associations (envious, innocent, ecological, etc.).

Try This 2.10: Distinguishing Evaluative from Nonevaluative Words

The dividing line between judgmental and nonjudgmental words is often more difficult to discern in practice than you might assume. Categorize each of the terms in the following list as judgmental or nonjudgmental, and be prepared to explain your reasoning: monstrous, delicate, authoritative, strong, muscular, automatic, vibrant, tedious, pungent, unrealistic, flexible, tart, pleasing, clever, slow.

Try This 2.11: Experiment with Adjectives and Adverbs

Write a paragraph of description—on anything that comes to mind—without using any evaluative adjectives or adverbs. Alternatively, analyze and categorize the adjectives and adverbs in a piece of your own recent writing.

3. GENERALIZING

Vagueness and generality are major blocks to learning because, like the other habits of mind discussed so far, they allow you to dismiss virtually everything you've read and heard except the general idea you've arrived at: What it all boils down to is . . . What this adds up to is . . . The gist of her speech was . . .

Most of us tend to remember our global impressions and reactions. The dinner was dull. The house was beautiful. The music was exciting. But we forget the specific, concrete causes of these impressions (if we ever fully noticed them). As a result, we deprive ourselves of material to think with—the data that might allow us to reconsider our initial impressions or share them with others.

Often, the generalizations that come to mind are so broad that they tell us nothing. To say, for example, that the economy of a particular emerging nation is inefficient, accomplishes very little, since the generalization could fit almost any economy.

Take My Word for It?

Generalizing is not always a bad habit. We generalize from our experience because this is one way of arriving at ideas. Summary writing, which you will do a lot of in college, is a useful form of generalizing. Summarizing materials helps you to learn and to share information with others.

The problem comes when generalizations omit any supporting details. Consider for a moment what you are actually asking others to do when you offer them a generalization such as "The proposed changes in immigration policy are a disaster." Unless the recipient of this observation asks a question—such as "Why do you think so?"—he or she is being required to take your word for it: the changes are a disaster because you say so.

What happens instead if you offer a few details that caused you to think as you do? Clearly, you are on riskier ground. Your listener might think that the details you cite lead to different conclusions and a different reading of the data, but at least conversation has become possible.

Antidotes to Habitual Generalizing

- Trace your general impressions back to the details that caused them. This tracing of attitudes back to their concrete causes is one of the most basic and necessary moves in the analytical habit of mind. Train yourself to become more conscious about where your generalizations come from (see the Five-Finger Exercise at the end of Chapter 1).
- Think of the words you use as steps on an abstraction ladder, and consciously climb down the ladder from abstract to concrete. "Mammal," for example, is higher on the abstraction ladder than "cow." A concrete word appeals to the senses. Abstract words are not available to our senses of touch, sight, hearing, taste, and smell.

"Peace-keeping force" is an abstract phrase. It conjures up a concept, but in an abstract and general way. "Submarine" is concrete. We know what people are talking about when they say there is a plan to send submarines to a troubled area. We can't be so sure what is up when people start talking about peace-keeping forces.

Try This 2.12: Locating Words on the Abstraction Ladder

Find a word above (more abstract) and a word below (more concrete) for each of the following words: society, food, train, taxes, school, government, cooking oil, organism, story, magazine.

Try This 2.13: Distinguishing Abstract from Concrete Words

Make a list of the first 10 words that come to mind and then arrange them from most concrete to most abstract. Then repeat the exercise by choosing key words from a page of something you have written recently.

4. NATURALIZING OUR ASSUMPTIONS (OVERPERSONALIZING)

It is surprisingly difficult to break the habit of treating our points of view as self-evidently true—not just for us but for everyone. The overpersonalizer assumes that because he or she experienced or believes X, everyone else does, too.

What is "common sense" for one person and so not even in need of explaining can be quite uncommon and not so obviously sensible to someone else. More often than not, "common sense" is a phrase that really means "what seems obvious to me and therefore should be obvious to you." This way of thinking is called **"naturalizing our assumptions."** The word *naturalize* in this context means we are representing—and seeing—our own assumptions as natural, as simply the way things are *and ought to be.*

Writers who naturalize their own assumptions tend to make personal experiences and prejudices an *unquestioned* standard of value. A person who has a nightmarish experience in the emergency room may lead him to reject a plan for nationalized health care, but his writing needs to examine in detail the holes in the plan, not simply evoke the three hours waiting to get seen by a doctor.

Try This 2.14: Fieldwork: Looking for Naturalized Assumptions

Take a day to research just how pervasive a habit of mind naturalizing assumptions is in the world around you. Start listening to the things people say in everyday conversation. (Lunch lines are a choice site for a little surreptitious overhearing.) Or read some newspaper editorials with your morning coffee (a pretty disturbing way to start the day in most cases). Jot down examples of people naturalizing their assumptions.

"I Didn't Know You Wanted My Opinion"

We cannot leave the topic of naturalizing assumptions—assuming our way of seeing the world is the only way—without contemplating the key term at the heart of the subject: opinions. Over the years, those of us who teach have heard our students say a million times, "I didn't know you wanted my opinion."

This classic student/teacher miscommunication warrants some analysis. What, in this context, does the word "opinion" mean? You may have already done some thinking on opinions and people's attitude toward them in the paraphrase × 3 section of this toolkit. There we asked you to paraphrase the assertion "I am entitled to my opinion." Now let's pursue the implications (which is what analysis does) of the exclamation—or complaint—"I didn't know you wanted my opinion."

- Paraphrase #1: You should have told me sooner that it is okay for me to talk about my personal beliefs!

- Paraphrase #2: I am pleasantly surprised to find that you are interested in my feelings and experience.

- Paraphrase #3: I had not anticipated that you might expect me to say what I think.

Paraphrases 1 and 2 reveal a common but problematic definition of opinion as personal beliefs and feelings. This way of thinking leads to the implicit ground rule that when a teacher asks for personal opinion, students believe they do not need to provide evidence or reasoning. They're in a "free zone," which is why another ground rule seems to be that "opinion pieces" should be graded more leniently or not at all.

The problem with this way of understanding opinion is that it assumes our opinions are merely personal. In fact, our opinions are never just our opinions. They are deeply embedded in the conceptual fabric of a culture, and they are always learned.

As contemporary cultural theorists are fond of pointing out, the "I" is not a wholly autonomous free agent who writes from a unique point of view. Rather, the "I" is shaped by forces outside the self—social, cultural, educational, historical, and so on. Chronic naturalizers will not see the extent to which they are socially constructed, sites through which dominant cultural ways of understanding the world (ideologies) circulate. To put it perhaps too strongly, they're like actors who don't know they're actors, reciting various cultural scripts they don't realize are scripts.

What about the third paraphrase, "I had not anticipated that you might expect me to say what I think"? Paraphrase #3 reveals a person who recognizes that she is being asked to share her thinking, not just her views.

She is ready to think more about what opinion means. Is an opinion the same as an idea or theory? Are most ideas just opinions? How do I figure out what I think about things other than simply consulting my ready store of familiar views?

What do faculty *really* want when they make assignments to which students respond, "I didn't know you wanted my opinion?" Faculty at our college tell us they want two things:

(1) for students to do more than merely transmit information

(2) for students to do more than merely react and instead find thoughtful ways to engage the information and develop a stake in it.

Opinions: Are They Counterproductive Habits of Mind?

So: are opinions counterproductive habits of mind? Not necessarily. It would be naïve to say that each of us should get rid of our opinions in order to think well. This simply is not possible nor is it desirable. To see opinions only in the negative would be to diminish the important role that they play in the lives of individuals and of cultures. Rather than trying to suppress opinions, we need to take responsibility as thinkers for having opinions about things and for respecting the fact that other people have opinions too. It's a civic duty.

We should examine our opinions, not primarily to assert and defend them, but to explore them for what they might reveal about ourselves and the communities to which we belong. Opinions as kneejerk reactions—reflexes—cannot help us. But thoughtful examination of our opinions can.

Habits of Mind in Psychology: A Psychologist Speaks

In the following Voice from Across the Curriculum, clinician and psychology professor Mark Sciutto notes that the problematic habits of mind identified in this chapter are also recognized as problems in the discipline of psychology. In cognitive behavior therapy, these habits are called automatic thoughts.

Voices From Across the Curriculum

o   Readers should not conclude that the "Counterproductive Habits of Mind" presented in this chapter are confined to writing. Psychologists who study the way we process information have established important links between the way we think and the way we feel. Some psychologists such as Aaron Beck have identified common "errors in thinking" that parallel the habits of mind discussed in this chapter. Beck and others have shown that falling prey to habits of mind is associated with a variety of negative outcomes. For instance, a tendency to engage in either/or thinking, overgeneralization, and personalization has been linked to higher levels of anger, anxiety, and depression. Failure to attend to these errors in thinking chokes off reflection and analysis. As a result, the person becomes more likely to "react" rather than think, which may prolong and exacerbate the negative emotions.

—Mark Sciutto, Professor of Psychology

To familiarize yourself further with the thinking errors identified by cognitive therapy, one place to look is *Cognitive Therapy: Basics and Beyond* by Judith S. Beck (the daughter of Aaron) (NY: The Guilford Press, 1995). There Dr. Beck lists 12 of the most common "automatic thoughts" that she labels "mistakes in thinking." These include "Emotional reasoning," about which she writes,

> "You think something must be true because you 'feel' (actually believe) it so strongly, ignoring or discounting evidence to the contrary'" (119).

Opinions—A Democratic Disease? A Political Science Professor Speaks

As a final word for the chapter, we turn to our colleague, Jack Gambino, who offers the view of a social scientist that everything is not opinion, nor are all opinions equal in weight.

Voices From Across the Curriculum

Many students taking political science courses come with the assumption that in politics, one opinion is as good as another. (Tocqueville thought this to be a peculiarly democratic disease.) From this perspective, any position a political science professor may take on controversial issues is simply his or her opinion to be accepted or rejected by students according to their own beliefs/prejudices. The key task, therefore, is not so much substituting knowledge for opinions, but rather substituting well-constructed arguments for unexamined opinions.

What is an argument, and how might it be distinguished from opinions? Several things need to be stressed: (1) The thesis should be linked to evidence drawn from relevant sources: polling data, interviews, historical material, and so forth. (2) The thesis should make as explicit as possible its own ideological assumptions. (3) A thesis, in contrast to mere statement of opinion, is committed to making an argument, which means that it presupposes a willingness to engage with others. To the extent that writers operate on the assumption that everything is an opinion, they have no reason to construct arguments; they are locked into an opinion.

—Jack Gambino, Professor of Political Science

Assignments: Using the Toolkit

1. **Do The Method on a Reading**. Look for repetitions, strands, and binaries in the paragraphs below, the opening of an article entitled "The End of Solitude" by William Deresiewicz, which appeared in *The Chronicle of Higher Education* on January 30, 2009 and at http://chronicle.com/article/The-End-of-Solitude/3708. After selecting the repetition, strand, or organizing contrast you find most important, try writing several paragraphs about it.

What does the contemporary self want? The camera has created a culture of celebrity; the computer is creating a culture of connectivity. As the two technologies converge—broadband tipping the Web from text to image, social-networking sites spreading the mesh of interconnection ever wider—the two cultures betray a common impulse. Celebrity and connectivity are both ways of becoming known. This is what the contemporary self wants. It wants to be recognized, wants to be connected: It wants to be visible. If not to the millions, on Survivor or Oprah, then to the hundreds, on Twitter or Facebook. This is the quality that validates us, this is how we become real to ourselves—by being seen by others. The great contemporary terror is anonymity. If Lionel Trilling was right, if the property that grounded the self, in Romanticism, was sincerity, and in modernism it was authenticity, then in postmodernism it is visibility.

So we live exclusively in relation to others, and what disappears from our lives is solitude. Technology is taking away our privacy and our concentration, but it is also taking away our ability to be alone. Though I shouldn't say taking away. We are doing this to ourselves; we are discarding these riches as fast as we can. I was told by one of her older relatives that a teenager I know had sent 3,000 text messages one recent month. That's 100 a day, or about one every 10 waking minutes, morning, noon, and night, weekdays and weekends, class time, lunch time, homework time, and toothbrushing time. So on average, she's never alone for more than 10 minutes at once. Which means, she's never alone.

2. **Paraphrase a Complicated Passage**. Paraphrasing can help you to understand sophisticated material by uncovering the implications of the language. As a case in point, consider this passage from an article about *Life* magazine by Wendy Kozol entitled, "The Kind of People Who Make Good Americans: Nationalism and *Life*'s Family Ideal." Rather than simply skipping those passages that seem unclear, the savvy analytical writer could confront them head-on through paraphrase. Try Paraphrase × 3 with this passage, from page 186:

> Traditional depictions of the family present it as a voluntary site of intimacy and warmth, but it also functions as a site of consumption. At the same time capitalism lauds the work ethic and the family as spheres of morality safe from the materialism of the outside world. These contradictions produce a 'legitimation crisis' by which capitalist societies become ever more dependent for legitimacy on the very sociocultural motivations that capitalism undermines. (186; rpt in *Rhetorical Visions* by Wendy Hesford, pp. 177–200).

3. **Experiment with Notice and Focus and The Method**. Find a subject to analyze using Notice and Focus and then The Method. Your aim here initially is not to write a formal paper but to do data-gathering on the page. Notice as much as you can about it. Then organize your observations using The Method: What details repeat? What is opposed to what?

   After you have written the paragraph that is the final part of The Method, revise and expand your work into a short essay. Don't worry too much at this point about form (introductory paragraph, for example) or thesis. Just write at greater length about what you noticed and what you selected as most revealing or interesting or strange or significant, and why.

   You can do this writing with either print or nonprint materials. For some suggestions, see Try This 2.2 and 2.4. The Method could yield interesting results applied to the architecture on your campus, the student newspaper, campus clothing styles, or the latest news about the economy.

4. **Analyze an Image in Relation to Text**. The Adrian Tomine *New Yorker* covers that we referred to in Try This 2.3 could produce a good short paper. You could do The Method on the two covers in order to write a comparative paper. Or, you could do The Method on the Tomine cover called "Double Feature" and the two paragraphs from "The End of Solitude" above, and write about them comparatively. (Note: the entire article is available online.)

What do you think Tomine's cover says about the issues raised in "The End of Solitude" by William Deresiewicz? How might Tomine see the issues differently? And how might Deresiewicz interpret Tomine's cover, and so what?

Chapter 3

Analysis: What It Is and What It Does

NOW THAT YOU HAVE acquired an overview of the study of writing (Chapter 1) and an acquaintance with some essential tools for doing analysis (Chapter 2), it is time to focus in on the process of analysis itself—how a writer uses these tools to produce better, smarter, more interesting thinking on the page.

This chapter defines analysis as the search for meaningful pattern. It asks how something does what it does or why it is as it is. Analysis is a form of detective work that typically pursues something puzzling, something you seek to understand rather than something you believe you already know. Analysis finds questions where there seemed not to be any, and it makes connections that might not have been evident at first. Analysis is, then, more than just a set of skills: it is a frame of mind, an attitude toward experience.

A. Five Analytical Moves

At the heart of this chapter are what we call the Five Analytical Moves. These represent our attempt to present a template for the analytical frame of mind.

> Move 1: Suspend judgment (understand before you judge).
>
> Move 2: Define significant parts and how they are related.
>
> Move 3: Look for patterns of repetition and contrast and for anomalies (aka The Method).
>
> Move 4: Make the implicit explicit (convert to direct statement meanings that are only suggested—make details "speak").
>
> Move 5: Keep reformulating questions and explanations (what other details seem significant? what else might they mean?).

We have seized upon analysis as the book's focus because it is the skill most commonly called for in college courses and beyond. When asked in faculty writing seminars to talk about what they want from student writing, faculty say that they want students to be able to arrive at ideas about information, rather than merely report it (neutral summary) or try to match information with personal experience. Control of information matters; engagement with the information also matters, but neither extreme is enough. Analysis occupies the middle ground between these two extremes.

What Faculty Seek in Student Writing

HAVING IDEAS
(doing something with the material)

versus

RELATING ◄ – – – – – – – – – – – – – – – – – – – ► REPORTING
(personal experience   (information
matters, but . . .)   matters, but . . .)

Metacognition

The word *metacognition* means thinking about thinking. The first step in improving as a writer is to press yourself to become more aware of your own thinking, not just *what* you think—your "database" of customary convictions—but *how* you think. Interestingly, most of us don't pay much attention to how we think. It just happens. Or does it?

An obstacle in learning to think well is that we are accustomed to being rewarded for having answers. This was the view advanced by one of America's greatest metacognitive philosophers, John Dewey, in his book *How We Think* (1933, rev. ed.). Dewey:

- located the origin of thinking in uncertainty and doubt;
- worked to understand understanding—the meaning-making process; and
- defined thinking as "systematic reflection and inquiry."

In this context, let's now return to the five analytical moves in more detail. These will add to the repertoire of observation and interpretation strategies you learned in Chapter 2—enhancing your ability to engage in what Dewey calls "systematic reflection."

MOVE 1: SUSPEND JUDGMENT

The first of these five moves, *suspending judgment*, is really more a pre-condition than an actual activity. We include it as an analytical move, however, because suspending judgment takes an act of will, and we need then to consciously substitute other ways of thinking.

As we suggested in our critique of the Judgment Reflex in Chapter 2, the tendency to judge everything—to respond with likes and dislikes, with agreeing and disagreeing—shuts down our ability to see and to think. Just listen in on the next three conversations around you to be reminded of the pervasiveness of this phenomenon.

Consciously leading with the word interesting (as in "What I find most interesting about this is ...") tends to deflect the judgment response into a more exploratory state of mind, one motivated by curiosity. As a general rule, you should seek to understand the subject you are analyzing before deciding how you feel about it. (*See the discussion of interesting, revealing, and strange under Notice and Focus in Chapter 2.*)

MOVE 2: DEFINE SIGNIFICANT PARTS AND HOW THEY'RE RELATED

Whether you are analyzing an awkward social situation, an economic problem, a painting, a substance in a chemistry lab, or your chances of succeeding in a job interview, the process of analysis is the same:

- Divide the subject into its defining parts, its main elements or ingredients.
- Consider how these parts are related, both to each other and to the subject as a whole.

One common denominator of all effective analytical writing is that it pays close attention to detail. We analyze because our global responses—to a play, for example, or to a speech or a social problem—are too general. Let's say you hear a local environmentalist give a public lecture on pollution. Afterward, you tell your friend, "I heard this great talk." This kind of generic response one could offer about almost anything. Such "one-size-fits-all" comments don't tell us much, except that you liked what you heard.

In order to say more, you'd need to become more analytical: you'd shift your attention to different elements of the talk and how they fit together. You might note that the talk began with a slide show of polluted creeks and that the speaker explained how different kinds of drain lines—sewer lines and storm water lines—are connected, so that when there are not enough water treatment plants in an area, a storm can cause the drains to overflow capacity and force officials to use "direct release," thus easing the pressure on the facility but fouling the creeks.

This move from generalization to analysis, from the larger subject to its key components, is characteristic of good thinking. To understand a subject, we need to get past our first, generic, evaluative response in order to discover what the subject is "made of," the particulars that contribute most strongly to the character of the whole.

The tendency of analysis to break things down into their component parts is sometimes thought of as destructive—as murdering to dissect (to paraphrase a famous poet). This point of view, however, fails to recognize that when people analyze, they break things down in order to see them more clearly and *construct* their understandings of the world they inhabit.

Some Everyday Examples If you find yourself being followed by a large dog, your first response, other than breaking into a cold sweat, will be to analyze the situation. What does being followed by a large dog mean for me, here, now? Does it mean the dog is vicious and about to attack? Does it mean the dog is curious and wants to play?

Similarly, if you are losing a game of tennis or you've just left a job interview or you are looking at a painting of a woman with three noses, you will begin to analyze. How can I play differently to increase my chances of winning? Am I likely to get the job, and why (or why not)? Why did the artist give the woman three noses?

In the case of the large dog, you might notice that he's dragging a leash, has a ball in his mouth, and is wearing a bright red scarf. Having broken your larger subject into these defining parts, you would try to see the connection among them and determine what they mean, what they allow you to decide about the nature of the dog: apparently somebody's lost pet, playful, probably not hostile, unlikely to bite me.

Analysis of the painting of the woman with three noses, a subject more like the kind you might be asked to write about in a college course, would proceed in the same way. Your result—ideas about the nature of the painting—would be determined, as with the dog, not only by your noticing its various parts but also by your familiarity with the subject. If you knew very little about art history, scrutinizing the painting's parts would not tell you, for instance, that it is an example of the movement known as Cubism. Even without this context, however, you would still be able to draw some analytical conclusions—ideas about the meaning and nature of the subject. You might conclude, for example, that the artist is interested in perspective or in the way we see, as opposed to realistic depictions of the world.

Try This 3.1: Description as a Form of Analysis

Describe something you wish to better understand. Initially, don't interpret; just record significant detail. Say what is there, what details you notice in your subject. Then write a paragraph in which you say what the description revealed to you about the nature of your subject. You might describe, for example, a painting or a photograph, a current event as reported in a newspaper or another source, a conversation overheard, a local scene (such as the college bookstore or a place where students congregate), a math problem, or your favorite song off a new CD.

Description as a Form of Analysis: Some Academic Examples

The act of describing is just as important to analytical writing—in fact to all kinds of writing—as it is to the writing of poems or fiction. Browse, for example, a history book, an economics textbook, the newspaper, any collection of essays, including those on scientific subjects, and you will find description (and narrative as well, since the two so often go hand in hand). We simply cannot think well without it. Although academic disciplines vary in the ways they use description, all of them call for keeping thinking in touch with telling detail.

It is also essential to recognize that virtually all forms of description are implicitly analytical. When we select particular details and call attention to them by describing them, we are more likely to begin noticing what these details suggest about the character of the whole. Description presents details so that analysis can make them speak.

Here are three excerpts of student papers from different academic disciplines, followed by one evocative example from a professional writer.

The first example, from a draft of an undergraduate honors thesis in biology, shows how a writer uses Move 2—defining significant parts and how they are related—to analyze the relationship between two kinds of aquatic snails. The writer, Emily Petchler Herstoff seeks to understand why a type of snail, *Crepidula adunca*, attaches itself selectively to one kind of grazing snail, *Calliostoma ligatum*, and not to other, similar snails.

> Studying the effects of predation on host choice can shed insight onto the symbiotic relationship between *Calliostoma ligatum* and *Crepidula adunca*, and may illuminate why *Calliostoma ligatum* is the preferred host for *Crepidula adunca* in the San Juan Islands. My first experimental goal was to determine if *Crepidula adunca* confers any benefits to *Calliostoma ligatum* in the form of predator defense. As *Crepidula adunca* has already been proven to harm its host *Calliostoma ligatum* (Vermeij et al, 1987), it may be that *Crepidula adunca* is in a parasitic, rather than mutualistic relationship with its host. To determine if *Crepidula adunca* may be mutualistic, I performed predation tests to see if *C. adunca* conferred any advantages, in the form of defense, to its host *Calliostoma ligatum*. I performed a series of predator preference experiments to determine if predators more frequently consumed *Calliostoma ligatum* without *Crepidula adunca*.

Here is another example, a rhetorical analysis of a commencement address delivered by novelist David Foster Wallace at Kenyon College in 2005 (later published as "This Is Water"). Notice how the writer isolates parts of the speech, such as its apologies and denials, in order to arrive at claims about the rhetoric of the speech as a whole. (*See Chapter 1, the short take called Rhetoric: What It Is and Why You Need It.*) The writer begins by listing four quotations from the address.

> "I am not the wise old fish" (1).
> "Please don't worry that I am getting ready to lecture you about compassion" (2)
> "Please don't think that I am giving you moral advice" (5).
> "Please don't dismiss it as just some finger-wagging Dr. Laura sermon" (7)
> A recurrent feature of the address is the author's imploring his audience ("Please") not to assume that he is offering moral instruction. The sheer repetition of this pattern suggests that he is worried about sounding like a sermonizer, that the writer is anxious about the didacticism of his speech.
> But obviously the piece does advance a moral position; it does want us to think about something serious, which is part of its function as a commencement address. What's most interesting is

the final apology, offered just as the piece ends (7). Here Wallace appears to shift ground. Rather than denying that he's "the wise old fish" (1), he denies that he is Dr. Laura, or rather, he pleads not to be dismissed as a Dr. Laura. So he's saying, in effect, that we should not see him as a TV personality who scolds ("finger wagging") and offers moral lessons for daily life ("sermon").

Why is he so worried about the didactic function? Obviously, he is thinking of his audience, fearful of appearing to be superior, and fearful that his audience does not want to be preached at. But he cannot resist the didactic impulse the occasion bestows. In these terms, what is interesting is the divided nature of the address: on the one hand, full of parables—little stories with moral intent—and on the other hand, full of repeated denials of the very moral impulse his narratives and the occasion itself generically decree.

In our next example, Michelle Bielko, a history and English major, isolates details in the writing of 19th-century poet Walt Whitman to theorize his celebratory treatment of the Civil War.

Of interest is the fact that an analysis of Whitman's poems and journalistic works from the period suggest that for the artist the Civil War was in some way a continuation of the noble Revolutionary War, providing Americans with the opportunity to exhibit heroism in the likeness of the fathers of the nation. A close examination of the language Whitman used in his Civil War poetry anthology *Drum Taps* and in *Memoranda During the War* demonstrates that the poet consciously sought ways to cast President Lincoln as the George Washington of the Civil War, *both* northerners and southerners as the virtuous patriots of the Civil War, and to curiously leave the loathsome loyalist of the American Revolution without a corresponding double in his literary representation of the 1861–1865 conflict. In doing so, Whitman was ironically able to reinvent the so called "Secession War," which threatened to divide and destroy the United States, as a unifying conflict as worthy of celebration as the American War for Independence from Britain.

Two parallel features drive this writer's analysis of Whitman: that he treats both northerners and southerners as Civil War patriots and that he focuses only on patriots in the Revolutionary War, ignoring colonists who remained loyal to the crown.

We take our final example from a classic early text in Urban Studies, *The Death and Life of Great American Cities* (1961), by Jane Jacobs. Notice how she weaves a pattern of descriptive detail to build her implicit argument that sidewalks in cities are sites where people police themselves, providing safety not only for friends but for strangers.

When I get home after work, the ballet is reaching its crescendo. This is the time of roller skates and stilts and tricycles, and games in the lee of the stoop with bottle tops and plastic cowboys; this is the time of bundles and packages, zigzagging from the drugstore to the fruit stand and back over to the butcher's; this is the time when teenagers, all dressed up, are pausing to ask if their slips show or their collars look right; this is the time when beautiful girls get out of MG's; this is the time when the fire engines go through; this is the time when anybody you know around Hudson Street will go by.

As darkness thickens and Mr. Halpert moors the laundry cart to the cellar door again, the ballet goes on under lights, eddying back and forth but intensifying at the bright spotlight pools of Joe's sidewalk pizza dispensary, the bars, the delicatessen, the restaurant and the drug store. The night workers stop now at the delicatessen, to pick up salami and a container of milk. Things have settled down for the evening but the street and its ballet have not come to a stop.

I know the deep night ballet and its seasons best from waking long after midnight to tend a baby and, sitting in the dark, seeing the shadows and hearing the sounds of the sidewalk. Mostly it is a sound like infinitely pattering snatches of party conversation and, about three in the morning, singing, very good singing. Sometimes there is sharpness and anger or sad, sad weeping, or a flurry of search for a string of beads broken. One night a young man came roaring along, bellowing terrible language at two girls whom he had apparently picked up and who were disappointing him. Doors opened, a wary semicircle formed around him, not too close, until the police came. Out came the heads, two, along Hudson Street, offering opinion, "Drunk . . . Crazy . . . A wild kid from the suburbs."

Writing that is not markedly academic in style, such as these paragraphs from Jane Jacobs, often makes its way into academic discussions. Descriptive detail is as valuable in academic writing as it is in more popular forms.

MOVE 3: LOOK FOR PATTERNS OF REPETITION AND CONTRAST AND FOR ANOMALIES (AKA THE METHOD)

We have been defining analysis as the understanding of parts in relation to each other and to a whole. But how do you know which parts to attend to? What makes some details in the material you are studying more worthy of your attention than others?

The heuristic we call The Method offers a tool for uncovering significant patterns. In its most reduced form, The Method organizes observation and then prompts interpretation by asking the following sequence of questions. (*See Chapter 2, The Method.*)

THE METHOD

What repeats?

What goes with what? (strands)

What is opposed to what? (binaries)

> (for all of these questions) ---> *SO WHAT?*

What doesn't fit? (anomalies) So what?

In virtually all subjects, repetition and close resemblance (strands) are signs of emphasis. In a symphony, for example, certain patterns of notes repeat throughout, announcing themselves as major themes. In Shakespeare's *King Lear,* references to seeing and eyes call attention to themselves through repetition, causing us to recognize that the play is *about* seeing. Binary oppositions, which often consist of two strands or repetitions in tension with each other, suggest what is at stake in a subject. We can understand *King Lear* by the way it opposes kinds of blindness to ways of seeing.

Along with looking for pattern, it is also fruitful to attend to anomalous details— those that seem not to fit the pattern. Anomalies help us to revise our assumptions. Picture a baseball player reading Dostoyevsky in the dugout: a TV commercial that did that to advertise a team was working through anomaly. In this case, the anomaly, a baseball player who reads serious literature, is used to subvert (question, unsettle) the stereotypical assumption that sports and intellectualism don't belong together.

People tend to avoid information that challenges (by not conforming to) views they already hold. Screening out anything that would ruffle the pattern they've begun to see, they ignore the evidence that might lead them to a better theory. Most advances in thought, for example, have arisen when someone has observed some phenomenon that does not fit with a prevailing theory.

Looking for Patterns: An Example

Examine the following excerpt from a draft of a paper about Ovid's *Metamorphoses,* a collection of short mythological tales dating from ancient Rome. We have included annotations in boldface to suggest how a writer's ideas evolve as she looks for pattern, contrast, and anomaly, constantly remaining open to reformulation.

The draft begins with two loosely connected observations: that males dominate females and that many characters in the stories lose the ability to speak and thus become submissive and dominated. In the excerpt, the writer begins to connect these two observations and speculate about what this connection means.

> 1. There are many other examples in Ovid's *Metamorphoses* that show the dominance of man over woman through speech control. In the Daphne and Apollo story, Daphne becomes a tree to escape Apollo, but her ability to speak is destroyed. Likewise, in the Syrinx and Pan story, Syrinx becomes a marsh reed, also a life form that cannot talk, although Pan can make it talk by playing it. *[The writer establishes a pattern of similar detail.]* Pygmalion and

Galatea is a story in which the male creates his rendition of the perfect female. The female does not speak once; she is completely silent. Also, Galatea is referred to as "she" and never given a real name. This lack of a name renders her identity more silent. *[Here the writer begins to link the contrasts of speech/silence with the absence/presence of identity.]*

2. Ocyrhoe is a female character who could tell the future but who was transformed into a mare so that she could not speak. One may explain this transformation by saying it was an attempt by the gods to keep the future unknown. *[Notice how the writer's thinking expands as she sustains her investigation of the overall pattern of men silencing women: here she tests her theory by adding another variable—prophecy.]* However, there is a male character, Tiresias, who is also a seer of the future and is allowed to speak of his foreknowledge, thereby becoming a famous figure. (Interestingly, Tiresias during his lifetime has experienced being both a male and a female.) *[Notice how the Ocyrhoe example has generated a contrast based on gender in the Tiresias example. The pairing of the two examples demonstrates that the ability to tell the future is not the sole cause of silencing because male characters who can do it are not silenced—though the writer pauses to note that Tiresias is not entirely male.]* Finally, in the story of Mercury and Herse, Herse's sister, Aglauros, tries to prevent Mercury from marrying Herse. Mercury turns her into a statue; the male directly silences the female's speech.

3. The woman silences the man in only two stories studied. *[Here the writer searches out an anomaly—women silencing men—that grows in the rest of the paragraph into an organizing contrast.]* In the first, "The Death of Orpheus," the women make use of "clamorous shouting, Phrygian flutes with curving horns, tambourines, the beating of breasts, and Bacchic howlings" (246) to drown out the male's songs, dominating his speech in terms of volume. In this way, the quality of power within speech is demonstrated: "for the first time, his words had no effect, and he failed to move them [the women] in any way by his voice" (247). Next the women kill him, thereby rendering him silent. However, the male soon regains his temporarily destroyed power of expression: "the lyre uttered a plaintive melody and the lifeless tongue made a piteous murmur" (247). Even after death Orpheus is able to communicate. The women were not able to destroy his power completely, yet they were able to severely reduce his power of speech and expression. *[The writer learns, among other things, that men are harder to silence; Orpheus's lyre continues to sing after his death.]*

4. The second story in which a woman silences a man is the
story of Actaeon, in which the male sees Diana naked, and she
transforms him into a stag so that he cannot speak of it: "he tried
to say 'Alas!' but no words came" (79). This loss of speech leads
to Actaeon's inability to inform his own hunting team of his true
identity; his loss of speech leads ultimately to his death. *[This
example reinforces the pattern that the writer had begun to notice
in the Orpheus example.]*

These paragraphs exemplify a writer in the process of discovering a workable idea. They begin with a list of similar examples, briefly noted. Notice, as the examples accumulate, how the writer begins to make more connections and to formulate trial explanations. In turn, the emerging patterns help her to see more significant details.

MOVE 4: MAKE THE IMPLICIT EXPLICIT

This move and the one that follows it (Keep reformulating questions and explanations) are the ones that push observations toward conclusions (the "So what?" part of the process).

One of the central activities and goals of analysis is to make explicit—overtly stated—what is implicit (suggested). When we do so, we are addressing such questions as "What follows from this?" and "If this is true, what else is true?" The pursuit of such questions—drawing out implications—moves our thinking and our writing *forward*.

We have already introduced in Chapter 2 several of the tools that spur the quest for implication: Asking So What? and Paraphrase × 3. Both of these heuristics enable a writer to examine evidence and draw conclusions about it that are not literally present but that follow from what the writer sees.

The word *implication* comes from the Latin *implicare*, which means "to fold in." The word *explicit* is in opposition to the idea of implication. It means "folded out." An act of mind is required to take what is folded in and fold it out for all to see. Paraphrasing is an especially useful tool in uncovering implications precisely because restating things in other words widens the range of meanings (folds them out) that are embedded in (folded in) the language and details under scrutiny.

This process of drawing out implications is also known as making inferences. *Inference* and *implication* are related but not synonymous terms. The term *implication* describes something suggested by the material itself; implications reside in the matter you are studying. The term *inference* describes your thinking process. In short, you infer what the subject implies.

Implication: An Example   Now, let's move on to an example, which will suggest not only how the process of making the implicit explicit works, but also how often we do it in our everyday lives. Imagine you are driving down the highway and find yourself analyzing a billboard advertisement for a brand of beer. Such an analysis might begin with your noticing what the billboard photo contains, its various "parts"—six young, athletic, and scantily clad men and women drinking beer while pushing kayaks into a fast-running river. At this point, you have produced not an analysis but a summary—a description of what the photo contains. If, however, you go on to consider what the particulars of the photo imply, your summary would become analytical.

You might infer, for example, that the photo implies that beer is the beverage of fashionable, healthy, active people. Your analysis would lead you to convert to direct statement meanings that are suggested but not overtly stated, such as the advertisement's goal of attacking common stereotypes about its product (that only lazy, overweight men drink beer). By making the implicit explicit (inferring what the ad implies) you can better understand the nature of your subject.

Try This 3.2: Making Inferences

This activity is suitable for in-class writing or small group work or to a longer writing assignment. Locate any magazine ad you find interesting. Ask yourself, *"What is this a picture of?"* Use our hypothetical beer ad as a model for rendering the implicit explicit. Don't settle for just one answer. Keep answering the question in different ways, letting your answers grow in length as they identify and begin to interpret the significance of telling details. Ask the implication-question: If the picture gives us this, what else is it asking us to believe? Also make sure to ask, after you have done some analysis, the *rhetoric*-question: "Why did the advertiser choose this particular image or set of images?" This question will help you to think about how the ad has been fashioned for consumption by a particular audience. You might then examine a second advertisement for the same product. Is there a pattern in the way certain items are marketed?

Then shift gears a bit by considering the implications of significant detail in the cover of a high-end magazine such as *The New Yorker*. First, describe the cover using analytical moves 2 and 3; then consider what the moves imply. You can easily find these covers online either by visiting *The New Yorker's* website or by going to the websites of particular artists who regularly produce *New Yorker* covers. You may have already experimented with a cover by Adrian Tomine in Chapter 2, Try This 2.3. You could look at more of his covers and read for patterns of subject matter and implication. You might also look at the covers of Harry Bliss—such as "Son of Kong," from August 1, 2005, cover #3632 at *The New Yorker* cover browser online.

Implications Versus Hidden Meanings

Two familiar phrases that reveal people's anxiety toward making the implicit explicit are *hidden meanings* and *reading between the lines*. Both phrases imply that meanings exist in places other than the literal words on the page: they are to be found either "under" or between the lines of text.

This is not a wholly unreasonable response because it recognizes that meanings are not always overt. But responding with these phrases does misrepresent the process of making inferences. It can also suggest some skeptical assumptions that a person may hold without fully realizing them. Let's spell some of these out.

For example, the charge that the meaning is hidden can imply for some people an act of conspiracy on the part of either an author, who chooses to deliberately obscure his or her meaning, or on the part of readers, who conspire to "find" things lurking below the surface that other readers don't know about and are unable to see. Another implicit assumption is that people probably know what they mean most of the time but, for some perverse reason, are unwilling to come out and say so.

"Reading between the lines" is a version of the hidden meaning theory in suggesting that we have to look for meanings elsewhere than in the lines of text themselves. At its most skeptical, the phrase "reading between the lines" means that an interpretation has come from nothing at all, from the white space between the lines and therefore has been imposed on the material by the interpreter.

Proponents of these views of analysis are, in effect, committing themselves to the position that everything in life means what it says and says what it means. It is probably safe to assume that most writers try to write what they mean and mean what they say. That is, they try to control the range of possible interpretations that their words could give rise to, but there is always more going on in a piece of writing (as in our everyday conversation) than can easily be pinned down and controlled. It is, in fact, an inherent property of language that it always means more than and thus other than it says.

The best evidence for the presence of implication in language itself (not under it or inserted into the white space) can be found by pondering statements that are rich in implication, for their unstated suggestions. We urge you take the time to work through Try This 3.3 below, an exercise demonstrating that implicit meanings are "really there."

Try This 3.3: Inferring Implications from Observations

Each of the statements below is rich in implication. Write a list of as many plausible implications as you can think of for each of the statements. After you have made your list of implications for each item, consider how you arrived at them. You might find it useful to do this exercise along with other people because part of its aim is to reveal the extent to which different people infer the same implications.

1. The sidewalk is disappearing as a feature of the American residential landscape. [Here are a couple of implications to prime the pump: people don't walk anywhere anymore; builders lack much sense of social responsibility.]

2. New house designs are tending increasingly toward open plans in which the kitchen is not separated from the rest of the house.

3. "Good fences make good neighbors."—Robert Frost

4. In the female brain, there are more connections between the right hemisphere (emotions, spatial reasoning) and the left hemisphere (verbal facility). In the male brain, these two hemispheres remain more separate.

5. In America, an increasing number of juveniles—people under the age of 18—are tried and convicted as adults, rather than as minors, resulting in more minors serving adult sentences for crimes they committed while still in their teens.

6. Neuroscientists tell us that the frontal cortex of the brain, the part responsible for judgment and especially for impulse control, is not fully developed in humans until roughly the age of 21. What are the implications of this observation relative to observation 5?

7. Linguists have long commented on the tendency of women's speech to use rising inflection at the end of statements as if the statements were questions. An actual command form—Be home by midnight!—thus becomes a question instead. What are we to make of the fact that in recent years, younger men (under 30) have begun to end declarative statements and command forms with rising inflections?

8. Shopping malls and grocery stores rarely have clocks.

9. List as many plausible implications as you can for this statement (which has been contested by other researchers).

> "In the eye-tracking test, only one in six subjects read Web pages linearly, sentence by sentence. In this study, Nielsen found that people took in hundreds of pages 'in a pattern that's very different from what you learned in school.' It looks like a capital letter F. At the top, users read all the way across, but as they proceed their descent quickens and horizontal sight contracts, with a slowdown around the middle of the page. Near the bottom, eyes move almost vertically, the lower-right corner of the page largely ignored."
>
> —Mark Bauerlein, "Online Literacy Is a Lesser Kind," *The Chronicle Review*, 9/19/08, http://chronicle.com/free/v55/i04/04b01001.htm.

(For an extended example of a writer who moves from implications, see "2:30," the commencement address by Bob Tarby, which is located after Move 5 on page 67.)

MOVE 5: KEEP REFORMULATING QUESTIONS AND EXPLANATIONS

Analysis, like all forms of writing, requires a lot of experimenting. Because the purpose of analytical writing is to figure something out, you shouldn't expect to know at the start of your writing process exactly where you are going, how all of your subject's parts fit together, and to what end. The key is to be patient and to know that there are procedures— in this case, questions—you can rely on to take you from uncertainty to understanding.

The following three groups of questions (organized according to the analytical moves they're derived from) are typical of what goes on in an analytical writer's head as he or she attempts to understand a subject. These questions will work with almost anything you want to think about. As you will see, the questions are geared toward helping you locate and try on explanations for the meaning of various patterns of details.

Which details seem significant? Why?

What does the detail mean?

What else might it mean?

    (Moves: Define Significant Parts; Make the Implicit Explicit)

How do the details fit together? What do they have in common?

What does this pattern of details mean?

What else might this same pattern of details mean? How else could it be explained?

    (Move: Look for Patterns)

What details don't seem to fit? How might they be connected with other details to form a different pattern?

What does this new pattern mean? How might it cause me to read the meaning of individual details differently?

    (Moves: Look for Anomalies and Keep Asking Questions)

The process of posing and answering such questions—the analytical process—is one of trial and error. One of the main things you acquire in the study of an academic discipline is knowledge of the kinds of questions the discipline typically asks. For example, an economics professor and a sociology professor might observe the same phenomenon, such as a sharp decline in health benefits for the elderly, and analyze its causes and significance in different ways. The economist might consider how such benefits are financed and how changes in government policy and the country's population patterns might explain the declining supply of funds for the elderly. The sociologist might ask about attitudes toward the elderly and about the social structures that the elderly rely on for support.

Science as a Process of Argument: A Biologist Speaks

In the following Voice from Across the Curriculum, molecular biologist Bruce Wightman argues that, as in other disciplines, scientific ideas are constantly tested and reformulated. He is responding to the misconception that science is all about facts and thus does not require analysis and interpretation.

Voices from Across the Curriculum

    I find it ironic that the discipline of science, which is so inherently analytical, is so difficult for students to think about analytically. Much of this comes from the prevailing view of society that science is somehow factual. Science students come to college to learn the facts. I think many find it comforting to think that everything they learn will be objective. None of the wishy-washy subjectivity that many perceive in other disciplines.

    Anyone who has ever done science knows that nothing could be further from the truth. Just like other academics, scientists spend endless hours patiently arguing over evidence that seems obscure or irrelevant to laypeople. There is rarely an absolute consensus. Science is an endless process of argument, obtaining evidence, analyzing evidence, and reformulating arguments. To be sure, we all accept gravity as a "fact." But to Newton, gravity was an argument for which evidence needed to be produced, analyzed, and discussed. It's important to remember that a significant fraction of his intellectual contemporaries were not swayed by his argument. Equally important is that many good scientific ideas of today will eventually be significantly modified or shown to be wrong.

—Bruce Wightman, Professor of Biology

"2:30": An Example of the Five Analytical Moves in Action

Printed below is a commencement address given on May 27, 2010 at Harvard University to medical and dentistry students and their families and friends. Students in both programs take their courses together for the first two years and then pursue separate tracks in the final two years before coming together again at graduation. The speaker, Bob Tarby, was a biology and English major at our college before going on to Harvard. HSDM is the Harvard School of Dental Medicine.

Study how this speech develops as a piece of thinking from its initial observation that "dentistry is the butt of a lot of jokes." Concentrate on moves 4 and 5—making the implicit explicit and reformulating questions. Throughout the piece, you will also notice how the writer has set up his primary questions by employing moves 1–3. He suspends judgment to explore a question. He locates significant parts and finds patterns, both in people's responses to dentists and in the way people think and feel about teeth.

Mark specific sentences in which the speaker makes the implicit explicit. Also mark places where he pauses to formulate and to reformulate questions. We have included a few analytical observations in square brackets to help you shift your attention from what the speech says to what it does—how it operates and moves.

2:30
by Bob Tarby

[1] Distinguished guests, deans, faculty, staff, and of course classmates, friends, and families—welcome! Welcome to the 138th HSDM-HMS Class Day. To my classmates— my friends and now my colleagues—thank you for the privilege to represent our class today.

[2] I'm not the most doggedly determined dental student that's graced Harvard's hallways. Therefore, as my classmates would only expect, I would like to start with an old joke:

[3] What's the best time to go see the dentist? Tooth hurty.

[4] If you didn't get it, just give it a few seconds to sink in. If you still don't get it, I can explain it later, although I'm pretty sure it's not going to be funny. But maybe it's better that way, because to all the dentists in the room, dental jokes are *never* funny. Anyone who's seen Seinfeld remembers the episode where Jerry tells another dental wisecrack: what's the difference between a dentist and a sadist? – Newer magazines.

His dentist, Dr. Whatley, seeks his revenge in an unnecessarily prolonged and painful procedure that is peppered with question upon question requiring narrative answers... Why is it, by the way, that dentists never ask simple yes or no questions when they've got their hands in your mouth?

[5] I'm sorry that Jerry's procedure was painful... but what do you think dentist jokes are to Dr. Whatley, or to us, the thirty-something individuals with purple lapels walking across the stage in about 20 minutes? "What do you call a doctor that didn't get into medical school? A dentist!?" Ouch.

[6] I'm certainly not here today solely to tell dentist jokes. Instead, I want to pose a nuanced idea about the intersection of humor and dentistry. Over the past couple of weeks, I've been thinking seriously about what makes dentistry unique. As we often cite, dentistry is a subspecialty of medicine, and our first two years in the medical school have been invaluable to who we have become as professionals. We are not medical doctors but doctors of dental medicine, and there is an important difference. Two things set dentistry apart from all other medical specialties:

1) dentistry deals (almost exclusively) with the oral cavity and maxillofacial region, and

2) dentistry is the butt of a lot of jokes

[7] There are plenty of other doctor jokes—I think proctology and urology probably bear the brunt of these—but I'll refrain from discussing other specialties and other orifices. Why do we care so much about the mouth? *[= primary question essay will explore]*

[8] Dentistry is not a contemporary construct. Thousands of years ago, Incans placed shell implants, and Egyptians inlaid their teeth with precious metals. Even the institution has been important enough to differentiate its educational system—dental school is different than medical school. History aside, the mouth is the only orifice that smiles back at us in the mirror every morning, indicating the implicit importance of dentistry. A smile goes beyond simply anatomy; its esthetic quality communicates health, well-being, and even status. This makes the mouth and the face—the orofacial structures, in dental lingo—important.

[9] As student clinicians, my classmates and I saw evidence of this everyday in the dental clinic: our patients sit in the chair, fidget anxiously, and say, apologetically, "I just ate lunch" or "I didn't have a chance to brush" or "I *try* to floss regularly". They

are embarrassed to open their mouths in front of people who chose mouths and teeth as their professional undertaking. Judging by their reticence to "open up", we can safely assume that this is an intensely personal space: the mouth runs the gamut from function and survival to social hierarchy. Put differently, you can't eat without teeth, and you can't get a job at a Top 10 company without a flawless line of pearly whites. Or at least that's the conception.

[10] If teeth serve such important functions, where do all these dental jokes come from? Everything is Freudian, and jokes are no exception. Among other ideas on humor, Freud presents a theory that jokes are structured like an inverted triangle: a straight line at the top and two sides coming down to a point. At each of the three points is a character: the teller, the witness, and at the bottom, the "butt." I know I promised not to speak on behalf of the proctologists, so we'll keep this brief.

[11] Looking at the language of jokes, especially ones that involve a butt, we see that the butt gets "sent up" or "knocked down a peg". Up or down, there is social movement implicit in the work of a joke. According to Freud, a joke is serious and subversive—read another way, it works to elevate the teller and denigrate the butt.

[12] So I pose a question: why are we constantly denigrating dentists? It might be because they cause us pain, but more likely, it's because they have a bizarre and special permission to probe one of our most personal anatomic spaces. We let dentists put needles, crowns and dentures, not to mention their hands, into a space that serves the dual function of nourishing our bodies and expressing our social status.

[13] More than just a highly sensitive observer, though, the dentist takes ownership of another person's mouth. By extension, he or she has control over the oral functions that make the mouth such an important orifice: the ability to eat, the ability to communicate and to express, and, perhaps most important for our argument here, the dentist has control over the esthetics of the mouth, which dictate so much of how we understand each other, and how we understand ourselves. Imposing on the oral cavity in such a way gives the dentist a transgressive power over our mouths, and a strange ownership of a very intimate space. No wonder dentists make us anxious.

[14] *[qualifies claim:]* But there are doctors who do the same thing—cardiac surgeons, for example, invade and transgress, and probably most people would be more than a little

anxious about having open-heart surgery. It would not, however, be a joking matter—a heart is among the few organs that are crucial for the very basis of life. Teeth on the other hand – well, who wants to admit that teeth are important? Certainly not as important as a heart, right?

[15] So we are anxious about the dentist smelling our breath or discovering bits of food stuck between our teeth, about having a smile that indicates social order, and, to further complicate matters, we are anxious about admitting all this. *[= ultimate claim]* Because teeth shouldn't be *that* important.

[16] Out of this anxiety, dentist jokes are born. Comedy is often a vehicle for truth: dentist jokes indicate that our fear of the dentist—physical discomfort or pain, the power the dentist holds over an important part of our body—is real. And jokes are a way to ease that fear, to make dentistry accessible and, occasionally, even funny.

[17] So today, on our inaugural day as dentists, let's embrace the dentist joke! Teeth are important, and we like them! We're going out into the world to change smiles and lives. And we're going to make jokes when opportunities arise—not because what we do isn't serious, but because we can't and shouldn't take ourselves too seriously.

Try This 3.4: Apply the Five Analytical Moves to a Speech

Speeches provide rich examples for analysis, and they are easily accessible on the Internet and on You Tube. We especially recommend a site called American Rhetoric (You can Google it for the URL). Choose any speech and analyze it for its use of the five analytical moves. Where, for example, does the speech locate pattern? How does it define significant parts and locate them in relation to the whole? Where does the speaker make inferences? To what extent does it reformulate its questions and explanations?

On the basis of your results, draw a few conclusions about the speech's point of view and its way of presenting that point of view, which is to say its rhetoric. Try to get beyond the obvious and the general. What does applying the moves cause you to notice that you might not have noticed before?

WHAT IT MEANS TO HAVE AN IDEA

In the final sections of this chapter, we will go on to distinguish analysis from other forms of writing: argument, summary, and personal response. We conclude this opening section of the chapter, on the Five Analytical Moves, with discussion of what counts as an idea in analytical writing.

Thinking, as opposed to reporting or reacting, should lead you to ideas. But what does it mean to have an idea? It's one thing to acquire knowledge, but you also need to learn how to produce knowledge, to think for yourself. The problem is that people get daunted when asked to arrive at ideas. They dream up ingenious ways to avoid the task. Or they get paralyzed with anxiety.

What is an idea? Must an idea be something entirely "original"? Must it revamp the way you understand yourself or your stance toward the world?

Such expectations are unreasonably grand. Clearly, a writer in the early stages of learning about a subject can't be expected to arrive at an idea so original that, like a Ph.D. thesis, it revises complex concepts in a discipline. Nor should you count as ideas only those that lead to some kind of life-altering discovery. Ideas are usually much smaller in scope, much less grand, than people seem to expect.

Some would argue that ideas are discipline-specific, that what counts as an idea in Psychology differs from what counts as an idea in History or Philosophy or Business. Surely the context does affect the way ideas are shaped and expressed. This book operates on the premise, however, that ideas across the curriculum share common elements. All of the items in the list below, for example, are common to ideas and to idea-making in virtually any context.

It is easiest to understand what ideas are by considering what ideas do and where they can be found. Most strong analytical ideas launch you in a process of resolving problems and bringing competing positions into some kind of alignment. They locate you where there is something to negotiate, where you are required not just to list answers but also to ask questions, make choices, and engage in reasoning about the significance of your evidence.

Here is a partial list of what it means to have an idea:

1. An idea usually starts with an observation that is puzzling, with something you want to figure out rather than something you think you already understand.

2. An idea may be the discovery of a question where there seemed not to be one.

3. An idea answers a question; it explains something that needs to be explained or provides a way out of a difficulty that other people have had in understanding something.

4. An idea may make explicit and explore the meaning of something implicit—an unstated assumption upon which an argument rests, or a logical consequence of a given position.

5. An idea may connect elements of a subject and explain the significance of that connection.

6. An idea often accounts for some *dissonance*, that is, something that seems to not fit together.

B. Distinguishing Analysis from Argument, Summary, and Expressive Writing

How does analysis differ from other kinds of thinking and writing? A common way of answering this question is to think of communication as having three possible centers of emphasis—the writer, the subject, and the audience. Communication, of course, involves all three of these components, but some kinds of writing concentrate more on one than on the others. Autobiographical writing, for example, such as diaries or memoirs or stories about personal experience, centers on the writer and his or her desire for self-expression. Argument, in which the writer takes a stand on an issue, advocating or arguing against a policy or attitude, is reader-centered; its goal is to bring about a change in its readers' actions and beliefs. Analytical writing is more concerned with arriving at an understanding of a subject than with either self-expression or changing readers' views.

These three categories of writing are not mutually exclusive. So, for example, expressive (writer-centered) writing is also analytical in its attempts to define and explain a writer's feelings, reactions, and experiences. And analysis is a form of self-expression since it inevitably reflects the ways a writer's experiences have taught him or her to think about the world. But even though expressive writing and analysis necessarily overlap, they also differ significantly in both method and aim. In expressive writing, your primary subject is your self, with other subjects serving as a means of evoking greater self-understanding. In analytical writing, your reasoning may derive from your personal experience, but it is your reasoning and not you or your experiences that matter. Analysis asks not just "what do I think?" but "how good is my thinking? how well does it fit the subject I am trying to explain?"

In its emphasis on logic and the dispassionate scrutiny of ideas ("what do I think about what I think?"), analysis is a close cousin of argument. But analysis and argument are not the same.

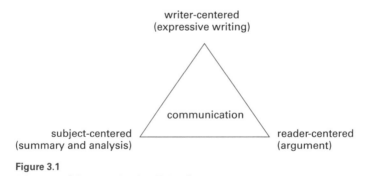

writer-centered
(expressive writing)

communication

subject-centered   reader-centered
(summary and analysis)   (argument)

Figure 3.1
Diagram of Communication Triangle

ANALYSIS AND ARGUMENT

Analysis and argument proceed in the same way. They offer evidence, make claims about it, and supply reasons that explain and justify the claims. In other words, in both analysis and argument, you respond to the questions "what have you got to go on?" (supply evidence) and "how did you get there?" (supply the principles and reasons that caused you to conclude what you did about the evidence).

Although analysis and argument proceed in essentially the same way, they differ in the kinds of questions they try to answer. Argument, at its most dispassionate, asks, "what can be said with truth about x or y?" In common practice, though, the kinds of questions that argument more often answers are more committed, directive, and should-centered, such as "which is better, x or y?," "how can we best achieve x or y?," and "why should we stop doing x or y?"

Analysis, by contrast, asks, "what does x or y mean"? In analysis of the evidence (your data) is something you wish to understand, and the claims are assertions about what that evidence means. The claim that an analysis makes is usually a tentative answer to a what, how, or why question; it seeks to explain why people watch professional wrestling or what a rising number of sexual harassment cases might mean, or how certain features of government health care policy are designed to allay the fears of the middle class.

The claim that an argument makes is often an answer to a "should" question: for example, readers should or shouldn't vote for bans on smoking in public buildings, or they should or shouldn't believe that gays can function effectively in the military. The writer of an analysis is more concerned with discovering how each of these complex subjects might be defined and explained than with convincing readers to approve or disapprove of them.

Analysis Versus Debate-Style Argument

A factor that sometimes separates argument and analysis is the closer association of argument with the desire to persuade. When the aim of argument is persuasion—to get the audience to accept the writer's position on a given subject—argument is likely to differ significantly from analysis. For one thing, a writer concerned with persuading others may feel the need to go into the writing process with considerable certainty about the position he or she advocates. The writer of an analysis, on the other hand, usually begins and remains for an extended period in a position of uncertainty.

Analytical writers are frequently more concerned with persuading themselves, with discovering what they believe about a subject, than they are with persuading others. The writer of an analysis is thus more likely to begin with the details of a subject he or she wishes to better understand, rather than with a position he or she wishes to defend.

Many of you may have been introduced to writing arguments through the debate model—arguing pro or con (for or against) on a given position, with the aim of defeating an imagined opponent and convincing your audience of the rightness of your position. The agree/disagree mode of writing and thinking that you often see in editorials, hear on radio or television, and even practice sometimes in school may incline you to focus all your energy on the bottom line—aggressively advancing a claim for or against some view—without first engaging in the exploratory interpretation of evidence that is so necessary to arriving at thoughtful arguments. But as the American College Dictionary says, "to argue implies reasoning or trying to understand; it does not necessarily imply opposition." It is this more exploratory, tentative, and dispassionate mode of argument that this book encourages you to practice.

Adhering to the more restrictive, debate-style definition of argument can create a number of problems for careful analytical writers:

1. By requiring writers to be oppositional, debate-style argument inclines them to discount or dismiss problems in the side or position they have chosen; they cling to the same static position rather than testing it as a way of allowing it to evolve.

2. It inclines writers toward either/or thinking rather than encouraging them to formulate more qualified (carefully limited, acknowledging exceptions, etc.) positions that integrate apparently opposing viewpoints.

3. It overvalues convincing someone else at the expense of developing understanding.

As should now be clear, the aims of analysis and argument can sometimes be in conflict. Nevertheless, it's important to remember that in practice, analysis and argument are inevitably linked. Even the most tentative and cautiously evolving analysis is ultimately an argument; it asks readers to accept a particular interpretation of a set of data.

Similarly, even the most passionately committed argument is an analysis. If you approach an argument with the primary goals of convincing others that you are right and defeating your opponents, you may neglect the more important goal of arriving at a fair and accurate assessment of your subject. In fact, you will be able to argue much more effectively from evidence if you first take the time to really consider what that evidence means, and thereby, to find valid positions to argue about it.

ETHOS AND ANALYSIS

Analysis, as we have been arguing, is interested in how we come to know things, how we make meaning. This focus privileges not just conclusions about a subject but sharing with readers the thought process that led to those conclusions. Rather than telling other people what to think, the best analytical writers encourage readers to think collaboratively with them. This is true of the best writers in the civic forum as well as in colleges and universities. *(See Chapter 1, the short take called "What's Different About Writing Arguments in College?")*

It follows that the character of the speaker (ethos) in an analysis will serve to create a more collaborative and collegial relationship with readers than might be the case in other kinds of writing.

Classical rhetoric thought of the impact that writers/speakers had on audiences in terms of three categories: logos, pathos, and ethos. These categories are very useful, especially as you go about trying to construct a written version of yourself that will allow you to succeed and grow as a college writer. The word *logos* (from Greek) refers to the logical component of a piece of writing or speaking. *Pathos* refers to the emotional component in writing, the ways it appeals to feelings in an audience. *Ethos* will be familiar to you as a term because of its relation to the word ethics. In classical rhetoric, ethos is the character of the speaker, which is important in determining an audience's acceptance or rejection of his or her arguments.

Much of this book is concerned with the logos of academic writing, with ways of deriving and arguing ideas in colleges, universities, and the world of educated discourse. Ethos matters, too. The thinking you do is hard to separate from the sense the audience has of the person doing the thinking. In fact, the personae (versions of ourselves) we assume when we write have a formative impact on what we think and say. Ethos is not just a mask we assume in order to appeal to a particular audience. The stylistic and thinking moves prescribed by the ethos of particular groups become, with practice, part of who we are and thus of how we think and interact with others.

Eventually, college writers need to learn how to adopt different self-presentations for different academic disciplines. The acceptable ethos of a Chemistry lab report differs in significant ways from the one you might adopt in a Political Science or English paper. For present purposes, we'll note that the ethoi of most analytical writing across the curriculum share certain significant traits:

- nonadversarial tone—is not looking for a fight
- collaborative and collegial—treats readers as colleagues who are worthy of respect and who share your interest
- carefully qualified—does not making overstated claims
- relative impersonality in self-presentation—keeps focus primarily on the subject, not the writer

ANALYSIS VERSUS SUMMARY: THE EXAMPLE OF *WHISTLER'S MOTHER*

One of the most common kinds of writing you'll be asked to do in college, other than analysis, is summary. Summary differs from analysis, because the aim of summary is to recount, in effect, to reproduce someone else's ideas. But summary and analysis are also clearly related and usually operate together. Summary is important to analysis because you can't analyze a subject without laying out its significant parts for your reader. Similarly, analysis is important to summary because summarizing is more than just copying someone else's words. To write an accurate summary, you have to ask analytical questions such as:

- Which of the ideas in the reading are most significant? Why?
- How do these ideas fit together? What do the key passages in the reading mean?

Summary Is a Focused Description

Like an analysis, an effective summary doesn't assume that the subject matter can speak for itself: the writer needs to play an active role. A good summary provides perspective on the subject as a whole by explaining, as an analysis does, the meaning and function of each of that subject's parts. Moreover, like an analysis, a good summary does not aim to approve or disapprove of its subject: the goal, in both kinds of writing, is to understand rather than to evaluate. (*For more on summary, see Chapter 7, Making Common Topics More Analytical, and Chapter 5, Writing About Reading.*)

So, summary, like analysis, is a tool of understanding and not just a mechanical task. But a summary stops short of analysis because summary typically makes much smaller interpretive leaps. A summary of the painting popularly known as *Whistler's Mother*, for example, would tell readers what the painting includes, which details are the most prominent, and even what the overall effect of the painting seems to be. A summary might say that the painting possesses a certain serenity and that it is somewhat spare, almost austere. This kind of language still falls into the category of *focused description,* which is what a summary is.

Analysis Makes an Interpretive Leap

An analysis would include more of the writer's interpretive thinking. It might tell us, for instance, that the painter's choice to portray his subject in profile contributes to our sense of her separateness from us and of her nonconfrontational passivity. We look at her, but she does not look back at us. Her black dress and the fitted lace cap that obscures her hair are not only emblems of her self-effacement, shrouds disguising her identity like her expressionless face, but also the tools of her self-containment and thus of her power to remain aloof from prying eyes. What is the attraction of this painting (this being one of the questions that an analysis might ask)? What might draw a viewer to the sight of this austere, drably attired woman, sitting alone in the center of a mostly blank space? Perhaps it is the very starkness of the painting, and the mystery of self-sufficiency at its center, that attracts us (see Figure 3.2).

Laying out the data is key to any kind of analysis not simply because it keeps the analysis accurate but also because, crucially, it is *in the act of carefully describing a subject that analytical writers often have their best ideas.* Observations of the sort just offered go beyond describing what the painting contains and enter into the writer's ideas about what its details imply, what the painting invites us to make of it and by what means. Notice in our analysis of the painting how intertwined the description (summary) is with the analysis.

REUNION DES MUSEES NATIONAUX, ART RESOURCE, NY. James Abbott McNeil Whistler.

Figure 3.2
Arrangement in Grey and Black: The Artist's Mother by James Abbott McNeill Whistler, 1871.

The writer who can offer a careful description of a subject's key features is likely to arrive at conclusions about possible meanings that others would share. You may not agree with the terms by which we have summarized the painting, and thus you may not agree with such conclusions as "the mystery of self-sufficiency." Nor is it necessary that you agree because there is no single, right answer to what the painting means. The absence of a single right answer does not, however, mean that all possible interpretations are equal and equally convincing to readers.

Here are two guidelines to be drawn from this discussion of analysis and summary:

1. Describe with care. The words you choose to summarize your data will contain the germs of your ideas about what the subject means.

2. In moving from summary to analysis, scrutinize the language you have chosen, asking, "why did I choose this word?" and "what ideas are implicit in the language I have used?"

Data	Analytical Moves	Interpretive Leaps (So What?)
subject in profile, not looking at us →	make implicit explicit (speculate about what the detail might suggest) →	figure strikes us as separate, nonconfrontational, passive
folded hands, fitted lace cap, contained hair, expressionless face →	locate pattern of same or similar detail; make what is implicit in pattern of details explicit →	figure strikes us as self-contained, powerful in her separateness and self-enclosure— self-sufficient?
patterned curtain and picture versus still figure and blank wall; slightly frilled lace cuffs and ties on cap versus plain black dress →	locate organizing contrast; make what is implicit in the contrast explicit →	austerity and containment of the figure made more pronounced by slight contrast with busier, more lively, and more ornate elements and with little picture showing world outside
slightly slouched body position and presence of support for feet →	anomalies; make what is implicit in the anomalies explicit →	these details destabilize the serenity of the figure, adding some tension to the picture in the form of slightly uneasy posture and figure's need for support: she looks too long, drooped in on her own spine

Figure 3.3
Summary and Analysis of *Whistler's Mother* Diagram

ANALYSIS AND PERSONAL ASSOCIATIONS

Although observations like those offered in the "Interpretive Leaps" column in Figure 3.3 go beyond simple description, they stay with the task of explaining the painting, rather than moving to private associations that the painting might prompt, such as effusions about old age, or rocking chairs, or the character and situation of the writer's own mother. Such associations could well be valuable as a means of prompting a searching piece of expressive writing. They might also help a writer to interpret some feature of the painting that he or she was working to understand. But the writer would not be free to use pieces of his or her personal history as conclusions about what the painting communicates, unless these conclusions could also be reasonably inferred from the painting itself.

Analysis is a creative activity, a fairly open form of inquiry, but its imaginative scope is governed by logic. The hypothetical analysis we have offered is not the only reading of the painting a viewer might make because the same pattern of details might lead to different conclusions. But a viewer would not be free to conclude anything he or she wished, such as that the woman is mourning the death of a son or is patiently waiting to die. Such conclusions would be unfounded speculations, since the black dress is not sufficient to support them. Analysis often operates in areas where there is no one right answer, but like summary and argument, it requires the writer to reason from evidence.

A few rules are worth highlighting here:

1. The range of associations for explaining a given detail or word must be governed by context.

2. It's fine to use your personal reactions as a way into exploring what a subject means, but take care not to make an interpretive leap stretch farther than the actual details will support.

3. Because the tendency to transfer meanings from your own life onto a subject can lead you to ignore the details of the subject itself, you need always to be asking yourself: "what other explanations might plausibly account for this same pattern of detail?"

As we began this chapter by saying, analysis is a form of detective work. It can surprise us with ideas that our experiences produce once we take the time to listen to ourselves thinking. But analysis is also a discipline; it has rules that govern how we proceed and that enable others to judge the validity of our ideas. A good analytical thinker needs to be the attentive Dr. Watson to his or her own Sherlock Holmes. That is what the remainder of this book will teach you to do. *(See Chapter 6, Making Interpretations Plausible, for more on the rules governing interpretation, again using* Whistler's Mother *as a primary example.)*

Rhetorical Analysis of an Advertisement: An Example

We have demonstrated how the five moves might work in the analysis of a painting. Our final example addresses a more popular form: advertising. The example is a student paper that uses the moves to produce a rhetorical analysis of a perfume advertisement that appeared in a magazine aimed at young women. Locate the Five Analytical Moves, especially making the implicit explicit.

The visual imagery of advertisements offers instructive opportunities for rhetorical analysis because advertising is a form of persuasion. Advertisers attend carefully to rhetoric by carefully targeting their audiences. This means advertisements are well suited to the questions that rhetorical analysis typically asks: how is the audience being invited to respond and by what means (in what context)? You'll notice that in the rhetorical analysis of the magazine ad, the writer occasionally extends her analysis to evaluative conclusions about the aims and possible effects (on American culture) of the advertisement.

Marketing the Girl Next Door: A Declaration of Independence?

[1] Found in *Seventeen* magazine, the advertisement for "tommy girl," the perfume manufactured by Tommy Hilfiger, sells the most basic American ideal of independence. Various visual images and text suggest that purchasing tommy girl buys freedom and liberation for the mind and body. This image appeals to young women striving to establish themselves as unbound individuals. Ironically, the advertisement uses traditional American icons as vehicles for marketing to the modern woman. Overall, the message is simple: American individualism can be found in a spray or nonspray bottle.

[2] Easily, the young woman dominates the advertisement. She has the look of the all-American "girl next door." Her appeal is a natural one, as she does not rely on makeup or a runway model's cheekbones for her beauty. Freckles frame her eyes that ambitiously gaze skyward; there are no limits restricting women in capitalist America. Her flowing brown hair freely rides a stirring breeze. Unconcerned with the order of a particular hairstyle, she smiles and enjoys the looseness of her spirit. The ad tells us how wearing this perfume allows women to achieve the look of self-assured and liberated indifference without appearing vain.

[3] The second most prevalent image in the advertisement is the American flag, which neatly matches the size of the young woman's head. The placement and size of the flag suggest that if anything is on her cloudless mind, it is fundamental American beliefs that allow for such self-determination. The half-concealed flag is seemingly continued in the young woman's hair. According to the ad, American ideals reside well within the girl as well as the perfume.

[4] It is also noticeable that there is a relative absence of all land surrounding the young woman. We can see glimpses of "fruited plains" flanking the girl's shoulders. This young woman is barely bound to earth, as free as the clouds that float beneath her head. It is this liberated image Americans proudly carry that is being sold in the product.

[5] The final image promoting patriotism can be found in the young woman's clothing. The young woman is draped in the blue jean jacket, a classic symbol of American ruggedness and originality. As far as we can see, the jacket is spread open, supporting the earlier claim of the young women's free and independent spirit. These are the very same ideals that embody American pride and patriotism. The ad clearly employs the association principle in linking the tommy girl fragrance with emotionally compelling yet essentially unrelated images of American nationalism and patriotism.

[6] A final obvious appeal to American nationalism is the tagline of the advertisement, the underlying message being "a declaration of independence." The young woman has already declared her independence, and now it is your turn. Doesn't every young woman want to be in that green field, hair blowing in the wind, wearing a confident look outlined against an American flag and clean, carefree, endless blue sky?

[7] Lastly, the advertisement utilizes several implicit arrows that point to the actual product of tommy girl perfume. The white writing against the dark blue jean jacket catches the eye first, encouraging the reader to continue in the traditional, left to right order. When the writing stops, we are naturally pointed

toward the product. In addition, the young woman's hair, seen earlier as an extension of the American flag, is flurrying out and somewhat downward. We follow the hair to its end, where it seemingly kisses the product's cap. All visual indications of direction in the advertisement lead the viewer to an inevitable end: the irresistible scent of tommy girl perfume.

[8] But we might also look beyond the ad's overt messages, and examine its effects on the viewer and our society as a whole. Returning to the ad's portrayal of the young woman, we are shown a girl with a natural beauty, free of worries or cares about conforming to the pressures of society as a female. Jean Kilbourne (2003) argues that countless ads tell women to search for freedom and independence through being thin, as echoed in the ad's skinny and attractive young woman. Kilbourne actually refers to another tommy girl ad that uses the same tagline: "'A declaration of independence,' proclaims an ad for perfume that features an emaciated model, but in fact the quest for a body as thin as the model's becomes a prison for many women and girls" (p. 263). She argues that ads encouraging a search for feminine independence often promote the worship of the thinness ideal, as well as the dilemma of being a successful and powerful woman while remaining "feminine" and unthreatening (pp. 262–264).

[9] Additionally, the ad for tommy girl perfume is also effective because it "takes on the trappings of a movement for social justice," according to Thomas Frank (1997, p. 187). Frank describes how advertisers constantly link products with the rebellious, revolutionary political and social movements of the past in order to conjure the vehement emotions associated with their resounding emotional content. The tommy girl ad emphasizes typical patriotic American images—like the American flag and denim clothing—as well as the phrase *a declaration of independence*, which explicitly creates a connection between the perfume and the American colonists' revolutionary pursuit of liberty in their beliefs and behavior during the American Revolution.

[10] Yet in reality, this marketing of liberation is paradoxical; although this freeing message promotes rebellion and nonconformity, it actually supports the market economy and feeds into capitalism and conformity. When advertisers employ political protest messages to be associated with products, they imply that buying the product is a form of political action.

[11] But lastly, the ad gives another paradoxical message with the portrayal of the beauty of the American, unspoiled, natural environment. Another typical American image is of the untouched landscapes, green pastures, and cloudless blue skies of the open frontier, which serves as the ad's backdrop.

The ad's clear blue sky with the American flag flying freely in the wind encourages the viewer to link the beauty of the natural American landscape with the purchase of tommy girl. Sut Jhally, editor of the video *Advertising and the End of the World* (1998), would argue that the ad's purpose—the consumption of the product—is paradoxically putting the environment at risk. Our "freedom" to buy all of what we need (and especially, what we don't need) is essentially spoiling the natural surroundings that we romanticize. And so the viewers are simply left to decide: Does this tommy girl ad truly portray a declaration of independence, or of *dependence?*

REFERENCES

Frank, T. (1997). Liberation marketing and the culture trust. In E. Barnouw et al. (Ed.), *Conglomerates and the media* (pp. 173–190). New York: The New Press.

Jhally, S. (Ed.). (1998). *Advertising and the end of the world* [Videotape]. Northampton, MA: Media Education Foundation.

Kilbourne, J. (2003). The more you subtract, the more you add: Cutting girls down to size. In G. Dines & J. Humez (Eds.), *Gender, race and class in media* (pp. 258–267). Thousand Oaks, CA: Sage.

GUIDELINES FOR ANALYSIS: WHAT IT IS AND WHAT IT DOES

1. Avoid deciding what your subject means before you analyze it, and remember that analysis often operates in areas where there is no one right answer.

2. As a general rule, analysis favors live questions—where something remains to be resolved—over inert answers, places where things are nailed down and don't leave much space for further thinking.

3. As you analyze a subject, ask not just "What are its defining parts?" but also "How do these parts help me to understand the meaning of the subject as a whole?"

4. Look for patterns of repetition and organizing contrasts in the data, as well as anomalies, and ask yourself questions about what these mean.

5. Make the implicit explicit: convert the suggested meanings of particular details into overt statements.

6. When you describe and summarize, attend carefully to the language you choose, since the words themselves will usually contain the germs of ideas.

7. The analytical process is one of trial and error. Learning to write well is largely a matter of learning how to frame questions. Whatever questions you ask, the answers will often produce more questions.

Assignments

1. **Expand a Try This into a Longer Essay**. Two of the Try This exercises in this chapter are suitable for more extended pieces of writing: Try This 3.2: Making Inferences and Try This 3.4: Apply the Five Analytical Moves to a Speech. Develop either into a piece of several pages in length.

2. **Analyze a Portrait or Other Visual Image**. Locate any portrait, preferably a good reproduction from an art book or magazine, one that shows detail clearly. Then do a version of what we've done with *Whistler's Mother*.

   Your goal is to produce an analysis of the portrait with the steps we included in analyzing *Whistler's Mother*. First, summarize the portrait, describing accurately its significant details. Do not go beyond a recounting of what the portrait includes; avoid interpreting what these details suggest.

   Then use the various methods offered in this chapter to analyze the data. What repetitions (patterns of same or similar detail) do you see? What organizing contrasts suggest themselves? In light of these patterns of similarity and difference, what anomalies do you then begin to detect? Move from the data to interpretive conclusions. This process will produce a set of interpretive leaps, which you may then try to assemble into a more coherent claim of some sort—a short essay about what the portrait "says."

3. **Describe a Neighborhood**. Revisit the paragraphs from Jane Jacobs' book, *The Death and Life of Great American Cities* (1961), which are offered earlier in this chapter under the heading Description as a Form of Analysis: Some Academic Examples. These paragraphs offer an implicitly analytical description of city life in Greenwich Village, a neighborhood in New York City, in the 1950s. Use these paragraphs as the basis of a writing assignment to be done in two steps.

   First, find an example of Jacobs' "go-to sentence," following the instructions offered in Chapter 2, the section entitled Identifying the "Go To" Sentence. Be sure to relate the shape of the sentence you select to Jacobs' way of thinking and of communicating her point of view in the piece.

   Second, write several descriptive paragraphs of your own in which you try to capture the character of a neighborhood by presenting significant detail.

   * * *

   We are offering you two further assignments, both taken from our colleagues. Either assignment might be adapted to materials in your writing course, but at least in part we share them with you to provide a glimpse of real life analytical assignments in writing-intensive courses in two different academic disciplines.

   * * *

4. **Analyze Two Representations of Inner City Life**. This assignment was designed by Political Science Professor Brian Mello for his course entitled *The Wire: Money, Drugs, & Life in Urban America*. You can adapt this assignment for your own use by comparing two representations of inner city life: photographs,

videos, songs, and so forth. Analyze these by locating patterns of significant detail and by making the implicit explicit. Dr. Mello's assignment follows:

> Your task is to find your own representation of inner city life, and bring it to the last week of class where you will be asked to share this with your peers. This representation could come in the form of a photograph (or series of photographs), a song (or a music video), a poem, a passage from a work of literature, or a passage from a non-fiction text.
>
> This assignment points us back to the central theme of this course—examining what assumptions are made by, and what implications should be drawn from the representation of socioeconomic concerns in *The Wire*. As Thomas Bender pointed out in his lecture, representations of urban life are never apolitical—they always create for the viewer certain assumptions and interpretations about life in urban America.
>
> Compare the story that gets expressed in the representation of urban life that you have selected to the story that gets told in any one of the following course texts—*The Wire, The Corner, Cop in the Hood,* or *Gang Leader for a Day*. You should focus in on specific passages or scenes from these texts. Insofar as a different interpretation of urban life emerges from the representations that you bring into class, what explains this difference? How can or should one reconcile these different interpretations? Insofar as there are similarities, what are they, and why might it be interesting or important that common representations emerge in multiple contexts? What do these representations tell us about who gets to represent urban life?

5. **Compare Two Cultural Documents That Reveal a Current Cultural Divide.** Here is an assignment designed by Communications Professor Dr. Jefferson Pooley for his writing-intensive course, *1968*. You can adapt this assignment by locating two contemporary documents that reveal a cultural divide in America now. Be sure to explain *how* the details of the documents disclose this cultural rift. You could also choose two political cartoons from different points of view on the same subject. Note: please refrain from taking a stand on the cultural divide that your documents embody. Focus instead on careful description and inferring implications. Here is the original assignment:

> In a three-page paper use the attached transcript from the "Chicago Seven" trial—the circus-like prosecution of prominent DNC protestors—to support the thesis that the exchange between Abbie Hoffman (Yippie leader) and Julius Hoffman (judge) represents, in microcosm, the cultural divide then gripping America. (The excerpt is a verbatim transcript from the infamous 1969 trial of Hoffman and six other New Left leaders.)
>
> Your task in this paper is to organize your evidence in some coherent way. The legal theatrics of the Hoffman-Hoffman exchange provide you with an abundance of material to work with. A strong paper will discuss the trial transcript according to some organizing logic, though the specific structure is up to you.

Chapter 4

Toolkit of Analytical Methods II: Going Deeper

A TEACHER COMMENT found in the margins of many essays and famous for bewildering students is the single word "develop"—or just "dev." Faculty who write that term seem to be saying they want more thinking, that what's on the page is too simple or uncomplicated. But it's no easy matter to develop your ideas. This chapter offers you tools for doing so—hence, the chapter's subtitle, Going Deeper.

This chapter is the logical next step to be taken. Where Chapter 2 equips you with foundational observational skills, and Chapter 3 incorporates them into a five-step analytical sequence, Chapter 4 offers you a set of analytical activities that can enable you to extend, complicate, and deepen your understanding of whatever you are analyzing. In effect, this new set of strategies seeks to give you more concrete ways of carrying out the last two of the five analytical moves featured in Chapter 3—to make what is implicit explicit and to reformulate questions and explanations.

Here is the list of the chapter's heuristics, each with a very brief summary of what it involves. We will go on to explain each in more detail.

1. Passage-Based Focused Freewriting

   (analyze a representative passage to understand better how the whole works)

2. Uncovering Assumptions

   (determine the givens, what must be believed first in order to posit what the thing you are analyzing has said)

3. Reformulating Binaries

   (question the accuracy of a basic contrast and determine the extent to which one side prevails over the other)

4. [Looking for] Difference within Similarity and Similarity Despite Difference

   (move beyond a mechanical matching exercise by exploring how two things are alike, and So What, and then different, and So What)

5. "Seems to Be About X, but Could Also Be (or Is 'Really') about Y"

   (assume that you got it wrong the first time to get somewhere new and interesting the second time)

Note: these heuristics, although not intended as formulae for organizing papers, can to some extent function in this way. They are primarily "thinking moves" designed to produce better, more in-depth thinking for essays, arguments or reports. The best way to learn these thinking skills is to practice them out repeatedly in your own work and with other writers.

1. PASSAGE-BASED FOCUSED FREEWRITING

WHAT IT DOES

Find an interesting passage
Sketch its context
Target and paraphrase key words and phrases
Explore why (so what that) the passage is interesting
Draw out implications
Ask how the passage is representative of the larger reading

WHAT IT DOES NOT DO

Voice reactions and criticisms
Free-associate with other subjects

Passage-based focused freewriting increases your ability to learn from what you read. The passage-based version differs from regular freewriting by limiting the focus to a piece of text. It prompts in-depth analysis of a representative example, on the assumption that you'll attain a better appreciation of the whole after you've explored how a piece of it works. *(Please review the short take from Chapter 1, Freewriting: How and Why to Do It.)*

The impromptu nature of passage-based focused freewriting encourages you to take chances, to think out loud on the page. It invites you to notice what you notice in the moment and take some stabs at what the passage might mean without having to worry about formulating a weighty thesis statement or maintaining consistency. It allows you to worry less about what you don't understand and instead start to work things out as you write.

A lot of great papers start as in-class writings—not as outlines.

Step 1: Choose a limited piece of concrete evidence to focus on and write about it without stopping for 10 to 20 minutes. Pick a passage you find interesting and that you probably don't quite understand. Copy out the passage at the beginning of your freewrite. This act will encourage attention to the words and induce you to notice more about the particular features of your chosen passage.

Step 2: Contextualize the evidence. Where does the passage come from in the text? Of what larger discussion is it a part? Briefly answering these questions will prevent you from taking things out of context.

Step 3: Focus on what the text is inviting you to think—its point of view—not on what you think, your point of view of that subject.

Step 4: Make observations about the evidence. Stay close to the data you've quoted, paraphrasing key phrases in the passage and teasing out the possible meanings of these words. Then reflect on what you've come to better understand through paraphrasing.

Step 5: Share your reasoning about what the evidence means. As you move from observation to implication, remember that you need to explain how the data mean what you claim they mean.

Step 6: Address how the passage is representative, how it connects to broader issues in the reading. Move from your analysis of local details to consider what the work as a whole may plausibly be "saying" about this or that issue or question. It's okay to work with the details for almost the entire time and then press yourself to an interpretive leap with the prompt, "I'm almost out of time but my big point is. . . ."

Discussion Passage-based focused freewriting is probably the single best way to arrive at ideas about what you are reading. The more you practice it, the better you will get—the easier you will find things to say about your chosen passage. Ask yourself:

- "What one passage in the reading do you think most needs to be discussed—is most useful and interesting for understanding the material?"
- "What one passage seems puzzling, difficult to pin down, anomalous, or even just unclear—and how might this be explained?"

The best passage-based focused freewrites usually do one or more of the following:

- **Interpretation**, which moves from restatement to what the sentence from the text means.
- **Implication**. A useful (and logical) next step is to go after implication. If X or Y is true, then what might follow from it? (Or "So what?")
- **Application**. A passage that is resonant in some way for the reader might lead him or her to write about some practical way of applying the reading—for example, as a lens for understanding other material *(see Chapter 5, Writing About Reading)*.
- **Assumptions**. We lay out implications by moving forward (so to speak). We unearth assumptions by moving backward. If a text asks us to believe X, what else must it already believe? From what unstated assumptions, in other words, would X follow?
- **Queries**. What questions, interpretive difficulties, and struggles are raised by the reading?

As the short take Freewriting: How and Why to Do It in Chapter 1 discusses, passage-based focused freewriting incorporates a number of the methods introduced in the opening chapters. So, for example:

- it often starts with observations discovered by doing Notice and Focus;
- it grows out of doing The Method, further developing the paragraph that explains why you chose one repetition, strand or binary as most important;

- in analyzing the chosen passage, writers normally paraphrase key words; and
- they keep the writing going by insistently asking "So what?" at the ends of paragraphs.

Notice how the writers use these tools in the examples that follow.

Passage-based Focused Freewriting: An Example

Sometimes, in-class writings are done in class in response to a prompt. The prompt for this freewrite was, "how does Obama's inaugural address compare with his election night victory speech?" Notice how the writer chooses to find most interesting.

> What was most interesting to me about Obama's inaugural speech was his use of the collective first person—"we," "our," "us," etc.—as opposed to the singular "I." This is especially different from his victory speech, which did not make use of the singular "I" and addressed the audience as "you." These pronoun choices are actually very conducive to the tone of each speech. Obama's victory speech was a *victory* speech—it was meant to be joyful, hopeful, optimistic, and of course thankful...so every use of "you" is not accusatory by rather congratulatory and proud—e.g., "this is because of you," "you have done this," "this is your victory."
>
> On the other hand, Obama's inaugural speech was by and large a more somber piece of writing—as the President said to George Stephanopolous, he wanted to capture that moment in history as exactly as possible. "You" here is not the American public as in the victory speech; rather, "you" is any "enemy" of America. And "I," it seems, has become "we." This choice automatically makes Obama the voice of society, as though speaking for every American. This is a really subtle but smart choice to make, because the listener or reader is hearing everything he says as his or her own position. Using that collective first person also puts Obama on the same level as everyone else, and when he does blame America for its own problems, the "our's" and "we's" soften the blow. The "you's" here are harsh and accusatory but meant for that great, terrible, unnamed enemy to "our" freedom and happiness.
>
> I found a lot more obvious echoes to Lincoln in this speech as compared to the victory speech, coupled with earth imagery—for example, "we cannot hallow this ground" (Lincoln) vs. "what the cynics fail to understand is that the ground has shifted" (Obama). This ties America to the actual physical land. It romanticizes and makes permanent the ideas of our country—a nice setting behind all of the nation's troubles—while simultaneously adding to the so-desired degree of "timelessness" of Obama's first inaugural address.

You can sense the writer, Molly Harper, gathering steam here as she begins to make connections in her evidence, yet her rhetorical analysis seems to spring naturally from simple observation of Obama's pronouns and then the significance of the contrast between them in the two speeches she is comparing.

Passage-based Focused Freewriting: Another Example

Below is an example of a student's exploratory writing on an essay by the twentieth-century African-American writer Langston Hughes. The piece is a twenty-minute reflection on two excerpts. Most notable about this piece, perhaps, is the sheer number of interesting ideas. That may be because the writer continually returns to the language of the original quotes for inspiration. She is not restricted by maintaining a single and consistent thread. It is interesting though, how as the freewrite progresses, a primary focus (on the second of her two quotes) seems to emerge.

Passages from "The Negro Artist and the Racial Mountain" by Langston Hughes

"But jazz to me is one of the inherent expressions of negro life in America; the eternal tom-tom beating in the Negro soul—the tom-tom of revolt against weariness in a white world, a world of subway trains, and work, work, work; the tom-tom of joy and laughter, and pain swallowed in a smile. Yet the Philadelphia clubwoman is ashamed to say that her race created it and she does not like me to write about it. The old subconscious "white is best" runs through her mind. . . . And now she turns up her nose at jazz and all its manifestations—likewise almost everything else distinctly racial."

"We build our temples for tomorrow, strong as we know how, and we stand on top of the mountain, free within ourselves."

Langston Hughes's 1926 essay on the situation of the Negro artist in America sets up some interesting issues that are as relevant today as they were in Hughes's time. Interestingly, the final sentence of the essay ("We build our temples. . .") will be echoed some four decades later by the Civil Rights leader, Martin Luther King, but with a different spin on the idea of freedom. Hughes writes "we stand on top of the mountain, free within ourselves." King says, "Free at last, free at last, my God almighty, we're free at last." King asserts an opening out into the world—a freeing of black people, finally, from slavery and then another century of oppression.

Hughes speaks of blacks in a more isolated position—"on top of the mountain" and "within ourselves." Although the mountain may stand for a height from which the artist can speak, it is hard to be heard from the top of mountains. It is one thing to be free. It is another to be free within oneself. What does this phrase mean? If I am free within myself I am at least less vulnerable to those who would restrict me from without. I can live with their restrictions. Mine is an inner freedom. Does inner freedom empower artists? Perhaps it does. It may allow them to say what they want and not worry about what others say or think. This is one thing that Hughes seems to be calling for. But he is also worried about lack of recognition of Negro artists, not only by whites but by blacks. His use of the repeated phrase, tom-tom, is interesting in this respect. It, like the word "mountain," becomes a kind of refrain in the essay—announcing both a desire to rise above the world and its difficulties (mountain) and a desire to be heard (tom-tom and mountain as pulpit).

The idea of revolt, outright rebellion, is present but subdued in the essay. The tom-tom is a "revolt against weariness" and also an instrument for expressing "joy and laughter." The tom-tom also suggests a link with a past African and probably Native American culture—communicating by drum and music and dance. White culture in the essay stands for a joyless world of "work work work." This is something I would like to think about more, as the essay seems to link the loss of soul with the middle and upper classes, both black and white.

And so the essay seeks to claim another space among those he calls "the low down folks, the so-called common element." Of these he says ". . . they do not particularly care whether they are like white folks or anybody else. Their joy runs, bang! into ecstasy. Their religion soars to a shout. Work maybe a little today, rest a little tomorrow. Play awhile. Sing awhile. O, let's dance!" In these lines Hughes the poet clearly appears. Does he say then that the Negro artist needs to draw from those of his own people who are the most removed from middle class American life? If I had more time, I would start thinking here about Hughes's use of the words "race" and "racial" . . . .

Try This 4.1: Do a Passage-based Focused Freewrite

Select a passage from any of the material you are reading and copy it at the top of the page. Remember to choose the passage in response to the question, "What is the single sentence that I think it is most important for us to discuss and why?" Then do a twenty-minute focused freewrite, applying the steps offered above. Discover what you think by seeing what you say.

It is often productive to take the focused freewrite and type it, revising and further freewriting until you have filled the inevitable gaps in your thinking that the time limit has created. (One colleague of ours has students revise and expand in a different font, so both can see how the thinking is evolving.) Eventually, you can build up, through a process of accretion, the thinking for an entire paper in this way.

An especially useful way of making pbff (as we shorthand it) productive academically is to freewrite for fifteen minutes every day on a different passage as you move through a book. If, for example, you are discussing a book over four class periods, prepare for each class by giving 15 minutes to a passage before you attend. You will not only discover things to say; you will begin to write your way to an essay.

2. UNCOVERING ASSUMPTIONS

WHAT IS AN ASSUMPTION?

An assumption is an underlying belief from which other statements spring.

Virtually all statements have underlying assumptions—especially claims.

Assumptions are usually unstated, which is why they need to be uncovered.

We generally reason forward to implications (what follows from X), but we reason backward to assumptions (what has led to X), which are a particular kind of implicit meaning.

The ability to uncover assumptions is a powerful analytical procedure to learn. It gives you insight into the root, the basic givens that a piece of writing has assumed are true. When you locate assumptions in a text, you understand the text better—where it's coming from, what else it believes that is more fundamental than what it is overtly declaring.

You also find things to write about. When analyzing the work of others, you are likely to discover related ideas or positions, and sometimes these are positions of which the writer is not aware. The same goes for developing and revising your own work. When you work back to your own premises from some statement you like that you have written, you will often find what else you believe, at a more basic level, that you did not realize you believed.

Step 1: Paraphrase the explicit statement. This will produce a range of related ideas and highlight the key terms in the original statement (*see Chapter 2, Paraphrase x 3*).

Step 2: List the implicit ideas that the statement seems to assume to be true. Ask yourself, "Given what is overtly stated, what must the writer also *already* believe?"

Step 3: Further analyze the original claim by drawing out implications of the underlying assumptions. What do you now recognize about the statement?

Discussion Uncovering assumptions is a version, with a difference, of Move 4 of the Five Analytical Moves from Chapter 3: it renders the implicit explicit. But in this case, what it is revealing is not what follows from a given statement, but rather, what precedes.

You should be aware that this tool gets used for different purposes. In argument, it is often used (and abused) to catch out the other guy: your opponent's undiscerned assumption is exposed in order to be attacked. But in analysis, the goal is not attack; as Chapter 1 discusses in the short takes entitled Analysis: A Quick Definition and What's Different About Writing Arguments in College, analysis can lead *eventually* to making an argument or claim, but it does not generally conduct search-and-destroy missions. It seeks instead primarily to understand other positions, and in this context, uncovering the assumptions of other writers can be an essential move in helping everyone comprehend more clearly what is involved in accepting or negotiating with another point of view.

Uncovering Assumptions: An Example

In the reference application sent to professors at our college for students seeking to enter the student-teaching program, the professor is asked to rank the student from one to four (unacceptable to acceptable) on the following criterion: *"The student uses his/her sense of humor appropriately."*

Step 1: To uncover the assumptions in that statement, we might first paraphrase it a few times:

> The student makes jokes in a way that is right for the situation.
>
> The student creates situations that invite others to laugh in ways that are not socially indecorous.
>
> The student has good manners in the way he or she does things that are funny.

The paraphrasing helps identify the key terms in the original statement that are open to interpretation: "uses" and "sense of humor" and especially, "appropriately."

Step 2: What are the implicit ideas that the claim assumes to be true? And what must the writers of the form also already believe if they have asked that question? Here is a partial list:

> students have a sense of humor;
>
> students use their sense of humor in class;
>
> some senses of humor are appropriate, and others are not;
>
> the teacher, the one asked to fill out the evaluation, can distinguish appropriate from inappropriate uses of humor in the classroom by students; and
>
> the teacher probably shares the values and attitudes of the teachers who sent out the form, and by extension, teachers in general have a consensus view on this issue.

Step 3: Let's return to analyze the original claim, drawing out implications of these underlying assumptions.

Interestingly, the predictive tool that the Education Department has devised to screen its applicants targets humor as a charged site—a classroom space in which a would-be teacher is likely to demonstrate his or her ability to conduct himself or herself modestly, to remain within the bounds of good taste as defined by the educational institution. Further, we see that the Education Department has done some thinking: they've figured out that humor is a site of potential danger and subversion. But they have also seen that humor is inevitable, and therefore that they can test their candidates' adequacy through this convenient focus. If there is going to be a problem, it's likely to show up there.

Uncovering Assumptions: Another Quick Example

Consider the claim, "Tax laws benefit the wealthy."

We might paraphrase the claim as "The rules for paying income tax give rich people monetary advantages" or "The rules for paying income tax help the rich get richer."

Now let's look at the implicit ideas that the claim assumes to be true. Because this sentence has been offered out of context, let's supply a range of possibilities:

Tax laws don't treat people equally.

Tax laws may have unintended consequences.

If we assume the speaker is worried about tax laws possibly benefitting the wealthy, then a few more assumptions can be inferred:

Tax laws shouldn't benefit anybody.

Tax laws shouldn't benefit those who are already advantaged.

This process of definition will help you see the key concepts upon which the claim depends. Regardless of the position you might adopt—attacking tax laws, defending them, showing how they actually benefit everyone, or whatever—you would risk arguing blindly if you failed to question what the purpose of tax law is in the first place. How does the writer intend "benefit"? Does he or she mean that tax laws benefit only the wealthy and presumably harm those who are not wealthy? Note by the way that the assumptions we might infer would differ depending on context. If this statement appeared at a rally for the Tea Party, it would suggest one set of underlying assumptions; if it appeared at the Democratic National Convention, it would suggest another set.

The wording of this claim seems to conceal an egalitarian premise: the assumption that tax laws should not benefit anyone, or, at least, that they should benefit everyone equally. But what is the purpose of tax laws? Should they redress economic inequities? Should they spur the economy by rewarding those who generate capital? Our point here is that you would need to move your thesis back to this point and test the validity of the assumptions upon which it rests.

Try This 4.2: Uncover Assumptions in Reviews

Say you read a review that praises a television show or film for being realistic but faults it for setting a bad example for the kids who watch it. What assumptions might we infer from such a review? Here is an example of one underlying assumption: Good and bad examples are clear and easily recognizable by everyone. List at least three more.

Then locate a review of any other cultural product—a film, a show, a CD, a book, a concert, and so forth. Isolate key claims and uncover assumptions, that is, reason back to premises.

Uncovering Assumptions: An Economist Speaks

In the following Voice from Across the Curriculum, economics professor James Marshall foregrounds the importance of uncovering assumptions in designing and answering research questions.

Voices From Across the Curriculum

What's beneath the question? On some occasions, students find that they have confronted an issue that cannot be resolved by the deductive method. This can be exciting for them. Will cutting marginal tax rates cause people to work more? The answer is yes or no, depending on the premises underlying the work-leisure preferences incorporated into your model.

—James Marshall, Professor of Economics

Try This 4.3: Uncovering Assumptions: Fieldwork

You can practice uncovering assumptions with all kinds of material—newspaper editorials, statements you see on billboards, ideas you are studying in your courses, jokes, and so forth. Try a little fieldwork: spend a week jotting down in your notebook interesting statements you overhear. Choose the best of these from the standpoint of the implied (but unstated) premises upon which each statement seems to rest. Then make a list of the uncovered assumptions.

---

3. REFORMULATING BINARIES

HOW TO REFORMULATE BINARIES

Step 1: Locate a range of opposing categories.

Step 2: Define and analyze the key terms.

Step 3: Question the accuracy of the binary and rephrase the terms.

Step 4: Substitute "to what extent?" for "either/or."

Binaries are an essential component of thinking and writing analytically. They have already figured significantly in earlier chapters—as part of The Method after locating repetitions and strands, and as Move 3 of the Five Analytical Moves, in searching for patterns. We wish now to focus on a new use of binaries, one that takes place in higher order analysis, when you are "going deeper." This move is reformulating binaries.

First, here is a quick reprise on the benefits and dangers of binary thinking. When you run into a binary opposition in your thinking, it is like a fork in the road, a place where two paths going in different directions present themselves and you pause to choose the direction you will take. Binary oppositions are sites of uncertainty, places where there is struggle among various points of view. As such, binaries are the breeding ground of ideas. And, as we suggested in our discussion of The Method in Chapter 2, when you determine the organizing contrast in whatever you are analyzing, you have found the structural beam that gives conceptual shape to a piece.

If you leap too quickly to a binary, however, one that is too general or inaccurate, you can get stuck in oversimplification, in rigidly dichotomized points of view. At that point, you are in the grasp of a reductive habit of mind called either/or thinking.

The solution is to remember that, when you find a binary opposition in an essay, film, political campaign, or anything else, you have located the argument that the film, essay, or campaign is having with itself, the place where something is at issue. Your next step is to immediately begin to ask questions about and complicate the binary. To "complicate" a binary is to discover evidence that unsettles it and to formulate alternatively worded binaries that more accurately describe what is at issue in the evidence.

Step 1: Locate a range of **opposing categories** (binaries). Finding binaries will help you find the questions around which almost anything is organized. Use The Method to help you uncover the binary oppositions in your subject matter that might function as organizing contrasts.

Step 2: Define and analyze the **key terms**. By analyzing the terms of most binaries, you should come to question them and ultimately arrive at a more complex and qualified position.

Step 3: Question the **accuracy** of the binary and **rephrase** the terms. Think of the binary as a starting point—a kind of deliberate overgeneralization—that allows you to set up positions you can then test in order to refine.

Step 4: Substitute **"to what extent?"** for "either/or." The best strategy in using binaries productively is usually to locate arguments **on both sides** of the either/or choice that the binary poses and then choose a position somewhere between the two extremes. Once you have arrived at what you consider the most accurate phrasing of the binary, you can rephrase the original either/or question in the more qualified terms that asking "To what extent?" allows. Making this move does not release you from the responsibility of taking a stand and arguing for it.

Discussion Thinking is not simply linear and progressive, moving from point A to point B to point C like stops on a train. Careful thinkers are always retracing their steps, questioning their first—and second—impressions, assuming that they've missed something. All good thinking is *recursive;* that is, it repeatedly goes over the same ground, rethinking connections. And that's why reformulating binaries is an essential analytical move.

As a general rule, analysis favors live questions over inert answers. It thrives where something remains to be resolved, not where things are already pretty much nailed down and don't leave much space for further thinking.

Reformulating binaries will cause you to do one or more of the following:

- Discover that you have not named the binary adequately and that another formulation of the opposition would be more accurate.

- Weigh one side of your binary more heavily than the other, rather than seeing the issue as all or nothing.

- Discover that the two terms of your binary are not really so separate and opposed after all but are actually parts of one complex phenomenon or issue. (This is a key analytical move known as "collapsing the binary.")

There is usually no single "right" answer about which of a number of binary oppositions is the primary organizing contrast. This is because analytical thinking involves interpretation. Interpretive conclusions are not matters of fact, but theories. It is in the nature of theories to be tentative and open to alternative readings of the same information. This is why good analytical thinking takes time and is inevitably open-ended.

Reformulating Binaries: An Example

Suppose you are analyzing the following topic in a management course: *Would the model of management known as Total Quality Management (TQM) that is widely used in Japan function effectively in the American automotive industry?*

Step 1: There are a range of opposing categories suggested by the language of the topic, the most obvious being function versus not function. But there are also other binaries here: Japanese versus American, and TQM versus more traditional and more traditionally American models of management. These binaries imply further binaries. The question requires a writer to consider the accuracy and relative suitability of particular traits commonly ascribed to Japanese versus American workers, such as communal and cooperative versus individualistic and competitive.

Step 2: Questions of definition might concentrate on what it means to ask whether TQM *functions effectively* in the American automotive industry? Does that mean "make a substantial profit"? "Produce more cars more quickly"? "Improve employee morale"? You would drown in vagueness unless you carefully argued for the appropriateness of your definition of this key term.

Step 3: How accurate is the binary? To what extent do American and Japanese management styles actually differ? Can you locate significant differences between these management styles that correspond to supposed differences between Japanese and American culture that might help you formulate your binary more precisely?

Step 4: To complicate the either/or formulation, you might suggest the danger of assuming that all American workers are rugged individualists and all Japanese workers are communal bees. Insofar as you are going to arrive at a qualified claim, it would be best stated in terms of the extent to which TQM might be adaptable to the auto industry.

Collapsing the Binary: A Brief Example

Let's consider a brief example in which a writer starts with the following binary: was the poet Emily Dickinson psychotic, or was she a poetic genius? This is a useful, if overstated, starting point for prompting thinking. Going over the same ground, the writer might next decide that the opposing terms *insanity* and *poetic genius* don't accurately name the issue. He or she might decide, as the poet Adrienne Rich did, that poetic genius is often perceived as insanity by the culture at large and, thus, it's not a viable either/or formulation. This move is known as *collapsing the binary*: coming to see that what had appeared to be an opposition is really two parts of one complex phenomenon.

Perhaps the insanity/poetic genius binary would be better reformulated in terms of conventionality/unconventionality—a binary that might lead the writer to start reappraising the ways in which Dickinson is not as eccentric as she at first appears to be.

Reformulating Binaries: Two More Examples

In the following two examples, writers Jonathan Franzen and James Howard Kunstler define a problem by locating, defining, analyzing, and reformulating binaries. The thinking in the Franzen paragraph moves by inverting readers' usual expectations. Notice how he does this with the binary public versus private. Kunstler's paragraph takes on the same issue but sets it up in slightly different terms. Notice how Kunstler reformulates the binary public versus private.

I. Walking up Third Avenue on a Saturday night, I feel bereft. All around me, attractive young people are hunched over their StarTacs and Nokias with preoccupied expressions, as if probing a sore tooth, or adjusting a hearing aid, or squeezing a pulled muscle; personal technology has begun to look like a personal handicap. All I really want from a sidewalk is that people see me and let themselves be seen, but even this modest ideal is thwarted by cell-phone users and their unwelcome privacy. They say things like "Should we have couscous with that?" and "I'm on my way to Blockbuster." They aren't breaking any laws by broadcasting these breakfast-nook conversations. There's no PublicityGuard that I can buy, no expensive preserve of public life to which I can flee. Seclusion, whether in a suite at the Plaza or in a cabin in the Catskills, is comparatively effortless to achieve. Privacy is protected as both commodity and right; public forums are protected as neither. Like old-growth forests, they're few and irreplaceable and should be held in trust by everyone. The work of maintaining them gets only harder as the private sector grows ever more demanding, distracting, and disheartening. Who has the time and energy to stand up for the public sphere? What rhetoric can possibly compete with the American love of "privacy"? [From Jonathan Franzen, "Imperial Bedroom" in *How to Be Alone* (Farrar, Straus, and Giroux, 2003)]

II. Civic life is what goes on in the public realm. Civic life refers to our relations with our fellow human beings—in short, our roles as citizens. Sometime in the past forty years we ceased to speak of ourselves as citizens and labeled ourselves consumers. That's what we are today in the language of the evening news—*consumers*—in the language of the Sunday panel discussion shows—*consumers*—in the blizzard of statistics that blows out of the U.S. Department of Commerce every month. Consumers, unlike citizens, have no responsibilities, obligations, or duties to anything larger than their own needs and desires, certainly not to anything like the common good. How can this be construed as anything other than an infantile state of existence? In degrading the language of our public discussion this way—labeling ourselves consumers—have we not degraded our sense of who we are? And is it any wonder that we cannot solve any of our social problems, which are problems of the public realm and the common good? [From James Howard Kunstler, *Home From Nowhere: Remaking Our Everyday World for the Twenty-First Century*, (Simon & Schuster, 1996)]

Try This 4.4: Reformulating Binaries in a Familiar Expression

Write a few paragraphs in which you work with the binaries suggested by the following familiar expression: "School gets in the way of one's education." Keep the focus on working through the binaries implicit in the quotation. What other terms would you substitute for "school" and "education"? Coming up with a range of synonyms for each term will clarify what is at stake in the binary. Remember to consider the accuracy of the claim. To what extent, and in what ways, is the expression both true and false?

Try This 4.5: Reformulating Binaries: More Practice

Apply the Strategies for Using Binaries Analytically to analyze the following statements (or questions), as we did with the TQM example. This does not mean that you must proceed step-by-step through the strategies, but, at the least, you should list all of the binaries you can find, isolate the key terms, and reformulate them. Even if the original formulation looks okay to you, assume that it is an overgeneralization that needs to be refined and rephrased.

a. It is important to understand why leaders act in a leadership role. What is the driving force? Is it an internal drive for the business or group to succeed, or is it an internal drive for the leader to dominate others?

b. Is nationalism good for emerging third-world countries?

c. The private lives of public figures should not matter in the way they are assessed by the public. What matters is how competently they do their jobs.

d. The Seattle sound of rock and roll known as Grunge was not original; it was just a rehash of Punk and New Wave elements.

Try This 4.6: Reformulating Binaries: Fieldwork

Locate some organizing contrasts in anything—something you are studying, something you've just written, something you saw on television last night, something on the front page of the newspaper, something going on at your campus or workplace, and so forth. Binaries pervade the way we think; therefore, you can expect to find them everywhere. Consider, for example, the binaries suggested by current trends in contemporary music or by the representation of women in birthday cards. Having selected the binaries you want to work with, pick one and transform the either/or thinking into a more qualified thinking using the extent to which formula.

4. DIFFERENCE WITHIN SIMILARITY

> When A & B are obviously similar,
> > look for unexpected difference.
> When A & B are obviously different,
> > look for unexpected similarity.

Too often, writers notice a fundamental similarity and stop there. But ideas tend to arise when a writer moves beyond this basic demonstration and complicates (or "qualifies") the basic similarity by also noting areas of difference, and accounting for the significance of that difference.

Step 1: Decide whether the similarities or differences are most obvious and easily explained.

Step 2: Briefly explain the relatively obvious similarity or difference by asking "So what?" Why is this similarity or difference significant?

Step 3: Then focus your attention on the less obvious but revealing difference within the similarity or similarity despite the difference.

Discussion   The phrase "difference within similarity" is to remind you that once you have started your thinking by locating apparent similarities, you can usually refine that thinking by pursuing significant, though often less obvious, distinctions among the similar things. In Irish studies, for example, scholars characteristically acknowledge the extent to which contemporary Irish culture is the product of colonization. To this extent, Irish culture shares certain traits with other former colonies in Africa, Asia, Latin America, and elsewhere. But instead of simply demonstrating how Irish culture fits the general pattern of colonialism, these scholars also isolate the ways that Ireland *does not fit* the model. They focus, for example, on how its close geographical proximity and racial similarity to England, its colonizer, have distinguished the kinds of problems it encounters today from those characteristic of the more generalized model of colonialism. In effect, looking for difference within similarity has led them to locate and analyze the anomalies.

A corollary of the preceding principle is that you should focus on *unexpected similarity rather than obvious difference*. The fact that in the Bush presidency Republicans differed from Democrats on environmental policy was probably a less promising focal point than their surprising agreement on violating the so-called lockbox policy against tapping Social Security funds to finance government programs. Most readers would expect the political parties to differ on the environment, and a comparison of their positions could lead you to do little more than summarizing. But a surprising similarity, like an unexpected difference, necessarily raises questions for you to pursue: do the parties' shared positions against the lockbox policy, for example, share the same motives?

Looking for Difference Within Similarity: An Example

Notice how in the following example, taken from an essay on George Orwell's book on the Spanish Civil War, *Homage to Catalonia:*, Lauren Artiles notes differences among political parties that shared an essential position.

> The forces that united against Franco in favor of the government were ragtag and unlikely; the resistance was made up of a slew of different factions of the political left, anarchists and socialists and communists all fighting together against the threat of a Fascist Spain. As Orwell said of the groups and their various acronyms, "It looked at first sight as though Spain was suffering from a plague of initials. I knew that I was serving in something called the P.O.U.M. but I did not realize that there were serious differences between the political parties. [...] I thought it idiotic that people fighting for their lives should *have* separate political parties; my attitude always was, 'Why can't we drop all this political nonsense and get on with the war?'" (47). [. . .]

> The conflict between the P.O.U.M. and the rest of the Communist parties was that the P.O.U.M. was staunchly dissident; they were anti-Stalinist and criticized his Purge Trials of the late '30s, a huge issue considering that the Soviet Union's support of the Spanish Communists' efforts was deemed so crucial. In addition, unlike their counterparts in the P.S.U.C. or Socialist Party of Catalonia, they were very much supporters of the revolution and believed it was a necessary end to the war already underway. The Communists' aim was to win the war and suppress the coming revolution, believing military efficiency to be superior to revolutionary chaos. These ideological differences, which seem so small to an outsider unfamiliar with party politics, led to the eventual persecution of the P.O.U.M. when the Communists seized power.

> [. . .] The question of revolution or no revolution became the biggest issue within the resistance movement and the failure to reach a consensus combined with the vicious power struggle this resulted in weakened the left critically; the war was no longer about defeating the evil of Fascism, but about petty ideological differences between those who were united by that noble, all-consuming cause.

Try This 4.7: Looking for Significant Difference or Unexpected Similarity

Choose any item from the list. After you've done the research necessary to locate material to read and analyze, list as many similarities and differences as you can: go for coverage. Then, review your list, and select the two or three most revealing similarities and the two or three most revealing differences. At this point, you are ready to write a few paragraphs in which you argue for the significance of a key difference or similarity. In so doing, try to focus on an *unexpected* similarity or difference—one that others might not initially notice.

1. accounts of the same event from two different newspapers or magazines or textbooks

2. two CDs (or even songs) by the same artist or group

3. two ads for the same kind of product, perhaps aimed at different target audiences

4. the political campaigns of two opponents running for the same or similar office

5. courtship behavior as practiced by men and by women

6. two clothing styles as emblematic of class or sub-group in your school, town, or workplace

5. SEEMS TO BE ABOUT X BUT COULD ALSO BE (IS "REALLY") ABOUT Y

Be suspicious of your first responses.

Use the formula "seems to be about X"
to try on alternative ways of understanding.

This is a useful freewriting prompt that helps students get beyond their first impressions and helps them to see that meanings are inevitably plural and that things mean differently in different contexts.

Like the other heuristics in this toolkit, this last one, "Seems to be about X," prompts you to move beyond potentially superficial explanations—to go deeper. When we begin to interpret something, we usually find that less obvious meanings are cloaked by more obvious ones, and so we are distracted from seeing them. In most cases, the less obvious and possibly unintended meanings are more telling and more interesting than the obvious ones we have been conditioned to see.

The person doing the interpreting too often stops with the first "answer" that springs to mind as he or she moves from observation to implication, usually landing upon a cliché. If this first response becomes the X, then he or she is prompted by the formula to come up with other, probably less commonplace interpretations as the Y.

Step 1: Start the interpretive process by filling in the blank (the X) in the statement "This subject seems to be about X." X should be an interpretive leap, not just a summary or description.

Step 2: Next, pose another interpretive possibility by finishing the sentence, "but it could also be (or is really) about Y."

Step 3: It's essential to repeat this process a number of times to provoke new, interpretive leaps. In effect, you are brainstorming alternative explanations for the same phenomenon.

Step 4: Choose what you think is the best formulation for Y, and write a paragraph or more explaining your choice.

Discussion This prompt is based on the conviction that understandings are rarely simple and overt. Completing the formula by supplying key terms for X and Y, writers get practice in making the implicit explicit and accepting the existence of multiple plausible meanings for something. "Seems to be about X" is especially useful when considering the *rhetoric* of a piece: its complex and various ways of targeting and appealing to an audience. It's also useful for "reading against the grain"—seeking out what something is about that it probably does not know it's about *(see Chapter 5, Writing About Reading)*.

Note: Don't be misled by our use of the word *really* in this formula ("Seems to be about X, is really about Y") into thinking that there should be some single, hidden, right answer. Rather, the aim of the formula is to prompt you to think recursively, to come up, initially, with a range of landing sites for your interpretive leap, rather than just one.

Seems to Be About X . . .: An Example

A classic and highly successful television ad campaign for Nike Freestyle shoes contains 60 seconds of famous basketball players dribbling and passing and otherwise handling the ball in dexterous ways to the accompaniment of court noises and hip-hop music. The ad seems to be about X (basketball or shoes) but could also be about Y. Once you've made this assertion, a rapid-fire (brainstormed) list might follow in which you keep filling in the blanks (X and Y) with different possibilities. Alternatively, you might find that filling in the blanks (X and Y) leads to a more sustained exploration of a single point. This is your eventual goal, but doing a little brainstorming first would keep you from shutting down the interpretive process too soon.

Here is one version of a rapid-fire list, any item of which might be expanded:

Seems to be about basketball but is "really" about dance

Seems to be about selling shoes but is "really" about artistry

Seems to be about artistry but is "really" about selling shoes

Seems to be about basketball but is "really" about race

Seems to be about basketball but is "really" about the greater acceptance of black culture in American media and society

Seems to be about the greater acceptance of black culture in American media but is "really" about representing black basketball players as performing seals or freaks

Seems to be about individual expertise but is "really" about working as a group

Here is one version of a more sustained exploration of a single Seems-to-Be-About-X statement.

> The Nike Freestyle commercial seems to be about basketball but is really about the greater acceptance of black culture in American media. Of course it is a shoe commercial and so aims to sell a product, but the same could be said about any commercial.
>
> What makes the Nike commercial distinctive is its seeming embrace of African-American culture. The hip-hop sound track, for example, which coincides with the rhythmic dribbling of the basketball, places music and sport on a par, and the dexterity with which the players (actual NBA stars) move with the ball — moonwalking, doing 360s on it, balancing it on their fingers, heads, and backs — is nothing short of dance.
>
> The intrinsic cool of the commercial suggests that Nike is targeting an audience of basketball lovers, not just African-Americans. If I am right, then it is selling blackness to white as well as black audiences. Of course, the idea that blacks are cooler than whites goes back at least as far as the early days of jazz and might be seen as its own strange form of prejudice. . . . In that case, maybe there is something a little disturbing in the commercial, in the way that it relegates the athletes to the status of trained seals. I'll have to think more about this.

Try This 4.8: Apply the Formula "Seems to Be About X, But Could Also Be (Is "Really") About Y"

As we have been saying, this formula is useful for quickly getting past your first responses. An alternative version of this formula is "Initially I thought X about the subject, but now I think Y." Take any reading or viewing assignment you have been given for class, and write either version of the formula at the top of a page. Fill in the blanks several times, and then explain your final choice for X and Y in a few paragraphs. You might also try these formulae when you find yourself getting stuck while drafting a paper. Seems to Be About X . . . is a valuable revision as well as interpretive tool.

Assignment: Using the Toolkit

Putting the Tools to Work: Composing an Analytical Portfolio. The heuristics introduced in this chapter have been included in the toolkit because they are "all-purpose" analytical moves. In a more extended assignment, try using several of them together. First, review the Try This exercises through the chapter, which suggest a variety of subjects to which you might apply the heuristics. Once you have selected a subject—which could be a film, an advertising campaign, a political campaign, a television series, something you are currently reading for a course or on your own, and so forth—do a series of passage-based focused freewritings as a way of generating ideas.

Try to use both reformulating binaries and uncovering assumptions in the same or consecutive freewrites. Alternatively, try to shake up your thinking by doing Seems to Be About X or Difference Within Similarity in the same or subsequent free writes.

Once you have produced at least four 20-minute free writes, survey them and choose the one you find most interesting. Then do the following:

*Type up three of the free writes, spending 10 or 15 minutes polishing each to achieve some kind of focus and coherence.

*Spend an hour or more expanding and revising your most interesting free write (or some combination of them) into a longer piece, perhaps 3–4 pages. Place this document at the front of the portfolio.

Chapter 5

Writing About Reading: More Moves to Make with Written Texts

THIS BOOK IS ABOUT ANALYZING two kinds of subjects, one of which we might call "the world" (anything and everything you want to better understand), and the other, the world of reading—that is, other people's ideas as these are developed in writing. Throughout the book's first four chapters, we have been concentrating, implicitly or explicitly, on ways of analyzing both worlds. In this chapter, we dwell on this second world—the world of reading.

Here is a list of the chapter's strategies for writing about reading, each with a brief summary of what it involves. We will then go on to explain each in more detail.

READING ANALYTICALLY

1. Find alternatives to reading for the gist: become conversant with the reading.
2. Go local—start with sentences (pointing, passage-based focused freewriting, paraphrasing, commonplace book)
3. Situate the reading rhetorically—find what it seeks to accomplish and what it is set against: the pitch, the complaint, and the moment
4. Seek to understand the reading fairly on its own terms—track the thinking of the piece as it moves through complication and qualification
5. Use the reading as a model
6. Apply the reading as a lens

THE THREE LIVES OF A READING

This chapter focuses on how to approach readings analytically, especially the kinds of complex reading you are likely to encounter in college and ultimately in the work-place. The chapter offers you ways to accomplish two primary tasks: (1) how to **own** a difficult reading, that is, how to make the thinking in a reading yours; and (2) how to use the reading, once you own it.

In practical terms, this chapter will focus on writing about reading in three contexts, which we refer to as the three lives of a reading. These are

- As an Object for Analysis
- As a Model for Imitating
- As a Lens for Viewing Other Material

For More on Writing About Reading Inevitably, not everything that we have to say about reading can be included in this chapter. The chapter assumes, first of all, that you will be using the heuristics in Chapters 2, 3, and 4 when you read. So, for example, when you read virtually anything, you will want to:

- look for patterns of repetition and contrast (aka The Method, Chapter 2),
- paraphrase (Chapter 2),
- make the implicit explicit (Chapter 3),
- uncover assumptions and reformulate binaries (Chapter 4), and
- do passage-based focused freewriting (Chapter 4).

Other essential reading-related skills will be treated in later chapters. These include

- writing analytical summaries (in Chapter 7, Making Common Topics More Analytical),
- writing reaction papers (also in Chapter 7),
- putting readings into conversation with other readings—research-based writing (in Chapter 13, Using Sources Analytically), and
- decoding disciplinary formats (in Chapter 15, Forms and Formats Across the Curriculum)

HOW TO READ: WORDS MATTER

The greatest enemies of reading analytically are "reading for the gist" and the transparent theory of language. Reading for the gist causes readers to leap to global (and usually unsubstantiated) impressions, attending only superficially to what they are reading. The transparent theory of language (first introduced in the discussion of paraphrase in Chapter 2) has a similar effect. This theory invites readers to see through the words as if they were clear windows, suggesting that there is a meaning that can be accessed without the language. Failure to arrest attention on the words causes readers to miss all but the vaguest impression of the ideas that the words embody.

Any child psychology textbook will tell you that as we acquire language, we acquire categories that shape our understanding of the world. Words allow us to ask for things, to say what's on our mind. This is not to say that words are the only reality, but to an enormous extent, we understand the world and our relation to it by working through language.

Considering how central language is in our lives, it's amazing how little we think about words. We tend to assume things mean simply or singly, but virtually all words have multiple meanings, and words mean differently depending on context. Consider the following examples of memorably silly headlines: "Teacher Strikes Idle Kids," "New Vaccines May Contain Rabies," "Local High School Drop-outs Cut in Half," and "Include Your Children When Baking Cookies" (or if you prefer, "Kids Make Nutritious Snacks"). Language is always getting away from us—in such sentences as "The bandage was wound around the wound," or in the classic, "Time flies like an arrow; fruit flies like a banana." The meanings of words and the kinds of sense a sentence makes are rarely stable.

BECOME CONVERSANT INSTEAD OF READING FOR THE GIST

Many readers operate under the mistaken impression that they are to read for the gist—for the main point, to be gleaned through a speed-reading. Although there are virtues to skimming, the vast majority of writing tasks you will encounter in college and in the workplace require your *conversancy* with material you have read. To become conversant means that

- after a significant amount of work with the material, you should be able to talk about it conversationally with other people and answer questions about it without having to look everything up; and
- you should be able to converse with the material—to be in some kind of dialogue with it, to see the questions the material asks, and to pose your own questions about it.

Few people are able to really understand things they read or see without making the language of that material in some way their own. We become conversant, in other words, by finding ways to actively engage material rather than moving passively through it.

Owning the Reading

The short take in Chapter 1, "Writing About Reading: Beyond Banking," lists four tasks that writing about reading at the college level normally requires:

- finding the questions rather than just the answers,
- putting key passages from a reading into conversation with each other,
- using an idea or methodology in a reading in order to generate thinking about something else, and
- gaining control of complex ideas on your own rather than expecting others (such as teachers) to do this work for you.

These tasks require you to change your orientation to reading. How, you might ask, do I make this change, given that I am reading difficult material produced by experts?

What does it mean to read actively and critically when I do not yet have enough knowledge to take issue with what the readings are saying?

There are two key acts of mind—positions you must accept—if you are to play this more active role in writing about reading:

1. *Learn to speak the language of the text.* Every course is in some sense a foreign language course: if a writer wishes to be heard, he or she needs to acquire the vocabulary of the experts. That's why it's so important to pay attention to the actual words in a reading and to use them when you write.

2. *Accept that good reading is a physical as well as a mental activity.* Passing your eyes or highlighter over the text or generalizing about it or copying notes from someone else's PowerPoint will not teach you the *skills* to become an independent thinker. These activities are too passive; they don't trigger your brain into engaging the material. To get physical with the reading, focus on particular words and sentences, copy them out, restate them, and clarify for yourself what you do and do not understand.

FOCUS ON INDIVIDUAL SENTENCES

GOING LOCAL

Pointing

Passage-based focused freewriting

Paraphrasing

Keep a commonplace book

Analyzing needs to be anchored, and anchoring to a general impression, a global sense of what the reading is about, is like putting a hook in a cloud. There is nothing specific to think about, to rephrase, to nudge towards implications or back to assumptions. The best way to remember what you read, and to have ideas about it, is to start with the local—individual sentences and short passages—and build up a knowledge base from there.

It does not matter which sentences you start with. What matters is to choose sentences that strike you as especially revealing, significant, or strange *(see Notice and Focus, Chapter 2)*. Good reading is *slow* reading: it stops your forward momentum long enough to allow you to dwell on individual sentences and make the effort necessary to understand them.

A second and related way that people neglect the actual words is that they approach the reading *looking to react.* They are so busy looking to respond to other people's statements that they don't listen to what the other person is saying. A recent article on reading by the literary and educational theorist Robert Scholes suggests that people read badly because they substitute for the words on the page some association or predetermined idea that the words accidentally trigger in them. As a result, they rehearse their own gestalts rather than taking in what the writer is actually saying (see Robert Scholes, "The Transition to College Reading," *Pedagogy*, volume 2, number 2, Duke UP, 2002, pp. 165–172).

We will now survey a few techniques for focusing on individual sentences.

Pointing

Pointing is a practice (associated with two writing theorists and master teachers, Peter Elbow and Sheridan Blau) in which members of a group take turns reading sentences aloud. Pointing provides a way of summarizing without generalizing, and it is one of the best ways to build community and to stimulate discussion.

1. Select sentences from a reading you are willing to voice.
2. Take turns reading aloud without raising hands. Read only one of your chosen sentences at a time. Later in the session, you may read again. Pointing usually lasts about five minutes and ends more or less naturally, when people no longer have sentences they wish to read.
3. No one comments on the sentences in any way during the pointing.
4. Some sentences in the reading repeat as refrains; others segue or answer the previously articulated line.

Pointing stirs our memories about the particular language of a piece. In reading aloud and hearing others do it, you hear key words and discover questions you'd not seen before; and the range of possible starting points for getting at what is central in the reading inevitably multiplies. Pointing is an antidote for the limiting assumption that a reading has only one main idea. It also remedies the tendency of group discussion to veer into general impressions and loose associations.

Passage-Based Focused Freewriting (PBFF)

Passage-based focused freewriting is probably the single best way to arrive at ideas about what you are reading. It is discussed at length in Chapter 4. Here is a quick reprise of the procedure.

PASSAGE-BASED FOCUSED FREEWRITING: WHAT IT DOES

Find an interesting passage
Sketch its context
Target and paraphrase key words and phrases
Explore why the passage is interesting
Draw out implications
Ask how the passage is representative of the larger reading

WHAT IT DOES NOT DO

Voice reactions and criticisms
Free-associate with other subjects

We cannot overstate how important we think it is to do this activity frequently. The practice will enhance your fluency and help you to trust writing as a tool of thought. It is the best place to practice the heuristics in this book. *(Also see the short take, Freewriting: How and Why to Do It, in Chapter 1.)*

Paraphrasing

Paraphrasing is an essential skill in reading closely. It is discussed at length in Chapter 2. Here is a quick reprise of the procedure.

PARAPHRASE FOR IMPLICATION

Locate a short key passage
Assume you **don't** understand it completely
Substitute other concrete language for **all** of the key words
Repeat the paraphrasing several times
Ponder the differences in implication among the versions
Return to the original passage and interpret its meanings

Successive restatement allows you to arrive at your own sense of the significance of the sentence. An essential last step in paraphrasing is to return to the original statement and take stock: "This is what I now understand the passage to mean, having done the paraphrase."

Keep a Commonplace Book

Professional writers have long kept commonplace books—essentially, records of their reading. Most such books consist primarily of quotations the writers have found striking and memorable. The goal of keeping a commonplace book in a course is to bring you closer to the language you find most interesting, which you inscribe in your memory as you copy it onto the page. It's remarkable what you will notice about a sentence (and the ideas in it) if you copy it out rather than just underline or highlight it. Moreover, you will find yourself remembering *the original language* that has struck you most forcefully in the reading. That way you can continue to ponder key words and phrases and to stay engaged, almost physically, with what the writers have said.

When we assign commonplace books in our courses, we stipulate that everyone copy at least two quotations (with citation) from each reading. (These often anchor pointing and passage-based focused freewriting—see the Try This on the next page.) By the end of the semester, every student will have produced a compressed history of his or her reading to supplement class notes and others' commentaries. Note: segregate your commonplace book, whether on paper or online, into a separate notebook or file. This makes the book sequential and browseable.

Try This 5.1: Writing & Reading with Others: A Sequence of Activities

We use this sequence of writing-about-reading activities regularly in our classes. It also works in small, self-directed groups, both in and outside the classroom.

1. Spend 5–10 minutes pointing on some piece of reading. Remember: no one should comment on his or her choice of sentences during the pointing exercise.

2. Without pausing for discussion, spend 10 minutes doing a passage-based focused freewrite on a sentence or several similar sentences from the reading. It is important to write nonstop and to keep writing throughout the appointed time.

3. Volunteers take turns reading all or part of their freewrites aloud to the group without comment. It is essential that people read rather than describe or summarize what they wrote. As each person reads, listeners should jot down words and phrases that catch their attention.

4. Listeners call out what they heard in the freewrite by responding to the question, "What did you hear?"

SITUATE THE READING RHETORICALLY: FIND THE PITCH, THE COMPLAINT, AND THE MOMENT

There is no such thing as "just information." Virtually all readings possess what speech-act theorists call "illocutionary force"—the goal of an utterance. Everything you read, to varying degrees, is aware of you, the audience, and is dealing with you in some way.

One of the most productive ways of analyzing a reading is to consider the frame within which a piece is presented: who its intended audience is, what it seeks to persuade that audience about, and how the writer presents himself or herself to appeal to that audience. Readings virtually never treat these questions explicitly, and thus, it is a valuable analytical move to infer a reading's assumptions about audience (*see the short take, Rhetoric: What It Is and Why You Need It, in Chapter 1*).

An element of situating a reading rhetorically is to locate what it seeks to accomplish and what it is set against at a given moment in time. We address these concerns as a quest to find what we call the pitch, the complaint, and the moment:

- the **pitch**, what the piece wishes you to believe;
- the **complaint**, what the piece is reacting to or worried about; and
- the **moment**, the historical and cultural context within which the piece is operating.

Here's a bit more on each.

The pitch: A reading is an argument, a presentation of information that makes a case of some sort, even if the argument is not explicitly stated. Look for language that reveals the position or positions the piece seems interested in having you adopt.

The complaint: A reading is a reaction to some situation, some set of circumstances, that the piece has set out to address, even though the writer may not say so openly. An indispensable means of understanding someone else's writing is to figure out what seems to have caused the person to write the piece in the first place. Writers write, presumably, because they think *something* needs to be addressed. What is that something? Look for language in the piece that reveals the writer's starting point. If you can find the position or situation he or she is worried about and possibly trying to correct, you will more easily locate the pitch, the position the piece asks you to accept.

The moment: A reading is a response to the world conditioned by the writer's particular moment in time. In your attempt to figure out not only what a piece says but where it is coming from (the causes of its having been written in the first place and the positions it works to establish), history is significant. When was the piece written? Where? What else was going on at the time that might have shaped the writer's ideas and attitudes?

The Pitch, the Complaint, and the Moment: Two Brief Examples

Here are two examples of student writing in response to the request that they locate the pitch, the complaint, and the moment for a famous essay in the field of Composition and Rhetoric, "Inventing the University" by David Bartholomae.

> Bartholomae's complaint seems to center around the idea that writing is typically taught at a grammatical, not intellectual level. 'Basic' writers are identified by their sentence level compositional errors, not by the content of their ideas or ability to present a complex argument. Bartholomae argues that students must be drawn into the language and mindset of academia before they have the authority to confidently expand upon more complicated ideas. Students are expected to fluently participate in academic discourse long before they have the authority to pull it off with ease. Therefore, students should be familiarized with the world of academia and led through the preliminary steps towards becoming proficient in its language. This is the only way to make them more authoritative writers.

And here is another example that treats the moment in particular:

> The moment, or the specific time in which the essay was written, offers some valuable insight into what might have shaped Bartholomae's perspective. First, it is important to note the other writers and thinkers Bartholomae cites throughout the essay. Take the author's frequent mention of writer Pat Bizzell whom Bartholomae deems "one of the most important scholars now writing on 'basic writers'" and whom he recognizes as "owing a

great debt to." He credits Bizzell with seeing how difficult it is for young writers to learn the complex vocabularies and conventions of academic discourse.

There are most likely other, more broadly cultural influences at work as well, such as the American political scene in 1985. In 1984 Ronald Reagan was re-elected president. His presidency and the conservative climate it fostered sparked change in Americans' attitude toward education. Reagan's policies mandated spending cuts and, it can reasonably be assumed, invited certain anti-academic and more pre-professional attitudes. In this moment, then, Bartholomae's concerns about higher education and the need for students to gain access into the privileged world of the educated begins to make more sense.

Audience Analysis: A Brief Example

Consider the following paragraph of student writing on the same essay, this time focused on how the essay's author establishes his relationship with his target audience. Here is the assignment the writer was responding to: Write a brief analysis of the essay's rhetoric—the various methods it employs to gain acceptance with its target audience. (a) Who is the target audience? How can you tell? Cite and analyze evidence. (b) What decisions has the author made on how best to "sell" his argument to this audience? How do you know?

Bartholomae often uses the inclusive "us" to describe academia, putting the reader (presumably, academics) above the level of those being discussed. Students must be taught "to speak our language, to speak as we do, to try on the peculiar ways of knowing, selecting, evaluating, reporting, concluding and arguing that define the discourse of our community" (3). He effectively builds up the reader, perhaps making him or her more open to absorbing the argument that follows. He refrains from criticizing, including his audience in his idea and putting them on the same level as he is. He refers to the students as 'our students' and writes almost as though the reader is separate from any flaws in the current system. He writes to colleagues, with the tone of one sharing something new and interesting.

Try This 5.2: Locating the Pitch and the Complaint

Go to aldaily.com (Arts & Letters Daily, the website sponsored by the Chronicle of Higher Education). Locate an article on a topic you find interesting. It should be a substantive piece of thinking, as opposed to an editorial or a piece of popular commentary.

It is easier to find the pitch if you first look for language that reveals the position or situation the writer is trying to correct. Once you have done this, find language that reveals the position or positions the piece seems interested in having you adopt. Type out these sentences, and be ready to explain your choices.

SEEK TO UNDERSTAND THE READING FAIRLY ON ITS OWN TERMS

Most good reading starts by giving the reading the benefit of the doubt: this is known as producing a *sympathetic reading*, or *reading with the grain*. This advice applies whether or not you are inclined to agree with the claims in the reading. When you are seeking to entertain the reading on its own terms, first you have to decide to suspend judgment as an act of mind, trying instead to think *with* the piece.

While giving the piece its most sympathetic reading, you may find yourself occasionally confused by disagreements that the reading appears to be having with itself. The back-and-forth movement of claims and qualifications can often be mistaken for contradiction or inconsistency. Rather than sit in judgment, follow the movement of mind in the writing as it tries to make sense of something complicated.

Notice, by the way, that this is a place where skimming for overall shape ("fast reading") is appropriate as a starting point. Browse first and last sentences of paragraphs, the introduction and conclusion, and transitional words such as "but" and "however."

ENTERING THE THINKING IN A READING: UNCOVERING ASSUMPTIONS AND REFORMULATING BINARIES (A REPRISE)

Here, we briefly revisit two items from Toolkit II, heuristics essential to seeing the thinking in a reading *(see Chapter 4).*

UNCOVERING ASSUMPTIONS

Isolate the key terms in the statement.
Ask what the statement rests on, the ideas underlying it.
Draw out implications of the underlying ideas.

All readings—virtually all statements—are built on assumptions. Uncovering the assumptions in a reading, also known as reasoning back to premises, enables you to understand the text better—where it's coming from, what else it believes that is more fundamental than what it is overtly declaring. The essential move is to ask, *"Given its overt claim, what must this reading also already believe?"* To answer this question, you need to make inferences from the primary claims to the ideas that underlie them. In effect, you are working backward, reinventing the chain of thinking that led the writer to the position you are now analyzing.

Once you begin looking at chains of thought, you will often discover that key binaries rise to the surface and need to be reconsidered. You will see examples of this phenomenon in two examples that follow: Christopher Borick's consideration of the term "liberal" and Anna Whiston's analysis of self-deprecation on late night talk shows.

REFORMULATING BINARIES

Step 1: Locate a range of opposing categories

Step 2: Define and analyze the key terms

Step 3: Question the accuracy of the binary and rephrase the terms

Step 4: Substitute "to what extent?" for "either/or"

At the heart of most seriously reflective thinking is some organizing binary. This is to say that thinking rarely looks like a steamroller paving the writer's way from a clear beginning to a predestined end. Rather, it consists of key terms in tension with each other, the tension providing organization and structure for the thought. Thus, the swiftest way to apprehend what's at stake in a reading is to discern its organizing contrasts. Analysis progresses when writers consider how accurately they have named the oppositions in their thinking and whether these should be named otherwise.

Tracking the Thinking Through Complication and Qualification: An Example

Notice how the writer of the following piece—an excerpt from "On Political Labels" by political scientist Christopher Borick—complicates the definition of liberalism by tracking it historically. Look in the first paragraph for the historical roots of liberalism as favoring public control over government actions. Then, in the second paragraph, see how this emphasis moves almost to its opposite—the belief that "government intervention in society is necessary." You'll learn a lot from the excerpt by seeing how it pivots around more than one sense of the word "freedom."

> Let's look at liberalism for a start. The term liberal can be traced at least back to17th-Century England, where it evolved from debates dealing with the voting franchise among English citizens. Proponents of including greater numbers of Englishmen in elections came to be known as liberals, thanks in part to the writings of John Locke, whose ideas about the social contract helped to build the philosophical underpinnings of this political ideology. Over time, liberalism has maintained its focus on public control over government actions, but there have been splits that have led to its current manifestation. In the 18th and 19th Centuries, liberalism began to stress the importance of individual freedom

and broader rights of the citizenry in terms of limits on government. In essence, this type of liberalism focused on "negative rights" or the restrictions on what government could do to its citizens. The First Amendment of the Constitution includes numerous examples of negative rights. The granting of the right to freedom of speech or the press is achieved through the prohibition of government from creating laws that abridge such freedoms. Thus negating an action of government creates rights for the people.

In the 20th Century, however, liberalism became synonymous with the view that government had to be much more active in helping citizens get to the point where they would be able to truly live a free life. In this expanding view of liberalism, government intervention in society is necessary to create a more level playing field on which individuals can then use their freedom to achieve desired goals. Such beliefs have been at the roots of government expansion into social welfare policies such as public housing, food stamps, and affirmative action, and have formed the core of government agendas such as Franklin Roosevelt's New Deal and Lyndon Johnson's Great Society.

As this piece progresses, you can expect that it will either resolve the significant gap between the two historical definitions of liberalism or that it will in various ways show us how the gap has continued to produce tensions or misunderstandings.

In the case of most academic writing, it is usually a mistake to assume that the piece is making a single argument. A smarter assumption is that the piece is interested in exploring an issue or a problem from multiple points of view.

THE PROBLEM OF CRITIQUE

Although you should not be expected simply to go along with all that you read, neither should you jump in and try to critique an expert from your too limited experience. So how do you go about doing the thing that people call "critical reading"?

1. Ultimately, your aim is to put the reading into conversation with other readings on the same subject. In this situation, you speculate, making inferences about what writer X would say about the position of writer Y, and vice versa, establishing a critical conversation in which you cast yourself as referee *(see Chapter 13, Using Sources Analytically for ways of making this move)*.

2. Usually, it is more important to learn how to use a complex theoretical lens than it is to arrive at a point from which you can launch an extended critique.

3. Even when an academic reading offers a single dominant claim, in most cases the writing will focus on limiting and qualifying that claim—categorizing it, dividing it into parts, tracing its implications, and so forth. So instead of approaching the reading with the question, "Where might this be wrong?", ask yourself, "How is the argument presented, and why is it presented in this way?"

What Do We Mean by Critical Reading? A Music Professor Speaks

In the following Voice from Across the Curriculum, music professor Ted Conner discusses ways of helping students develop more sophisticated reading skills.

Voices From Across the Curriculum

As a first step, we consider what we mean by a "critical reading." Because the term itself has become so ingrained in our consciousness, we rarely think critically about what it means. So, we discuss moving beyond a summary of the content and cursory judgment. I ask students to take notes on each reading (content and commentary) and conclude with three points. These points may include a main idea of the article or a part of the author's argument they found particularly interesting. We try to locate insights into the author's reason for writing the essay and rhetorical gestures or techniques used by the author to influence the reader.

Does the author make his or her objectives and biases explicit? If not, we examine the rhetorical strategies authors employ to convince us of their objectivity. We observe the ways that language colors the presentation of facts—how "a bitter civil war that pitted the slave-holding Southern states against the rest of the country" was probably not written by an author sympathetic to the Confederacy.

Much of our time is spent investigating how authors construct their narratives: the mode of emplotment (comedy, tragedy, romance, satire), the way the argument is formed, and its ideological position—liberal, conservative, radical, anarchist. These various frames for viewing the reading help us to move beyond content, delay judgment, and evaluate readings on a more sophisticated level.

—Ted Conner, Professor of Music

READING AGAINST THE GRAIN

When we ask ourselves what a work (and, by implication, an author) might not be aware of communicating, we are *reading against the grain*. When we ask ourselves what a work seems aware of, what its (and, by implication, its author's) conscious intentions are, we are *reading with the grain.*

Surely you have had the experience of looking back on something you wrote and wondering where it came from. You didn't plan to say it that way ahead of time. This suggests that writers can never be fully in control of what they communicate—that words always, inescapably, communicate more (and less) than we intend. Any of us who has had what we thought a perfectly clear and well-intentioned letter misinterpreted (or so we thought) by its recipient can understand this idea. When we look at the letter again, we usually see what it said that we hadn't realized (at least not consciously) we were saying.

Communication of all kinds takes place both directly and indirectly. Reading against the grain—looking for what a work is saying that it might not know it is saying, that it might not mean to say—requires us to notice and emphasize implicit patterns and make their significance explicit. So, for example, in the classic novel *Jane Eyre*, the narrator Jane repeatedly remarks on her own plain appearance, with the implication that physical beauty is transient and relatively insignificant. Reading against the grain, we'd see the novel's very obsession with plainness as a symptom of how worried it is about the subject, how much it actually believes (but won't admit) that looks matter. *(See also Chapter 9 for methods of analyzing the logic of an argument.)*

USE A READING AS A MODEL

Most of the critical activities with readings involve assimilating and thinking about the information conveyed. But to use a reading as a model is to focus instead on presentation. This represents a change in orientation for most readers, and it takes a little practice to learn how to do it. A useful guideline to remember is *look beyond content* (or subject matter). To focus on presentation is to focus on what a piece of writing does rather than just on what it says.

There are two primary reasons for using a reading as a model:

1. It can provide a way of approaching and organizing your own material.
2. Additionally, it can lead you to see features of a reading that you might otherwise overlook. We are, for the most part, "seduced" by the content of what we read, and so we do not see how the piece is "behaving"—how it sets us up, how it repeats certain phrases, how it is patterned.

If, for example, you were to do an analysis of programs designed to help smokers quit by using an analysis of programs designed to help drinkers quit, the latter might be used as a model for the former. And, if the drinking cessation piece began with a long anecdote to phrase some central problem in program design, and you then began your piece with an analogous problem serving the same aim for your piece, that would represent a still closer use of a reading as a model.

To use a reading as a model, detach your attention from the pure information-assimilation mode to observe *how* the reading says *what* it says. Where does it make claims? What kind of evidence does it provide? Does the writer overtly reveal his or her premises? How and when does she use metaphors or analogies?

And what about the overall organization of the piece you are reading? Not all reading proceeds in a straight narrative line from A to B to C. Some pieces are organized like quilts, a series of patches or vignettes operating as variations on a theme. Others favor a radial organization—locating some central issue or example in the center, and then spiraling out to connect it to other matters, then returning to it again and spiraling out again.

APPLY A READING AS A LENS

This final section of the chapter shows how to apply a reading to other material you are studying. Using a reading as a lens means literally looking at things as the reading does, trying to think in its terms.

As with using a reading as a model, when you use a reading as a lens, you first need to separate its analytical method from the particular argument to which it leads.

Not that the argument should be ignored, but your emphasis rests on *extracting the methodology* in order to apply it to your own analytical ends. For example, you can learn a lot about looking at spaces from one of Mike Davis' urban studies articles on the relocation of the homeless in Los Angeles without necessarily focusing on either L.A. or the homeless. Most college campuses, for example, offer significant opportunities to observe the manipulation of public space either to encourage or deter use by certain populations.

Your first goal when working with a reading as a lens is to fully explore its usefulness for explaining features of your subject. Of course, the match between lens and new material will never be perfect. Thus, you need to remember that whenever you apply the lens A to a new subject B, you are taking lens A from its original context and using its ideas in somewhat different circumstances for at least somewhat different purposes. Using the lens in a different context on a different kind of information will often require you to adjust the lens—to refocus it a bit to bring this new content into clear focus.

Let's say, for example, that you read a smart review essay on the representation of black/white race relations in contemporary films in the 1970s, and you decide to use the review as a lens for exploring the spate of black/white buddy films that emerged in the 1990s.

"Yes, but …," you find yourself responding: there are places where the 1990s films appear to fit within the pattern that the article claims, but there are also exceptions to the pattern. What do you do? What *not* to do is either choose different films that "fit better" or decide that the article is wrong-headed. Instead, start with the "yes": talk about how the film accords with the general pattern. Then focus on the "but," the claims in the reading (the lens) that seem not to fit, or material in your subject not adequately accounted for by the lens.

Because cultural climates and trends are constantly shifting and reconfiguring themselves, particularly in popular culture, you will learn from examining the films how the original review might be usefully extended to account for phenomena that were not present when it was originally written.

Using a Reading as a Lens: "Self-Deprecation on Late Night Television"

The following student paper by Anna Whiston was a culminating project for a first-year seminar. The assignment was to use concepts from two books by sociolinguist Deborah Tannen—*You Just Don't Understand: Women and Men in Conversation* and *That's Not What I Meant: How Conversational Style Makes or Breaks Relationships*—to explore a conversational topic of the student's choice, in this case, conversations among male celebrities on late night talk shows. The essay won an award at our college for best writing by a first-year student. The faculty reviewers praised the essay for its analytical depth, its respect for complexity, and its sophisticated use of secondary sources as lenses.

Throughout the essay, the writer deliberately seeks out evidence that might initially seem to contradict theories supplied by her lens. But rather than finding fault with the lens or dismissing the apparent contradictions, she deftly locates the complexity in Tannen's thinking and in her primary material, refusing to oversimplify either.

As you read the essay (which we have excerpted slightly), notice how the writer

- locates significant patterns in her primary material (her transcripts of conversations on late night talk shows) and asks "So what?";
- uses restatement to infer implications;
- uncovers assumptions;
- formulates and reformulates binaries; and
- uses both data and lens to repeatedly qualify and complicate her claims.

We have included annotations in square brackets to suggest how the writer uses various analytical methods for writing about reading.

"I think my cooking, uh, sucks": Self-Deprecation on Late Night Television
by Anna Whiston

Low confidence is not exactly typical in Hollywood. Celebrities are known just as much for their egos as they are for the movies that they headline and the scandals that they induce. And yet, late night talk shows, such as *The Tonight Show with Jay Leno, Late Night with Conan O'Brien, The Late Show with David Letterman,* and *Jimmy Kimmel Live*, include endless examples of self-deprecation on the parts of both the male hosts and the male celebrity guests. Self-deprecation is, on the surface, a way of belittling oneself. However, examination of the conversations that take place on these television programs helps show that this strand of apparent humility is actually a much more nuanced conversational technique. Conversations on late night talk shows reveal that self-deprecation does not necessarily pit one man as inferior to another.

In *You Just Don't Understand*, linguist Deborah Tannen explores conversation as a process affected largely by the gender of the speaker. For men, according to Tannen, "…life is a contest in which they are constantly tested and must perform, in order to avoid the risk of failure" (178). This sense of competition often manifests itself in "one-upsmanship," a strategy in which men attempt to outdo each other in order to achieve a hierarchical position within a conversation (Tannen 26). However, there are certain situations in which hierarchy is not necessarily desirable. The interactions between men on late night talk shows serve as one example of this situation.

In another one of her works on conversation, *That's Not What I Meant*, Tannen discusses framing, the idea that "everything about the way we say something contributes to establishing the footing that frames our relationships to each other "(75).

The guests on talk shows are entering a frame, or conversational alignment, that is inherently asymmetrical. Though both guest and host are technically celebrities, the guest is presented as the centerpiece of the program, the man who answers the questions, while the host is simply the asker. This frame is not always one that is appealing for the guest, who may want to create a persona that is not that of an elite star, but of a likable and approachable everyman. In order to cultivate this persona, the guest can use conversation to downplay his star status and success in order to establish a more symmetrical alignment to the host, thereby changing the frame of the conversation. As we will see, however, this reframing is complicated, since it essentially shifts the asymmetry to a different ground. An example of this technique can be found in actor Paul Rudd's interview with NBC late night talk show host Conan O'Brien:

Rudd: I'm great, how are you?
O'Brien: I'm very good. You know things are going very well for you. You've been in so many successful movies. You have this new film *Role Models*. People love this movie, very funny, big hit for you, you've gotta be excited. I mean you you're a big, big star.
Rudd: It...I don't know about that, but it's very exciting. Oh God, I'm still out of breath! I swear to God.

By negating O'Brien's compliment, Rudd downplays his fame and thus reframes the conversation. By saying, "Oh God, I'm still out of breath," Rudd draws attention away from his stardom to some goofy dancing that O'Brien and Rudd did at the beginning of the interview. When O'Brien again tries to draw attention to Rudd's star power, Rudd again dodges the compliment.

O'Brien: But I would have to think by now that it's reaching critical mass, so many successful movies you must be getting the star treatment now. I bet you're treated like—
Rudd: I met Bruce Springsteen. I met him but it wasn't a...I snuck backstage at a Police concert and he was there.

Rudd's move, which allows him to segue into a self-deprecating anecdote about his encounter with Bruce Springsteen, represents an effort to resist the frame that O'Brien attempts to establish. Instead of accepting the frame that situates Rudd as a star and O'Brien as an average fan, Rudd strategically reframes the conversation by invoking a third party, a star whom both O'Brien and Rudd admire. Now, the conversation is not taking place between a "big star" and his fan, but rather between two fans.

[The writer sets up and queries binaries:] To help understand Rudd's move, we can use Tannen's conversational categories of "report-talk" and "rapport-talk," the former being a way of "exhibiting knowledge and skill" and the latter being a way of "establishing connections" by "displaying similarities and matching experiences" (*Understand* 77). While men are generally associated with report talk rather than rapport talk, the two categories are not necessarily gender exclusive. Humility, which often takes the form of self-deprecation, can help to remove asymmetry from a conversation. Such a move allows the men to capitalize on their similarities rather than emphasize their differences. We see Rudd do just that by transforming his conversational role from that of the star to that of the fan, a fan that must sneak backstage to meet his musical idols, just like the proverbial rest of us.

[The writer uses her lens to reformulate binaries and uncover assumptions:] If the goal of a conversation is to achieve a sense of equality between speakers, one speaker reinforcing the other's self-deprecation may appear to be detrimental to a relationship. Surely, if one makes a comment that he or she is not funny enough, not smart enough, or not brave enough, it is only polite for the other speaker to contradict this statement. However, when the conversation is between men, such a negation would likely be interpreted as sympathy, and may actually undermine rapport. According to Tannen, "Showing elaborate concern for others' feelings frames you as the social worker who has it all together, and them as your patients" (*Understand* 173). Sympathy or pity, as a result, creates a conversational hierarchy. The sympathizer is in a superior position; he is the one with answers while the other man is the one with the problems.

The men conversing on late night talk shows, rather than offering sympathy on hearing another man's self-deprecating anecdote, frequently endorse and even augment the other's self-deprecation. Take, for example, Rudd's story about a wedding he attended, paying special attention to O'Brien's responses.

Rudd: I had a horrible one happen a few years ago where I actually got, um, thrown out of a wedding.
O'Brien: You got thrown out of a wedding?
Rudd: Yeah.
O'Brien: Did you know the people well, I mean these were friends of yours?
Rudd: Yeah, um—
O'Brien: And they threw you out?

Rudd goes on to describe a slightly embarrassing but very humorous video that he made for the bride and groom, with the conversation continuing as follows:

O'Brien: But you didn't think—you didn't know they were gonna show it at the wedding? And so all these people are there, hundreds of people?
Rudd: Well yeah...and uh, uh I'm not even gonna...yeah.
O'Brien: And what happened?
Rudd: Well I—she like, you know—people got kind of freaked out and the bride ran out. I mean it's not the way you imagine your wedding day—
O'Brien: The bride ran away?! That's terrible!
Rudd: I felt horrible.

O'Brien does nothing to soothe Rudd's worries about Rudd's disastrous experience; he urges his guest to divulge all the painful details and seems to relish Rudd's embarrassment. But then, Rudd's purpose was probably not to earn sympathy. O'Brien supported Rudd by *not* showing sympathy, as "refraining from giving sympathy is generous, insofar as it [sympathy] potentially condescends" (*Understand* Tannen 61). Had O'Brien responded that he was sure that Rudd's friends would forgive him and that the incident was not remarkably embarrassing, he would have undermined the purpose of Rudd's story. Instead, O'Brien complies with Rudd by emphasizing the "terrible" nature of his guest's experience. [...]

*[The writer moves next to another of Tannen's theories, which reformulate the binaries in the Rudd and O'Brien example:]*Tannen suggests that while women look for understanding for their problems, men look for solutions: "Yet another man commented that women seem to wallow in their problems, wanting to talk about them forever, whereas he and other men want to get them out and be done with them, either by finding a solution or by laughing them off" (*Understand* 52). The men in these examples did not want sympathy for their problems, nor did they want their problems dismissed—they sought validation. But, unlike the women Tannen described, such validation does not come from sympathy or identification, but from laughter and reinforcement. The self-deprecator is laughing at a problem of his own, and needs the other man to acknowledge that his problem is funny, and is, indeed, a problem, for the two men to achieve equal status within the conversation.

[The writer then moves on to another pattern in her data, instances where two men in a conversation both use self-deprecation:] Self-deprecation is not always used by only one party; it is also sometimes used by both parties to negotiate footing within a conversation. The following excerpt comes from a conversation between ABC late night host Jimmy Kimmel and comedian Artie Lange in which the two men discuss a celebrity wedding both men attended.

Kimmel: I know, right. Well you said something—
Lange: Wasn't that a great event though?
Kimmel: It was great and you did a great job with the toast. What was it you said with the toast about—
Lange: Well it's a, it's an older guy marrying a model way too young for him…

Notice how Lange attempts to avoid accepting Kimmel's assertion that Lange said something funny at the wedding, drawing attention instead to the event as a whole when he senses that Kimmel is about to be complimentary. Later in the same conversation, Lange retaliates and attempts to reframe the conversation.

Lange: But you upstaged me because you—when—I didn't know—I didn't know any other funny people were gonna talk. And then you went up and killed it before they married each other and—
Kimmel: Well you should have known about that. They asked me to do a little thing at the ceremony—
Lange: Right.
Kimmel: Like the day before so I did a little prayer for them.
Lange: That was nice—it was—you were funny.
Kimmel: I didn't mean to, uh, step on your toes there, I didn't want to ruin it. But you do owe me and I'll tell you why…

Lange attempts to reframe the conversation by saying that Kimmel upstaged him. Kimmel, like Lange, dismisses the praise, saying that the prayer that Lange labeled "very funny" was really a "little thing" that he had put together the "day before." Kimmel then clumsily changes the subject in order to draw attention away from himself. This presents a case in which a compliment comes across more as an accusation than a statement of praise. *[The writer has offered an alternative explanation for a possible contradiction with her lens:]* One possible explanation for the desire to dismiss and minimize praise is that compliment-giving is not the selfless act in may appear to be, but is, in fact, pure one-upmanship.

[The writer locates a theory in her lens that would support the explanation:] According to Tannen, "Giving praise, like giving information is also inherently asymmetrical. It too frames the speaker as one-up, in a position to judge someone else's performance" (*Understand* 69). Thus, accepting praise may force the man on the receiving end of the praise to surrender supremacy to the praise-giver. By negating or avoiding praise, hierarchy can be reserved.

The type of combative self-deprecation that Kimmel and Lange display in this conversation, in which one man accuses the other of "upstaging" him, also indicates that self-deprecation is used to display magnanimity. In *That's Not What I Meant*, Tannen writes, "It's an ironic twist by which you want to be magnanimous but want credit for it too—and taking credit for being magnanimous reframes the other person's behavior as depriving you" (89). Self-deprecating humor operates in a similar way. One is not merely telling an embarrassing personal anecdote or using himself as the target of a joke, but, on the "metamessage" level, which looks beyond the surface of a statement to determine "what we're doing when we speak" (*Understand* 32), he is telling his partner (and in the case of talk shows, the audience as well) that he is being generous, sacrificing his own pride in order to compliment the other man. This is evident in Kimmel and Lange's conversation. Both men combine compliments of the other man with denunciations of themselves, suggesting that such a combination is a generous and giving gesture. *[The writer ably concludes her analysis with a compressed restatement about competition:]* The real competition is not about which man was funnier at the wedding, but over which man can better compliment the other's performance.

In Conan O'Brien's conversation with actor Kiefer Sutherland, O'Brien repeatedly pokes fun at his own weakness in order to emphasize Sutherland's toughness, a trait for which the actor is known. It may appear that O'Brien is putting himself down, but at the same time he displays one-upmanship. When O'Brien is being self-deprecating, downplaying his own skills in relation to Sutherland's, Sutherland becomes the recipient of O'Brien's generosity. O'Brien, thus, comes out of the conversation in a hierarchical position to Sutherland, for he was the one giving, and not receiving, the praise and generosity.

[The writer now extends her category of self-deprecation to include another form, teasing:] Teasing and self-deprecation may appear to go hand-in-hand. In teasing, man A makes fun of man B, and in self-deprecation, man B makes fun of man B. Either

way, man B is made fun of. However, the target of the humor is not always as important as the source. If man A teases man B, man A has the upper hand. But if man B teases himself, it is man B who gains dominance in the conversation. On the topic of the wedding that Jimmy Kimmel and Artie Lange attended, Lange says, "Um, but I was glad you were at my table, man, cause it was all good looking people. You uglied it up a bit." Kimmel responds, "I know, yeah. That's uh...yeah we make quite an imposing pair." The men go on, both making fun of what they describe as mutual ugliness. Later in the conversation, Lange begins to tease Kimmel about the host's girlfriend, saying that the couple was engaging in frequent displays of public affection at the wedding. In this situation, Kimmel does *not* transform Lange's teasing into self-deprecation, but instead tries to remove the teasing altogether.

Lange: And so I'm thinking I'm not gonna be the only single loser there and then you and Sarah—I look over and it's like you were shooting *Nine and a Half Weeks* or something.
Kimmel: Oh, no it wasn't.
Lange: You oughta, you oughta see these two.
Kimmel: That's not true.
Lange: "So Jim there's a broad over there we could dance with" he's like (kissing face).
Kimmel: Stop it. That wasn't me—
Lange: I'm telling you, she—
Kimmel: That's really embarrassing cause that wasn't me. Maybe you're confusing me with Corolla, people do that from time to time.

In this excerpt, Lange shatters the mutual self-deprecation that the two had been enjoying earlier, teasing Kimmel about something that Kimmel is clearly not comfortable being teased nor teasing himself about. As a result, Lange has dominance in this conversation. Kimmel struggles to recapture a sense of control, telling Lange that *he* is the one who should be embarrassed, at which point he bring ups a third party, actor Adam Corolla, to be the subject of the teasing. *[The writer is seeing the questions and making them explicit; then characteristically, she seeks out points of connection with the lens:]* Why did Kimmel choose to be self-deprecating about his looks but not his relationship? One possibility, as Tannen suggests, is that men are uncomfortable discussing "personal relationships and feelings" (*Understand* 276). Whatever Kimmel's reasons were, his shifting behavior in this conversation depicts the varying forms and uses of teasing. Teasing can be transformed into self-deprecation, providing the self-deprecator with dominance. But, when the teasing is resisted, the teaser has the opportunity to gain the upper hand. This sheds light on the nature of teasing as a move that provides the teaser with control, regardless of if the teaser is another man or the target of the teasing himself.

Perhaps, then, self-deprecating humor also functions as a sort of pre-emptive move in which one man points out his own flaws before the other man has the chance to do so. If a man makes fun of himself, he still has control. He refuses to surrender this power to another man and thus surrender a hierarchical position in the conversation. Take, for example, this excerpt from Senator John McCain's conversation with NBC host Jay Leno:

Leno: And you went up to the mountains too?
McCain: We went up to our place near Sedona and had a very nice time and—
Leno: Now which house is that, number twel—
McCain: You know that's uh let's see it's a very...let's see... twenty-seven.

Leno was on the verge of making a dig about the senator's many homes, but McCain, seeing this coming, beat Leno to the punch, cutting him off before he even finished the word "twelve." McCain then goes on to exaggerate the number of homes that he owns. This shows that McCain not only understands the public's perception of him, he also is aware that his surplus of homes is a funny, and perhaps even embarrassing, subject. Thus, McCain uses self-deprecation to control the conversation, taking away Leno's opportunity to laugh at him before he laughs at himself.

Perhaps the most frequent and telling place in which self-deprecation pops up is in stories. Late night television is an excellent medium through which to study storytelling; in addition to the release dates of the projects they are promoting, celebrities always come equipped with an anecdote or two. Tannen includes a study of the differences found in stories told by men from those told by women. Her findings indicated that "the stories the men told made them look good" while the women were more likely to tell stories "in which they [women] violate social norms and are scared or embarrassed as a result" (*Understand* 177). The behavior of men on late night talk shows would seem to contradict these findings: the men's stories usually involve them telling of an incident in which, they were, indeed, "embarrassed as a result." However, when we look at the content of these stories, it becomes apparent that these stories function on a more sophisticated level than simple self-effacement.

[This paragraph begins the writer's summation and culmination of her analysis. Notice how deftly she uses Tannen's key terms rather than just relying on quotation.] Whether it is Paul Rudd's story about showing an embarrassing movie at a friend's wedding or Steve Carrell's anecdote about his parents flying on a plane with a Thanksgiving turkey because his cooking "sucks," the men doing the self-deprecating do not ultimately portray themselves in an embarrassing or pathetic light. The stories that they tell at their own expense draw laughs—and the story teller is laughing with them. In this regard, the stories told are actually more flattering than they are embarrassing. The stories send the message, or metamessage, that the storyteller is able not only to laugh at himself, but also to draw laughs from his audience, all the while coming across as likable and humble. What appears to be humility or lack of self-confidence actually serves a purpose more akin to a joke. And when a joke is told, conversational asymmetry is unavoidable as one man is doing the joke telling while the other functions as the audience (*Understand* 90). Thus, what seems like a way to put one's self down is, in fact, one-upmanship.

Self-deprecation is a complex conversational tool. On the surface, it seems to be simply a way for the speaker to disparage himself. It also, however, can function as a tool for humility and compromise, a way to create conversational symmetry from a situation of asymmetry. The most subtle and fascinating way in which self-deprecation functions, however, is a bit of a paradox: by putting himself down, a man can actually build himself up. This is revealing of the extent to which conversation operates in ways that can be very deceptive. People, whether rich and famous or otherwise, can use conversation not just as a way to transmit information, but as a means to an end. Although this study involved individuals whose job it is to use words to play a character or keep a reputation in check, one need not be an Oscar-winning actor to reap the benefits of being a smart conversationalist. Conversation is not merely a straightforward exchange of words; it is a skill, that when used strategically and with great awareness, can help a speaker to get ahead—often without anyone else realizing that he is doing it.

GUIDELINES FOR WRITING ABOUT READING

1. Get beyond reading for the gist. Always mark a few key passages in whatever you read.

2. Whenever you read critically, actively look for the pitch and the complaint—what the writer wants to convince you of, and the position that he or she is reacting against. Also be aware of the moment—how the historical context qualifies the way we interpret the reading.

3. Experiment with passage-based focused freewriting. Find out what you think by seeing what you say.

4. Alternatively, keep a commonplace book. The act of copying out key sentences from a reading and perhaps jotting a few notes will inevitably lead you to remember more and discover more about what you are reading.

5. Paraphrase key passages to open up the language and reveal complexities you may not have noticed. Paraphrasing three times is sure to help get you started interpreting a reading, moving you beyond just repeating pieces of it as answers.

6. In applying a reading as a lens, think about how lens A both fits and does not fit subject B: use the differences to develop your analysis.

7. Uncover unstated assumptions by asking, "Given its overt claim, what must this reading also already believe?"

8. A provocative way to open up interpretation is to try reading against the grain of a reading. Ask, "what does this piece believe that it does not know it believes?" Using The Method to uncover obsessive repetitions will sometimes provide the evidence to formulate against-the-grain claims.

Assignments: Writing Analytically About Reading

1. **Apply a Reading as a Lens**. Use a reading as a lens for examining a subject. For example, look at a piece of music or a film through the lens of a review that does not discuss the particular piece or film you are writing about. Or you might read about a particular theory of humor and use that as a lens for examining a comic play, film, story, television show, or stand-up routine.

2. **Analyze a Challenging Paragraph and Apply It as a Lens**. In a recent book on representations of the public and the private in contemporary American life, law professor Jeffrey Rosen offers the following discussion of political scientist Daniel Boorstin's analysis of heroes and celebrities:

> In *The Image*, Daniel Boorstin explored the way the growth of movies, radio, print, and television had transformed the nature of political authority, which came to be exercised not by distant and remote heroes but instead by celebrities,

whom Boorstin defined as 'a person who is known for his well-knownness.' 'Neither good nor bad,' a celebrity is 'morally neutral,' 'the human pseudo-event,' who has been 'fabricated on purpose to satisfy our exaggerated expectations of human greatness' (11). While the heroes of old exercised authority by being remote and mysterious, modern celebrities exercise authority by being familiar and intelligible, creating the impression—but not the reality—of emotional accessibility. Heroes were distinguished by their achievement, celebrities by their image or trademarks or 'name brands' (*The Naked Crowd*, Random House, 2004).

Bring the tools for reading analytically to bear on this passage in the following sequence:

a.   Use paraphrase to restate both Boorstin's claims and Rosen's exposition of it.

b.   Then locate the dominant binaries in the paragraph and articulate these to help you determine what is at stake there.

c.   Once you've done these tasks, take Boorstin's theory and use it as a lens to examine the presentation of a public figure of your choice, whether a politician, a contemporary hero, a celebrity, a musician, a sports star, and so forth. As you write about this figure, seek to explore not only how your subject fits the lens but also how he or she does not fit. Use the Whiston essay on talk shows as a model for negotiating complication in both the lens and the primary material.

3.   **Apply the Lens of Ritual to Daily Life**. In her book, *The Rituals of Dinner* (1991), Margaret Visser discusses table manners as a form of ritual:

> Rules of politeness tend to cluster round moments of transition, of meeting others, making decisions, conferring, parting, commemorating. Rituals are there to make difficult passages easier. They include the gestures—waving, nodding, smiling, speaking set phrases—which daily smooth our meetings with other people; the attitudes and postures we adopt when standing or sitting in the presence of others, especially when we are talking to them; the muttering of 'excuse me' when interrupting others or squeezing past them. Full-dress celebrations of coming together, of marking transitions and recollections, almost always require food, with all the ritual politeness implied in dining—the proof that we all know how eating should be managed. We eat whenever life becomes dramatic: at weddings, birthdays, funerals, at parting and at welcoming home, or at any moment which a group decides is worthy of remark. Festivals and feasts are solemn or holy days; they are so regularly celebrated by people meeting for meals that 'having a feast' has actually come to mean 'eating a lot.'

As this paragraph suggests, rituals depend on rules and conventional behaviors that provide order and stability, thereby easing "difficult passages." Use the tools you've acquired in this and previous chapters to uncover the implications in this paragraph. Then use it as a lens to analyze some ritual from everyday life. Obviously, Visser is concentrating on the ritual functions surrounding food—which you can use as a model for your investigation of some other ritual, perhaps one that you never noticed as a ritual before. It could be any system regulated by manners:

- handling a pet in public,
- ordering drinks for a group of friends,
- visiting a professor during office hours,
- participating in class discussion,
- attending a baseball game, or
- socializing in the library.

And the list is endless. Choose any ritual activity, and use Visser as a model and a lens to analyze it. Describe carefully its rules, and explore what these rules control and why such control is useful.

Chapter 6

Making Interpretations Plausible

IN THIS CHAPTER, we focus on the move from description to interpretation and address some of the issues that interpretation typically raises. What makes some interpretations better than others? What makes interpretations more than a matter of personal opinion?

The book has so far offered two kinds of prompts for making interpretive leaps: ranking (what is most important, or interesting, or revealing and why?) and asking "So what?" We've also demonstrated that the writer who can offer careful description of a subject's key features is likely to arrive at conclusions about possible meanings that others would share. We will now add another necessary move: specifying and arguing for a context in which the evidence might be best understood—the **interpretive context**.

Here are two key principles:

- *Everything means*; that is, everything in life calls on us to interpret—even when we are unaware of doing so.
- *Meaning is contextual*; that is, meaning-making always occurs inside of some social or cultural or other frame of reference.

> **WHAT INTERPRETATION DOES**
>
> Offers a theory of what X means, not fact
>
> Supplies a context for understanding X that is suggested by the details
>
> Strives for the plausible, not the certain: explains individual details and patterns of evidence
>
> Supplies reasons for why evidence means what you claim it means

MOVING FROM DESCRIPTION TO INTERPRETATION

Throughout this book, we have been defining analysis as a search for meaning, a search conducted primarily through discovery of significant patterns in your evidence. In Chapter 3, Analysis: What It Is and What It Does, we noted that the process of noticing, of recording selected details and patterns of detail (analysis), is already the beginning of interpretation. Analysis differs from description and summary because it triggers larger interpretive leaps.

As we also argued in Chapter 3, the first step toward arriving at and persuading others to accept your interpretation is to make the most of the observation stage by following these two rules:

1. **Describe with care.** The words you choose to summarize your data will contain the germs of your ideas about what the subject means.

2. **In moving from summary to analysis and interpretation, look consciously at the language you have chosen,** asking, "Why did I choose this word? What ideas are implicit in the language I have used?"

Your readers' willingness to accept an interpretation is powerfully connected to their ability to see its *plausibility*, that is, how it follows from both the supporting details you selected and the language you used in characterizing those details. *An interpretive conclusion is not a fact, but a theory.* Interpretive conclusions stand or fall not so much on whether they can be proved right or wrong, but on whether they are demonstrably plausible. Often, the best you can hope for with interpretive conclusions is not that others will say, "Yes, that is obviously right," but "Yes, I can see where it might be possible and reasonable to think as you do."

A major point of this chapter is that interpretive contexts are suggested by the material you are studying; they aren't simply imposed on it by a writer. Explaining why you think a subject should be seen through a particular interpretive "lens" is an important part of making interpretations reasonable and plausible. Our discussion will illustrate how, once an interpretive context is selected, a writer goes about analyzing evidence to test—as well as support—the usefulness of that context.

Different interpretations will account better for some details than others, which is why it enriches our view of the world to try on different interpretations. Ultimately, you will have to decide which possible interpretation, as seen through which plausible interpretive context, best accounts for what you think is most important and interesting to notice about your subject.

HOW TO INTERPRET

Organize the data (do The Method)
Move from observation to implication (ask So what?)
Select an appropriate interpretive context
Determine a range of plausible interpretations
Assess the extent to which one interpretation explains the most

MAKING INTERPRETATIONS PLAUSIBLE ACROSS THE CURRICULUM

As we note at various points in this book, the practices governing data gathering, analysis, and interpretation differ as you move from one academic division to another. In the humanities, the data to be analyzed are usually textual—visual or verbal details.

In the social sciences, data are sometimes textual, as would be the case, for example, if you were analyzing the history of a particular political theory or practice such as free speech. But much analytical thinking in the social sciences and the natural sciences involves arriving at plausible conclusions about the significance of quantitative (numerical) and experimental data. This book's primary interpretive prompt, "So what?" (where do these research data get me, and why does this data set mean what I say it means?) still applies in the sciences, though the interpretive leaps are typically worded differently.

Interpretation in the natural and social sciences considers the extent to which data either confirm or fail to confirm the expectations defined in a hypothesis, which is a theory the writer proposes in response to a research question. This chapter's examples demonstrate analytical thinking as it typically operates in the humanities. The emphases, however, on careful description of evidence and on arguing for the appropriateness of a particular interpretive context are common to all three academic divisions. *(For more on the language and methods of interpretation in the natural and social sciences, see Chapter 15, Forms and Formats Across the Curriculum.)*

PLAUSIBLE VERSUS IMPLAUSIBLE INTERPRETATIONS: THE SOCIAL CONTEXT

Meanings must be reasoned from sufficient evidence if they are to be judged plausible. Meanings can always be refuted by people who find fault with your reasoning or can cite conflicting evidence. Let's refer back briefly to a hypothetical question raised in Chapter 3's discussion of *Whistler's Mother*—that the woman in the painting who is clad in black is mourning the death of a loved one, perhaps a person who lived in the house represented in the painting on the wall. It is true that black clothes often indicate mourning. This is a culturally accepted, recognized sign. But with only the black dress, and perhaps the sad facial expression (if it is sad) to go on, this "mourning theory" gets sidetracked from what is actually in the painting into storytelling. Insufficient evidence would make this theory implausible.

Now, what if another person asserted that Whistler's mother is an alien astronaut, for example, her long black dress concealing a third leg? Obviously, this interpretation would not win wide support, and for a reason that points up another of the primary limits on the meaning-making process: meanings, to have value outside one's own private realm of experience, have to make sense to other people. The assertion that Whistler's mother is an alien astronaut is unlikely to be deemed acceptable by enough people to give it currency.

This is to say that the relative value of interpretive meanings is to some extent socially (culturally) determined. Although people are free to say that things mean whatever they want them to mean, saying doesn't make it so. The mourning theory has more evidence than the alien astronaut theory, but it still relies too heavily on what is not there, on a narrative for which there is insufficient evidence in the painting itself.

In experimental science, it is especially important that a writer/researcher can locate his or her work in the context of other scientists who have achieved similar results. Isolated results and interpretations, those that are not corroborated by others' research, have much less credibility. In this respect, the making of meaning is collaborative and communal. The collaborative nature of scientific and scholarly work is one of the reasons that writing about reading is so important in college-level writing. In order to interpret evidence in a way that others will find plausible, you first have to have some idea of what others in the field are talking about.

INTERPRETIVE CONTEXTS AND MULTIPLE MEANINGS

There are, however, other possible interpretations that would satisfy the two criteria of sufficient evidence and broad cultural acceptance. And it is valuable to recognize that evidence usually will support more than one plausible interpretation. Consider, for example, a reading of *Whistler's Mother* that a person might produce if he or she began with noticing the actual title, *Arrangement in Grey and Black: The Artist's Mother*. From this starting point, a person might focus observation on the disposition of color exclusively and arrive at an interpretation that the painting is about painting (which might then explain why there is also a painting on the wall).

The figure of the mother then would have meaning only insofar as it contained the two colors mentioned in the painting's title, black and gray, and the painting's representational content (the aspects of life that it shows us) would be assigned less importance. This is a promising and plausible idea for an interpretation. It makes use of different details from previous interpretations that we've suggested, but it would also address some of the details already targeted (the dress, the curtain) from an entirely different context, focusing on the use and arrangement of color.

To generalize: two equally plausible interpretations can be made of the same thing. It is not the case that our first reading (in Chapter 3), focusing on the profile view of the mother and suggesting the painting's concern with mysterious separateness, is right, whereas the painting-about-painting (or aesthetic) view, building from the clue in the title, is wrong. They operate within different contexts.

An interpretive context is a lens. Depending on the context you choose—preferably a context suggested by the evidence itself—you will see different things. Regardless of how the context is arrived at, an important part of getting an interpretation accepted as plausible is to argue for the appropriateness of the interpretive context you use, not just the interpretation it takes you to.

Specifying an Interpretive Context: A Brief Example

Notice how, in the following analysis, the student writer's interpretation relies on his choice of a particular interpretive context, post–World War II Japan. Had he selected another context, he might have arrived at some different conclusions about the same details. Notice also how the writer perceives a pattern in the details and queries his own observations ("So what?") to arrive at an interpretation.

The series entitled "Kamaitachi" is a journal of the photographer Hosoe's desolate childhood and wartime evacuation in the Tokyo countryside. He returns years later to the areas where he grew up, a stranger to his native land, perhaps likening himself to the legendary Kamaitachi, an invisible sickle-toothed weasel, intertwined with the soil and its unrealized fertility. "Kamaitachi #8" (1956), a platinum palladium print, stands alone to best capture Hosoe's alienation from and troubled expectation of the future of Japan. *[Here, the writer chooses the photographer's life as his interpretive context.]*

The image is that of a tall fence of stark horizontal and vertical rough wood lashed together, looming above the barren rice fields. Straddling the fence, half-crouched and half-clinging, is a solitary male figure, gazing in profile to the horizon. Oblivious to the sky above of dark and churning thunderclouds, the figure instead focuses his attentions and concentrations elsewhere. *[The writer selects and describes significant detail.]*

It is exactly this *elsewhere* that makes the image successful, for in studying the man we are to turn our attention in the direction of the figure's gaze and away from the photograph itself. He hangs curiously between heaven and earth, suspended on a makeshift man-made structure, in a purgatorial limbo awaiting the future. He waits with anticipation—perhaps dread?—for a time that has not yet come; he is directed away from the present, and it is this sensitivity to time which sets this print apart from the others in the series. One could argue that in effect this man, clothed in common garb, has become Japan itself, indicative of the post-war uncertainty of a country once-dominant and now destroyed. What will the future (dark storm clouds) hold for this newly-humbled nation? *[Here, the writer notices a pattern of in-between-ness and locates it in an historical context in order to make his interpretive leap.]*

Remember that regardless of the subject you select for your analysis, you should directly address not just "What does this say?" but also, as this writer has done, *"What are we invited to make of it, and in what context?"*

The Role of Context in Interpreting Numerical Data

In the previous example, the writer chose an interpretive context that seemed to best explain a pattern of detail in his evidence. In order to make a case for his interpretation, the writer needed to demonstrate the appropriateness and relevance of his chosen context, including his reasons for choosing one possible interpretive context over another.

The process is similar when a writer seeks to interpret numerical data. The writer must decide the extent to which his or her numerical data confirm or fail to confirm an expectation defined in the study's hypothesis. Here is a brief example of statistical analysis from a political science course on public opinion research. The study uses a data set generated to test the hypothesis that "Republican defectors who have been members of the party for over 11 years are less likely to change party affiliation to Democrat because of the Republican Party's policies than Republican defectors registered with the party for under 10 years." Note how the writer integrates quantitative data into her discussion of the findings, a move characteristic of interpretation in the social sciences, and how she establishes the context in which this data might be best understood. Notice too how her findings complicate her original research question.

> The data suggest that the longer a Republican defector was a member of the Republican Party, the more likely that person was to switch party affiliation to Democrat because of the Republican Party's policies as opposed to changes in his or her own belief system. For example, 35% of Republican defectors who had been members of the party for 1-5 years agreed with the statement 'the Republican Party's policies led me to leave the party,' while 35% said it was due to changes in their personal beliefs. Thus, it appears as though both reasons have equal influence on an individual's decision to switch parties.
>
> However, when you look at the defectors who were members of the party for over 6 years, roughly 20% more of them left because of the party's policies than because of a change in their personal beliefs. This suggests that people don't change their views—it is the party's change of views that prompts defection by even long-time members.

In the case of statistical data, an interpretive problem arises when writers attempt to determine whether a statistical correlation between two things—blood cholesterol level and the likelihood of dying of a heart attack, for example—can be interpreted as causal. Does a statistical correlation between high cholesterol levels and heart attack suggest that higher levels of cholesterol cause heart attacks, or might it only suggest that some other factor associated with cholesterol is responsible? Similarly, if a significantly higher percentage of poor people treated in hospital emergency rooms die than their more affluent counterparts, do we conclude that emergency room treatment of the poor is at fault? What factors, such as inability of poor people to afford regular preventive health care, might need to be considered in interpretation of the data? *(For more on interpreting numerical data, see "Interpreting the Numbers: A Psychology Professor Speaks" in Chapter 8, Reasoning from Evidence to Claims.)*

INTENTION AS AN INTERPRETIVE CONTEXT

An interpretive context that frequently creates problems in analysis is intention. People relying on authorial intention as their interpretive context typically assert that the author—not the work itself—is the ultimate and correct source of interpretations.

FIGURE 6.1

The Dancers **by Sarah Kersh. Pen-and-Ink Drawing, 6″ × 13.75″**

Look at the drawing titled *The Dancers* in Figure 6.1. What follows is the artist's statement about how the drawing came about and what it came to mean to her.

> This piece was created completely unintentionally. I poured some ink onto paper and blew on it through a straw. The ink took the form of what looked like little people in movement. I recopied the figures I liked, touched up the rough edges, and ended with this gathering of fairy-like creatures. I love how in art something abstract can so suddenly become recognizable.

In this case, interestingly, the artist initially had no intentions beyond experimenting with materials. As the work evolved, she began to arrive at her own interpretation of what the drawing might suggest. Most viewers would probably find the artist's interpretation plausible, but this is not to say that the artist must have the last word and that it is somehow an infraction for others to produce alternative interpretations.

Suppose the artist had stopped with her first two sentences. Even this explicit statement of her lack of intention would not prohibit people from interpreting the drawing in some of the ways that she later goes on to suggest. The artist's initial absence of a plan doesn't require viewers to interpret *The Dancers* as only ink on paper.

Whenever an intention is ascribed to a person or an act or a product, this intention contributes significantly to meaning; but the intention, whatever its source, does not outrank or exclude other interpretations. It is simply another context for understanding.

Why is this so? In our earlier discussion of personalizing, we suggested that people are not entirely free agents, immune to the effects of the culture they inhabit. It follows that when people produce things, they are inevitably affected by that culture in ways of which they are both aware and unaware. The culture, in other words, speaks through them. In the early 1960s, for example, a popular domestic sitcom, *Leave It to Beaver,* portrayed the mother, June Cleaver—usually impeccably dressed in heels, dress, and pearls—doing little other than dusting the mantle and making tuna fish sandwiches for her sons. Is the show then intentionally implying that the proper role for women is that of domestic helper? Well, in the context of post–women's movement thinking, the show's representation of Mrs. Cleaver might plausibly be read this way, but not as a matter of intention. To conclude that *Leave It to Beaver* promoted a particular stereotype about women does not mean that the writers got together every week and thought out ways to do so.

It is interesting and useful to try to determine from something you are analyzing what its makers might have intended. But, by and large, you are best off concentrating on what the thing itself communicates as opposed to what someone might have wanted it to communicate.

WHAT IS AND ISN'T "MEANT" TO BE ANALYZED

What about analyzing things that were not intended to "mean" anything, like entertainment films and everyday things like blue jeans and shopping malls? Some people believe it is wrong to bring out unintended implications. Let's take another example: Barbie dolls. These are just toys intended for young girls, people might say. Clearly, the intention of the makers of Barbie is to make money by entertaining children. Does that mean Barbie must remain outside of interpretive scrutiny for such things as her built-in earrings, high-heeled feet, and heavily marketed lifestyle?

What the makers of a particular product or idea intend is only a part of what that product or idea communicates. The urge to cordon off certain subjects from analysis on the grounds that they weren't meant to be analyzed unnecessarily excludes a wealth of information—and meaning—from your range of vision. It is right to be careful about the interpretive contexts we bring to our experience. It is less right—less useful—to confine our choice of context in a too literal-minded way to a single category. To some people, baseball is only a game and clothing is only there to protect us from the elements.

What such people don't want to admit is that things communicate meaning to others whether we wish them to or not; that is, the meanings of most things are socially determined. What, for example, does the choice of wearing a baseball cap to a staff meeting or to a class "say"? Note, by the way, that a communicative gesture such as the wearing of a hat need not be premeditated to communicate something to other people. The hat is still "there" and available to be "read" by others as a sign of certain attitudes and a culturally defined sense of identity—with or without intention.

Meaning and Social Contexts

Baseball caps, for example, carry different associations from berets or wool caps because they come from different social contexts. Baseball caps convey a set of attitudes associated with the piece of American culture they come from. They suggest, for example, popular rather than high culture, casual rather than formal, young—perhaps defiantly so, especially if worn backward—rather than old, and so on.

We can, of course, protest that the "real" reason for turning our baseball cap backward is to allow more light in, making it easier to see than when the bill of the cap shields our faces. This practical rationale makes sense, but it does not explain away the social statement that the hat and a particular way of wearing it might make, whether or not this statement is intentional. Because meaning is, to a significant extent, socially determined, we can't entirely control what our clothing, our manners, our language, or even our way of walking communicates to others.

The social contexts that make gestures like our choice of hats carry particular meanings are always shifting, but some such context is always present. As we asserted at the beginning of this chapter, everything means, and meaning is always contextual.

We turn now to two common problems writers encounter in interpretation. These problems are so widespread that we have fancifully labeled them "schools."

THE FORTUNE COOKIE SCHOOL OF INTERPRETATION

The theory of interpretation that we call the Fortune Cookie School believes that things have a single, hidden, "right" meaning, and that if a person can only "crack" the thing, it will yield an extractable and self-contained "message." There are several problems with this conception of the interpretive process *(see Chapter 3, Implications Versus Hidden Meanings)*.

First, the assumption that things have single hidden meanings interferes with open-minded and dispassionate observation. Adherents of the Fortune Cookie School look solely for clues pointing to *the* hidden message and, having found these clues, discard the rest, like the cookie in a Chinese restaurant once the fortune has been extracted. The fortune cookie approach forecloses on the possibility of multiple plausible meanings, each within its own context. When you assume only one right answer exists, you are also assuming there is only one proper context for understanding and, by extension, that anybody who happens to select a different starting point or context and who thus arrives at a different answer is necessarily wrong.

Most of the time, practitioners of the fortune cookie approach aren't even aware they are assuming the correctness of a single context because they don't realize a fundamental truth about interpretations: they are always limited by contexts. In other words, we are suggesting that claims to universal truths are always problematic. Things don't just mean in some simple and clear way for all people in all situations; they always mean within a network of beliefs, from a particular point of view. The person who claims to have access to some universal truth, beyond context and point of view, is either naïve (unaware) or, worse, a bully—insisting that his or her view of the world is obviously correct and must be accepted by everyone.

THE ANYTHING GOES SCHOOL OF INTERPRETATION

At the opposite extreme from the single-right-answer Fortune Cookie School lies the completely relativist Anything Goes School. The problem with the Anything Goes approach is that it tends to assume that *all* interpretations are equally viable, and that meanings are simply a matter of individual choice, regardless of evidence or plausibility. Put another way, it overextends the creative aspect of interpretation to absurdity, arriving at the position that you can see in a subject whatever you want to see. But such unqualified relativism is not logical. It is simply not the case that meaning is entirely up to the individual; some readings are clearly better than others. The better interpretations have more evidence and rational explanation of how the evidence supports the interpretive claims—qualities that make these meanings more public and negotiable.

MAKING AN INTERPRETATION: THE EXAMPLE OF A *NEW YORKER* COVER

A major point of this section is that interpretive contexts are suggested by the material you are studying; they aren't simply imposed. Explaining why you think a subject should be seen through a particular interpretive "lens" is an important part of making interpretations reasonable and plausible. Our discussion illustrates a writer's decision-making process in choosing an interpretive context and how, once that context has been selected, the writer goes about analyzing evidence to test as well as support the usefulness of that context.

The example on which we focus is a visual image, a cover from the *New Yorker* magazine (see Figure 6.2). The cover of the October 9, 2000 issue is by Ian Falconer and is entitled "The Competition." To see the image in color, you can easily access it online by following these steps: (1) visit the *New Yorker* store website; (2) click on Browse by Artist; (3) choose Ian Falconer; and (4) page forward to October 9, 2000.

Producing a close description of anything you analyze is one of the best ways to begin because the act of describing causes you to notice more and triggers analytical thinking. Here is our description of the *New Yorker* cover:

The picture contains four women, visible from the waist up, standing in a row in semi-profile, staring out at some audience other than us, since their eyes look off to the side. All four gaze in the same direction. Each woman is dressed in a bathing suit and wears a banner draped over one shoulder in the manner of those worn in the swimsuit competition at beauty pageants. Three of the women are virtually identical. The banners worn by these three women show the letters *gia, rnia,* and *rida,* the remainder of the letters being cut off by the other women's shoulders, so that we have to fill in the missing letters to see which state each woman represents.

The fourth woman, who stands third from the left in line, tucked in among the others who look very much alike, wears a banner reading *york.* This woman's appearance is different in just about every respect from the other three. Whereas they are blonde with long flowing hair, she is dark with her hair up in a tight bun. Whereas their mouths are wide open, revealing a wall of very white teeth, her mouth is closed, lips drawn together. Whereas their eyes are wide open and staring, hers, like her mouth, are nearly closed, under deeply arched eyebrows.

The dark woman's lips and eyes and hair are dark. She wears dark eye makeup and has a pronounced dark beauty mark on her cheek. Whereas the other three women's cheeks are high and round, hers are sharply angular. The three blonde women wear one-piece bathing suits in a nondescript gray color. The dark-haired woman, whose skin stands out in stark contrast to her hair, wears a two-piece bathing suit, exposing

FIGURE 6.2
"The Competition" by Ian Falconer

her midriff. Like her face, the dark-haired woman's breast, sticking out in half profile in her bathing suit, is pointed and angular. The other three women's breasts are round and quietly contained in their high-necked gray bathing suits.

Using the Method to Identify Patterns of Repetition and Contrast

As we discussed in Chapter 2, looking for patterns of repetition and contrast (aka The Method) is one of your best means of getting at the essential character of a subject. It will prevent you from generalizing, instead involving you in hands-on engagement with the details of your evidence. Step 1, looking for things that repeat exactly, tends to suggest items for step 2, repetition of the same or similar kinds of words or details (strands), and step 2 leads naturally to step 3, looking for binary oppositions and organizing contrasts.

Here are our partial lists of exact repetitions and strands and binary oppositions in the *New Yorker* cover:

Some Details That Repeat Exactly

Large, wide open, round eyes (3 pairs)

Long, blonde, face-framing hair (3)

Small, straight eyebrows (3 pairs)

Wide-open (smiling?) mouths with expanses of white teeth (3)
    (but individual teeth not indicated)

banners (4) but each with different lettering

round breasts (3)

states that end in *a* (3)

Some Strands (groups of the same or similar kinds of details)

Lots of loose and flowing blonde hair/large, fully open, round eyes/large, open, rather round (curved) mouths:

Connecting logic = open, round

Skin uniformly shaded on three of the figures/minimal color and shading contrasts/mouths full of teeth but just a mass of white without individual teeth showing:

Connecting logic = homogenous, undifferentiated, indistinct

Binary Oppositions

Blonde hair/black hair

Open mouths/closed mouth

Straight eyebrows/slanted (arched) eyebrows

Round breasts/pointed breast

Covered midriff/uncovered midriff

Notice that we have tried hard to stick with "the facts" here—concrete details in the picture. If we were to try, for example, to name the expression on the three blonde women's faces and the one on the black-haired woman (expressionless versus knowing? vapid versus shrewd? trusting versus suspicious? and so on), we would move from data gathering—direct observation of detail—into interpretation. The longer you delay interpretation in favor of noticing patterns of like and unlike detail, the more thoughtful and better grounded your eventual interpretation will be.

Anomalies

Miss New York

Pushing Observations to Conclusions: Selecting an Interpretive Context

As we argued throughout this chapter, the move from observations to conclusions depends on context. You would, for example, come up with different ideas about the significance of particular patterns of detail in the *New Yorker* cover if you were analyzing them in the context of the history of the *New Yorker* cover art than you might if your interpretive context was other art done by Ian Falconer, the cover's artist. Both of these possibilities suggest themselves, the first by the fact that the title of the magazine, the *New Yorker*, stands above the women's heads, and the second by the fact that the artist's last name, Falconer, runs across two of the women.

What other interpretive contexts might one plausibly and fairly choose, based on what the cover offers us? Consider the cover's date—October 9, 2000. Some quick research into what was going on in the country in the early fall of 2000 might provide some clues about how to read the cover in a **historical context**. November 2000 was the month of a presidential election. At the time the cover was published, the long round of presidential primaries, with presidential hopefuls courting various key states for their votes, had ended, but the last month of campaigning by the presidential nominees—Al Gore and George W. Bush—was in full swing.

You might wish to consider whether and how the cover speaks to the country's political climate during the Gore/Bush competition for the presidency. The banners and the bathing suits and the fact that the women stand in a line staring out at some implied audience of viewers, perhaps judges, reminds us that the picture's narrative context is a beauty pageant, a competition in which women representing each of the states compete to be chosen the most beautiful of them all. Choosing to consider the cover in the context of the presidential campaign would be reasonable; you would not have to think you were imposing a context on the picture in an arbitrary and ungrounded way. Additionally, the table of contents identifies the title of Falconer's drawing as "The Competition."

Clearly, other information on the cover might allow you to interpret the picture in some kind of political and/or **more broadly cultural context**. A significant binary opposition is New York versus Georgia, California, and Florida. The three states having names ending in the same letter are represented by look-alike, virtually identical blondes. The anomalous state, New York, is represented by a woman, who, despite standing in line with the others, is about as different from them as a figure could be.

So what that the woman representing New York looks so unlike the women from the other states? And why those states?

If you continued to pursue this interpretive context, you might want more information. Which presidential candidate won the primary in each of the states pictured? How were each of these states expected to vote in the election in November? Since timing would matter in the case of a topical interpretive context, it would also be interesting to know when the cover art was actually produced and when the magazine accepted it. If possible, you could also try to discover whether other of the cover artist's work was in a similar vein. (He has a website.)

Making the Interpretation Plausible

As we have been arguing, the picture will "mean" differently, depending on whether we understand it in terms of American presidential politics in the year 2000, or in terms of American identity politics at the same point, specifically attitudes of and about New Yorkers, and the *New Yorker* magazine's place among these attitudes—and influence on them. Analytical thinking involves interpretation, and interpretive conclusions are tentative and open to alternative possibilities.

What makes an interpretation plausible? Your audience might choose not to accept your interpretation for a number of reasons. They might, for example, be New Yorkers and, further, inclined to think that New Yorkers are cool and that this is what the picture "says." They might be from one of the states depicted on the cover in terms of look-alike blondes and, further, inclined to think that New Yorkers are full of themselves and forever portraying the rest of the country as shallowly conformist and uncultured.

But none of these personal influences ultimately matters. What matters is that you share your data, show your reasons for believing that it means what you say it means, and do this well enough for a reader to find your interpretation reasonable (whether he or she actually believes it or not).

Arriving At an Interpretive Conclusion: Making Choices

Let's try on one final interpretive context, and then see which of the various contexts (lenses) through which we have viewed the cover produces the most credible interpretation, the one that seems to best account for the patterns of detail in the evidence. We will try to push our own interpretive process to a choice by selecting one interpretive context as the most revealing: the *New Yorker* magazine itself.

In this context, the dark-haired figure wearing the New York banner stands, in a sense, for the magazine or, at least, for a potential reader—a representative New Yorker. What, then, does the cover "say" to and about New Yorkers and to and about the magazine and its readers?

So what that the woman representing New York is dark when the other women are light, is closed (narrowed eyes, closed mouth, hair tightly pulled up and back) when the others are open (wide-open eyes and mouths, loosely flowing hair), is pointed and angular when the others are round, sports a bared midriff when the others are covered?

As with our earlier attempt to interpret the cover in the context of the 2000 presidential campaign, interpreting it in the context of other *New Yorker* covers would require a little research. How do *New Yorker* covers characteristically represent New Yorkers? What might you discover by looking for patterns of repetition and contrast in a set of *New Yorker* covers rather than just this one?

The covers are all online. A cursory review of them would make evident the magazine's fondness for simultaneously sending up and embracing the stereotype of New Yorkers as sophisticated, cultured, and cosmopolitan. How does the cover read in the context, for example, of various jokes about how New Yorkers think of themselves relative to the rest of the country, such as the cover depicting the United States as two large coastlines, east and west, connected by an almost nonexistent middle?

Armed with the knowledge that the covers are not only characteristically laughing at the rest of the country but also at New Yorkers themselves, you might begin to make explicit what is implicit in the cover.

Here are some attempts at making the cover speak. Is the cover in some way a "dumb blonde" joke in which the dark woman with the pronounced beauty mark and calculating gaze participates in but also sets herself apart from some kind of national "beauty" contest? Are we being invited (intentionally or not) to invert the conventional value hierarchy of dark and light so that the dark woman—the sort that gets represented as the evil stepmother in fairy tales such as "Snow White"—becomes "the fairest of them all," and nobody's fool?

Let's end this sample analysis and interpretation with two possibilities—somewhat opposed to each other, but both plausible, at least to certain audiences (East and West Coast Americans, and readers of the *New Yorker*). At its most serious, the *New Yorker* cover may speak to American history in which New York has been the point of entry for generations of immigrants, the "dark" (literally and figuratively) in the face of America's blonde northern European legacy. Within the context of other *New Yorker* covers, however, we might find ourselves wishing to leaven this dark reading with comic overtones—that the magazine is also admitting, yes America, we do think that we're cooler and more individual and less plastic than the rest of you, but we also know that we shouldn't be so smug about it.

GUIDELINES FOR MAKING INTERPRETATIONS PLAUSIBLE

1. Laying out the data is key to any kind of analysis, not simply because it keeps the analysis accurate but because, crucially, it is in the act of carefully describing a subject that analytical writers often have their best ideas. The words you choose to summarize your data will contain the germs of your ideas about what the subject means.

2. All explanations and interpretations occur in a context, which functions like a lens for focusing your subject. An important part of getting an interpretation accepted as plausible is to *argue for the appropriateness of the interpretive context you use*, not just the interpretation it takes you to.

3. Look for a range of plausible interpretations rather than assuming only one right answer exists. Control the range of possible interpretations by attending carefully to context.

4. It is interesting and sometimes useful to try to determine from something you are analyzing what its makers might have intended. But, by and large, you are best off concentrating on what the thing itself communicates as opposed to what someone might have wanted it to communicate. Besides, intentions can rarely be known with much accuracy.

Assignments: Making Interpretations Plausible

1. **Build a Paper from Implications**. Begin this assignment by making observations and drawing out implications for one of the topics below. Then use your list as the starting point for a longer paper.

   Having done the preceding exercise with inferring implications, you could now make up your own list of observations and pursue implications. Make some observations, for example, about the following, and then suggest the possible implications of your observations:

   • changing trends in automobiles today;

   • what your local newspaper chooses to put on its front page (or editorial page) over the course of a week;

   • shows (or advertisements) that appear on network television (as opposed to cable) during one hour of evening prime time; and

   • advertisements for scotch whiskey in highbrow magazines.

2. **Analyze a Magazine Cover by Researching an Interpretive Context**. Choose a magazine that, like *The New Yorker*, has interesting covers. Write an analysis of one such cover by studying other covers from the same magazine. Follow the model offered at the end of this chapter:

   a. Apply The Method—looking for patterns of repetition and contrast—to the cover, so that you arrive at key repetitions, strands, and organizing contrasts and begin to ponder a range of possible interpretive leaps to what they signify.

   b. Use these data to suggest plausible interpretive contexts for the cover. Remember that interpretive contexts are not simply imposed from without; they're suggested by the evidence.

   c. Then move to the other covers. Perform similar operations on them to arrive at an awareness of common denominators among the covers, and to analyze what those shared traits might reveal or make more evident in the particular cover you are studying. You will be trying to figure out how the magazine conceives of itself and its audience by the way it characteristically represents its "face."

It might be illuminating to survey a range of covers by a single artist, such as Ian Falconer, who created the cover we analyze in the chapter.

3. **Write an Essay in Which You Make Observations About Some Cultural Phenomenon, Some Place and Its Social Significance, or an Event** (in terms of its significance in some context of your choice) and then push these observations to tentative conclusions by repeatedly asking "So what?"

Be sure to query your initial answers to the "So what?" question with further "So what?" questions, trying to push further into your own thinking and into the meaning of whatever it is you have chosen to analyze. Trends of some sort are good to work with. Marketing trend? So what? Trends in movies about unmarried women or married men or… So what? And so forth.

Since the chapter offers sample analyses of paintings and advertisements, you might choose one of these. Cartoons are interesting subjects. Here you would really have to think a lot about your choice of interpretive context. Gender? Politics? Humor? Family life? American stereotypes? What are we invited to make of this, by what means, and in what context?

Chapter 7

Making Common Topics More Analytical

THE FIRST UNIT OF THIS BOOK, The Analytical Frame of Mind, has sought to persuade you that analysis is worth the challenge—that you can unlearn less productive ways of thinking and take on fresh habits that will make you smarter. In this final chapter of Unit 1, we offer concrete advice about how to succeed in creating writing that fulfills some of the most common basic writing tasks you will be asked to produce at the undergraduate level and beyond.

A unifying element of the chapters in this unit is their focus on the stage of the composing process that rhetoricians call *invention*. This chapter takes up several of classical rhetoric's "topics of invention." These are "places" (from the Greek *topoi*) from which a writer or orator might discover the things he or she needs to say. These topics include comparison/contrast and definition to which we have added summary, reaction papers, and agree/disagree topics because these are such common forms in college and other writing settings. The chapter offers you strategies for making the best use of these topics as analytical tools.

The remainder of the chapter offers strategies for upping the analytical quotient of the staple forms of academic and so-called "real world" writing. We can't guarantee these strategies will succeed, but if you follow them, you are likely to have more and better ideas and to achieve greater success in writing inside the traditional forms.

COMMON TOPICS

Summary

Personal Response: The Reaction Paper

Agree/Disagree

Comparison/Contrast

Definition

SUMMARY

Summary and analysis go hand-in-hand; the primary goal for both is to understand rather than evaluate. Summary is a necessary early step in analysis because it provides perspective on the subject as a whole by explaining the meaning and function of each of that subject's parts. Within larger analyses—papers or reports—summary performs the essential function of contextualizing a subject accurately. It creates a fair picture of what's there.

Summarizing isn't simply the unanalytical reporting of information; it's more than just shrinking someone else's words. To write an accurate summary, you have to ask analytical questions, such as the following:

- Which of the ideas in the reading are most significant? Why?
- How do these ideas fit together?
- What do the key passages in the reading mean?

Summarizing is, then, like paraphrasing, a tool of understanding and not just a mechanical task.

When summaries go wrong, they are just lists, a simple "this and then this" sequence. Often lists are random, as in a shopping list compiled from the first thing you thought of to the last. Sometimes they are organized in broad categories: fruit and vegetables here, dried goods there. At best, they do very little logical connecting among the parts beyond "next." Summaries that are just lists tend to dollop out the information monotonously. They omit the *thinking* that the piece is doing—the ways it is connecting the information, the contexts it establishes, and the implicit slant or point of view.

Writing analytical summaries can teach you how to read for the connections, the lines that connect the dots. And when you're operating at that level, you are much more likely to have ideas about what you are summarizing.

Strategies for Making Summaries More Analytical

Strategy 1: Look for the underlying structure. Use The Method to find patterns of repetition and contrast (*see Chapter 2*). If you apply it to a few key paragraphs, you will find the terms that get repeated, and these will suggest strands, which in turn make up organizing contrasts. This process works to categorize and then further organize information and, in so doing, to bring out its underlying structure.

Strategy 2: Select the information that you wish to discuss on some principle other than general coverage. Use Notice and Focus to rank items of information in some order of importance (*see Chapter 2*). Let's say you are writing a paper on major changes in the tax law or on recent developments in U.S. policy toward the Middle East. Rather than simply collect the information, try to arrange it into hierarchies. What are the least or most significant changes or developments, and why? Which are most overlooked or most overrated or most controversial or most practical, and why? All of these terms—significant, overlooked, and so forth—have the effect of focusing the summary, guiding your decisions about what to include and exclude.

Strategy 3: Reduce scope and say more about less. Both The Method and Notice and Focus involve some loss of breadth; you won't be able to cover everything. But this is usually a trade-off worth making. Your ability to rank parts of your subject or choose a revealing feature or pattern to focus on will give you surer control of the material than if you just reproduce what is in the text. You can still begin with a brief survey of major points to provide context, before narrowing the focus. Reducing scope is an especially efficient and productive strategy when you are trying to understand a reading you find difficult or perplexing. It will move you beyond passive summarizing and toward having ideas about the reading.

If, for example, you are reading Chaucer's *Canterbury Tales* and start cataloguing what makes it funny, you are likely to end up with unanalyzed plot summary—a list that arranges its elements in no particular order. But narrowing the question to "How does Chaucer's use of religious commentary contribute to the humor of 'The Wife of Bath's Tale'"? reduces the scope to a single tale and the humor to a single aspect of humor. Describe those as accurately as you can, and you will begin to notice things.

Strategy 4: Get some detachment: shift your focus from what? to how? and why? Most readers tend to get too single-minded about absorbing the information. That is, they attend only to the *what*: what the reading is saying or is about. They take it all in passively. But you can deliberately shift your focus to *how* it says what it says, and *why*.

To focus on how and why something is presented in a given way—whether it be a sign on a subway or the language of a presidential speech—is to focus rhetorically. Like analysis in general, rhetorical analysis asks what things mean, why they are as they are and do what they do. But rhetorical analysis asks these questions with one primary question always foregrounded: how does the thing achieve its effects on an audience? Rhetorical analysis asks not just what do I think, but *what am I being invited to think (and feel) and by what means?*

One way to distinguish a summary is to concentrate on rhetorical matters. If, for example, you were asked to discuss the major discoveries that Darwin made on *The Beagle,* you could avoid simply listing his conclusions by redirecting your attention to *how* he proceeds. You could choose to focus, for example, on Darwin's use of the scientific method, examining how he builds and, in some cases, discards hypotheses. Or you might select several passages that illustrate how Darwin proceeded from evidence to conclusion and then *rank* them in order of importance to the overall theory. Notice that in shifting the emphasis to Darwin's thinking—the how and why—you would not be excluding the what (the information component) from your discussion.

PERSONAL RESPONSE: THE REACTION PAPER

The biggest advantage of reaction papers is that they give you the freedom to explore where and how to engage your subject. They bring to the surface your emotional or intuitive response, allowing you to experiment with placing the subject in various contexts.

Interestingly, a response paper is not actually asking for your response, at least not primarily. Instead, it is asking you to locate something you think is interesting, revealing, especially significant, and/or perhaps difficult (and thus in need of discussion) in the reading (or observing), and to analyze what you locate. You are allowed to talk about how you responded to the subject, but you are expected to do so in terms of how you found a way to understand and think about the material—as opposed to your gut-level evaluative judgment (like/dislike) of it.

Personal response becomes a problem, however, when it distracts you from analyzing the subject. When you are invited to respond personally, you are being asked for more than your endorsement or critique of the subject. If you find yourself constructing a virtual list—I agree with this point, or I disagree with that point—you are probably doing little more than matching your opinions with the points of view encountered in a reading. At the very least, you should look for places in the reaction paper where you find yourself disagreeing with yourself.

In most cases, you will be misinterpreting the intent of a personal response topic if you view it as an invitation either to

1. assert your personal opinions unreflectively, or
2. substitute narratives of your own experience for careful consideration of the subject. In an academic setting, an opinion is more than simply an expression of your beliefs; it's a conclusion that you earn the rights to through a careful examination of evidence.

Strategies for Making Personal Responses More Analytical

Strategy 1: Trace your responses back to their causes. As we noted in the first two chapters, tracing your impressions back to their causes is the key to making personal response analytical—because you focus on the details that gave you the response rather than on the response alone. In the planning stage, you may find it useful to brainstorm some of your reactions/responses—the things you might say about the material if asked to talk about it with a sympathetic friend. You would then take this brainstorm and use it to choose the key sentences, passages, and so forth in the reading that you want to focus on in your analysis.

Let's say you are responding to an article on ways of increasing the numbers of registered voters in urban precincts. You find the article irritating; your personal experience working with political campaigns has taught you that getting out the vote is not as easy as this writer makes it seem. From that starting point, you might analyze one (to you) overly enthusiastic passage, concentrating on how the writer has not only overestimated what campaign workers can actually do but also condescends to those who don't register—assuming, perhaps, that they are ignorant rather than indifferent or disillusioned. Tracing your response back to its cause may help to defuse your emotional response and open the door to further investigation of the other writer's rationale. You might, for example, discover that the writer has in mind a much more long-term effect or that urban models differ significantly from the suburban ones of your experience.

Strategy 2: Assume that you may have missed the point. It's difficult to see the logic of someone else's position if you are too preoccupied with your own. Similarly, it is difficult to see the logic, or illogic, of your own position if you already assume it to be true. Although an evaluative response (approve/disapprove) can sometimes spur analysis, it can also lead you to prejudge the case. If, however, you habitually question the validity of your own point of view, you will sometimes recognize the possibility of an alternative point of view, as was the case in the voter registration example (see Figure 7.1). Assuming that you have missed the point is a good strategy in all kinds of analytical writing. It causes you to notice details of your subject that you might not otherwise have registered.

Strategy 3: Locate your response within a limiting context. Suppose you are asked in a religion course to write your religious beliefs. Although this topic would naturally lead you to think about your own experiences and beliefs, you would probably do best to approach it in some more limiting context. The reading in the course could provide this limit. Let's say that thus far you have read two modern religious thinkers, Martin Buber and Paul Tillich. Using these as your context, "What do I believe?" would become "How does my response to Buber and Tillich illuminate my own assumptions about the nature of religious faith?" An advantage of this move, beyond making your analysis less general, is that it would help you to get perspective on your own position.

Another way of limiting your context is to consider how one author or recognizable point of view you have encountered in the course might respond to a single statement from another author or point of view. If you used this strategy to respond to the topic "Does God exist?" you might arrive at a formulation such as "How would Martin Buber critique Paul Tillich's definition of God?" Although this topic appears to exclude personal response entirely, it does not. Your opinion would necessarily enter because you would be actively formulating something not already evident in the reading (how Buber might respond to Tillich).

Evaluative Personal Response: *"The article was irritating."* This response is too broad and dismissively judgmental. Make it more analytical by tracing the response back to the evidence that triggered it.

A More Analytical Evaluative Response: *"The author of the article oversimplifies the problem by assuming the cause of low voter registration to be voters' ignorance rather than voters' indifference."* Although still primarily an evaluative response, this observation is more analytical. It takes the writer's initial response ("irritating") to a specific cause.

A Non-evaluative Analytical Response: *"The author's emphasis on increased coverage of city politics in local/neighborhood forums such as the churches suggests that the author is interested in long-term effects of voter registration drives and not just in immediate increases."* Rather than simply reacting ("irritating") or leaping to evaluation ("oversimplifies the problem"), the writer here formulates a possible explanation for the difference between his or her point of view on voter registration drives and the article's.

FIGURE 7.1
Making Personal Response More Analytical

AGREE/DISAGREE

We offer here only a brief recap of this kind of topic because it is discussed at length in earlier chapters. *(In particular, see the discussion of the Judgment Reflex Under Counterproductive Habits of Mind in Chapter 2.)* Topics are frequently worded as agree/disagree, especially on essay exams, but the wording is potentially misleading because you are rarely being asked for as unqualified an opinion as agree or disagree.

In most cases, your best strategy in dealing with agree/disagree questions is to choose *neither* side. Instead, question the terms of the binary so as to arrive at a more complex and qualified position to write about. In place of choosing one side or the other, decide to what extent you agree and to what extent you disagree. You are still responsible for coming down more on one side than the other, but this need not mean that you have to locate yourself in a starkly either/or position. The code phrase for accomplishing this shift *(as we've suggested in the discussion of Reformulating Binaries in Chapter 4)* is "the extent to which": "To what extent do you agree (or disagree)?"

COMPARISON/CONTRAST

Although comparison/contrast is meant to invite analysis, it is too often treated as an end in itself. The fundamental reason for comparing and contrasting is that you can usually discover ideas about a subject much more easily when you are not viewing it in isolation. When executed mechanically, however, without the writer pressing to understand the significance of a similarity or difference, comparison/contrast can suffer from pointlessness. The telltale sign of this problem is the formulaic sentence beginning, "Thus we see there are many similarities and differences between X and Y"—as "chaos" and "cream cheese" might fit that formula (both begin with the letter "c").

Comparison/contrast topics produce pointless essays if you allow them to turn into matching exercises—that is, if you match common features of two subjects but don't get beyond the equation stage (a, b, c = x, y, z). Writers fall into this trap when they have no larger question or issue to explore and perhaps resolve by making the comparison. If, for example, you were to pursue the comparison of the representations of the Boston Tea Party in British and American history textbooks, you would begin by identifying similarities and differences. But simply presenting these and concluding that the two versions resemble and differ from each other in some ways would be pointless. You would need to press your comparisons with the So what? question (*see Chapter 2*) in order to give them some interpretive weight.

Strategies for Making Comparison/Contrast More Analytical

Strategy 1: Argue for the significance of a key comparison. Rather than simply covering a range of comparisons, focus on a key comparison. Although narrowing the focus might seem to eliminate other important areas of consideration, it usually allows you to incorporate at least some of these other areas in a more tightly connected, less list-like fashion. So, for example, a comparison of the burial rites of two cultures will probably reveal more about them than a much broader but more superficial list of cultural similarities and differences. In the majority of cases, covering less is covering more.

You can determine which comparison is key by ranking—designating one part of your topic as especially important or revealing. Suppose you are asked to compare General David Petraeus's strategy in the current Afghanistan conflict with General Douglas MacArthur's strategy in World War II. As a first move, you could limit the comparison to some revealing parallel, such as the way each man dealt with the media, and then argue for its significance above other similarities or differences. You might, for instance, claim that in their treatment of the media, we get an especially clear or telling vantage point on the two generals' strategies. At this point, you are on your way to an analytical point—for example, that because MacArthur was more effectively shielded from the media at a time when the media was a virtual instrument of propaganda, he could make choices that Petraeus might have wanted to make but could not.

Strategy 2: Use one side of the comparison to illuminate the other. Usually, it is not necessary to treat each part of the comparison equally. It's a common misconception that each side must be given equal space. In fact, the purpose of your comparison governs the amount of space you'll need to give to each part. Often, you will use one side of the comparison primarily to illuminate the other. For example, in a course on contemporary military policy, the ratio between the two parts would probably be roughly 70 percent on Petraeus to 30 percent on MacArthur rather than 50 percent on each.

Strategy 3: Imagine how one side of your comparison might respond to the other. This strategy, a variant of the preceding one, is a particularly useful way of helping you to respond to comparison/contrast topics more purposefully. This strategy can be adapted to a wide variety of subjects. If you were asked to compare Sigmund Freud with one of his most important followers, Jacques Lacan, you would probably be better off focusing the broad question of how Lacan revises Freud by considering how and why he might critique Freud's interpretation of a particular dream in *The Interpretation of Dreams*. Similarly, in the case of the Afghanistan example, you could ask yourself how MacArthur might have handled some key decision in dealing with Kabul and why. Or you might consider how he would have critiqued Petraeus's decisions and why.

Strategy 4: Focus on difference within similarity (or similarity within difference). The typical move when you are asked to compare two subjects is to collect a number of parallel examples and show how they are parallel, which can lead to bland tallying of similarities without much analytical edge. In the case of obvious similarities, you should move quickly to significant differences within the similarity and the implications of these differences. In this way, you will better define your subject, and you will be more likely to offer your readers something that is not already clear to them. For example, the Carolingian and Burgundian Renaissances share an emphasis on education, but if you were asked to compare them, you could reveal the character of these two historical periods more effectively by concentrating on the different purposes and origins of this emphasis on education. *(Here we are reprising the final heuristic presented in Chapter 4, Toolbox II.)*

A corollary of the difference-within-similarity formula is that you can focus on unexpected similarity rather than obvious difference. So, for example, we would probably expect that, given the vast differences in terrain and in government between Iraq and Afghanistan, significant differences would exist in the United States' military campaigns in these two locales. But as David Petraeus used to command forces in Iraq and now does so in Afghanistan, we might productively look for some revealing similarities despite obvious differences.

DEFINITION

Definition becomes meaningful when it serves some larger purpose. You define "rhythm and blues" because it is essential to any further discussion of the evolution of rock-and-roll music or because you need that definition in order to discuss the British Invasion spearheaded by groups such as the Beatles, the Rolling Stones, and the Yardbirds in the late 1960s, or because you cannot classify John Lennon or Mick Jagger or Eric Clapton without it.

Like comparison/contrast, definition can produce pointless essays if the writer gets no further than assembling information. Moreover, when you construct a summary of existing definitions with no clear sense of purpose, you tend to list definitions indiscriminately. As a result, you are likely to overlook conflicts among the various definitions and overemphasize their surface similarities. Definition is in fact a site at which there is some contesting of authorities—different voices who seek to make their definition triumph.

Strategies for Making Definition More Analytical

Strategy 1: Test the definition against evidence. One common form of definition asks you to apply a definition to a body of information. It is rare to find a perfect fit. Therefore, as a general rule, you should use the data to assess the accuracy and the limitations of the definition, rather than simply imposing it on your data and ignoring or playing down the ways in which it does not fit. Testing the definition against evidence will evolve your definition. The definition, in turn, will serve as a lens to better focus your thinking about the evidence.

Suppose you were asked to define capitalism in the context of third world economies. You might profitably begin by matching some standard definition of capitalism with specific examples from one or two third-world economies, with the express purpose of detecting where the definition does *and does not* apply. In other words, you would respond to the definition topic by assaying the extent to which the definition provides a tool for making sense of the subject.

Strategy 2: Use a definition from one source to critique and illuminate another. As a general rule, you should attempt to identify the points of view of the sources from which you take your definitions, rather than accepting them as uncontextualized answers. It is essential to identify the particular slant because otherwise you will tend to overlook the conflicting elements among various definitions of a key term.

A paper on alcoholism, for example, will lose focus if you use all of the definitions available. If, instead, you convert the definition into a comparison and contrast of competing definitions, you can more easily generate a point and purpose for your definition. By querying, for example, whether a given source's definition of alcoholism is moral or physiological or psychological, you can more easily problematize the issue of definition.

Strategy 3: Problematize as well as synthesize the definition. To explore competing definitions of the same term requires you to attend to the difficulties of definition. In general, analysis achieves direction and purpose by locating and then exploring a problem. You can productively make a problem out of defining. This strategy is known as *problematizing*, which locates and then explores the significance of the uncertainties and conflicts. It is always a smart move to problematize definitions, as this tactic reveals complexity that less careful thinkers might miss.

The definition of capitalism that you might take from Karl Marx, for example, will differ in its emphases from Adam Smith's. In this case, you would not only isolate the most important of these differences but also try to account for the fact that Marx's villain is Smith's hero. Such an accounting would probably lead you to consider how the definition has been shaped by each of these writers' political philosophies or by the culture in which each theory was composed.

Strategy 4: Shift from "what?" to "how?" and "why?" questions. It is no accident that we earlier offered the same strategy for making summary more analytical: analytical topics that require definition also depend on "why?" or "how?" questions, not "what?" questions (which tend simply to call for information).

If, for example, you sought to define the meaning of darkness in Joseph Conrad's *Heart of Darkness* and any two other modern British novels, you would do better to ask why the writers find darkness such a fertile term than simply to accumulate various examples of the term in the three novels. You might start by isolating the single best example from each of the works, preferably ones that reveal important differences as well as similarities. Then, in analyzing how each writer uses the term, you could work toward some larger point that would unify the essay. You might show how the conflicts of definition within Conrad's metaphor evolve historically, get reshaped by woman novelists, change after World War I, and so forth.

GUIDELINES FOR MAKING COMMON TOPICS MORE ANALYTICAL

1. Find ways to move beyond passive summary (what questions). Use information to develop some idea (how and why questions) rather than just repackaging what others have written.

2. Drastically reduce scope. Concentrate on what seems the most important or revealing part of your subject (ranking) rather than trying to cover everything.

3. Avoid turning comparisons into pointless matching exercises. Only set up similarities and differences in order to discuss the significance of that comparison.

4. You needn't devote equal space to both sides of a comparison. If one side is used primarily to illuminate the other, a 30–70 ratio (or 20–80 or 40–60) makes more sense than 50–50.

5. Rather than answering a question of definition with inert summary, test the definition against evidence and/or explore its competing parts.

6. For agree/disagree questions, the best move is to choose *neither* side. Question the terms of the binary so as to arrive at a more complex and qualified position. Decide to what extent you agree and to what extent you disagree.

Assignments: Making Common Topics More Analytical

1. **Write Two Summaries of the Same Article or Book Chapter**. Make the first one consecutive (the so-called "coverage" model), that is, try to cover the piece by essentially listing the key points as they appear. Limit yourself to a typed page. Then rewrite the summary, doing the following:

   - rank the items in order of importance according to some principle that you designate, explaining your rationale;
   - eliminate the last few items on the list, or at most, give each a single sentence; and
   - use the space you saved to include more detail about the most important item or two.

   The second half of this assignment will probably require closer to two pages.

2. **Explore Significant Differences and Similarities**. This assignment first appeared as a Try This in Chapter 4. If you did not do it then, try it now.

   Use any item from the list below. List as many similarities and differences as you can: go for coverage. Then review your list and select the two or three most revealing similarities and the two or three most revealing differences. At this point, you are ready to write a few paragraphs in which you argue for the significance of a key difference or similarity. In so doing, you may find it interesting to focus on an *unexpected* similarity or difference—one that others might not initially notice.

   1. Accounts of the same event from two different newspapers or magazines or textbooks;

   2. two CDs (or even songs) by the same artist or group;

   3. two ads for the same kind of product, perhaps aimed at different target audiences;

   4. the political campaigns of two opponents running for the same or similar office;

5. courtship behavior as practiced by men and by women; or

6. two clothing styles as emblematic of class or sub-group in your school, town, or workplace.

3. **Write a Comparative Definition**. Seek out different and potentially competing definitions of the same term or terms. Begin with a dictionary such as the *Oxford English Dictionary* (popularly known as the *OED*, available in most library reference rooms or online) that contains both historically based definitions tracking the term's evolution over time and etymological definitions that identify the linguistic origins of the term (its sources in older languages). Be sure to locate both the etymology and the historical evolution of the term or terms.

Then look up the term in one or preferably several specialized dictionaries. We offer a list of some of these in Chapter 14, "Finding, Citing, and Integrating Sources," but you can also ask your reference librarian for pertinent titles. Generally speaking, different disciplines generate their own specialized dictionaries.

Summarize key differences and similarities among the ways the dictionaries have defined your term or terms. Then write a comparative essay in which you argue for the significance of a key similarity or difference, or an unexpected one.

Here is the list of words: hysteria, ecstasy, enthusiasm, witchcraft, leisure, gossip, bachelor, spinster, romantic, instinct, punk, thug, pundit, dream, alcoholism, aristocracy, atom, ego, pornography, conservative, liberal, entropy, election, tariff. Some of these words are interesting to look at together, such as ecstasy/enthusiasm or liberal/conservative or bachelor/spinster. Feel free to write on a pair instead of a single word.

UNIT II

WRITING ANALYTICAL PAPERS: HOW TO USE EVIDENCE, EVOLVE CLAIMS, AND CONVERSE WITH SOURCES

Chapter 8

Reasoning from Evidence to Claims

> Most of what goes wrong in using a thesis is the result of a writer leaping too quickly to a generalization that would do as a thesis, and then treating evidence only as something to be mustered in support of that idea.

THIS CHAPTER IS ABOUT EVIDENCE—what it is, what it is meant to do, and how to recognize when you are using it well. The chapter's overall argument is that you should use evidence to test, refine, and develop your ideas, rather than just to prove they are correct.

Evidence is usually suggestive rather than conclusive. The interesting and important questions are to be found not in the facts but in our hypotheses about what the facts mean. Finding solid evidence—the facts—is only part of the problem. The larger question is always interpretive: what do the facts really tell us?

Theories—ways of seeing and understanding things—are what cause us to accept some things as facts. So, for example, once observers and theorists had demonstrated that the sun rather than the earth was at the center of the (then) known universe, people had to reconsider what was and wasn't a fact. This is why good writing uses evidence to test and qualify claims as well as support them. And this is also why this book argues against the narrow view of evidence as "the stuff that proves I'm right." Rather than arriving at demonstrably true claims from definite facts, writers more often arrive at plausible theories about evidence. Most thinking about evidence, in other words, is inevitably interpretive and tentative (*see Chapter 6, Making Interpretations Plausible*).

THE FUNCTIONS OF EVIDENCE

To substantiate claims

To test and refine ideas

To define key terms more precisely

To qualify (restrict the scope) of claims, making them more accurate

The chapter's first section addresses two common problems: claims without evidence (unsubstantiated claims) and evidence without claims (pointless evidence). The chapter's second section then offers examples of the kinds of evidence most commonly encountered in academic writing.

HOW TO MAKE EVIDENCE SPEAK

Select telling pieces of concrete data
Explain clearly what you take the data to mean
Show why the evidence might support the claim
Focus on how the evidence complicates (qualifies) the claim

A. Linking Evidence and Claims

Evidence matters because it always involves authority: the power of evidence is, well, *evident* in the laboratory, the courtroom, the classroom, and just about everywhere else. Your SAT scores are evidence, and they may have worked for or against you. If they worked against you—if you believe yourself smarter than the numbers on this standardized test indicate—then you probably offered alternative evidence, such as class rank or extracurricular achievements when you applied to college. As this example illustrates, there are many kinds of evidence; and whether or not something qualifies as acceptable evidence, as well as what it may show or prove, is often debatable. Are high school grades a more reliable predictor of success in college than a 600 on the Verbal? What exactly is an SAT score evidence of?

The types and amounts of evidence necessary for persuading readers and building authority also vary from one discipline to another, as does the manner in which the evidence is presented. While some disciplines—the natural sciences, for example—require you to present your evidence first and then interpret it, others (the humanities and some social sciences) will expect you to interpret your evidence as it is presented. But in all disciplines, and virtually any writing situation, it is important to support claims with evidence, to make your evidence lead to claims, and especially to be explicit about *how you've arrived at the connection between your evidence and your claims* (see Figure 8.1).

The relationship between evidence and claims is rarely self-evident: that relationship virtually always needs to be explained. The word *evident* comes from a Latin verb meaning "to see." To say that the truth of a statement is "self-evident"

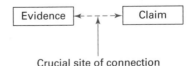

Crucial site of connection

FIGURE 8.1
Linking Evidence and Claims.

means that it does not need proving because its truth can be plainly seen by all. One of the Five Analytical Moves discussed in Chapter 3 was making the implicit explicit. This move is critical for working with evidence. The thought connections that have occurred to you about what the evidence means will not automatically occur to others. Persuasive writing always makes the connections between evidence and claim overt.

The first step in learning to explain the connection between your evidence and your claims is to remember that *evidence rarely, if ever, can be left to speak for itself.* When you leave evidence to speak for itself, you are assuming it can be interpreted in only one way and that others will necessarily think as you do.

Writers who think that evidence speaks for itself generally do very little with it. Sometimes they will present it without making any overt claims, stating, for example, "There was no alcohol at the party," and expecting the reader to understand this statement as a sign of approval or disapproval. Alternatively, they may simply place the evidence next to a claim: "The party was terrible—there was no alcohol," or "The party was great—there was no alcohol." Juxtaposing the evidence with the claim (just putting them next to each other) leaves out the thinking that connects them, thereby implying that the logic of the connection is obvious. But even for readers prone to agreeing with a given claim, simply pointing to the evidence is rarely enough.

Of course, before you can attend to the relationship between evidence and claims, you first have to make sure to include both of them. But before we examine the problems posed by leaving either one out (evidence or claims), let's first consider what it is that evidence is meant to do.

THE FUNCTION OF EVIDENCE

A common assumption about evidence is that it is "the stuff that proves I'm right." Although this way of thinking about evidence is not wrong, it is much too limited. Corroboration (proving the validity of a claim) is one of the functions of evidence—but not the only one.

It helps to remember that the word *prove* actually comes from a Latin verb meaning "to test." The noun form of prove, proof, has two meanings: (1) evidence sufficient to establish a thing as true or believable and (2) the act of testing for truth or believability. When you operate on the first definition of proof alone, you are far more likely to seek out evidence that supports only your point of view, ignoring or dismissing other evidence that could lead to a different and possibly better idea. You might also assume that you can't begin writing until you have arrived at an idea you're convinced is right, since only then could you decide which evidence to include. Both of these practices close down your thinking instead of leading you to a more open process of formulating and testing ideas.

The advantage to following the second definition of the word proof—in the sense of testing—is that you will be better able to negotiate among competing points of view. Doing so will predispose your readers to consider what you have to say because you are offering them not only the thoughts a person has had, but also a person in the act of thinking. Writing well means sharing your thought process with your readers, telling them why you believe the evidence means what you say it does.

"BECAUSE I SAY SO": UNSUBSTANTIATED CLAIMS

Problem: Making claims that lack supporting evidence.

Solution: Use concrete details to support and sharpen the claim.

Unsubstantiated claims occur when a writer concentrates only on conclusions, omitting the evidence that led to them. At the opposite extreme, pointless evidence results when a writer offers a mass of detail attached to an overly general claim. Both of these problems can be solved by offering readers the evidence that led to the claim and explaining how the evidence led there.

The word *unsubstantiated* means "without substance." An unsubstantiated claim is not necessarily false; it just offers none of the concrete "stuff" upon which the claim is based. When a writer makes an unsubstantiated claim, he or she has assumed that readers will believe it just because the writer put it out there.

Perhaps more important, unsubstantiated claims deprive you of details. If you lack some actual "stuff" to analyze, you tend to overstate your position and leave your readers wondering exactly what you mean. The further away your language gets from concrete, physical details—things that you can see, hear, count, taste, smell, and touch—the more abstract it becomes.

You can see the problem of unsubstantiated assertions not only in papers but in everyday conversation. It occurs when people get in the habit of leaping to conclusions—forming impressions so quickly and automatically that they have difficulty even recalling what triggered a particular response. Ask such people why they thought a new acquaintance is pretentious, and they will rephrase the generalization rather than offer the evidence that led to it: the person is pretentious because he puts on airs.

Rephrasing your generalizations rather than offering evidence starves your thinking; it also shuts out readers. If, for example, you defend your judgment that a person is pretentious by saying that he puts on airs, you have ruled on the matter and dismissed it. (You have also committed a logical flaw known as a circular argument; because "pretentious" and "putting on airs" mean virtually the same thing, using one in support of the other is arguing in a circle.) If, by contrast, you include the grounds upon which your judgment is based—that he uses words without regard to whether his listeners will understand or that he always wears a bow tie—you have at least given readers a glimpse of your evaluative criteria. Readers are far more likely to accept your views if you give them the chance to think with you about the evidence. The alternative—offering groundless assertions—is to expect them to take your word for it.

There is, of course, an element of risk in providing the details that have informed your judgment. You leave yourself open to attack if, for example, your readers wear bow ties. But this is an essential risk to take, for otherwise, you leave your readers wondering why you think as you do, or worse, unlikely to credit your point of view.

Most importantly, taking care to substantiate your claims will make you more inclined to think openly and carefully about your judgments. And precisely because what people have taken to be common knowledge ("women can't do math," for example, or "men don't talk about their feelings") so often turns out to be wrong, you should take care to avoid unsubstantiated claims.

DISTINGUISHING EVIDENCE FROM CLAIMS

To check your drafts for unsubstantiated assertions, you first have to know how to recognize them. It is sometimes difficult to separate facts from judgments, data from interpretations of the data. Writers who aren't practiced in this skill can believe that they are offering evidence when they are really offering only unsubstantiated claims. In your own reading and writing, pause once in a while to label the sentences of a paragraph as either evidence (E) or claims (C). What happens if we try to categorize the sentences of the following paragraph in this way?

> The owners are ruining baseball in America. Although they claim they are losing money, they are really just being greedy. Some years ago, they even fired the commissioner, Fay Vincent, because he took the players' side. Baseball is a sport, not a business, and it is a sad fact that it is being threatened by greedy businessmen.

The first and last sentences of the paragraph are claims. They draw conclusions about as yet unstated evidence that the writer will need to provide. The middle two sentences are harder to classify. If particular owners have said publicly that they are losing money, the existence of the owners' statements is a fact. But the writer moves from evidence to unsubstantiated claims when he suggests that the owners are lying about their financial situation and are doing so because of their greed. Similarly, it is a fact that Commissioner Fay Vincent was fired, but it is only an assertion that he was fired "because he took the players' side," an unsubstantiated claim. Although many of us might be inclined to accept some version of this claim as true, we should not be asked to accept his opinion as self-evident truth. What is the evidence in support of the claim? What are the reasons for believing that the evidence means what he says it does?

The writer of the baseball paragraph, for example, offers as fact that the owners claim they are losing money. If he were to search harder, however, he would find that his statement of the owners' claim is not entirely accurate. The owners have not unanimously claimed that they are losing money; they have acknowledged that the problem has to do with poorer "small-market" teams competing against richer "large-market" teams. This more complicated version of the facts might at first be discouraging to the writer, since it reveals his original thesis ("greed") to be oversimplified. But then, as we have been saying, the function of evidence is not just to corroborate your claims; it should also help you to *test* and *refine* your ideas and to *define* your key terms more precisely.

Try This 8.1: Distinguishing Evidence from Claims

Take an excerpt from your own writing, at least two paragraphs in length—perhaps from a paper you have already written, or a draft you are working on—and, at the end of every sentence, label it as either evidence (E) or claim (C). For sentences that appear to offer both, determine which parts of the sentence are evidence and which are claim, and then decide which one, E or C, predominates. What is the ratio of evidence to claim, especially in particularly effective or weak paragraphs? This is also an instructive way of working with other writers in small groups or pairs. It is often much easier to distinguish (E) from (C) in someone else's writing first.

If none of your writing is immediately handy, try this exercise with a few paragraphs of Anna Whiston's essay on talk shows included in Chapter 5, the section entitled "Using a Reading as a Lens: An Extended Example."

GIVING EVIDENCE A POINT: MAKING DETAILS SPEAK

Problem: Presenting a mass of evidence without explaining how it relates to the claims.

Solution: Make details speak. Explain how evidence confirms and qualifies the claim.

Your thinking emerges in the way that you follow through on the implications of the evidence you have selected. You need to interpret it for your readers. You have to make the details speak, conveying to your readers why they mean what you claim they mean. The following example illustrates what happens when a writer leaves the evidence to speak for itself.

> Baseball is a sport, not a business, and it is a sad fact that it is being threatened by greedy businessmen. For example, Eli Jacobs, the previous owner of the Baltimore Orioles, recently sold the team to Peter Angelos for one hundred million dollars more than he had spent ten years earlier when he purchased it. Also, a new generation of baseball stadiums have been built in the last few decades—in Baltimore, Chicago, Arlington (Texas), Cleveland, San Francisco, Milwaukee, Houston, Philadelphia, and most recently, in Washington. These parks are enormously expensive and include elaborate scoreboards and luxury boxes. The average baseball players, meanwhile, now earn more than a million dollars a year, and they all have agents to represent them. Alex Rodriguez, the third baseman for the New York Yankees, is paid more than twenty million dollars a season. Sure, he continues to set records for homers by a player at his age, but is any ballplayer worth that much money?

Unlike the previous example, which was virtually all claims, this paragraph, except for the opening claim and the closing question, is all evidence. The paragraph presents what we might call an "evidence sandwich": it encloses a series of facts between two claims. (The opening statement blames "greedy businessmen," presumably owners, and the closing statement appears to indict greedy, or at least overpaid, players.) Readers are left with two problems. First, the mismatch between the opening and concluding claims leaves it not altogether clear what the writer is saying that the evidence suggests. And second, he has not told readers why they should believe that the evidence means what he says it does. Instead, he leaves it to speak for itself.

If readers are to accept the writer's implicit claims—that the spending is too much and that it is ruining baseball—he will have to show how and why the evidence supports these conclusions. The rule that applies here is that *evidence can almost always be interpreted in more than one way.*

We might, for instance, formulate at least three conclusions from the evidence offered in the baseball paragraph. We might decide that the writer believes baseball will be ruined by going broke or that its spirit will be ruined by becoming too commercial. Worst of all, we might disagree with his claim and conclude that baseball is not really being ruined, since the evidence could be read as signs of health rather than decay. The profitable resale of the Orioles, the expensive new ballparks (which, the writer neglects to mention, have drawn record crowds), and the skyrocketing salaries all could testify to the growing popularity rather than the decline of the sport.

How to Make Details Speak: A Brief Example

The best way to begin making the details speak is to take the time to look at them, asking questions about what they imply.

1. Say explicitly what you take the details to mean.
2. State exactly how the evidence supports your claims.
3. Consider how the evidence complicates (qualifies) your claims.

The writer of the baseball paragraph leaves some of his claims and virtually all of his reasoning about the evidence implicit. What, for example, bothers him about the special luxury seating areas? Attempting to uncover his assumptions, we might speculate that he intends it to demonstrate how economic interests are taking baseball away from its traditional fans because these new seats cost more than the average person can afford. This interpretation could be used to support the writer's governing claim, but he would need to spell out the connection, to reason back to his own premises. He might say, for example, that baseball's time-honored role as the all-American sport—democratic and grassroots—is being displaced by the tendency of baseball as a business to attract higher box office receipts and wealthier fans.

The writer could then make explicit what his whole paragraph implies, that baseball's image as a popular pastime in which all Americans can participate is being tarnished by players and owners alike, whose primary concern appears to be making money. In making his evidence speak in this way, the writer would be practicing step 3 above—using the evidence to complicate and refine his ideas. He would discover which specific aspect of baseball he thinks is being ruined, clarifying that the "greedy businessmen" to whom he refers include both owners and players.

Let's emphasize the final lesson gleaned from this example. When you focus on tightening the links between evidence and claim, the result is almost always a "smaller" claim than the one you set out to prove. This is what evidence characteristically does to a claim: it shrinks and restricts its scope. This process, also known as *qualifying a claim*, is the means by which a thesis develops.

Sometimes it is hard to give up on the large, general assertions that were your first responses to your subject. But your sacrifices in scope are exchanged for greater accuracy and validity. The sweeping claims you lose ("Greedy businessmen are ruining baseball") give way to less resounding but also more informed, more incisive, and less judgmental ideas ("Market pressures may not bring the end of baseball, but they are certainly changing the image and nature of the game").

B. Kinds of Evidence: What Counts?

Thus far, this chapter has concentrated on how to use evidence after you've gathered it. In many cases, though, a writer has to consider a more basic and often hidden question before collecting data: what counts as evidence? This question raises two related concerns:

> *Relevance*: in what ways does the evidence bear on the claim or problem you are addressing? Do the facts really apply in this particular case, and if so, how?

> *Framing assumptions*: in what ways is the evidence colored by the point of view that designated it as evidence? At what point do these assumptions limit its authority or reliability?

To raise the issue of framing assumptions is not to imply that all evidence is merely subjective, somebody's impressionistic opinion. We are implying, however, that even the most apparently neutral evidence is the product of some way of seeing that qualifies the evidence as evidence in the first place. In some cases, this way of seeing is embedded in the established procedure of particular disciplines. In the natural sciences, for example, the actual data that go into the results section of a lab report or formal paper are the product of a highly controlled experimental procedure. As its name suggests, the section presents the results of seeing in a particular way.

The same kind of control is present in various quantitative operations in the social sciences, in which the evidence is usually framed in the language of statistics. And in somewhat less systematic but nonetheless similar ways, evidence in the humanities and in some projects in the social sciences is always conditioned by methodological assumptions. A literature student cannot assume, for example, that a particular fate befalls a character in a story because of events in the author's life (it is a given of literary study that biography may inform but does not explain a work of art). As the professors' comments in this section of the chapter make clear, evidence is never just some free-floating, absolutely reliable, objective entity for the casual observer to sample at random. It is always a product of certain starting assumptions and procedures that readers must take into account.

Questions of Relevance and Methodology: A Political Science Professor Speaks

In the following Voice from Across the Curriculum, political science professor Jack Gambino suggests that it is always useful to try to figure out the methodological *how* behind the *what,* especially since methodology is always based in certain assumptions as opposed to others.

Voices from Across the Curriculum

What counts as evidence? I try to impress upon students that they need to substantiate their claims with evidence. Most have little trouble with this. However, when I tell them that evidence itself is dependent upon methodology—that it's not just a question of gathering "information," but also a question of how it was gathered—their eyes glaze over. Can we trust the source of information? What biases may exist in the way questions are posed in an opinion poll? Who counts as an authority on a subject? (No, Rush Limbaugh cannot be considered an authority on women's issues, or the environment, or, for that matter, anything else!) Is your evidence out of date? (In politics, books on electoral behavior have a shelf life only up to the next election. After two years, they may have severe limitations.)

Methodological concerns also determine the relevance of evidence. Some models of, say, democratic participation define as irrelevant certain kinds of evidence that other models might view as crucial. For instance, a pluralist view of democracy, which emphasizes the dominant role of competitive elites, views the evidence of low voter turnout and citizen apathy as a minor concern. More participatory models, in contrast, interpret the same evidence as an indication of the crisis afflicting contemporary democratic practices.

In addition to this question of relevance, methodology makes explicit the game plan of research: how did the student conduct his or her research? Why did he or she consider some information more relevant than others? Are there any gaps in the information? Does the writer distinguish cases in which evidence strongly supports a claim from evidence that is suggestive or speculative?

Finally, students need to be aware of the possible ideological nature of evidence. For instance, Americans typically seek to explain such problems as poverty in individualistic terms, a view consistent with our liberal heritage, rather than in terms of class structure, as a Marxist would. Seeking the roots of poverty in individual behavior simply produces a particular kind of evidence different from that which would be produced if we began with the assumption that class structure plays a decisive influence in shaping individual behavior.

—Jack Gambino, Professor of Political Science

The preferences of different disciplines for certain kinds of evidence notwithstanding, most professors share the conviction that the evidence you choose to present should not be one-sided. They also understand that the observation and use of evidence is never completely neutral.

A useful example for thinking about evidence-gathering in this context is Werner Heisenberg's famous formulation, the Uncertainty Principle. A theoretical physicist, Heisenberg hypothesized a subatomic particle orbiting the nucleus of an atom that could be observed only when it passed through a concentrated beam of light. At the instant of its illumination, however, the direction of the particle would necessarily be skewed by the beam. From this model, Heisenberg concluded that the act of observation invariably alters whatever is observed.

This insight has made its way across the academic disciplines. In anthropology, for example, Clifford Geertz has written extensively on the ways that researchers into other cultures not only impose their own cultural assumptions onto their subjects, but also, by their very presence, cause change in the behavior of the people they are observing.

The challenge of determining what counts as evidence is also at issue when you start with a given problem or question and then must decide what you should look at. Say you are looking into the causes of child abuse. How do you decide what to look at? How do you even define what it is you are studying, since what conceivably constitutes child abuse now might have been considered normal child-rearing practices in the past? If you are searching for causes, what is the important evidence? In the past, the physical environment lay outside what sociologists usually considered, but what if the height of buildings in which child abuse occurs provides better data than the size of families? As this hypothetical example suggests, the relationship between cause and effect is always slippery, and the assumptions about what is and isn't evidence are potentially blinding.

We are, to a significant degree, a society obsessed with evidence—from UFO fanatics to conspiracy theorists to those who avidly follow the latest leaks in the press about the peccadilloes of the famous. This raises the question of the kinds of evidence that can be used to support claims.

MORE THAN JUST THE FACTS

As we have been suggesting for most of this chapter, evidence is virtually never simply a matter of "the facts." It is no accident that one often hears the phrase "questions of evidence" because evidence is perennially subject to question—for its accuracy, its veracity, and so forth. When we hear that mellifluous voiceover in the TV commercial assuring us that "3 out of 4 dentists recommend a fluoride toothpaste," how are we to take that remark? Why are lie detector tests "inadmissible as evidence" in some cases?

Nor is established practice a guarantee that the evidence is reliable. About 15 years ago, sportswriter Bill James levied a powerful attack on the accepted way of providing data for assessing a baseball player's fielding—the fielding average, which was a ratio of the total number of balls hit to a fielder (his "chances") as against his errors. James pointed out that fielding percentage didn't take into account the greater number of balls that a superior fielder might get to in the first place, adding that the more difficult the chance, the more likely the player was to make an error. So the number of errors was not a reliable index of a player's proficiency. Consequently, James invented a new statistical measure, the range factor, which more heavily weights the number of chances and devalues the number of errors. In effect, he redefines the pool of evidence.

What follows are some passages from student and professional writing, each of which illustrates a different kind of evidence. The list is not comprehensive, but we have tried to select a few of the most common categories.

STATISTICAL EVIDENCE

Statistics are a primary tool—a virtual language—for those writing in the natural and especially the social sciences. They have the advantage of greater objectivity, and, in the social sciences, of offering a broad view of a subject. Remember, though, that like other forms of evidence, statistics do not speak for themselves; their significance must be overtly elucidated. And, as the fielding average example suggests, it should never simply be assumed that statistics are valid representations of the reality they purport to measure.

The following brief excerpt is from a study of factors that determine Americans' views on global warming, written by Christopher Borick and Barry Rabe (in *Issues in Governance Studies*, No.18, July, 2008).

Excerpt from "A Reason to Believe: Examining the Factors That Determine Americans' Views on Global Warming"

Since the 1980s, there has been a growing body of data that examines the perceptions of Americans regarding the issue of global warming. This data paints a picture of generally increasing recognition, acceptance, and concern in the United States regarding atmospheric heating of the earth (Nisbet and Myers, 2007).

In the past two decades, the number of Americans who have heard of the "greenhouse effect" has steadily increased. In 1986, less than one in four respondents said they had heard of global warming. By 2006, over nine out of ten recognized the issue (Nisbet and Myers, 2007). A growing number of Americans believe that the Earth is already experiencing increased heating as Table One shows. [...]

Public opinion research shows Americans are increasingly acknowledging global warming (Nisbet and Myers, 2007); however, what isn't seen are the underlying causes of these beliefs. In particular, what type of evidence do Americans cite as having an important effect on their perceptions of global warming? Recent Pew Research Center polls have shown fairly significant short-term shifts in the number of Americans who believe there is evidence of global warming. Between June 2006 and January 2007, there was a 7% increase (70% to 77%) among U.S. residents who indicated there was "solid evidence" that the Earth is warming. However, between January 2007 and April 2008, the percentage decreased by 6% (77% to 71%). This decline in public acceptance of the evidence of global warming may be an aberration in a long-term trend of increasing belief. However, the shift does raise questions regarding the underlying factors affecting public acknowledgement of global warming. What types of evidence are individuals reacting to? *[The writers note a significant short-term shift in views of Americans on global warming but then go on to frame a new research question about the kinds of evidence upon which individuals are basing their claims. This will in turn lead to further opinion polling and statistical analysis.]*

Interpreting the Numbers: A Psychology Professor Speaks

In the following Voice from Across the Curriculum, psychology professor Laura Edelman offers advice on how to read statistically. She expresses respect for the value of numbers as evidence, as opposed to relying on one's own experience or merely speculating. But she also advises students to be aware of the various problems of interpretation that statistical evidence can invite.

Voices from Across the Curriculum

The most important advice we offer our psychology students about statistical evidence is to look at it critically. We teach them that it is easy to misrepresent statistics and that you really need to evaluate the evidence provided. Students need to learn to think about what the numbers actually mean. Where did the numbers come from? What are the implications of the numbers?

In my statistics course, I emphasize that it is not enough just to get the "correct" answer mathematically. Students need to be able to interpret the numbers and the implications of the numbers. For example, if students are rating satisfaction with the textbook on a scale of one (not at all satisfied) to seven (highly satisfied) and we get a class average of 2.38, it is not enough to report that number. You must interpret the number (the class was generally not satisfied) and again explain the implications (time to choose a new text).

Students need to look at the actual numbers. Let's say I do an experiment using two different stat texts. Text A costs $67 and text B costs $32. I give one class text A and one class text B, and at the end of the semester I find that the class using text A did statistically significantly better than the class using text B. Most students at this point would want to switch to the more expensive text A. However, I can show them an example where the class using text A had an average test grade of 87 and the class with text B had an average test grade of 85 (which can be a statistically significant difference): students see the point that even though it is a statistical difference, practically speaking it is not worth double the money to improve the class average by only two points.

There is so much written about the advantages and limitations of empirical information that I hardly know where to begin. Briefly, if it is empirical, there is no guesswork or opinion (Skinner said "the organism is always right"—that is, the data are always right). The limitations are that the collection and/or interpretation can be fraught with biases and error. For example, if I want to know if women still feel that there is gender discrimination in the workplace, I do not have to guess or intuit this (my own experiences are highly likely to bias my guesses): I can do a survey. The survey should tell me what women think (whether I like the answer or not). The limitations occur in how I conduct the survey and how I interpret the results. You might remember the controversy over the Hite Report on sexual activities (whom did she sample, and what kind of people answer those kinds of questions, and do they do so honestly?).

Despite the controversy over the problems of relying on empirical data in Psychology, I think that it is the only way to find answers to many fascinating questions about humans. The patterns of data can tell us things that we have no other access to without empirical research. It is critically important for people to be aware of the limitations and problems, but then to go on and collect the data.

—Laura Edelman, Professor of Psychology

EXPERIMENTAL EVIDENCE

Experimental evidence is a form of empirical evidence. Empirical evidence is derived from experience, the result of observation and experiment, as opposed to theory. It is usually associated with the bodily senses; the word *empirical* means "capable of being observed, available to the senses," and the word comes from the Greek word for experience.

Experimental evidence is usefully distinguished from other forms of evidence by the careful attention to procedure it requires. Evidence in the sciences is usually recorded in particular predetermined formats, both because of the importance of methodology, and because the primary test of validity in the sciences is that the experiment must be repeatable, so that another experimenter can follow the same procedure and achieve the same results (*see Chapter 15, Forms and Formats Across the Curriculum*).

The concern with procedure is present throughout writing in the sciences, though, not just in the Methods section of a lab report. Scientific writing constantly begins by asking the question, "How do we know what we think we know?" And, since experiments inevitably take a scientist into the unknown, it then asks, "On the basis of what we know, what else might be true, and how can we find out?" The concern with procedure in scientific writing is ultimately, then, a matter of clearly articulating the means of verifying and explaining what we think we know.

The treatment of evidence in the following example of scientific writing, a review of existing research on a given phenomenon, explores the adequacy of competing hypotheses.

Excerpt from "Hypotheses about Rev Function"

Two major hypotheses for Rev function have been proposed. One is that Rev may inhibit splicing or interfere with the assembly of the spliceosome. This hypothesis would imply that inhibiting spliceosome activity would release pre-mRNA for transport to the cytoplasm (Fischer et al. 1995). The other hypothesis is that Rev might directly target viral pre-mRNA to the cytoplasm through the interaction of its domains with cellular cofactors. *[States hypotheses and their implications]* While there is evidence to support both models, there seems to be stronger support in favor of the second hypothesis. The finding that

functional inactivation of the Rev activation domain always
resulted in the inability of the protein to exit the nucleus provides
significant evidence that the activation domain is a nuclear export
signal (NES) and Rev is indeed actively involved in the direct
transport of viral mRNAs (Meyer et al. 1996). *[Offers as rationale
for preferred hypothesis that it better explains evidence]*
Additionally, Rev was able to directly promote nuclear export
of RRE-containing mRNAs after nuclear injection into Xenopus
oocytes independently of the presence of introns in these RNAs
and thus presumably in the absence of spliceosome formation
(Fischer et al. 1994). *[Adds additional evidence from second
source to support preferred hypothesis]*

USING AUTHORITIES AS EVIDENCE

A common way of establishing support for a claim is to invoke an authority—to call
in as evidence the thinking of an expert in the subject area you are writing about. The
practice of invoking authorities as evidence can be heard in TV advertising ("three out
of four doctors recommend...," etc.) as well as in scholarly books and articles, where
a writer may offer as partial support for a claim the thinking of a better-known writer.
Much academic writing consists of evaluating and revising views that people have
come to believe are authoritative. The building of knowledge involves in large part the
ongoing consideration of who or what will be accepted as authoritative.

Later in this unit of the book, we offer a whole chapter on the matter of using
authorities as evidence *(Chapter 13, Using Sources Analytically: The Conversation
Model)*. In that chapter, we explain how to use—rather than just include and agree
with—other writers on your subject. In the meantime, we offer the following passage
from a student paper on ancient art. In it, you will see how the writer calls on the
authority of his sources, putting them into evidence for his case, but also how he offers
alternatives to their claims on the basis of his own review of the primary evidence (the
art objects themselves).

Note that he does not simply import his sources' claims but their evidence as well.
Calling in the support of an authority, an expert witness, can be very useful, but it's no
substitute for logic: the fact that somebody has gotten a claim printed doesn't mean
it's a good conclusion. Sharing the source's evidence and reasoning with your readers
will help them to understand your use of the source.

Notice as well how the writer is refereeing a range of possible interpretations by
juxtaposing the ways that different experts theorize the significance of empirical evidence—such as their all having ears and all being naked females. (As noted earlier, the
word "empirical" means capable of being observed, available to the senses; the word
comes from the Greek word for experience.)

The paper from which we took the following excerpt is a study of a group of white
marble statues from the Cycladic Islands in the Aegean Sea. Designated as part of the
"Early Spedos" stylistic group, the statues date from 2700–2500 B.C. After a careful

description of the figures themselves, the writer uses a blend of his own analysis and theories by art history authorities to speculate about the significance of the figures.

Excerpt from "Early Spedos Cycladic Idols"

The function of the figurines is still unclear; there is no specific accepted doctrine or theory on why these figures were created, though many hypotheses and interpretations have been offered. *[Writer states problem.]* It is commonly known that statues were placed facing the deceased, or the deceased were placed facing the statues in the tomb itself. Most statues are female in the folded arm pose, about hand size for perhaps a daily use, like a child's doll, and accompanied tools and jewelry in the tomb. *[Writer offers empirical analysis by summarizing potentially revealing details in the evidence. He next begins to cite the theories of three authorities on the function of the figures.]*

Bigwood notes that, "The different qualities of the carving suggest that the sculptures were not just in the possession of an elite but were accessible to the whole culture" (250–251). Along with a widespread class base, figures occurred in tombs regardless of a person's sex. With these facts in mind, a few theories on function seem more acceptable than others. Take Fitton, who states in her book,

> Figures were put into graves for a variety of reasons. They [may have been] servants who would attend the dead in the after-life, sometimes with special roles—female figures [may have been] concubines, musicians who played for the deceased, and so on. Alternatively, they [may have been] personal possessions, thought to protect the owner in life before accompanying him or her to the grave. As such, they may represent their owners, or a deity (67).

In his book, Thimme suggests that the figures were conceived as images of divine beings and specifically intended for the grave: the female figures represent a divine mistress of life and death who will secure for the deceased rebirth in another world (42).

The occurrence of female figures in both women's and men's graves best suits Thimme's hypothesis that the figures represent a being quite independent of the deceased, a divine or daemonic being (Thimme 43). *[Writer cites empirical evidence to support one of his authority's claims.]* Fitton offers some words on the attractive possibility of the female deity theory:

> A female deity, perhaps with worshippers represented in her own image, is an attractive possibility. While the once-fashionable assumption that the prehistoric Aegean peoples worshipped a 'Great Mother' goddess is demonstrably simplistic, there can be no doubt that some explanation is needed to account for the fact

that the majority of Cycladic figures are in the form of a naked female, and a female deity remains a possible identification (69). *[Includes not just another authority's claim but also the supporting evidence]*

The theories put forth by Fitton and Thimme seem to be most confirming since other interpretations, including substitute mother, nurse mother, concubine, and magical midwife are weakened by our knowledge that, for the first two mother theories, there was a rarity of child tombs and, with the last two sexual/procreative theories, the inclusion of figurines in graves occurred irrespective of the individual's sex. *[Writer uses empirical evidence to dismiss claims of authorities conflicting with those he is advocating.]* In respect to the particular figurines examined above, the presence of ears suggests a divine being who was designed to listen to prayers, a point to reinforce the validity of a female mother goddess theory. *[Writer uses more empirical evidence to justify chosen claim]*

ANECDOTAL EVIDENCE

An anecdote is a little story (a narrative), a piece of experience. The word comes from a Greek term meaning "things unpublished." At its best, anecdotal evidence involves the close examination of particular instances. At its worst, it misrepresents fairly isolated anecdotes as if they were truly representative instances, but without any substantiating evidence. In effect, these inadequately contextualized examples take cheap shots at others' positions—a common practice during political campaigns.

Often it includes the writer/researcher's own experience with whatever he or she is studying. So, for example, a historian wishing to understand the origins and development of the Latino community in a small east coast American city might use as a large part of her evidence interviews that she has conducted with local Latino residents.

Anecdotal evidence is in some ways at the opposite extreme from statistical evidence. Statistical research often attempts to locate broad trends and patterns by surveying large numbers of instances and tries to arrive at reliable information by deliberately controlling the kind and amount of questions it asks. In fact, one of the most important tasks for someone using statistical research is the careful crafting of the questions to guarantee that they don't, for example, predispose the respondent to choose a particular response. By contrast, the kind of thinking based on anecdotal evidence is less concerned with verifiable trends and patterns than with a more detailed and up-close presentation of particular instances.

Given the difficulty of claiming that a single case (anecdote) is representative of the whole, researchers using anecdotal evidence tend to achieve authority through a large number of small instances, which begin to suggest a trend. Authority can also be acquired through the audience's sense of the analytical ability of the researcher—her skill, for example, at convincingly connecting the evidence with the claim.

Sometimes, statistical and anecdotal evidence operate hand-in-hand; they tend to need each other. A certain number of closely examined particular instances may be necessary in order to determine what questions to ask for a larger statistical survey. Statistical evidence is occasionally seen as incomplete and can even be misleading without more in-depth examination. Thus, for example, one of the most popular research tools in both business and the academic world is the combining of a questionnaire with follow-up discussion by a focus group. The focus group usually consists of a representative sample of respondents to a questionnaire who are selected for a more detailed follow-up discussion of the questions than the statistical format could ever allow. Often the researcher will learn from the focus group that the questionnaire was asking the wrong questions, or that respondents had been generally misunderstanding the questions.

While it is a central claim of this book that evidence cannot and should not be expected to speak for itself, and thus needs analysis, there is another side to this argument, especially in certain kinds of research. Historians, for example, are especially sensitive to the problem of distorting evidence by offering too much interpretation of it before they have adequately presented it—in effect, filtering it prematurely though their own conclusions. While they take care to frame the evidence in a context that makes its range of meanings apparent, they try not to put too much of themselves between the reader and the data. Rather than speaking for their subjects, such historians give them a space to speak.

Here is an example in which a historian presents the experience of a representative individual, one of the first Puerto Rican immigrants to Allentown, Pennsylvania. Note that she allows us to hear his "voice"—his experience—more than hers, although, if you look for it, you will see her presence as well.

Excerpt from *Hidden from History: The Latino Community of Allentown, PA* by Anna Adams

Jesus Ramos, the oldest of nine children of a Puerto Rican migrant worker, came to New Jersey in the early 1950s to pick fruit. He worked in the fields for two summers, returning to Puerto Rico for the winters. After visiting a Puerto Rican friend who had settled in Allentown, Ramos decided to move there himself. He recalls that by the late 1950s there were approximately 500 Latinos living in Allentown with no place to buy Spanish foods. *[Writer uses subject as statistical source]* Ramos and Juan Acevedo opened La Famosa grocery store where he sold Goya products upstairs and had pool tables in the basement. When Puerto Ricans began to congregate and socialize in the store, the police accused them of loitering and arrested Mr. Ramos for running a gambling establishment. *[Writer embeds narrative of racism without commenting on it; notice that she sticks to the vividly evoked facts]* After clearing himself of those charges, he went to work in the cutoff department of the Greif/Genesco Corporation where he stayed for twenty-eight years. He and his wife Carmen have raised nine children in Allentown. As one of the pioneers of the Puerto Rican community, Jesus tried to smooth the way for others. *[Here, the writer generalizes about her subject, turning him into a representative figure]* He lobbied for Genesco to hire more Spanish speaking people and was one of the founders of Casa Guadalupe, a community center dispensing social services. Despite his efforts, things weren't always easy. "As long as you spoke Spanish, they looked at you different, and you had to work three times harder than the others," he says in fluent, heavily accented English. *[Notice the implied commentary in the fact that after 40 years Ramos continues to sound Puerto Rican but also to speak his new language fluently: he inhabits two worlds, whether out of reluctance to deny his Puerto Rican heritage or inability to do so]* He recalls one occasion when a subordinate co-worker quit rather than take orders from a Puerto Rican. *[Although use of the word "recalls" tells us that the whole account was told to the writer by Ramos, she is selective about what she actually quotes and exerts her influence in this way]*

Try This 8.2: Finding Kinds of Evidence

Find and examine a piece of writing that makes use of anecdotal evidence. Such evidence can take the form of stories or brief story-like examples in which the writer reports his or her own or others' experience and observations. You might look for examples of this kind of evidence in a magazine like *the New York*er, in a feature article of a newspaper's Sunday magazine section, in a chapter from a nonfiction book on some feature of contemporary life and culture, in a historical account (since history-writing often makes use of anecdotal evidence), in a transcript of a radio interview such as the kind Terry Gross conducts in her program "Fresh Air" on public radio, and so forth.

You could also look at a textbook you are using, or seek out a textbook on economics or sociology or anthropology. Try to determine what in a given section of the book might be categorized as anecdotal evidence. Also try to name and categorize the other kinds of evidence the book uses.

Remember that there are more kinds of evidence than we have named and illustrated in this chapter. Start getting into the habit of asking yourself, "What kind of evidence is this, and how is it used?"

Case Studies: Two Examples

The case study is a cousin of anecdotal evidence in that it relies on in-depth and careful description of a particular case in point. The case study is a common form of what is known as qualitative research, as opposed to quantitative (numerical) research, in the social sciences. Each discipline has its own rules governing the method of conducting a case study.

The first example is a piece of what's called ethnographic writing wherein the writer uses description to come to terms with and understand some kind of cultural experience. This piece, by Elissa Davidowitz, was written for a course on research methodologies in education. Notice how, in the words of her professor, Pearl Rosenberg, the excerpt combines "ongoing data collection, self-reflexive thinking, and socio-cultural analysis" and captures "her humility in the face of an unfamiliar task in relation to real people."

> I didn't understand how Kent could give the other students such a hard time for dropping out of school when he did the same thing. Yes, they dropped out of school, but they are here five days a week at 8:30 in the morning to get their GED. Doesn't that make them somewhat credible? I thought so. After working with Kent I was left with many questions. I knew from my short time with him that he was a man struggling to maintain his self-worth and self-respect. His constant need to "prove" himself made it clear that he thought of me as someone who held power over him. What did it mean for me to take on the role of educator and Kent to be the student? *[Writer frames the case—helping to teach a GED class to inner city people]*
>
> As Kent felt the need to prove himself to me, I felt the need to prove to Kent that the teaching in that room was going both ways. Anne Ferguson describes in her ethnography, *Bad Boys*, the need for teachers to classify students as "good" or "bad." Ferguson goes on to explain that, "Even though we treat it this way, the category 'child' does not describe and contain a homogeneous and naturally occurring group of individuals at a certain stage of human development . . . What it means to be a child varies dramatically by virtue of location in cross-cutting categories of class, gender, and race" (Ferguson, 81). The same can be said for adults. We cannot classify all adults in one way. Yes, it may be easy to say that all of the adult learners attending the GED class dropped out of school because they were lazy kids, but it is never that simple. Each individual is a complex being filled with multiple dimensions living in a world where people are constantly trying to simplify things. As an educator, it is crucial to understand the many aspects that make up a child or person. Coming to terms with the truth of the complexity of people's lives is the first step towards helping them grow both as an individual and a student. *[Writer uses secondary source to contextualize the study and foreground her assumptions about complexity]*
>
> Throughout my time volunteering at the GED class, I have learned how motivation varies greatly from individual to individual. I always knew that people were motivated by different factors, internal or external, sometimes both. It became clear to

me that Vissilios and Kent were internally motivated. Although Kent was affected by the need to provide for his family, he was also getting his GED to prove to himself that he was capable. In my interview with Vissilios the same idea of "proving oneself" became evident. Vissilios told me that he was not pushed by his mother to stay in school when he was younger, and was not pushed to go back to school. He explained that he wanted his GED to prove to people that it wasn't lack of ability that kept him from getting a high school diploma; rather it was his own laziness as a kid. After talking with Mrs. Cooper about the issue of motivation for adult learners, I gained a new insight into the field. Mrs. Cooper explained to me from the beginning that this is a GED class, and that her students are adults. They are not required to show up to class; they come by choice. She explained that there is an attendance policy and if the students are falling below the amount of hours they are required to attend, it is the teacher's choice whether or not to drop the student from the class. Mrs. Cooper said that in her 15 years of teaching at the Literacy Center she has never officially dropped a student. She explained that in order to keep her students motivated she feels that focusing on their personal needs is the most effective. She makes a point to make herself available for extra help as often as possible. Mrs. Cooper also tries to make the class interesting by discussing current events when relevant. *[Writer presents the point of view of one of her students and then quotes an authority to help her assess his motives]*

The second example is a case study in which psychology students were asked to analyze data suggestive of particular kinds of mental illnesses as they are represented in contemporary films. The difference between the following case study and the preceding one is that the psychology case study has prescribed categories (subheads) under which the information is recorded. The assignment here is to give examples of some of the behaviors exhibited by the character Roy in *Matchstick Men* that might lead to a diagnosis of obsessive-compulsive disorder.

Matchstick Men

Patient Evaluation: Roy

Presenting Problem:

Patient describes extreme discomfort when placed in outdoor settings. He fears dirt, germs, insects, and pollen. He becomes extremely distracted by these fears when he is outdoors. Patient also reports that he feels the need to open and close each door through which he enters or leaves a room three times while counting out loud (often in a language other than English).

He reports extreme anxiety at the thought of his home being anything less than perfectly clean and is plagued by constant thoughts of cleanliness. Patient fears shoes on the carpet of his home and is at times overwhelmed by anxiety if in fact someone walks on the carpet with shoes on. Patient reports muscular ticks in his face, neck and head in certain situations. These often become prominent when he is nervous, outdoors, or in a new or unfamiliar setting.

History of Present Illness:

Patient reports that he has noticed his symptoms and has attempted to self-medicate utilizing illegally obtained prescription drugs. He does not know the name of this medication. Symptoms seem to have been present for at least fifteen years but may stretch as far back as adolescence. Patient reports that on one occasion he felt suicidal because of his overwhelming feelings about his symptoms but that fear of staining his carpet prevented him from taking his own life with a handgun.

Past Psychiatric Illness, Treatments, Outcomes:

No known history

Medical History:

Patient reports anxiety-induced spells of hyperventilation and lightheadedness.

Psychosocial History:

Patient reports that his last romantic relationship ended nearly fifteen years ago. He describes this relationship as abusive and states that he was physically aggressive toward his ex-wife Heather. At the end of this relationship Heather was pregnant; patient knows nothing about the whereabouts of the child. Patient's only close relationship is that which he holds with his "business partner" Frank with whom he conducts illegal and fraudulent business endeavors. Although he works with Frank on a daily basis and considers him a close partner, Roy claims that he does not fully trust Frank because of their line of work.

Drug and Alcohol History:

Patient reports that he has a history of alcoholism beginning over fifteen years ago. Patient is known to have utilized some sort of illegally conjured prescription drug to self medicate for his symptoms. Patient smokes as many as eight packs of cigarettes each day.

Behavioral Observations:

Patient is alert and coherent however, he displays nervous behavior, fidgeting and ticks in his face and neck. Patient seems eager to leave the office and his eyes repeatedly dart around the room. He repeatedly and urgently requests a prescription for his symptoms and is hesitant to answer questions.

Mental Status Exam:

Speech pattern is urgent. Patient refuses to answer questions but seems capable of doing so when pressed. Patient seems to have high intellectual capacity and is completely conscious of his surroundings. Patient seems to have no control over obsessive thoughts.

Functional Assessment:

Patient does not recognize the severity of his illness. He believes that he must live with his illness but that only medication has the capability to help him. The patient is involved with illegal activity and has very little social interaction beyond that with his partner Frank. He does not function well in new environments and cannot go outside without becoming extremely uncomfortable. Without treatment the patient may be a suicide risk.

Strengths:

Patient is extremely intelligent and creative. He is organized, meticulous, and values cleanliness. Although his work is criminal, he excels in his ability to talk to people and persuade them into doing what he wants them to do.

Diagnosis:

Obsessive Compulsive Disorder

Treatment Plan:

It is recommended that patient begin a carefully monitored drug therapy and Cognitive therapy program. Patient will be strongly encouraged in therapy to withdraw from his criminal lifestyle in order to apply his talents and strengths toward more productive work.

Prognosis:

If the patient is treated cognitively and chemically through drug therapy, vast improvement may be achieved. However, if criminal behavior persists, treatment may not be as effective. Similarly, if patient does not continue consistent treatment indefinitely, a relapse of symptoms is highly probable.

TEXTUAL EVIDENCE

Types of evidence, as we've been noting, can be divided into two broad categories: quantitative (numerically based) and qualitative (based on interviews and other kinds of non-numerical data). Those who work with qualitative data tend to focus closely on words. We are using the term "textual evidence" to designate instances in which the language itself is of fundamental importance: both how things are worded and the range of meanings that key words might possess. Insofar as the actual language of a document counts, you are in the domain of textual evidence.

Perhaps the profession that most commonly uses textual evidence is the law, which involves interpreting the language of contracts, wills, statutes, statements of intention, etc. Similarly, diplomats, accountants, people in business—all those who must rely on written documents to guarantee understanding—need to be adept at textual analysis. People in such fields as literary study, media studies, and public relations also engage in textual analysis.

Notice in the following excerpt from a student paper how the writer focuses on particular words as evidence.

Excerpt from "Women and Nature in Lessing and Chopin"

Susan tends to fear everything connected to the natural world *[General claim about feature of text she wishes to understand]*. The heroine first shows signs of irrationality as she refuses to sit in her garden. Lessing describes, "She was filled with tension, like a panic: as if an enemy was in the garden with her" (Doris Lessing, "To Room 19" 2306) *[Writer selects evidence]*. This "enemy" is a threat to Susan's carefully planned and structured life, and so she attempts to avoid nature. This becomes an interesting idea as the story clearly shows that Susan longs to yield to that "enemy" and to destroy her ordered existence. *[Explains quoted evidence, selecting a particular word that organizes thinking in the text and that she proceeds to apply to the text as a whole]* Susan decides she must have a holiday to free herself from the bondage that her children represent, and so she goes on a walking tour of Wales. But she never can truly be unfettered; even on a mountainside, her family is capable of dragging her back to her obligations. In this case, the telephone becomes Susan's downfall, as Lessing writes, "Susan prowled over wild country with the telephone wire holding her to her duties like a leash" (2313). *[Distinguishes organizing contrast in the language of additional evidence (freedom in nature vs. entrapment in domesticity) and uses it to develop claim]* [...] Susan is forced to deal with an unfaithful spouse instead of being the adulterous one herself. In her mind, sex does have close ties to nature, but she chooses to ignore it as her husband has hurt her by acting upon his passions. It does not seem to be a coincidence that room 19 is entirely green; the curtains, the bed, and the wicker chair all share the same hue. And when Matthew practically forces Susan to create an imaginary lover, she selects the name Michael Plant, an obvious reference to the natural equaling the sensual. *[Locates additional evidence to confirm the pattern and further develop her claim]*

Try This 8.3: Using Textual Evidence

Here is another excerpt from the paper on women and nature. Study the passage and answer the following questions. Where do we see the writer's general claim about the evidence? Where does she select the feature of the text she wants to focus on? How does the cited evidence organize her thinking—on what pattern or organizing contrast?

Chopin also applies the imagery of birds to her heroine, symbolically alluding to Edna's wish to fly, in a sense, from all her responsibilities. Edna refers to her new home as the "pigeon house," a place where she thinks she has evaded her husband and children. She asserts her independence in this new dwelling, throwing parties and working on her art. Perhaps the greatest reference to Edna's tie to birds occurs right before she kills herself. Chopin portrays the scene on page 108, "A bird with a broken wing was beating the air above, reeling, fluttering, circling disabled down, down to the water." This bird comes to represent everything Edna has endured up until her breakdown, her suicide "down, down to the water." Edna can never reconcile her natural sexual instincts, her "broken wing," with the civilized world she inhabits; society will not let her merge the two domains, and so she resolves to die.

WHAT DO THE FACTS REALLY TELL US?

In the realm of analysis, there are precious few smoking guns and absolutely reliable eyewitnesses. When there are, you have an open-and-shut case that probably does not need to be argued. It makes sense, then, to avoid thinking that a particular use of evidence is strong and good because the evidence is clearly true and factual, whereas another use of evidence is weak and inadequate because it's possibly untrue and not factual. Most analytical uses of evidence are a matter of making inferences, interpreting the evidence with subtlety and respect.

To a significant extent, decisions about the value of evidence depend on the kind of claim you are making (how broad, for example, and how conclusive) and the genre you are writing in. What could be appropriate and valid for writing a magazine profile of residents trying to rebuild a poor urban neighborhood might not be appropriate and valid for supporting policy decisions or sociological theories about people in such neighborhoods. The strength of such a profile, however, should not be underestimated, because it may be rich in suggestion, in questions and angles of approach for further research.

Whatever kind of evidence you're using, the emphasis rests on how you use what you have: how you articulate what it means and how carefully you link the evidence to your claims. When you find yourself asking, "How good is my argument?" here are two working criteria from the chapter:

- Am I oversimplifying the implications of my evidence?
- Does my use of evidence go beyond mere corroboration of an overly general claim?

Another guiding principle, perhaps the chapter's most important point, is to think with the evidence; keep it before you. If you start to move too far afield, return to the source, the evidence itself, to refresh your thinking.

GUIDELINES FOR REASONING FROM EVIDENCE TO CLAIMS

1. Learn to recognize unsubstantiated assertions, rather than treating claims as self-evident truths. Whenever you make a claim, offer your readers the evidence that led you to it.

2. Make the evidence speak. Explain how it supports the claim; offer your reasons for believing the evidence means what you say it does.

3. Use evidence to advance your claim, not just confirm it. Explore how the evidence does not fit the claim, and use what you learn to reshape the claim, making it more accurate.

4. Consider what counts as evidence in a given field or context, or as one of the Voices puts it, remember that "evidence itself is dependent upon methodology—that it's not just a question of gathering 'information,' but also a question of how it was gathered."

5. Most professors agree that evidence is never completely neutral, simply a matter of "the facts," so you need to determine the slant—the principles of selection—that have produced this evidence. And as a corollary, try to gather evidence from more than one side of a topic.

Assignments: Reasoning from Evidence to Claims

1. **Distinguishing Evidence from Claims**. Take an excerpt from your own writing, at least two paragraphs in length—perhaps from a paper you have already written or a draft you are working on—and at the end of every sentence label the sentence as either evidence (E) or claim (C). For sentences that appear to

offer both, determine which parts of the sentence are evidence and which are claim, and then decide which one, E or C, predominates. What is the ratio of evidence to claim, especially in particularly effective or weak paragraphs?

2. **Find Examples of Using Authorities as Evidence**. How are the authorities used? What other kinds of evidence appear in the piece? It might be interesting with this assignment to compare a piece of academic writing with a piece of nonacademic writing on the same subject.

3. **Linking Evidence with Claims**. Study a piece of writing, yours or something you come across in your reading. Locate the places where the writer explicitly explains the connection between the evidence and the claim. If you are studying your own writing, this exercise could be the basis of a revision in which you more fully explain the thought process that caused you to say your evidence means what you say it does.

Chapter 9

Analyzing Arguments

THIS CHAPTER addresses different schools of thought on the nature and purpose of argument along with a brief introduction to the rules of argument through which the linking of evidence and claims has traditionally been tested. The chapter ends with a glossary of the most common logical fallacies.

THREE VIEWPOINTS ON ARGUMENT
- Formal Argument Analysis: The Syllogism and the Toulmin Model
- Rogerian Argument and Practical Reasoning
- Figurative Logic: Reasoning with Metaphors

Argument analysis and the definition of argument depend on what a person wants to know, and by what means. In some academic disciplines, the means are primarily quantitative. In most disciplines, the means are empirical in one way or another—based on observation.

As this chapter and later ones (*especially Chapter 15, Forms and Formats Across the Curriculum*) demonstrate, each division and discipline of the academic world has its own way of knowing. This way of knowing—called an *epistemology*—carries with it a particular way of assessing the value of evidence and of determining the relative validity of claims. No one discipline has the last word on thinking.

Psychology departments, for example, concentrate much less on the soundness of an argument than they do on factors that influence the way people think. We offer one example of thinking about thinking in psychology in the Voice from Across the Curriculum appearing at the end of Chapter 2. There psychologist Mark Sciutto speaks about cognitive behavior therapy and the problem of various kinds of automatic thoughts, such as globalizing and fortune-telling, that distort the way people think. In Chapter 2, we argue that the deeply ingrained habits of overgeneralizing, judging, and leaping prematurely to conclusions are the most fundamental causes of poor thinking.

Neuroscience departments study thinking in a more materially empirical way, by trying to isolate the various biochemical and other mechanisms in the brain that determine how we process experience. History, religion, English, and art history departments, among others, study the various traditions of thought, including traditions in language that shape and condition thinking in individuals and cultures.

We now turn to the long tradition of analyzing arguments that has evolved from the thinking of Aristotle and other early Greek philosophers. This necessarily brief discussion cannot do justice to the methods of argument analysis employed by philosophers, especially logicians. But it is possible to provide a skeletal version of how these methods operate and also to locate them in the context of other ways of thinking about argument.

THE RULES OF ARGUMENT: SYLLOGISM AND ENTHYMEME

Philosophers have long quested for forms that might lend to human argument some greater clarity and certainty, more like what is possible with formulas in math. As you will see and as most philosophers readily admit, the reality of evaluating arguments in day-to-day life is necessarily a less tidy process than the rules of argument might make it seem. The kinds of certainty that are sometimes possible with formulas in math are not so easily available when using words to make claims about human experience. Nevertheless, the rules of argument described here offer a set of specific guidelines for discovering things that go right—and wrong—in the construction of an argument.

Probably the most common way of talking about logical argumentation goes back to Aristotle. This approach doesn't always have direct applications in the kinds of analytical writing described in this book, but knowing the ways that philosophers have devised for evaluating arguments can expand your ability to assess your own and others' reasoning about claims and evidence.

There are a number of rules for evaluating the validity of a syllogism's conclusion. In this short section, we cannot offer enough of the details about argument analysis to equip you with the necessary skills. But we will give you enough detail so that you can understand the basic principles and methods of this way of thinking about argument.

At the heart of the Aristotelian model is the syllogism, which consists of three parts:

1. Major premise: a general proposition presumed to be true;
2. Minor premise: a subordinate proposition also presumed to be true; and
3. Conclusion: a claim that follows logically from the two premises, if the argument has been properly framed.

Here is a frequently cited example of a syllogism:

All men are mortal (major premise).

Socrates is a man (minor premise).

Therefore, Socrates is mortal (conclusion).

A premise is a proposition (assumption) upon which an argument is based and from which a conclusion is drawn. In the syllogism, if both of the premises have been stated in the proper form (both containing a shared term), then the conclusion must be valid.

An important thing to know about syllogisms is that they are only as true as the premises they are made of. It is not, however, the business of the syllogism to test the truth of the premises. Syllogisms can only demonstrate that the form of the argument is valid. As you will see, this word "valid" is a key term in argument evaluation, a term that does not mean the same thing as right or true.

If a writer follows the prescribed steps of the syllogism without violating any of the rules on proper wording and on the way the steps may be put together, then the conclusion arrived at in step 3 is valid. An argument evaluated in this way can be valid and still be false. For example:

All politicians are corrupt.

The mayor of Chicago is a politician.

Therefore, the mayor of Chicago is corrupt.

The problem here is not with the form of the syllogism but with the fact that the major premise is untrue.

To make good use of syllogistic reasoning, you need to get into the habit of recasting arguments that you write or read or hear into the proper syllogistic form. The way most people articulate claims—often without even recognizing that they are making claims—is rarely if ever syllogistic. Claims, for example, if they are to be most easily assessed for validity, usually need to be recast using forms of "to be" rather than other kinds of verbs (as in the Chicago example above).

While arguments as formulated in formal logic are grounded in abstract, universal terms, most arguments as we encounter them in daily life involve statements about values and beliefs. These real-life arguments typically appear in a form that philosophers call the "enthymeme." An enthymeme is an incomplete syllogism. One of its premises has been left unstated, usually because the person offering the argument takes the unstated assumption to be a given, something so obviously true that it doesn't even need to be made explicit.

Sample Enthymeme: Cats make better pets than dogs because cats are more independent.

Unstated Assumption: Independent animals make better pets.

Sample Enthymeme: Charter schools will improve the quality of education because they encourage competition.

Unstated Assumption: Competition improves the quality of education.

TOULMIN'S ALTERNATIVE MODEL OF THE SYLLOGISM

British philosopher Steven Toulmin offered a competing model of argument in his influential book, *The Uses of Argument* (1958). Toulmin's model was motivated by his belief that the philosophical tradition of formal logic, with its many rules for describing and evaluating the conduct of arguments, conflicts with the practice and idiom (ways of phrasing) of arguers. To radically simplify Toulmin's case, it is that the

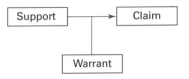

FIGURE 9.1
The Toulmin Model.

syllogism does not adequately account for what really happens when thinkers try to frame and defend various claims. Toulmin tried to describe the structure of argument in a way that he thought came closer to what actually happens in practice when we try to take a position.

The Toulmin model of argument renames and reorders the process of reasoning described in the Aristotelian syllogism as follows:

1. Data: the evidence appealed to in support of a claim; data respond to the question "What have you got to go on?"

2. Warrant: a general principle or reason used to connect the data with the claim; the warrant responds to the question "How did you get there?" (from the data to the claim).

3. Claim: a conclusion about the data (see Figure 9.1).

Consider this model in terms of the chapter's opening discussion of linking evidence and claims. In the Toulmin model, the warrant is the link. It supplies the reasoning that explains why the evidence (support) leads to the conclusion (claim).

Let's look briefly at how this reasoning structure works in practice by looking at one of Toulmin's examples.

data: Harry was born in Bermuda.

warrant: The relevant statutes provide that people born in the colonies of British parents are entitled to British citizenship (reason for connecting data to claim);

claim: So, presumably, Harry is a British citizen. (conclusion)

We can now follow Toulmin a little further in his critique and revision of syllogistic ways of describing thinking. A syllogism, as you saw above, is designed to reveal its soundness through the careful framing and arrangement of its terms:

All men are mortal. (All x's are y.)

Socrates is a man. (Socrates is an x.)

Therefore, Socrates is mortal. (Socrates is a y.)

At what price, asks Toulmin, do we simplify our phrasing of complex situations in the world in order to gain this appearance of truth? In how many situations, he asks, can we say that "all x's are y"?

The strictness of the rules necessary for guaranteeing formal validity, Toulmin argues, leaves out the greater amount of uncertainty that is a part of reasoning about most questions, issues, and problems. Toulmin observes, using his own argument structure as a case in point, that as soon as an argument begins to add information in support of its premises, the complexity and inevitable tentativeness of the argument become apparent, rather than its evident truth.

Here is Toulmin's explanation of what must happen to the form of an argument when a person begins to add more supporting information, which Toulmin calls *backing*. The backing for the warrant in the example above about the British citizenship of people born in Bermuda would inevitably involve mentioning "the relevant statutes"—acts of Parliament, statistical reports, and so forth—to prove its accuracy. The addition of such information, says Toulmin, would "prevent us from writing the argument so that its validity shall be manifest from its formal properties alone" (*The Uses of Argument,* 123).

Not everyone agrees with Toulmin's revision or his reasoning. The rhetorician Edward Corbett, for example, argues that the Toulmin system lacks rules and guidelines for assessing the "logicality of the argument" (*The Elements of Reasoning,* Macmillan, 1991, p. 44). Corbett also argues that Toulmin's system is less easy to use than it appears, noting that recognizing claims, data, warrants, and backing in an argument may not be any easier than finding conclusions, minor premises, and major premises in a syllogism.

The rules of argument are important for clarifying and testing our thinking. And, of course, many more forms and structures are available in logic than this brief account could begin to suggest. There are, for example, a number of rules for arriving at claims about evidence inductively. Syllogistic reasoning is deductive; it works by bringing premises into accord with some larger governing premise.

To use an analogy, if the Aristotelian syllogism appears to offer us the promise of never mistaking the forest for the trees, Toulmin's revision of that model is to never let us forget that the forest is in fact made up of trees.

As a writer, you will naturally want some guidelines and workable methods for selecting evidence and linking it to claims. But what you can't expect to find is a set of predetermined slots into which you can drop any piece of evidence and find the truth. Rather, analyses and arguments operate within the complex set of details and circumstances that are part of life as we live it. An argument depends not only on whether or not its premises follow logically but on the quality of the thinking that produces those premises in the first place and painstakingly tests their accuracy. This is the job of analysis.

ROGERIAN ARGUMENT AND PRACTICAL REASONING

Most people want to be reasonable and have others think of them as reasonable. It has long been hoped by some people that we might devise a foolproof system for demonstrating that one person's argument is clearly right and another's is clearly wrong. Certainty is an attractive goal for many people.

The kind of formal argument analysis we have been considering is a piece of this hope. The rules of argument—whichever model you try to apply—do have a significant capacity for discriminating sound arguments from less sound ones. Moreover, the challenge of translating real world propositions into the forms required by this or that argumentative system is not insurmountable. A number of books out there can teach you to do it.

Our discussion, however, has disclosed the problems that logical analysis of the forms of argument faces. It is difficult to incorporate into the prescribed forms much of the detail that is actually significant in making the argument sound. Even these problems can be negotiated, though, if you don't expect too much and if you take a practical approach, such as focusing on enthymemes (the form that everyday arguments most often take) and learning to supply the missing assumptions.

There are, however, other objections to prioritizing the rules of argument. These objections come from contemporary rhetoricians who are less concerned about testing the adequacy of arguments than they are with making argument better serve the needs of people in everyday life and in the larger arena of public discourse. The view of argument offered throughout this book—for example, in the discussion of counterproductive habits of mind in the latter half of Chapter 2—is aligned with the thinking of two such rhetoricians, Carl Rogers and Wayne Booth. For these rhetoricians, the aim is not primarily to defeat opponents but to locate common ground. (Many have noticed the presence of militaristic rhetoric in argument analysis.)

Both Rogers and Booth place their emphasis on listening. They stress the need to be able to understand and accurately represent the positions of "opponents" in an argument. This goal is very much the norm in academic writing, where people try to put different points of view into conversation rather than set out to have one view defeat another. As Zachary Dobbins has argued, "For Booth, reasoning equates not just with rational thought but instead with inquiry, a term that more expansively describes the process all of us are daily engaged in to shape and make sense of the world—a process the ends of which are seldom certain or empirically measurable" ("Wayne Booth, Narrative, and the Rhetoric of Empathy"—an unpublished talk delivered at the 2010 Conference on College Composition and Communication). Dobbins quotes Booth to the effect that "The supreme purpose of persuasion [...] should not be to talk someone else into a preconceived view; rather it must be to engage in mutual inquiry or exploration [...]" (*Modern Dogma and the Rhetoric of Dissent*).

TWO WAYS TO IMPROVE AN ARGUMENT: CHECK FOR UNSTATED ASSUMPTIONS AND QUALIFY CLAIMS

Many of the arguments we encounter in daily life succumb to overly rigid and unqualified categorical thinking. Of course, putting things into categories is not unto itself a bad practice. In order to generalize from particular experiences, we try to put those experiences into meaningful categories. Analytical thought is quite unthinkable without categories. But these can mislead us into oversimplification when the categories are too broad or too simply connected.

This is especially the case with the either/or choices to which categorical thinking is prone: approve/disapprove, real/unreal, accurate/inaccurate, believable/unbelievable. The writer who evaluates leadership in terms of its selflessness/selfishness, for example, needs to pause to consider why we should evaluate leadership in these terms in the first place.

We will refer to the following two examples to illustrate how (1) qualifying your claims and (2) checking for the unstated assumptions upon which your claims depend can remedy the two primary problems created by categorical thinking: unqualified claims and overstated positions. *(For more on methods of uncovering unstated assumptions and reformulating binaries, see Chapter 4, Toolkit of Analytical Methods II.)*

> **Example I:** I think that there are many things shown on TV that are damaging for people to see. But there is no need for censorship. No network is going to show violence without the approval of the public, obviously for financial reasons. What must be remembered is that the public majority will see what it wants to see in our mass society.

> **Example II:** Some members of our society feel that [the televised cartoon series] *The Simpsons* promotes wrong morals and values for our society. Other members find it funny and entertaining. I feel that *The Simpsons* has a more positive effect than a negative one. In relation to a real-life marriage, Marge and Homer's marriage is pretty accurate. The problems they deal with are not very large or intense. As for the family relationships, the Simpsons are very close and love each other.

The main problem with Example I is the writer's failure to qualify his ideas, a problem that causes him to generalize to the point of oversimplification. Note the writer's habit of stating his claims absolutely (we have italicized the words that make these claims unqualified):

"there is *no* need for censorship"

"*no* network is going to show violence without"

"*obviously* for financial reasons"

"what *must* be remembered"

"the majority *will* see"

Such broad, pronouncement-like claims cannot be supported. The solution is to more carefully limit the claims, especially the key premise about public approval. The assertion that a commercial television industry will, for financial reasons, give the public "what it wants" is true *to an extent* (our key phrase for reformulating either/ors)—but it is not true as globally as the writer wishes us to believe.

Couldn't it also be argued, for example, that given the power of television to shape people's tastes and opinions, the public sees not just what it wants but what it has been taught to want? This complication of the writer's argument about public approval undermines the credibility of his global assertion that "there is no need for censorship."

Example II would appear to be more qualified than Example I because it acknowledges the existence of more than one point of view. Rather than broadly asserting that the show is positive and accurate, she tempers these claims (as italics show): "I *feel* that *The Simpsons* has a *more* positive effect *than* a negative one"; "Marge and Homer's marriage is *pretty* accurate." These qualifications, however, are superficial.

Before she could convince us to approve of *The Simpsons* for its accuracy in depicting marriage, she would have to convince us that accuracy is a reasonable criterion for evaluating TV shows (especially cartoons) rather than assuming the unquestioned value of accuracy. Would an accurate depiction of the life of a serial killer, for example, necessarily make for a "positive" show? Similarly, if a fantasy show has no interest in accuracy, is it necessarily "negative" and without moral value?

When writers present a debatable premise as if it were self-evidently true, the conclusions built upon it cannot stand. At the least, the writer of Example II needs to recognize her debatable premise, articulate it, and make an argument in support of it. She might also precede her judgment about the show with more analysis. Before deciding that the show is "more positive than negative" and thus does not promote "wrong morals and values for our society," she could analyze what the show says about marriage and how it goes about saying it.

Likewise, if the writer of Example I had further examined his own claims before rushing to argue an absolute position on censorship, he would have noticed how much of the thinking that underlies them remains unarticulated and thus unexamined. It would also allow him to sort out the logical contradiction with his opening claim that "there are many things shown on TV that are damaging for people to see." If television networks will only broadcast what the public approves of, then apparently the public must approve of being damaged or fail to notice that it is being damaged. If the public either fails to notice it is being damaged or approves of it, aren't these credible arguments for rather than against censorship?

FIGURATIVE LOGIC: REASONING WITH METAPHORS

To understand reasoning only in terms of propositional logic is to ignore how much of our day-to-day thinking is conducted indirectly, not in the form of explicit claims but in metaphors. Many people assume that figurative thinking—the kind conducted in metaphors and similes—is confined only to poems and that it is not really thinking but is instead primarily emotional and irrational.

There are some problems with these charges against figurative thinking that lie beyond the scope of this discussion—for example, that emotions are the enemy of rationality, an assumption that neuroscience researchers like Antonio Damasio have challenged. What is important for present purposes is to consider challenges that can reasonably be made to the assumption that one of our most common ways of thinking is not, in fact, a way of reasoning about evidence.

THE LOGIC OF METAPHOR

- Metaphors pervade our ways of thinking
- Metaphor is a way of thinking by analogy
- The logic of metaphors is implicit

- The implicit logic of metaphors can be made explicit by scrutinizing the language
- We can recast figurative language to see and evaluate its arguments just as we recast language to examine its logic in syllogistic form

Everyday Thinking

Metaphors are deeply engrained in the language we use everyday; they are far from being solely the concern of poets. George Lakoff, professor of linguistics and cognitive science, and English professor Mark Turner, among others, have demonstrated that metaphors are built into the way we think. (See Lakoff and Turner's book, *More than Cool Reason, a Field Guide to Poetic Metaphor*, University of Chicago Press, 1989.) As such, metaphors routinely constitute our assumptions about the world and our place in it. Life, for example, is a journey. To become successful, you climb a ladder. Being up is a good thing. To be down is to be unhappy and blue. These are all metaphors. If we accept their implicit arguments in an unexamined way, they call the shots in our lives more than we should allow them to.

Although figurative logic does not operate in the same way as claims-based (propositional) logic, it nevertheless produces arguments, the reasoning of which can be analyzed and evaluated. Let's start with a definition. A metaphor works by **analogy**— a type of comparison that often finds similarities between things that are otherwise unlike. Consider the simile "My love is like a red red rose." A simile, identifiable by its use of the words "like" or "as," operates like a metaphor except that both sides of the analogy are explicitly stated. The subject of the simile, love, is called the tenor; the comparative term brought in to think about love, rose, is called the vehicle.

In metaphors, the thought connection between the vehicle (rose) and the tenor (my love) is left unstated. But for our purposes, the clearer and more explicit simile will do. It is the nature of the resemblance between the speaker's "love" and roses that we are invited to infer.

What are the characteristics of red roses—especially red red (very red) roses—that might be relevant in this piece of thinking by analogy? Well, most people find roses to be beautiful. Most people associate red with passion. In fact, science can now measure the body's response to different colors. Red produces excitement. Red can even make the pulse rate go up. Roses are also complicated flowers. Their shape is convoluted. Roses are thought of as female. Rose petals are fragile. Many roses have thorns. So, the simile is actually a piece of thinking about love and about women.

It is not a very deep piece of thinking, and probably many women would prefer that the thorn part not be made too prominent. In fact, a reader would have to decide in the context of other language in the poem whether thorniness, as a characteristic of some roses, is significant and ought to be considered. The point is that the simile does make an argument about women that could be stated overtly, analyzed, and evaluated. The implication that women, like roses, might have thorns—and thus be hard to "pick," defending them from male intruders, and so forth is part of the argument.

Here is the procedure for exploring and decoding the logic of metaphor—what we have to do, more or less automatically, to understand the thinking that the metaphor suggests.

Step 1: Isolate the vehicle—the language in the metaphor that states one side of the analogy.

Step 2: Articulate the characteristics of the vehicle, its defining traits.

Step 3: Select the characteristics of the vehicle that seem most significant in context.

Step 4: Use these significant characteristics of the vehicle to prompt interpretive leaps to what the metaphor communicates. Make the implicit explicit.

Notice how, in the rose example, our recasting of the original simile has made explicit the implicit meanings inside the figurative language. This recasting is a useful act of thinking, one that makes evident the thought process that a metaphor sets in motion.

What such recasting reveals is not only that metaphors do, in fact, make claims, but that they are remarkably efficient at doing so. A metaphor can say a lot in a little by compressing a complex amalgam of thought and feeling into a single image.

What objections might remain to thinking that figurative language has an implicit logic and is a way of thinking and making arguments? People who pride themselves on being logical thinkers and place great value on rationality are inclined to think of metaphorical language as imprecise and too little available to any systematic way of arriving at meaning that all who encounter the metaphor might share. This is a reasonable objection, but one that can be answered in the terms that we introduced in our discussion of Practical Reasoning above.

As we argue at some length in Chapter 6, Making Interpretations Plausible, certainty and single right answers are very rarely available, especially when our evidence consists of words. Even in areas, however, where it is not possible to prove beyond a doubt that one statement of meaning is truer and more accurate than another, people will usually accept some reasoning from evidence as better—truer to the meaning of the words in context—than others. The meaning-making process is social and consensual. To put a Rogerian slant on this point, understanding figurative logic involves careful listening to language, an openness to multiple possibilities, and it also requires empathy—much like what is required of us in understanding people's arguments in everyday life.

Skepticism about the logic and usefulness of metaphorical language is especially common among people who like to think of themselves as completely out-front (a metaphor!) and practical—always saying what they mean, as though it were possible for everything that mattered to be made entirely overt and equally understandable by all, regardless of background and experience.

The fact that metaphors require interpretation—as do most uses of language— does not take away from the fact that metaphors are a way of thinking. Being able to articulate the implicit arguments embodied in metaphors, making their meanings explicit so that they can be opened to discussion with others—is an important thinking and language skill to acquire.

A BRIEF GLOSSARY OF COMMON LOGICAL FALLACIES

This last section of the chapter offers a brief discussion of common fallacies—false moves—that can subvert argument and interpretation. If you can recognize these fallacies, you can more easily avoid them both in constructing arguments and in analyzing the arguments of others.

The logical fallacies share certain characteristics. First of all, they are forms of cheating in an argument, which is to say that, however false and misleading they may be, and however intentional or unintentional, these tactics are often quite successful. They offer cheap and unethical ways of "winning" an argument—usually at the cost of shutting down the possibility of negotiation among competing views and discovery of common ground that are the goals of Rogerian argument.

The most noticeable feature of arguments based on the logical fallacies is sloganizing—or slogan-slinging, which is a suitably graphic way of putting it. In sloganizing, each side tries to lay claim to various of a culture's honorific words, which then are repeated so often and so much out of context that they evoke little more than a warm glow that each side hopes to attach to its cause. Words and phrases often used in this way are "liberty," "freedom," "the individual," and "the American people," to name a few.

Words like these are sometimes referred to as "weasel" words, along with words like "natural" and "real." The analogy with weasels goes to the notion that weasels suck out the contents of eggs, leaving empty shells behind.

The sloganizing move gets made when each side tries to attach to the other side various labels that evoke fear, even though the words have been repeated so often, in reference to so many different things, that they have become virtually meaningless. This type of sloganizing almost always takes complex circumstances and reduces them to clear-cut goods and evils. Prominent examples in the current contentious political environment are "socialist," "big government," and "capitalist."

It is usual to organize the fallacies into the categories Pathos, Ethos, and Logos from classical rhetoric *(see Chapter 3, the section on Analysis and Argument)*. Appeals to the audience's emotions, for example, such as the fallacy called "bandwagon," fall under pathos. Attacks on the character of one's opponent, such as the fallacy called *ad hominem*, are located under ethos. Various kinds of deceptive and erroneous thinking, such as *post hoc ergo propter hoc*, come under Logos.

Here is another useful way to think about the fallacies. The categories overlap somewhat, but it is helpful to differentiate diversionary tactics from moves that misrepresent the issues.

- Fallacies that derail an argument by distracting audience attention to a mostly irrelevant topic (e.g., red herring, *ad hominem*)
- Fallacies that oversimplify and polarize positions, often through the use of slogans or scare words (e.g., slippery slope, equivocation, false dichotomies, false analogies, straw man).

Some of the fallacies in this second category appear to make a show of substantiality and logicality, while actively misrepresenting things (e.g., simple cause/complex effect, confusing a correlation with a cause—especially when statistics are involved).

Recognizing fallacies in other people's arguments all too often leads to games of "gotcha." Pointing out others' dubious moves can help you "win;" A better alternative is the Rogerian one, to restate what another person is saying in a manner that he or she is willing to accept. This difficult but rewarding tactic can bring both sides in the argument out from behind the barriers, so to speak, where real discussion might be possible. As you will see, many of these errors involve the root problem of oversimplification.

1. ***Ad hominem***. Literally, the Latin phrase means "to the person." When an argument is aimed at the character of another person rather than at the quality of his or her reasoning or performance, we are engaging in an *ad hominem* argument. If a political candidate is attacked because he or she is rich, rather than on the basis of his or her platform, he or she is the victim of an ad hominem attack. In some cases, an *ad hominem* argument is somewhat pertinent—e.g., if a political candidate is discovered to have mob connections.

2. **Bandwagon (*ad populum*)**. Bandwagon arguments appeal to the emotions of a crowd, as in "everyone's doing it." A bandwagon argument is a bad argument from authority, because no reasons are offered to demonstrate that "everybody" is an informed and reliable source.

3. **Begging the question (circular reasoning)**. When you beg the question, you attempt to prove a claim by offering an alternative wording of the claim itself. To beg the question is to argue in a circle by asking readers to accept without argument a point that is actually at stake. This kind of fallacious argument hides its conclusion among its assumptions. For example, "*Huckleberry Finn* should be banned from school libraries as obscene because it uses dirty language" begs the question by presenting as obviously true issues that are actually in question: the definition of obscenity and the assumption that the obscene should be banned because it is obscene.

4. **Equivocation**. Equivocation confuses an argument by using a single word or phrase in more than one sense. For example: "Only man is capable of religious faith. No woman is a man. Therefore, no woman is capable of religious faith." Here the first use of "man" is generic, intended to be gender neutral, while the second use is decidedly masculine.

5. **False analogy**. A false analogy misrepresents matters by making a comparison between two things that are more unlike than alike. The danger that arguing analogically can pose is that an inaccurate comparison, usually one that oversimplifies, prevents you from looking at the evidence. Flying to the moon is like flying a kite? Well, it's a little bit like that, but . . . in most ways that matter, sending a rocket to the moon does not resemble sending a kite into the air.

   An analogy can also become false when it becomes overextended: there is a point of resemblance at one juncture, but the writer then goes on to assume that the two items compared will necessarily resemble each other in most other respects. To what extent is balancing your checkbook really like juggling? On the other hand, an analogy that first appears overextended may not be: how far, for example, could you reasonably go in comparing a presidential election to a sales campaign, or an enclosed shopping mall to a village main street?

When you find yourself reasoning by analogy, ask yourself two questions: (1) are the basic similarities greater and more significant than the obvious differences? and (2) am I over-relying on surface similarities and ignoring more essential differences?

6. **False cause**. This is a generic term for questionable conclusions about causes and effects. Here are three versions of this fallacy:

   a. **Simple cause/complex effect**. This fallacy occurs when you assign a single cause to a complex phenomenon that cannot be so easily explained. A widespread version of this fallacy is seen in arguments that blame individual figures for broad historical events, for example, "Eisenhower caused America to be involved in the Vietnam War." Such a claim ignores the cold war ethos, the long history of colonialism in Southeast Asia, and a multitude of other factors. When you reduce a complex sequence of events to a simple and single cause—or assign a simple effect to a complex cause—you will virtually always be wrong.

   b. ***Post hoc, ergo proctor hoc***. This term is the Latin for **after this, therefore because of this**. The fallacy rests in assuming that because *A* precedes *B* in time, *A* causes *B*. For example, it was once thought that the sun shining on a pile of garbage caused the garbage to conceive flies.

      This error is the stuff that superstition is made of. "I walked under a ladder, and then I got hit by a car" becomes "Because I walked under a ladder, I got hit by a car." A more dangerous form of this error goes like this:

      Evidence: A new neighbor moved in downstairs on Saturday. My television disappeared on Sunday.

      Conclusion: The new neighbor stole my TV.

      As this example also illustrates, typically in false cause some significant alternative has not been considered, such as the presence of flies' eggs in the garbage. Similarly, it does not follow that if a person watches television and then commits a crime, television watching necessarily causes crime; there are other causes to be considered.

   c. **Mistaking correlation for cause**. This fallacy occurs when a person assumes that a correlation between two things—some kind of connection—is necessarily causal. Philosopher David Hume called this problem "the constant conjunction of observed events." If you speed in a car and then have a minor accident, it does not follow that speeding caused the accident. If an exit poll reveals that a large number of voters under the age of 25 voted for candidate X, and X loses, it does not follow that X lost because he failed to appeal to older voters. There is a correlation, but the candidate may have lost for a number of reasons.

7. **False dilemma**. When the options are reduced to only two often sharply opposed alternatives, you have committed a false dilemma. An obvious example appears

in the case often made for Intelligent Design: because the universe is very complexly organized, it had to have been created by an intelligent life force. Are there no alternative explanations?

8. **Hasty generalization**. A conclusion derived from only one or two examples produces the fallacy known as hasty generalization. It is also known as an unwarranted inductive leap because the conclusion lacks sufficient evidence. When a child concludes that all orange food tastes bad because he dislikes carrots, he has run afoul of this fallacy. Give him an orange popsicle.

9. *Non sequitur*. Latin for "it does not follow," *non sequiturs* skip logical steps in arriving at a conclusion. For example: "If we mandate a new tax on people who work downtown but do not live there, businesses will all leave the city." Really?

10. **Oversimplification/overgeneralization** is an inadequately qualified claim. It may be true that some heavy drinkers are alcoholics, but it would not be fair to claim that all heavy drinking is or leads to alcoholism. As a rule, be wary of "totalizing" or global pronouncements; the bigger the generalization, the more likely it will admit of exceptions.

11. **Poisoning the well**. This fallacy occurs when a person uses loaded language to trivialize or dismiss an argument before even mentioning it. For example: "No reasonable person would swallow that left-wing, tax-and-spend position."

12. **Red herring**. The name comes from the practice of using herring, a smelly fish, to distract dogs from the scent they are supposed to be tracking. A red herring diverts the attention of the audience from the matter at hand, often by provoking them with some loaded or controversial topic not really related to the matter at hand. For example, if you are talking about the quality of different kinds of computers, the issue of whether or not they were made in America would be a red herring.

13. **Slippery slope**. This error is based on the fear that once a move is made in one direction, we will necessarily continue to "slide" in that direction. So, for example, if the U.S. approves medicinal uses of marijuana, soon there will be no control of what is now illicit drug use across the nation. A classic case is offered by the Vietnam War: if a single country was allowed to fall under communist rule, soon all the other countries in the region would follow.

14. **Straw man**. This move involves oversimplifying and even caricaturing another person's argument or position in order to make it easier to refute. For example, opponents of health care reform treat it as a straw man when they claim that such reform would deny benefits to the elderly and perhaps even result in so-called "death panels"—groups who would choose which people will live and which will die.

15. **Weasel word**. A specialized form of equivocation results in what are sometimes called weasel words. As we note earlier, a weasel word is one that has been used so much and so loosely that it ceases to have much meaning (the term derives from the weasel's reputed practice of sucking the contents from an egg without destroying the shell). The word "natural," for example, can mean good, pure, and unsullied, but it can also refer to the ways of nature (flora and fauna). Such

terms ("love," "reality," and "experience" are others) invite equivocation because they mean so many different things to different people.

GUIDELINES FOR ANALYZING ARGUMENTS

1. Make unstated premises (assumptions) explicit.
2. Look for the general principle or reason (warrant) that connects your data ("what have I got to go on?") with your claim.
3. Remember that argument need not be mortal combat: "mutual inquiry or exploration" (as Wayne Booth puts it) is a constructive goal.
4. Be able to state another's position to his or her satisfaction before you agree or disagree with it, as Carl Rogers counsels.
5. Beware of excessively categorical thinking, which produces overstated claims. To remedy, make sure to qualify your claims and check for unstated assumptions.

Assignments: Analyzing Arguments

1. **Find Examples of Any Two of the Logical Fallacies**. You might look in newspapers, online web pages, blogs, and so forth. Copy out the language that contains the fallacy and explain why it is what you say it is.
2. **Find Examples of Figurative Thinking**. Look at prose rather than poetry so that you can locate figurative thinking as it operates in everyday writing. You can choose a piece of academic writing to see how figurative thinking operates there. Or you might look at a magazine feature article or other essay or even in your college catalog. Copy out the relevant language and explain how the figurative thinking works. Use the four-step procedure for exploring the logic of metaphor.
3. **Apply Toulmin's Scheme to an Editorial**. Choose any editorial from your local newspaper and run it through Toulmin's scheme, which we have repeated below:

   - Data: what evidence does the editorial offer in support of its position? (Data respond to the question "What have you got to go on?")
   - Warrant: what general principle or reason is used to connect the data with the claim? (The warrant responds to the question "How did you get there?")
   - Claim: what conclusion does the writer draw?

   After you have anatomized the editorial in these terms, assess its strength more carefully. What do you find most and least convincing about it, and why? Do you detect any logical lapses—into categorical thinking, say, if not actual logical fallacies? Write up your assessment in a few paragraphs.

Chapter 10

Using Evidence to Build a Paper: 10 on 1

IN THIS CHAPTER, WE ARGUE for the importance of saying more about less. The phrase we use for this idea is 10 on 1. The term 10 on 1 was briefly mentioned in Chapter 2, Toolkit of Analytical Methods I, as a variant of Notice and Focus, an observation strategy. In this chapter, 10 on 1 is used to talk about essay structure as well as the analysis of selected data.

The phrase 10 on 1 stands for the principle that it is better to make 10 observations or points about a single representative issue or example (10 on 1) than to make the same basic point about 10 related issues or examples (1 on 10). Doing 10 on 1 teaches writers to narrow their focus and then analyze in depth, drawing out as much meaning as possible from their best examples.

ORGANIZING PAPERS USING 10 ON 1

1. Use The Method or Notice and Focus to find a revealing pattern or tendency in your evidence (see Chapter 2).
2. Select a representative example.
3. Do 10 on 1 to produce an in-depth analysis of your example.
4. Test your results in similar cases.

DEVELOPING A THESIS IS MORE THAN REPEATING AN IDEA

When the time comes to compose a formal paper with a thesis, it is very common for writers to abandon the wealth of data and ideas they have accumulated in the exploratory writing stage, panic, and revert to old habits: "Now I better have my one idea and be able to prove to everybody that I'm right." Out goes careful attention to detail. Out goes any evidence that doesn't fit. Instead of analysis, they substitute the kind of paper we call a *demonstration;* that is, they cite evidence to prove that a generalization is generally true. The problem with the demonstration lies with its too limited notions of what a thesis and evidence can do in a piece of analytical thinking.

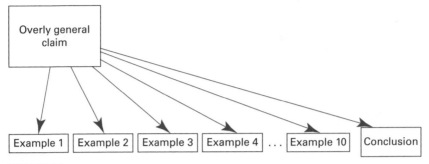

FIGURE 10.1
Doing 1 on 10. The horizontal pattern of 1 on 10 (in which "10" stands arbitrarily for any number of examples) repeatedly makes the same point about every example. Its analysis of evidence is superficial.

A paper produced by repeating a single unchanging idea generally follows the form we call 1 on 10: the writer makes a single and usually very general claim ("History repeats itself," "Exercise is good for you," and so forth) and then proceeds to affix it to 10 examples (see Figure 10.1). A writer who reasserts the same idea about each example is going to produce a list, not a piece of developed thinking. By contrast, in nearly all good writing the thesis evolves by gaining in complexity and, thus, in accuracy as the paper progresses.

The 1 on 10 demonstration results from a mistaken assumption about the function of evidence, that it exists only to demonstrate the validity of (corroborate) a claim. Beyond corroborating claims, evidence should serve to test and develop and evolve the thesis. This is one of the most important points of this chapter.

When and How to Use 1 on 10

Doing 1 on 10 is not always a counterproductive habit of mind. Although collecting a bunch of similar examples of the same phenomenon is unlikely to produce an analytically acute paper, there are occasions when gathering evidence to develop a thesis is essential. It makes sense to do 1 on 10 in order to find an example worth developing because in effect you will be locating a pattern of evidence. The search for repetition that is the first step in The Method is essentially a form of doing 1 on 10.

Noticing a repetition is a key way of ascertaining if a particular kind of evidence is important. If, for example, you discover that revolutionary movements at vastly different historical moments and geographical locales produce similar kinds of violence, it would be essential to demonstrate that pattern before you settled down to analyze one such instance as exemplary. Similarly, when a writer is trying to determine whether there is sufficient evidence to make a claim, it is useful to collect a group of related examples before focusing on the most interesting or revealing ones. If, for example, you were writing about the failure of faith in the biblical book of Exodus, you would do well to chart repeated instances of its failure to substantiate that it is a recurrent feature. But to get beyond this general demonstration, you would need to look more closely at a representative instance.

Sometimes doing 1 on 10 can be valuable in itself, not just as a step in some larger analytical procedure. Demonstrations have their place—short speeches, for example, in situations where the audience has to follow a chain of thought in spite of interference from noise or other distractions.

STUCK IN 1 ON 10: THE PROBLEM OF FIVE-PARAGRAPH FORM

In Chapter 1, we argued that five-paragraph form, an organizational scheme still taught in many high schools, blocks thought. In this chapter, we will be more specific about why this happens and how you can move on to better organizational schemes. *(See Chapter 1, the short take entitled Breaking Out of 5-Paragraph Form.)*

Perhaps the best way to explain the problem with 5-paragraph form can be found in Greek mythology. On his way to Athens, the hero Theseus encounters a particularly surly host, Procrustes, who offers wayfarers a bed for the night but with a catch. If they do not fit his bed exactly, he either stretches them or lops off their extremities until they do. This story has given us the word "procrustean," which the dictionary defines as "tending to produce conformity by violent or arbitrary means." Five-paragraph form is a procrustean formula that most students learn in high school. Although it has the advantage of providing a mechanical format that will give virtually any subject the appearance of order, it usually lops off a writer's ideas before they have the chance to form, or it stretches a single idea to the breaking point.

A complex idea is one that has many sides. To treat such ideas intelligently, writers need a form that will not require them to cut off all of those sides except the one that most easily fits the bed. Most of you will find the basic 5-paragraph form familiar:

1. An introduction that ends with a thesis listing three points (the so-called tripartite thesis)
2. Three body paragraphs, each supporting one of the three points
3. A conclusion beginning "Thus, we see" or "In conclusion" that essentially repeats the thesis statement as it was in paragraph one.

Here is an example in outline form:

Introduction: The food in the school cafeteria is bad. It lacks variety, it's unhealthy, and it is always overcooked. In this essay, I will discuss these three characteristics.

Paragraph 2: The first reason cafeteria food is bad is that there is no variety. (Plus one or two examples—no salad bar, mostly fried food, and so forth)

Paragraph 3: Another reason cafeteria food is bad is that it is not healthy. (Plus a few reasons—high cholesterol, too many hot dogs, too much sugar, and so forth)

Paragraph 4: In addition, the food is always overcooked. (Plus some examples—the vegetables are mushy, the "mystery" meat is tough to recognize, and so forth)

Conclusion: Thus, we see ... (Plus a restatement of the introductory paragraph)

Most high school students write dozens of themes using this basic formula. They are taught to use 5-paragraph form because it seems to provide the greatest good—a certain minimal clarity—for the greatest number of students. But the form does not promote logically tight and thoughtful writing. It is a meat grinder that can turn any content into sausages.

The two major problems it typically creates are easy to see.

1. *The introduction reduces the remainder of the essay to redundancy.* The first paragraph tells readers, in an overly general and list-like way, what they're going to hear; the succeeding three paragraphs tell the readers the same thing again in more detail, carrying the overly general main idea along inertly; and the conclusion repeats what the readers have just been told (twice). The first cause of all this redundancy lies with the thesis. As in the example above, the thesis (cafeteria food is "bad") is too broad—an unqualified and obvious generalization—and substitutes a simple list of predictable points for a complex statement of idea.

2. *The form arbitrarily divides content:* why are there three points (or examples or reasons) instead of five or one? A quick look at the three categories in our example reveals how arbitrarily the form has divided the subject. Isn't overcooked food unhealthy? Isn't a lack of variety also conceivably unhealthy? The format invites writers to list rather than analyze, to plug supporting examples into categories without examining them or how they are related. Five-paragraph form, as is evident in our sample's transitions ("first," "second," "in addition"), counts things off but doesn't make logical connections. At its worst, the form prompts the writer to simply append evidence to generalizations without saying anything about it.

The subject, on the other hand, is not as unpromising as the format makes it appear. It could easily be redirected along a more productive pathway. (If the food is bad, what are the underlying causes of the problem? Are students getting what they ask for? Is the problem one of cost? Is the faculty cafeteria better? Why or why not?)

Now let's look briefly at the introductory paragraph from a student's essay on a more academic subject. Here we can see a remarkable feature of 5-paragraph form—its capacity to produce the same kind of say-nothing prose on almost any subject.

> Throughout the film *The Tempest*, a version of Shakespeare's play *The Tempest*, there were a total of nine characters. These characters were Calibano, Alonso, Antonio, Aretha, Freddy, the doctor, and Dolores. Each character in the film represented a person in Shakespeare's play, but there were four people who were greatly similar to those in Shakespeare, and who played a role in symbolizing aspects of forgiveness, love, and power.

The final sentence of the paragraph reveals the writer's addiction to 5-paragraph form. It signals that the writer will proceed in a purely mechanical and superficial way, producing a paragraph on forgiveness, a paragraph on love, a paragraph on power, and a conclusion stating again that the film's characters resemble Shakespeare's in these three aspects. The writer is so busy *demonstrating* that the characters are concerned with forgiveness, love, and power that she misses the opportunity to analyze the significance of her own observations. Instead, readers are drawn wearily to a conclusion; they get no place except back where they began. Further, the demonstration mode prevents her from analyzing connections among the categories. The writer might consider, for example, how the play and the film differ in resolving the conflict between power and forgiveness (focusing on difference within similarity) and to what extent the film and the play agree about which is the most important of the three aspects (focusing on similarity despite difference).

These more analytical approaches lie concealed in the writer's introduction, but they never get discovered because the 5-paragraph form militates against sustained analytical thinking. Its division of the subject into parts, which is only one part of analysis, has become an end unto itself. The procrustean formula insists on a tripartite list in which each of the three parts is separate, equal, and above all, inert.

Here are two quick checks for whether a paper of yours has closed down your thinking through a scheme such as 5-paragraph form:

1. *Look at the paragraph openings.* If these read like a list, each beginning with an additive transition like "another" followed by a more or less exact repetition of your central point ("another example is…," "yet another example is…"), you should suspect that you are not adequately developing your ideas.

2. *Compare the wording in the last statement of the paper's thesis (in the conclusion) with the first statement of it in the introduction.* If the wording at these two locations is virtually the same, you will know that your thesis has not responded adequately to your evidence.

ANALYZING EVIDENCE IN DEPTH: "10 ON 1"

The practice called 10 on 1 focuses analysis on a representative example. In doing 10 on 1, you are taking one part of the whole, putting it under a microscope, and then generalizing about the whole on the basis of analyzing a single part.

- The phrase 10 on 1 means 10 observations and implications about one representative piece of evidence (where 10 is an arbitrary number meaning "many").
- The phrase 1 on 10 means one general point attached to 10 pieces of evidence.

As a guideline, 10 on 1 will lead you to draw out as much meaning as possible from your best example—a case of narrowing the focus and then analyzing in depth (see Figure 10.2). Eventually, you will move from this key example to others that usefully extend and qualify your point, but first you need to let analysis of your representative example produce more thinking.

You can use 10 on 1 to accomplish various ends: (1) to locate the range of possible meanings your evidence suggests; (2) to make you less inclined to cling to your first

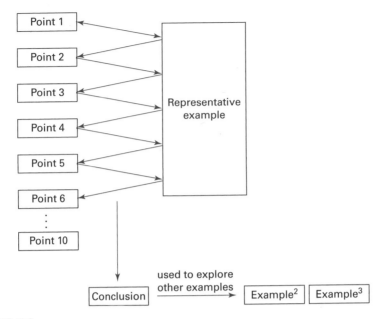

FIGURE 10.2
Doing 10 on 1. The pattern of 10 on 1 (in which "10" stands arbitrarily for any number of points) successively develops a series of points about a single representative example. Its analysis of evidence is in depth.

claim; (3) to open the way for you to discover the complexity of your subject; and (4) to slow down the rush to generalization and thus help to ensure that when you arrive at a working thesis, it will be more specific and better able to account for your evidence.

Demonstrating the Representativeness of Your Example

Focusing on your single best example has the advantage of economy, cutting to the heart of the subject, but it runs the risk that the example you select might not in fact be representative. Thus, to be safe, you need to demonstrate its representativeness overtly. This means showing that your example is part of a larger pattern of similar evidence and not just an isolated instance. To establish that pattern, it is useful to do 1 on 10—locating 10 examples that share a trait—as a preliminary step and then select one of these for in-depth analysis.

In terms of logic, the problem of generalizing from too little and unrepresentative evidence is known as an unwarranted inductive leap. The writer leaps from one or two instances to a broad claim about an entire class or category. Just because you see an economics professor and a biology professor wearing corduroy jackets, for example, you would not want to leap to the conclusion that all professors wear corduroy jackets. Most of the time, unwarranted leaps result from making too large a claim and avoiding examples that might contradict it.

10 on 1 and Disciplinary Conventions

In some cases, the conventions of a discipline appear to discourage doing 10 on 1. The social sciences in particular tend to require a larger set of analogous examples to prove a hypothesis. Especially in certain kinds of research, the focus of inquiry rests on discerning broad statistical trends over a wide range of evidence. But some trends deserve more attention than others, and some statistics similarly merit more interpretation than others. The best writers learn to choose examples carefully—each one for a reason—and to concentrate on developing the most revealing ones in depth.

For instance, proving that tax laws are prejudiced in particularly subtle ways against unmarried people might require a number of analogous cases along with a statistical summary of the evidence. But even with a subject such as this, you could still concentrate on some examples more than others. Rather than moving through each example as a separate case, you could use your analyses of these primary examples as lenses for investigating other evidence.

PAN, TRACK, AND ZOOM: USING 10 ON 1 TO BUILD A PAPER

How can 10 on 1 generate the form of a paper? The language of filmmaking offers a useful way for understanding the different ways a writer can focus evidence. The writer, like the director of a film, controls the focus through different kinds of shots.

The pan—The camera pivots around a stable axis, giving the viewer the big picture. Using a pan, we see everything from a distance. Pans provide a context, some larger pattern, the "forest" within which the writer can also examine particular "trees." Pans establish the representativeness of the example the writer later examines in more detail, showing that it is not an isolated instance.

The track—The camera no longer stays in one place but follows some sequence of action. For example, whereas a pan might survey a room full of guests at a cocktail party, a track would pick up a particular guest and follow along as she walks across the room, picks up a photograph, proceeds through the door, and throws the photo in a trash can. Analogously, a writer tracks by moving in on selected pieces of the larger picture and following them to make telling connections among them.

The zoom—The camera moves in even closer on a selected piece of the scene, allowing us to notice more of its details. For example, a zoom might focus in on the woman's hand as she crumples the photograph she's about to throw away or on her face as she slams the lid on the trash can. A writer zooms in by giving us more detail on a particular part of the evidence and making the details say more. The zoom is the shot that enables you to do 10 on 1.

In a short paper (three to five pages), you might devote as much as 90 percent of your writing to exploring what one example (the "1"—your zoom) reveals about the larger subject. Even in a paper that uses several examples, however, as much as 50 percent might still be devoted to analysis of and generalization from a single case. The remaining portion of the paper would make connections with other examples, testing and applying the ideas you arrived at from your single case. In-depth analysis of your best example thus creates a center from which you can move in two directions: (1) toward generalizations about the larger subject and (2) toward other examples, using your primary example as a tool of exploration.

Doing 10 on 1: A Brief Example (Tiananmen Square)

Note how the writer of the following discussion of the people's revolt in China in 1989 sets up his analysis. He first explains how his chosen example—a classic photograph (shown in Figure 10.3) from the media coverage of the event—illuminates his larger subject. The image is of a Chinese man in a white shirt who temporarily halted a line of tanks on their way to quell a demonstration in Tiananmen Square in Beijing.

> The tank image provided a miniature, simplified version of a larger, more complex revolution. The conflict between man and tank embodied the same tension found in the conflict between student demonstrators and the Peoples' Army. The man in the white shirt, like the students, displayed courage, defiance, and rebellious individuality in the face of power. Initially, the peaceful revolution succeeded: the state allowed the students

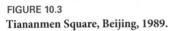

FIGURE 10.3
Tiananmen Square, Beijing, 1989.

to protest; likewise, the tank spared the man's life. Empowered, the students' demands for democracy grew louder. Likewise, the man boldly jumped onto the tank and addressed the soldiers. The state's formerly unshakable dominance appeared weak next to the strength of the individual. However, the state asserted its power: the Peoples' Army marched into the square, and the tanks roared past the man into Beijing.

The image appeals to American ideology. The man in the white shirt personifies the strength of the American individual. His rugged courage draws on contemporary heroes such as Rambo. His defiant gestures resemble the demonstrations of Martin Luther King Jr. and his followers. American history predisposes us to identify strongly with the Chinese demonstrators: we have rebelled against the establishment, we have fought for freedom and democracy, and we have defended the rights of the individual. For example, the *New York Times* reported that President George [H. W.] Bush watched the tank incident on television and said, "I'm convinced that the forces of democracy are going to overcome these unfortunate events in Tiananmen Square." Bush represents the popular American perspective of the Chinese rebellion; we support the student demonstrators.

This analysis is a striking example of doing 10 on 1. In the first paragraph, the writer constructs a detailed analogy between the particular image and the larger subject of which it was a part. The analogy allows the writer not just to describe but also to interpret the event. In the second paragraph, he develops his focus on the image as an image, a photographic representation tailor-made to appeal to American viewing audiences. Rather than generalizing about why Americans might find the image appealing, he establishes a number of explicit connections (does 10 on 1) between the details of the image and typical American heroes. By drawing out the implications of particular details, he manages to say more about the significance of the American response to the demonstrations in China than a broader survey of those events would have allowed.

Try This 10.1: Doing 10 on 1 with Newspaper Visuals

Search out photographs in the newspaper and do 10 on 1. Or alternatively, spend some time doing 10 on 1 on a comic strip. What perspectives emerge once you have restricted the focus? List details, but also list multiple implications. Remember to ask not just What do I notice? but What else do I notice? And not just What does it imply? but What else might it imply?

Try This 10.2: Doing 10 on 1 with a Reading

Take a piece of reading—a representative example—from something you are studying and do 10 on 1. The key to doing 10 on 1 successfully is to slow down the rush to conclusions so that you can allow yourself to notice more about the evidence and make the details speak. The more observations you assemble about your data before settling on your main idea, the better that idea is likely to be. Remember that a single, well-developed paragraph from something you are reading can be enough to practice on, especially because you are working on saying more about less rather than less about more.

CONVERTING 1 ON 10 INTO 10 ON 1: A STUDENT PAPER (FLOOD STORIES)

The following student paper, about the recurrence of flood stories in religious texts and myth, shows what happens when a writer falls into doing 1 on 10. That is, rather than zooming in on representative examples to test and refine his ideas, he attaches the same underdeveloped point to each of his examples. Typical of the 1-on-10 pattern, the flood paper views everything from the same relatively unrevealing distance.

In the essay that follows, we have used boldface to track the "one" point—the as-yet-underdeveloped thesis idea—that the writer has attached to each of his examples (1 on 10). Brackets and ellipses [...] indicate where we have abridged the essay.

Flood Stories

[1] **The role of people**, as reflected in Genesis, Ovid's *Metamorphoses*, and the *Epic of Gilgamesh*, **is solely to please the gods**. Men, as the gods' subordinates, exist to do right in the gods' eyes **and make them feel more like gods**; for without men, whom could the gods be gods of? [...]

[2] In Genesis, for example, God created humans in his own image or likeness, and **when they displeased Him**, He destroyed them. If God could see wickedness in his creations, perhaps it was like seeing wickedness in himself. Further, the idea of having evidence of God being able to create an imperfect, "wicked" race of humans may have been a point God wasn't willing to deal with: "The Lord saw that the wickedness of man was great in the earth, and that every imagination of the thoughts of his heart was only evil continually. And the Lord was sorry that he had made man on the earth and it grieved him to his heart." It seems as though **God had become unhappy with his creations** so they

were to be destroyed. Like a toy a child no longer has use for, humankind was to be wasted.

[3] Similarly, in Ovid's *Metamorphoses*, God made humanity and "fashioned it into the image of the all-governing gods." Again here, humans were made in the gods' image to serve as an everlasting monument of their glorification, to honor them and do good by them. In other words, **humans spent less time making the gods happy and therefore made them unhappy.** Some men even questioned the reality of the gods' existence and the strength of their power. Lyacon, for example, had a driving tendency to try to belittle the gods and make them look like fools. **The gods were very displeased** with this trend, and now the entire race had to be destroyed. A flood would be sent to wipe out the race of men. *[The writer then summarizes several examples in which the wicked are destroyed and a few upstanding citizens are preserved and arrives at the following conclusion:]*Thus, the justification of yet another flood to appease the gods' egos.

[4] Further evidence of **humans as being a mere whim of the gods to make them happy** lies in the flood story in the *Epic of Gilgamesh.* It is obvious **the gods weren't concerned with humankind, but rather with their own comfort.** As the story goes, Enlil, the god of earth, wind, and air, couldn't bear the noise humans were making while he tried to sleep, so he gathered all the gods together, and thus they jointly decided to get rid of their grief of having all the humans around by destroying them. Ea [the god of wisdom], however, warned one man (Utnapishtim) of the flood to come. He told him to build a boat for himself and his wife and for the "seeds of all living creatures." [...]

[5] Enlil later repented the harshness of his actions, deified Utnapishtim and his wife and then had the two live far away "on the distance of the rivers' mouths." It possibly **could have been belittling** to have Utnapishtim and his wife speaking to the new race of humans in terms of how rash and mindlessly the gods were capable of acting, so he immortalized them and had them live far out of the reach of human ears—"the secret of the gods."

[6] It seems that the **main objective of the gods was to remain gods; for that is what made them happy. And humanity's role, then, was as the gods' stepping-stone to their happiness.** [...] Witnessing the fall of humankind, for the gods, was like witnessing imperfection in themselves, and thus their fall;

anything causing these feelings didn't do the gods any good and therefore could be terminated without a second thought. **It was the job of human beings to make the gods happy**, and upon failure at this task, they could be "fired" (death), only to be replaced later—it wasn't a position which the gods could hold vacant for long. Thus were the great flood stories.

The essay starts with a pan on the "big picture." Panning on all three stories has allowed the writer to discover similarities among his blocks of evidence and to demonstrate that the examples he has chosen are representative of his generalization—his claim—that in all three flood stories men exist "solely to please the gods."

The writer then constructs a series of tracks, summaries of each of the three stories that isolate some interesting parallels for readers to ponder. But at this point, rather than allowing his tracks to set up zooms, the writer returns again and again to versions of his original pan. In other words, a reflex move to 1-on-10 leads him to repeatedly match the evidence to his one governing claim.

To develop his central claim, the writer needs to devote much less space to repeating that claim, and more to actually looking at key pieces of evidence, zooming in on significant variations within the general pattern. In his second paragraph, for example, the writer allows the 1-on-10 pattern to rush his thinking and distract him from his evidence. He claims that the God of Genesis "had become unhappy with his creations so they were to be destroyed. Like a toy a child no longer has use for, humankind was to be wasted."

This claim fits Enlil, the god in *Gilgamesh* who, as we are later told, decides to get rid of humans because they make too much noise. But it does not so easily fit the God of Genesis, about whom the writer has just told us that "the wickedness of man...grieved him to his heart." If he did 10 on 1 on this passage, slowing down to think about the evidence, the writer would likely see that the difference between the two gods is significant. The grief that his evidence mentions suggests that God's decision to flood the earth was possibly ethical rather than childishly selfish and rash. And the statement from Genesis that "every imagination of the thoughts of [man's] heart was only evil continually" might lead him to see that humans were not simply victims of divine prerogative, but rather that they deserved punishment.

The writer doesn't consider these other possible interpretations because his reliance on pans—the general pattern—has predisposed him to see his evidence only as another sign of the gods' egotism, their desire to remain "happy" at any cost.

Revising the Draft Using 10 on 1 and Difference Within Similarity

How might the writer make better use of the evidence he has collected, using the principle of looking for difference within similarity?

Revision Strategy 1: *Assume that the essay's "answer"—its conclusion about the evidence—does not yet go far enough.* Rather than having to throw out his thinking, the writer should consider, as is almost always the case in revision, that he hasn't refined his initial idea enough. As an interpretation of the evidence, it leaves too much unaccounted for.

Revision Strategy 2: *Find a "1" to use with 10 on 1—a piece of the evidence sufficiently revealing to be analyzed in more detail; then zoom in on it.* In the case of the writer of "Flood Stories," that 1 might be a single story, which he could examine in more detail. He could then test his claims about this story through comparison and contrast with the other stories. In the existing draft, the writer has not used comparison and contrast to refine his conclusion; he has just imposed the same conclusion on the other stories. Alternatively, the 1 might be the single most interesting feature that the three stories share.

Revision Strategy 3: *To find the most revealing piece or feature of the evidence, keep asking, What can be said with some certainty about the evidence?* This question will induce a writer to rehearse the facts to keep them fresh, so that his or her first impressions don't "contaminate" or distort consideration of subsequent evidence.

If the writer were to apply these strategies, he might have a conversation with himself that sounded something like this:

"What can I say with some certainty about my evidence?"

"In all three of these stories, a first civilization created by a god is destroyed by the same means—a flood."

Notice that this is a factual description of the evidence rather than a speculation about it. You are always better off to report the facts in your evidence carefully and fully before moving to conclusions. (This is harder to do than you might think.)

"What else is certain about the evidence?"

"In each case the gods leave a surviving pair to rebuild the civilization rather than just wiping everybody out and inventing a new kind of being. Interestingly, the gods begin again by choosing from the same stock that failed the first time around."

Mulling over the evidence in this way—taking care to lay out the facts and distinguish them from speculation—can help you decide what evidence to zoom in on. One of the chief advantages of zooms is that they get you in close enough to your evidence to see the questions its details imply.

Revision Strategy 4: *Examine the evidence closely enough to see what questions the details imply and what other patterns they reveal.* So far, the writer has worked mostly from two quite general questions: Why did the gods decide to wipe out their creations? And why do the gods need human beings? But there are other questions his evidence might prompt him to ask. In each story, for example, the gods are disappointed by humankind, yet they don't invent submissive robots who will dedicate their lives to making the deities feel good about themselves. Why not? This question might cause the writer to uncover a shared feature of his examples (a pattern) that he has thus far not considered—the surviving pairs.

Revision Strategy 5: *Uncover implications in your zoom that can develop your interpretation further.* Having selected the surviving pairs for more detailed examination, what might the writer conclude about them? One interesting fact that the surviving pairs reveal is that the flood stories are not only descriptions of the end of a world but also creation accounts, because they also tell us how a new civilization, the existing one, got started.

Revision Strategy 6: *Look for difference within similarity to better focus the thesis.* Given the recurrence of the survival pairs in the three stories, where might the writer locate a significant difference? One potentially significant difference involves the survival pair in the story of Gilgamesh, who are segregated from the new world and granted immortality. Perhaps this separation suggests that the new civilization will not be haunted by the painful memory of a higher power's intervention, leaving humans less fearful of what might happen in the future. This distinction could focus the argument in the essay; it does not distract from the writer's overall generalization but rather develops it.

Revision Strategy 7: *Constellate the evidence to experiment with alternative thesis options.* Notice how the hypothetical revision we've been producing has made use of looking for difference within similarity to explore alternative ways of connecting the evidence—a selected set of zooms—into an overall explanation. We call this activity *constellating the evidence*: like the imaginary lines that connect real stars into a recognizable shape, your thinking configures the examples into some larger meaning. In this case, instead of repeatedly concluding that the gods destroy humans when humans fail to make them happy, the writer might be on his way to a thesis about the relative optimism or skepticism of the way the flood stories represent change.

- Possible thesis #1: The flood stories propose the view that real change is necessarily apocalyptic rather than evolutionary.

- Possible thesis #2: The flood stories present qualified optimism about the possibility of new starts.

Try This 10.3: Describing Evidence

Have a conversation with yourself (on paper) about some piece of evidence you are studying. Start with the question we proposed for the student writer of the flood stories essay: What can be said with some certainty about this evidence? What, in other words, is clearly true of the data? What can be reported about it as fact without going on to interpretation of the facts?

This distinction between fact and interpretation can be a tricky one, but it is also essential because, if you can't keep your data separate from what you've begun to think about them, you risk losing sight of the data altogether. Press yourself to keep answering the same question—What can be said with some certainty about this evidence? or a variant of the question, such as What's clearly true of this evidence is....

You may find it helpful to do this exercise with a partner or in a small group. If you work in a small group, have one member record the results as these emerge. You might also try this exercise as a freewrite and then share your results with others by reading aloud your list of facts or putting them on a blackboard along with other people's results. Once you've assembled a list of what can fairly be stated as fact about your evidence, you are ready to start on some version of the question, What do these facts suggest? or What features of these data seem most to invite/require interpretation?

DOING 10 ON 1: A STUDENT PAPER (*GOOD BYE LENIN!*)

The essay below is an exploratory draft on a film, using a single scene to generate its thinking. As you read the essay, watch how the writer uses 10 on 1. Unlike "Flood Stories," in which the writer felt compelled to make all of his evidence fit a narrow thesis, here the writer repeatedly tests her tentative conclusions against the evidence until she arrives at a plausible *working thesis* that might organize the next draft.

Think of the working thesis as an ultimate So what?—the product of other, smaller interpretive leaps along the way. As we did in Chapter 6 Interpretation, we have written in the So what? prompt where the writer has used it to move from observation to implication to conclusions. Notice how the writer allows her evidence to complicate and stimulate her thinking rather than just confirm (corroborate) her general idea.

On the Edge: A Scene from *Good Bye Lenin!*

[1] The movie shows us Alex and Lara's first date, which is to a sort of underground music club where the performers wear costumes made of plastic tubing and leather, and play loud hard-core rock music. At first, the musicians look surreal, as though they are part of a strange dream from which, at any moment, Alex will awake. The Western rock is real, though, as are the sci-fi costumes, and the scene moves forward to show Alex and Lara climbing a stairway out onto what looks like a fire escape and then through a window and into an apartment.

[2] Here, Alex and Lara settle down into conversation. The young couple sits, hand in hand, and gazes together into the night sky; yet, as the camera pans away, we see that the apartment where the two have retreated is missing its façade. Inside, three walls are still decorated, complete with furniture, wallpaper, and even working lamps; yet, the two sit on the ledge of the fourth wall, which has crumbled away completely.

[3] *[So what?:]* On the surface, I think the movie invites us to read this as a visual representation of the new lives Alex, Lara, and the other characters face now that the wall has fallen. As a Westerner, at first I read this scene as a representation of the

new relationship between Lara and Alex. In other words, I imagined the movie's placement of the couple on the ledge of a domestic space as a representation of where their lives were going together—toward some shared domestic life, toward living together, toward becoming a family. I also thought this was a clever representation of the collapse of communism— this wall has also fallen down.

[4] *[Complicating evidence:]* I don't think, however, that the movie lets us entertain this one romanticized reading of the scene for long—the image is too frightening. As the camera pans away, we see that this isn't a new Westernized apartment; this is an East German flat decorated in much the same way as Alex's home was only months before. The image is alarming; the wall here has been ripped down, *[so what?:]* and we are forced to ask, did the fall of communism violently blow apart domestic and daily living of East German people?

[5] The movie allows us this dichotomy and, I think, fights to sustain it. On one hand, Alex and Lara would not be on this date if the wall hadn't come down, and yet the scene is more than just another representation of East Germany torn between Communism and the new Westernization. *[Working thesis:]* The movie tries hard to remind us that the rapid Westernization of East Germany devastated while it liberated in other ways. This scene uses space to represent Alex and Lara's (and East Germany's) dilemma: Alex and Lara gaze out at the night sky but only because the wall has been blown apart. The exposed apartment is uninhabitable and yet the lights still work, the pictures are still hung, and a young couple leans against one another inside.

This draft is a good example of a writer using evidence to complicate as well as support her claims. Her thinking evolves through successive complications; that is, she complicates a previous claim that was a complication. When the writer arrives at tentative answers, she tests them rather than just adding more evidence to prove she is right.

Try This 10.4: Marking Claims, Evidence, and Complications in a Draft

As a check on the range of concepts that this and the previous chapter have introduced, mark the student draft as follows:

- *Mark claims—assertions made about the evidence—with the letter C.* Claims are ideas that the evidence seems to support. An example of a claim is in paragraph 4: "I don't think, however, that the movie lets us entertain this one romanticized reading of the scene for long."

- *Underline evidence.* The evidence is the pool of primary material (data)—details from the film, rather than the writer's ideas about it. An example of evidence is in paragraph 2: "The young couple sits, hand in hand, and gazes together into the night sky; yet, as the camera pans away, we see that the apartment where the two have retreated is missing its façade." This piece of evidence is the 1 of the 10 on 1. In effect, the whole draft goes after the range of possible implications that may be inferred from the image of the young couple sitting at the edge of an apartment that is missing one of its walls, presumably a result of war damage.

- *Circle complications.* Complications can be found both in the evidence a writer cites and in the claims a writer makes about it. Complicating evidence is evidence that does not fit the claims the writer has been making. For example, in paragraph 4: "As the camera pans away, we see that this isn't a new Westernized apartment; this is an East German flat decorated in much the same way as Alex's home was only months before. The image is alarming; the wall here has been ripped down." This evidence causes the writer to reconsider an earlier claim from paragraph 3, that the scene is about the couple moving "toward some shared domestic life, toward living together, toward becoming a family."

A TEMPLATE FOR ORGANIZING PAPERS USING 10 ON 1: AN ALTERNATIVE TO FIVE-PARAGRAPH FORM

Here is a template for writing papers using 10 on 1. It brings together much of the key terminology introduced in this chapter. Think of it not as a rigid format but as an outline for moving from one phase of your paper to the next. Unlike five-paragraph form, the template will give you room to think and to establish connections among your ideas.

1. In your introduction, start by noting (panning on) an interesting pattern or tendency you have found in your evidence. (As explained at the beginning of the chapter, you may find it useful to do 1 on 10 in order to discover the pattern.) Explain what attracted you to it—why you find it potentially significant and worth looking at. This paragraph would end with a tentative theory (working thesis) about what this pattern or tendency might reveal or accomplish.

2. Zoom in on your representative example, some smaller part of the larger pattern and argue for its representativeness and usefulness in coming to a better understanding of your subject.

3. Do 10 on 1—analyze your representative example—sharing with your readers your observations (what you notice) and your tentative conclusions (answers

to the So what? question). Then use complicating evidence to refine your claims.

4a. In a short paper, you might at this point move to your conclusion, with its qualified, refined version of your thesis and brief commentary on what you've accomplished, that is, the ways in which your analysis has illuminated the larger subject.

4b. In a longer paper, you would begin constellating—organizing the essay by exploring and elaborating the connections among your representative examples analyzed via 10 on 1. In the language of the film analogy, you would move from your initial zoom to another zoom on a similar case, to see the extent to which the thesis you evolved with your representative example needed further adjusting to better reflect the nature of your subject as a whole. This last move is a primary topic of our next chapter.

GUIDELINES FOR USING EVIDENCE TO BUILD A PAPER: 10 ON 1

1. Learn to recognize unsubstantiated assertions, rather than treating claims as self-evident truths. Whenever you make a claim, offer your readers the evidence that led you to it.

2. Make details speak. Explain how evidence confirms or qualifies your claim, and offer your reasons for believing the evidence means what you say it does.

3. Say more about less rather than less about more, allowing a carefully analyzed part of your subject to provide perspective on the whole.

4. It is generally better to make ten points on a representative issue or example than to make the same basic point about ten related issues or examples; this axiom we call 10 on 1.

5. Argue overtly that the evidence on which you choose to focus is representative. Be careful not to generalize on the basis of too little or unrepresentative evidence.

6. Use your best example as a lens through which to examine other evidence. Analyze subsequent examples to test and develop your conclusions, rather than just confirming that you are right.

7. Look for difference within similarity as a way of doing 10 on 1. Rather than repeating the same overly general claim (i.e., doing 1 on 10), use significant variation within the general pattern to better develop your claim.

8. To find the most revealing piece or feature of the evidence, keep asking yourself, "What can I say with some certainty about the evidence?" If you continually rehearse the facts, you are less likely to let an early idea blind you to subsequent evidence.

Assignment: Writing a Paper Using the 10 on 1 Template

Write a paper in which you do 10 on 1 with a single representative example of something you are trying to think more carefully about. The template should work with virtually any content. It could be an in-depth look at a particular kind of film (vampire films or feel-good sports stories or tragic death at an early age films), or the advertisements for a particular product (cars, make-up, hair care, sports equipment, suntan lotion). It could be a more academic subject: economic stimulus packages, government bail-outs, intelligence tests, failed revolutions, successful fascist dictatorships. You might choose a representative passage from a story or a representative story from a volume of stories by a single author—or a representative poem from a short volume of poetry or a representative passage from a nonfiction book or article. It could be a passage from a favorite columnist or a single representative song from a CD. It could be a single scene or moment or character from a film or play or other performance. It could be one picture or work of art that is representative of a larger exhibit.

Brainstorm your "1" on the page, making observations and asking, So what? Draw out as much meaning as possible from your representative example. Go for depth. Then use this example as a lens for viewing similar examples. Remember to use the template in the previous section as a model for organizing the paper.

Chapter 11

Making a Thesis Evolve

THIS CHAPTER IS AT THE HEART of what we have to say about essay writing, especially about the function of thesis statements. The chapter argues that even in a final draft a thesis develops through successive complications; it doesn't remain static, as people tend to believe. Even in cases such as the report format of the natural and social sciences, where the thesis itself cannot change, there is still development between the beginning of the paper and the end. The thesis, usually called a hypothesis, is tested in various ways in order to evaluate its adequacy.

Formulating a claim, seeking conflicting evidence, and then using these conflicts to revise the claim is a primary movement of mind in analytical writing. Here's the mantra: *the complications you encounter are an opportunity to make your thesis evolve*, not a problem. An evolving thesis is one that responds more fully and accurately to evidence.

This chapter contains one heuristic, Six Steps for Making a Thesis Evolve Through Successive Complications. Here is a skeletal version of this process, which the chapter will demonstrate and define in more detail.

SIX STEPS FOR MAKING A THESIS EVOLVE THROUGH SUCCESSIVE COMPLICATIONS

1. Formulate an idea about your subject, a working thesis.
2. See how far you can make this thesis go in accounting for confirming evidence.
3. Locate evidence that is not adequately accounted for by the thesis.
4. Make explicit the apparent mismatch between the thesis and selected evidence, asking and answering "so what?"
5. Reshape your claim to accommodate the evidence that hasn't fit.
6. Repeat steps 2, 3, 4, and 5 several times.

Your ability to discover ideas and improve on them in revision, as we've argued in the preceding chapters, depends largely on your attitude toward evidence—on your ability to use it as a means of testing and developing your ideas rather than just (statically) confirming and reasserting them.

MOVING FROM IDEA TO THESIS STATEMENT: WHAT A GOOD THESIS LOOKS LIKE

Considerable misunderstanding exists about thesis statements among students—and among many teachers. We have chosen to use the term "thesis" because, by and large, it is the most common term across the academic disciplines for what might otherwise be called a "controlling idea" or "primary claim" or "hypothesis." The term has a long history, going back to classical rhetoric wherein a thesis involved taking a position on some subject. The term "thesis" named general questions with wide applications. The term "hypothesis" was used "to name a specific question that involved actual persons, places, or events" (Crowley 57). (For an excellent discussion of the history of these terms, see Sharon Crowley and Debra Hawhee, *Ancient Rhetorics for Contemporary Students.*)

This idea of "taking a position," as in an argument, is what some faculty members dislike about the term, mistaking it perhaps for an invitation to writers to express their views on a subject rather than closely examining it. For every faculty member who wishes student writers to organize their thinking around a clearly-defined central claim (thesis), other faculty members argue that thesis-driven writing and reflective writing differ in methods and goals.

In the meantime, we will continue to use the term thesis, though not in the way it is often described in writing textbooks, where it is presented as a static idea that a writer sets out to prove. Our use of the term is probably closer to the idea of a "hypothesis," which has come to mean a theory to be tested.

Arriving at Thesis Statements: When and Where

The most disabling misunderstanding for students is that a writer needs to have a thesis before he or she begins writing. Good thesis statements are the product of writing, not its precursor. Worrying about having a thesis statement too early in the writing process will just about guarantee papers that support overly general and often obvious ideas. Arriving prematurely at claims also blinds writers to complicating evidence (evidence that runs counter to the thesis) and so deprives them of their best opportunities to arrive at better ideas.

Another disabling assumption is that the thesis of a paper must always appear at or near the end of the first paragraph, preferably in the form of a single-sentence claim. The fact is that the governing idea of most analytical writing is too complex to be asserted as a single-sentence claim that could be understood at the beginning of the paper. *Nevertheless*, it is true that a writer has not moved from the exploratory writing phase to the writing of a paper until he or she has discovered an idea around which his or her thinking can cohere. Without a governing idea to hold onto, readers will not understand why you are telling them what you are telling them. In order for a paper to make sense to readers, a thesis, or, in the case of inductively organized papers, a thesis "trail" (some sense of the issues and questions that are generating the paper's forward momentum) must be evident. (See *The Shaping Force of Common Thought Patterns: Deduction and Induction* in Chapter 15.)

The best way to learn about thesis statements is to look for them in published writing. You will find that the single-sentence thesis statement as prescribed in writing textbooks is a rather rare specimen. It is most common in argument, wherein a writer has a proposition that he or she wants readers to either adopt or dismiss. In analytical writing, the thesis is more likely to become evident in phases, guided by some kind of opening claim sufficient to get the paper started. This claim is commonly known as the **working thesis**. Sometimes as much as the first third of a paper will explore an idea that the rest of the paper will subsequently replace with a different, though not necessarily opposing perspective. If you look closely, however, you will see the trail that lets readers anticipate a shift from one possible way of seeing things to another.

Strong versus Weak Thesis Statements

A thesis is an idea. It is a thought that you have arrived at about your evidence, rather than something you can expect to find, ready-made, in whatever you are studying. A strong thesis is a theory about the meaning and significance of your evidence that would not have been immediately obvious to your readers. A weak thesis either makes no claim or makes a claim that doesn't need proving, such as a statement of fact or an opinion with which virtually all of your readers would most likely agree before reading your essay (for example, "exercise is good for you").

Analytical writing begins with something puzzling that the writer wishes to better understand. Strong thesis statements enable exploration. Weak thesis statements disable exploration by closing things down way too tightly at the outset.

Here are two characteristics that an idea needs to possess in order to work as a thesis.

- the thesis of an analytical paper is an idea about what some feature or features of your subject *means*
- a thesis should be an idea in need of argument; that is, it should not be a statement of fact or an idea with which most readers would already agree.

Finding the Tension in Good Thesis Statements

In the Try This on the next page are six examples of good thesis statements, that is, good translations of ideas into forms that could direct the development of an essay. The first thing you should notice about all of these thesis statements is the presence of tension—the pressure of one idea against another idea, of one potentially viable way of seeing things against another viable, but finally less satisfactory way of seeing things. Good ideas usually take place with the aid of some kind of back pressure, by which we mean that the idea takes shape by pushing against (so to speak) another way of seeing things. This is not the same as setting out to overturn and completely refute one idea in favor of another (although thesis statements sometimes work in this way too). More often what happens is that the thesis statement's primary idea emerges as some kind of clarification or reworking of another idea. The forward momentum of the thesis comes from playing the newer idea off of the older one.

Try This 11.1: Spotting the Tension in Good Thesis Statements

Look at the thesis statements below, all of which were taken from published analytical essays. Find the tension in each, or the defining pressure of one idea against another possibility. In the first thesis sentence, for example, the primary idea is that the new advertising campaign for Docker trousers is radical. The back pressure against which this idea takes shape is that this new campaign may not seem radical. The writer will demonstrate the truth of both of these claims, rather than overturning one and then championing the other. The same can be said of the parts of the second thesis statement. The primary idea, recognizable by the syntax of the second sentence, is that cosmetic surgery will make life worse for everyone. The back pressure against which this idea will take shape is the claim that cosmetic surgery has psychologicial benefits; it makes individual people happier.

Notice that the thesis statement does not simply say: "Cosmetic surgery is bad." The writer's job will be to demonstrate that the potential harm of cosmetic surgery outweighs the benefits, but the benefits won't be just summarily dismissed. Both of the two ideas are to some extent true. Neither idea, in other words, is **a straw man**—the somewhat deceptive argumentative practice of setting up a dummy position solely because it is easy to knock down. A straw man does not strengthen a thesis statement because it fails to provide genuine back pressure.

1) It may not seem like it, but "Nice Pants" is as radical a campaign as the original Docker series.

2) If opponents of cosmetic surgery are too quick to dismiss those who claim great psychological benefits, protesters are far too willing to dismiss those who raise concerns. Cosmetic surgery might make individual people happier, but in the aggregate it makes life worse for everyone.

3) The history of thought in the modern era of history of thinking about the self may be an exaggeration, but the consequences of this vision of a self set apart have surely been felt in every field of inquiry.

4) We may join with the modern builders in justifying the violence of means—the sculptor's hammer and chisel—by appealing to ends that serve the greater good. Yet too often modern planners and engineers would justify the creative destruction of habitat as necessary for doubtful utopias.

5) The derogation of middlebrow, in short, has gone much too far. It's time to bring middlebrow out of its cultural closet, to hail its emollient properties, to trumpet its mending virtues. For middlebrow not only entertains, it educates—pleasurably training us to appreciate high art.

6) There is a connection between the idea of place and the reality of cellular telephones. It is not encouraging. Places are unique—or at least we like to believe they are—and we strive to experience them as a kind of engagement with particulars. Cell phones are precisely the opposite.

If you have been taught to write in 5-paragraph form in school, you will initially have some difficulty writing thesis statements of the sort you have just seen. This is because the "thesis statement plus three supporting paragraphs" format of 5-paragraph form invites listing rather than the articulation of ideas. The typical three-part thesis of 5-paragraph form offers a short list of broadly stated topics (rather than well-defined claims about the topics) and then offers examples of each of these in the body paragraphs.

There is nothing wrong with partitioning the development of a subject into manageable parts, but there is a lot wrong with a thesis that makes no claim or an overly general and obvious claim such as "Television causes adolescents to become violent, lazy, and ill-read." All three parts of this general claim may be true, but nothing much of substance can be said about them in a short paper that is trying to cover all three. And notice the lack of tension in this sample thesis statement. Try writing a better thesis statement—one that has tension—about the impact of some aspect of television on teenagers.

A Note on the Syntax of Good Thesis Statements

Before we move on to concentrated applications of the procedure for making a thesis evolve, take a look at the shape of imprecise thesis statements:

Environmentalism prevents economic growth.

Tax laws benefit the wealthy.

The economic situation today is bad.

Women in contemporary films are more sensitive than men.

All four are simple, declarative sentences that offer very broad assertions. They are both grammatically and conceptually simple. More than that, they're *slack*—especially the first three, in which the primary claim stands alone, not in relation to anything else.

The very *shape* of these weak thesis statements is a warning sign. Most effective working theses, though they may begin more simply, achieve both grammatical and conceptual complexity as they evolve. Such theses contain tension in their syntax, the balance of this against that. Thus, they begin with "although" or incorporate "however" or use an "appears to be about *x* but is actually about *y*" kind of formulation. *(See "Appears to be about X..." in Chapter 4.)*

Here, by contrast, are three possible versions of the fourth weak thesis above:

Although women more readily cry in contemporary films, the men, by not crying, seem to win the audience's favor.

The complications that fuel the plots in today's romantic comedies arise because women and men express their sensitivity so differently; the resolutions, however, rarely require the men to capitulate.

A spate of recent films has witnessed the emergence of the new "womanly" man as hero, and not surprisingly, his tender qualities seem to be the reason he attracts the female love interest.

THE RECIPROCAL RELATIONSHIP BETWEEN THESIS AND EVIDENCE: THE THESIS AS LENS

What we have said so far about the thesis does not mean that all repetition of ideas in an essay is bad or that a writer's concluding paragraph should have no reference to the way the paper began. One function of the thesis is to provide the connective tissue, so to speak, that holds together a paper's three main parts—beginning, middle, and end. Periodic reminders of your paper's thesis, its unifying idea, are essential for keeping both you and your readers on track.

As we've also argued, though, developing an idea requires more than repetition. It is in light of this fact that the analogy of thesis to connective tissue proves inadequate. A better way of envisioning how a thesis operates is to think of it as a camera lens. This analogy more accurately describes the relationship between the thesis and the subject it seeks to explain. While the lens affects how we see the subject (what evidence we select, what questions we ask about that evidence), the subject we are looking at also affects how we adjust the lens.

Here is the principle that the camera lens analogy allows us to see: the relationship between thesis and subject is *reciprocal*. In good analytical writing, especially in the early, investigatory stages of writing and thinking, the thesis not only directs the writer's way of looking at evidence; the analysis of evidence should also direct and redirect (bring about revision of) the thesis. Even in a final draft, writers are usually fine-tuning their governing idea in response to their analysis of evidence. (See Figure 11.1.)

The enemy of good analytical writing is the fuzzy lens—imprecisely worded thesis statements. Very broad thesis statements, those that are made up of imprecise (fuzzy) terms, make bad lenses. They blur everything together and muddy important distinctions. If your lens is insufficiently focused, you are not likely to see much in your evidence. If you say, for example, that the economic situation today is bad, you will at least have some sense of direction, but the imprecise terms "bad" and "economic situation" don't provide you with a focus clear enough to distinguish significant detail in your evidence. Without significant detail to analyze, you can't develop your thesis, either by showing readers what the thesis is good for (what it allows us to understand and explain) or by clarifying its terms.

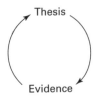

FIGURE 11.1
The Reciprocal Relationship Between Thesis and Evidence. Like a lens, the thesis affects the way a writer sees evidence. Evidence should also require the writer to readjust the lens.

A writer's thesis is usually fuzzier in a paper's opening than it is in the conclusion. As we argued in our critique of five-paragraph form in Chapter 10, a paper ending with a claim worded almost exactly as it was in the beginning has not made its thesis adequately responsive to evidence. The body of the paper should not only substantiate the thesis by demonstrating its value in selecting and explaining evidence, but also bring the opening version of the thesis into better focus.

Making a Thesis Evolve: A Brief Example

More often than not, when inexperienced writers face a situation in which evidence seems to be unclear or contradictory, they tend to make one of two unproductive moves: they either ignore the conflicting evidence, or they abandon the problem altogether and look for something more clear-cut to write about. Faced with evidence that complicates your thesis, the one thing not to do is run away.

The savvy writer will actively seek out complicating evidence, taking advantage of chances to bring out complications in order to make the thesis more fully responsive to evidence. Let's revisit a sample thesis from the discussion of uncovering assumptions in Chapter 4, "tax laws benefit the wealthy." If you were to seek out data that would complicate this overstated claim, you would soon encounter evidence that would press you to make some distinctions that the initial formulation of this claim leaves obscure. You would need, for example, to distinguish different sources of wealth and then to determine whether all or just some wealthy taxpayers are benefited by tax laws.

Do people whose wealth comes primarily from investments benefit less (or more) than those whose wealth comes from high wages? Evidence might also lead you to consider whether tax laws, by benefiting the wealthy, also benefit other people indirectly. Both of these considerations would necessitate some reformulation of the thesis. By the end of the paper, the claim that tax laws benefit the wealthy would have evolved into a more carefully defined and qualified statement that would reflect the thinking you have done in your analysis of evidence. This, by and large, is what good concluding paragraphs do—they reflect back on and reformulate your paper's initial position in light of the thinking you have done about it. (See Figure 11.2.)

But, you might ask, isn't this reformulating of the thesis something a writer does before he or she writes the essay? Certainly some of it is accomplished in the early exploratory writing and note-taking stage. But your finished paper will necessarily do

FIGURE 11.2
A strong thesis evolves as it confronts and assimilates evidence; the evolved thesis may expand or restrict the original claim. The process may need to be repeated a number of times.

more than list conclusions. Your revision process will have weeded out various false starts and dead ends that you may have wandered into on the way to your finished ideas, but the main routes of your movement from a tentative idea to a refined and substantiated theory should remain visible for readers to follow. To an extent, all good writing reenacts the chains of thought that led you to your conclusions.

Try This 11.2: Qualifying Overstated Claims

Making a thesis evolve is to make that thesis more accurate. To do so is almost always to qualify (limit) the claim. Using the model of inquiry in the treatment of the example "Tax laws benefit the wealthy," seek out complications in one of the overstated claims listed below. These complications should include conflicting evidence (which you should specify) and questions about the meaning or appropriateness of key terms. Illustrate a few of these complications, and then reformulate the claim in language that is more carefully qualified and accurate.

Welfare encourages recipients not to work.

Religious people are more moral than those who are not.

Herbal remedies are better than pharmaceutical ones.

The book is always better than the film.

Women are more sensitive than men.

We learn from the lessons of history.

The Evolving Thesis as Hypothesis and Conclusion in the Natural and Social Sciences

A thesis functions differently depending on the academic discipline—whether it must be stated in full at the outset, for example, and what happens to it between the beginning of the paper and the end. The differences appear largest as you move back and forth between courses in the humanities and courses in the natural and certain of the social sciences.

The natural and social sciences generally use a pair of terms, *hypothesis* and *conclusion*, for the single term *thesis*. Because writing in the sciences is patterned according to the scientific method, writers in disciplines such as biology and psychology must report how the original thesis (hypothesis) was tested against empirical evidence and then conclude on this basis whether or not the hypothesis was confirmed.

The gap between this way of thinking about the thesis and the concept of an evolving thesis is not as large as it may seem. The scientific method is in sync with one of the chapter's main points—that something must happen to the thesis between the introduction and the conclusion—so that the conclusion does more than just restate what had already been claimed in the beginning.

Analogously, in a scientific paper, the hypothesis is tested against evidence, the results of which allow the writer to draw conclusions about the hypothesis's validity. Although the hypothesis does not change (or evolve), the testing of it and subsequent interpretation of those results produce commentary on and, often, qualifications of the paper's central claim.

In the natural and social sciences, successive reformulations of the thesis are less likely to be recorded and may not even be expressly articulated. But, as in all disciplines, the primary analytical activity in the sciences is to repeatedly reconsider the assumptions on which a conclusion is based. *(See Chapter 15, Forms and Formats Across the Curriculum.)*

The Hypothesis in the Natural and Social Sciences: Four Professors Speak

The following Voices from Across the Curriculum explain how a hypothesis functions in writing in their disciplines. Notice that in each case, although the hypothesis itself does not change, something does happen to it between introduction and conclusion.

Voices from Across the Curriculum

○ If the empirical evidence doesn't confirm your hypothesis, you rethink your hypothesis, but it's a complex issue. Researchers whose hypotheses are not confirmed often question their *method* ("if I had more subjects," or "a better manipulation of the experimental group," or "a better test of intelligence," etc.) as much as their hypothesis. And that's often legitimate. Part of the challenge of psychological research is its reliance on a long array of assumptions. Failure to confirm a hypothesis could mean a problem in any of that long array of assumptions. So failure to confirm your hypothesis is often difficult to interpret.
—Alan Tjeltveit, Professor of Psychology

○ The thesis in experimental psychology papers is the statement of the hypothesis. It is always carefully and explicitly stated in the last few sentences of the introduction. The hypothesis is usually a deductive statement such as: if color does influence mood, then an ambiguous picture printed on different colors of paper should be interpreted differently, depending on the color of the paper. Specifically, based on the results of Jones (1997), the pink paper should cause participants to perceive the picture as a more calm and restful image, and the green paper should cause the picture to be interpreted as a more anxious image.
—Laura Edelman, Professor of Psychology

○ The thesis is usually presented in the abstract and then again at the end of the introduction. Probably the most frequent writing error is not providing a thesis at all. Sometimes this is because the student doesn't *have* a thesis; other times, it is because the student wants to maintain a sense of mystery about the paper, as if driving toward a dramatic conclusion. This actually makes it harder to read. The best papers are clear and up front about what their point is, then use evidence and argument to support and evaluate the thesis. I encourage students to have a sentence immediately following their discussion of the background on the subject that can be as explicit as: "In this paper, I will argue that while research on toxic effects of methyl bromide provides troubling evidence for severe physiological effects, conclusive proof of a significant environmental hazard is lacking at this time."

I try to avoid the use of the term "hypothesis." I think it gives the false sense that scientists always start with an idea about how something works. Frequently, that is not the case. Some of the best science has actually come from observation. Darwin's work on finches is a classic example. His ideas about adaptation probably derived *from* the observation.

—Bruce Wightman, Professor of Biology

Economists do make pretense to follow scientific methodology. Thus, we are careful not to mix hypothesis and conclusion. I think it's important to distinguish between what is conjectured, the working hypothesis, and what ultimately emerges as a result of an examination of the evidence. Conclusions come only after some test has been passed.

—James Marshall, Professor of Economics

So, in the natural and social sciences, successive reformulations of the thesis are less likely to be recorded and may not even be expressly articulated. But, as in all disciplines, the primary analytical activity in the sciences is to repeatedly reconsider the assumptions on which a conclusion is based.

SIX STEPS FOR MAKING A THESIS EVOLVE

As an overarching guideline, *acknowledge the questions that each new formulation of the thesis prompts you to ask.* The thesis develops through successive complications. Allowing your thesis to run up against potentially conflicting evidence ("but what about this?") enables you to build on your initial idea, extending the range of evidence it can accurately account for by clarifying and qualifying its key terms.

1. Formulate an idea about your subject. This working thesis should be some claim about the meaning of your evidence that is good enough to get you started.

2. See how far you can make this thesis go in accounting for evidence. Use the thesis to explain as much of your evidence as it reasonably can. Try it on.

3. Locate evidence that is not adequately accounted for by the thesis. Actively search for such evidence because the initial version of the thesis will incline you to see only what fits and not to notice the evidence that doesn't fit.

4. Make explicit the apparent mismatch between the thesis and selected evidence. Explain how and why some pieces of evidence do not fit the thesis.

5. Reshape your claim to accommodate the evidence that hasn't fit. This will mean rewording your thesis to resolve or explain apparent contradictions.

6. Repeat steps two, three, four, and five several times, until you are satisfied that the thesis statement accounts for your evidence as fully and accurately as possible.

EVOLVING A THESIS IN AN EXPLORATORY DRAFT: THE EXAMPLE OF *LAS MENINAS*

The example is a student writer's exploratory draft on a painting called *Las Meninas* (Spanish for "the ladies-in-waiting") by the seventeenth-century painter Diego Velázquez. The method of analysis used here will, however, work with anything, print or non-print.

Look at the painting in Figure 11.3, and then read the student's draft. As you read, you will notice that much of the essay consists of list-like description, which leaves it somewhat unfocused. But careful description is a necessary stage in moving toward interpretations of evidence, especially in an exploratory draft where the writer is not yet committed to any single position. Notice how the writer's word choice in her

SCALA/Art Resource, NY. Diego Rodrigues Velázquez. Las Meninas. 1656.

FIGURE 11.3
Las Meninas by Diego Velázquez, 1656 Approximately 10'5" x 9'. Museo del Prado, Madrid.

descriptions prompts various kinds of interpretive leaps. We have added in brackets our observations about how the writer's thinking is proceeding, and we have used underlining to track her various attempts at formulating a thesis.

Velázquez's Intentions in *Las Meninas*

[1] Velázquez has been noted as being one of the best Spanish artists of all time. It seems that as Velázquez got older, his paintings became better. Toward the end of his life, he painted his masterpiece, *Las Meninas*. Out of all his works, *Las Meninas* is the only known self-portrait of Velázquez. There is much to be said about *Las Meninas*. The painting is very complex, but some of the intentions that Velázquez had in painting *Las Meninas* are very clear. *[The writer opens with background information and a broad working thesis (underlined).]*

[2] First, we must look at the painting as a whole. The question that must be answered is, Who is in the painting? The people are all members of the Royal Court of the Spanish monarch Philip IV. In the center is the king's daughter, who eventually became Empress of Spain. Around her are her *meninas* or ladies-in-waiting. These *meninas* are all daughters of influential men. To the right of the *meninas* are dwarfs who are servants, and the family dog who looks fierce but is easily tamed by the foot of the little dwarf. The more unique people in the painting are Velázquez himself, who stands to the left in front of a large canvas; the king and queen, whose faces are captured in the obscure mirror; the man in the doorway; and the nun and man behind the *meninas*. To analyze this painting further, the relationship between characters must be understood. *[The writer describes the evidence and arrives at an operating assumption—focusing on the relationship among characters.]*

[3] Where is this scene occurring? Most likely it is in the palace. But why is there no visible furniture? Is it because Velázquez didn't want the viewers to become distracted from his true intentions? I believe it is to show that this is not just a painting of an actual event. This is an event out of his imagination. *[The writer begins pushing observations to tentative conclusions by asking So what?]*

[4] Now, let us become better acquainted with the characters. The child in the center is the most visible. All the light is shining on her. Maybe Velázquez is suggesting that she is the next light for Spain and that even God has approved her by shining all the available light on her. Back in those days there was a belief in the divine right of kings, so this just might be what Velázquez is saying. *[The writer starts ranking evidence for importance and continues to ask,*

So what?; she arrives at a possible interpretation of the painter's intention.]

[5] The next people of interest are the ones behind the *meninas*. The woman in the habit might be a nun and the man a priest.

[6] The king and queen are the next group of interesting people. They are in the mirror, which is to suggest they are present, but they are not as visible as they might be. Velázquez suggests that they are not always at the center where everyone would expect them to be. *[The writer continues using Notice and Focus plus asking So what?; the writer has begun tackling evidence that might conflict with her first interpretation.]*

[7] The last person and the most interesting is Velázquez. He dominates the painting along with the little girl. He takes up the whole left side along with his gigantic easel. But what is he painting? As I previously said, he might be painting the king and queen. But I also think he could be pretending to paint us, the viewers. The easel really gives this portrait an air of mystery because Velázquez knows that we, the viewers, want to know what he is painting. *[The writer starts doing 10 on 1 with her selection of the most significant detail.]*

[8] The appearance of Velázquez is also interesting. His eyes are focused outward here. They are not focused on what is going on around him. It is a steady stare. Also interesting is his confident stance. He was confident enough to place himself in the painting of the royal court. I think that Velázquez wants the king to give him the recognition he deserves by including him in the "family." And the symbol on his vest is the symbol given to a painter by the king to show that his status and brilliance have been appreciated by the monarch. It is unknown how it got there. It is unlikely that Velázquez put it there himself. That would be too outright, and Velázquez was the type to give his messages subtly. Some say that after Velázquez's death, King Philip IV himself painted it to finally give Velázquez the credit he deserved for being a loyal friend and servant. *[The writer continues doing 10 on 1 and asking So what?; she arrives at three tentative theses (underlined).]*

[9] I believe that Velázquez was very ingenious by putting his thoughts and feelings into a painting. He didn't want to offend the king who had done so much for him. It paid off for Velázquez because he did finally get what he wanted, even if it was after he died. *[The writer concludes and is now ready to redraft to tighten links between evidence and claims, formulate a better working thesis, and make this thesis evolve.]*

Description to Analysis: The Exploratory Draft

The purpose of an exploratory draft is to use writing as a means of arriving at a working thesis that the next draft can more fully evolve. Most writers find that potential theses emerge near the end of the exploratory draft—which is the case in this student draft (see the three claims underlined in paragraph 8).

This is a good exploratory draft. The writer has begun to interpret details and draw plausible conclusions from what she sees, rather than just describing (summarizing) the scene depicted on the canvas or responding loosely to it with her unanalyzed impressions.

The paper is typical of an early draft in several ways:

- It is written more for the writer as a form of inquiry than for readers. The writer reports her thoughts as they occur, but she doesn't always explain how she arrived at them or how they connect to each other.
- recognizable thesis doesn't emerge until near the end (in paragraph 8).
- The paper contains more than one potential thesis. The paper ignores the conflicts among its various theses and some of its evidence.
- The writer tends to end paragraphs with promising observations and then walk away, leaving the observations undeveloped. Rather than draw out the implications of her observations, she halts her thinking too soon in order to move on to the next piece of evidence. See, for example, this writer's repeated return to paragraph openings using "next" and "also," which traps her into listing parallel examples rather than building connections among them. As we will illustrate later, the writer can remedy this problem by querying her observations with the question "So what?"

What is especially good about the draft is that it reveals the writer's willingness to push on from her first idea (reading the painting as an endorsement of the divine right of kings, expressed by the light shining on the princess) by seeking out complicating evidence. This first idea does not account for enough of the evidence and is undermined by evidence that clearly doesn't fit, such as the small size and decentering of the king and queen, and the large size and foregrounding of the painter himself.

Rather than ignoring these potentially troublesome details, the writer instead zooms in on them, making the painter's representation of himself and of his employers the 1 for doing 10 on 1 (making a number of observations about a single representative piece of evidence and analyzing it in depth).

Starting a Revision by Looking Again at the Details: The Method

Now what? The writer is ready to rewrite the paper in order to choose and better define her thesis. She might first wish to step back a bit from her initial formulations by using The Method to again survey the details of the painting, looking for patterns of repetition and contrast.

Examples of exact or nearly exact **repetitions**:

the pictures in the background

the fact that both the dwarf and the painter, each on his own side of the painting, stare confidently and directly at the viewer

Examples of **strands** (repetition of the same or similar kind of detail):

details having to do with family

servants: dwarf, *meninas*, dog? painter?

details having to do with art and the making of art: easel, brush, paintings on wall

Examples of organizing **contrasts**—binaries:

royalty/commoners

employers/servants

large/small

foreground/background

central (prominent)/marginalized (less prominent)

Having used The Method to see the evidence anew, the writer would be ready to try the Six Steps for Making the Thesis Evolve. She'd begin by noticing that, as is the case in most exploratory drafts, she has several potential thesis statements vying for control of the paper.

Applying the Six Steps to *Las Meninas*

Step 1: *Formulate a working thesis.*

As a general rule, you should *assume the presence of multiple, often competing theses*, some of which you may not have yet detected. In the *Las Meninas* paper, as is often the case in early drafts, no single idea emerges clearly as the thesis. Instead, we get three related but not entirely compatible ideas vying for control of the paper (all in paragraph 8):

"I think that Velázquez wants the king to…"

Thesis 1: give Velázquez "the recognition he deserves by including him in the 'family.'"

Thesis 2: "show that his [Velázquez's] status and brilliance [as an artist] have been appreciated."

Thesis 3: give Velázquez "the credit he deserved for being a loyal friend and servant."

These three ideas about the painter's intentions could be made to work together, but at present the writer is left with an uneasy fit among them.

Step 2: *See how far you can make each thesis go in accounting for evidence.*

Each of the three potential thesis ideas explains some of the evidence. The writer should try on each one to see what it helps to explain.

> **Thesis 1:** painting as bid for inclusion in the family
>
> > **Evidence:** the painter's inclusion of himself with the family—the king, queen, and princess—in a fairly domestic scene
>
> **Thesis 2:** painting as bid for appreciation of painter's status and brilliance as an artist
>
> > **Evidence:** prominence of easel and brush and painter himself in the painting; painter's confident stare and the apparent decentering of king and queen; painting set in artist's studio—his space
>
> **Thesis 3:** painting as bid for credit for being loyal friend and servant
>
> > **Evidence:** painter's location of himself among other loyal servants at court (ladies in waiting, dog, and large dwarf)

Step 3: *Locate evidence that is not adequately accounted for by each thesis.*

Step 4: *Make explicit the apparent mismatch between the thesis and selected evidence.*

What happens when the writer begins to search for evidence that doesn't seem to be adequately accounted for by her various thesis formulations?

> **Thesis 1:** painting as bid for inclusion in the family
>
> > **Evidence mismatches:** presence of painter among servants; foregrounding of servants in image and in painting's title *(The Ladies in Waiting)*—painter's large size (larger than king and queen) does not go with the idea of "inclusion," and emphasis on servants does not go with inclusion in royal family
>
> **Thesis 2:** painting as bid for appreciation of painter's status and brilliance as an artist
>
> > **Evidence mismatches:** prominence of other servants in the painting; emphasis on family as much as or more than on artist himself—if bidding for status, painter would not present himself as just one of the servants, nor might he give so much attention to the princess (and the king and queen's regard for her)
>
> **Thesis 3:** painting as bid for credit for being loyal friend and servant
>
> > **Evidence mismatches:** painter's prominence; his confident stare; prominence of easel and brush; small size of king and queen (smaller than servants)—if painter wished to emphasize loyalty and service, his subordinate relationship to the more powerful at court, he would have made himself and the tools of his trade less important

Step 5: *Choose the claim that seems to account for the most evidence and then reshape that claim to better accommodate evidence that doesn't fit.*

When you've found conflicting or inadequately explained evidence, try using it to evolve your existing thesis rather than beating a too-hasty retreat. The direction in which the writer's thinking is moving—that the painting asks for someone's strengths to be recognized—is not an entirely new start. The shift she is apparently making but not yet overtly articulating is from the painting as showcase of royal power to the painting as showcase of the painter's own power.

In order to better formulate this claim, the writer should query what she is emphasizing as the primary feature of her evidence: size, especially that of the king and queen versus the painter. She could do this by pushing her thinking with the question So what?

- **So what** that the king and queen are small, but the painter, princess, and dwarf (another servant) are all large and fairly equal in size and/or prominence?
- **So what** that there are size differences in the painting? What might large or small size mean?

Here are possible answers to the "So what?" questions:

- Perhaps the relative size and/or prominence of figures in the painting can be read as indicators of their importance or of what the painter wants to say about their importance.
- Perhaps the king and queen have been reduced so that Velázquez can showcase their daughter, the princess.
- Perhaps the size and physical prominence of the king and queen are relatively unimportant. In that case, what matters is that they are a presence, always overseeing events (an idea implied but not developed by the writer in paragraph 6).
- Perhaps the painter is demonstrating his own ability to make the king and queen any size—any level of importance—he chooses. Although the writer does not overtly say so, the king and queen are among the smallest as well as the least visible figures.

Given these answers to the So what? questions, the writer should probably choose Thesis 2—that the painting is a bid for recognition of the painter's status and brilliance as an artist—because this thesis explains more of the evidence than anything else the writer has come up with so far. It explains, for example, the painter's prominence and the relative insignificance of the monarchs: that the painter, in effect, creates their stature (size, power) in the world through his paintings. Framed in a mirror and appearing to hang on the wall, the king and queen are, arguably, suspended among the painter's paintings, mere reflections of themselves—or, rather, the painter's reflection of them.

Step 6: *Repeat steps 2 through 5 as necessary.*

The writer would probably want to concentrate on repeating Step 2, seeing how far she can go in making her revised thesis account for additional evidence.

Thesis: painting as bid for appreciation of painter's status and brilliance as an artist

Step 2 repeated: *See how far you can make each thesis go in accounting for evidence.*

Evidence:

- The painter is demonstrating that he can make the members of the royal family any size he wants, then the painting not only is a bid for recognition, but also can be seen as a playful though not-so-subtle threat: be aware of my power and treat me well, or else suffer the consequences. As an artist, the painter decides how the royal family will be seen. The king and queen depend on the painter, as they do in a different way on the princess, with whom Velázquez makes himself equal in prominence, to extend and perpetuate their power.

- In subverting viewers' expectations both by decentering the monarchs and concealing what is on the easel, the painter again emphasizes his power, in this case, over the viewers (among whom might be the king and queen if their images on the back wall are mirror reflections of them standing, like us, in front of the painting). He is not bound by their expectations and in fact appears to use those expectations to manipulate the viewers: he can make them wish to see something he has the power to withhold.

- The presence of the large dwarf in the right-hand foreground is positioned in a way that links him with the painter. The dwarf arguably furthers the painting's message and does so, like much else in the painting, in the form of a loaded joke: the small ("dwarfed" by the power of others) are brought forward and made big.

Knowing When to Stop: How Much Revising Is Enough?

We emphasize before leaving this example that the version of the thesis we have just proposed is not necessarily the "right" answer. Looked at in a different context, the painting might have been explained primarily as a demonstration of the painter's mastery of the tools of his trade—light, for example, and perspective. But our proposed revision of the thesis for the *Las Meninas* paper meets two important criteria for evaluating thesis statements:

1. It unifies the observations the writer has made.
2. It is capable of accounting for a wide range of evidence.

The writer has followed through on her original desire to infer Velázquez's intentions in the painting. As we argued in Chapter 6 (Making Interpretations Plausible), whether or not Velázquez consciously intended to make his painting a tongue-in-cheek self-advertisement, there is clearly enough evidence to claim plausibly that the painting can be understood in this way.

How do you know when you've done enough reformulating of your thesis and arrived at the best possible idea about your evidence? Getting the thesis to account for (respond to) all rather than just some of your evidence does not mean you need to discuss every detail of the subject. Writers must take care not to ignore important evidence, especially if it would alter their "case," but no analysis can address everything—nor should it. Your job as a writer is to select those features of your subject that seem most significant and to argue for their significance. An analysis says to readers, in effect, "These are the details that best reveal the nature and meaning of my subject, or at least the part of the subject that I am trying to address."

EVOLVING A THESIS IN A LATER-STAGE DRAFT: THE EXAMPLE OF *EDUCATING RITA*

In this example, we will apply the Six Steps in order to make a thesis evolve within the draft, rather than to select among various as yet unformed competitors for the role of thesis (as was the case with *Las Meninas*). The process of thesis evolution we will trace here would remain visible in the writer's final draft as a means of sharing her thought processes with her readers. By contrast, the writer of *Las Meninas* would probably not include in her final draft the competition among her three potential thesis statements—only the evolution of the "winning" one.

In the film *Educating Rita*, a working-class English hairdresser (Rita) wants to change her life by taking courses from a professor (Frank) at the local university, even though this move threatens her relationship with her husband (Denny), who burns her books and pressures her to quit school and get pregnant. Frank, she discovers, has his own problems: he's a divorced alcoholic who is bored with his life, bored with his privileged and complacent students, and bent on self-destruction. The film follows the growth of Frank's and Rita's friendship and the changes it brings about in their lives. By the end of the film, each has left a limiting way of life behind and has set off in a seemingly more promising direction. Rita leaves her constricting marriage, passes her university examinations with honors, and begins to view her life in terms of choices; Frank stops drinking and sets off, determined but sad, to make a new start as a teacher in Australia.

Step 1: *Formulate an idea about your subject, a working thesis.*

Working thesis: *Educating Rita* celebrates the liberating potential of education. The film's relatively happy ending and the presence of the word *educating* in the film's title make this thesis a reasonable opening claim.

Step 2: *See how far you can make this thesis go in accounting for evidence.*
The working thesis seems compatible, for example, with Rita's achievement of greater self-awareness and independence. She becomes more articulate, which allows her to free herself from otherwise disabling situations. She starts to think about other kinds of work she might do, rather than assuming that she must continue in the one job she has always done. She travels, first elsewhere in England and then to the Continent. So, the thesis checks out as viable: there is enough of a match with evidence to stick with and evolve it.

Steps 3 & 4: *Locate evidence that is not adequately accounted for by the thesis, and ask So what? about the apparent mismatch between the thesis and selected evidence.*
Some evidence reveals that the thesis as stated is not the whole picture. Rita's education causes her to become alienated from her husband, her parents, and her social class; at the end of the film, she is alone and unsure about her direction in life. In

Frank's case, the thesis runs into even more problems. His boredom, drinking, and alienation seem to have been caused, at least in part, by his education rather than by his lack of it. He sees his book-lined study as a prison, not a site of liberation. Moreover, his profound knowledge of literature has not helped him control his life: he comes to class drunk, fails to notice or care that his girlfriend is having an affair with one of his colleagues, and asks his classes whether it is worth gaining all of literature if it means losing one's soul.

Step 5: *Reshape your claim to accommodate the evidence that hasn't fit.*

The idea that the film celebrates the liberating potential of education still fits a lot of significant evidence. Rita is arguably better off at the end of the film than at the beginning: we are not left to believe that she should have remained resistant to education, like her husband, Denny, whose world doesn't extend much beyond the corner pub. But the thesis also leaves some significant evidence unaccounted for, so the writer would need to bring out the complicating evidence—the film's seemingly contradictory attitudes about education—and then modify the wording of the thesis in a way that might resolve or explain these contradictions.

Education as represented by the film seems to be of two kinds: enabling and stultifying. The next step in the development of the thesis would be to elaborate on how the film seeks to distinguish enabling forms of education from debilitating ones (as represented by the self-satisfied and status-conscious behavior of the supposedly educated people at Frank's university). Perhaps this difference is what the film is primarily interested in—not just education's potential to liberate.

Revised thesis: *Educating Rita* celebrates the liberating potential of enabling—in contrast to stultifying—education.

Step 6: *Repeat steps 2, 3, 4, and 5.*

Having refined the thesis in this way, the writer would then repeat the step of seeing what the new wording allows him or her to account for in the evidence. The revised thesis would foreground a contest in the film between two different kinds of and attitudes toward education. This thesis as lens would cause us to see Frank's problems as being less a product of his education than of the cynical and pretentious versions of education that surround him in his university life. It would also explain the film's emphasis on Frank's recovery of at least some of his idealism about education, for which Rita has provided the inspiration.

What else does this revised thesis account for in the evidence? What about Frank's emigration to Australia? If we can take Australia to stand for a newer world, one where education would be less likely to become the stale and exclusive property of a self-satisfied elite, then the refined version of the thesis would seem to be working well. In fact, given the possible thematic connection between Rita's working-class identity and Australia (associated, as a former frontier and English penal colony, with lower-class vitality as opposed to the complacency bred of class privilege), the thesis about the film's celebration of the contrast between enabling and stultifying forms of education could be sharpened further. It might be proposed, for example, that the film presents institutional education as desperately in need of frequent doses of "real life" (as represented by Rita and Australia)—infusions of working-class pragmatism, energy, and optimism—if it is to remain healthy and open, as opposed to becoming the oppressive property of a privileged social class. This is to say that the film arguably exploits stereotypical assumptions about social class.

Revised thesis: *Educating Rita* celebrates the liberating potential of enabling education, defined as that which remains open to healthy doses of working-class, real-world infusions.

Repeat steps 3 and 4, locating evidence not adequately accounted for and ask so what?

At the end of the film, Frank and Rita walk off in opposite directions down long, empty airport corridors. Though promising to remain friends, the two do not become a couple. This closing emphasis on Frank's and Rita's alienation from their respective cultures, and the film's apparent insistence on the necessity of each going on alone, significantly qualifies the happiness of the "happy ending."

Having complicated the interpretation of the ending, the writer would again need to modify the thesis in accord with new observations. Does the film simply celebrate education if it also presents it as being, to some degree, incompatible with conventional forms of happiness? By emphasizing the necessity of having Frank and Rita each go on alone, the film may be suggesting that to be truly liberating, education—as opposed to its less honest and more comfortable substitutes—inevitably produces and even requires a certain amount of loneliness and alienation. Shown in Figure 11.4 are the successive revisions of the thesis.

Repeat step 5, reshaping the claim.

Final version of thesis: *Educating Rita* celebrates the liberating potential of enabling education (kept open to real-world, working-class energy) but also acknowledges its potential costs in loneliness and alienation.

Note: this last version of the thesis is the one that would appear in the writer's final paragraph, the product of qualifying and refining the paper's claim by repeatedly confronting and assimilating complicating evidence. In effect, the Six Steps have produced a reasonably complete draft in outline form.

Try This 11.3: Tracking a Thesis

As should be clear now, various versions of the thesis recur throughout a piece of writing, usually with increasing specificity, complication, and grammatical complexity. The four evolutions of the thesis statement on *Educating Rita* illustrate this pattern of recurrence clearly. One of the best ways to teach yourself how and where to locate statements of the thesis in your own writing is to track the thesis in a piece of reading. Use a highlighter to mark the evolutions. Where in the essay do you find the thesis? How has it changed in each recurrence? In response to what complication?

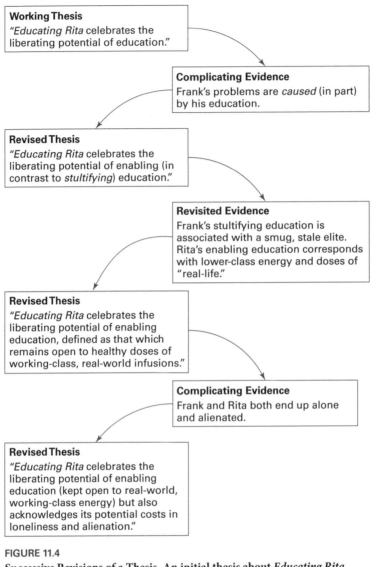

FIGURE 11.4
**Successive Revisions of a Thesis. An initial thesis about *Educating Rita*
evolves through successive complications as it reexamines evidence in the
film.**

The Evolving Thesis in Outline Form: Superman

We borrow this example from the website of the First Year Writing Program at
Ohio State University, for which we offer much thanks. Like the evolving thesis in
Educating Rita, some of the various reformulations of the thesis would appear in the
final draft.

Original Thesis:
"Superman is an unchanging icon because he stands for Truth, Justice, and the American way."

Complicating Evidence:
Superman has made dramatic body-image changes in his "career."

Revised Thesis: "Though Superman's body-image has changed, his status as an icon and his message have remained steady."

Complicating Evidence:
Older body-images are met with boredom and distaste by the new generation of viewers. He has become younger and more sexual.

Revised Thesis:
"The new young, sexy Superman liberates him from past images, and caters his message to a new, more sexually sophisticated generation of viewers."

Complicating Evidence:
If Superman's body-image changes so much, doesn't this change his message automatically? What does his body-image say? Does his body speak loader than his message?

Revised Thesis:
"A young, sexy Superman liberates his image from a wholesome, community-oriented image and celebrates more explicitly a message of individuality and sexual power."

Complicating Evidence:
It is the viewers who place these demands on Superman's image. He is the "offspring" of consumers.

Revised Thesis:
"A younger and more sexualized generation of consumers has liberated Superman's image from a wholesome, community-oriented image to reflect more readily its own values of individuality and sexual power."

LOCATING THE EVOLVING THESIS IN THE FINAL DRAFT

Having achieved a final version of a thesis, what next? Why wouldn't a writer just relocate the last and fullest statement of the thesis to his or her first paragraph and then prove it?

Usually it's neither possible nor desirable to encapsulate in the opening sentences what it will take the whole paper to explain. The position articulated in the fully evolved thesis is typically too complex to be stated intelligibly and concisely in the introduction. If you approach an essay as an act of thinking, then the evolutions of the thesis record the history of your various changes in thinking as you encounter evidence. If your readers get to see these, they are far more likely to go along with you, literally to follow your trains of thought. Rather than imposing your conclusions, you will be sharing your thought process with the reader, which is what good writing does.

Normally, you lead (usually at the end of the first paragraph or at the beginning of the second) with the best version of your thesis you can come up with that will be understandable to your readers without a lengthy preamble. If you find yourself writing a page-long introductory paragraph to get to your initial statement of thesis, try settling for a simpler articulation of your central idea in its first appearance.

The first paragraph does not need to—and usually can't—offer your conclusion; it will take the body of your paper to accomplish that. It should, however, provide a quick look at particular details that set up the issue. Use these details to generate a theory, a working hypothesis, about whatever it is you think is at stake in the material. The rest of the paper will test and develop this theory.

The *Educating Rita* paper might open, for example, by using a version of the Seems-to-Be-About-X gambit (see Chapter 4), claiming that at first glance the film seems to celebrate the liberating potential of education. You could then lay out the evidence for this view and proceed to complicate it in the ways we've discussed.

Your concluding paragraph should offer the more carefully qualified and evolved version of your thesis that the body of your paper has allowed you to arrive at. Rather than just summarize and restate what you said in your introduction, the concluding paragraph leaves readers with what you take to be your single best insight. It should put what you have had to say into some kind of perspective.

Recognizing and Relocating Your Thesis: A History Professor Speaks

In the following Voice from Across the Curriculum, history professor Ellen Poteet offers suggestions on how writers might best prompt themselves to arrive at and recognize a thesis in their writing.

Voices from Across the Curriculum

For an analytical or interpretive historical essay, *thesis* is a conventional term and one of much value. The thesis usually is that point of departure from the surfaces of evidence to the underlying significance, or problems, a given set of sources reveal to the reader and writer. In most cases, the thesis is best positioned up front, so that the writer's audience has a sense of what lies ahead and why it is worth reading on. I say *usually* and *in most cases* because the hard and fast rule should not take precedence over the inspirational manner in which a thesis comes to be formulated and recognized by the writer. It is my experience, in fact, that if inspiration strikes, one realizes it only after the fact.

Recognizing a thesis can be extremely difficult. It can often be a lot easier to talk "about" what one is writing than to say succinctly what the thrust of one's discussion is. I sometimes ask students to draw a line at the end of a paper after they have finished it, and then write one, at most two sentences, saying what they most want to tell their readers. My comment on that postscript frequently is "Great statement of your thesis. Just move it up to your first paragraph where it could begin to develop."

—Ellen Poteet, Professor of History

Try This 11.4: Moving from Observations to a Thesis

The following piece of writing is a student's exploratory draft analyzing a place—a chain restaurant located in a Boston shopping mall. It is an early draft; the writer has not yet been expected to attend to organization, style, and so on. One purpose of such idea-gathering drafts is to survey the data in order to discover one or more possible working theses.

For our purposes, the draft offers an opportunity to identify claims and assess how they connect to the evidence presented. It can also give you practice in reformulating claims on the basis of careful examination of evidence. The steps listed below are a version of the Six Steps for Making a Thesis Evolve. These steps also work well for pairs or small groups of writers working on each others' drafts.

1. Underline all of the paper's claims about the meaning of the details the writer has noticed. Star the claims that seem to be potential thesis formulations.

2. Examine the match between evidence and claims, focusing on the claims. Where do you find mismatches? Try in a sentence or two to explain the mismatch.

3. Reformulate one of the writer's potential thesis statements in a way that better accounts for the evidence. Be sure that the thesis has tension—that it generates forward momentum by casting its primary claim against another possibility. Try starting the thesis with the word "although" or use the formulation, "Seems to be about X, but is also (or really) about Y."

Mall Cuisine

[1] At the outer reaches of an enclosed shopping mall near downtown Boston's Copley Square there is an interesting restaurant named Bon Marche. The mall is huge, connecting several high-rise hotels, and it offers dozens of upscale shops.

[2] My friend and I entered Bon Marche just to look around; we were hungry for some breakfast, and it looked promising. Almost immediately a Latino guy about twenty wearing a green beret stopped us to give us a check. He told us that there was one for take-out and one for eating there, and then he explained how the restaurant worked. There were a number of different stations serving food, and you were supposed to give them your ticket to be stamped when you got food there. The ticket, by the way, which was designed to look like a passport, included a comical warning that if you lost it, you would be required to wash dishes there for two days.

[3] The stations were scattered all over this enormous room, and each one offered a different kind of food. (We later learned that they had a market downstairs too, where they sold the food uncooked.) A lot of the foods were international in flavor. There was lots of seafood, especially

shellfish of various kinds. Other stations offered omelettes, sushi, wood-oven cooked pizza, fresh squeezed juices (including carrot!), soups such as chowders and bouillabaisse, crepes, Oriental stir fries, and various kinds of bread and pastries. I did notice, though, that there was no lox, though plenty of fresh salmon they would cook for you.

[4]   I noticed that at a number of these stations, you could basically design your food choice. For example, you would choose what "innards" you wanted in your omelette from a variety of ingredients in silver bowls at the front of the station. The same went for the stir fry station and the pizza station, where you chose among toppings. And most of the stations also offered vegetarian options.

[5]   We decided to have breakfast, and that's when we discovered one drawback to this station idea. We had to wait in line for about fifteen minutes before we were able to order our omelettes. They looked and smelled great, and they came with hash browns, but when we asked for some bacon, the Latina girl who was cooking told us that we had to go to another station where they cook breakfast meats. That would mean waiting in line again, while our food was getting cold. And then we'd have to wait in line again if we wanted juice, which was at another station.

[6]   Just as there is a great variety of exotic foods, there are a lot of diverse seating areas at Bon Marche. One area was glassed-in, like a French bistro, with small white tables that had multicolored umbrellas in them. Another seemed Indonesian—rattan furniture and hay bales. We chose an area by the windows looking out over downtown Boston. It was decorated with lattices like a grape arbor at an Italian villa.

[7]   Once we noticed the international character of Bon Marche's food and settings, we began to see it in other aspects of the place. First of all, there's the French name of the place. And virtually all of the staff were members of ethnic minorities—especially Latinos, African-Americans, and Asians. Plus the place was awash in the upbeat rhythms of Latino music—a kind of nouveau sound. While most of the staff were young, the sushi counter proved an exception. That station featured two middle-aged Asian women, bent over their sushi mats, making mostly Boston rolls and California rolls, one after another after another. We were struck with how boring the job must be. How many omelettes was that woman cooking an hour, with the line getting longer every minute?

[8]   Still, the food was tasty (and inexpensive!), and the atmosphere was really interesting. I had the overall impression that Bon Marche was all about youth and choice and feeling optimistic. Considering its great location and how busy it was, the staff must make pretty good money, and so they are getting to participate in the American dream of opportunity and freedom as well.

[9]   That's when I realized that maybe what makes Bon Marche so great is that it embodies democracy. It has everything for everybody, and the individual gets to choose what he or she wants, down to the last

detail. And the whole place was just bursting with food—there seemed to be abundance for all. It makes available to everyone the experience of international cuisines at affordable prices, whereas in the past you would have had to travel abroad, or at least to expensive restaurants all over the city, to get this diversity. Mall culture offers the world in one convenient location, as Bon Marche exemplifies.

[10] As we were leaving, we saw more evidence for this democracy idea in the uniforms that the staff were wearing. They all had full-length aprons matching the color of their berets—the men all wore green berets while the women wore red ones. This uniform was bright and happy, and the berets seemed to symbolize that everyone was equal. Also the berets seem to go with the restaurant's French name, except that the berets themselves had these fitted leather bases that made them seem stiffer than traditional French berets.

[11] The cashier was located at the front of the restaurant, and when she gave us our receipts, we also received what they called "exit visas" that we then had to hand to a guy standing about four feet away, just at the interface of the restaurant and the rest of the mall. It was as if we were leaving this fantasy world behind.

GUIDELINES FOR FINDING AND DEVELOPING A THESIS

1. A thesis offers a theory about the meaning of evidence that would not have been immediately obvious to your readers.

2. A thesis is made, not found. It is the result of a process of thinking of about the evidence but is not itself present in the evidence, like a golden egg.

3. Treat your thesis as a hypothesis to be tested rather than an obvious truth.

4. Most effective theses contain tension. They are conceptually complex, and that is reflected in their grammatical shape—often they will begin with "although" or incorporate "however."

5. The body of your paper should serve not only to substantiate the thesis by demonstrating its value in selecting and explaining evidence, but also to evolve the thesis—move it forward—by uncovering the questions that each new formulation of it prompts you to ask.

6. When you encounter potentially conflicting evidence (or interpretations of that evidence), don't simply abandon your thesis. Use the complications to refine your thesis until you arrive at the most accurate explanation of the evidence that you can manage.

7. To check that your thesis has evolved, locate and compare the various versions of it throughout the draft. Have you done more than demonstrate the general validity of an unqualified claim?

Assignment: Making a Thesis Evolve

Formulate and Evolve a Thesis on a Film, Painting, or Other Visual Image.
Using the models of either *Las Meninas* or *Educating Rita*, produce an interpretation of the film or painting or other visual image of your choice.

First, begin by formulating a variety of possible statements about the film
or painting that could serve as a working thesis. These might be in answer to
the question "What is the film/painting about?" or "What does it 'say'?" Or
you might begin by doing The Method to uncover pattern of repetition or
contrast you have observed and can then explain.

Obviously, this assignment could be adapted to other subjects—an
essay, the coverage of a current event, and so forth. Here are some specific
suggestions:

- The contemporary appeal of a cartoon or other popular television
  character
- Differences in political rhetoric between Democrats and Republicans
  on the same issue
- The rhetoric of a popular print or television ad campaign for a familiar
  product, such as an insurance company or a soft drink or an automobile

Next, follow the procedure for making the thesis evolve, listed again here
for convenience:

1. Formulate an idea about your subject, a working thesis.
2. See how far you can make this thesis go in accounting for confirming
   evidence.
3. Locate evidence that is not adequately accounted for by the thesis.
4. Make explicit the apparent mismatch between the thesis and selected
   evidence, asking and answering "So what?"
5. Reshape your claim to accommodate the evidence that hasn't fit.
6. Repeat steps 2, 3, 4, and 5 several times.

Chapter 12

Recognizing and Fixing Weak Thesis Statements

BY WAY OF REVIEW, a strong thesis makes a claim that (1) requires analysis to support and evolve it and (2) offers some point about the significance of your evidence that would not have been immediately obvious to your readers. By contrast, a weak thesis either makes no claim or makes a claim that does not need proving. This chapter offers advice on how to recognize a weak thesis statement—and how to fix it. The chapter consists largely of examples of weak thesis statements taken from actual student papers, followed by discussion of how to recognize and rethink and rephrase them.

Weak thesis statements don't give the writer enough to do in his or her essay. Typically, a weak thesis is an unproductive claim because it doesn't actually require further thinking or proof, as, for example, "An important part of one's college education is learning to better understand others' points of view" (a piece of conventional wisdom that most people would already accept as true, and thus not in need of arguing).

FIVE KINDS OF WEAK THESIS STATEMENTS

1. A thesis that makes no claim ("This paper examines the pros and cons of . . .")
2. A thesis that is obviously true or a statement of fact ("Exercise is good for you")
3. A thesis that restates conventional wisdom ("Love conquers all")
4. A thesis that offers personal conviction as the basis for the claim ("Shopping malls are wonderful places")
5. A thesis that makes an overly broad claim ("Individualism is good")

Solutions? Be suspicious of your first responses to a subject. Privilege live questions over inert answers. Find ways to bring out the complexity of your subject. Look again at the What It Means to Have an Idea section in Chapter 3, which tells you to start with something puzzling that you want to figure out rather than with something you already believe to be clearly and obviously true. Look back as well to Chapter 11, which guides you to use evidence to complicate your claims and to compose thesis statements that contain inherent tension. When in doubt, do more exploratory writing to trigger better ideas.

FIVE KINDS OF WEAK THESIS STATEMENTS AND HOW TO FIX THEM

WEAK THESIS TYPE 1: THE THESIS MAKES NO CLAIM

Problem Examples

> I'm going to write about Darwin's concerns with evolution in *The Origin of Species.*

> This paper addresses the characteristics of a good corporate manager.

Both problem examples name a subject and link it to the intention to write about it, but they don't make any claim about the subject. As a result, they direct neither the writer nor the reader toward some position or plan of attack. Even if the second example were rephrased as "This paper addresses why a good corporate manager needs to learn to delegate responsibility," the thesis would not adequately suggest why such a claim would need to be argued or defended. *There is, in short, nothing at stake, no issue to be resolved.*

Solution: Raise specific issues for the essay to explore.

Solution Examples

> Darwin's concern with survival of the fittest in *The Origin of Species* initially leads him to neglect a potentially conflicting aspect of his theory of evolution—survival as a matter of interdependence.

> The very trait that makes for an effective corporate manager—the drive to succeed—can also make the leader domineering and, therefore, ineffective.

Some disciplines expect writers to offer statements of method and/or intention in their papers' openings. Generally, however, these openings also make a claim: for example, "In this paper, I examine how Congressional Republicans undermined the attempts of the Democratic administration to legislate a fiscally responsible health care policy for the elderly," *not* "In this paper, I discuss America's treatment of the elderly."

WEAK THESIS TYPE 2: THE THESIS IS OBVIOUSLY TRUE OR IS A STATEMENT OF FACT

Problem Examples

> The jean industry targets its advertisements to appeal to young adults.

> The flight from teaching to research and publishing in higher education is a controversial issue in the academic world. I will show different views and aspects concerning this problem.

A thesis needs to be an assertion with which it would be possible for readers to disagree.

In the second example, few readers would disagree with the fact that the issue is "controversial." In the second sentence of that example, the writer has begun to identify a point of view—that the flight from teaching is a problem—but her declaration that she will "show different views and aspects" is a broad statement of fact, not an idea. The phrasing of the claim is noncommittal and so broad that it prevents the writer from formulating a workable thesis.

> **Solution:** Find some avenue of *inquiry*—a question about the facts or an issue raised by them. Make an assertion with which it would be possible for readers to disagree.

Solution Examples

> By inventing new terms, such as "loose fit" and "relaxed fit," the jean industry has attempted to normalize, even glorify, its product for an older and fatter generation.

> The "flight from teaching" to research and publishing in higher education is a controversial issue in the academic world. As I will attempt to show, the controversy is based to a significant degree on a false assumption, that doing research necessarily leads teachers away from the classroom.

WEAK THESIS TYPE 3: THE THESIS RESTATES CONVENTIONAL WISDOM

Problem Examples

> An important part of one's college education is learning to better understand others' points of view.

> "*I was* supposed to bring the coolers; *you* were supposed to bring the chips!" exclaimed ex-Beatle Ringo Starr, who appeared on TV commercials for Sun County Wine Coolers a few years ago. By using rock music to sell a wide range of products, the advertising agencies, in league with corporate giants such as Pepsi, Michelob, and Ford, have corrupted the spirit of rock and roll.

"Conventional wisdom" is a polite term for cultural cliché. Most clichés were fresh ideas once, but over time they have become trite, prefabricated forms of nonthinking. Faced with a phenomenon that requires a response, inexperienced writers sometimes resort to a small set of culturally approved "answers." Because conventional wisdom is so general and so commonly accepted, however, it doesn't teach anybody—including the writer—anything. Worse, because the cliché looks like an idea, it prevents the writer from engaging in a fresh exploration of his or her subject.

There is some truth in both of the preceding problem examples, but neither complicates its position. A thoughtful reader could, for example, respond to the advertising example by suggesting that rock and roll was highly commercial long before it colonized the airwaves. The conventional wisdom that rock and roll is somehow pure and honest while advertising is phony and exploitative invites the savvy writer to formulate a thesis that overturns these clichés. It could be argued that rock has actually improved advertising, not that ads have ruined rock—or, alternatively, that rock has shrewdly marketed idealism to gullible consumers. At the least, a writer committed to the original thesis would do better to examine what Ringo was selling—what he/wine coolers stand for in this particular case—than to discuss rock and advertising in such predictable terms.

> **Solution:** Seek to complicate—see more than one point of view on—your subject. Avoid conventional wisdom unless you can qualify it or introduce a fresh perspective on it.

Solution Examples

> While an important part of one's college education is learning to better understand others' points of view, a persistent danger is that the students will simply be required to substitute the teacher's answers for the ones they grew up uncritically believing.

> While some might argue that the presence of rock and roll soundtracks in TV commercials has corrupted rock's spirit, this point of view not only falsifies the history of rock but also blinds us to the ways that the music has improved the quality of television advertising.

WEAK THESIS TYPE 4: THE THESIS BASES ITS CLAIM ON PERSONAL CONVICTION

Problem Examples

> Sir Thomas More's *Utopia* proposes an unworkable set of solutions to society's problems because, like communist Russia, it suppresses individualism.

> Although I agree with Jeane Kirkpatrick's argument that environmentalists and business should work together to ensure the ecological future of the world, and that this cooperation is beneficial for both sides, the indisputable fact is that environmental considerations should always be a part of any decision that is made. Any individual, if he looks deeply enough into his soul, knows what is right and what is wrong. The environment should be protected because it is the right thing to do, not because someone is forcing you to do it.

Like conventional wisdom, personal likes and dislikes can lead inexperienced writers into knee-jerk reactions of approval or disapproval, often expressed in a moralistic tone. The writers of the preceding problem examples assume that their primary job is to judge their subjects, or testify to their worth, not to evaluate them analytically. They have taken personal opinions for self-evident truths. *(See Naturalizing Our Assumptions in Chapter 2.)*

The most blatant version of this tendency occurs in the second problem example, which asserts, "Any individual, if he looks deeply enough into his soul, knows what is right and what is wrong. The environment should be protected because it is the right thing to do." Translation (only slightly exaggerated): "Any individual who thinks about the subject will obviously agree with me because my feelings and convictions feel right to me and therefore they must be universally and self-evidently true." Testing an idea against your own feelings and experience is not an adequate means of establishing whether something is accurate or true.

It is fine, of course, to write about what you believe and to consult your feelings as you formulate an idea. But the risk you run in arguing from your unexamined feelings and convictions is that you will continue to play the same small set of tunes in response to everything you hear. And without the ability to think from multiple perspectives, you are less able to defend your convictions against the ideas that challenge them because you won't really have examined the logic of your own beliefs—you just believe them.

> **Solution:** Try on other points of view honestly and dispassionately; treat your ideas as hypotheses to be tested rather than obvious truths. In the following solution examples, we have replaced opinions (in the form of self-evident truths) with ideas—theories about the meaning and significance of the subjects that are capable of being supported and qualified by evidence.

Solution Examples

> Sir Thomas More's *Utopia* treats individualism as a serious but remediable social problem. His radical treatment of what we might now call "socialization" attempts to redefine the meaning and origin of individual identity.

> Although I agree with Jeane Kirkpatrick's argument that environmentalists and business should work together to ensure the ecological future of the world, her argument undervalues the necessity of pressuring businesses to attend to environmental concerns that may not benefit them in the short run.

WEAK THESIS TYPE 5: THE THESIS MAKES AN OVERLY BROAD CLAIM

Problem Examples

> Violent revolutions have had both positive and negative results for man.

> There are many similarities and differences between the Carolingian and the Burgundian Renaissances.
>
> *Othello* is a play about love and jealousy.

Overly generalized theses avoid complexity. Such statements usually lead either to say-nothing theses or to reductive either/or thinking. Similar to a thesis that makes no claim, theses with overly broad claims say nothing in particular about the subject at hand and so are not likely to guide a writer's thinking beyond the listing stage. One of the best ways to avoid drafting overly broad thesis statements is to sensitize yourself to the characteristic phrasing of such theses: "both positive and negative," "many similarities and differences," or "both pros and cons." Virtually everything from meatloaf to taxes can be both positive and negative.

Solution: Convert broad categories and generic claims to more specific, more qualified assertions; find ways to bring out the complexity of your subject.

Solution Examples

> Although violent revolutions begin to redress long-standing social inequities, they often do so at the cost of long-term economic dysfunction and the suffering that attends it.
>
> The differences between the Carolingian and Burgundian Renaissances outweigh the similarities.
>
> Although *Othello* appears to attack jealousy, it also supports the skepticism of the jealous characters over the naïveté of the lovers.

Getting Beyond the All-Purpose Thesis: A Dance Professor Speaks

In the following Voice from Across the Curriculum, dance professor Karen Dearborn offers examples of thesis statements that do more than offer standard "different but alike" phrasing.

Voices from Across the Curriculum

Making the Thesis Specific

Not so good thesis/question: "What were Humphrey's and Weidman's reasons behind the setting of *With My Red Fires,* and of what importance were the set and costume design to the piece as a whole?"

Good thesis: "While Graham and Wigman seem different, their ideas on inner expression (specifically subjectivism versus objectivism) and the incorporation of their respective countries' surge of nationalism bring them much closer than they appear."

What I like about the good thesis is that it moves beyond the standard "they are different, but alike" (which can be said about anything) to actually tell the reader what specific areas the paper will explore. I can also tell that the subject is narrow enough for a fairly thorough examination of one small slice of these two major choreographers' work rather than some over-generalized treatment of these two historic figures.

—Karen Dearborn, Professor of Dance

Try This 12.1: Revising Weak Thesis Statements

You can learn a lot about writing strong thesis statements by analyzing and rewriting weak ones. For the following example, first identify the type of problem for each thesis. Then rewrite them, providing solutions as we have done. Revising will require you to add information and thinking—to come up with some interesting claims that most readers would not already have thought of.

1. In this paper, I discuss police procedures in recent domestic violence cases.
2. The way that the media portrayed the events of April 30, 1975, when Saigon fell, greatly influenced the final perspectives of the American people toward the end result of the Vietnam War.
3. From cartoons in the morning to adventure shows at night, there is too much violence on television.
4. The songs of the punk rock group Minor Threat relate to the feelings of individuals who dare to be different. Their songs are just composed of pure emotion. Pure emotion is very important in music because it serves as a vehicle to convey the important message of individuality. Minor Threat's songs are meaningful to me because I can identify with them.
5. It is important to understand why leaders act in a leadership role. What is the driving force? Is it an internal drive for the business or group to succeed, or is it an internal drive for the leader to dominate over others?

HOW TO REPHRASE THESIS STATEMENTS: SPECIFY AND SUBORDINATE

Weak thesis statements can be quickly identified by their word choice and syntax (sentence structure). Each of the first three problem examples for Weak Thesis Type 5, for example, relies mostly on nouns rather than verbs; the nouns announce a broad heading, but the verbs don't do anything with or to the nouns. In grammatical terms, these thesis statements don't *predicate* (affirm or assert something about the subject of a proposition). Instead, they rely on anemic verbs like *is* or *are,* which function as equal signs that link general nouns with general adjectives rather than specify more complex relationships.

By replacing the equal sign with a more active verb, you can force yourself to advance some sort of claim, as in one of our solutions: "The differences between the Carolingian and Burgundian Renaissances *outweigh* the similarities." While this reformulation remains quite general, it at least begins to direct the writer along a more particular line of argument. Replacing *is* or *are* (verbs that function only as equal signs) with stronger verbs usually impels you to rank ideas in some order of importance and to assert some conceptual relation among them.

The best way to remedy the problem of overgeneralization is to move toward specificity in word choice, in sentence structure, and in idea. If you find yourself writing "The economic situation is bad," consider revising it to "The tax policies of the current administration threaten to reduce the tax burden on the middle class by sacrificing education and health care programs for everyone."

Here's the problem/solution in schematic form:

Broad Noun	**+ Weak Verb**	**+ Vague, Evaluative Modifier**
economic situation	is	bad

Specific Noun	**+ Active Verb**	**+ Specific Modifier**
(The) tax policies (of the current administration)	threaten to reduce (the tax burden on the middle class)	by sacrificing education and health care programs for everyone

By eliminating the weak thesis formula—broad noun plus *is* plus vague evaluative adjective—a writer is compelled to qualify, or define carefully, each of the terms in the original proposition, arriving at a more particular and conceptually rich assertion.

A second way to rephrase overly broad thesis statements, in tandem with adding specificity, is to *subordinate* one part of the statement to another. The both-positive-and-negative and both-similarity-and-difference formulae are recipes for say-nothing theses because they encourage pointless comparisons. Given that it is worthwhile to notice both strengths and weaknesses—that your subject is not all one way or all another—what, then, can you do to convert the thesis from a say-nothing to a say-something claim? Generally, there are two strategies for this purpose that operate together. The first we have already discussed.

1. *Specify:* Replace the overly abstract terms—terms like *positive* and *negative* (or *similar* and *different*)—with something specific; *name* something that is positive and something that is negative instead.

2. *Subordinate:* Rank one of the two items in the pairing underneath the other.
   When you subordinate, you put the most important, pressing, or revealing side of the comparison in what is known as the main clause and the less important side in what is known as the subordinate clause, introducing it with a word like *while* or *although*. (*See Glossary of Grammatical Terms in Chapter 19 for the definitions of main and subordinate clauses.*)

In short, specify to focus the claim, and subordinate to qualify (further focus) the claim still more. This strategy produces the remedies to both the *Othello* and the violent revolution examples in Weak Thesis Type 5. As evidence of the refocusing work that fairly simple rephrasing accomplishes, consider the following version of the violent revolution example, in which we merely invert the ranking of the two items in the pair.

Although violent revolutions often cause long-term economic dysfunction and the suffering that attends it, such revolutions at least begin to redress long-standing social inequities.

Is it Okay to Phrase a Thesis as a Question?

A question frequently asked about thesis statements is: Is it okay to phrase a thesis as a question? The answer is both yes and no. Phrasing a thesis as a question makes it more difficult for both the writer and the reader to be sure of the direction the paper takes because a question doesn't make an overt claim. Questions, however, can clearly imply claims. And many writers, especially in the early, exploratory stages of drafting, begin with a question, as we note in the discussion of What It Means to Have an Idea in Chapter 3.

As a general rule, use thesis questions cautiously, especially in final drafts. Although a thesis question often functions well to spark a writer's thinking, it can too often muddy the thinking by leaving the area of consideration too broad. Make sure that you do not let the thesis-question approach allow you to evade the responsibility of making some kind of claim. Especially in the drafting stage, a question posed overtly by the writer can provide focus, but only if he or she then proceeds to answer it with what would become a first statement of thesis.

Try This 12.2: Determining What the Thesis Requires You to Do Next

Learning to diagnose the strengths and weaknesses of thesis statements is a skill that comes in handy as you read the claims of others and revise your own. A good question for diagnosing a thesis is *What does the thesis require the writer to do next?* This question should help you to figure out what the thesis actually wants to claim, which can then direct you to possible rephrasings that would better direct your thinking.

Using this question as a prompt, list the strengths and weaknesses of the following two thesis statements, and then rewrite them. In the first statement, just rewrite the last sentence (the other sentences have been included to provide context).

1. Many economists and politicians agree that, along with the Environmental Protection Agency's newest regulations, a global-warming treaty could damage the American economy. Because of the great expense that such environmental standards require, domestic industries would financially suffer. Others argue, however, that severe regulatory steps must be taken to prevent global warming, regardless of cost. Despite both legitimate claims, the issue of protecting the environment while still securing our global competitiveness remains critical.

2. Regarding promotion into executive positions, women are continually losing the race because of a corporate view that women are too compassionate to keep up with the competitiveness of a powerful firm.

GUIDELINES FOR RECOGNIZING AND FIXING WEAK THESIS STATEMENTS

1. Your thesis should make a claim with which it would be possible for readers to disagree. In other words, move beyond defending statements that your readers would accept as obviously true.

2. Be skeptical of your first (often semiautomatic) response to a subject: it will often be a cliché (however unintentional). Avoid conventional wisdom unless you introduce a fresh perspective on it.

3. Convert broad categories and generic (fits anything) claims to more specific assertions. Find ways to bring out the complexity of your subject.

4. Submit the wording of your thesis to this grammatical test: if it follows the "abstract noun + is + evaluative adjective" formula ("The economic situation is bad"), substitute a more specific noun and an active verb that will force you to predicate something about a focused subject ("Tax laws benefit the rich").

5. Routinely examine and question your own key terms and categories rather than simply accepting them. Assume that they mean more than you first thought.

6. Always work to uncover and make explicit the unstated assumptions (premises) underlying your thesis. Don't treat debatable premises as givens.

7. As a rule, be suspicious of thesis statements that depend on words such as "real," "accurate," "believable," "right," and "good." These words usually signal that you are offering personal opinions—what "feels" right to you—as self-evident truths for everybody.

8. One way to assess the adequacy of a thesis statement is to ask yourself where the writer would need to go next to develop his or her idea. If you can't answer that question, then the thesis is still too weak.

9. Qualify your claims; you will avoid the global pronouncements—typical of the dangers of overly categorical thinking—that are too broad to be of much use (or true).

Assignment: Recognizing and Fixing Weak Thesis Statements

Analyzing Cliches: "Love Is the Answer"

Clichés are not necessarily untrue; they just are not worth saying (even if you're John Lennon, who offered this sodden truism in one of his more forgettable tunes).

One of the best ways to inoculate yourself against habitually resorting to clichés to provide easy and safe answers to all the problems of the planet—easy because they fit so many situations generically, and safe because, being so common, they *must* be true—is to go out and collect them, and then use this data-gathering to generate a thesis. Spend a day doing this, actively listening and looking for clichés—from overheard conversations (or your own), from reading matter, from anywhere (talk radio and TV are exceptionally rich resources) that is part of your daily round.

Compile a list, making sure to write down not only each cliché but the context in which it is used. From this data, and applying what you have learned from the chapters in this unit, formulate a thesis and write a paper about one or more of the clichés that infect some aspect of your daily life. You might find it useful to use The Method to identify key shared traits among the clichés and/ or among the contexts in which you have discovered them. And you might apply the advice provided under Weak Thesis Type 3 to work out alternative formulations to certain clichés to discover what that might teach us about the ways clichés function in given situations—how, for example, they do and don't fit the facts of the situation. If you can find a copy of Paul Muldoon's short poem, "Symposium," which is composed entirely of clichéd expressions, it might anchor an analysis or provide a lens for uncovering aspects of your data.

Chapter 13

Using Sources Analytically: The Conversation Model

THIS CHAPTER SHOWS you how to integrate secondary sources into your writing. That is often a daunting task because it requires you to negotiate with authorities who generally know more than you do about the subject at hand. Simply ignoring sources is a head-in-the-sand attitude and, besides, you miss out on learning what people interested in your subject are talking about. But what role can you invent for yourself when the experts are talking? Just agreeing with a source is an abdication of your responsibility to present your thinking on the subject. But taking the opposite tack by disagreeing with an expert who has studied your subject and written books about it would also appear to be a fool's game. So what are you to do?

This chapter attempts to answer that question. It lays out the primary trouble spots that arise when writers use secondary materials, and it suggests remedies—ways of using sources as points of departure for your own thinking rather than using them as either "The Answer" or a straw man. We call this approach *conversing with sources.*

Six Strategies for Analyzing Sources

Strategy 1: Make Your Sources Speak

Strategy 2: Attend Carefully to the Language of Your Sources by Quoting or Paraphrasing

Strategy 3: Supply Ongoing Analysis of Sources (Don't Wait until the End)

Strategy 4: Use Your Sources to Ask Questions, Not Just to Provide Answers

Strategy 5: Put Your Sources into Conversation with One Another

Strategy 6: Find Your Own Role in the Conversation

The kind of writing you are doing will affect the way you use sources. Analytical writing uses sources to expand understanding—often to allow readers to view a subject from a range of plausible points of view. This approach differs from the kind of research based writing wherein the goal is to locate a single position that beats out the others in a combative mode. One way sources are often used in an academic setting is as lenses for examining other sources and primary materials. *(For using a source as a lens, see Chapter 5, Writing About Reading: More Moves to Make with Written Texts.)*

We use the terms *source* and *secondary source* interchangeably to designate ideas and information about your subject that you find in the work of other writers. Secondary sources allow you to gain a richer, more informed, and complex vantage point on your *primary sources*. Here's how primary and secondary sources can be distinguished: if you were writing a paper on the philosopher Nietzsche, his writing would be your primary source, and critical commentaries on his work would be your secondary sources. If, however, you were writing on the poet Yeats, who read and was influenced by Nietzsche, a work of Nietzsche's philosophy would become a secondary source on your primary source, Yeats's poetry.

"SOURCE ANXIETY" AND WHAT TO DO ABOUT IT

Typically, inexperienced writers either use sources as "answers"—they let the sources do too much of their thinking—or ignore them altogether as a way of avoiding losing their own ideas. Both of these approaches are understandable but inadequate.

Confronted with the seasoned views of experts in a discipline, you may well feel there is nothing left for you to say because it has all been said before or, at least, it has been said by people who greatly outweigh you in reputation and experience. This anxiety explains why so many writers surrender to the role of conduit for the voices of the experts, providing conjunctions between quotations. So why not avoid what other people have said? Won't this avoidance ensure that your ideas will be original and that, at the same time, you will be free from the danger of getting brainwashed by some expert?

The answer is no. If you don't consult what others have said, you run at least two risks: you will waste your time reinventing the wheel, and you will undermine your analysis (or at least leave it incomplete) by not considering information and ideas commonly discussed in the field. By remaining unaware of existing thinking, you choose, in effect, to stand outside of the conversation that others interested in the subject are having.

It is possible to find a *middle ground* between developing an idea that is entirely independent of what experts have written on a subject and producing a paper that does nothing but repeat other people's ideas. A little research—even if it's only an hour's browse in the relevant databases on your library's website—will virtually always raise the level of what you have to say above what it would have been if you had consulted only the information and opinions that you carry around in your head.

A good rule of thumb for coping with source anxiety is to formulate a tentative position on your topic before you consult secondary sources. In other words, give yourself time to do some preliminary thinking. Try writing informally about your topic, analyzing some piece of pertinent information already at your disposal. That way, you will have your initial responses written down to weigh in relation to what others have said.

THE CONVERSATION ANALOGY

Now, let's turn to the major problem in using sources—a writer leaving the experts he or she cites to speak for themselves. In this situation, the writer characteristically makes a generalization in his or her own words, juxtaposes it to a quotation or other reference from a secondary source, and assumes that the meaning of the reference will be self-evident. This practice not only leaves the connection between the writer's thinking and his or her source material unstated but also substitutes mere repetition of someone else's viewpoint for a more active interpretation. The source has been allowed to have the final word, with the effect that it stops the discussion and the writer's thinking.

First and foremost, then, you need *to do something* with the reading. Clarify the meaning of the material you have quoted, paraphrased, or summarized and explain its significance in light of your evolving thesis.

It follows that the first step in using sources effectively is to reject the assumption that sources provide final and complete answers. If they did, there would be no reason for others to continue writing on the subject. As in conversation, we raise ideas for others to respond to. Accepting that no source has the final word does not mean, however, that you should shift from unquestioning approval to the opposite pole and necessarily assume an antagonistic position toward all sources. Indeed, a habitually antagonistic response to others' ideas is just as likely to bring your conversation with your sources to a halt as is the habit of always assuming that the source must have the final word.

Most people would probably agree on the attributes of a really good conversation. There is room for agreement and disagreement, for give and take, among a variety of viewpoints. Generally, people don't deliberately misunderstand each other, but a significant amount of the discussion may go into clarifying one's own as well as others' positions. Such conversations construct a genuinely collaborative chain of thinking: Karl builds on what David has said, which induces Jill to respond to Karl's comment, and so forth.

There are, of course, obvious differences between conversing aloud with friends and conversing on paper with sources. As a writer, you need to construct the chain of thinking, orchestrate the exchange of views with and among your sources, and give the conversation direction. A good place to begin in using sources is to recognize that you need not respond to everything another writer says, nor do you need to come up with an entirely original point of view—one that completely revises or refutes the source. You are using sources analytically, for example, when you note that two experiments (or historical accounts, or whatever) are similar but have different priorities or that they ask similar questions in different ways. Building from this kind of observation, you can then analyze what these differences imply.

TWO METHODS FOR CONVERSING WITH SOURCES

- Choose one sentence from a secondary source and one from a primary source, and put these into conversation. What does each reveal about the other?
- Pick one sentence from one source (A) and one from another (B): how does A speak to B? How does B speak to A?

Remember: go local, not global. You will be better off if you bring together two representative moves or ideas from the sources rather than trying to compare a summary of one source with a summary of another. A useful phrase here is "points of contact": look for ways that an idea or observation in source A appears to intersect with one in source B. Then stage the conversation you can imagine taking place between them.

Conversing with a Source: A Brief Example

Consider, for example, the following quotation, the opening sentences of an essay, "Clichés," by Christopher Ricks, which is ostensibly a review of a reissued book on the subject:

> The only way to speak of a cliché is with a cliché. So even the best writers against clichés are awkwardly placed. When Eric Partridge amassed his *Dictionary of Cliches* in 1940 (1978 saw its fifth edition), his introduction had no choice but to use the usual clichés for clichés. Yet what, as a metaphor, could be more hackneyed than *hackneyed,* more outworn than *outworn,* more tattered than *tattered?* Is there any point left to—or in or on—saying of a cliché that its "original point has been blunted"? Hasn't this too become blunted? (Christopher Ricks, "Cliches" in *The State of the Language,* University of California Press, 1980, p. 54)

A writer would not want to cite this passage simply to illustrate that clichés are "bad"—language uses to be avoided—or to suggest, as a dictionary might, that a cliché is a form of expression one might call "hackneyed" or "outworn" or "tattered," even though this information is clearly included in Ricks's sentences. Nor would a writer simply want to reiterate Ricks's leading claim, that "The only way to speak of a cliché is with a cliché," because Ricks already said that.

Instead, you'd need to talk about how Ricks treats the topic—that he has uncovered a paradox, for example, in that first sentence. You might go on to say that his point of view provides a useful warning for those who wish to talk about clichés. And then you might make some inferences you could build on: that simply dismissing clichés on vaguely moral grounds as unoriginal (hackneyed) does not add anything to our knowledge, and so perhaps, it's time to rethink our usual response to clichés and to see them afresh. In any case, as a rule of thumb, only include a quotation if you plan to say something about it.

WAYS TO USE A SOURCE AS A POINT OF DEPARTURE

There are many ways of approaching secondary sources, but these ways generally share a common goal: to use the source as a point of departure. Here is a partial list of ways to do that.

- Make as many points as you can about a single representative passage from your source, and then branch out from this center to analyze other passages that "speak" to it in some way. (*See 10 on 1 and Pan, Track and Zoom in Chapter 10.*)

- Use Notice and Focus to identify what you find most strange in the source; this will help you cultivate your curiosity about the source and find the critical distance necessary to thinking about it.

- Use The Method to identify the most significant organizing contrast in the source; this will help you see what the source itself is wrestling with, what is at stake in it.

- Apply an idea in the source to another subject. (*See Applying a Reading as a Lens in Chapter 5.*)

- Uncover the assumptions in the source, and then build upon the source's point of view, extending its implications. (*See Uncovering Assumptions in Chapter 4.*)

- Agree with most of what the source says, but take issue with one small part that you want to modify.

- Identify a contradiction in the source, and explore its implications, without necessarily arriving at a solution.

In using a source as a point of departure, you are in effect using it as a stimulus to have an idea. If you quote or paraphrase a source with the aim of conversing rather than allowing it to do your thinking for you, you will discover that sources can promote rather than stifle your ability to have ideas. Try to think of sources not as answers but as voices inviting you into a community of interpretation, discussion, and debate.

SIX STRATEGIES FOR ANALYZING SOURCES

Many people never get beyond like/dislike responses with secondary materials. If they agree with what a source says, they say it's "good," and they cut and paste the part they can use as an answer. If the source somehow disagrees with what they already believe, they say it's "bad," and they attack it or—along with readings they find "hard" or "boring"—discard it. As readers, they have been conditioned to develop a point of view on a subject without first figuring out the conversation (the various points of view) that their subject attracts. They assume, in other words, that their subject probably has a single meaning—a gist—disclosed by experts, who mostly agree. The six strategies that follow offer ways to avoid this trap.

Strategy 1: Make Your Sources Speak

Quote, paraphrase, or summarize *in order to* analyze—not in place of analyzing. Don't assume that either the meaning of the source material or your reason for including it is self-evident. Stop yourself from the habit of just stringing together citations for which you provide little more than conjunctions. Instead, explain to your readers what the quotation or paraphrase or summary of the source means. What elements of it do you find interesting or revealing or strange? Emphasize how those affect your evolving thesis.

In making a source speak, focus on articulating how the source has led to the conclusion you draw from it. Beware of simply putting a generalization and a quotation next to each other (juxtaposing them) without explaining the connection. Instead, fill the crucial site between claim and evidence with your thinking. Consider this problem in the following paragraph from a student's paper on political conservatism.

> Edmund Burke's philosophy evolved into contemporary American conservative ideology. There is an important distinction between philosophy and political ideology: philosophy is "the knowledge of general principles that explain facts and existences." Political ideology, on the other hand, is "an overarching conception of society, a stance that is reflected in numerous sectors of social life" (Edwards 22). Therefore, conservatism should be regarded as an ideology rather than a philosophy.

The final sentence offers the writer's conclusion—what the source information has led him to—but how did it get him there? The writer's choice of the word "therefore" indicates to the reader that the idea following it is the result of a process of logical reasoning, but this reasoning has been omitted. Instead, the writer assumes the reader will be able to connect the quotations with his conclusion. The writer needs to make the quotation speak by analyzing its key terms more closely. What is "an overarching conception of society," and how does it differ from "knowledge of general principles"? More important, what is the rationale for categorizing conservatism as either an ideology or a philosophy?

Here, by contrast, is a writer who makes her sources speak. Focus on how she integrates analysis with quotation.

> Stephen Greenblatt uses the phrase "self-fashioning" to refer to an idea he believes developed during the Renaissance—the idea that one's identity is not created or born but rather shaped, both by one's self and by others. The idea of self-fashioning is incorporated into an attitude toward literature that has as its ideal what Greenblatt calls "poetics of culture." A text is examined with three elements in mind: the author's own self, the cultural self-fashioning process that created that self, and the author's reaction to that process. Because our selves, like texts, are "fashioned," an author's life is just as open to interpretation as that of a literary character.
>
> If this is so, then biography does not provide a repository of unshakeable facts from which to interpret an author's work. Greenblatt criticizes the fact that the methods of literary interpretation are applied just to art and not to life. As he observes, "We wall off literary symbolism from the symbolic structures operative elsewhere, as if art alone were a human creation" (Begley 37). If the line between art and life is indeed blurred, then we need a more complex model for understanding the relationship between the life and work of an author.

In this example, the writer shows us how her thinking has been stimulated by the source. At the end of the first paragraph and the beginning of the second, for example, she not only specifies what she takes to be the meaning of the quotation but also draws a conclusion about its implications (that the facts of an author's life, like his or her art, require interpretation). And this manner of proceeding is habitual: the writer repeats the pattern in the second paragraph, moving beyond what the quotation says to explore what its logic suggests.

Strategy 2: Attend Carefully to the Language of Your Sources by Quoting or Paraphrasing Them

Rather than generalizing broadly about ideas in your sources, you should spell out what you think is significant about their keywords. In those disciplines in which it is permissible, *quote sources if the actual language they use is important to your point.* Generally, disciplines in the humanities expect you to quote as well as paraphrase, while in the social sciences, students are encouraged to paraphrase, not quote.

Quoting and paraphrasing has the benefit of helping writers to represent the views of their sources fairly and accurately. In situations where quoting is not allowed—such as in the report format in psychology—you still need to attend carefully to the meaning of keywords in order to arrive at a summary or paraphrase that is not overly general. As we have suggested repeatedly, paraphrasing provides an ideal way to begin interpreting because the act of careful rephrasing usually illuminates attitudes and assumptions implicit in a text. It is almost impossible not to have ideas and not to see the questions when you start paraphrasing.

Another reason quoting and paraphrasing are important is because your analysis of a source will nearly always benefit from attention to the way the source represents its position. Although focusing on the manner of presentation matters more with some sources than with others—more with a poem or scholarly article in political science than with a paper in the natural sciences—the information is never wholly separable from how it is expressed. If you are going to quote *Newsweek* on Pakistan, for example, you will be encountering not "the truth" about American involvement in this Asian nation but rather one particular representation of the situation—in this case, one crafted to meet or shape the expectations of mainstream popular culture. Similarly, if you quote President Bush on terrorism, what probably matters most is that the president chose particular words to represent—and promote—the government's position. It is not neutral information. The person speaking and the kind of source in which his or her words appear usually acquire added significance when you make note of these words rather than just summarizing them.

Strategy 3: Supply Ongoing Analysis of Sources (Don't Wait Until the End)

Unless disciplinary conventions dictate otherwise, analyze *as* you quote or paraphrase a source, rather than summarizing everything first and leaving your analysis for the end. A good conversation does not consist of long monologues alternating among the speakers. Participants exchange views, query, and modify what other speakers have said. Similarly, when you orchestrate conversations with and among your sources, you need to integrate your analysis into your presentation of them.

In supplying ongoing analysis, you are much more likely to explain how the information in the sources fits into your unfolding presentation, and your readers will be more likely to follow your train of thought and grasp the logic of your organization. You will also prevent yourself from using the sources simply as an answer. A good rule of thumb in this regard is to force yourself to ask and answer "So what?" at the ends of paragraphs. In laying out your analysis, however, take special care to distinguish your voice from the sources'.

Bringing Sources Together: A Psychology Professor Speaks

In the following Voice from Across the Curriculum, psychology professor Alan Tjeltveit offers a tip about how members of his discipline orchestrate a number of sources on more than one topic.

Voices from Across the Curriculum

Avoid serial citation summaries; that is, rather than discussing what Author A found, then what Author B found, then what Author C found, and so forth, *integrate* material from all of your sources. For instance, if writing about the cause and treatment of a disorder, discuss what all authors say about cause, then what all authors say about treatment, and so forth, addressing any contradictions or tensions among authors.

—Alan Tjeltveit, Professor of Psychology

Strategy 4: Use Your Sources to Ask Questions, Not Just To Provide Answers

Use your selections from sources as a means of raising issues and questions. Avoid the temptation to plug in such selections as answers that require no further commentary or elaboration. You will no doubt find viewpoints you believe to be valid, but it is not enough to drop these answers from the source into your own writing at the appropriate spots. You need to *do* something with the reading, even with those sources that seem to have said what you want to say.

As long as you consider only the source in isolation, you may not discover much to say about it. Once you begin considering it in other contexts and with other sources, you may begin to see aspects of your subject that your source does not adequately address. Having recognized that the source does not answer all questions, you should not conclude that the source is "wrong"—only that it is limited in some ways. Discovering such limitations is in fact advantageous because it can lead you to identify a place from which to launch your own analysis.

It does not necessarily follow that your analysis will culminate in an answer to replace those offered by your sources. Often—in fact, far more often than many writers suspect—it is enough to discover issues or problems and raise them clearly. Phrasing explicitly the issues and questions that remain implicit in a source is an important part of what analytical writers do, especially with cases in which there is no solution, or at least none that can be presented in a relatively short paper. Here, for example, is how the writer on Stephen Greenblatt's concept of self-fashioning concludes her essay:

> It is not only the author whose role is complicated by New Historicism; the critic also is subject to some of the same qualifications and restrictions. According to Adam Begley, "it is the essence of the new-historicist project to uncover the moments at which works of art absorb and refashion social energy, an endless process of circulation and exchange" (39). In other words, the work is both affected by and affects the culture. But if this is so, how then can we decide which elements of culture (and text) are causes and which are effects? If we add the critic to this picture, the process does indeed appear endless. The New Historicists' relationship with their culture infuses itself into their assessment of the Renaissance, and this assessment may in turn become part of their own self-fashioning process, which will affect their interpretations, and so forth....

Notice that this writer incorporates the quotation into her own chain of thinking. By paraphrasing the quotation ("In other words"), she arrives at a question ("how then") that follows as a logical consequence of accepting its position ("but if this is so"). Note, however, that she does not then label the quotation right or wrong. Instead, she tries to figure out to what position it might lead and to what possible problems.

By contrast, the writer of the following excerpt, from a paper comparing two films aimed at teenagers, settles for plugging in sources as answers and consequently does not pursue the questions implicit in her quotations.

> In both films, the adults are one-dimensional caricatures, evil beings whose only goal in life is to make the kids' lives a living hell. In *Risky Business*, director Paul Brickman's solution to all of Joel's problems is to have him hire a prostitute and then turn his house into a whorehouse. Of course, as one critic observes, "the prostitutes who make themselves available to his pimply faced buddies are all centerfold beauties: elegant, svelte, benign and unquestionably healthy (after all, what does V.D. have to do with prostitutes?)" (Gould 41)—not exactly a realistic or legal solution. Allan Moyle, the director of *Pump Up the Volume*, provides an equally unrealistic solution to Mark's problem. According to David Denby, Moyle "offers self-expression as the cure to adolescent funk. Everyone should start his own radio station and talk about his feelings" (59). Like Brickman, Moyle offers solutions that are neither realistic nor legal.

This writer is having a hard time figuring out what to do with sources that offer well-phrased and seemingly accurate answers (such as "self-expression is the cure to adolescent funk"). She settles for the bland conclusion that films aimed at teenagers are not "realistic"—an observation that most readers would already recognize as true. But unlike the writer of the previous example, she does not ask herself, "If this is true, then what follows?" Some version of the So what? question might have led her to inquire how the illegality of the solutions is related to their unrealistic quality. So what, for example, that the main characters in both films are not marginalized as criminals and made to suffer for their illegal actions, but rather are celebrated as heroes? What different kinds of illegality do the two films apparently condone, and how might these be related to the different decades in which each film was produced? Rather than use her sources to think with, in order to clarify or complicate the issues, the writer has used them to confirm a fairly obvious generalization.

Strategy 5: Put Your Sources Into Conversation with One Another

Rather than limiting yourself to agreeing or disagreeing with your sources, aim for conversation with and among them. Although it is not wrong to agree or disagree with your sources, it is wrong to see these as your only possible moves. This practice of *framing the discussion* typically locates you either for or against some well-known point of view or frame of reference; it's a way of sharing your assumptions with the reader. You introduce the source, in other words, to succinctly summarize a position that you plan to develop or challenge in a qualified way. This latter strategy—sometimes known as straw man, because you construct a "dummy" position specifically in order to knock it down—can stimulate you to formulate a point of view, especially if you are not accustomed to responding critically to sources.

As this boxing analogy suggests, however, setting up a straw man can be a dangerous game. If you do not fairly represent and put into context the straw man's argument, you risk encouraging readers to dismiss your counterargument as a cheap shot and to dismiss you for being reductive. On the other hand, if you spend a great deal of time detailing the straw man's position, you risk losing momentum in developing your own point of view.

In any case, if you are citing a source in order to frame the discussion, the more reasonable move is both to agree *and* disagree with it. First, identify shared premises; give the source some credit. Then, distinguish the part of what you have cited that you intend to develop or complicate or dispute. This method of proceeding is obviously less combative than the typically blunt straw man approach; it verges on conversation.

In the following passage from a student's paper on Darwin's Theory of Evolution, the student clearly recognizes that he needs to do more than summarize what Darwin says, but he seems not to know any way of conversing with his source other than indicating his agreement and disagreement with it.

> The struggle for existence also includes the dependence of one being on another being to survive. Darwin also believes that all organic beings tend to increase. I do not fully agree with Darwin's belief here. I cannot conceive of the fact of all beings increasing in number. Darwin goes on to explain that food, competition, climate, and the location of a certain species contribute to its survival and existence in nature. I believe that this statement is very valid and that it could be very easily understood through experimentation in nature.

This writer's use of the word "here" in his third sentence is revealing. He is tagging summaries of Darwin with what he seems to feel is an obligatory response—a polite shake or nod of the head: "I can't fully agree with you there, Darwin, but here I think you might have a point." The writer's tentative language lets us see how uncomfortable, even embarrassed, he feels about venturing these judgments on a subject too complex for this kind of response. It's as though the writer moves along, talking about Darwin's theory for a while, and then says to himself, "Time for a response," and lets a particular summary sentence trigger a yes/no switch. Having pressed that switch, which he does periodically, the writer resumes his summary, having registered but not analyzed his own interjections. There is no reasoning in a chain from his own observations, just random insertions of unanalyzed agree/disagree responses.

Here, by contrast, is the introduction of an essay that uses summary to frame the conversation that the writer is preparing to have with her source.

> In *Renaissance Thought: The Classic, Scholastic and Humanist Strains,* Paul Kristeller responds to two problems that he perceives in Renaissance scholarship. The first is the haze of cultural meaning surrounding the word "humanism": he seeks to clarify the word and its origins, as well as to explain the apparent lack of religious concern in humanism. Kristeller also reacts to the notion of humanism as an improvement upon medieval Aristotelian scholasticism.

Rather than leading with her own beliefs about the source, the writer emphasizes the issues and problems she believes are central in it. Although the writer's position on her source is apparently neutral, she is not summarizing passively. In addition to making choices about what is especially significant in the source, she has also located it within the conversation that its author, Kristeller, was having with his own sources—the works of other scholars whose view of humanism he wants to revise ("Kristeller responds to two problems").

As an alternative to formulating your opinion of the sources, try constructing the conversation you think the author of one of your sources might have with the author of another. How might they recast each other's ideas, as opposed to merely agreeing or disagreeing with those ideas? Notice how, farther on in the paper, the writer uses this strategy to achieve a clearer picture of Kristeller's point of view:

> Unlike Kristeller, Tillyard [in *The Elizabethan World Picture*] also tries to place the seeds of individualism in the minds of the medievals. "Those who know most about the Middle Ages," he claims, "now assure us that humanism and a belief in the present life were powerful by the 12th century" (30). Kristeller would undoubtedly reply that it was scholasticism, lacking the humanist emphasis on individualism that was powerful in the Middle Ages. True humanism was not evident in the Middle Ages.
>
> In Kristeller's view, Tillyard's attempts to assign humanism to medievals are not only unwarranted, but also counterproductive. Kristeller ends his chapter on "Humanism and Scholasticism" with an exhortation to "develop a kind of historical pluralism. It is easy to praise everything in the past that appears to resemble certain favorable ideas of our own time, or to ridicule and minimize everything that disagrees with them. This method is neither fair nor helpful" (174). Tillyard, in trying to locate humanism within the medieval world, allows the value of humanism to supersede the worth of medieval scholarship. Kristeller argues that there is inherent worth in every intellectual movement, not simply in the ones that we find most agreeable.
>
> Kristeller's work is valuable to us primarily for its forthright definition of humanism. Tillyard has cleverly avoided this undertaking: he provides many textual references, usually with the companion comment that "this is an example of Renaissance humanism," but he never overtly and fully formulates the definition in the way that Kristeller does.

As this excerpt makes evident, the writer has found something to say about her source by putting it into conversation with another source with which she believes her source, Kristeller, would disagree ("Kristeller would undoubtedly reply"). Although it seems obvious that the writer prefers Kristeller to Tillyard, her agreement with him is not the main point of her analysis. She focuses instead on foregrounding the problem that Kristeller is trying to solve and on relating that problem to different attitudes toward history. In so doing, she is deftly orchestrating the conversation between her sources. Her next step would be to distinguish her position from Kristeller's. Having used Kristeller to get perspective on Tillyard, she now needs somehow to get perspective on Kristeller. The next strategy addresses this issue.

Strategy 6: Find Your Own Role in the Conversation

Even in cases in which you find a source's position entirely congenial, it is not enough simply to agree with it. This does not mean you should feel compelled to attack the source but rather that you need to find something of your own to say about it.

In general, you have two options when you find yourself strongly in agreement with a source. You can (1) apply it in another context to qualify or expand its implications. Or you can (2) seek out other perspectives on the source in order to break the spell it has cast on you. To break the spell means you will necessarily become somewhat disillusioned but not that you will then need to dismiss everything you previously believed.

How, in the first option, do you take a source somewhere else? Rather than focusing solely on what you believe your source finds most important, locate a lesser point, not emphasized by the reading, that you find especially interesting and develop it further. This strategy will lead you to uncover new implications that depend on your source but lie outside its own governing preoccupations. In the preceding humanism example, the writer might apply Kristeller's principles to new geographic (rather than theoretical) areas, such as Germany instead of Italy.

The second option, researching new perspectives on the source, can also lead to uncovering new implications. Your aim need not be simply to find a source that disagrees with the one that has convinced you and then switch your allegiance because this move would perpetuate the problem from which you are trying to escape. Instead, you would use additional perspectives to gain some critical distance from your source. An ideal way of sampling possible critical approaches to a source is to consult book reviews on it found in scholarly journals. Once the original source is taken down from the pedestal through additional reading, there is a greater likelihood that you will see how to distinguish your views from those it offers.

You may think, for example, that another source's critique of your original source is partly valid and that both sources miss things you could point out; in effect, you *referee* the conversation between them. The writer on Kristeller might play this role by asking herself: "So what that subsequent historians have viewed his objective—a disinterested historical pluralism—as not necessarily desirable and in any case impossible? How might Kristeller respond to this charge, and how has he responded already in ways that his critics have failed to notice?" Using additional research in this way can lead you to situate your source more fully and fairly, acknowledging its limits as well as its strengths.

In other words, this writer, in using Kristeller to critique Tillyard, has arrived less at a conclusion than at her next point of departure. A good rule to follow, especially when you find a source entirely persuasive, is that if you can't find a perspective on your source, you haven't done enough research.

Evaluating Sources in the Sciences: A Biology Professor Speaks

In the following Voice from Across the Curriculum, molecular biologist Bruce Wightman suggests the range of tasks he expects students to do when they engage a source—not only to supply ongoing analysis of it and to consider its contributions in light of other research, but also to locate themselves in relation to the questions their analysis of the source has led them to discover.

Voices from Across the Curriculum

One of the problems with trying to *read* critical analyses of scientific work is that few scientists want to be in print criticizing their colleagues. That is, for political reasons, scientists who write reviews are likely to soften their criticism or even avoid it entirely by reporting the findings of others simply and directly.

What I want from students in molecular biology is a critical analysis of the work they have researched. This can take several forms.

First, *analyze* what was done. What were the assumptions (hypotheses) going into the experiment? What was the logic of the experimental design? What were the results?

Second, *evaluate* the results and conclusions. How well do the results support the conclusions? What alternative interpretations are there? What additional experiments could be done to strengthen or refute the argument? This is hard, no doubt, but it is what you should be doing every time you read anything in science or otherwise.

Third, *synthesize* the results and interpretations of a given experiment in the context of the field. How does this study inform other studies? Even though practicing scientists are hesitant to do this in print, everyone does it informally in journal clubs held usually on a weekly basis in every lab all over the world.

—Bruce Wightman, Professor of Biology

USING SOURCES ANALYTICALLY: AN EXAMPLE

In a recent article on thinking entitled "The Other You" that appeared in the journal *New Scientist*, the writer introduces sources in sequence, wherein each source offers a different researcher's angle on the same central question: how is the subconscious related to the conscious activities of the mind? The writer, Kate Douglas, discusses the implications of each source without choosing any one as "the answer":

- "Shadlin sees the subconscious and conscious as two parts of the same system, rather than two separate thought processors working in the same machine" (45).

- "Others want to further subdivide conscious and subconscious thought and have come up with alternative descriptions to replace the old two-part model" (45)

- "Peter Dayan [and colleagues] see the mind as comprising four systems."
- "Dayan says that our behavior is often driven by more than one of the four controllers."

At the end of this phase of the article, Douglas then states, "Importantly, the subconscious isn't the dumb cousin of the conscious, but rather a cousin with different skills" (Kate Douglas, "The Other You," *New Scientist*, December 1–7, 2007. vol. 196, no. 2632, p. 45).

As this example demonstrates, often in conversing with sources, a writer is not staging conflicts or debates, but bringing together multiple points of view and offering a final synthesis. Those familiar with the popular journalist Malcolm Gladwell may recognize that he is fond of this method. In books such as *Blink*, Gladwell presents one piece of research, and in making inferences about it, leads us to the next and often unexpectedly related piece of research. Part of the appeal of Gladwell's method is how he quilts together a range of disparate voices into one unfolding narrative. The thinking in a Gladwell piece is presented in the way he connects the parts, not in the way that he is critiquing them, finding shortcomings, or emphasizing the differences.

GUIDELINES FOR CONVERSING WITH SOURCES

1. Avoid the temptation to plug in sources as answers. Aim for a *conversation* with them. Think of sources as voices inviting you into a community of interpretation, discussion, and debate.

2. Quote, paraphrase, or summarize *in order to* analyze. Explain what you take the source to mean, showing the reasoning that has led to the conclusion you draw from it.

3. Quote sparingly. You are usually better off centering your analysis on a few quotations, analyzing their key terms, and branching out to aspects of your subject that the quotations illuminate. Remember that not all disciplines allow direct quotation.

4. Don't underestimate the value of close paraphrasing. You will almost invariably begin to interpret a source once you start paraphrasing its key language.

5. Locate and highlight what is at stake in your source. Which of its points does the source find most important? What positions does it want to modify or refute, and why?

6. Look for ways to develop, modify, or apply what a source has said, rather than simply agreeing or disagreeing with it.

7. If you challenge a position found in a source, be sure to represent it fairly. First, give the source some credit by identifying assumptions you share with it. Then, isolate the part that you intend to complicate or dispute.

8. Look for sources that address your subject from different perspectives. Avoid relying too heavily on any one source. Aim at the end to synthesize these perspectives: what is the common ground?

9. When your sources disagree, consider playing mediator. Instead of immediately agreeing with one or the other, clarify areas of agreement and disagreement among them.

Assignments: Conversing with Sources

1. **Make One Source Speak to Another.** Choose two articles or book chapters by different authors or by the same author at different points in his or her career. The overriding aim of the assignment is to give you practice in getting beyond merely reacting and generalizing, and instead, participating in your sources' thinking.

   Keep in mind that your aim is not to arrive at your opinion of the sources, but to construct the conversation you think the author of one of your sources might have with the author of another. How might they recast each other's ideas, as opposed to merely agreeing or disagreeing with those ideas? It's useful to confine yourself to thinking as impartially as you can about the ideas found in your two sources.

2. **Use Passage-Based Focused Freewriting to Converse with Sources.** Select a passage from a secondary source that appears important to your evolving thinking about a subject you are studying, and do a passage-based focused freewrite on it. You might choose the passage in answer to the question "What is the one passage in the source that I need to discuss, that poses a question or a problem or that seems, in some way difficult to pin down, anomalous or even just unclear?" Copy the passage at the top of the page, and write without stopping for 20 minutes or more. As noted in the discussion of freewriting in Chapter 4, paraphrase key terms as you relentlessly ask "So what?" about the details.

3. **Use a Source as a Lens on Another Source.** Apply a brief passage from a secondary source to a brief passage from a primary source, using the passage from the secondary source as a lens. Choose the secondary source passage first—one that you find particularly interesting, revealing, or problematic. Then locate a corresponding passage from the primary source to which the sentence from the first passage can be connected in some way. Copy both passages at the top of the page, and then write for 20 minutes. You should probably include paraphrases of key phrases in both—not just the primary text—but your primary goal is to think about the two together, to allow them to interact.

Chapter 14

Finding, Citing, and Integrating Sources

THIS CHAPTER SHIFTS ATTENTION to more technical matters associated with writing the researched paper. More than just mechanically gathering information, research continues to be a primary means of discovering the ongoing conflicts about a subject and having ideas about it. Engaging the information sparks thinking—not just arranging.

THIS CHAPTER IS DIVIDED INTO FIVE SECTIONS

A. Research Methods
B. Plagiarism and the Logic of Citation
C. Citing Sources: Four Documentation Styles
D. Integrating Quotations Into Your Paper
E. Preparing an Abstract

The core of this chapter is a discussion of research methods written by a reference librarian at our college, Kelly Cannon. It offers a wealth of insider's tips for making more productive use of your research time.

A. A Guided Tour of Research Methods by Reference Librarian Kelly Cannon

THREE RULES OF THUMB FOR GETTING STARTED

- A half-hour spent with a reference librarian can save you half a day wandering randomly through the stacks selecting sources.
- Start your research in the present and work backward. Usually the most current materials include bibliographical citations that can help you identify the most important sources in the past. Along the same lines, you are usually better off starting with journal articles rather than books because articles are more current.

- Consistently evaluate the reliability of the source, looking for its potential bias or agenda. Evidence is always qualified by how it is framed. For example, *Newsweek* can be a useful source if you want evidence about popular understanding of a subject or issue. The fact that the material comes from *Newsweek* and thus represents a position aimed at a mainstream, nonacademic audience provides the central reason for citing it.

The challenge of doing research in the Information Age is that there is so much information available. How do you know which information is considered authoritative in a particular discipline and which isn't? How can you avoid wasting time with source materials that have been effectively refuted and replaced by subsequent thinking? A short answer to these questions is that you should start in the reference room of your library or with its electronic equivalent. Many if not all of the resources listed below are now available online through your college library website. Your reference librarian can advise you on availability.

Start with Indexes, Specialized Dictionaries, Abstracts, and Bibliographies

These reference sources can rapidly provide you with both a broad perspective on your subject and a summary of what particular sources contain. An **index** offers a list of titles directing you to scholarly journals; often this list is sufficient to give you a clearer idea of the kinds of topics about which writers in the field are conversing. **Compilations of abstracts** and **annotated bibliographies** provide more information—anywhere from a few sentences to a few pages that summarize each source. *(See the section at the end of this chapter on abstracts and how to write them.)*

Here are a few of the most commonly used indexes, bibliographies, and abstracts:

Art Abstracts

Business Source Elite

ERIC (Education)

MLA (Modern Language Association)

PubMed

SocAbs

Specialized dictionaries and encyclopedias are sometimes extraordinarily useful in sketching the general terrain for a subject, and they often include bibliographical leads as well. Here are some titles, ranging from the expected to the eccentric:

Dictionary of the History of Ideas	*Encyclopedia of Economics*
Dictionary of Literary Biography	*Encyclopedia of Native American*
Encyclopedia of American History	*Religions*
Encyclopedia of Bioethics	*Encyclopedia of Philosophy*
Encyclopedia of Crime and Justice	*Encyclopedia of Psychology*

Encyclopedia of Unbelief

Encyclopedia of World Art

Encyclopedic Dictionary of Mathematics

Macmillan Encyclopedia of Computers

Encyclopedia of Medical History

McGraw Hill Encyclopedia of Science and Technology

New Grove Dictionary of Music and Musicians

Oxford English Dictionary

Most of the resources just listed also include book reviews. In addition, the *Reader's Guide to Periodical Literature* locates reviews as well as articles in popular—general audience—publications such as *Time* and *Newsweek*. For a broader range of titles, you might also consult *Book Review Index, Book Review Digest,* and *Subject Guide to Books in Print.*

Indexes of Scholarly Journals

Nearly every discipline has its own major index, one most consulted by scholars. Here are just a few: *MLA* (literary criticism), *ERIC* (education), *PsycInfo* (psychology), *Historical Abstracts* (non-U.S. history), *Sociological Abstracts* (sociology), and *PubMed* (medicine).

When professors refer to bibliographic research, they probably mean research done with indexes. Again, these indexes are specific to particular subject areas. Their coverage is not broad, but deep and scholarly. These are the indexes to consult when seeking the most scholarly information in your area of study. Although the full text is often not included, the indexing provides information sufficient to track down the complete article.

These indexes are a great aid in evaluating the scholarly merit of a publication, as they usually eliminate any reference that isn't considered scholarly by the academy. For example, *MLA* only indexes literary criticism that appears in peer-reviewed journals and academically affiliated books. So, consider the publications that appear in these indexes to have the academic "seal of approval."

For more information on this crucial aspect of research, see the headings later in this chapter entitled "Subscriber-Only Databases" and "Four Steps Toward Productive Research Across the Disciplines."

Finding Your Sources: Articles and Books

The resources above will not only provide you with an excellent overview of your topic, but also direct you to authoritative books and journal articles. The next step is to find out how to access the full text of those books and articles online or in print form. Your library's online catalog will direct you to books in your local library. You may wish to take advantage of this time in the catalog to run a keyword search on your topic. Watch the subject headings that appear at the bottom of catalog records. You can click on these subject headings to guide you to more books highly relevant to your topic.

Don't be concerned if many of the books that have been recommended in specialized dictionaries, encyclopedias, and indexes don't appear in your library's online catalog. The reference librarian can direct you to *WorldCat*, where you can request on interlibrary loan any book to be sent to you from another library for your perusal. This is a valuable service, as it makes available to you the research collections of large universities, all with the stroke of a key.

Journal articles are likely to be the next step in your research. You will need to find which articles are available in-house, online or in print, and which you will need to submit an interlibrary loan request for (in this case, unlike with books, you will receive a photocopy of the interlibrary loaned article to keep—no need to return it to the lending library). Your library's online catalog will generally—though not always—provide you with a complete list of journals available electronically or in print. Just title search on the journal name, not the article title, in order to locate the journal. Ask a reference librarian for assistance in locating journals. He or she can also assist you in requesting on interlibrary loan any articles from journals your library does not have.

Finding Quality Sources: Two Professors Speak

In the following Voices from Across the Curriculum, a business professor and a psychology professor offer useful tips for searching under more than one heading in order to find more information.

Voices from Across the Curriculum

A critical part of the bibliographic effort is to find a topic on which materials are available. Most topics can be researched. The key is to choose a flexible keyword/phrase and then try out different versions of it. For example, a bibliography on "women in management" might lead you to look up *women, females, business* (women in), *business* (females in), *gender in the workplace, sexism and the workplace, careers* (of men, of women, in business), *women and CEOs, women in management, affirmative action and women, women in corporations, female accountants,* and so forth. Be imaginative and flexible. A little bit of time with some of the indexes will provide you with a wealth of sources.

Here is a sampling of indexes heavily used in the social sciences, for instance: *Social Science Index, SocAbs, Wall Street Journal Index* (for *WSJ* stories), *New York Times Index* (for *NYT* stories), *Business Source Elite,* and the *Public Affairs Information Service (PAIS).*

—Frederick Norling, Professor of Business

Use quality psychological references, that is, use references that professional psychologists use and regard highly. *Psychology Today* is not a good reference; *Newsweek* and *Reader's Digest* are worse. APA journals, such as the *Journal of Abnormal Psychology,* on the other hand, are excellent.

In looking for reference material, be sure to search under several headings. For example, look under *depression, affective disorders,* and *mood disorders.* Books (e.g., *The Handbook of Affective Disorders*) are often very helpful, especially for giving a general overview of a topic. Books addressing a professional audience are generally preferable to those addressing a general, popular audience.

Finally, references should be reasonably current. In general, the newer, the better. For example, with rare exceptions (classic articles), articles from before 1970 are outdated and so should not be used.

—Alan Tjeltveit, Professor of Psychology

FINDING QUALITY ON THE WEB

Imagine a megalibrary to which anyone has access any time of day or night and to which anyone can contribute material, to inform, but perhaps more so to sell and to promote, no matter how questionable the cause or idea. So it is with the web. A general caveat to this "library of the Internet" might well be User Beware.

Take as an example the website *Martin Luther King: A True Historical Examination* (www.martinlutherking.org). This site appears prominently in any web search for information about Martin Luther King, Jr. The site is visually appealing, claiming to include "essays, speeches, sermons, and more." But who created the site? As it turns out, after a little digging (see Tips #1 and #2 later in the chapter), the site is sponsored by Stormfront, Inc. (http://stormfront.org), an organization out of West Palm Beach, Florida, serving "those courageous men and women fighting to preserve their White Western culture, ideals and freedom of speech." This author is concealed behind the work, a ghost writer of sorts. While the site is at one's fingertips, identifying the author is a challenge, more so than in the world of conventional publishing, where protocols are followed such as author and publisher appearing on the same pages as the title. For those websites with no visible author, no publishing house, no recognized journal title, no peer-review process, and no library selection process (the touchstones of scholarship in the print world), seemingly easy Internet research is now more problematic: the user must discern what is—and is not—authoritative information.

Understanding Domain Names

But how is the user to begin evaluating a web document? Fortunately, there are several clues to assist you through the Internet labyrinth. One clue is in the web address itself. For example, the *Internet Movie Database* has www.imdb.com as its web address (also known as URL, or uniform resource locator). One clue lies at the very end of the URL, in what is known as the domain name, in this case the abbreviation ".com." Websites ending in .com are commercial, often with the purpose of marketing a product. Sites ending in .org generally signal nonprofits, but many have a veiled agenda, whether it is marketing or politics. Like the .coms, .org addresses are sold on a first-come first-served basis. (The organization that oversees the many vendors of .com and .org domain names is The Internet Corporation for Assigned Names and Numbers, or ICANN [www.icann.org/].)

On the other hand, .edu and .gov sites may indicate less bias, as they are ostensibly limited exclusively to educational and government institutions, and they are often the producers of bonafide research. In particular, .gov sites contain some of the best information on the Internet. This is in part because the U.S. government is required by an act of Congress to disseminate to the general public a large portion of its research.

The U.S. government, floated by tax dollars, provides the high-quality, free websites reminiscent of the precommercial Internet era. This means that government sites offer high-quality data, particularly of a statistical nature. Scholars in the areas of business, law, and the social sciences can benefit tremendously, without subscription fees, from a variety of government databases. Prime examples are the legislative site known as *Thomas* (http://thomas.loc.gov) and data gathered at the website of the Census Bureau (www.census.gov).

Print Corollaries

But a domain name can be misleading; it is simply one clue in the process of evaluation. Another clue is the correlation between a website and the print world. Many websites correlate with a print edition, such as the web version of the *Economist* (economist.com), offering some unique information, some identical, as that offered in the print subscription. (Access to some web articles may be limited to subscribers.) Moreover, some websites are the equivalents of their print editions. For example, Johns Hopkins University Press now publishes its journals, known and respected for years by scholars, in both print and electronic formats. Many college and university libraries subscribe to these Johns Hopkins journals electronically, collectively known as *Project Muse* (http://muse.jhu.edu). In both cases—the *Economist* and *Project Muse*—the scholar can expect the electronic form of the publication to have undergone the same editorial rigor as the print publication.

Web-Published Gems

Building a reputation of high quality takes time. But the Internet has been around long enough now that some publications with no pre-web history have caught the attention of scholars who turn to these sites regularly for reliable commentary on a variety of subject areas.

These high-quality sites can best be found by tapping into scholarly web directories such as the *ipl2* (www.ipl.org) and *intute* (www.intute.ac.uk) that work like mini search engines but are managed by humans who sift through the chaff, including in these directories only what they deem to be gems.

The student looking specifically for free, peer-reviewed journals original to the web can visit a highly specific directory called the *Directory of Open Access Journals* (www.doaj.org), listing several hundred journals in a variety of subject areas. Many libraries have begun to link to these journals to promote their use by students and faculty.

Then there are the web treasures that compare to highbrow magazines or newspapers such as *The New Yorker*. Two celebrated examples are *Salon.com* (salon.com) and *Slate* (slate.com), both online literary reviews. Once tapped into, these sites do a good job of recommending other high-quality websites. Scholars are beginning to cite from these web-based publications just as they would from any print publication of long-standing reputation.

An excellent site for links to all kinds of interesting articles from journals and high level general interest magazine is *Arts and Letters Daily.com* (http://aldaily.com), sponsored by *The Chronicle of Higher Education*. You should also be aware of websites run by special interest organizations, such as the *American Academy of Poets* (http://poets.org), which offers bibliographic resources, interviews, reviews, and the like.

Wikipedia, Google, and Blogs

Three tools have in recent years dramatically altered the nature of web-based research. First and foremost, the search engine *Google*, through a proprietary search algorithm, has increased the relevance and value of search results. Relevance in *Google* is determined by text-matching techniques, while value is determined by a unique "PageRank" technology that places highest on the list those results that are most often linked to from other websites.

However, the determination of value is by no means fool-proof. *Google's* ranking of value assesses less a website's authoritativeness than its popular appeal. For example, a recent search on "marijuana" yielded as its second result (*Wikipedia's* entry on marijuana is first) a private website promoting the use of marijuana and selling marijuana paraphernalia. This site could be useful in any number of ways in a research paper (i.e., as a primary resource reflecting public perceptions and use of marijuana in the United States). That it appears so high on the list suggests *Google's* algorithm of popularity over authoritativeness. This is not necessarily a bad thing, just something to be aware of. It is a little like picking a pebble off the ground. Its value is not inherent: responsibility rests with the user to discover its value. Finding information in *Google* is never the challenge. Discerning appropriateness and authoritativeness is the bigger task.

High on the list of most search results in *Google*—if not first—is *Wikipedia*. Is this an authoritative source? Certainly, *Wikipedia* has revolutionized the way web pages are authored. The world is the author of every entry. That is the beauty and the hazard and the secret to its broad scope and thus to its popularity. Anyone can write and edit in *Wikipedia*. In this way, *Wikipedia* is infinitely democratic. All opinions count equally, for better or worse—while authority languishes. Consequently, *Wikipedia* is likely to contribute little to a scholarly research project. In fact, it could detract from an assertion of authority. In short, use *Wikipedia* entries judiciously. Like any encyclopedia, *Wikipedia* will be viewed by the informed reader as introductory, not as the hallmark of thorough research.

Just as *Wikipedia* invites all of us to be writers, so too do blogs. But unlike *Wikipedia*, blogs typically reveal the identity or at least the assumed identity of the author, and are written by a closed group of people, often one individual. As such, over time the identity and politics of the author(s) show through. In the best tradition of the World Wide Web, blogs have extended the sphere of publication, inviting everyone to be published authors, possibly achieving popularity and authority on a topic no matter how narrow by being at the right place at the right time, with access to the right information written in a voice of confidence. Blogs invite outside comment, but lack the formal structure of a peer review. As such, use blogs sparingly in academic research, being attentive to the credentials of the author(s), and to the wider acceptance of a particular blog in the scholarly community.

Asking the Right Questions

In the end, it is up to the individual user to evaluate each website independently. Here are some critical questions to consider:

Question: Who is the author?

Response: Check the website's home page, probably near the bottom of the page.

Question: Is the author affiliated with any institution?

Response: Check the URL to see who sponsors the page.

Question: What are the author's credentials?

Response: Check Google Scholar (scholar.google.com) to see if this person is published in scholarly journals or books.

Question: Has the information been reviewed or peer-edited before posting?

Response: Probably not, unless the posting is part of a larger scholarly project; if so, the submission process for publication can be verified at the publication home page.

Question: Is the page part of a larger publication that may help to assess authoritativeness?

Response: Try the various links on the page to see if there is an access point to the home page of the publication. Or try the backspacing technique mentioned later in the chapter.

Question: Is the information documented properly?

Response: Check for footnotes or methodology.

Question: Is the information current?

Response: Check the "last update," usually printed at the bottom of the page.

Question: What is the purpose of the page?

Response: Examine content and marginalia.

Question: Does the website suit your purposes?

Response: Review what the purpose of your project is. Review your information needs: primary vs. secondary, academic vs. popular. And always consult with your instructor.

Subscriber-Only Databases

An organized and indexed collection of discreet pieces of information is called a *database*. Two examples of databases are a library's card catalogue and online catalogue. The World Wide Web is full of databases, though they are often restricted to subscribers. Subscription fees can be prohibitive, but fortunately for the average researcher, most college and university libraries foot the bill. The names of these databases are now well known and, arguably, contain the most thoroughly reviewed (i.e., scholarly) full text available on the web. Inquire at your library to see if you have access to these databases:

Academic Search Premier from EBSCO (www.ebscohost.com)

Academic ASAP/Onefile from Gale, Cengage Learning (www.gale.cengage.com)

JSTOR from ITHAKA (www.jstor.org)

Project Muse from Johns Hopkins (muse.jhu.edu/)

Proquest Central from ProQuest (www.proquest.com)

Omnifile from Wilson (www.hwwilson.com).

Each of these databases contains its own proprietary search engine, allowing refinement of searches to a degree unmatched by search engines on the Internet at large. More is not better in an information age. The fact that information is at your fingertips, and sometimes "in your face," can be a problem. Well-organized databases are shaped and limited by human hands and minds, covering only certain media types or subject areas.

Second, databases allow searching by subject heading, in addition to keyword searching. This means that a human has defined the main subject areas of each entry, consequently allowing the user much greater manipulation of the search. For example, if I enter the words "New York City" in a simple keyword search, I will retrieve everything that simply mentions New York City even once; the relevance will vary tremendously. On the other hand, if subject headings have been assigned, I can do a subject search on New York City and find only records that are devoted to my subject. This may sound trivial, but in the age of information overload, precision searching is a precious commodity.

The most specialized databases are those whose primary purpose is not to provide full text but to index all of the major journals, along with books and/or book chapters, in a discipline, regardless of where the full text to that journal can be found. These electronic indexes provide basic bibliographic information and sometimes an abstract (summary) of the article or book chapter. (*See Scholarly Indexes earlier in the chapter.*)

Try This 14.1: Tuning in to Your Research Environment: Four Exercises

Every university and college is different, each with its own points of access to information. Following are some exercises to help you familiarize yourself with your own scholarly environment.

Exercise #1: Go to your library's reference desk and get a list of all the scholarly journal indexes available electronically at your school. Then get a list of all online, full-text databases available to you.

Exercise #2: Contact your reference librarian to get a list of all the journals the library subscribes to electronically. Then get a list of all journals available at your library either in print or electronically in your major area of study.

Exercise #3: Ask the reference librarian about web access in general for your major area of study. What tips can the librarian give you about doing electronic research at your academic institution? Are there any special databases, web search engines/directories, or indexes you should consult in your research?

Exercise #4: Try out some or all of the full-text databases available on your campus. Now try the same searches in a scholarly index. What differences do you see in the quality/scope of the information?

Eight Tips for Locating and Evaluating Electronic Sources

Tip #1: Backspacing "Backspacing" a URL can be an effective way to evaluate a website. It may reveal authorship or institutional affiliation. To do this, place the cursor at the end of the URL and then backspace to the last slash and press Enter. Continue backspacing to each preceding slash, examining each level as you go.

Tip #2: Using WHOIS WHOIS (www.networksolutions.com/whois/index.jsp) is an Internet service that allows anyone to find out who's behind a website.

Tip #3: Beware of the ~ in a Web Address Many educational institutions allow the creation of personal home pages by students and faculty. While the domain name remains .edu in these cases, the fact that they are personal means that pretty much anything can be posted and so cannot assure academic quality.

Tip #4: Phrase Searching Not finding relevant information? Try using quotation marks around key phrases in your search string. For example, search in *Google* for this phrase, enclosed in quotation marks: "whose woods these are I think I know."

Tip #5: Title Searching Still finding irrelevant information? Limit your search to the titles of web documents. A title search is an option in several search engines, among them *Yahoo* (advanced search) (http://search.yahoo.com) and *Google* (advanced search) (www.google.com).

Tip #6: *Wikipedia* Discussion Tab Use *Wikipedia* to full advantage by clicking on the discussion tab located at the top of *Wikipedia* entries. The discussion tabs expose the often intense debates that rage behind the scenes on topics like marijuana, genocide, and Islam. The discussion tab is an excellent source for locating paper topics because it highlights ongoing sources of controversy—those areas worthy of additional writing and research. To find the most controversial topics at any given moment, visit *Wikipedia*'s Controversial Issues page (http://en.wikipedia.org/wiki/Wikipedia:List_of_controversial_issues).

Tip #7: Full Text The widest selection of previously published full text (newspapers, magazines, journals, book chapters) is available in subscription databases via the web.

Inquire at your library to see if you have access to *Academic Search Premier* from EBSCO(www.ebscohost.com), *Academic ASAP/Onefile* from Gale Cengage (www. gale.cengage.com), *JSTOR* from ITHAKA (www.jstor.org), *Project Muse* from Johns Hopkins (muse.jhu.edu/), *Proquest Central* from ProQuest (www.proquest.com), *Omnifile* from Wilson (www.hwwilson.com), or other full-text databases.

The leading free full-text site for magazines and newspapers is BNET's *FindArticles* (http://findarticles.com). This database of "hundreds of thousands of articles from more than 300 magazines and newspapers" can be searched by all magazines, magazines within categories, or specific magazine or newspaper.

For the full text of books, try the *Internet Archive Text Archive* (hwww.archive.org/ details/texts)), pointing to the major digital text archives.

Tip #8: Archives of Older Published Periodicals Full text for newspapers, magazines, and journals published prior to 1990 is difficult to find on the Internet. One subscription site your library may offer is *JSTOR* (www.jstor.org), an archive of scholarly full-text journal articles dating back in some cases into the late 1800s. *LexisNexis Academic* (www. lexisnexis.com), also a subscription service, includes the full text of popular periodicals such as the *New York Times* as far back as 1980.

Two free sites offer the full text of eighteenth- and nineteenth-century periodicals from Great Britain and the United States, respectively: *Internet Library of Early Journals* (www.bodley.ox.ac.uk/ilej) and *Nineteenth Century in Print* (http://memory. loc.gov/ammem/ndlpcoop/moahtml/snchome.html).

Use your library's interlibrary loan service to acquire articles from periodicals not freely available on the web. Electronic indexing (no full text) for older materials is readily available, back as early as 1900, sometimes earlier. Inquire at your library.

Four Steps Toward Productive Research Across the Disciplines

The steps below include a few of the sites most relied on by academic librarians. For the subscription databases, you will need to inquire at your library for local availability.

Step 1: search at least one of these multidisciplinary subscription databases; check your library's website for availability.

- *Academic Search Premier* (EBSCOhost) for journals
- *Academic ASAP/Onefile* (Gale Cengage) for journals
- *JSTOR* for journals
- *Omnifile* (WilsonWeb) for journals
- *Project Muse* for journals
- *Proquest Central* for journals
- *WorldCat* (OCLC FirstSearch) for books

Step 2: search subject-specific databases. These too are mostly subscription databases; check your library's website for availability.

- Anthropology: *Anthropological Abstracts*
- Art: *Art Abstracts*
- Biology: *Biological Abstracts, Biological and Agricultural Index*
- Business: *ABI Inform, Business Source Elite/Premier, Business & Company Resource Center, Dow Jones Factiva, LexisNexis*
- Chemistry: *SciFinder Scholar, Science Direct*
- Communication: *Communication and Mass Media, Communication Abstracts*
- Computer Science: *Inspec*
- Economics: *EconLit*
- Education: *ERIC* (free)
- Film Studies: *MLA*
- Geography/Geology: *GEOBASE*
- History: *America History and Life, Historical Abstracts*
- Language, Literature: *MLA, Literature Online*
- Law: *LexisNexis, Westlaw*
- Mathematics: *MathSciNet*
- Medicine: *PubMed, Science Direct* (free)
- Music: *RILM*
- Philosophy: *Philosopher's Index*
- Physics: *Inspec*
- Political Science: *PAIS*
- Psychology: *PsycINFO*
- Religion: *ATLA Religion*
- Sociology: *Sociological Abstracts*

Step 3: visit these not-to-be-missed free websites and meta-sites that lead to a variety of materials relevant to a discipline:

- All subjects: *Google Scholar* scholar.google.com (books and journals)
- Anthropology: *Anthropological Index Online* http://aio.anthropology.org.uk/aiosearch/ (journals) *Anthropology Resources on the Internet* www.anthropology-resources.net
- Art: *ArtCyclopedia* www.artcyclopedia.com (images and critical bibliographies)
- Biology: *Biology Browser* www.biologybrowser.org (gateway to digital archives of colleges and universities, *Agricola* http://agricola.nal.usda.gov (journals)
- Business: *EDGAR* www.sec.gov/edgar.shtml (company annual reports), *Hoover's Online* www.hoovers.com/free (company reports)
- Chemistry: *Chemdex.org* www.chemdex.org (chemical compounds), *World of Chemistry* scienceworld.wolfram.com/chemistry (encyclopedia)

- Communication: *Television News Archive: Vanderbilt University* tvnews.vanderbilt.edu (index to television news)
- Computer Science: *arXiv.org* arxiv.org/ non-peer-reviewed but moderated scholarly e-print submissions), *CompInfo* www.compinfo-center.com (magazines and downloads)
- Economics: *Intute: Economics* www.intute.ac.uk/economics/ (reviewed websites associated with economics)
- Education: *Educator's Reference Desk* eduref.org (resource guides and lesson plans)
- Film Studies: *Film Studies Resources* www.lib.berkeley.edu/MRC/filmstudies/index.html (index to reviews and criticism)
- Geography/Geology: *GeoSource* www.library.uu.nl/geosource (gateway to reviewed web resources)
- History: *American Memory* memory.loc.gov/ammem/index.html (primary documents)
- Language, Literature: *Online Literary Criticism Collection* www.ipl.org/div/litcrit (biography and criticism)
- Law: *FindLaw* www.findlaw.com (free legal information)
- Mathematics: *arXiv.org* arxiv.org/ (non-peer-reviewed but moderated scholarly e-print submissions), Mathworld mathworld.wolfram.com (encyclopedia),
- Medicine: *BioMed Central* www.biomedcentral.com (journals)
- Music: *Online Resources for Music Scholars* hcl.harvard.edu/research/guides/music/resources/index.html (gateway to music resources on the web)
- Philosophy: *Stanford Encyclopedia of Philosophy* plato.stanford.edu
- Physics: *arXiv.org* arxiv.org/ (non-peer-reviewed but moderated scholarly e-print submissions), *World of Physics* http://scienceworld.wolfram.com/physics
- Political Science: *Intute: Politics* www.intute.ac.uk/politics/ (web resources), *THOMAS* http://thomas.loc.gov (U.S. government documents)
- Psychology: *Intute: Psychology* www.intute.ac.uk/psychology/ (web resources)
- Religion: *Religion Online* http://www.religion-online.org/ (articles and book chapters), *Hartford Institute forReligion Research* www.hartfordinstitute.org (surveys and statistics)
- Sociology: *Intute: Sociology* www.intute.ac.uk/sociology (web resources)

Step 4: search the web using these selective search engines:

- *Intute* www.intute.ac.uk/

Intute is arguably the most academically oriented of all the search engines. The creators of *Intute* have carefully screened and summarized websites for inclusion.

- *ipl2* www.ipl.org/

ipl2 contains a lower percentage of academic websites than *Intute*.

B. Plagiarism and The Logic of Citation

It is impossible to discuss the rationale for citing sources without reference to plagiarism, even though the primary reason for including citations is not to prove that you haven't cheated. It's essential that you give credit where it's due as a courtesy to your readers. Along with educating readers about who has said what, citations enable them to find out more about a given position and to pursue other discussions on the subject. Nonetheless, plagiarism is an important issue: academic integrity matters. And because the stakes are very high if you are caught plagiarizing, we will now offer some guidelines on how to avoid it.

In recent years, there has been a significant rise in the number of plagiarism cases nationally. Many commentators blame the Internet, with its easily accessible, easy to cut-and-paste information, for increasing the likelihood of plagiarism. Others cite a lack of clarity about what plagiarism is and why it is a serious problem. So, let's start by clarifying.

Most people have some idea of what plagiarism is. You already know that it's against the rules to buy a paper from an Internet "paper mill" or to download others' words verbatim and hand them in as your own thinking. And you probably know that even if you change a few words and rearrange the sentence structure, you still need to acknowledge the source. Plagiarism gives the impression that you have written or thought something you have in fact borrowed from someone else. It is a form of theft and fraud. Borrowing from someone else, by the way, also includes taking and not acknowledging words and ideas from your friends or your parents. Put another way, any assignment with your name on it signifies that you are the author—that the words and ideas are yours—with any exceptions indicated by source citations and, if you're quoting, by quotation marks.

Knowing what plagiarism is, however, doesn't guarantee that you'll know how to avoid it. Is it okay, for example, to cobble together a series of summaries and paraphrases in a paragraph, provided you include the authors in a bibliography at the end of the paper? Or how about if you insert a single footnote at the end of the paragraph? The answer is that both are still plagiarism because your reader can't tell where your thinking starts and others' thinking stops. As a basic rule of thumb, readers must be able to distinguish your contribution from that of your sources, and exactly which information came from which source.

WHY DOES PLAGIARISM MATTER?

A recent survey indicated that 53 percent of Who's Who High Schoolers thought that plagiarism was no big deal (Sally Cole and Elizabeth Kiss, "What Can We Do About Student Cheating?" *About Campus*, May–June 2000, p. 6). So why should institutions of higher learning care about it? Here are two great reasons:

- Plagiarism poisons the environment. Students who don't cheat are alienated by students who do and get away with it, and faculty can become distrustful of students and even disillusioned about teaching when constantly driven to track down students' sources. It's a lot easier, by the way, than most students think for faculty to recognize language and ideas that are not the student's own. And now there are all those search engines provided by firms like Turnitin.com that have been generated in response to the Internet paper-mill boom. Who wants another cold war?

- Plagiarism defeats the purpose of going to college, which is learning how to think. You can't learn to think by just copying others' ideas; you need to learn to trust your own intelligence. Students' panic about deadlines and their misunderstandings about assignments sometimes spur plagiarism. It's a good bet that your professors would much rather take requests for help and give extra time on assignments than have to go through the anguish of confronting students about plagiarized work.

So, plagiarism gets in the way of trust, fairness, intellectual development, and, ultimately, the attitude toward learning that sets the tone for a college or university community.

FREQUENTLY ASKED QUESTIONS (FAQS) ABOUT PLAGIARISM

Is it still plagiarism if I didn't intentionally copy someone else's work and present it as my own; that is, if I plagiarized it by accident?
Yes, it is still plagiarism. Colleges and universities put the burden of responsibility on students for knowing what plagiarism is and then making the effort necessary to avoid it. Leaving out the quotation marks around someone else's words or omitting the attribution after a summary of someone else's theory may be just a mistake—a matter of inadequate documentation—but faculty can only judge what you turn in to them, not what you intended.

If I include a list of works consulted at the end of my paper, doesn't that cover it?
No. A works-cited list (bibliography) tells your readers what you read but leaves them in the dark about how and where this material has been used in your paper. Putting one or more references at the end of a paragraph containing source material is a version of the same problem. The solution is to cite the source at the point that you quote or paraphrase or summarize it. To be even clearer about what comes from where, also use what are called in-text attributions. See the next FAQ on these.

What is the best way to help my readers distinguish between what my sources are saying and what I'm saying?
Be overt. Tell your readers in the text of your paper, not just in citations, when you are drawing on someone else's words, ideas, or information. Do this with phrases like "According to X" or "As noted in X"—called in-text attributions.

Are there some kinds of information that I do not need to document?
Yes. Common knowledge and facts you can find in almost any encyclopedia or basic reference text generally don't need to be documented (such as, John F. Kennedy became president of the United States in 1960). This distinction can get a little tricky because it isn't always obvious what is and is not common knowledge. Often, you need to spend some time in a discipline before you discover what others take to be known to all. When in doubt, cite the source.

If I put the information from my sources into my own words, do I still need to include citations?
Yes. Sorry, but rewording someone else's idea doesn't make it your idea. Paraphrasing is a useful activity because it helps you to better understand what you are reading, but paraphrases and summaries have to be documented and carefully distinguished from ideas and information you are representing as your own.

If I don't actually know anything about the subject, is it okay to hand in a paper that is taken entirely from various sources?
It's okay if (1) you document the borrowings and (2) the assignment called for summary. Properly documented summarizing is better than plagiarizing, but most assignments call for something more. Often comparing and contrasting your sources begins to give you ideas so that you can have something to contribute. If you're really stumped, go see the professor.

You also reduce the risk of plagiarism if you consult sources after—not before—you have done some preliminary thinking on the subject. If you have become somewhat invested in your own thoughts on the matter, you will be able to use the sources in a more active way, in effect, making them part of a dialogue.

Is it plagiarism if I include things in my paper I thought of with another student or a member of my family?
Most academic behavior codes, under the category called "collusion," allow for students' cooperative efforts only with the explicit consent of the instructor. The same general rule goes for plagiarizing yourself—that is, for submitting the same paper in more than one class. If you have questions about what constitutes collusion in a particular class, be sure to ask your professor.

What about looking at secondary sources when my professor hasn't asked me to? Is this a form of cheating?
It can be a form of cheating if the intent of the assignment was to get you to develop a particular kind of thinking skill. In this case, looking at others' ideas may actually retard your learning process and leave you feeling that you couldn't possibly learn to arrive at ideas on your own.

Professors usually look favorably on students who are willing to take the time to do extra reading on a subject, but it is essential that, even in class discussion, you make it clear that you have consulted outside sources. To conceal that fact is to present others' ideas as your own. Even in class discussion, if you bring up an idea you picked up on the Internet, be sure to say so explicitly.

C. CITING SOURCES: Four Documentation Styles by Reference Librarian Kelly Cannon

The four most common styles of documentation are those established by:

- the *American Psychological Association (APA),*
- the *Council of Science Editors (CSE),*
- the *University Press of Chicago,* and
- the *Modern Language Association (MLA).*

Note: The University of North Carolina at Chapel Hill Libraries offer authoritative examples of basic citations of electronic and print resources in all four styles at http://www.lib.unc.edu/instruct/citations/.

For citation examples not given at the University of North Carolina at Chapel Hill Libraries website, it is advisable to consult the various organizations' printed manuals—*Publication Manual of the American Psychological Association* (6th edition), the *Chicago Manual of Style* (15th edition), *Scientific Style and Format: The CSE Manual for Authors, Editors, and Publishers,* and the *MLA Handbook for Writers of Research Papers* (7th edition). It is important to use the most recent edition available of each of these manuals.

You have probably already discovered that some professors are more concerned than others that students obey the particulars of a given documentation style. Virtually all faculty across the curriculum agree, however, that *the most important rule for writers to follow in documenting sources is formal consistency.* That is, all of your in-text citations or footnotes/endnotes should follow the same format, and all of your end-of-text citations should follow the same format.

Once you begin doing most of your writing in a particular discipline, you may want to purchase or access on the Internet the more detailed style guide adhered to by that discipline. Because documentation styles differ not only from discipline to discipline but also even from journal to journal within a discipline, you should consult your professor about which documentation format he or she wishes you to use in a given course.

THE FOUR DOCUMENTATION STYLES: SIMILARITIES AND DIFFERENCES

The various styles differ in the specific ways that they organize the bibliographical information, but they also share some common characteristics.

1. They place an extended citation for each source, including the author, title, date, and place of publication, at the end of the paper (though in *Chicago*, this end-of-text list is optional when employing footnotes/endnotes: consult with your professor). These end-of-text citations are organized in a list, usually alphabetically.

2. All four styles distinguish among different kinds of sources—providing slightly differing formulas for citing books, articles, encyclopedias, government documents, interviews, and so forth.

3. They all ask for these basic pieces of information to be provided whenever they are known: author, title of larger work along with title of article or chapter as appropriate, date of publication, and publisher or institutional affiliation.

To briefly distinguish the styles:

- the APA style employs the author-date format of parenthetical in-text citation and predominates in the social sciences;
- the *Chicago* style, best known for its use of footnotes or endnotes, is employed in history, the fine arts, and some other humanities disciplines;
- the CSE (aka CBE) style, which employs alternately the citation-sequence system and the name-year system, is commonly used throughout the sciences, especially the natural sciences; and
- the MLA style, which uses the author-page format of parenthetical in-text citation, prevails in the humanities disciplines of language, literature, film, and cultural studies.

Here are a few basic examples of in-text and end-of-text citations in the four most commonly used styles, followed by a brief discussion of the rules that apply.

1. *APA* STYLE

In-text citation: Studies of students' changing attitudes toward the small colleges they attend suggest that their loyalty to the institution declines steadily over a four-year period, whereas their loyalty to individual professors or departments increases "markedly, by as much as twenty-five percent over the last two years" (Brown, 1994, p. 41).

For both books and articles, include the author's last name, followed by a comma, and then the date of publication. If you are quoting or referring to a specific passage, include the page number as well, separated from the date by a comma and the abbreviation "p." (or "pp."), followed by a space. If the author's name has been mentioned in the sentence, include only the date in the parentheses immediately following the author's name.

In-text citation: Brown (1992) documents the decline in students' institutional loyalty.

End-of-text book citation: Tannen, D. (1991). *You just don't understand: Women and men in conversation.* New York: Ballantine Books.

End-of-text journal article citation: Baumeister, R. (1987). How the self became a problem: A psychological review of historical research. *Journal of Personality and Psychology, 52,* 163–176.

End-of-text website citation: Hershey Foods Corporation. (2001, March 15). *2001 Annual Report.* Retrieved from http://www. hersheysannualreport.com/2000/index.htm

End-of-text citation of a journal article retrieved from a website or database: Paivio, A. (1975). Perceptual comparisons through the mind's eye. *Memory & Cognition, 3,* 635-647. doi:10.1037/0278-6133.24.2.225

Note that citations of journal articles retrieved on the web include a DOI, a unique code that allows easy retrieval of the article. The DOI is typically located on the first page of the electronic journal article near the copyright notice. When a DOI is used in your citation, no other retrieval information is needed. Use this format for the DOI in references: doi:xxxxxxx

If no DOI has been assigned to the content, provide the home page URL of the journal or report publisher. If you retrieve an article from a library (subscription) database, in general it is not necessary to include the database information in the citation. Do not include retrieval dates unless the source material has changed over time.

APA style requires an alphabetical list of references (by author's last name, which keys the reference to the in-text citation). This list is located at the end of the paper on a separate page and entitled "References." Regarding manuscript form, the first line of each reference is not indented, but all subsequent lines are indented three spaces.

In alphabetizing the references list, place entries for a single author before entries he or she has co-authored, and arrange multiple entries by a single author by beginning with the earliest work. If there are two or more works by the same author in the same year, designate the second with an "a," the third with a "b," and so forth, directly after the year. For all subsequent entries by an author after the first, substitute three hyphens followed by a period [---.] for his or her name. For articles by two or more authors, use commas to connect the authors, and precede the last one with a comma and an ampersand (&).

The APA style divides individual entries into the following parts: author (using initials only for first and middle names), year of publication (in parentheses), title, and publication data. Each part is separated by a period from the others. Note that only the first letter of the title and subtitle of books is capitalized (although proper nouns would be capitalized as necessary).

Journal citations differ from those for books in a number of small ways. The title of a journal article is neither italicized (nor underlined) nor enclosed in quotation marks, and only the first word in the title and subtitle is capitalized. The name of the journal is italicized (or underlined), however, and the first word and all significant words are capitalized. Also, notice that the volume number (which is separated by a comma from the title of the journal) is italicized (or underlined) to distinguish it from the page reference. Page numbers for the entire article are included, with no "p." or "pp." and are separated by a comma from the preceding volume number. If the journal does not use volume numbers, then p. or pp. is included.

2. *CHICAGO* STYLE

Footnote or endnote citation: The earliest groups to explore that part of the country spent much of their time finding out of the way places to "hide their families and cache their grain."[1]

The raised numeral indicates a footnote at the bottom of the page or an endnote at the conclusion of a chapter. Following is an example of what that note would look like, assuming this is the first note to have appeared in the paper, thus listed as note number one:

Footnote/endnote book citation: 1. Juanita Brooks, *The Mountain Meadows Massacre* (Norman, OK: University of Oklahoma Press), 1991, 154.

Here are some examples of other types of notes, numbered consecutively as if each were appearing in the same paper, in this order:

Footnote/endnote journal article citation: 2. Richard Jackson, "Running Down the Up-Escalator: Regional Inequality in Papua New Guinea," *Australian Geographer* 14 (May 1979): 180.

Footnote/endnote website citation: 3. Baha'i International Community. "The Baha'i Faith." *The Baha'i World*. http://www. bahai.org/article1201.html (accessed July 20, 2010).

Footnote/endnote citation of a journal article retrieved from a website: 4. Linda Belau, "Trauma and the Material Signifier," *Postmodern Culture* 11, no. 2 (2001): par. 6, http://www.iath. virginia.edu/pmc/text-only/issue.101/11.2belau.txt (accessed July 20, 2010).

Footnote/endnote library (subscription) database journal article citation: 5. Ilan Rachun, "The Meaning of 'Revolution' in the English Revolution (1648–1660)," *Journal of the History of Ideas* 56, no. 2, 196, http://www.jstor.org (accessed July 10, 2010).

In addition to footnotes/endnotes, the *Chicago* style recommends but does not require an alphabetical list of references (by author's last name). This list is located at the end of the paper on a separate page and is entitled "Bibliography." Listed below are the same references employed above, formatted for the bibliography:

End-of-text book citation: Brooks, Juanita. *The Mountain Meadows Massacre*. Norman, OK: University of Oklahoma Press, 1991.

End-of-text journal article citation: Jackson, Richard. "Running Down the Up-Escalator: Regional Inequality in Papua New Guinea." *Australian Geographer* 14 (May 1979): 175–84.

End-of-text website citation: Baha'i International Community. "The Baha'i Faith." *The Baha'i World*. http://www.bahai.org/article1201.html (accessed July 20, 2010).

End-of-text citation of a journal article retrieved from a website: Belau, Linda. "Trauma and the Material Signifier." *Postmodern Culture* 11, no. 2 (2001), http://www.iath.virginia.edu/pmc/text-only/issue.101/11.2belau.txt (accessed July 20, 2010).

End-of-text library (subscription) database journal article citation: Rachun, Ilan. "The Meaning of 'Revolution' in the English Revolution (1648-1660)." *Journal of the History of Ideas* 56, no. 2 (1995):195–215. http://www.jstor.org (accessed July 10, 2010).

Each entry in the bibliography is divided into three parts: author, title, and publication data. Each of these parts is separated by a period from the others. Titles of book-length works are italicized. Journal citations differ slightly: article names go inside quotations, no punctuation follows the titles of journals, and a colon precedes the page numbers when pagination is known.

3A. *CSE* STYLE EMPLOYING NAME-YEAR (AUTHOR-DATE) SYSTEM

In-text citation: Soap works as a cleaning agent because of the distinctiveness of each end of the soap molecule, that is their "opposing tendencies" (McMurry and others 2010, p 768).

For both books and articles, include the author's last name followed by the date of publication. For two authors, include the two last names (Smith and Jones 2009). For more than two authors, as in the case above, employ the phrase "and others." If you are quoting or referring to a specific passage, include the page number as well, separated from the date by a comma and the abbreviation "p" (or "pp") followed by a space. If the author's name has been mentioned in the sentence, include only the date in the parentheses immediately following the author's name wherever it appears in the sentence.

In-text citation: Romero (2008) reviews the transformation of scientific knowledge about the polymer.

End-of-text book citation: McMurry J, Castellion ME, Ballantine DS. 2010. **Fundamentals of general, organic, and biological chemistry.** New York: Prentice Hall.

End-of-text journal article citation: Healy R, Cerio R, Hollingsworth A, Bewley A. 2010. Acquired perforating dermatosis associated with pregnancy. Clin Exp Dermatol 35(6): 621–623.

End-of-text website citation: Hilton-Taylor C, compiler. 2000. 2000 IUCN red list of threatened species [Internet]. Gland, Switzerland and Cambridge, UK: IUCN. [cited 2002 Feb 12]. Available from: http://www.redlist.org/

End-of-text citation of journal article retrieved from a website: Philippi TE, Dixon PM, Taylor BE. 1998. Detecting trends in species composition. Ecol Appl [Internet]. [cited 2010 Feb 12]; 8(2): 300–308. Available from: http://www.esajournals.org/esaonline/?request=get-pdf&file=i1051-0761-008-02-0300.pdf

End-of-text library (subscription) database journal article citation: Kenny G, Yardley J, Brown C, Sigal R, Jay O. 2010. Heat stress in older individuals and patients with common chronic diseases. Can Med Assoc J [Internet]. [cited 2010 June 12]; 182(10): 1053–1060. Available from Health Source: Academic/Nursing Edition: http://0-search.ebscohost.com.library.muhlenberg.edu/login.aspx?direct=true&db=hch&AN=522266 11&site=ehost-live&scope=site. System requirements: Adobe Acrobat. Subscription required for access.

CSE style requires an alphabetical list of references (by author's last name, which keys the reference to the in-text citation). This list is located at the end of the paper on a separate page and is titled "Cited References." Regarding manuscript form, the first line of each reference is not indented, but all subsequent lines are indented three spaces.

In alphabetizing the references list, place entries for a single author before entries that he or she has co-authored, and arrange multiple entries by a single author by beginning with the earliest work.

The *CSE* style divides individual entries into the following parts: author (using initials only for first and middle names), year of publication, title, and publication data. Each part is separated by a period from the others. Note that only the first letter of the title and subtitle of books is capitalized (although proper nouns would be capitalized as necessary).

Journal citations differ from those for books in a number of small ways. The title of a journal article is neither italicized (nor underlined) nor enclosed in quotation marks, and only the first word in the title and subtitle is capitalized. CSE style requires that journal titles be abbreviated in the standard manner used by science researchers, found at ISI Journal Title Abbreviations http://www.efm.leeds.ac.uk/~mark/ISIabbr/. This is followed by a volume number and an issue number if available. Page numbers for the entire article are included, with no "p." or "pp.," and are separated by a colon from the preceding volume or issue number.

3B. *CSE* STYLE EMPLOYING CITATION SEQUENCE SYSTEM

In-text citation: Soap works as a cleaning agent because of the distinctiveness of each end of the soap molecule, that is their "opposing tendencies."[1]

Page numbers are generally not included in this system of CSE, but point to the source generally.

End-of-text book citation: 1. McMurry J, Castellion ME, Ballantine DS. Fundamentals of general, organic, and biological chemistry. New York: Prentice Hall; 2010.

End-of-text journal article citation: 2. Healy R, Cerio R, Hollingsworth A, Bewley A. 2010. Acquired perforating dermatosis associated with pregnancy. Clin Exp Dermatol. 2010; 35(6): 621–623.

End-of-text website citation: 3. Hilton-Taylor C, compiler. 2000 IUCN red list of threatened species [Internet]. Gland, Switzerland and Cambridge, UK: IUCN; 2000 [cited 2002 Feb 12]. Available from: http://www.redlist.org/

End-of-text citation of journal article retrieved from a website: 4. Philippi TE, Dixon PM, Taylor BE. Detecting trends in species composition. Ecol Appl [Internet]. 1998 [cited 2010 Feb 12]; 8(2): 300–308. Available from: http://www.esajournals.org/esaonline/?request=get-pdf&file=i1051-0761-008-02-0300.pdf

End-of-text library (subscription) database journal article citation: 5. Kenny G, Yardley J, Brown C, Sigal R, Jay O. Heat stress in older individuals and patients with common chronic diseases. Can Med Assoc J [Internet]. 2010 [cited 2010 June 12]; 182(10): 1053–1060. Available from Health Source: Academic/Nursing Edition: http://0-search.ebscohost.com.library.muhlenberg.edu/login.aspx?direct=true&db=hch&AN=52226611&site=ehost-live&scope=site. System requirements: Adobe Acrobat. Subscription required for access.

In the CSE style, end-of text citations appear in a list titled "Cited References," and correspond to the superscript numeral appearing in the text, in the order of their introduction in the text.

The *CSE* style in according to this system divides individual entries into the following parts: author (using initials only for first and middle names), title, and publication data. Each part is separated by a period from the others. Note that only the first letter of the title and subtitle of books is capitalized (although proper nouns would be capitalized as necessary).

Journal citations differ from those for books in a number of small ways. The title of a journal article is neither italicized (nor underlined) nor enclosed in quotation marks, and only the first word in the title and subtitle is capitalized. *CSE* style requires that journal titles be abbreviated in the standard manner used by science researchers, found at ISI Journal Title Abbreviations http://www.efm.leeds.ac.uk/~mark/ISIabbr/. This is followed by a volume number and an issue number if available. Page numbers for the entire article are included, with no "p." or "pp." and are separated by a colon from the preceding volume or issue number.

4. *MLA* STYLE

In-text citation: The influence of Seamus Heaney on younger poets in Northern Ireland has been widely acknowledged, but Patrick Kavanagh's "plain-speaking, pastoral" influence on him is "less recognized" (Smith 74).

"(Smith 74)" indicates the author's last name and the page number on which the cited passage appears. If the author's name had been mentioned in the sentence—had the sentence begun "According to Smith"—you would include only the page number in the citation. Note that there is no abbreviation for "page," that there is no intervening punctuation between name and page, and that the parentheses precede the period or other punctuation. If the sentence ends with a direct quotation, the parentheses come after the quotation marks but still before the closing period. Also note that no punctuation occurs between the last word of the quotation ("recognized") and the closing quotation mark.

End-of-text book citation: Douglas, Ann. *Terrible Honesty: Mongrel Manhattan in the 1920s.* New York: Farrar, Straus, and Giroux, 1995. Print.

End-of-text journal article citation: Cressy, David. "Foucault, Stone, Shakespeare and Social History." *English Literary Renaissance* 21 (1991): 121–33. Print.

End-of-text website citation: Landow, George, ed. *Contemporary Postcolonial and Postimperial Literature in English.* Brown University, 2002. Web. 25 June 2010.

End-of-text citation of a journal article retrieved from a website: Nater, Miguel. "El beso de la Esfinge: La poética de lo sublime en *La amada inmóvil* de Amado Nervo y en los *Nocturnos* de José Asunción Silva." *Romanitas* 1.1 (2006): n. pag. Web. 25 June 2010.

End-of-text library (subscription) database journal article citation: Arias, Judith H. "The Devil at Heaven's Door." *Hispanic Review* 61.1 (Winter 1993): n. pag. *Academic Search Premier.* Web. 25 June 2010.

Note that the above citations all indicate a format type (print or web) and the web citations end with the date the researcher accessed the website or database.

MLA style stipulates an alphabetical list of references (by author's last name, which keys the reference to the in-text citation). This list is located at the end of the paper on a separate page and entitled "Works Cited."

Each entry in the Works Cited list is divided into three parts: author, title, and publication data. Each of these parts is separated by a period from the others. Titles of book-length works are italicized, unless your instructor prefers underlining. (Underlining is a means of indicating italics.) Journal citations differ slightly: article names go inside quotations, no punctuation follows the titles of journals, and a colon precedes the page numbers when pagination is known.

D. Integrating Quotations into Your Paper

Writers lose authority and readability when they fail to correctly integrate quotations into their own writing. The following guidelines should help, but keep in mind that not all disciplines encourage (or even permit) writers to include quotations. In those disciplines, such as psychology and the natural sciences, the comments below would then apply to integrating paraphrase or summary.

1. **Acknowledge sources in your text, not just in citations.** When you incorporate material from a source, attribute it to the source explicitly in your text—not just in a citation. In other words, when you introduce the material, *frame* it with a phrase such as "according to Marsh" or "as Gruen argues."

   Although it is not required, you are usually much better off making the attribution overtly, even if you have also cited the source within parentheses or with a footnote at the end of the last sentence quoted, paraphrased, or summarized. If a passage does not contain an attribution, your readers will not know that it comes from a source until they reach the citation at the end. Attributing upfront clearly distinguishes what one source says from what another says and, perhaps more important, what your sources say from what you say. Useful verbs for introducing attributions include the following: notes, observes, argues, comments, writes, says, reports, suggests, and claims. Generally speaking, by the way, you should cite the author by last name only—as "Gruen," not as "William Gruen" or "Mr. Gruen."

2. **Splice quotations onto your own words.** Always attach quotations to some of your own language; don't let them sit in your text as independent sentences with quotation marks around them. You can normally satisfy this rule with an attributive phrase—commonly known as a tag phrase—that introduces the quotation.

   According to Paul McCartney, "All you need is love."

   Note that the tag phrase takes a comma before the quote.
   Alternatively, you can splice quotations into your text with a setup: a statement followed by a colon.

> Patrick Henry's famous phrase is one of the first that American schoolchildren memorize: "Give me liberty, or give me death."

The colon, you should notice, usually comes at the end of an independent clause (that is, a subject plus verb that can stand alone), at the spot where a period normally goes. It would be incorrect to write "Patrick Henry is known for: 'Give me liberty, or give me death.'"

The rationale for this guideline is essentially the same as that for the previous one: if you are going to move to quotation, you first need to identify its author so that your readers will be able to put it in context quickly.

Spliced quotations frequently create problems in grammar or punctuation for writers. Whether you include an entire sentence (or passage) of quotation or just a few phrases, you need to take care to integrate them into the grammar of your own sentence.

One of the most common mistaken assumptions is that a comma should always precede a quotation, as in "A spokesperson for the public defender's office demanded, 'an immediate response from the mayor.'" The sentence structure does not call for any punctuation after "demanded."

3. **Cite sources after quotations.** In MLA style, locate citations in parentheses after the quotation and before the final period. This information appears at the end of the sentence, with the final period following the closing parenthesis.

> A recent article on the best selling albums in America claimed that "Ever since Elvis, it has been pop music's job to challenge the mores of the older generation" (Hornby 168).

Note that in MLA style there is normally *no punctuation* at the end of the quotation itself, either before or after the closing quotation mark. A quotation that ends either in a question mark or an exclamation mark is an exception to this rule because the sign is an integral part of the quotation's meaning.

> As Hamlet says to Rosencrantz and Guildenstern, "And yet to me what is this quintessence of dust?" (2.2.304–05).

See the section entitled "How to Cite Sources" earlier in this chapter for the appropriate formats for in-text citations in various documentation styles.

4. **Use ellipses to shorten quotations.** Add ellipses to indicate that you have omitted some of the language from within the quotation. Form ellipses by entering three dots (periods) with spaces in between them, or use four dots to indicate that the deletion continues to the end of the sentence (the last dot becomes the period). Suppose you wanted to shorten the following quotation from a recent article about Radiohead by Alex Ross:

> The album "OK Computer," with titles like "Paranoid Android," "Karma Police," and "Climbing Up the Walls," pictured the onslaught of the information age and a young person's panicky embrace of it (Ross 85).

Using ellipses, you could emphasize the source's claim by omitting the song titles from the middle of the sentence:

The album "OK Computer" ... pictured the onslaught of the information age and a young person's panicky embrace of it (Ross 85).

In most cases, the gap between quoted passages should be short, and in any case, you should be careful to preserve the sense of the original. The standard joke about ellipses is helpful here: A reviewer writes that a film "will delight no one and appeal to the intelligence of invertebrates only, but not average viewers." An unethical advertiser cobbles together pieces of the review to say that the film "will delight ... and appeal to the intelligence of ... viewers."

5. **Use square brackets to alter or add information within a quotation.** Sometimes it is necessary to change the wording slightly inside a quotation to maintain fluency. Square brackets indicate that you are altering the original quotation. Brackets are also used when you insert explanatory information, such as a definition or example, within a quotation. Here are a few examples that alter the original quotations previously cited.

According to one music critic, the cultural relevance of Radiohead is evident in "the album 'OK Computer' ... [which] pictured the onslaught of the information age and a young person's panicky embrace of it" (Ross 85).

Popular music has always "[challenged] the mores of the older generation," according to Nick Hornby (168).

Note that both examples respect the original sense of the quotation; they have changed the wording only to integrate the quotations gracefully within the writer's own sentence structure.

E. Preparing an Abstract

There is one more skill essential to research-based writing that we need to discuss: how to prepare an abstract. The aim of the nonevaluative summary of a source known as an abstract is to represent a source's arguments as fairly and accurately as possible, not to critique them. Learning how to compose an abstract according to the conventions of a given discipline is a necessary skill for academic researched writing. Because abstracts differ in format and length among disciplines, you should sample some in the reference section of your library or via the Internet to provide you with models to imitate. Some abstracts, such as those in *Dissertation Abstracts,* are very brief—less than 250 words. Others may run as long as two pages.

Despite disciplinary differences, abstracts by and large follow a generalizable format. The abstract should begin with a clear and specific explanation of the work's governing thesis (or argument). In this opening paragraph, you should also define the work's purpose, and possibly include established positions that it tries to refine, qualify, or argue against. What kind of critical approach does it adopt? What are its aims? On what assumptions does it rest? Why did the author feel it necessary to write the work—that is, what does he or she believe the work offers that other sources don't? What shortcomings or misrepresentations in other criticism does the work seek to correct? *(For specifics on writing abstracts in the Natural Sciences, see Chapter 16, Introductions and Conclusions Across the Curriculum.)*

You won't be able to produce detailed answers to all of these questions in your opening paragraph, but in trying to answer some of them in your note-taking and drafting, you should find it easier to arrive at the kind of concise, substantive, and focused overview that the first paragraph of your abstract should provide. Also, be careful not to settle for bland, all-purpose generalities in this opening paragraph. And if you quote there, keep the selections short, and remember that quotations don't speak for themselves.

In summary, your aim in the first paragraph is to define the source's particular angle of vision and articulate its main point or points, including the definition of key terms used in its title or elsewhere in its argument.

Once you've set up this overview of the source's central position(s), you should devote a paragraph or so to the source's *organization* (how it divides its subject into parts) and its *method* (how it goes about substantiating its argument). What kind of secondary material does the source use? That is, how do its own bibliographic citations cue you to its school of thought, its point of view, its research traditions?

Your concluding paragraph should briefly recount some of the source's conclusions (as related to, but not necessarily the same as, its thesis). In what way does it go about culminating its argument? What kind of significance does it claim for its position? What final qualifications does it raise? The following model is a good example of an abstract:

Abstract of "William Carlos Williams," *An Essay*

By Christopher MacGowan in The Columbia History of American Poetry, pp. 395–418, Columbia University Press, 1993.

MacGowan's is a chronologically organized account of Williams' poetic career and of his relation to both modernism as an international movement and modernism as it affected the development of poetry in America. MacGowan is at some pains both to differentiate Williams from some features of modernism (such as the tendency of American writers to write as well as live away from their own cultural roots) and to link Williams to modernism. MacGowan argues, for example, that an essential feature of Williams's commitment as a poet was to "the local—to the clear presentation of what was under his nose and in front of his eyes" (385).

But he also takes care to remind us that Williams was in no way narrowly provincial, having studied in Europe as a young man (at Leipzig), having had a Spanish mother and an English father, having become friendly with the poets Ezra Pound and H. D. while getting his medical degree at the University of Pennsylvania, and having continued to meet important figures in the literary and art worlds by making frequent visits to New York and by traveling on more than one occasion to Europe (where Pound introduced him to W. B. Yeats, among others). Williams corresponded with Marianne Moore, he continued to write to Pound and to show Pound some of his work, and he wrote critical essays on the works of other modernists. MacGowan reminds us that Williams also translated Spanish works (ballads) and so was not out of contact with European influences.

Williams had a long publishing career—beginning in 1909 with a self-published volume called *Poems* and ending more than fifty years later with *Pictures from Brueghel* in 1962. What MacGowan emphasizes about this career is not only the consistently high quality of work, but also its great influence on other artists (he names those who actually corresponded with Williams and visited with him, including Charles Olson, Robert Creeley, Robert Lowell, Allen Ginsberg, and Denise Levertov). MacGowan observes that Williams defined himself "against" T. S. Eliot—the more rewarded and internationally recognized of the two poets, especially during their lifetimes—searching for "alternatives to the prevailing mode of a complex, highly allusive poetics," which Williams saw as Eliot's legacy (395). MacGowan depicts Williams as setting himself "against the international school of Eliot and Pound—Americans he felt wrote about rootlessness and searched an alien past because of their failure to write about and live within their own culture" (397).

GUIDELINES FOR FINDING, CITING, AND INTEGRATING SOURCES

1. Examine bibliographies at the end of the articles and books you've already found. Remember that one quality source can, in its bibliography, point to many other resources.

2. Citing sources isn't just about acknowledging intellectual or informational debts; it's also a courtesy to your readers, directing them how to find out more about the subjected cited.

3. Before you settle in with one author's book-length argument, use indexes and bibliographies and other resources to achieve a broader view.

4. URLs with domain names ending in .edu and .gov usually offer more reliable choices than the standard .com.

5. When professors direct you to do bibliographic research, they usually are referring to research done with indexes; these are available in print, online, and CD-ROM formats.

6. In evaluating a website about which you don't know much, try "backspacing" a URL to trace back to its authorship or institutional affiliation.

7. Tell your readers in the text of your paper, not just in citations, when you are using someone else's words, ideas, or information; rewording someone else's idea doesn't make it your idea.

8. Always attach a quotation to some of your own language; never let it stand as its own sentence in your text. Attribution—"According to Walden"—before the quote fulfills this function nicely.

Assignments: A Research Sequence

The traditional sequence of steps for building a research paper—or for any writing that relies on secondary materials—is *summary, comparative analysis, and synthesis*. The following sequence of four exercises addresses the first two steps as discrete activities. (You might, of course, choose to do only some of these exercises.)

1. **Compose an Informal Prospectus.** Formulate your initial thinking on a subject before you do more research. Include what you already know about the topic, especially what you find interesting, particularly significant, or strange. This exercise helps deter you from being overwhelmed by and absorbed into the sources you later encounter.

2. **Conduct a "What's Going on in the Field" Search, and Create a Preliminary List of Sources.** This exercise is ideal for helping you to find a topic or, if you already have one, to narrow it. The kinds of bibliographic materials you consult for this portion of the research project depend on the discipline within which you are writing. Whatever the discipline, start in the reference room of your library with specialized indexes (such as the *Social Sciences Index* or the *New York Times Index*), book review indexes, specialized encyclopedias and dictionaries, and bibliographies (print version or CD-ROM) that give you an overview of your subject or topic. If you have access to databases through your school or library, you should also search them. (See the section in this chapter entitled Electronic Research: Finding Quality on the Web.)

   The "what's going on in the field" search has two aims:

   1. to survey materials to identify trends—the kinds of issues and questions that others in the field are talking about (and, thus, find important)

   2. to compile a bibliography that includes a range of titles that interest you, that could be relevant to your prospective topic, and that seem to you representative of research trends associated with your subject (or topic)

You are not committed at this point to pursuing all of these sources but rather to reporting what is being talked about. You might also compose a list of keywords (such as Library of Congress headings) that you have used in conducting your search. If you try this exercise, you will be surprised how much value there is in exploring indexes *just for titles,* to see the kinds of topics people are currently conversing about. And you will almost surely discover how *narrowly* focused most research is (which will get you away from global questions).

Append to your list of sources (a very preliminary bibliography) a few paragraphs of informal discussion of how the information you have encountered (the titles, summaries, abstracts, etc.) has affected your thinking and plans for your paper. These paragraphs might respond to the following questions:

a. In what ways has your "what's going on in the field" search led you to narrow or shift direction in or focus your thinking about your subject?

b. How might you use one or more of these sources in your paper?

c. What has this phase of your research suggested you might need to look for next?

3. **Write an Abstract of an Article (or Book Chapter).** Use the procedure offered in the preceding section, "How to Prepare an Abstract." Aim for two pages in length. If other members of your class are working on the same or similar subjects, it is often extremely useful for everyone to share copies of their abstracts. Remember, your primary concern should lie with representing the argument and point of view of the source as fairly and accurately as possible.

    Append to the end of the abstract a paragraph or two that addresses the question, "How has this exercise affected your thinking about your topic?" Objectifying your own research process in this way helps move you away from the cut-and-paste–provide-only-the-transitions mode of writing research papers.

4. **Write a Comparative Summary.** Choose two reviews of a single source. Most writers, before they invest the significant time and energy required to study a book-length source, take the much smaller amount of time and energy required to find out more about the book. Although you should always include in your final paper your own analytical summary of books you consult on your topic, it's extremely useful also to find out what experts in the field have to say about the source.

    Select from your "what's going on" list one book-length source that you've discovered is vital to your subject or topic. As a general rule, if a number of your indexes, bibliographies, and so forth, refer you to the same book, it's a good bet that this source merits consultation.

    Locate two book reviews on the book, and write a summary that compares the two reviews. Ideally, you should locate two reviews that diverge in their points of view or in what they choose to emphasize. Depending on the length and complexity of the reviews, your comparative summary should require two or three pages.

In most cases, you will find that reviews are less neutral in their points of view than are abstracts, but they always do more than simply judge. A good review, like a good abstract, should communicate the essential ideas contained in the source. It is the reviewer's aim also to locate the source in some larger context, by, for example, comparing it to other works on the same subject and to the research tradition the book seeks to extend, modify, and so forth. Thus, your summary should try to encompass how the book contributes to the ongoing conversation on a given topic in the field.

Append to your comparative summary a paragraph or two that explains how this exercise has affected your thinking about your topic.

Obviously, you could choose to do a comparative summary of two articles, two book chapters, and so forth, rather than two book reviews. But in any event, if you use books in your research, you should always find a means of determining how these books are received in the relevant critical community.

The next step, if you were writing a research paper, would involve the task known as *synthesis,* in which you essentially write a comparative discussion that includes more than two sources. Many research papers start with an opening paragraph that synthesizes prevailing, perhaps competing, interpretations of the topic being addressed. Few good research papers consist only of such synthesis, however. Instead, writers use synthesis to frame their ideas and to provide perspective on their own arguments; the synthesis provides a platform or foundation for their own subsequent analysis.

It is probably worth adding that bad research papers fail to use synthesis as a point of departure. Instead, they line up their sources and agree or disagree with them. To inoculate you against this unfortunate reflex, review the section in Chapter 13 entitled Six Strategies for Analyzing Sources, especially Strategy 6: Find Your Own Role in the Conversation.

UNIT III

MATTERS OF FORM:
THE SHAPES
THAT THOUGHT TAKES

Chapter 15

Forms and Formats Across the Curriculum

THIS IS A CHAPTER ABOUT ORGANIZATION—the forms and formats writers use to structure their ideas. The first section of the chapter concentrates on *disciplinary formats*—the prescribed structures for finished papers in the academic disciplines. The best way to learn these formats is from professors in specific disciplines, but this book can teach you what these look like, their purpose, and more generally, how to analyze them so you can better understand what they do.

The rest of the chapter will then broaden the focus from specific disciplinary formats to more general matters of form:

- ways of grasping the overall shape of a paper
- how and where to locate the thesis
- how and where to use transitions
- ways of organizing paragraphs

Overall, the chapter overall seeks to increase your **rhetorical awareness**, that is, your awareness of how an audience's attitudes and needs can affect the shape of your writing.

It's important to recognize that all organizational schemes are conventional—which is to say, they are agreed-upon protocols with social functions. They show you how to write in a way that will allow you to be heard by others in a particular discourse community, such as an academic discipline. But it's also important to recognize that these protocols embody ways of thinking that help people to arrive at ideas. Formats are not just containers for information; they are tools of invention. They show you the accepted ways of finding things out in a discipline.

A. Disciplinary Forms and Formats

Two Functions of Formats: Rhetorical and Heuristic

- Rhetorical: formats make communication among members of a discipline easier and more efficient.
- Heuristic: formats offer writers a means of finding and exploring ideas.

THE TWO FUNCTIONS OF DISCIPLINARY FORMATS

Most of the writing (and thinking) we do is generated by some kind of format, even if we are not aware of it. Writers virtually never write in the absence of conventions. Accordingly, you should not regard the formats you encounter simply as *prescriptive* (that is, strictly required) sets of artificial rules. Rather, try to think of them as descriptive accounts of the various *heuristics*—sets of questions and categories—that humans typically use to guide and stimulate their thinking.

Because formats offer a means not only of displaying thinking in a discipline but also of shaping it, the format a discipline requires (whether tacitly or overtly) conditions its members to think in particular ways. Learning to use the format that scientists use predisposes you to think like a scientist. Although knowing the required steps of a discipline's writing format won't write your papers for you, not knowing how writers in that discipline characteristically proceed can keep you from being read.

Academic disciplines differ in the extent to which they adhere to prescribed organizational schemes. In biology and psychology, for example, formal papers and reports generally follow an explicitly prescribed pattern of presentation. Some other disciplines are less uniform and less explicit about their reliance on formats, but writers in these fields—economics, for example, or history—usually operate within fairly established forms as well. Thus, we also use the term "format" for organizational schemes that lay out the form of prospective papers in a series of steps.

The writing strategies and heuristics in this book are formats in the sense that most prescribe a series of steps. Our emphasis rests more on the process of invention than it does on the organization of the finished paper, but, as we have been suggesting, the two are not really separate. See, for example, "A Template for Organizing Papers Using 10 on 1: An Alternative to 5-Paragraph Form" (end of Chapter 10) and "Six Steps for Making a Thesis Evolve Through Successive Complications" (Chapter 11). The book's heuristics can be used as organizational models and can be adapted to disciplinary forms. They are especially useful in the many disciplines that do not prescribe a specific format.

USING FORMATS HEURISTICALLY: AN EXAMPLE

To lose sight of the heuristic value of formats is to become preoccupied with formats merely as disciplinary etiquette. The solution to this problem probably sounds easier than it is: you need to find the spaces in a format that will allow it to work as a heuristic. Consider how you might go about using even a highly specified organizational scheme like the following:

1. State the problem.
2. Develop criteria of adequacy for a solution.
3. Explore at least two inadequate solutions.
4. Explicate the proposed solution.
5. Evaluate the proposed solution.
6. Reply to anticipated criticisms.

The best reason not to ignore any of the six steps in this problem/solution format is that the format does have a logic, although it leaves that logic unstated. The purpose of including at least two inadequate solutions (step 3), for example, is to protect the writer against moving to a conclusion too quickly on the basis of too little evidence. The requirements that the writer evaluate the solution and reply to criticisms (steps 5 and 6) press the writer toward complexity, preventing a one-sided and uncritical answer. In short, heuristic value in the format is there for a writer to use if he or she doesn't allow a premature concern with matters of form to take precedence over thinking. It would be a mistake, in other words, to assume that one must move through the six steps consecutively; the writer would only need to arrange his or her thinking in that order when putting together the final product.

FORMS AND FORMATS ACROSS THE CURRICULUM: SOME COMMON ELEMENTS

As you read this chapter's discussion of differences among disciplinary formats, also look for features they share. Differences in surface features—sentence style, organization—tend to obscure the fact that a common underlying structure and set of aims unites most kinds of academic writing across the curriculum.

You can train yourself to start seeing this underlying structure by first recognizing that academic writing in all disciplines is **problem-oriented**, which is to say that academic writing typically starts by noting something that is missing from previous writing and research. As you will see, disciplines differ in how overtly writers may single out problems in other writers' thinking. And yet, in one way or another, most academic writing begins by locating something that needs to be done—why there is a need for more study—and why this new work might matter. The introductory sections of most kinds of academic writing tell readers what the writer found interesting, worth pursuing, and why.

Science Format (IMRAD) Compared with Other Academic Formats

Here is a quick overview of the organizational scheme prescribed in the natural sciences and for some kinds of papers in the social sciences, such as reports on research in psychology and political science. Although not all writing in these disciplines follows this format, most does—especially lab reports and articles based on the experimental method and quantitative research. The structure is commonly referred to as IMRAD:

I   introduction

M   methods

R   results

A

D   discussion

You can think of this format as two descriptions of the research (methods and results) framed by two sections (introduction and discussion) that locate it in the context of existing knowledge in the field. The introduction locates the new work in terms of what has already been done (which points to what still needs to be done). The discussion section considers how knowledge in the field might be changed by addition of the new results. (See LabWrite Program sponsored by NSF at www.ncsu.edu/labwrite. Also see advice from the Council of Science Editors—CSE.)

The IMRAD format, which we will define in more detail in a moment, lays out a sequence that you can locate as the underlying structure of much academic writing. Here is a restatement of the format that makes the common denominators easier to recognize.

The Common Format of Academic Writing

1. Begin with some kind of problem or question or uncertainty. Say why the new study might matter, why it needs doing. Offer a theory to be tested (working thesis/hypothesis).
2. Test the adequacy of the theory by conducting some kind of experimental procedure or other way of analyzing evidence.
3. Report resulting data—what was revealed by the experiment or other analytical method such as close reading of textual evidence or statistical analysis.
4. Interpret the results and draw conclusions about their significance. How might the results change current thinking and/or open the way to new questions and further study?

If you are just learning to write and think in an academic discipline, you cannot be expected to offer in the opening paragraph the state of knowledge in the field on a particular question. Nor can you be expected to arrive at something that will alter thinking in a discipline—although sometimes this does in fact happen. Nevertheless, college writers and their teachers across the curriculum write with similar goals: *ask and answer a new question, offer alternatives to existing ideas or evidence, or provide a new perspective or better evidence on something already known.*

Writing in the Sciences: A Biochemistry Professor Speaks

The following Voice from Across the Curriculum is taken from a presentation that biochemistry professor Keri Colabroy delivered to a group of undergraduate writing tutors at our college. The talk aimed at enabling the tutors, many of whom are not science majors, to work more confidently with writing that science students bring to the college's Writing Center. We are grateful to Professor Colabroy for making her material available to us and to the tutors we train. You will find more of this material in the next chapter, Introductions and Conclusions Across the Curriculum.

Voices from Across the Curriculum

The lab report as taught in college science courses teaches students to mimic the process of thinking required to write a scientific paper. The governing question of the lab report is, "To what extent is my data consistent with what I was supposed to get?" Like most scientific writing, the lab report has four parts (five if you include the abstract):

The Parts of Lab Reports and Scientific Papers

Abstract

The short synoptic version of essentially the entire paper: What you did, what you found and how you did it

Introduction/Purpose/Objective

What you are trying to accomplish and why it is important

Methods/Experimental Procedures

The details of how you performed the experiments

Results/Data

Reporting of the data without commentary, often done with tables, graphs and figures rather than text

Primarily summative and descriptive, like a Notice and Focus exercise without the implications (See *Writing Analytically,* Chapter 2)

Discussion/Conclusions

This is where the analysis happens. Cite the data, then make qualified, evidence-based claims from the data; draw implications.

In the written accounts of scientific experiments, some information is repeated across sections. This repetition is deliberate. No scientist reads a paper in order, and so every section has to stand by itself.

In scientific papers, introductions serve two purposes:

(1) to orient your readers to the scientific context of your work while showing them the inherent need for new (your) information to solve an *uncertainty* or *problem,* something you or the community doesn't quite understand (in Writing Analytically, the prompts "interesting, significant or strange" focus writers on problems and areas of uncertainty); and

(2) to state succinctly what the paper/study has accomplished and what that means for the big picture you outlined in point #1.

The introduction of a scientific paper is full of references to primary literature (other scientific papers). In most undergraduate science courses, students are not asked to write the introduction section. Instead, the professor provides a paraphrase of the question/problem that the experiment is meant to solve.

It is not until the discussion section that the science writer analyzes the data. The discussion section is not a summary; rather, the writer makes qualified claims and backs them up with evidence. The discussion section completes the frame set up by the introduction by arguing for the significance of the study within its scientific context. A discussion section concludes by looking backwards to summarize implications, then looking forward to articulate what this particular study means for the whole field.

The conclusion explains how questions have been answered and how knowledge in the field might be changed because of the new information.

Word choice in scientific papers—especially the choice of verbs—is important. Scientific writing never "proves," for example. It "implies" and "indicates." The science writer chooses verbs to make carefully qualified claims based on an accumulation of evidence.

Scientific writing is corporate, by which I mean that scientific writers speak to and about the community of other science writers. To name a particular scientist is considered pretentious. It is appropriate to point out inconsistencies in thinking as in, "a lot of work has been done here, but we still don't understand X." It is not considered appropriate to locate shortcomings in the work of particular scientists.

—Keri Colabroy, Professor of Biochemistry

How to Write—and Read—Scientific Formats: Three Professors Speak

Note that the observations in the following Voices from Across the Curriculum apply to much but certainly not all of the writing that goes on in the sciences. Writing in physics, for example, where research is more theoretical, often takes a different form. There are other exceptions. Writing in psychology can appear in the form of the case study rather than in reports on experiments.

It is necessary, a biology professor asserts, to recognize the need for flexibility when using the scientific format. Although the format has a clear defining logic, the distinctions among the various parts are not always as clear-cut as some students may think they are. (*For examples of science writing, see Chapter 16, Introductions and Conclusions Across the Curriculum.*)

Voices from Across the Curriculum

In writing in the social sciences, there is a standard plot with three alternative endings. The "Introduction" (a standard section of APA style) sets forth the problem, which the "Methods" section promises to address. The "Results" section "factually" reports the outcome of the study, with the "Discussion" section interpreting the results. "The data" are given the starring role in determining which ending is discussed in the "Discussion" section: hypothesis confirmed, hypothesis rejected, or hard to say. (I would say "which ending the author chooses" versus "which ending is discussed," but the data are supposed to be determinative, and the role of the author/investigator neutral.) Analytical thinking comes in setting up the problem and making sense of the results in conjunction with existing literature on the subject.

—Alan Tjeltveit, Professor of Psychology

O Experimental Psychology uses a very rigid format. I explain to the students the functions of the different sections for the reader. Once students start to read journal articles themselves, the functions of the sections become clear. Readers do not always want to read or reread the whole article. If I want to replicate someone's research, I may read just the "Methods" section to get the technical details I need. I may read just the "Results" section to get a sense of the numerical results I might expect. On the other hand, I may not care about the details of how the experiment was run. I might just want to know if it worked, in which case I would read the first few sentences of the "Discussion" section. The format lets me know exactly where to find whatever I might be looking for, without having to read through the whole article.

—Laura Edelman, Professor of Psychology

O Scientific format appears highly formulaic at first glance. Papers are generally broken into four sections: "Introduction" (What is this all about, what do we already know, why do we care?), "Experimental Procedures" (What did you actually do?), "Results" (What happened in your experiments?), and "Discussion" (What do you think it means, what are the remaining questions?). This breakdown is useful because it emphasizes the process of argument (introduction and results), providing evidence (results), and analysis (discussion). However, although this may seem different from writing in other disciplines, I think of it as a codification of basic analytical writing that is common in most disciplines.

A common mistake made by beginning and intermediate students is taking this breakdown too literally. In order to be comprehensible, the rules must be broken periodically. For example, results frequently must be referred to in the "Experimental Procedures" section in order to understand *why* the next procedure was performed. Similarly, the "Results" section frequently must include some discussion, so that the reader understands the immediate significance of the results, if not the broader implications. For example, the following sentences might appear in a "Results" section: "These data suggest that the p53 protein may function in repressing cell division in potential cancer cells. In order to test this possibility, we overexpressed p53 protein in a transformed cell line." The first sentence provides an interpretation of the results that is necessary to understand why the next experiment was performed.

—Bruce Wightman, Professor of Biology

B. The Shaping Force of Common Thought Patterns

DEDUCTION AND INDUCTION

According to the usual definitions of the terms deduction and induction, you might expect that a fairly full-fledged version of the thesis would appear at the beginning of a deductive paper but at the end of an inductive one. But as we will go on to show, papers don't neatly fit these two abstract models of thinking. In practice, all writing combines the two patterns. In virtually all essays, the paper

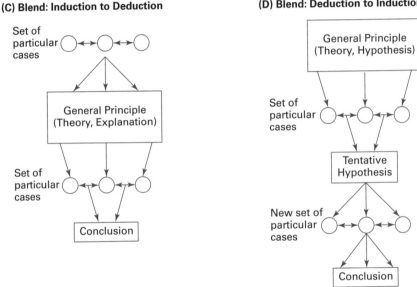

(A) Deduction

(B) Induction

(C) Blend: Induction to Deduction

(D) Blend: Deduction to Induction

FIGURE 15.1
Deduction and Induction. Deduction (A) uses particular cases to exemplify general principles and analyze their implications. Induction (B) constructs general principles from the analysis of particular cases. In practice, analytical thinking and writing blend deduction and induction and start either with particular cases (C) or a general principle (D).

begins with some kind of organizing claim; this is not delayed until the end. And in virtually all essays, the opening claim is not simply repeated at the end but occurs there in its duly tested and evolved form. To clarify these claims we need to offer some definitions. (See Figure 15.1, A and B).

Deduction

As a thought process, deduction reasons from a general principle (assumed to be true) to the particular case. It introduces this principle up front and then uses it to select and interpret evidence. For example, a deductive paper might state in its first paragraph that attitudes toward and rules governing sexuality in a given culture can be seen, at least in part, to have economic causes. The paper might then apply this principle, already assumed to be true, to the codes governing sexual behavior in several cultures or several kinds of sexual behavior in a single culture.

A good deductive argument is, however, more than a mechanical application or matching exercise of general claim and specific details that are explained by it. Deductive reasoning uses the evidence to draw out the implications—what logicians term *inferring the consequences*—of the claim. The general principle explains selected features of particular cases, and *reciprocally,* the evidence brings out implications in the principle.

Thus, the general principle stated at the beginning of the paper and the idea stated as the paper's conclusion are not the same. Rather, the conclusion presents the (evolved) idea that the writer has arrived at through the application of the principle.

Induction

An inductively organized paper typically begins not with a principle already accepted as true but with particular data for which it seeks to generate some explanatory principle. Whereas deduction moves by applying a generalization to particular cases, induction moves from the observation of individual cases to the formation of a general principle. Because all possible cases can obviously never be examined— every left-handed person, for example, if one wishes to theorize that left-handed people are better at spatial thinking than right-handers—the principle (or thesis) arrived at through inductive reasoning always remains open to doubt.

Nevertheless, the thesis of an inductive paper is generally deemed acceptable if a writer can demonstrate that the theory is based on a reasonably sized sampling of representative instances. Suffice it to say that a child who arrives at the thesis that all orange food tastes bad on the basis of squash and carrots has not based that theory on an adequate sampling of available evidence.

The Overlap

In most cases, induction and deduction operate in tandem (see Figure 15.1, C and D). Analysis by nature moves between the particular and the general, regardless of which comes first. Whether the overall shape of the analysis—its mode of progression—is primarily inductive or deductive, it will still gain in complexity from beginning to end as it confronts evidence.

It's true that in some disciplines (philosophy, for example) the deductive pattern of argument prevails, but not exclusively. The analysis of evidence, though clearly designed to reflect a general principle, will also lead to new formulations that will modify the general principle in various ways.

THESIS SLOTS

Even in the most inductive forms of essay development, readers are guided by various formulations of the thesis. Here is a short list of the places in an essay that readers typically expect some version of the thesis to occur:

- The first articulation of the working thesis usually occurs late in the opening paragraph or early in the second paragraph of a piece. This first articulation comes after the writer has presented the problem or question that establishes the tension the thesis aims to resolve, and after he or she has provided some kind of context for it.

- Subsequent articulations of the thesis usually occur at points of transition, typically at paragraph openings following the analysis of complicating evidence. This kind of updating has the added benefit of providing unity to the essay, using the thesis as a kind of spine.

- The final statement of the thesis occurs in the concluding paragraph, or perhaps the next to last one. It is usually offered in clear relationship to the terms offered in the introduction, so the reader is offered a last vision of where the essay has traveled.

THE SHAPING FORCE OF THESIS STATEMENTS

A sentence is the shape that thought takes. The shape of the thought in thesis statements has shaping force in the way the paper develops. Some thesis shapes are more effective than others.

- A strong thesis usually contains **tension**, the balance of this against that
- Thesis statements often begin with a grammatically subordinate idea that will get outweighed by a more pressing claim: "Although X appears to account for Z, Y accounts for it better."
- A less effective thesis shape is the *list*

The order of clauses in a thesis statement often predicts the shape of the paper. A thesis that begins with a subordinate clause ("Although X ....."), for example, might lead to a paper in which the first part of the paper deals with the claims for X and then moves to a fuller embrace of Y.

The advantage of the subordinate construction (and the reason that so many theses are set up this way) is that the subordinate idea helps you to define your own position by giving you something to define it against. The subordinate clause of a thesis helps you to demonstrate that there is in fact an issue involved—that is, more than one possible explanation exists for the evidence you are considering. In practice, using this shape will often lead you to arrive at some compromise position between the claims of both X and Y. What appeared to be a *binary opposition*—"not X but Y"—emerges as a more complex combination of the two.

A less effective thesis shape that can predict the shape of a paper is the *list*. This shape, in which a writer might offer three points and then devote a section to each, often leads to sloppier thinking than one having a thesis statement containing both subordinate and independent clauses, because the list often does not sufficiently specify the connections among its various components. As a result, it fails to assert a relationship among ideas.

Try This 15.1: Predicting Essay Shapes from Thesis Shapes

It is a useful skill, both in reading and writing, to predict paper shapes from thesis shapes. For each of the theses below, what shape is predicted? That is, what will probably be discussed first, what second, and why? Which words in the thesis are especially predictive of the shape the paper will take?

1. The reforms in education, created to alleviate the problems of previous reforms, have served only to magnify the very problems they were meant to solve.

2. Although women more readily cry in contemporary films, the men, by not crying, seem to win the audience's favor.

3. The complications that fuel the plots in today's romantic comedies arise because women and men express their sensitivity so differently; the resolutions, however, rarely require the men to capitulate.

THE SHAPING FORCE OF TRANSITIONS

The linkage between where you've been and where you're going is usually a point in your writing at which thinking is taking place. This is especially the case in the evolving rather than the static model of thesis development in which the writer continually *updates* the thesis as it moves through evidence.

- Thinking tends to occur at points of transition.
- A good transition articulates a paper's logical links—how each phase of the paper leads to the next.
- Too many additive transitions ("also," "another example of") produce papers that list, an overly loose form of organization

It is useful to think of transitions as *directional indicators*, especially at the beginnings of paragraphs but also within them. "And," for example, is a plus sign. It indicates that the writer will add something, continuing in the same direction. The words "but," "yet," "nevertheless," and "however" are among the many transitional words that alert readers to changes in the direction of the writer's thinking. They might indicate the introduction of a qualification, or a potentially contradictory piece of evidence, or an alternative point of view.

Some additive transitions do more work than "also" or "another." The word "moreover" is an additive transition, but it adds emphasis to the added point. The transitional sequence "not only... but also" restates and then adds information in a way that clarifies what has gone before.

Too many additive transitions can pose a problem for your writing. A list is a slack form of organization, one that fails to identify how this is related to that. Although transitional wording such as "another example of" or "also" at the beginning of paragraphs does tell readers that a related point or example will follow, it does not specify that relationship beyond piling on another "and." Essentially, these words just list.

If you find yourself relying on "another" and "also" at points of transition, force yourself to substitute other transitional wording that indicates more precisely the nature of the relationship with what has gone before in the paper. Language such as "similarly" and "by contrast" can sometimes serve this purpose. Often, some restatement is called for to keep your reader on track—brief repetition is not necessarily redundant. A good transition reaches backward, telling where you've been, as the grounds for making a subsequent move forward.

The first step toward improving your use of transitions (and thereby, the organization of your writing) is to become conscious of them. If you notice that you are beginning successive paragraphs with "Another reason," for example, you can probably conclude that you are listing rather than developing your ideas. If you notice a number of sentences that start with the vague referent "This," you probably need to name the thing "This" refers to.

Think of transitions as echoes in the service of continuity. If you study the transitions in a piece, you will usually find that they echo either the language or the ideas of something that precedes them as they point to what is ahead.

Try This 15.2: Tracking Transitions

As an exercise in becoming more conscious of how transitions shape thinking, track the transitions in a piece of writing. Take a few pages of something you are reading (preferably a complete piece, such as a short article) and circle or underline all of the directional indicators. Remember to check not only the beginnings of paragraphs but within them. Then, survey your markings. What do you notice now about the shape of the piece? This exercise is also useful for expanding your repertoire of transitional words to use in your own writing. As an alternative, track the transitional wording in the next section of this chapter.

C. The Rhetoric of Form

Thus far, we have talked about form primarily in relation to the search for meaning. We've demonstrated that some forms of arranging ideas (5 paragraph form, for example) interfere with a writer's ability to have ideas in the first place. Whatever form one uses, we've argued, it has to be flexible enough to allow ideas to evolve. The point is that there are various factors influencing a writer's decisions about forms and formats. These include both the demands of the subject itself and those of the discourse community within which the writing seeks to communicate.

We now wish to expand on the role that a writer's sense of his or her *audience* plays in determining the formal presentation of ideas. We have entitled this section "The Rhetoric of Form" to emphasize the effects that a chosen form has on an audience—on its receptiveness to a writer's ideas, for example.

The study of rhetoric is primarily concerned with the various means at a writer's (or speaker's) disposal for influencing the views of an audience. In early rhetorics, Greek and Roman writers divided these means into three large categories—ethos, logos, and pathos—that you encountered earlier in this book in our definition of analysis (*see Chapter 3*). We'll use these categories for organizing what we wish to say about the relationship between formal structures and audience.

1. **Ethos** refers to the character of the speaker or writer. If an audience perceives a speaker to be ethical and rational, it will be inclined to perceive her or his argument as ethical and rational too. Thus, writers attend to the kind of *persona* they become on the page, the personality conveyed by the words and the tone of the words. In classical orations—the grandparent of virtually all speech and essay formats—the first section was always allotted to particular means of establishing an appealing persona, one whom an audience would want to listen to and believe. *(See the next section, "The Classical Oration Format".)*

2. **Logos** refers to the character of the thinking itself: the rational component, evident in the presence and development of the ideas.

3. **Pathos** includes appeals to the audience's emotions—which writing does all of the time, whether a writer wants it to or not. It is possible to think of the form of a paper in terms of how it might negotiate the likes and dislikes, the hopes and fears, of its assumed audience. If, for instance, you were to present an argument in favor of a position with which you knew in advance that your audience was predisposed to disagree, you would probably choose to delay making a case for this position until you had found various ways of earning that audience's trust. By contrast, when presenting an argument to an audience of like-minded people, you would be much more likely to start out with the position you planned to advance.

THE CLASSICAL ORATION FORMAT

All-purpose formats have been around a long time. Some are very simple. Others are more elaborate. The simplest organizing scheme consists of three parts: introduction, body, and conclusion. The format of the classical oration has a more elaborate form:

- *exordium*, introduction
- *narratio*, statement of facts
- *divisio*, outline of the points or steps in the argument
- *confirmatio*, proof of the case
- *confutatio*, refutation of opposing arguments
- *peroratio*, conclusion

If you read or listen to (for example) political speeches, you will find that many of them follow this order. This is because the form of the classical oration is suited primarily to argument—to the kind of writing in which the writer makes a case for or against something and refutes opposing arguments. As we have been demonstrating throughout this book, analytical thinking does not fit well into formats calling for an upfront statement of a predetermined claim, which is then simply proven to be correct. And so the book offers alternative organizational schemes that allow the space necessary for the recursive (back and forth between evidence and claims) thinking that analytical writing involves. These forms include some of the elements of the classical oration but without its emphasis on proof and refutation.

THREE COMMON ORGANIZING STRATEGIES

The following organizational patterns are determined more by rhetorical consider-ations—the desired effect on an audience—than by their idea-generating potential. As you will see, however, each also has potential for shaping thought. The first two pat-terns, climactic order and comparison/contrast, are common in all forms of writing. The third pattern, which concerns locating refutations and concessions, is particular to argument.

Climactic Order: Saving the Best for Last

Climactic order arranges elements from least to most important. The idea is to build to your best points, rather than leading with them and thereby allowing the paper to trail off from your more minor and less interesting observations. But what are your best points? A frequent mistake writers make in arranging their points climactically—and one that has much to do with the rhetoric of form—is to assume that the best point is the most obvious, the one with the most data attached to it and the one least likely to produce disagreement with readers. Such writers end up giving more space than they should to ideas that really don't need much development because they are already evident to most readers.

If you follow the principle of climactic order, you would begin with the most obvious and predictable points—and ones that, psychologically speaking, would get readers assenting—and then build to the more revealing and less obvious ones. So, for example, if the comparisons between film A and film B are fairly mundane but the contrasts are really provocative, you'd get the comparisons out of the way first and build to the contrasts, exploiting difference within similarity (see Chapter 4).

If, for example, there are three important reasons for banning snowmobiling in your town, you might choose to place the most compelling one last. If you were to put it first, you might draw your readers in quickly (a principle used by news stories) but then lose them as your argument seemed to trail off into less interesting rationales.

Comparisons/Contrasts: Two Formats

In Chapter 7, we discuss comparison as an invention strategy. We now want to address this subject from the perspective of organizing a paper. The first decision a writer has to make when arranging comparisons and contrasts is whether to address the two items being compared and contrasted in sequential blocks (A and then B) or point by point

- Organize by subjects being compared (subject A and then subject B), or
- Organize the comparison under a series of topics (Topic 1: A and B, Topic 2: A and B, etc.)

If you are comparing subject A with subject B, you might first make all the points you wish to make about A and then make points about B by explicitly referring back to A as you go. The advantage of this format is that it will allow you to use comparing and contrasting to figure out what you wish to say as you are drafting.

The disadvantage of this "subject-A-then-subject-B" format is that it can easily lose focus. If you don't manage to keep the points you raise about each side of your comparison parallel, you may end up with a paper comprised of two loosely connected halves. The solution is to make your comparisons and contrasts in the second half of the paper connect explicitly with what you said in the first half. What you say about subject A, in other words, should set the subtopics and terms for discussion of subject B.

The alternative pattern of organization for comparisons and contrasts is to organize by topic—not A and then B but A1 and B1, A2 and B2, A3 and B3, and so forth. That is, you talk about both A and B under a series of subtopics. If, for example, you were comparing two films, you might organize your work under such headings as directing, script, acting, special effects, and so forth.

The advantage of this format is that it better focuses the comparisons, pressing you to use them to think with. The disadvantage is that organizing in this way is sometimes difficult to manage until you've already done quite a bit of thinking about the two items you're comparing. The solution, particularly in longer papers, is sometimes to use both formats. You begin by looking at each of your subjects separately to make the big links and distinctions apparent and then focus what you've said by further pursuing selected comparisons one topic at a time.

Concessions and Refutations: Giving and Taking Away

In the language of argument, you *concede* whenever you acknowledge that a position at odds with your own does indeed have merit, even though you continue to believe that your position overall is the more reasonable one. When making a concession, a writer needs to represent this competing point of view as genuinely creditable—rather than only seemingly creditable until he or she lays out a means of opposing it. Another option is to argue against these views so as to *refute* their reasonableness. (*For a misuse of concessions and refutations, see Straw Man under Logical Fallacies in Chapter 9, Analyzing Arguments.*)

As a rule of thumb, avoid making your readers wait too long before you either concede or refute a view that you can assume will already have occurred to them. If you delay too long, you may inadvertently suggest either that you are unaware of the competing view or that you are afraid to bring it up.

In the case of short and easily managed concessions and refutations, you can often house these within the first several paragraphs and, in this way, clear a space for the position you wish to promote. In the case of more complicated and potentially more threatening alternative arguments, you may need to express your own position clearly and convincingly first. But to avoid the rhetorical problem of appearing to ignore the threat, you will probably need to give it a nod, telling readers that they will return to a full discussion of it later, once you have laid out your own position in some detail.

The placement of arguments has much to do with their relative complexity. Reasonably straightforward and easily explained concessions and refutations can often all be grouped in one place, perhaps as early as the second or third paragraph of a paper. The approach to concession and refutation in more complex arguments does not allow for such grouping. For each part of your argument, you will probably need to concede and refute as necessary, before moving to the next part of your argument and repeating the procedure.

Try This 15.3: Locating Concessions and Refutations

The following passage from a student essay on the relation between gender inequality and language makes skillful use of concessions and refutations. The excerpt is part of an introductory paragraph, after the writer has set up the issue: whether or not the elimination of sexism in language (the use of male pronouns and words like "mankind," for example, in circumstances applying to both men and women) through the use of generic pronouns (those that do not indicate gender, such as "they" rather than "he") can help to eliminate gender exclusion in the culture. The paragraph names the two sides of the issue and moves from there to a tentative thesis.

Study the paragraph to answer the following questions: (1) What language functions as concession? (2) What language functions as refutation? (3) What part of the competing argument does the refutation still appear willing to concede? (4) How is the refutation that the writer offers different from the position to which he concedes?

Gender Inequality and Linguistic Bias

The more conservative side on this issue questions whether the elimination of generic pronouns can, in fact, change attitudes, and whether intentionally changing language is even possible. The reformist side believes that the elimination of generic pronouns is necessary for women's liberation from oppression and that reshaping the use of male pronouns as generic is both possible and effective. Although the answer to the debate over the direct link between a change in language and a change in society is not certain, it is certain that the attitudes and behaviors of societies are inseparable from language. Language conditions what we feel and think. The act of using "they" to refer to all people rather than the generic "he" will not automatically change collective attitudes toward women. These generic pronouns should be changed, however, because 1) the struggle itself increases awareness and discussion of the sexual inequalities in society, and subsequently, this awareness will transform attitudes and language, and 2) the power of linguistic usage has been mainly controlled by and reserved for men. Solely by participating in linguistic reform, women have begun to appropriate some of the power for themselves.

D. The Idea of the Paragraph

Throughout this section of the chapter, we will focus on what are sometimes called "body" paragraphs, as opposed to the more special-function paragraphs that serve as the beginning and end of papers. *(For discussion of introductory and concluding paragraphs, see the next chapter, Introductions and Conclusions Across the Curriculum.)*

HOW A PARAGRAPH SAYS

It is useful to think of any piece of writing as consisting of parts or blocks. The paragraph is a fundamental building block, bigger than the sentence, smaller than the section or paper. Paragraphs can be thought of by analogy with the paper. Like papers, paragraphs have parts: they make opening gambits, they put forward evidence and analyze it, and they arrive at some kind of summarizing or culminating closure. They have, in short, a beginning, a middle, and an end. But unlike the paper, the paragraph does not stand alone as an independent entity. For a paragraph to be effective, readers need to be able to understand its role in unfolding the thinking of the paper as a whole.

The two primary characteristics of virtually all strong paragraphs are unity and development.

- **unity**: all the sentences in the paragraph should be related to some central idea or focus. Normally, the sentence that serves this function in the paragraph is the topic sentence.
- **development**: the sentences in a paragraph need to connect to each other in some way; a paragraph needs to go somewhere, to build. Normally, the sentences in a paragraph either offer a series of observations about the main idea or build one upon the next to offer a more sustained analysis of one element of the main idea.

Notice that we don't say here that a paragraph offers a claim plus examples and reasons. This model of the paragraph is true in some cases, but paragraphs typically do more than make simple claims and then back them up with one or more examples.

Once you begin paying attention to paragraphs, you will see that they are far less uniform in their shapes and procedures than you may have been asked to believe. The paragraph police will not haul you away for producing a paragraph that lacks a topic sentence, or places it at the end of the paragraph instead of the front, or contains several claims instead of one, or delays the substantiating evidence till later. Nonetheless, most of the paragraphs you encounter—and most that you should write—have unity and development. They are about one thing, and they tell you why it is important.

HOW LONG? PARAGRAPHS, READERS, AND WRITERS

Paragraphing is a kindness to your reader, since it divides your thinking into manageable bites. If you find a paragraph growing longer than half a page—particularly if it is your opening or second paragraph—find a place to make a paragraph break. More frequent paragraphing provides readers with convenient resting points from which to relaunch themselves into your thinking.

Long paragraphs are daunting—rather like mountains—and they are easy to get lost in, for both readers and writers. When writers try to do too much in a single paragraph, they often lose focus and lose contact with the larger purpose or point that got them into the paragraph in the first place. Remember that old rule about one idea to a paragraph? Well, it's not a bad rule, though it isn't exactly right because sometimes you need more space than a single paragraph can provide to lay out a complicated phase of your overall argument. In that case, just break wherever it seems reasonable to do so in order to keep your paragraphs from becoming ungainly. Two paragraphs can be about the same thing, the first half and then the second half. This paragraph, for example, might have been easier to process if we had broken it right before the question about that old rule.

Paragraphs are a relief not just for your readers: they also give the writer a break. When you draft, start a new paragraph whenever you feel yourself getting stuck: it's the promise of a fresh start. Paragraph breaks are like turning a corner to a new view, even when the thinking is continuous. They also force the writer to make transitions, overt connections among the parts of his or her thinking, and to state or restate key ideas. Paragraph indentations allow readers to scan essays, searching for connecting words and important ideas.

It can be extraordinarily useful to draft a paper in phases, as a series of paragraphs:

- Break up the larger interpretation or argument into more manageable pieces.
- Give yourself space to think in short sections that you can then sequence.
- When you revise, use paragraphs to clean up your thinking by dividing it into its most logical parts.

A short paragraph will always provide emphasis, for which most readers will thank you. (You should, however, use very short paragraphs sparingly.)

Paragraphs need to justify their existence. A paragraph break should remind you to check that you have suggested to the readers why they need to know this information. Ask yourself why you are telling them what you are telling them. How does the thinking in the paragraph relate to the overall idea that your paper is developing?

A good way to check if your paragraph is really advancing your claims is to ask and answer "So what?" at the end of the paragraph.

PARAGRAPHS ACROSS THE CURRICULUM: SOME COMMON PATTERNS

The simplest way of thinking about paragraph organization draws on a slightly extended version of what is known as the traditional rhetorical modes: Exemplification, Narration, Description, Process, Comparison/Contrast, Classification/Division, Definition, Cause/Effect, Problem/Solution, and, of course, Analysis.

You have been studying the characteristic shape of analytical thinking throughout this book. It consists of seeing the parts of something in relation to the whole. In practice, this means finding a significant pattern of detail and explaining what this pattern reveals about the nature and purpose of whatever it is you are studying. The practice we call 10 on 1 (see Chapter 10) is typical of analytical paragraphs. It consists of close scrutiny of a single representative example wherein the writer notices as much as possible about the example and then interprets his or her observations by asking and answering the question "So what?"

Because analysis typically focuses on relationships among the parts and between those parts and the whole, classification and division are well-suited to analytical writing. In the organizational pattern called division, the writer breaks a subject into its component parts. Classification explains how the parts relate to each other by putting them into categories. In practice, classification and division tend to occur together, often in conjunction with definition. When we define something we locate its defining traits, the features that make it what it is.

Here is a brief example of classification and division going on in the same paragraph:

> The United States has never had a pure growth-directed model of education. Some distinctive and by-now-traditional features of our system resist being cast in those terms. Unlike virtually every nation of the world, we have a liberal-arts model of university education: instead of entering college to study a single subject, students are required to take a wide range of courses in their first two years, prominently including courses in the humanities. That model influences secondary education: nobody is tracked too early into a nonhumanities stream. (Martha C. Nussbaum, "The Liberal Arts Are Not Elitist," *The Chronicle of Higher Education*, February 28, 2010).

Although most paragraphs employ a mix of these modes of organization, the patterns are usually easy to see. For purposes of illustration, we will focus on narrative organization. A surprising amount of writing in the disciplines is **narrative**; that is, writers often find themselves needing to explain sequences of action (as in the methods and results sections of a scientific paper or lab report) or events or behaviors or ideas. Notice, for example, how profoundly narrative the writing is in the following excerpt from a lab report.

A set of electrophilic aromatic substitution reactions was performed using two monosubstituted benzenes so as to describe substitution patterns as a function of substrate. Samples of toluene and ethylbenzene each underwent a nitration via a 1:1 mixture of sulfuric and nitric acid. The acid mixture formed a strongly electrophilic nitronium ion which attacked the mono-substituted benzene ring and replaced a proton. Upon mixing the reagents, both nitration reactions turned yellow. The toluene reaction darkened somewhat over the reaction period, while the ethylbenzene reaction turned brown. The color change is evidence of a reaction occurring. The products of each reaction were isolated via a liquid extraction with MTBE and dried. The isolated products were analyzed via GC-MS (gas chromatography – mass spectroscopy) which separates compounds based on their volatility. This was used to both identify the products and determine their respective ratios.

A good piece of writing—at the level of the paragraph as well as at the level of the paper as a whole—tells a story. It explains how and why the writer came to focus on an issue or question or problem. It also narrates for readers how the writer came to understand the meaning and significance of his or her evidence.

LINKING THE SENTENCES IN PARAGRAPHS: MINDING THE GAPS

It helps to think of the space between the period at the end of a sentence and the beginning of the next sentence as a gap that the reader has to cross. Start thinking in this way as you follow the train of thought in this paragraph and those that follow it. Keep asking yourself: what is the connection between each sentence and the one that follows it? What keeps the reader from falling out of the paper at the gaps between sentences, losing sight of the thought connections that make a paragraph more than just a collection of sentences?

In many paragraphs, the connections between and among sentences are made apparent by the repetition of **key words**. This idea of key words brings us back to a core principle of this book: that both writers and readers make meaning by locating significant patterns of repetition and contrast. What is the pattern of repeated words in the paragraph above this one, for example? Notice the repetition of the key word "gap," which goes with the idea of falling and which is in opposition to such words as "connection" and "train of thought." The other connecting feature of the paragraph comes with its repeated use of questions. The paragraph you are now reading gets its sense of purpose from the previous paragraph's questions. Here we start answering them.

Sometimes (but not always) the connecting logic that helps readers negotiate the gaps between sentences must be made explicit. So, for example, some sentences begin with the words, "So, for example." The function of this type of connection is illustration. Some other words that operate in this gap-bridging way are "thus," "furthermore," "in addition," "similarly," "in other words," and "on the contrary."

When the organizing principle of a paragraph is sufficiently evident, explicit transitional words are often not needed. If parallelism is the paragraph's organizing principle, for example, readers will be able to see the relationship among the paragraph's sentences without a lot of repetition of connecting words.

WHAT A PARAGRAPH DOES: THE PARAGRAPH AS MOVEMENT OF MIND

The key to understanding how to write paragraphs, as well as how to analyze what you read in them, is to focus on what the various sentences in a paragraph *do*. To follow what a paragraph *does* is to follow its succession of sentences as a movement of mind, an unfolding of consciousness on the page that conveys to readers the relationships among its various pieces of information. If you can keep this idea in mind, seeing paragraphs as possessing behavior—actively shaping thought and communicating it to imagined readers—your writing will improve.

The sentences in a paragraph have different jobs; there is a distribution of labor. To see this element of paragraphing, it is essential that you "look beyond content"; that is, you need to focus on what the sentences are doing, not just on what they are saying. In Chapter 8, Reasoning from Evidence to Claims, we ask you to distinguish which sentences in a paragraph were evidence and which were claims, and to mark these with an E or a C. Those are two functions of sentences in paragraphs—two tasks that sentences in a paragraph can perform.

As this chapter has already suggested, there are other functions as well. Here are some roles sentences play in paragraphs:

- link one idea to another
- link evidence to a claim
- qualify the major claim (the thesis)
- paraphrase the major claim (restating and querying the key terms in order to figure out what they imply)
- operate as transitions, linking the paragraph to the one that precedes it and to the overall idea the paper is developing

Paragraph Structure #1: Topic Sentence, Restriction, Illustration

One model for thinking about paragraph structure comes from the rhetorician Alton Becker: Topic sentence (T), Restriction (R) and Illustration (I). The topic sentence states some kind of claim—an idea that the paragraph will develop in some way. This may or may not appear as the first sentence of the paragraph, and there may be more than one claim in the paragraph, although one of these is usually primary. Restriction limits the claim in some way. Illustration supplies examples in support of the claim.

As our earlier discussions of thesis and evidence have suggested, evidence does more than just support claims; when we consider how evidence does not match the claim, we are led to qualify (shrink, restrict) the claim. This process of asserting ideas and then restricting them also goes on, often repeatedly, at the level of the paragraph.

The TRI model does not cover everything that goes on in various kinds of paragraphs, but it is a good way to start looking at paragraphs in order to begin thinking about what the sentences do. Here is a somewhat expanded list of jobs that sentences may do inside paragraphs.

What Sentences Do Inside Paragraphs

T = topic sentence -> announces the main idea of the paragraph

R = restriction -> qualifies, further defines, limits claims; happens at various points in the paragraph

P = paraphrasing -> restates claims and evidence to analyze them

I = illustration -> provides substantiating evidence

EXP = explains the illustrations, draws out meaning of evidence

Th = thesis restatement -> offers versions of an evolving thesis

Tr = transitional wording -> links sentences, connects ideas inside paragraph but also connects paragraph to what precedes and follows it

SW = answers "So what?"-> tells readers the purpose of the paragraph, why the writer bothered to tell them this

Let's look at a paragraph to see what some of the sentences are doing. We have labeled some of the sentences (in square brackets) according to our expanded version of Becker's marking scheme.

> [T:] Armin Schnider, a neurologist from the Cantonal University Hospital in Geneva, Switzerland, says that the vast majority of confabulations he has heard from his patients over the years relate directly to their earlier lives. [I:] One of his patients, a retired dentist, worried while in hospital that he was keeping his patients waiting. [I:] Another, an elderly woman, talked regularly about her baby in the present tense. [EXP:] Most of these patients had damage to the temporal lobes of the brain, particularly the memory regions of the hippocampus, so it seemed likely that they had somehow lost the ability to make new memories and were retrieving old ones instead. [EXP:] The intriguing thing was that they didn't realize these memories were old — they seemed convinced by their stories, and sometimes even acted on them. [SW:] So Schnider decided to study their memory in more detail. (Helen Phillips, "Everyday Fairytales," New Scientist, 7 October 2006)

Try This 15.4: Label the Function of the Sentences in a Paragraph

One of the best ways to understand how paragraphs work—to apprehend them as tools of thought and to be able to deploy them to work for you—is to assign the abbreviations in our list above to any paragraph in anything you have written or read, including this book.

Paragraph Structure #2: Observation -> Implication -> Conclusion

One of the models described in this book for the analytical movement of mind is as follows: *Observation → So what? → implication → So what? → tentative conclusions.* This sequence goes beyond the simplest kind of paragraph development—idea + illustration—because it contains more of the writer's thinking on how he or she reasons to the claim from evidence. Explicitly drawing out the implications of evidence complicates, but also more accurately represents the process of thinking, than does simply attaching examples to the idea they support.

   One example of this model of mental movement appears earlier in this book, in the section of Chapter 2 entitled "Asking So What?" Not all paragraphs in an analytical paper move in this way, but a significant number of them do. We reprint the paragraph here, adding annotations about what the paragraph does.

   [Paragraph opens with empirical observation:] If you look closely at Camilo Vergara's photo of Fern Street, Camden, 1988, you'll notice a sign on the side of a dilapidated building that reads "Danger: Men Working - W. Hargrove Demolition."

   [Implication:] Perhaps that warning captures the ominous atmosphere of these very different kinds of photographic documents by Camilo Vergara and Edward Burtynsky: "Danger: Men Working." Watch out—human beings are at work! *[Topic sentence:]* But the work that is presented is not so much a building-up as it is a tearing-down—the work of demolition. *[Qualification of claim:]* Of course, demolition is often necessary in order to construct anew: old buildings are leveled for new projects, whether you are building a highway or bridge in an American city or a dam in the Chinese countryside.

   [Paraphrasing—interpretive restatement:] You might call modernity itself, as so many have, a process of creative destruction, a term used variously to describe modern art, capitalism, and technological innovation. *[Topic sentence:]* The photographs in this exhibit, however, force us to pay attention to the "destructive" side of this modern equation. *[Writer asks So what? and concludes:]* What both Burtynsky and Vergara do in their respective ways is to put up a warning sign—they question

whether the reworking of our natural and social environment leads to a sustainable human future. *[Restatement:]* And they wonder whether the process of creative destruction may not have spun recklessly out of control, producing places that are neither habitable nor sustainable. *[Supporting observation:]* In fact, a common element connecting the two photographic versions is the near absence of people in the landscape. *[Observation:]* While we see the evidence of the transforming power of human production on the physical and social environment, neither Vergara's urban ruins nor Burtynsky's industrial sites actually show us "men working." *[Observation:]* Isolated figures peer suspiciously out back doors or pick through the rubble, but they appear out of place. *[Writer asks So what? and concludes in reference to the paragraph's opening observation:]* It is this sense of displacement—of human beings alienated from the environments they themselves have created—that provides the most haunting aspect of the work of these two photographers. (Jack Gambino, "Demolition Zones: Contemporary Photography by Edward Burtynsky and Camilo Jose Vergara")

Paragraph Structure #3: Coordinate and Subordinate Paragraphs

Here is a third way of thinking about how paragraphs develop. In his influential essay, "A Generative Rhetoric of the Paragraph," Francis Christensen defines the topic sentence as "the one the other sentences depend from, the one they develop or amplify, the one they are a comment on" (*Notes Toward a New Rhetoric*, 1967, page 80). Christensen posits two kinds of paragraphs: coordinate and subordinate. In coordinate structures, all of the sentences following the topic sentence are equal in weight, or as he puts it, "all children of the same mother" (61).

Consider the following example of a (primarily) coordinate paragraph, taken from earlier in this chapter. Most of the sentences relate back to the topic sentence in some way. A number 1 indicates that the sentence is coordinate with the topic sentence, operating on the same level of importance and repeatedly clarifying the topic sentence. The number 2 indicates that the sentence is a subordinate structure, which will be explained below.

> **[T:]** Paragraphs are a relief not just for your readers: they also give the writer a break.
> 1 When you draft, start a new paragraph whenever you feel yourself getting stuck: it's the promise of a fresh start.
> 1 Paragraph breaks are like turning a corner to a new view, even when the thinking is continuous.
> 1 They also force the writer to make transitions, overt connections among the parts of his or her thinking, and to state or restate key ideas.
> 1 Paragraph indentations allow readers to scan essays, searching for connecting words and important ideas.

The paragraph above best fits the pattern that Christensen calls coordinate because all of the sentences that come after the topic sentence "develop or amplify" it. Each offers reasons for thinking that paragraphs are a relief not just for readers but also for writers.

In what Christensen identifies as subordinate structures, each sentence clarifies or comments on the one before it, as for example in this short sequence that he cites:

1   The process of learning is essential to our lives.

  2   All higher animals seek it deliberately.

    3   They are inquisitive and they experiment.

      4   An experiment is a sort of harmless trial run...(60).

Note how each sentence generates the one that follows it, rather than primarily relating back to the topic sentence.

Here is another example of a subordinate paragraph to contemplate:

1   Another startling conclusion from the science of consciousness is that the intuitive feeling we have that there's another executive "I" that sits in a control room of our brain, scanning the screens of the senses and pushing the buttons of the muscles, is an illusion.

  2   Consciousness turns out to consist of a maelstrom of events distributed across the brain.

    3   These events compete for attention, and as one process outshouts the others, the brain rationalizes the outcome after the fact and concocts the impression that a single self was in charge all along. (Steven Pinker, "The Mystery of Consciousness," *Time*, January 19, 2007)

Go back now and look at our first example (above) of a coordinate paragraph—the one about paragraph breaks being a relief. Are there any sentences in that paragraph that we might have classified as subordinate? What about the last sentence, for example? Notice that it clearly refers back to the topic sentence because it explains what paragraph indentations do to help readers. But it is also true that this last sentence evolves out of the sentence that immediately precedes it by developing the idea of transitions ("connecting words" "overt connections") and restatement of "key ideas." So we might have labeled that last sentence as level 2.

This kind of ambiguity should not concern you. It is less important to be able to accurately and precisely locate each sentence in a paragraph as coordinate or subordinate than it is to begin to recognize that most paragraphs are some kind of mix of these two thought patterns. In practice, as Christensen observes, most paragraphs combine coordinate and subordinate sequences, although one of the two structures often predominates. Consider, for example, the following paragraph, where we have explained in square brackets our reasons for labeling the sentences as we did.

[*Topic sentence:*] Imagery may be necessary for human imagination.

1 It has been suggested that all the products of the imagination are derived from imagery, following some transformation of the basic imagery. [*restates and slightly expands topic sentence*]

1 For example, Rutgers' psychologist Alan Leslie, when he worked in London in the 1980s, proposed that imagination essentially involves three steps: *[sets up example of the transformation process that is necessary for the human imagination]*

[The next moves in the paragraph lay out the psychologist's three steps; they are still supporting the topic sentence, but refer back more directly to the sentence immediately above them. Christensen describes this move as a subordinate sequence.]

2 Take what he called a 'primary' representation (which, as we have already established, is an image that has truth relations to the outside world).

2 Then make a copy of this primary representation (Leslie calls this copy a 'second-order' representation).

2 Finally, one can then introduce some change to this second-order representation, playing with its truth relationships to the outside world without jeopardising the important truth relationships that the original, primary representation needs to preserve.

1 For Leslie, when you use your imagination, you leave your primary representation untouched (for important evolutionary reasons that we will come onto), but once you have a photocopy of this (as it were), you can do pretty much anything you like with it." *[Having laid out the transformative process in the middle of the paragraph, the writer is now free to finish the paragraph with a summative sentence that more fully spells out why imagery is necessary to the imagination.]*(Simon Baron-Cohen, "The Biology of Imagination," Entelechy: Mind & Culture summer/fall 2007 no. 9)

You do not need to ponder these relationships each time you write a new sentence in a paragraph, but, when you find yourself getting stuck in your writing, you can help yourself to move forward by thinking about which sentence in the paragraph is the actual generator (or jumping off point) for the next one.

Try This 15.5: Arrange Coordinate and Subordinate Sequences

Go back to the paragraph on page 338 that we used to illustrate our expanded version of Becker's TRI model. Try to arrange the sentences according to levels—coordinate and subordinate. Which sentences in the paragraph form a coordinate sequence with the topic sentence? Are there any sentences in the paragraph that, rather than being generated by the topic sentence instead clarify or comment on the one that precedes it?

Try This 15.6: Identify the Structure of Paragraphs

Take each of the paragraphs below and apply the terms offered in this section to describe what various sentences do. Look for coordinate versus subordinate structures, but more specifically, label the mental moves performed by individual sentences. We have numbered the sentences to make the paragraphs easier to work with.

Paragraph A:

1. What does it mean for a nation to advance?

2. In one view, it means to increase its gross domestic product per capita.

3. For decades that measure has been the standard used by development economists, as if it were a proxy for a nation's overall quality of life.

4. Never mind about distribution and social equality; never mind about the preconditions of stable democracy; never mind about the quality of race and gender relations; never mind about the improvement of other aspects of a human being's quality of life that are not well linked to economic growth.

5. (Empirical studies have by now shown that political liberty, health, and education are all poorly correlated with growth.)

6. One sign of what that model leaves out is the fact that South Africa under apartheid used to shoot to the top of development indexes.

7. There was a lot of wealth in the old South Africa, and the old model of development rewarded that achievement (or good fortune), ignoring the staggering distributional inequalities, the brutal apartheid regime, and the health and educational deficiencies that went with it.

(Martha C. Nussbaum, "The Liberal Arts Are Not Elitist" *The Chronicle of Higher Education*, February 28, 2010)

Paragraph B:

1. What does the contemporary self want?

2. The camera has created a culture of celebrity; the computer is creating a culture of connectivity.

3. As the two technologies converge—broadband tipping the Web from text to image, social-networking sites spreading the mesh of interconnection even wider—the two cultures betray a common impulse.

4. Celebrity and connectivity are both ways of becoming known.

5. This is what the contemporary self wants.

6. It wants to be recognized, wants to be connected: it wants to be visible.

7. If not to the millions, on Survivor or Oprah, then to the hundreds, on Twitter or Facebook.

8. This is the quality that validates us, this is how we become real to ourselves—by being seen by others.

9. The great contemporary terror is anonymity.

10. If Lionel Trilling was right, if the property that grounded the self, in Romanticism, was sincerity, and in modernism it was authenticity, then in postmodernism it is visibility.

(William Deresiewicz, "The End of Solitude," *The Chronicle of Higher Education*, January 30, 2009)

Paragraph C:

1. White might not have succeeded in completely ridding his life of modern civilization, but Strunk's manual in White's hands became a successful *primitivist* tract.

2. Perhaps that seems like an overstatement, but in fact what counts as primitivist is flexible, Marianna Torgovnick reminded us, entirely dependent on what bugs one about the modern.

3. The key feature of primitivism, Torgovnick offered, is defining the primitive in reaction to the present: "Is the present too majestic? Primitive life is not—it is a precapitalist utopia in which only use value, never exchange value, prevails. Is the present sexually repressed? Not primitive life—primitives live life whole, without fear of the body" (8).

4. For Strunk and White, modern life was verbose and obscure, so primitive life must be brief, direct, and clear.

5. New things are bad things, new words the worst of all.

6. The words *offputting* and *ongoing* appear in the third and subsequent editions of The *Elements of Style* as "newfound adjectives, to be avoided because they are inexact and clumsy" (*Third Edition* 54).

7. The suffix oriented is lambasted as "a clumsy, pretentious device, much in vogue" (*Third Edition* 55).

8. *The Elements of Style* thus had become, over a period of nearly unprecedented technological progress, the perfect complement to the manual typewriter—a deliberate rejection of "books with permissive steering and automatic transitions" that made our lives easier but rendered our prose impotent and our character lax (xvi).

9. For impotence and laxity, *The Elements of Style* offers a program of stylistic and moral restitution, word by word.

(Catherine Prendergast, "The Fighting Style: Reading the Unabomber's Strunk and White," *College English*, Volume 72, No 1, September 2009)

FINDING THE SKELETON OF AN ESSAY: AN EXAMPLE

We end this chapter with a skeletal version of an essay by one of our colleagues (available in the anthology version of this text). We have included only the first sentence of each paragraph, and in some cases the last, the working thesis as it appears at the end of paragraph 2, and the evolved thesis as it appears in the next to final paragraph. As you will see, each paragraph does begin with some kind of assertion. You will also see that writers allow themselves some flexibility on where they locate the working thesis and its later evolution. This way of looking at essays is a practice we recommend: it can teach you a lot about paragraphing and essay structure in a hurry.

September 11th: A National Tragedy?

By James Peck

Paragraph 1, sentence 1: Since the events of September 11th, I've been pursued by thoughts and images of tragedy.

Paragraph 1, last sentence: A voluminous literature theorizes the limits of tragic form, and I admit it rankles me to hear the word "tragic" used as a generic modifier for anything really bad that happens.

Paragraph 2, sentence 1: With the events of September 11th, however, I have found myself using the language of tragedy pretty indiscriminately.

Paragraph 2, last two sentences [Working thesis]: But I am coming to the conviction that tragedy offers a demanding, stark paradigm that at least accounts for some of the emotional force of these events and may even suggest some generative ways to think about them. Beyond simply capturing a bit of the devastation wrought by the attacks, can the form of tragedy help us narrate, image, or otherwise represent these horrors?

Paragraph 3, sentence 1: I acknowledge that it may seem frivolous, even blasphemous, to discuss these overwhelming and all too real events in a matrix borrowed from the relatively rarified topic of dramatic form.

Paragraph 4, sentence 1: I'm suggesting that the form of tragedy might accommodate some of the affective power of September 11th, and even point towards some of its moral claims.

Paragraph 5, sentence 1: I think this ought to be the tenor of our discourse in the wake of September 11th.

Paragraph 6, sentence 1: A tragic witnessing of September 11th must also preserve outrage at these callous acts.

Paragraph 7, sentence 1: Finally, a tragic witnessing of these events should squarely face some awful truths, dwell in the full weight of those truths, and try to see ourselves anew as a result of doing so.

Paragraph 8, sentence 1: The cornerstone of Aristotle's theory of tragedy is the dual principle of peripety and recognition.

Paragraph 9, sentence 1: I worry that my discussion may seem tasteless, or worse, coy.

Paragraph 10, sentence 1: I don't want to live in a melodrama.

Paragraph 11, sentence 1: It deeply worries me that the dominant national discourse in the aftermath of September 11th is melodramatic.

Paragraph 12, sentence 1: I'd like to close by evoking the function of tragedy in Athenian democracy.

Paragraph 13, sentence 1: Given this avowedly patriotic context, the most remarkable thing about the City Dionysia was its frank criticism of Athenian public life.

Paragraph 13, final sentence [The evolved thesis]: In this moment of national crisis, I think we would benefit from bringing the same questioning, restless, self-critical spirit to our own national conversation.

Paragraph 14 (entire): I hope we take seriously our casual language, and witness September 11th as a tragedy. Remember the dead. Pursue their killers. Interrogate ourselves.

GUIDELINES FOR FORMS AND FORMATS ACROSS THE CURRICULUM

1. Find the space in a format that will allow it to work as a heuristic, a set of steps designed not just to organize but to stimulate and guide your thinking. Avoid the slot-filler mentality.

2. Look for and expect to find the common denominators among the various formats you learn to use across the curriculum. You can master—and benefit from—virtually any format if you approach it not as a set of arbitrary and rigid rules, but as a formalized guide to having ideas.

3. Don't make your readers wait too long before you concede or refute a view that you can assume will already have occurred to them. Otherwise, they may assume you are unaware of the competing view or afraid to bring it up.

4. Always treat opposing views fairly. A good strategy is to concede their merits but argue that, in the particular context you are addressing, your position is more important or appropriate.

5. Use climactic order to organize your points, building to your best ones. The best ones are usually the most revealing and thought-provoking, not the most obvious or commonly agreed upon.

6. Phrasing your thesis to include a subordinate construction—"although X appears to account for Z, Y accounts for it better"—will give your paper a ready-made organizational shape, along with giving you something to define your own position against.

7. A good transition reaches backward, telling where you've been, as the grounds for making a subsequent move forward. Opt for "similarly" and "by contrast," for example, which specify connections for your readers, rather than merely additive transitions such as "another" and "also."

8. Half a page is a healthy length for most paragraphs, long enough to launch an idea but short enough to give your reader time to rest.

9. To keep your paragraphs healthy, focus at some point in your writing process on what they do—not just what they say. Here are five questions to ask yourself:

   • Do your readers know why you are telling them what you are telling them?

   • Can readers see the connection between the paragraph and your evolving thesis?

   • Has your paragraph moved backwards before moving forward?

   • Have you buried your best ideas, the main claims of the paragraph, in the middle, rather than leading or concluding with them?

   • Have you asked and answered "so what?" at the end of the paragraph?

Assignments: Forms and Formats

1. **Infer the Format of a Published Article.**
   Often the format governing the organization of a published piece is not immediately evident. That is, it is not subdivided according to conventional disciplinary categories that are obeyed by all members of a given discourse community. Especially if you are studying a discipline in which the writing does not follow an explicitly prescribed format, such as history, literature, or economics, you may find it illuminating to examine representative articles or essays in that discipline, looking for an implicit format. In other words, you can usually discern some underlying pattern of organization: the formal conventions, the rules that are being followed even when these are not highlighted.

   The following assignment works well whether you tackle it individually or in a group. It can lead to a paper, an oral report, or both. First, you need to assemble several articles from the same or a similar kind of journal or magazine. "Journal" is the name given to publications aimed at specialized, usually scholarly, audiences, as opposed to general or popular audiences. *Time, Newsweek,* and the *New Yorker* are called "magazines" rather than "journals" because they are aimed at a broader general audience. *Shakespeare Quarterly* is a journal; *Psychology Today* is a magazine.

   Having found at least three journal or magazine articles, study them in order to focus on the following question: *Insofar as there appears to be a format that articles in this journal adhere to, what are its parts?*

   How, for example, does an article in this journal or magazine typically begin and end? Does there seem to be a relatively uniform place in which these articles include opposing arguments? You will, in other words, be analyzing the articles inductively (reasoning from particular details to general principles). Begin with the product and reason backward to the skeleton beneath the skin.

Note that if your professor directs you to work with magazines rather than journals, you should probably further narrow the focus—to a *Time* cover story, to the *New Yorker*'s "Letter from [the name of a city]," or another such recurring feature. Even gossip columns and letters of advice to the lovelorn in teen magazines adhere to certain evident, though not explicitly marked, formats.

Write up your results. Cite particular language from at least two articles in support of your claims about the implicit format. In presenting your evidence, keep the focus on the underlying form, showing how the different articles proceed in the same or similar ways. Don't let yourself get too distracted by the articles' content, even though there may be similarities here as well. Instead, work toward formulating a rationale for the format—what you take to be its rhetoric of form. You will need, for example, both to lay out the typical form of the introduction and to account for its taking that typical form. Devote several paragraphs to this rationale, either at the end of your report or integrated within it.

2. **Find the Organizing Principles of an Essay**
   Excerpt a skeletal version of an essay, using the model of the 9/11 essay by James Peck located at the end of the chapter. Copy out the opening sentence of each paragraph as well as sentences that state the essay's working thesis and its final form in or near the concluding paragraph. Your aim is to discern the shape of the thinking in the essay at a glance.

3. **Practice Induction**
   Study a group of like things inductively. You might, for example, use greeting cards aimed at women versus greeting cards aimed at men, a group of poems by one author, or ads for one kind of product (jeans) or aimed at one target group (teenage girls).

   Compile a set of significant details about the data, and then leap to a general claim about the group that you think is interesting and reasonably accurate. This generalization is your inductive principle. Then use the principle to examine deductively more data of the same kind, exploring its implications as you evolve it more accurately.

Chapter 16

Introductions and Conclusions Across the Curriculum

THIS CHAPTER ADDRESSES two perennial trouble-spots in all kinds of writing—introductions and conclusions. The chapter gives special attention to strategies for solving two problems: trying to do too much in the introduction and not doing enough in the conclusion.

There are no absolute rules for writing introductions and conclusions, but there does seem to be a consensus across the disciplines that introductions should raise issues rather than settle them and that conclusions should go beyond merely restating what has already been said. Insofar as disciplinary conventions permit, in introductions you should play an ace but not your whole hand; and in conclusions, don't just summarize—culminate.

Throughout the chapter, we will point to differences in the language that the various disciplines use in their prescriptions for introductions and conclusions, but once you have learned to see past differences in style, you will recognize that the jobs introductions and conclusions do are actually quite similar across the curriculum.

> The introduction isolates a specific question or issue and explains why, in a specified context, this question or issue matters.
>
> Think of the concluding paragraph as the site of the paper's final So what?, which is shorthand for "Where does this get us?" or "Why does this matter?"
>
> Rather than just restate and summarize, the concluding paragraph should leave readers with your single best insight and put it into some kind of broader perspective.

INTRODUCTIONS AND CONCLUSIONS AS SOCIAL SITES

When you read, you enter a world created of written language—a textual world—and to varying degrees, you leave the world "out there." Even if other people are around, we all read in relative isolation; our attention is diverted from the social and physical world upon which the full range of our senses normally operates.

Your introduction takes the reader from the everyday world of sights and sounds and submerges him or her into a textual one. And your conclusion returns the reader to his or her nonwritten reality. Introductions and conclusions **mediate**—they carry the reader from one way of being to another. They function as the most social parts of any written communication, the passageways in which you need to be most keenly aware of your reader.

At both sites, there is a lot at stake. The introduction gives the reader his or her first impression, and we all know how indelible that can be. The conclusion leaves the reader with a last—and potentially lasting—impression of the written world you have constructed.

HOW MUCH TO SAY UPFRONT

Most of the difficulties in composing introductions and conclusions arise in deciding how you should deal with the thesis. How much of it should you put in the introduction?

The first paragraph does not need to—and usually can't—offer your conclusion; it will take the body of your paper to accomplish that. It should, however, provide a quick look at particular details that set up the issue. Use these details to generate a theory, a working hypothesis, about whatever it is you think is at stake in the material. The rest of the paper will test and develop this theory.

The most important thing to do in the introductory paragraph of an analytical paper is to lay out a genuine issue, something that seems to be at stake in whatever it is you are studying. Preferably, you should select a complex issue—one not easily resolved, seeming to have some truth on both sides—and not an overly general one. Otherwise, you run the risk of writing a paper that proves the obvious or radically oversimplifies.

Set up this issue as quickly and concretely as you can. As a general rule, you should assume that readers of your essay will need to know on page one—preferably by the end of your first paragraph—what your paper is attempting to resolve or negotiate.

In the sciences, the standard instructions for composing an introduction are worded somewhat differently, but with similar intent: create a context by citing all previous work relevant to your study, show the need for new information by pointing to an uncertainty or problem in existing knowledge, and say what you are trying to accomplish and why it is important.

WHAT INTRODUCTIONS DO: "WHY WHAT I'M SAYING MATTERS"

The primary challenge in writing introductions lies in occupying the middle ground between saying too much too soon (overassertive prejudgment) and saying too little upfront (avoidance of taking a position).

A rule of thumb is *start fast*. The introduction should give your reader a quick (a third of a typed page or a half-page at most) sampling of some feature or features in your evidence that initially aroused your curiosity. Avoid unnecessary throat-clearing, and cut immediately to something interesting that you have observed and that your paper will put into context and explain. Your introduction is saying: "Look at this, reader; it is worth thinking about, and here's why."

As the Latin roots of the word suggest—*intro,* meaning "within," and *ducere,* meaning "to lead or bring"—an introduction brings the reader into a subject. Its length varies, depending on the scope of the writing project. An introduction may take a paragraph, a few paragraphs, a few pages, a chapter, or even a book. In most academic writing, one or two paragraphs is a standard length. In that space, you should try to accomplish some or all of the following objectives:

- Define your topic—the issue, question, or problem—and say why it matters.
- Indicate your method of approach to the topic.
- Provide necessary background or context.
- Offer the working thesis (hypothesis) your paper will develop.

An objective missing from this list that you might expect to find is the directive to engage the reader. Clearly, all introductions need to engage the reader, but this advice is too often misinterpreted as an invitation to be entertaining or cute. In academic writing, you don't need a gimmick to engage your readers; you can assume they care about the subject. You will engage them if you can articulate why your topic matters, doing so in terms of existing thinking in the field.

Especially in a first draft, the objectives just listed are not so easily achieved, which is why many writers wisely defer writing the polished version of the introduction until they have completed at least one draft of the paper. At that point, you will usually have a clearer notion of why your subject matters and which aspect of your thesis to place first. Often, the conclusion of a first draft becomes the introduction to the second draft.

In any case, the standard shape of an introduction is a *funnel*. It starts wide, providing background and generalization and then narrows the subject to a particular issue or topic. Here is a typical example from an essay entitled "On Political Labels" by Christopher Borick.

> One of the first things you should think about when you see or hear a political label is where it came from. Common political labels such as "liberal" or "conservative" have long histories that shed light on their contemporary use. It's important to recognize that a label's meaning differs from place to place and over time. A conservative in Texas may believe much differently from a conservative in New York, just as an American conservative varies in view points from a conservative in Norway. Similarly, someone calling herself a conservative in 2005 would significantly differ from someone calling himself a conservative in 1905 or even 1975. You may wonder, with such variation over time and place, how can we attach meaning to key political terms at all? While not always easy to see, at least part of the answer can be discovered through an examination of the history of the terms.

The paragraph begins with a generalization in the first sentence (about standard responses to the subject at hand) and funnels down in the last sentence to a qualified working thesis (that some of the meaning lies in the linguistic history of the terms themselves). This does not mean that the first sentence of the paragraph is a throwaway, something broad and bland. Make the first sentence count. Say something incisive and substantive.

PUTTING AN ISSUE OR QUESTION IN CONTEXT

Rather than leaping immediately to the paper's issue, question, or problem, most effective introductions provide some broader context to indicate why the issue matters. Although the various models we offer here differ in small ways from discipline to discipline, the essential characteristics they share suggest that most professors across the curriculum want the same things in an introduction: the locating of a problem or question within a context that provides background and rationale, culminating in a working thesis.

It is important for writers to be conscious of their choice of interpretive context. As we argued in Chapter 6, things don't just "mean" in the abstract; they mean in particular contexts. Thus, to a significant extent, context shapes and determines what we see. Whether we are aware of it or not, we are always locating things in some context. An interpretive context is a lens through which we scrutinize what we are trying to understand. The best writers defend their choice of interpretive context and make their readers aware of it from the start.

Providing an Introductory Context: A Political Science Professor Speaks

In the following Voice from Across the Curriculum, political science professor Jack Gambino notes the usefulness of anomalies for contextualizing papers in his discipline. The discovery of an anomaly, something that does not fit with conventional ways of thinking, can serve as a useful point of departure in a paper that goes on to revise an existing theory or opinion.

Voices from Across the Curriculum

An introduction is not simply the statement of a thesis but also the place where the student needs to set a context, a framework that makes such a thesis statement interesting, timely, or in some other way important. It is common to see papers in political science begin by pointing out a discrepancy between conventional wisdom (what the pundits say) and recent political developments, between popular opinion and empirical evidence, or between theoretical frameworks and particular test cases. Papers, in other words, often begin by presenting *anomalies*.

I encourage students to write opening paragraphs that attempt to elucidate such anomalies by:

1. Stating the specific point of departure: Are they taking issue with a bit of conventional wisdom? Popular opinions? A theoretical perspective? This provides the context in which a student is able to "frame" a particular problem, issue, and so forth.

2. Explaining why the wisdom/opinion/theory has become problematic or controversial by focusing on a particular issue, event, test case, or empirical evidence.

3. Formulating a brief statement of the tentative thesis/position to be pursued in the paper. This can take several forms, including the revising of conventional wisdom/theory/opinion, discarding it in favor of alternative conceptions, or calling for redefinition of an issue and question.

—Jack Gambino, Professor of Political Science

INTRODUCTIONS AND ABSTRACTS IN THE SCIENCES

The natural and social sciences both rely on a fairly tightly defined format for reports on research. The professors quoted in the remainder of this chapter emphasize the importance of isolating a specific question or issue and locating it within a wider context. Notice, as you read these voices, how little the model for an introduction changes in moving from social science to natural science.

In the sciences, the introduction is an especially important and somewhat challenging section of the report to compose because it requires a writer not merely to assemble but also to assimilate the background of information and ideas that frame his or her hypothesis.

One distinctive feature of scientific papers is that a separate prefatory section called the *abstract* precedes the introduction. Authors also produce abstracts for papers in many other disciplines, but these are usually published separately—for example, in a bibliography, in a journal's table of contents, and so forth.

The abstract provides a very concise summary of the paper. Here is a brief definition from a professor of biochemistry at our college, Keri Colabroy: "what you did (experimental approach), why you did it (the problem, some background), and what you found (major findings and conclusions). You might want to know that there are subtle differences in the format of abstracts depending on the journal." *(For more on science writing, see Chapter 15, Forms and Formats Across the Curriculum.)*

Introductions in the Sciences: Three Professors Speak

In the following Voices from Across the Curriculum, biology professor Richard Niesenbaum and psychology professors Laura Edelman and Mark Sciutto address the challenges of introducing and contextualizing research in science writing. Introductions in the IMRAD format (Introduction, Methods, Results, and Discussion/Conclusions), the standard form for lab reports and other kinds of science writing, must do a lot of work in a small space.

Voices from Across the Curriculum

A paper usually starts by making some general observation or a description of known phenomena and by providing the reader with some background information. The first paragraphs should illustrate an understanding of the issues at hand and should present an argument for why the research should be done. In other words, a context or framework is established for the entire paper. This background information must lead to a clear statement of the objectives of the paper and the hypothesis that will be experimentally tested. This movement from broad ideas and observations to a specific question or test starts the deductive scientific process.

—Richard Niesenbaum, Professor of Biology

The introduction is one of the hardest sections to write. In the introduction, students must summarize, analyze, and integrate the work of numerous other authors and use that to build their own argument.

The task is to read each article and *summarize* it in their own words. The key is to analyze rather than just repeat material from the articles so as to make clear the connections among them. (It is important to note that experimental psychologists almost never use direct quotes in their writing. Many of my students have been trained to use direct quotation for their other classes, and so I have to spend time explaining how to summarize without directly quoting or plagiarizing the work that they have read.)

Finally, in the introduction the students must show explicitly how the articles they have summarized lead to the hypothesis they have devised. Many times the students see the connection as implicitly obvious, but I require that they explicitly state the relationships between what they read and what they plan to do.

—Laura Edelman, Professor of Psychology

The format of the empirical paper in psychology resembles an hourglass. It starts reasonably broad, narrows, and then broadens again to the larger perspective: "Now that we know this, where can we go with it? What are the implications?" As in other kinds of science writing, the empirical psychology paper consists of abstract, introduction, methods, results, and discussion. The introduction is especially difficult to write because it must contextualize the new research by pulling together a lot of reading from a variety of sources. This part of the introduction, the literature review, answers the question, "What do we know?"

In order to efficiently locate the new study in the context of others' work on the subject, writers must **integrate** citations. Rather than summarize what Johnson found and then what Smith found and then what Moore found, the writer needs to bring these together into a more concise summary. All three studies might be summarized and cited in one paragraph or even a single sentence. As a rule of thumb, citations should include more than one source. Single citations don't allow enough integration.

—Mark Sciutto, Professor of Psychology

Integration of Citations in a Literature Review: A Brief Example

Note in the following paragraph—from a 1999 article in *Personality and Social Psychology Bulletin*—how the citations (in parentheses) include more than one study:

Self-presentational motives play a role in a variety of potentially dangerous health-related behaviors, including behaviors that lead to risk of HIV infection; accidental death and injury; and alcohol, tobacco, and drug use (Leary, Tchividjian, & Kraxberger, 1994; Martin, Leary, & Rejeski, in press). The desire to be perceived as a risk-taker, brave, or one of the crowd (or conversely, concerns about being viewed as overly cautious or neurotic) may lead people to take chances with their health to create the desired image (Denscombe, 1993; Finney, 1978).

Introductions in Scientific Papers: A Brief Example

The following example comes from a set of excerpted introductions that biochemistry professor Keri Colabroy uses to teach her students how to write concise, focused sentences of two types: Type #1: sentences that orient readers to the scientific context of a new study while also showing the need for it, and Type #2: sentences that succinctly state what the paper/study has accomplished. The sentences come from a paper published in *Nature Chemical Biology* 2006.

> #1 Although the antitumor activity of these two compounds has been shown to involve binding to microtubules, the targets and modes of actions for many other bioactive cyanobacterial metabolites remain elusive.

Dr. Colabroy comments: *This is a great sentence. You can see the tension. Some activity has been shown, but there is still something we don't understand . . . and that is the problem this paper will solve.*

> #2 Here we examine the mode of action of apratoxin A using a number of approaches based on functional genomics, including mRNA expression analysis and genome-wise, arrayed cDNA overexpression. These and other studies suggest that apratoxin A acts in part by blocking the FGFR signaling pathway.

Dr. Colabroy comments: *The use of "here" focuses your attention on the action that immediately follows—"we examine." That is different from "we found" or "we propose," and it implies that the authors didn't really have a hypothesis going in. They were just trying to learn some stuff, and in the process, they came up with some "implications" from the data.*

Framing Research Questions and Hypotheses: A Political Science Professor Speaks

In the following Voice from Across the Curriculum, political science professor Chris Borick explains effective and less effective ways of stating research questions and hypotheses in the introduction.

Voices from Across the Curriculum

Different fields within political science—legal writing, political theory, political policy and behavior—prescribe different forms of writing. Political policy and political behavior papers adhere to a version of the format used in science writing. This format has six parts: statement of the research question, literature review (context), statement of hypothesis, measurement of variables, description of tests, and analysis of findings. The literature review describes the conversation that is going on in the field on the paper's topic. It explains what others know. The research question tells readers what the writer is trying to do. The hypothesis states a claim that is specific enough to test.

The research question sets up the hypothesis; it is the point from which everything flows. Consider the following two versions of a research question on capital punishment. 1) In this study I seek to examine the capital punishment laws used at the state level. 2) In this study I seek to explain why some states adopt capital punishment and others do not. The second version is clearly better. It gives much better direction.

The hypothesis needs to indicate some direction for the research. Although general in scope, it must be specific enough to test. Here again are two examples. Which do you think would make the better hypothesis? 1) The greater the percentage of college educated individuals in a state, the more likely that state will be to allow same sex marriage. 2) The more educated a society, the more liberal it will be.

—Chris Borick, Professor of Political Science

INTRODUCTIONS IN THE HUMANITIES

We have devoted considerable attention in this chapter and the previous one to the prescribed formats for writing lab reports, scientific articles, and empirical studies in the social sciences. As we have suggested throughout these chapters, the surface differences you will encounter as you move across the curriculum can too easily obscure the underlying structure that the disciplines share.

Nevertheless, there are some striking differences. In the sciences, for example, it is inappropriate to name and especially to criticize particular pieces of research or their authors. Writers in the humanities are much more likely to name names, to quote other studies, and to be explicit on where these studies seem to fall short. Relatively broad claims about consensus views on the writer's topic are okay. In fact, papers in the humanities often begin that way. But these highly compressed generalizations are typically followed with more detail on who said what, why they may have said it, and what needs revising.

Because most writing in the humanities is grounded in textual analysis, humanities writers think it important to attend to the actual language of other people's writing. Words and their meanings are data to humanities writers. For this reason, writers in the humanities quote and then paraphrase key statements, rather than summarizing and paraphrasing without the original language, as is the rule in psychology and other science and social science writing. It is a habit of mind in the humanities to share the evidence—the language being phrased and cited—with readers, rather than asking them to take the writer's word for it.

As in the sciences, methods of analysis in the humanities are empirical—grounded in close observation of evidence. But, as we argued in Chapter 6, "Making Interpretations Plausible," the authority of a writer's interpretation of evidence relies on other scholars accepting it as plausible. This is true in the sciences as well, a fact somewhat hidden by the nature of scientific evidence and the very detailed character of the process of investigation.

Here is a typical set of guidelines for writing introductory paragraphs in a humanities paper—in this case, in English. Introductions are not the same across all disciplines in the humanities, but much in the following guidelines is representative.

1. **An introduction is not a conclusion**. You do not need to announce, in short form, your whole argument. In English papers, the intro paragraph is an opening gambit. The thesis you state at the end of paragraph one should be an idea, not a statement of fact. For example, you might offer an idea about what you think is the most important difference and/or similarity between the poem you have chosen to analyze and "Ode to a Nightingale." This statement will get qualified and expanded and tested in the paper. You should not simply march the statement through the paper and prove you are right.

2. **The intro offers readers some representative piece of your evidence**—some data from your poem: perhaps a binary that you see in both poems or some other tendency of the language in both that you found interesting and that you think is worth exploring. *The reader should come away from your opening paragraph knowing what you found interesting and worth pursuing and why.*

3. **Resist dumping a great lump of background into the intro**. You should do some contextualizing in the opening, but don't overdo it. Stay focused on the poem and what you notice about the kind of thinking it is inviting us to do.

4. **Resist what is known as "freshman omniscience"**—recognizable by sweeping claims and a grandiose tone . . . "Since the beginning of time poets have been . . ."

5. **The last sentence of the paragraph should make some kind of claim**. It should not be the standard tri-partite thesis of the 5-paragraph form essay.

HOW MUCH TO INTRODUCE UPFRONT: TYPICAL PROBLEMS

Introductions need to do a lot in a limited space. To specify a thesis and locate it within a larger context, to suggest the plan or outline of the entire paper, and to negotiate first relations with a reader—that's plenty to pack into a paragraph or two. In deciding how much to introduce up front, you must make a series of difficult choices about what to include and exclude.

The danger is trying to turn the introduction into a miniature essay. Consider the three problems discussed next as symptoms of overcompression, telltale signs that you need to reconceive, and probably reduce, your introduction.

Digression

Digression results when you try to include too much background. If, for example, you plan to write about a recent innovation in video technology, you'll need to monitor the amount and kind of technical information you include in your opening paragraphs. You'll also want to avoid starting at a point that is too far away from your immediate concerns, as in "Communication has always been a necessary part of being human."

As a general rule in academic writing, don't assume your readers know little or nothing about the subject. Instead, use the social potential of the introduction to set up your relationship with your readers and make clear what you are assuming they do and do not know.

Incoherence

Incoherence results when you try to preview too much of your paper's conclusion in the introduction. Such introductions move in too many directions at once, usually because the writer is trying to conclude before going through the discussion that will make the conclusion comprehensible. The language you are compelled to use in such cases tends to be too dense, and the connections between the sentences tend to get left out, because there isn't enough room to include them. After having read the entire paper, your readers may be able to make sense of the introduction, but in that case, the introduction has not done its job.

The following introductory paragraph is incoherent, primarily because it tries to include too much. It neither adequately connects its ideas nor defines its terms.

> Twinship is a symbol in many religious traditions. The signifi-
> cance of twinship will be discussed and explored in the Native
> American, Japanese Shinto, and Christian religions. Twinship
> can be either in opposing or common forces in the form of dei-
> ties or mortals. There are several forms of twinship that show
> duality of order versus chaos, good versus evil, and creation
> versus destruction. The significance of twinship is to set moral
> codes for society and to explain the inexplicable.

Prejudgment

Prejudgment results when you appear to have already settled the question to be pursued in the rest of the paper. The problem here is logical. In an effort to preview your paper's conclusion at the outset, you risk appearing to assume something as true that your paper will in fact need to test. In most papers in the humanities and social sciences, where the thesis evolves in specificity and complexity between the introduction and conclusion, writers and readers can find such assumptions prejudicial. Opening in this way, in any event, can make the rest of the paper seem redundant. Even in the sciences, where a concise statement of objectives, plan of attack, and hypothesis are usually required up front, separate "Results" and "Discussion" sections are reserved for the conclusion.

Avoiding Strong Claims in the Introduction: An Economics Professor Speaks

In the following Voice from Across the Curriculum, economics professor James Marshall argues that strong claims in the form of conclusions don't belong in the introduction.

Voices from Across the Curriculum

I might be careful about how tentative conclusions should play in the opening paragraph, because this can easily slide into a prejudging of the question at hand. I would be more comfortable with a clear statement of the prevailing views held by others. For example, a student could write on the question, "Was Franklin Delano Roosevelt a Keynesian?" What purpose would it serve in an opening paragraph to reveal without any supporting discussion that FDR was or was not a Keynesian?

What might be better would be to say that in the public mind FDR is regarded as the original big spender, that some people commonly associate New Deal policies with general conceptions of Keynesianism, but that there may be some surprises in store as that common notion is examined.

In sum, I would discourage students from making strong claims at or near the beginning of a paper. Let's see the evidence first. We should all have respect for the evidence. Strong assertions, bordering on conclusions, too early on are inappropriate.

—James Marshall, Professor of Economics

USING PROCEDURAL OPENINGS

In the interests of clear organization, some academic disciplines require students to include in the introduction an explanation of how the paper will proceed. Such a general statement of method and/or intention is known as a *procedural opening*. Among the disciplines in which you are most likely to find this format are philosophy, political science, and sociology. The danger of procedural openings is that the writer will avoid making a claim at all.

The statement of a paper's plan is not and cannot take the place of a thesis (an idea about the topic that the paper will explore and defend). Consider the deficiencies of the following procedural opening.

> In this paper I will first discuss the strong points and weak points in America's treatment of the elderly. Then I will compare this treatment with that in other industrial nations in the West. Finally, I will evaluate the various proposals for reform that have been advanced here and abroad.

This paragraph identifies the subject, but it neither addresses why the subject matters nor suggests the writer's approach. Nor does it provide background to the topic or suggest a hypothesis that the paper will pursue. In some kinds of essays, especially those that move (inductively) from specific observations to more general claims, there is little need for procedural openings, with their declaration of intention and method at the outset. As the following Voice from Across the Curriculum reveals, however, there is real difference on this matter across disciplines.

Using Procedural Openings: A Political Science Professor Speaks

In the following Voices from Across the Curriculum box, political science professor Jack Gambino explains a common organizational strategy used to orient readers, particularly in social science papers.

Voices from Across the Curriculum

      I encourage students to provide a "road map" paragraph early in the paper, perhaps the second or third paragraph. (This is a common practice in professional journals.) The "road map" tells the reader the basic outline of the argument. Something like the following: "In the first part of my paper I will present a brief history of the issue. . . . This will be followed by an account of the current controversy. . . . Part III will spell out my alternative account and evidence. . . . I then conclude. . . ." I think such a paragraph becomes more necessary with longer papers.

              —Jack Gambino, Professor of Political Science

GOOD WAYS TO BEGIN

All of the following ways to begin a paper enable you to play an ace, establishing your authority with your readers, without having to play your whole hand. They offer a starting position rather than a miniaturized version of the entire paper. Remember that the aim of the introduction is to answer the question, Why does what I'm about to say matter? What makes it especially interesting or revealing, and in what context? Here are a few methods of accomplishing this aim.

Challenge a Commonly Held View

This move provides you with a framework against which to develop your ideas; it allows you to begin with some back pressure, which will help you to define your position. Because you are responding to a known point of view, you have a ready way of integrating context into your paper. As the economics professor notes of the FDR example, until we understand what the prevailing view is on FDR, it is pointless to start considering whether or not he was a Keynesian.

Begin with a Definition

Beginning with a definition is a reliable way to introduce a topic, so long as that definition has some significance for the discussion to follow. If the definition doesn't do any conceptual work in the introduction, the definition gambit becomes a pointless cliché.

    You are most likely to avoid a cliché if you cite a source other than a standard dictionary for your definition. The reference collection of any academic library contains a range of discipline-specific lexicons that provide more precise and authoritative definitions than Webster ever could. A useful alternative is to quote a particular author's definition of a key term because you want to make a point about his or her particular definition: for example, "Although the *Dictionary of Economics* defines Keynesianism as *XYZ*, Smith treats only *X* and *Y*" (or substitutes *A* for *Z*, and so forth).

Lead with Your Second-Best Example

Another versatile opening gambit, where disciplinary conventions allow, is to use your *second-best example* to set up the issue or question that you later develop in depth with your best example. This gambit is especially useful in papers that proceed inductively on the strength of representative examples, an organizational pattern common in the humanities. As you are assembling evidence in the outlining and prewriting stage, in many cases you will accumulate a number of examples that illustrate the same basic point. For example, several battles might illustrate a particular general's military strategy; several political primaries might exemplify how a particular candidate tailors his or her speeches to appeal to the religious right; several scenes might show how a particular playwright romanticizes the working class, and so on.

Save the best example to receive the most analytical attention in your paper. If you were to present this example in the introduction, you would risk making the rest of the essay vaguely repetitive. A quick close-up of another example will strengthen your argument or interpretation. By using a different example to raise the issues, you suggest that the phenomenon exemplified is not an isolated case and that the major example you will eventually concentrate on is indeed representative.

Exemplify the Topic with a Narrative

An occasional gambit in the humanities and social sciences, the narrative opening introduces a short, pertinent, and vivid story or anecdote that exemplifies a key aspect of a topic. Although generally not permissible in the formal reports assigned in the natural and social sciences, narrative openings turn up in virtually all other kinds of writing across the curriculum.

As the introduction funnels to its thesis, the readers receive a graphic sense of the issue that the writer will now develop nonnarratively. Nonnarrative treatment is necessary because by itself anecdotal evidence can be seen as merely personal. Storytelling is suggestive but usually does not constitute sufficient proof; it needs to be corroborated.

WHAT CONCLUSIONS DO: THE FINAL "SO WHAT?"

Like the introduction, the conclusion has a key social function: it escorts the readers out of the paper, just as the introduction has escorted them in. What do readers want as they leave the textual world you have taken them through? The concluding paragraph presents the paper's final "So what?"

Implicit here is the notion that conclusions always state (or restate) the thesis in its most fully evolved form. (See Chapter 11.) In addition, the conclusion usually makes all of the following moves:

- *It comes full circle.* That is, it creates a sense of closure by revisiting the way the paper began. Often, it returns to some key phrase from the context established in the introduction and updates it.

- *It pursues implications.* That is, it reasons from the particular focus of the essay to broader issues, such as the study's practical consequences or applications, or future-oriented issues, such as avenues for further research. To unfold implications in this way is to broaden the view from the here and now of the paper by looking outward to the wider world and forward to the future.

- *It identifies limitations.* That is, it acknowledges restrictions of method or focus in the analysis, and qualifies the conclusion (and its implications) accordingly.

These moves are quite literally movements—they take the thinking in the essay, and the readers with it, both backward and forward. The backward thrust we call *culmination*; the forward thrust we call *send-off*.

When you culminate a paper, you bring together things you have already said, establishing their connection and ascending to one final statement of your thinking. The word *culminate* is derived from the Latin "*columen*," meaning "top or summit." To culminate is to reach the highest point, and it implies a mountain (in this case, of information and analysis) you have scaled.

The climactic effects of culmination provide the basis for the send-off. The send-off is both social and conceptual, a final opening outward of the topic that leads the reader out of the paper with something further to think about. Here, the thinking moves beyond the close analysis of data that has occupied the body of the paper into a kind of speculation that the writer has earned the right to formulate. Simply put, you culminate with the best statement of your big idea, and your send-off gets you and the reader out of the paper.

Beyond Restatement: Two Professors Speak

The professors in the following Voices from Across the Curriculum suggest ways of ending on a note of expanded implication, bringing the paper's more focused analysis to a larger perspective.

Voices from Across the Curriculum

I tell my students that too many papers "just end," as if the last page or so were missing. I tell them the importance of ending a work. One could summarize main points, but I tell them this is not heavy lifting.

I believe the ending should be an expansion of possibilities, sort of like an introduction to some much larger "mental" paper out there. I sometimes encourage students to see the concluding section as an option to introduce ideas that can't be dealt with now. Sort of a "Having done this, I would want to explore boom, boom, boom if I were to continue further." Here the students can critique and recommend ("Having seen 'this,' one wonders 'that'").

—Frederick Norling, Professor of Business

o   The conclusion does not appear simply as a restatement of a thesis, but rather as an attempt to draw out its implications and significance (the "So what?"). This is what I usually try to impress upon students. For instance, if a student is writing on a particular proposal for party reform, I would expect the concluding paragraph to consider both the significance of the reform and its practicality.

I should note that professional papers often indicate the tentativeness of their conclusions by stressing the need for future research and indicating what these research needs might be. Although I haven't tried this, maybe it would be useful to have students conclude papers with a section entitled "For Further Consideration" in which they would indicate those things that they would have liked to have known but couldn't, given their time constraints, the availability of information, and lack of methodological sophistication. This would serve as a reminder of the tentativeness of conclusions and the need to revisit and revise arguments in the future (which, after all, is a good scholarly habit).

—Jack Gambino, Professor of Political Science

CONCLUSIONS IN THE SCIENCES: THE DISCUSSION SECTION

As is the case with introductions, the conclusions of reports written in the natural and in some social sciences are regulated by formalized disciplinary formats. Conclusions, for example, occur in a section entitled "Discussion." There, the writer analyzes conclusions and qualifies them in relation to some larger experimental context, "the big picture."

First, specific results are interpreted (but not restated), and then their implications and limitations are discussed. At the end, the writer should rephrase the original research question and discuss it in light of the results presented. It is at this point that alternative explanations may be considered and new questions posed.

Writing Conclusions in the Sciences: Two Professors Speak

In the following Voices from Across the Curriculum, a psychology professor and a biochemistry professor explain how the discussion section of a scientific paper locates its conclusions in the context of other research—that which came before and that which will follow.

Voices from Across the Curriculum

o   The conclusion occurs in a section labeled "Discussion" and, as specified by the *Publication Manual of the American Psychological Association*, is guided by the following questions:

- What have I contributed here?
- How has my study helped to resolve the original problem?
- What conclusions and theoretical implications can I draw from my study?

In a broad sense, a particular research report should be seen as but one moment in a broader research tradition that *preceded* the particular study being written about and that will *continue after* this study is published. And so the conclusion should tie this particular study into both previous research considering implications

for the theory guiding this study and (when applicable) practical implications of this study. One of the great challenges of writing a research report is thus to place this particular study within that broader research tradition. That's an analytical task.
—Alan Tjeltveit, Professor of Psychology

The Discussion section is where the scientist finally gets to analyze the data. The previous two sections of a science paper—Methods and Results—report rather than analyze. In the Discussion section, the writer makes claims and backs them with evidence (data). Analysis of the data tells readers what the study found in the context of current knowledge in the field and the researcher's expectations. The paper's conclusions, which usually appear in the last paragraph of the Discussion, always look back and then forward—first back to previous research and then forward to remaining questions.
—Keri Colabroy, Professor of Biochemistry

Conclusions in Scientific Papers: A Brief Example

As you read this sample Discussion/Conclusion section of a scientific paper, refer back to Dr. Colabroy's preceding comments.

> The rapid and sustained elevations in 2-AG induced by JZL 184 were accompanied by an array of CB1-dependent behavioral effects, including analgesia, hypomotility and hypothermia. This collection of phenotypes qualitatively resembles those induced by direct CB1 agonists. Overall these data suggest that MAGL-regulated 2-AG pathways endogenously modulate several behavioral processes classically associated with the pharmacology of cannabinoids . . . .
>
> In summary, we believe that the properties of JZL184 warrant inclusion of this compound among the growing arsenal of efficacious and selective pharmacological probes used to examine the endocannabinoid system. JZL184 could itself serve as a lead scaffold for the development of such dual inhibitors, given that at high concentrations this compound inhibited both MAGL and FAAH without affecting other brain serine hydrolases.

SOLVING TYPICAL PROBLEMS IN CONCLUSIONS

The primary challenge in writing conclusions, it should now be evident, lies in finding a way to culminate your analysis without claiming either too little or too much. There are a number of fairly common problems to guard against if you are to avoid either of these two extremes.

Redundancy

In Chapter 10, we lampooned an exaggerated example of the 5-paragraph form for constructing its conclusion by stating "Thus, we see" and then repeating the introduction verbatim. The result is redundancy. It's a good idea to refer back to the opening, but it's a bad idea just to reinsert it mechanically. Instead, reevaluate what you said there in light of where you've ended up, repeating only key words or phrases from the introduction. This kind of selective repetition is a desirable way of achieving unity and will keep you from making one of two opposite mistakes—either repeating too much or bringing up a totally new point in the conclusion.

Raising a Totally New Point

Raising a totally new point can distract or bewilder a reader. This problem often arises out of a writer's praiseworthy desire to avoid repetition. As a rule, you can guard against the problem by making sure you have clearly expressed the conceptual link between your central conclusion and any implications you may draw. An implication is not a totally new point but rather one that follows from the position you have been analyzing.

Similarly, although a capping judgment or send-off may appear for the first time in your concluding paragraph, it should have been anticipated by the body of your paper. Conclusions often indicate where you think you (or an interested reader) may need to go next, but you don't actually go there. In a paper on economist Milton Friedman, for example, if you think another economist offers a useful way of critiquing him, you probably should not introduce this person for the first time in your conclusion.

Overstatement

Many writers are confused over how much they should claim in the conclusion. Out of the understandable (but mistaken) desire for a grand (rather than a modest and qualified) culmination, writers sometimes overstate the case. They assert more than their evidence has proven or even suggested. Must a conclusion arrive at some comprehensive and final answer to the question your paper has analyzed?

Depending on the question and the disciplinary conventions, you may need to come down exclusively on one side or another. In a great many cases, however, the answers with which you conclude can be more moderate. Especially in the humanities, good analytical writing seeks to unfold successive layers of implication, so it's not even reasonable for you to expect neat closure. In such cases, you are usually better off qualifying your final judgments, drawing the line at points of relative stability.

Anticlimax

The end of the conclusion is a "charged" site because it gives the reader a last impression of your paper. If you end with a concession—an acknowledgement of a rival position at odds with your thesis—you risk leaving the reader unsettled and possibly confused. The term for this kind of letdown is "anticlimax." In most cases, you will flub the send-off if you depart the paper on an anticlimax.

There are many forms of anticlimax besides ending with a concession. If your conclusion peters out in a random list or an apparent afterthought or a last-minute qualification of your claims, the effect is anticlimactic. And for many readers, if your final answer comes from quoting an authority in place of establishing your own, that, too, is an anticlimax.

At the beginning of this section, we suggested that a useful rule for the introduction is to play an ace but not your whole hand. In the context of this card-game analogy, it is similarly effective to save an ace for the conclusion. In most cases, this high card will provide an answer to some culminating "So what?" question—a last view of the implications or consequences of your analysis.

Try This 16.1: Analyze Paired Introductions and Conclusions

The best way to learn about introductions and conclusions is to study them separated out from the larger articles or essays they frame. Once they are isolated in this way, you can begin to focus on the form, noticing how the introductions raise an issue, provide minimal context, and perhaps start down a particular thesis path. And looking at the paired conclusion, you can see where each writer ends up and how he or she gets us there, culminating the journey in the context of its beginning.

What follows are eight introductions paired with their conclusions, taken from various kinds of published writing. Study the pairings to identify how particular sentences function, in terms of both organization and rhetoric. The following questions should help.

- Where in each of the introductions does the working thesis or other indication of the paper's probable direction appear?
- Which words and sentences in each of the conclusions bring the paper full circle?
- What seems to have happened to the paper's opening claims by the time the writer arrives at his or her conclusion?
- What strategies does each writer use to begin and end his or her writing?
- Where and how do the concluding paragraphs seem to culminate and provide readers with some kind of send-off?

Your goal is to get in the practice of noticing what writers do in their introductions and conclusions.

1. From Jessica Love, "They Get to Me" in *The American Scholar* (July 2, 2010). [http://www.theamericanscholar.org/they-get-to-me/]

Introduction:

I used to be a normal psycholinguistics graduate student. I wanted to study how the mind parses improbable metaphors, unintelligible accents, and quirky syntax. Sexy things. Things that would play out well at parties. I imagined myself magnanimously explaining how sentences like "The bartender served the bourbon fell down the stairs" were truly grammatical. I imagined myself dropping newspaper headlines like "Iraqi Head Seeks Arms" into conversations with beautiful people. I would defend Internet chatroom slang on local radio. I would exchange holiday cards with Steven Pinker.

But something has happened. I am in my third year of graduate school, and I have fallen in love. I have fallen for pronouns. It's hard to shut me up about them.

Conclusion:

Lucky for me, there are plenty of pronouns in need of more study—the diectics (here, there), the reflexives (himself, themselves), the interrogatives (who, what), the possessives (his, mine), the indefinites (somebody, anything)—each with its own relatively unexamined life. Or, for the freshest pronoun around, I could always coin one myself.

In Baltimore, some teenagers already have: their candidate, yo, is a new gender-neutral third-person personal pronoun. As in Yo was tuckin' in his shirt or Yo sucks at magic tricks. If yo sticks around—and if it spreads—maybe we can put the ever-awkward he or she to rest forever. And what would that mean? What consequences could that have for how we think about our world? Empirical question. Send in the psycholinguists.

2. From "Energy in the European Union, Gas Wars" in *The Economist* 390.8613 (January 10, 2009). (*The Economist* does not publish the names of the authors of its articles.)

Introduction:

A gas row between Russia and Ukraine has become a Christmas ritual. That may explain why, until this week, the European Union seemed to pay the latest tiff so little heed. Indeed, the people in Brussels talked of it as a normal bilateral commercial dispute in which the EU should neither interfere nor take sides. Yet Russia's abrupt decision on January 5th to cut off almost all the gas it supplies to the EU countries via Ukraine has sharply raised the stakes, inviting the Europeans to intervene more directly. The shutdown should force a rethink of the EU's overall energy policy as well.

Conclusion:

Beyond this, Europe needs to work harder to diversify its sources of energy, something that it must do anyway if it is to meet its ambitious climate-change targets. And it cannot be repeated too often that a fully liberalized energy market, with better linkages between countries, offers all of Europe not only a more efficient energy future but also a more secure one.

3. From Germaine Greer, "Beaten to the Punchline" in *The Guardian* (February 3, 2009). [http://www.guardian.co.uk/stage/2009/mar/02/germaine-greer-comedy-women]

Introduction:

I should probably not have said, in so few words on television recently, that women aren't as funny as men. Put so baldly, the observation sounds like deliberate provocation, as if I was baiting feminists, or looking for some kind of a knee-jerk response. I was actually trying to present an aspect of the psychopathology of everyday life that strikes me as interesting and important. Women are at least as intelligent as men, and they have as vivid and ready a perception of the absurd; but they have not developed the arts of fooling, clowning, badinage, repartee, burlesque and innuendo into a semi-continuous performance as so many men have.

Conclusion:

At the heart of the judgment that women are not as funny as men is another far less inflammatory observation: that women are less competitive. Competition drives men to more and more outrageous and bizarre mental acrobatics, to stay ahead of the game and have the last laugh. The greater the pressure, the faster the firing of neurons in the male brain. You get your best results from women when you take the pressure off. Men do the inspired lunacy; women do droll.

4. From Robert Kagan, "Why the United States and Europe See the World Differently" in *Policy Review* 113 (2002). [http://www.hoover.org/publications/policyreview/3460246.html] Accessed March 10, 2009.

Introduction:

It is time to stop pretending that Europeans and Americans share a common view of the world, or even that they occupy the same world. On the all-important question of power—the efficacy of power, the morality of power, the desirability of power—American and European perspectives are diverging. Europe is turning away from power, or to put it a little differently, it is moving beyond power into a self-contained world of laws and rules and transnational negotiation and cooperation. It is entering a post-historical paradise of peace and relative prosperity, the realization of Kant's "Perpetual Peace." The United States, meanwhile, remains mired in history, exercising power in the anarchic Hobbesian world where international laws and rules are unreliable and where true security and the defense and promotion of a liberal order still depend on the possession and use of military might. That is why on major strategic and international questions today, Americans are from Mars and Europeans are from Venus: They agree on little and understand one another less and less. And this state of affairs is not transitory—the product of one American election or one catastrophic event. The reasons for the transatlantic divide are deep, long in development, and likely to endure. When it comes to setting national priorities, determining threats, defining challenges, and fashioning and implementing foreign and defense policies, the United States and Europe have parted ways.

Conclusion:

These are small steps, and they will not address the deep problems that beset the transatlantic relationship today. But, after all, it is more than a cliché that the United States and Europe share a set of common Western beliefs. Their aspirations for humanity are much the same, even if their vast disparity of power has now put them in very different places. Perhaps it is not too naïvely optimistic to believe that a little common understanding could still go a long way.

5. From Jerry A. Coyne, " in *The New Republic* (February 4, 2009). [http://www.tnr.com/article/books/seeing-and-believing] Accessed February 23, 2011

Introduction:

Charles Darwin was born on February 12, 1809—the same day as Abraham Lincoln—and published his magnum opus, On the Origin of Species, fifty years later. Every half century, then, a Darwin Year comes around: an occasion to honor his theory of evolution by natural selection, which is surely the most important concept in biology, and perhaps the most revolutionary scientific idea in history. 2009 is such a year, and we biologists are preparing to fan out across the land, giving talks and attending a multitude of DarwinFests. The melancholy part is that we will be speaking more to other scientists than to the American public. For in this country, Darwin is a man of low repute. The ideas that made Darwin's theory so revolutionary are precisely the ones that repel much of religious America, for they imply that, far from having a divinely scripted role in the drama of life, our species is the accidental and contingent result of a purely natural process.

Conclusion:

This disharmony is a dirty little secret in scientific circles. It is in our personal and professional interest to proclaim that science and religion are perfectly harmonious. After all, we want our grants funded by the government, and our schoolchildren exposed to real science instead of creationism. Liberal religious people have been important allies in our struggle against creationism, and it is not pleasant to alienate them by declaring how we feel. This is why, as a tactical matter, groups such as the National Academy of Sciences claim that religion and science do not conflict. But their main evidence—the existence of religious scientists—is wearing thin as scientists grow ever more vociferous about their lack of faith. Now Darwin Year is upon us, and we can expect more books like those by Kenneth Miller and Karl Giberson. Attempts to reconcile God and evolution keep rolling off the intellectual assembly line. It never stops, because the reconciliation never works.

6. From John Cassidy, "Harder Times" in *The New Yorker* (March 16, 2009).

Introduction:

As an exercise in political symbolism, the release of the White House's $3.6-trillion budget for 2010 was an important moment. President Obama, by putting some numbers behind his plans to reform health care, limit carbon emissions, and tackle rising inequality, confirmed his intention to lead the country in a new direction. Republican jibes that the budget was "socialist" should be treated with the respect they deserve, which is to say none: after a major rise in outlays this year, due to the stimulus package, federal spending as a share of the gross domestic product is projected to fall back to twenty-two percent by 2013, which represents a rise of just one percent over last year's figure.

Conclusion:

Last week, Christina Romer, the head of the Council of Economic Advisers, expressed the hope that the Administration's policies would lead to a "Rooseveltian moment," by which she meant a sharp economic upturn, like the one that occurred from 1933 to 1937. Acting in a Rooseveltian manner involves defying orthodoxy, challenging powerful interests, and giving voice to the public's disgust at the corrupt financial establishment. F.D.R. was called a lot worse names than socialist. He didn't let it stop him.

7. From Blight S. K., Larue R. C., Mahapatra A., Longstaff D. G., Chang E., Zhao G., Kang P. T., Green-Church K. B., Chan M. K., Krzycki J. A., "Direct Charging of tRNAcua with pyrrolysine in vitro and in vivo" in *Nature* 439 (2004).

Introduction:

Most organisms employ UAG as a stop codon, but translation is not terminated at in-frame UAGs in some methyltransferases of methanogenicArchaea. Rather, these codons serve as sense codons and, as determined by crystal structure analysis, UAG encodes pyrrolysine, that is, lysine with the epsilon nitrogen in amide linkage to (4R, 5R)-4-substituted-pyrroline-5-carboxylate, the 22nd amino acid found to be genetically encoded in nature. A key question is whether the UAG-translating tRNAcua is first charged with lysine and then modified to pyrrolysine for incorporation into the growing polypeptide or whether pyrrolysine is attached as the fully synthesized amino acid to tRNAcua. Here we show that the latter possibility is feasible by demonstrating the direct pyrrolysylation of tRNAcua in vitro. This is the first example found in nature of specific aminoacylation of tRNA with a non-canonical amino acid. The results reported show further that the expression of only two genes, pylT and pylS, which encode tRNAcua and pyrrolysyl-tRNAsynthetase, can expand the genetic code of E. coli to include pyrrolysine. This procedure could potentially be used to immediately expand the genetic code of any species that can incorporate exogenously added pyrrolysine.

Conclusion:

The current data indicate that pyrrolysine is encoded in DNA using the general mechanism employed for the common set of 20 amino acids. Direct charging of pyrrolysine onto tRNAconstrasts with selenocysteine, a genetically encoded non-canonical amino acid synthesized only on tRNA. Several systems have been recently developed to expand and manipulate the genetic code to generate recombinant proteins containing unnatural amino acids. By adding pylS and pylT genes, it should now be possible to generate proteins with the 22nd amino acid incorporated at UAG targeted sites in any species that can incorporate added pyrrolysine, thereby adding a unique natural amino acid with electrophilic properties. We are now focusing on the pyrrolysine biosynthetic pathway, which offers the possibility of also adding genes that will generate pyrrolysine internally in recombinant organisms.

8. From Aviya Kushner, "McCulture" in *The Wilson Quarterly* (2009).

Introduction:

As a child, I lived in a house where we spoke only Hebrew. I remember relatives from the American side of the family complaining about my parents' language policy when they visited our house in New York. "She'll suffer if she doesn't speak English at home," one worried. "She won't be able to write well enough to get into college." But something unexpected happened as my Israeli mother sang the Psalms to my siblings and me while we bathed: empires fell. The Berlin Wall literally came down. Droves of immigrants and

refugees—huddled masses who had long yearned to be free—
changed London, Berlin, Tel Aviv, and New York. India rose, China
skyrocketed, and four young Israelis invented instant messaging.
Bilingual kids like me, toting odd foods at lunch and speaking with
their mothers in something unintelligible, were suddenly not the
problem, but the glittering future.

Conclusion:

This is not to discount the value of bilingual writers. There are bilingual writers who feel a special freedom in English: a rebirth, they
say, without the weight of culture or history, the taste of prayer or
the memory of genocide. Olga Grushin, at the end of our conversation, quoted Charlemagne, who said that to have a second language
is to possess a second soul.

I was moved by the idea of another soul. But then I thought it
over, as reader instead of writer. As praise is heaped on people who
have mastered English, we are rewarding writers for selling their
first soul. A culture with a healthier translation climate would create a space between languages, a space between souls. As readers,
we'd win. We'd be able to hear the sound of all sorts of souls on the
page—whether a first soul or, as Charlemagne claimed, a second
soul, trying to speak, or perhaps, with luck, sing.

GUIDELINES FOR WRITING INTRODUCTIONS AND CONCLUSIONS

Introductions

1. The introduction seeks to raise the issue, not settle it. Articulate why, in the context of existing thinking on the subject, your topic matters.

2. Don't try to do too much. Offer only the most relevant context, the most essential parts of your road map, and (disciplinary conventions permitting) a first rather than last claim.

3. Always introduce a working (hypo)thesis, frame it with (appropriately cited) background or other context, and indicate your method or angle of approach.

4. Especially in longer papers, you can use a procedural opening to forecast the organization clearly, but don't let it distract you from also stating your claim.

5. Experiment with opening gambits: challenge a common view, use your second best example to set up the issue, or exemplify the problem with a narrative opening.

Conclusions

6. Culminate—don't just summarize. Offer your most fully evolved and quali-fied statement of the thesis or your final judgment on the question posed in the introduction.

7. Come full circle: revisit the introductory hypothesis and context. This strat-egy will unify your paper and locate it within an ongoing conversation on your topic.

8. Your conclusion should not unqualifiedly claim more than your evidence has established, but it should leave the reader with further implications or speculations to ponder (a send-off).

9. Let your conclusion gradually escort the reader out of the paper. Like the introduction, it is a social site, so try to leave the reader with a positive last impression.

Assignments: Analyzing Introductions and Conclusions

1. **Introductions and Audience.** Compare and contrast introductory para-graphs from a popular magazine with those from an academic journal aimed at a more specialized audience. Select one of each and analyze them to determine what each author assumes the audience knows. Where in each paragraph are these assumptions most evident? If you write out your analy-sis, it should probably take about a page, but this exercise can also be done productively with others in a small group.

2. **Analyzing Introductions.** One of the best ways to learn about introductions is to gather some sample introductory paragraphs and, working on your own or in a small group, figure out how each one works, what it accomplishes. Here are some particular questions you might pose:

   • Why does the writer start in this way—what is accomplished?

   • What kind of relationship does this opening establish with the audience and to what ends?

   • How does the writer let readers know why the writing they are about to read is called for, useful, and necessary?

   • Where and by what logic does the introduction funnel?

3. **Analyzing Conclusions.** Find some examples of concluding paragraphs from published writing. First, compare the conclusion with the introduction, looking for the way the conclusion comes full circle. Which elements of the

introduction are repeated to accomplish this? Then look for the statement of the essay's thesis in its final, culminating form. Finally, locate the send-off by finding implications and limitations that the writer has noted as part of his final *So what?* On the basis of your findings, write a few paragraphs in which you describe the writer's approach to conclusions.

At this point, you will be ready to repeat this exercise with some of your own work. Only this time, rather than describing the writer's approach, write an improved version of one of your conclusions based on what you learned from your analysis.

Chapter 17

Revising for Style: Word Choice

THIS FIRST CHAPTER ON STYLE ADDRESSES WORD CHOICE, also known as diction, and its effect on style. The chapter seeks to make you more self-conscious about the kinds of words you habitually use and to expand your range of choices. Chapter 18 attempts to do the same with sentence shapes (syntax). The unit's final chapter moves from stylistic questions—a matter of choice—to common grammatical errors, a matter of correct versus incorrect forms. For this chapter and the next, we'll be asking you to think rhetorically, that is, in terms of appropriate choices for particular contexts rather than right versus wrong.

Most people simply don't pay attention to words. They use words as if their sounds were inaudible, their shapes were invisible, and their meanings were single and self-evident. One goal of this chapter is to interest you in words themselves—as *things* with particular qualities, complex histories, and varied shades of meaning.

STYLE: THE BASICS

Style is not merely decorative.
Simplicity does not necessarily equal clarity.
A matter of words is always a matter of meaning.

STYLE IS MEANING

A key concept throughout this unit is that style is not merely decorative. It is often mistakenly assumed that style is separate from meaning and in that sense largely cosmetic. From this perspective, paying close attention to style seems finicky, or worse, cynical—a way of dressing up the content to sell it to readers or listeners. The problem with this perspective is that it subscribes to what we have earlier referred to as *the transparent theory of language.* This is the idea that meaning exists outside of language—that we somehow see *through* words to meaning and can then address that meaning without addressing the words that embody it. In the transparent theory of language, words are merely pointers to get past.

Another key concept of this unit is that simplicity does not necessarily equal clarity. This chapter targets the unexamined cultural bias in favor of "straight talk." The assumption seems to be that people who use too many words, especially big ones, are needlessly complicating what would otherwise be obvious to anyone's common sense. *Not so.* (Those imperious arbiters of style, Strunk and White, are sometimes correct when they say in *The Elements of Style*—"Never use six words when three will do"—but not always.) Strunk and White also say, for example, never to use the "not un-" formation. So they summarily rule that it is always better to say "I am happy" rather than "I am not unhappy." The second sentence, however, does not mean the same thing as the first. The difference is not just a matter of words but of meaning. This chapter seeks to persuade you that a matter of words is always a matter of meaning.

STYLE: A MATTER OF CHOICES

And what is style? Well, it's not just icing on the cake—cosmetic, a matter of polishing the surface. Broadly defined, *style* refers to all of a writer's decisions in selecting, arranging, and expressing what he or she has to say. Many factors affect your style: your aim and sense of audience, the ways you approach and develop a topic, the kinds of evidence you choose, and, particularly, the kinds of syntax (word order) and diction (word choice) you characteristically select.

In this sense, style is personal. The foundations of your style emerge in the dialogue you have with yourself about your topic. When you revise for style, you consciously reorient yourself toward communicating the results of that dialogue to your audience. Stylistic decisions, then, are a mix of the unconscious and conscious, of chance and choice. You don't simply impose style onto your prose; it's not a mask you don or your way of icing the cake. Revising for style is more like sculpting. As a sculptor uses a chisel to "bring out" a shape from a block of walnut or marble, a writer uses style to bring out the shape of the conceptual connections in a draft of an essay. This bringing out demands a certain detachment from your own language. It requires that you become aware of your words as words and of your sentences as sentences.

You may have been taught that you should always avoid the first-person *I* in academic writing, steer clear of jargon, and never start a sentence with *and* or *but*. There are occasions when all three rules, and others like them, should be rejected. These are matters of usage, not hard-and-fast rules of grammar. This chapter seeks to persuade you that all writing is *contextual*, its appropriateness dependent on the rhetorical situation.

It is commonly assumed that "getting the style right" is a task that begins at the editing stage of producing a paper, as part of polishing the final draft. This assumption is only partly true. Getting the style right is not as simple as proofreading for errors in grammar or punctuation. Proofreading occurs in the relatively comfortable linguistic world of simple right and wrong. Stylistic considerations, by contrast, take place in the more exploratory terrain of *making choices* among more and less effective ways of formulating and communicating your meaning. Most writers do delay a full-fledged stylistic revision until a late stage of drafting, but that doesn't mean that they totally ignore stylistic questions as they draft. The decisions you make about how to phrase your meaning inevitably exert a powerful influence on the meaning you make.

If stylistic considerations are not merely cosmetic, then it follows that rethinking the way you have said something can lead you to rethink the substance of what you have said.

HOW STYLE SHAPES THOUGHT: A BRIEF EXAMPLE

How does the difference in sentence structure affect the meaning of the following two sentences?

> **Draft:** The history of Indochina is marked by colonial exploitation as well as international cooperation.

> **Revision:** The history of Indochina, *although* marked by colonial exploitation, testifies to the possibility of international cooperation.

In the draft, the claim that Indochina has experienced colonial exploitation is equal in weight to the claim that it has also experienced international cooperation. But the revision ranks the two claims. The "although" clause makes the claim of exploitation secondary to the claim of cooperation. The first version of the sentence would probably lead you to a broad survey of foreign intervention in Indochina. The result would likely be a static list in which you judged some interventions to be "beneficial" and others "not beneficial." The revised sentence redirects your thinking, tightens your paper's focus to prioritize evidence of cooperation, and presses you to make decisions, such as whether the positive consequences of cooperation outweigh the negative consequences of colonialism. In short, the revision leads you to examine the dynamic relations between your two initial claims.

Rethinking what you mean is just as likely to occur when you attend to word choice. Notice how the change of a single word in the following sentences could change the entire paper.

> **Draft:** The president's attitude toward military spending is ambiguous.

> **Revision:** The president's attitude toward military spending is ambivalent.

In the draft, the use of the word "ambiguous" (meaning "open to many interpretations") would likely lead to a paper on ways that the president's decisions are unclear. If the president's policies aren't unclear—hard to interpret—but are conflicted over competing ways of thinking, then the writer would want the word "ambivalent." This recognition would lead not only to reorganizing the final draft but also to refocusing the argument, building to the significance of this ambivalence (that the president is torn between adopting one of two stances) rather than to the previous conclusion (that presidential policy is incoherent).

"RIGHT" AND "WRONG" WORDS: SHADES OF MEANING

The nineteenth-century English statesman Benjamin Disraeli once differentiated between *misfortune* and *calamity* by using these words in a sentence describing his political rival William Gladstone: "If Mr. Gladstone fell into the Thames, it would be a misfortune; but if someone dragged him out, it would be a calamity." Misfortune and calamity might mean the same thing to some people, but in fact the two words allow a careful writer to discriminate fine shades of meaning.

One of the best ways to pay attention to words as words is to practice making subtle distinctions among related words. The "right" word contributes accuracy and precision to your meaning. The "wrong" word, it follows, is inaccurate or imprecise. The most reliable guide to choosing the right word and avoiding the wrong word is a dictionary that includes not only concise definitions but also the origin of words (known as their *etymology*). A dicey alternative is a thesaurus (a dictionary of synonyms, now included in most word processing software). A thesaurus can offer you a host of choices, but you run a fairly high risk of choosing an inappropriate word because the thesaurus lists words as synonyms that really have different shades of meaning and connotation.

Many of the most common diction errors happen because the writer has not learned the difference between similar terms that actually have different meanings. A common error of this kind is use of the word "notorious" when what the writer means to say is "famous." A *notorious* figure is widely but unfavorably known, whereas a *famous* person is usually recognized for accomplishments that are praiseworthy. Referring to a famous person as notorious—a rather comic error—could be an embarrassing mistake.

A slightly less severe version of getting the wrong word occurs when a writer uses a word with a shade of meaning that is inappropriate or inaccurate in a particular context. Take, for example, the words *assertive* and *aggressive*. Often used interchangeably, they don't really mean the same thing—and the difference matters. Loosely defined, both terms mean forceful. But assertive suggests being bold and self-confident, whereas aggressive suggests being eager to attack. In most cases, you compliment the person you call assertive but raise doubts about the person you call aggressive (whether you are giving a compliment depends on the situation: aggressive is a term of praise on the football field but less so if used to describe an acquaintance's behavior during conversation at the dinner table).

One particularly charged context in which shades of meaning matter involves the potentially sexist implications of using one term for women and another for men. If, for example, in describing a woman and a man up for the same job, the employer were to refer to the woman as *aggressive* but the man as *assertive,* his diction would deservedly be considered sexist. It would reveal that what is perceived as poised and a sign of leadership potential in a man is construed as unseemly belligerence in a woman. The sexism enters when word choice suggests that what is assertive in a man is aggressive in a woman.

Word Histories and the *OED*

In choosing the right shade of meaning, you will get a sharper sense for the word by knowing its etymological history—the word or words from which it evolved. In the preceding example, *aggressive* derives from the Latin *aggressus,* meaning "to go to or approach"; and *aggressus* is itself a combination of *ad,* a prefix expressing motion, and *gradus,* meaning "a step." An aggressive person, then, is "coming at you." *Assertive,* on the other hand, comes from the Latin *asserere,* combining *ad* and *serere,* meaning "to join or bind together." An assertive person is "coming to build or put things together"—certainly not to threaten.

The best dictionary for pursuing word histories, by the way, is the *Oxford English Dictionary,* which commonly goes by its initials, *OED.* Available in every library reference collection and usually online at colleges and universities as well, it provides examples of how words have been used over time.

Try This 17.1: Tracing Word Histories

One of the best ways to pay attention to words as words is to practice making fine distinctions among related words, as we did with aggressive and assertive. The following exercise will not only increase your vocabulary but also acquaint you with that indispensable reference work for etymology: the *OED.*

Look up one of the following pairs of words in the *OED.* Write down the etymology of each word in the pair, and then, in a paragraph for each, summarize the words' linguistic histories—how their meanings have evolved across time. (The *OED's* examples of how the word has been used over time will be helpful here.)

ordinal/ordinary

explicate/implicate

tenacious/stubborn

induce/conducive

enthusiasm/ecstasy

adhere/inhere

monarchy/oligarchy

overt/covert

What's Bad About "Good" and "Bad"

Broad evaluative terms such as *good* and *bad* can seduce you into stopping your thinking while it is still too general and ill-defined—a matter discussed at length in The Judgment Reflex section of Chapter 2. If you train yourself to select more precise words whenever you encounter *good* and *bad* in your drafts, not only will your prose become clearer but also the search for new words will probably start you thinking again, sharpening your ideas. If, for example, you find yourself writing a sentence such as "The subcommittee made a *bad* decision," ask yourself *why* you called it a bad decision. A revision to "The subcommittee made a shortsighted decision" indicates what in fact is bad about the decision and sets you up to discuss why the decision was myopic, further developing the idea.

Be aware that often evaluative terms are disguised as neutrally descriptive ones—*natural,* for instance, and *realistic.* Realistic according to whom, and defined by what criteria? Something is natural according to a given idea about nature—an assumption—and the same goes for *moral*. These are not terms that mean separately from a particular context or ideology, that is, an assumed hierarchy of value. Similarly, in a sentence such as "Society disapproves of interracial marriage," the broad and apparently neutral term *society* can blind you to a host of important distinctions about social class, about a particular culture, and so on.

Concrete and Abstract Diction

At its best, effective analytical prose uses both concrete and abstract words. Simply defined, concrete diction brings things to life by offering readers words that play on their senses. *Telephone, eggshell, crystalline, azure, striped, kneel, flare,* and *burp* are examples of concrete diction. You need concrete language whenever you are describing what happens or what something looks like—in a laboratory experiment, in a military action, in a painting or film sequence. The language of evidence consists of concrete diction. It allows us to see for ourselves the basis of a person's convictions in the stuff of lived experience.

By contrast, abstract diction refers to words that designate concepts and categories. *Virility, ideology, love, definitive, desultory, conscientious, classify,* and *ameliorate* are examples of abstract diction. So are *democracy, fascism, benevolence,* and *sentimentality.* Abstract words give us the language of ideas. We cannot do without abstract terms, and yet writing made up only of such words loses contact with experience, with the world that we can apprehend through our senses.

The line between abstract and concrete is not always as clear as these examples may suggest. You may recall the ladder of abstraction that we discuss in the section entitled Generalizing in Chapter 2. There, we propose that abstract and concrete are not hard-and-fast categories so much as a continuum, a sliding scale. Word A (for example, machine) may be more abstract than word B (computer) but more concrete than word C (technology).

Concrete and abstract diction need each other. Concrete diction illustrates and anchors the generalizations that abstract diction expresses. Notice the concrete language used to define the abstraction *provinciality* in this example:

> There is no cure for *provinciality* like traveling abroad. In America, the waiter who fails to bring the check promptly at the end of the meal we rightly convict for not being watchful. But in England, after waiting interminably for the check and becoming increasingly irate, we learn that only an ill-mannered waiter would bring it without being asked. We have been rude, not he.

In the following example, the abstract terms *causality, fiction,* and *conjunction* are integrated with concrete diction in the second sentence:

> According to the philosopher David Hume, *causality* is a kind of *fiction* that we ascribe to what he called "the constant *conjunction* of observed events." If a person gets hit in the eye and a black semicircle develops underneath it, that does not necessarily mean the blow caused the black eye.

A style that omits concrete language can leave readers lost in a fog of abstraction that only tangible details can illuminate. The concrete language helps readers see what you mean, much in the way that examples help them understand your ideas. Without the shaping power of abstract diction, however, concrete evocation can leave you with a list of graphic but ultimately pointless facts. The best writing integrates concrete and abstract diction, the language of showing and the language of telling (explaining).

Try This 17.2: Two Experiments with Abstract and Concrete Diction

1. Compose a paragraph using only concrete diction and then one using only abstract diction. Compare results with another person who has done the same task, as this can lead to an interesting discussion of kinds of words, where they reside on the ladder of abstraction, and why.

2. Rewrite the sentences listed below, substituting more concrete language and/or more precise abstractions. Support any abstractions you retain with appropriate detail. Just for the challenge, try to rewrite so that your sentences include no abstract claims, that is, use only concrete details to convey the points.

> It was a great party; everybody had fun.
>
> It was a lousy party; everybody disliked it.
>
> The book was really boring.
>
> The film was very interesting.
>
> His morals were questionable.
>
> Social Security is not an entitlement.
>
> He became extraordinarily angry.

Latinate Diction

One of the best ways to sensitize yourself to the difference between abstract and concrete diction is to understand that many abstract words are examples of what is known as Latinate diction. This term describes words in English that derive from Latin roots, words with such endings as *–tion, –ive, –ity, –ate,* and *–ent.* (Such words are designated by an *L* in the etymological section of dictionary definitions.) Taken to an extreme, Latinate diction can leave your meaning vague and your readers confused. This is not because there is something dubious about words that come into English from Latin. A large percentage of English words have Latin or Greek roots, words like *pentagon* (Greek for five sides), *anarchy* (Latin for without order), and *automobile* (Latin for self-moving).

The problem with Latinate diction lies in the way it is sometimes used. Latin endings such as *–tion* make it too easy for writers to construct sentences made up of a high percentage of vague nouns, as in the following example:

> The examination of different perspectives on the representations of sociopolitical anarchy in media coverage of revolutions can be revelatory of the invisible biases that afflict television news.

This sentence actually makes sense, but the demands it makes on readers will surely drive off most of them before they have gotten through it. Reducing the amount of Latinate diction can make it more readable:

> Because we tend to believe what we see, the political biases that afflict television news coverage of revolutions are largely invisible. We can begin to see these biases when we focus on how the medium reports events, studying the kinds of footage used, for example, or finding facts from other sources that the news has left out.

Although the preceding revision retains a lot of Latinate words, it provides a ballast of concrete, sensory details that allows readers to follow the idea. Although many textbooks on writing argue against using Latinate terms where shorter, concrete terms (usually of Anglo-Saxon origin) might be used instead, such an argument seems needlessly limiting in comparison with the advantages offered by a thorough mixture of the two levels of diction. It's fine to use Latinate diction; just don't make it the sole staple of your verbal diet.

CHOOSING WORDS: SOME RHETORICAL CONSIDERATIONS

We don't wish to make too firm a distinction between writing to make things clear and writing that is considerate of the needs of an audience beyond just clarity. And yet it is the case that when you begin to imagine the response of an audience, an actual listener to or reader of your prose, some additional considerations do come into play. The most important of these is tone.

Tone

Tone is the *implied attitude* of a piece of language toward its subject and audience. Whenever you revise for style, your choices in syntax and diction affect the tone. There are no hard-and-fast rules to govern matters of tone, and your control of it depends on your sensitivity to the particular context—your understanding of your own intentions and your readers' expectations.

Let's consider, for example, the tonal implications of the warning signs in the subways of London as compared with New York.

London: Leaning out of the window may cause harm.

New York: Do not lean out of the window.

Initially, you may find the English injunction laughably indirect and verbose in comparison with the shoot-from-the-hip clarity of the American sign. But that is to ignore the very thing we are calling *style*. The American version appeals to authority, commanding readers what not to do without telling them why. The English version, by contrast, appeals to logic; it is more collegial toward its readers and assumes they are rational beings rather than children prone to misbehave.

In revising for tone, you need to ask yourself if the attitude suggested by your language is appropriate to the aim of your message and to your audience. Your goal is to keep the tone *consistent* with your rhetorical intentions. The following paragraph, from a college catalogue, offers a classic mismatch between the overtly stated aim and the tonal implications:

> The student affairs staff believes that the college years provide a growth and development process for students. Students need to learn about themselves and others and to learn how to relate to individuals and groups of individuals with vastly different backgrounds, interests, attitudes and values. Not only is the tolerance of differences expected, but also an appreciation and a celebration of these differences must be an outcome of the student's experience. In addition, the student must progress toward self-reliance and independence tempered by a concern for the social order.

The explicit content of this passage—*what* it says—concerns tolerance. The professed point of view is student-friendly, asserting that the college exists to allow students "to learn about themselves and others" and to support the individual in accord with the "appreciation . . . of . . . differences." But note that the implicit tone—*how* the passage goes about saying *what* it says—is condescending and intolerant. Look at the verbs. An imperious authority lectures students about what they "*need* to learn," that tolerance is "*expected*," that "celebration . . . *must* be an outcome," and that "the student *must* progress" along these lines. Presumably, the paragraph does not intend to adopt this high-handed manner, but its deafness to tone subverts its desired meaning.

Try This 17.3: Analyzing Tone-Deaf Prose

Using the example from the college catalogue as a model, locate and bring to class examples of tonal inconsistency or inappropriateness that you encounter in your daily life. If you have difficulty finding examples, try memos from those in authority at your school or workplace, which often contain excruciating examples of officialese. Type one of your passages, and underneath it compose a paragraph of analysis in which you single out particular words and phrases and explain how the tone is inappropriate. Then rewrite the passage to remedy the problem.

Formal and Colloquial Styles: Who's Writing to Whom, and Why Does It Matter?

Generalizations About Style

- There are many ways of conveying a message.
- The way you phrase a message constitutes a significant part of its meaning.
- Your phrasing gives your reader cues that suggest your attitude and your ways of thinking.
- There are no transparent (absolutely neutral) delivery systems.
- All stylistic decisions depend on your sensitivity to context—who's talking to whom about what subject and with what aims.

The last of these generalizations concerns what is called the *rhetorical situation*. *Rhetoric* is the subject that deals with how writers and speakers behave in given situations and, more specifically, how they can generate language that produces the effects they desire on a particular audience. Obviously, as you make stylistic choices, you need to be aware of the possible consequences of making certain statements to a certain audience in a certain fashion.

How you say something is always a significant part of *what* you say. To look at words as words is to focus on the *how* as well as the *what*. Imagine that you call your friend on the phone, and a voice you don't recognize answers. You ask to speak with your friend, and the voice responds, "With whom have I the pleasure of speaking?" By contrast, what if the voice instead responds, "Who's this?" What information do these two versions of the question convey, beyond the obvious request for your name?

The first response—"With whom have I the pleasure of speaking?"—tells you that the speaker is formal and polite. He is also probably fastidiously well educated: he not only knows the difference between "who" and "whom" but also obeys the etiquette that outlaws ending a sentence with a preposition ("Whom have I the pleasure of speaking *with*?"). The very formality of the utterance, however, might lead you to label the speaker pretentious. His assumption that conversing with you is a "pleasure" suggests empty flattery. On the other hand, the second version—"Who's this?"—while also grammatically correct, is less formal. It is more direct but also terse to a fault; the speaker does not seem particularly interested in treating you politely.

The two hypothetical responses represent two different levels of style. Formal English obeys the basic conventions of standard written prose, and most academic writing is fairly formal. An informal style—one that is conversational and full of slang—can have severe limitations in an academic setting. The syntax and vocabulary of written prose aren't the same as those of speech, and so attempts to import the language of speech into academic writing can result in your communicating less meaning with less precision. Let's look at one brief example:

> Internecine quarrels within the corporation destroyed morale and sent the value of the stock plummeting.

The phrase "internecine quarrels" may strike some readers as a pretentious display of formal language, but consider how difficult it is to communicate this concept economically in more colloquial (talk-like, conversational) terms. "Fights that go on between people related to each other" is awkward; "brother against brother" is sexist and a cliché; and "mutually destructive disputes" is acceptable but long-winded and less precise.

It is arguably a part of our national culture to value the simple and the direct as more genuine and democratic than the sophisticated, which is supposedly more aristocratic and pretentious. This "plain-speaking" style, however, can hinder your ability to develop and communicate your ideas. In the case of internecine, the more formal diction choice actually communicates more, and more effectively, than the less formal equivalents.

When in doubt about how your readers will respond to the formality or informality of your style, you are usually better off opting for some version of "With whom have I the pleasure of speaking?" rather than "Who's this?" The best solution usually lies somewhere in between: "May I ask who's calling?" would protect you against the imputation of either priggishness or piggishness.

Try This 17.4: Analyzing Effective Tone

Find an example of tone that you think is just about perfect for the message and audience. Type it, and underneath discuss why it succeeds. Be as specific as you can about how the passage functions stylistically. Talk about particular phrasings and the match between what is being said and how it is said. Factor into your discussion the relationship between levels of style in the example and its presumed audience.

First Person, Second Person or Third Person?

The person question concerns which of the three basic forms of the pronoun you should use when you write. Here are the three forms, with brief examples.

First person: I believe Heraclitus is an underrated philosopher.

Second person: You should believe that Heraclitus is an underrated philosopher.

Third person: He or she believes that Heraclitus is an underrated philosopher.

Which person to use is a stylistic concern because it involves a writer's *choices* as regards to level of formality, the varying expectations of different audiences, and overall tone.

As a general rule, in academic writing you should discuss your subject matter in the third person and avoid the first and second person. There is logic to this rule: most academic analysis focuses on the subject matter rather than on you as you respond to it. If you use the third person, you keep the attention where it belongs.

"I": Pro and Con

Using the first-person "I" can throw the emphasis on the wrong place. Repeated assertions of "in my opinion" actually distract your readers from what you have to say. Omit them except in the most informal cases. You might, however, consider using the first person in the drafting stage if you are having trouble bringing your own point of view to the forefront. In this situation, the "I" becomes a strategy for loosening up and saying what you really think about a subject rather than adopting conventional and faceless positions. In the final analysis, though, most analytical prose is more precise and straightforward in the third person. When you cut "I am convinced that" from the beginning of any claim, what you lose in personal conviction you gain in concision and directness by keeping the focus on the main idea in a main clause.

Using the First-Person "I": Three Professors Speak

Are there cases when you should use "I"? Contrary to the general rule, some professors actually prefer the first-person pronoun in particular contexts, as noted in the accompanying Voices from Across the Curriculum. It is a general rule, however, in the formal products of science and social science writing, to avoid personal pronouns. (*See Chapter 15, Forms and Formats Across the Curriculum.*)

Voices From Across the Curriculum

o   Avoid phrases like "*The author* believes (or will discuss)." Except in the paper's abstract, "*I* believe (or will discuss)" is okay, and often best.
—Alan Tjeltveit, Professor of Psychology

o   I prefer that personal opinion or voice (for example, "I this" or "I that") appear throughout. I like the first person. No "the author feels" or "this author found that," please! Who is the author? Hey, it's you!
—Frederick Norling, Professor of Business

o   The biggest stylistic problem is that students tend to be too personal or colloquial in their writing, using phrases such as the following: "Scientists all agree," "I find it amazing that," "The thing that I find most interesting." Students are urged to present data and existing information in their own words, but in an objective way. My preference in writing is to use the active voice in the past tense. I feel this is the most direct and least wordy approach: "I asked this," "I found out that," "These data show."
—Richard Niesenbaum, Professor of Biology

Note that these are not blanket endorsements; they specify a limited context within which "I" is preferred. The biology professor's cautioning against using an overly personal and colloquial tone is also probably the consensus view.

Although a majority of professors may prefer the first-person "I think" to the more awkward "the writer (or 'one') thinks," we would point out that, in the service of reducing wordiness, you can often avoid both options. For example, in certain contexts and disciplines, the first-person-plural, we, is acceptable usage: "The president's speech assumes that *we* are all dutiful but disgruntled taxpayers." The one case in which the first person is particularly appropriate occurs when you are citing an example from your own experience. Otherwise, if you are in doubt about using I or we, avoid these first-person pronouns.

"You": Pro and Con

Proceed with caution. Using "you" is a fairly assertive gesture. Many readers will be annoyed, for example, by a paper about advertising that states, "When you read about a sale at the mall, you know it's hard to resist." Most readers resent having a writer airily making assumptions about them or telling them what to do. Some rhetorical situations, however, call for the use of "you." Textbooks, for example, use "you" frequently because it creates a more direct relationship between authors and readers. Yet, even in appropriate situations, directly addressing readers as "you" may alienate them by ascribing to them attitudes and needs they may not have.

The conventional argument for using the first and second person is that "I" and "you" are personal and engage readers. It is not necessarily the case, however, that the third person is therefore impersonal. Just as film directors put their stamps on films by the way they organize the images, move among camera viewpoints, and orchestrate the sound tracks, so writers, even when writing in the third person, have a wide variety of resources at their disposal for making the writing more personal and accessible for their audiences. See, for example, the discussion of the passive voice in Chapter 18.

Jargon

Many people assume that all jargon—the specialized vocabulary of a particular group—is bad: pretentious language designed to make most readers feel inferior. Many writing textbooks attack jargon in similar terms, calling it either polysyllabic balderdash or a specialized, gate-keeping language designed by an in-group to keep others out.

Yet, in many academic contexts, jargon is downright essential. It is conceptual shorthand, a technical vocabulary that allows the members of a group (or a discipline) to converse with one another more clearly and efficiently. Certain words that may seem odd to outsiders in fact function as connective tissue for a way of thought shared by insiders.

The following sentence, for example, although full of botanical jargon, is also admirably cogent:

> In angiosperm reproduction, if the number of pollen grains
> deposited on the stigma exceeds the number of ovules in the
> ovary, then pollen tubes may compete for access to ovules, which
> results in fertilization by the fastest growing pollen tubes.

We would label this use of jargon acceptable because it is written, clearly, *by* insiders *for* fellow insiders. It might not be acceptable language for an article intended for readers who are not botanists, or at least not scientists.

The problem with jargon comes when this insiders' language is directed at outsiders as well. The language of contracts offers a prime example of such jargon at work:

> The Author hereby indemnifies and agrees to hold the Publisher, its licensees, and any seller of the Work harmless from any liability, damage, cost, and expense, including reasonable attorney's fees and costs of settlement, for or in connection with any claim, action, or proceeding inconsistent with the Author's warranties or representations herein, or based upon or arising out of any contribution of the Author to the Work.

Run for the lawyer! What does it mean to "hold the Publisher . . . harmless"? To what do "the Author's warranties or representations" refer? What exactly is the author being asked to do here—release the publisher from all possible lawsuits that the author might bring? We might label this use of jargon obfuscating; although it may aim at precision, it leaves most readers bewildered. Although nonprofessionals are asked to sign them, such documents are really written by lawyers for other lawyers.

As the botanical and legal examples suggest, the line between acceptable and obfuscating jargon has far more to do with the audience to whom the words are addressed than with the actual content of the language. Because most academic writing is addressed to insiders, students studying a particular area need to learn its jargon. Using the technical language of the discipline is a necessary skill for conversing with others in that discipline. Moreover, by demonstrating that you can "talk the talk," you will validate your authority to pronounce an opinion on matters in the discipline.

Here are two guidelines that can help you in your use of jargon: (1) when addressing *insiders,* use jargon accurately ("talk the talk"); and (2) when addressing *outsiders*—the general public or members of another discipline—either define the jargon carefully or replace it with a more generally known term, preferably one operating at the same level of formality.

The Politics of Language

We cannot leave this chapter without reflecting on its place in what we earlier labeled the culture of inattention and cliché that surrounds us. Style has political and ethical implications. A little over a half-century ago, in his famous essay "Politics and the English Language," George Orwell warns of the "invasion of one's mind by ready-made phrases... [which] can only be prevented if one is constantly on guard against them." The worst modern writing, he declares, "consists in gumming together long strips of words which have already been set in order by someone else, making the results presentable by sheer humbug."

Insofar as style is an expression of the writer's self, Orwell implies, (1) we are under attack from broad cultural clichés and sentimental nostrums that do our thinking for us, and (2) it is thus a matter of personal integrity and civic responsibility to ask ourselves a series of questions about the sentences that we write. As Orwell says,

> What am I trying to say? What words will express it? What image
> or idiom will make it clearer? Is this image fresh enough to have
> an effect? [...] Could I put it more shortly? Have I said anything
> that is avoidably ugly?

Words matter. They matter in how we name things, in how we phrase meanings—but also in how we are shaped by the words we read and hear in the media. Words don't simply reflect a neutral world that is out there in some objective way that offers self-evident meanings we can universally agree upon. Words don't reflect—they constitute; they call the world into being. They call us into being when we write them.

Earlier in this chapter we noted, for example, that the decision to call a woman "aggressive" as opposed to "assertive" matters. There are examples all around you of language creating rather than merely reflecting reality. Start looking for these on the front page of your newspaper, in political speeches, in advertising, even in everyday conversation. Does it matter, for instance, that there are no equivalents to the words "spinster" or "whore" for men? Does it change things to refer to a bombing mission as a "containment effort" or, by way of contrast, to call an enthusiastic person "a fanatic"?

An article in the journal *Foreign Affairs* by Peter van Ham (October 2001) offers one last dispatch from the frontier of the culture of inattention and cliché. The article is about the rise of the so-called brand state—about how nations market themselves not only to consumers but to other nations. A brand, defined as "a customer's idea about a product," is a powerful tool to replace what a thing is with what other people, for reasons of their own, would have you think it is. This is the world we inhabit, and style can be its adversary or its accomplice. In the last analysis, that's what's at stake in choosing to care about style.

GUIDELINES FOR WORD CHOICE

1. Remember first and foremost that revision is not merely cosmetic: to change the words is to change the meaning.

2. Strive for distance from your own prose as you edit for diction: place yourself in the position of the audience. Is the tone appropriate to the rhetorical context?

3. There are always shades of meaning. Strive to choose the best—the most accurate and appropriate—word for the situation. When in doubt, consult etymology, the history of the word, as the most reliable guide to its usage.

4. Avoid "good," "bad," "real," and other broad, judgmental terms that prematurely close off analysis.

5. Blend concrete and abstract diction, which is generally the language of details and the language of abstractions, respectively. In particular, go easy on those Latinate-*tion* words.

6. In given contexts, jargon is useful shorthand, but there is always the danger of getting used by it. Make sure you know what the words mean, and don't over-rely on them.

Assignment: Thinking About Word Choice

Analyze the Style of a Particular Group Write a paper that analyzes the style of a particular group or profession (for example, sports, advertising, bureau-cracy, show business, or music reviewing). Or as an alternative, adopt the voice of a member of this group, and write a parody that critiques or analyzes the language practices of the group. If you choose the latter, be aware that there is always a risk in parody of belittling in an unduly negative way a style that is not your own.

Obviously, you will first need to assemble and make observations about a number of samples of the style you are analyzing or parodying. Use The Method to help you uncover the kinds of words that are repeated, the most common strands, and so forth. Look at the level of formality, the tone, the use of concrete and abstract diction, and the predilection for Latinate as opposed to Anglo-Saxon words. Who's writing to whom about what, and so what that the writing adopts this style? Also, see the assignments at the end of Chapter 18.

Chapter 18

Revising for Style: The Rhetoric of the Sentence

ONE OF THE MOST DISTINCTIVE WAYS of identifying a really good writer is by the way he or she puts together a sentence. A writer who understands how to build sentences is a writer who understands the key concept of sentence style: that there is a powerful link between the shape of a sentence and the shape of a thought. We summarize this key idea with the phrase, *a sentence is the shape thought takes.* The slide below bullets what shape can do.

A SENTENCE IS THE SHAPE THOUGHT TAKES

What the shape can do:
- indicate where to find the important meanings in the sentence
- reveal how the other information in the sentence is related to the most important meanings
- get readers to follow you and understand you in the way you desire
- slow readers down when they need the extra time to understand more complex points
- keep them on track, so they know where they are going and they remember where they've come from

OPERATING ASSUMPTIONS

In order to compose sentences that will work for you and help your readers access your meaning as you wish them to, it's necessary for many writers to re-orient the way they think about sentences. This means unlearning some old habits—discarding some unhelpful beliefs—that interfere with writing fluent sentences and replacing these habits with new assumptions about how to construct sentences. The following three "laws" are corollaries of our primary mantra—that every sentence is a shape thought takes.

- **Every sentence is a delivery system**. *Stop thinking that a sentence is a neutral carrier of meanings.* There's a good chance you've never really thought much about your sentences as sentences—that is, as arrangements of words that always carry rhythm and emphasis, whether you intend them to or not. The sentence always affects, is always part of the content it carries. If you care about the meanings you are asking your sentences to convey, don't let yourself look past them; train yourself to *see* them. This takes practice, but it is a very worthwhile skill to acquire.

- **Every sentence possesses style**. *Start focusing on what makes sentences right rather than on what makes them wrong.* Yes, it matters if you commit lots of sentence-level errors, but temporarily stop worrying about such errors and the rules of grammar (which the next chapter will focus on). Instead, focus on style, the choices a writer makes as he or she fashions meaning for a particular purpose in a particular setting. Start looking actively for sentences you like. Then analyze what you like about them. Imitate them. Try making one a go-to sentence. *(See Chapter 2, Toolkit I on Go-To Sentences.)*

- **Every sentence is composed of interchangeable parts**. *And you can rearrange the parts.* This rearranging lies at the heart of revision—a process of seeing again to make your meanings more accurate or clear or memorable. Assembling and reassembling the parts is not a cosmetic act. It is an act of thinking.

There's a surprisingly small amount of specialized vocabulary to master in order to see and talk about sentence shapes. We can best illustrate this vocabulary and how it works by looking at one comma rule and then four basic sentence shapes. We will then build on this foundation for the rest of the chapter, adding more technical terms as we need them.

Please be aware that all of these terms have been collected in the Glossary of Grammatical Terms located at the end of Chapter 19. In particular, see entries for the following terms: *clause, conjunction, conjunctive adverb, coordination, direct object, phrase, preposition, subject, subordination,* and *verbals.* Earlier in that chapter, you will also find a brief guide to punctuation entitled "What Punctuation Marks Say: A Quick-Hit Guide." Punctuation makes sentence shapes visible.

THE PRIMARY COMMA RULE: IDENTIFYING THE MAIN CLAUSE

The main idea of most sentences resides in the main clause, the subject + verb that can stand by itself (aka independent clause). The main clause generally gets the most emphasis and carries the most meaning. Sentences are built around main clauses, and writers (as well as readers) will benefit from developing the ability to find the main clause in any sentence. Here's one:

The cat / was happy.

The diagonal line separates the subject from the predicate. "Cat" is the subject, "was" is the verb, and "happy" is an adjective that modifies (describes) "cat."

Let's say we wish to add some modifying information to this sentence, such as "despite not having enough for breakfast." There are three places (slots) in sentences where this modifying phrase might be added. In each sample sentence below we have underlined the main clause and italicized the modifying information.

beginning: *Despite not having enough for breakfast,* <u>the cat was happy.</u>

middle: <u>The cat,</u> *despite not having enough for breakfast,* <u>was happy.</u>

end: <u>The cat was happy,</u> *despite not having enough for breakfast.*

These "slots" for adding information at the beginning, middle, and end are generally separated from the main clause by commas. *The commas are there to help the reader easily find and recognize the main clause.*

The first example, with the modifying phrase at the end, doesn't absolutely need a comma; we won't misread the sentence without it, though the comma does help to clarify matters. And, what if we raise the level of complexity by adding more modifiers to a more complicated idea?

modifying phrase at beginning: *Although both candidates claimed to be running clean races and blamed the other for the mud-slinging,* <u>the campaign was ugly.</u>

modifying phrase at middle: <u>The campaign,</u> *although both candidates claimed to be running clean races and blamed the other for the mud-slinging,* <u>was ugly.</u>

modifying phrase at end: <u>The campaign was ugly,</u> *although both candidates claimed to be running clean races and blamed the other for the mud-slinging.*

Now let's build on this primary comma rule by applying it to the four basic sentence shapes.

HOW TO RECOGNIZE THE FOUR BASIC SENTENCE TYPES & WHAT THEY DO

To see sentence shapes, always start by finding the clauses. A clause is any subject + verb combination. There are two types of clauses:

- **independent clauses,** which can stand alone, such as <u>The dog was depressed</u>

- **dependent clauses,** which cannot stand alone, such as <u>Because the dog was depressed</u>. A dependent clause literally depends (hangs on) another clause.

Sentences can be divided into four basic types depending on the kind and relation of clauses.

Consumers shop.

Consumers shop, and producers manufacture.

Consumers shop in predictable ways, so producers manufacture with different target groups in mind.

> Consumers shop in ways that can be predicted by such determinants as income level, sex, and age; consequently, producers use market research to identify different target groups for their products.

These four sentences become progressively longer, and the information they contain becomes increasingly detailed, but they also differ in their structure—specifically, in the number of independent and dependent clauses they contain.

The Simple Sentence: One Statement at a Time

How and why to use the simple sentence: The *simple sentence* consists of a single independent clause. Simple sentences are the most effective choice when you wish to say something clearly and forcefully. They are especially effective in contrast to longer and more complicated sentences that may surround them. They give the reader—and the writer—a chance to get grounded. It's as if the sentence structure itself—the **syntax**—says: "simply put." If you find yourself getting confused while writing something complicated, it's probably time for a simple sentence. On the other hand, if you string together too many simple sentences in a row, you are probably not adequately connecting your ideas. At its most basic, the simple sentence contains a single subject and verb.

> Consumers shop.

Other words and phrases can be added to this sentence, but it will remain simple so long as "Consumers shop" is the only clause.

> Most consumers shop unwisely.

Even if the sentence contains more than one grammatical subject or more than one verb, it remains simple in structure.

> Most consumers **shop** unwisely and **spend** more than they can afford. *[two verbs]*

> Both female **consumers** and their **husbands** shop unwisely. *[two subjects]*

The sentence structure in the example that uses two verbs ("shop" and "spend") is known as a *compound predicate*. The sentence structure in the example that uses two subjects ("consumers" and "husbands") is known as a *compound subject*. If, however, you were to add both another subject and another verb to the original simple sentence, you would have the next sentence type, a compound sentence.

The Compound Sentence: Two Items of Equal Weight

How and why to use the compound sentence: The *compound sentence* consists of at least two independent clauses and no subordinate clauses. The information conveyed in these clauses should be of roughly equal importance. Use compound sentences when you are grouping in twos, both pairing likes and balancing oppositions. There should probably be some kind of conceptual linkage between the two clauses. Using compound sentences helps both you and your readers to organize the information.

In most cases, the two independent clauses in a compound sentence are bound by a *coordinating conjunction* (*and, or, but* are the most common), preceded by a comma. This comma is extremely useful, for it lets your readers know as they move across the sentence that you are about to add a second independent clause. Compound sentences put equal grammatical weight on each independent clause.

> Producers manufacture, and consumers shop.

As with the simple sentence, you can also add qualifying phrases to the compound sentence, and it will remain compound, as long as no dependent clauses are added.

> Consumers shop in predictable ways, so producers manufacture with different target groups in mind.

> Consumers shop recklessly during holidays; marketers are keenly aware of this fact.

Note that a compound sentence can connect its independent clauses with a semicolon as an alternative to the comma + coordinate conjunction. This is the primary use of the semicolon—to link two independent clauses that are closely related in some way. *(See What Punctuation Marks Say: A Quick-Hit Guide in Chapter 19.)* If you were to substitute a **subordinating conjunction** for either of these connectors, however, you would have a sentence with one independent clause and one dependent clause. For example:

> *Because consumers shop in predictable ways*, <u>producers manufacture</u> with different target groups in mind.

This revision changes the compound sentence into the next sentence type, the complex sentence.

The Complex Sentence: Ranking the Value of Ideas or Information

How and why to use the complex sentence: The *complex sentence* consists of a single independent clause and one or more dependent clauses: "Before the President did X, he did Y, because he was forced to do so." The information conveyed in the dependent clauses are subordinated to the more important independent clause. Complex sentences are invaluable when you are establishing emphasis and assigning different values to different pieces of information. In the following example, the subject and verb of the main clause are underlined, and the subordinating conjunctions are italicized:

> *Although mail-order merchandising has increased*, most <u>consumers</u> still <u>shop</u> unwisely, buying on impulse rather than deliberation.

This sentence contains one independent clause ("consumers shop"). Hanging on it are one introductory dependent clause ("although merchandising has increased") and one participial phrase ("buying on impulse"). If your sentence had two independent clauses (compound) and one or more dependent clauses, it would become the next sentence type: compound-complex. In the following example, the subjects and verbs of the two main clauses are underlined, and the conjunctions are italicized:

> Mail-order <u>merchandising</u>—*which* generally saves shoppers money—<u>has</u> <u>increased</u>, *but* <u>consumers</u> still <u>shop</u> unwisely, buying on impulse rather than deliberation.

The Compound-Complex Sentence: Using Syntax to Convey Complexity

How and why to use the compound-complex sentence: The *compound-complex sentence* consists of two or more independent clauses and one or more dependent clauses. This syntactic shape is essential in representing complex relationships and so is frequently put to use in various forms of analytical writing, especially in academic writing. It is also probably true that the ability to use compound-complex sentences elevates a writer's credibility: it demonstrates that he or she can bring together in a single sentence a range of different pieces of information and order them in relationship to each other. This is not to say that the compound-complex sentence invites confusion: on the contrary, when handled carefully, it has the opposite effect—it clarifies the complexity and enables readers to see it clearly. See the discussion of parallel structure later in this chapter for one mode of achieving this clarity when you build complicated sentences.

See if you can find and identify the parts of the following compound-complex sentence. List separately the main clauses, the subordinate clauses, and the various coordinating and subordinating conjunctions. (See the *conjunction* entry in the Glossary of Grammatical Terms at the end of Chapter 19 for a list of these.)

> Consumers shop in ways that can be predicted by such determinants as income level, sex, and age; consequently, producers use market research that aims to identify different target groups for their products.

As we end this survey of the four sentence types, let us reinforce a key point about sentence style: it is not simply good or bad. Every stylistic choice a writer makes (consciously or not) has implications. This chapter aims to equip you with the information you need in order to see the range of your choices and thus make appropriate decisions.

Try This 18.1: Compose the Four Sentence Types

As we have done with the consumers-shop example, compose a simple sentence and then a variety of expansions: a compound subject, a compound predicate, a compound sentence, a complex sentence, and a compound-complex sentence.

To prevent this exercise from becoming merely mechanical, keep in mind how different sentence shapes accomplish different ends. In other words, make sure your compound sentence balances two items of information, that your complex sentence emphasizes one thing (in the main clause) over another (in the subordinate clause), and that your compound-complex sentence is capable of handling and organizing complexity.

Try This 18.2: Identify the Four Sentence Types in Sentences You Like

As one of the operating assumptions for this chapter, we suggested that "Every sentence possesses style" and so you should *"Start focusing on what makes sentences right rather than on what makes them wrong."* We use these propositions as the basis for an exercise in which we direct students to locate in their reading any sentences whose shape they like, and to use these as the basis for practicing their ability to name sentence features.

In the following list of sentences, all taken from our students' lists, do the following:

- identify which of the four types it is
- underline the subject and verb of the main clause(s)
- double-underline the subordinate clauses
- circle the coordinating conjunctions and subordinating conjunctions

1. "Since the Martians were evidently, in spite of their repulsive forms, intelligent creatures, it had been resolved to show them, by approaching them with signals, that we too were intelligent." (H. G. Wells, *The War of the Worlds*)

2. "Latin American societies have not transcended racism by embracing indigenous American and African elements in their national mix, but they have gotten further than many other multiracial societies, including, many believe, the United States." (John Charles Chasteen, *Born in Blood and Fire*)

3. "Chwa was in her late eighties at the time of the interview, had poor eyesight, though good hearing, and could still walk." (Richard B. Lee, *The Dobe Ju/'hoansi*)

4. "John Darnielle, leader of a veteran band called the Mountain Goats, writes songs that unspool like short stories, and his new album, "Heretic Pride," is full of desperate characters and evocative settings." (John Jurgensen, *The Washington Post*)

5. "As it is undeniable that portions of the human family have existed in a state of savagery, other portions in a state of barbarism, and still other portions in a state of civilization, it seems equally so that these three distinct conditions are connected with each other in a natural as well as necessary sequence of progress." (R. Jon McGee and Richard L. Warms, *Anthropological Theory: An Introductory History*)

Alternatively, you might do these operations on sentences of your own choice. Also please note that there will be an opportunity to repeat and expand this Try This in the end-of-chapter assignments. We recommend, in any case, that you might start your own list of sentences you like. It's one of the very best ways to learn about style.

USING COORDINATION AND SUBORDINATION TO EMPHASIZE MEANINGS

As we trust you are beginning to see, sentence structure operates as a form of implicit logic. The syntax defines relationships among the clauses—subject + verb combinations—in a sentence according to the choices you make about coordination and subordination. A third factor in according emphasis is the order of clauses, as we shall discuss in what follows. All three—coordination, subordination, and the order of clauses—are tools of logic and emphasis that help to rank your meanings and convey this ranking to the reader.

Using Coordination to Balance This with That

Coordination uses grammatically equivalent constructions to link ideas. These ideas should carry roughly equal weight as well. Sentences that use coordination connect clauses with coordinating conjunctions (such as *and, but,* and *or*). Here are two examples.

> Historians organize the past, *and* they can never do so with absolute neutrality.

> Homegrown corn is incredibly sweet, *and* it is very difficult to grow.

If you ponder these sentences, you may begin to detect the danger of the word *and.* It does not specify a precise logical relationship between the things it connects but instead simply adds them. Notice that the sentences get more precise if we substitute *but* for *and.*

> Historians organize the past, *but* they can never do so with absolute neutrality.

> Homegrown corn is incredibly sweet, *but* it is very difficult to grow.

These sentences are still coordinate in structure; they are still the sentence type known as compound. But they achieve more emphasis than the *and* versions. In both cases, the *but* clause carries more weight, because *but* always introduces information that qualifies or contradicts what precedes it.

Emphasis Rests at the End of Coordinate Clauses

In both the *and* and *but* examples of coordinate clauses, the second clause tends to be stressed. The reason is simple: *the end is usually a position of emphasis.* You can see the effect of clause order more starkly if we reverse the clauses in our examples.

> Historians are never absolutely neutral, but they organize the past.

> Homegrown corn is very difficult to grow, but it is incredibly sweet.

Note how the meanings have changed in these versions because emphasis tends to fall on whatever comes last in a sentence. Rather than simply having their objectivity undermined ("Historians are never absolutely neutral"), historians are now credited with at least providing organization ("they organize the past"). Similarly, whereas the previous version of the sentence about corn was likely to dissuade gardeners from trying to grow it ("it is very difficult to grow"), the new sentence is more likely to lure them to nurture corn ("it is incredibly sweet").

Nonetheless, all of these sentences are examples of coordination because the clauses are grammatically equal. As you revise, notice when you use coordinate syntax, and think about whether you really intend to give the ideas equal weight. Consider as well whether reversing the order of clauses will more accurately convey your desired emphasis to your readers.

Try This 18.3: Rearrange Coordinate Clauses for Emphasis

Rearrange the parts of the following coordinate sentence, which is composed of four sections, separated by commas. Construct at least three versions, and jot down how the meaning changes in each version.

> I asked her to marry me, two years ago, in a shop on Tremont Street, late in the fall.

Then subject two sentences of your own, perhaps taken from your papers, to the same treatment. Make sure to describe how the meaning changes in each case, because it will get you accustomed to seeing the effects of the rearrangements.

Using Subordination to Adjust Emphasis

In sentences that contain *subordination,* there are two "levels" of grammar—the main clause and the subordinate clause—that create two levels of meaning. When you put something in a main clause, you emphasize its significance. When you put something in a subordinate clause, you make it less important than what is in the main clause.

As noted in the discussion of complex sentences, a subordinate clause is linked to a main clause by words known as *subordinating conjunctions*. Here is a list of the most common ones: *after, although, as, as if, as long as, because, before, if, rather than, since, than, that, though, unless, until, when, where, whether,* and *while*. All of these words define something *in relation to* something else:

> *If* you study hard, you will continue to do well.

> You will continue to do well, *if* you study hard.

In both of these examples, *if* subordinates "you study hard" to "you will continue to do well," regardless of whether the *if* clause comes first or last in the sentence.

How the End Affects Emphasis When Using Subordinate Clauses

Unlike the situation with coordinate clauses, the emphasis in sentences that use subordination virtually always rests on the main clause, regardless of the clause order. Nevertheless, the principle of end-position emphasis still applies, though to a lesser extent than among coordinate clauses. Let's compare two versions of the same sentence.

> Although the art of the people was crude, it was original.

> The art of the people was original, although it was crude.

Both sentences emphasize the idea in the main clause ("original"). Because the second version locates the "although" clause at the end, however, the subordinated idea ("crude") has more emphasis than it does in the first version.

You can experiment with the meaning and style of virtually any sentence you write by reversing the clauses. Here, taken almost at random, is an earlier sentence from this chapter, followed by two such transformations.

> When you put something in a subordinate clause, you make it less important than what is in the main clause.

> Put information in a subordinate clause if you want to make it less important than what is in the main clause.

> If you want to make information less important than what is in the main clause, put it in a subordinate clause.

As we hope you can see, the ordering of clauses is one way of according emphasis, the decision to subordinate or coordinate is another, and the two modes of emphasizing can work in tandem. Thus, a sentence that ends with a subordinate clause gives that clause more force than a sentence that contains a subordinate clause but does not end with it.

> **Try This 18.4: Experiment with Coordination, Subordination, and the Order of Clauses**
>
> Do two rewritings of the following sentence, changing the order of clauses and subordinating or coordinating as you wish. We recommend that you make one of them end with the word *friendly.*
>
> > Faculty members came to speak at the forum, and they were friendly, but they were met with hostility, and this hostility was almost paranoid.
>
> How does each of your revisions change the meaning and emphasis?

Parallel Structure: Put Parallel Information into Parallel Form

One of the most important and useful devices for shaping sentences is *parallel structure* or, as it is also known, *parallelism.* Parallelism is a form of symmetry: it involves placing sentence elements that correspond in some way into the same (that is, parallel) grammatical form. Consider the following examples, in which the parallel items are underlined or italicized:

> The three kinds of partners in a law firm who receive money from a case are popularly known as <u>finders</u>, <u>binders</u>, and <u>grinders</u>.

> The Beatles acknowledged their musical debts <u>to</u> American rhythm and blues, <u>to</u> English music hall ballads and ditties, and later <u>to</u> classical Indian ragas.

> There was <u>no way that</u> the President <u>could gain</u> the support of party regulars *without alienating* the Congress, and <u>no way that</u> he <u>could appeal</u> to the electorate at large *without alienating* both of these groups.

> In the entertainment industry, the money that <u>goes out</u> to hire *film stars* or *sports stars* <u>comes back</u> in increased ticket sales and video or television rights.

As all of these examples illustrate, at the core of parallelism lies repetition—of a word, a phrase, or a grammatical structure. Parallelism uses repetition to organize and emphasize certain elements in a sentence, so that readers can perceive more clearly the shape of your thought. In the Beatles example, each of the prepositional phrases beginning with *to* contains a musical debt. In the President example, the repetition of the phrase *no way that* emphasizes his entrapment.

Parallelism has the added advantage of economy: each of the musical debts or presidential problems might have had its own sentence, but in that case the prose would have been wordier and the relationships among the parallel items more obscure. Along with this economy come balance and emphasis. The trio of rhyming words (finders, binders, and grinders) that concludes the law-firm example gives each item equal weight; in the entertainment-industry example, "comes back" answers "goes out" in a way that accentuates their symmetry.

Try This 18.5: Find Examples of Parallelism

List all of the examples of parallelism in the following famous passage from the beginning of the Declaration of Independence:

> We hold these truths to be self-evident: that all men are
> created equal; that they are endowed by their Creator with
> certain inalienable rights; that, among these, are life, liberty,
> and the pursuit of happiness.

Remember that parallelism can occur with clauses and phrases, especially prepositional phrases. You might find it useful to review the entries for these three terms in the glossary in Chapter 19. After you have completed your list, what do you notice about the way that the parallel structures accumulate? And what is the effect of the placement and phrasing of these parallelisms? In other words, try to describe how this famous passage develops stylistically.

When you employ parallelism in revising for style, there is one grammatical rule to obey. It is important to avoid what is known as *faulty parallelism,* which occurs when the items that are parallel in content are not placed in the same grammatical form.

Faulty: *To study* hard for four years and then *getting* ignored once they enter the job market is a hard thing for many recent college graduates to accept.

Revised: *To study* hard for four years and then *to get* ignored once they enter the job market is a hard thing for many recent college graduates to accept.

Try This 18.6: Correct Errors in Parallelism

Rewrite the following examples of faulty parallelism using correct parallel structure. In the last of these sentences, you will need to contemplate the thinking behind it as well as its form.

1. The problems with fast food restaurants include the way workers are exploited, eating transfatty acids, and that the food can damage your liver.

2. Venus Williams likes to play tennis and also designing clothes.

3. In the 1960s the use of drugs and being a hippie were ways for some people to let society know their political views and that they were alienated from the mainstream.

Two Powerful Forms of Parallelism: Antithesis and Chiasmus

One particularly useful form of balance that parallel structure accommodates is known as *antithesis* (from the Greek word for "opposition"), a conjoining of contrasting ideas. Here, the pattern sets one thing against another thing, as in the following example:

> Where bravura failed to settle the negotiations, tact and patience succeeded.

"Failed" is balanced antithetically against "succeeded," as "bravura" against "tact and patience." Antithesis commonly takes the form of "if not *x*, at least *y*" or "not *x*, but *y*."

Another specialized form of parallelism known as *chiasmus* is a rhetorical pattern that organizes elements in an ABBA structure. The most famous chiasmus known to most Americans comes from a speech by John F. Kennedy: "Ask not [A] what your country can do for you [B]; ask what you [B] can do for your country [A]."

Note how this form also uses antithesis—the JFK example moves from "ask not" to "ask"—which is why it is known as a form of inverted parallelism, the second half of the expression balanced against the first, with the parts reversed. You can more easily remember the term chiasmus once you realize that it derives from the Greek letter *chi*, meaning X, as that is the shape of the AB -> BA structure. Here is another example of chiasmus from Matthew 19:30: "But many that are *first* shall be *last*; and the *last* shall be *first*." The effect is memorable.

As you write, and especially as you revise for style, search for opportunities to place sentence elements in parallel structure. Remember that parallelism can occur with *clauses and phrases, especially prepositional phrases*. Often, the parallels will be hidden in the sentences of your draft, but they can be brought out with a minimum of labor. After you've acquired the habit of casting your thinking in parallel structures, they will rapidly become a staple of your stylistic repertoire, making your prose more graceful, clear, and logically connected.

PERIODIC AND CUMULATIVE SENTENCES: TWO EFFECTIVE SENTENCE SHAPES

The shape of a sentence governs the way it delivers information. The order of clauses, especially the placement of the main clause, affects what the sentence means.

There are two common sentence shapes defined by the location of their main clauses; these are known as *periodic* and *cumulative* sentences. The periodic sentence is built on suspense and delay: it puts maximum emphasis on the way the sentence ends. The cumulative sentence aims for upfront impact; there is no suspense, but rather, the rolling momentum of an extended follow-through.

The Periodic Sentence: Delay Closure to Achieve Emphasis

The main clause in a periodic sentence builds to a climax that is not completed until the end. Often, a piece of the main clause (such as the subject) is located early in the sentence, as in the example on the next page.

> The <u>way</u> that beverage companies market health—"No
> Preservatives," "No Artificial Colors," "All Natural," "Real
> Brewed"—<u>is</u> often, because the product also contains a high
> percentage of sugar or fructose, <u>misleading</u>.

We have underlined parts of the main clause to clarify how various modifiers interrupt it. The effect is suspenseful: not until the final word does the sentence consummate its fundamental idea. Pieces of the main clause are spread out across the sentence.

Another version of the periodic sentence locates the entire main clause at the end, after introductory modifiers.

> Using labels that market health—such as "No Preservatives,"
> "No Artificial Colors," "All Natural," and "Real Brewed"—while
> producing drinks that contain a high percentage of sugar or
> fructose, <u>beverage companies are misleading</u>.

As previously discussed, the end of a sentence normally receives emphasis. When you use a periodic construction, the pressure on the end intensifies because the sentence needs the end to complete its grammatical sense. In both of the preceding examples, the sentences "snap shut." They string readers along, delaying *grammatical closure*—the point at which the sentences can stand alone independently—until they arrive at climactic ends. (Periodic sentences are also known as *climactic sentences.*)

You should be aware of one risk that accompanies periodic constructions. If the delay lasts too long because there are too many "interrupters" before the main clause gets completed, your readers may forget the subject being predicated. To illustrate, let's add more subordinated material to one of the preceding examples.

> The way that beverage companies market health—"No
> Preservatives," "No Artificial Colors," "All Natural," "Real
> Brewed"—is often, because the product also contains a high
> percentage of sugar or fructose, not just what New Agers
> would probably term "immoral" and "misleading" but what a
> government agency such as the Food and Drug Administration
> should find illegal.

Arguably, the additions (the "not just" and "but" clauses after "fructose") push the sentence into incoherence. The main clause has been stretched past the breaking point. If readers don't get lost in such a sentence, they are at least likely to get irritated and wish the writer would finally get to the point.

Nonetheless, with a little care, periodic sentences can be extraordinarily useful in giving emphasis. If you are revising and want to underscore some point, try letting the sentence snap shut upon it. Often the periodic *potential* will already be present in the draft, and stylistic editing can bring it out more forcefully. Note how minor the revisions are in the following example:

> **Draft:** The novelist Virginia Woolf suffered from acute anxieties for most of her life. She had several breakdowns and finally committed suicide on the eve of World War II.

> **Revision:** Suffering from acute anxieties for most of her life, the novelist Virginia <u>Woolf</u> not only <u>had</u> several <u>breakdowns but</u>, finally, on the eve of World War II, <u>committed suicide</u>.

This revision has made two primary changes. It has combined two short sentences into a longer sentence, and it has made the sentence periodic by stringing out the main clause (italicized). What is the effect of this revision? Stylistically speaking, the revision radiates a greater sense of its writer's authority. The information has been arranged for us. After the opening dependent clause ("Suffering…"), the subject of the main clause ("Woolf") is introduced, and the predicate is protracted in a *not only/ but* parallelism. The interrupters that follow "had several breakdowns" ("finally, on the eve of World War II") increase the suspense, before the sentence snaps shut with "committed suicide."

In general, when you construct a periodic sentence with care, you can give readers the sense that you are in control of your material. You do not seem to be writing off the top of your head, but rather from a position of greater detachment, rationally composing your meaning.

The Cumulative Sentence: Start Fast to Build Momentum

The cumulative sentence is in many respects the opposite of the periodic. Rather than delaying the main clause or its final piece, the cumulative sentence begins by presenting the independent clause as a foundation and then *accumulates* a number of modifications and qualifications. As the following examples illustrate, the independent clause provides quick grammatical closure, freeing the rest of the sentence to amplify and develop the main idea.

> <u>Robert F. Kennedy was assassinated</u> by Sirhan B. Sirhan, a twenty-four-year-old Palestinian immigrant, prone to occultism and unsophisticated left-wing politics and sociopathically devoted to leaving his mark in history, even if as a notorious figure.

> <u>There are two piano concerti</u> composed solely for the left hand, one by Serge Prokofiev and one by Maurice Ravel, and both commissioned by Paul Wittgenstein, a concert pianist (and the brother of the famous philosopher Ludwig Wittgenstein) who had lost his right hand in combat during World War I.

Anchored by the main clause, a cumulative sentence moves serially through one thing and another thing and the next thing, close to the associative manner in which people think. To an extent, then, cumulative sentences can convey more immediacy and a more conversational tone than can other sentence shapes. Look at the following example:

> The film version of *Lady Chatterley's Lover* changed D. H. Lawrence's famous novel a lot, omitting the heroine's adolescent experience in Germany, making her husband much older than she, leaving out her father and sister, including a lot more lovemaking, and virtually eliminating all of the philosophizing about sex and marriage.

Here, we get the impression of a mind in the act of thinking. Using the generalization of changes in the film as a base, the sentence then appends a series of parallel participial phrases ("omitting," "making," "leaving," "including," "eliminating") that moves forward associatively, gathering a range of information and laying out possibilities. Cumulative sentences perform this outlining and prospecting function very effectively. On the other hand, if we were to add four or five more changes to the sentence, readers would likely find it tedious, or worse, directionless. As with periodic sentences, overloading the shape can short-circuit its desired effect.

Try This 18.7: Write Periodic and Cumulative Sentences

If you consciously practice using periodic and cumulative constructions, you will be surprised how quickly you can learn to produce their respective effects in your own writing. You will also discover that both of these sentence shapes are already present in your prose in some undiscovered and thus unrefined way. It is often simply a case of bringing out what is already there. Try including at least one of each in the next paper you write.

Toward that end, compose a simple sentence on any subject, preferably one with a direct object. Then construct two variations expanding it, one periodic and one cumulative. Here, as a model, is an example using the core sentence "James Joyce was a gifted singer."

> **Periodic:** Although known primarily as one of the greatest novelists of the twentieth century, James Joyce, the son of a local political functionary who loved to tip a few too many at the pub, was also a gifted—and prizewinning—singer.

> **Cumulative:** James Joyce was a gifted singer, having listened at his father's knee to the ballads sung in pubs, having won an all-Ireland prize in his early teens, and having possessed a miraculous ear for the inflections of common speech that was to serve him throughout the career for which he is justly famous, that of a novelist.

Can't think of a core sentence? Okay, here are a few:

> Why do airlines show such mediocre films?

> Madison Bumgarner and friends brought a flag to San Francisco.

> Every senator is a millionaire.

CUT EXTRA WORDS TO ACHIEVE GREATER DIRECTNESS

If you can reduce verbiage, your prose will communicate more directly and effectively. In cutting the fat, you need to consider both the diction and the syntax. When it comes to diction, the way to eliminate superfluous words is deceptively simple: ask yourself if you need all of the words you've included to say what you want to say. Such revision requires an aggressive attitude. *Expect* to find unnecessary restatements or intensifiers such as "quite" and "very" that add words but not significance.

Sometimes, by the way, the problem is not just a matter of syntax but a matter of confidence. A lot of writing becomes obscure because the writer is trying to hide what he or she has to say with various "throat clearings" and other defensive verbiage. If you don't say anything clearly enough to be understood, you can't be accused of being wrong. If you find yourself bogged down in language, take a moment to write as directly as possible an answer to the question, "What I'm really trying to say here is…"

BEGINNING WITH "IT IS" OR "THERE IS": ADVANTAGES AND DISADVANTAGES

Sentences that begin with "It is" or "There is" are known as *expletive* constructions. The term *expletive* comes from a Latin word that means "serving to fill out." Most of the time, you can streamline your prose by getting rid of expletive constructions. Consider how the expletives function in the following examples:

> *There* are several prototypes for the artificial heart.

> *It* is obvious that the American West exerted a profound influence on the photography of Ansel Adams.

Compare these with versions that simply eliminate the expletives.

> The artificial heart has several prototypes.

> The American West exerted a profound influence on the photography of Ansel Adams.

The "It is obvious that" opening, for example, causes the grammar of the sentence to subordinate its real emphasis.

In some cases, though, an expletive can provide useful emphasis, as in the following example: "There are three primary reasons that you should avoid litigation." Although this sentence grammatically subordinates its primary content (avoiding litigation), the expletive provides a useful frame for what is to follow.

In an excellent book entitled *Rhetorical Grammar* (Longman, 2009), Martha Kolln and Loretta Gray make the case for using what they term "the there-transformation" as a strategy for adding emphasis. They do so by focusing on what they call "the rhythm pattern" of the sentence. Compare "There's a stranger standing on the porch," where the accent falls on "stranger," with the end focus of "The stranger stands on the porch." Here are two more examples of their advice on using rhythm patterns to provide emphasis, which we offer in part to demonstrate how easily you can begin attuning yourself to shapes:

- **End focus:** a common rhythm pattern in which, if you read aloud, you can hear the stress near the end, in the last or next to last unit of information. Kolln offers as examples "Barbara wrecked her motorcycle yesterday" and "My book for chemistry class cost almost 60 dollars." Note how the pressure falls on the "yes" in yesterday and the "six" in sixty and "dol" in dollars.
- **Interrupting the rhythm pattern:** a sentence marked by an inserted interrupter—Kolln offers "Other ways, in fact, are much more common." Here, the interrupter attracts emphasis by standing out.

STATIC VERSUS ACTIVE VERBS: "TO BE" OR "NOT TO BE"

Verbs energize a sentence. They do the work, connecting the parts of the sentence with each other. In a sentence of the subject–verb–direct object pattern, the verb—known as a *transitive verb*—functions as a kind of engine, driving the subject into the predicate, as in the following examples.

John F. Kennedy effectively *manipulated* his image in the media.

Thomas Jefferson *embraced* the idea of America as a country of yeoman farmers.

By contrast, "is" and other forms of the verb "to be" provide an equal sign between the subject and the predicate but otherwise tell us nothing about the relationship between them. "To be" is an *intransitive* verb; it cannot take a direct object. Compare the two preceding transitive examples with the following versions of the same sentences using forms of the verb "to be."

John F. Kennedy *was* effective at the manipulation of his image in the media.

Thomas Jefferson's idea *was* for America to be a country of yeoman farmers.

Rather than making things happen through an active transitive verb, these sentences let everything just hang around in a state of being. In the first version, Kennedy did something—*manipulated* his image—but in the second he just *is* (or *was*), and the energy of the original verb has been siphoned into an abstract noun, "manipulation." The revised Jefferson example suffers from a similar lack of momentum compared with the original version: the syntax doesn't help the sentence get anywhere.

Certain situations, however, dictate the use of forms of "to be." For definitions in particular, the equal sign that an "is" provides works well. For instance, "Organic gardening *is* a method of growing crops without using synthetic fertilizers or pesticides." As with choosing between active and passive voices, the decision to use "to be" or not should be just that—a conscious decision on your part.

Table 18.1 Static and Active Verbs

Action Hidden in Nouns and "To Be" Verbs	Action Emphasized in Verbs
The <u>cost</u> of the book *is* ten dollars.	The book *costs* ten dollars.
The <u>acknowledgment</u> of the fact *is* increasingly widespread that television *is* a <u>replacement</u> for reading in American culture.	People increasingly *acknowledge* that television *has replaced* reading in American culture.
A computer *is* ostensibly a labor-<u>saving</u> device—until the hard drive *is* the victim of a <u>crash</u>.	A computer ostensibly *saves* labor—until the hard drive *crashes*.
In the <u>laying</u> of a flagstone patio, the important preliminary steps to remember *are* the <u>excavating</u> and the <u>leveling</u> of the area and then the <u>filling</u> of it with a fine grade of gravel.	To *lay* a flagstone patio, first *excavate* and *level* the area and then *fill* it with a fine grade of gravel.

If you can train yourself to eliminate every unnecessary use of "to be" in a draft, you will make your prose more vital and direct. In most cases, you will find the verb that you need to substitute for "is" lurking somewhere in the sentence in some other grammatical form. In the preceding sentence about Kennedy, "manipulate" is implicit in "manipulation." In Table 18.1, each of the examples in the left-hand column uses a form of "to be" for its verb (italicized) and contains a potentially strong active verb lurking in the sentence in some other form (underlined). These "lurkers" have been converted into active verbs (italicized) in the revisions in the right-hand column.

Clearly, the examples in the left-hand column have problems other than their reliance on forms of "to be"—notably wordiness. But as Richard Lanham first articulated in his excellent *Revising Prose* (Longman, 2006), "to be" syntax tends to encourage circumlocution and verbosity. Lanhan named this kind of writing "The Official Style," and he attacked it for its flabbiness, which he traced to its addiction to forms of "to be," the passive voice, and strings of prepositions in place of concrete verbs in the active voice (see the next section). Lanham's proposes a series of steps, which he calls The Paramedic Method, for doing triage on Official Style sentences. He instructs writers to mark all of the prepositions, identify the forms of *to be*, find the action buried in the sentence and make it into an active verb.

Try This 18.8: Finding the Active Verb

Take a paper you've written and circle the sentences that rely on forms of "to be." Then, examine the other words in these sentences, looking for "lurkers." Rewrite the sentences, converting the lurkers into vigorous verbs. You will probably discover many lurkers, and your revisions will acquire more energy and directness.

ACTIVE AND PASSIVE VOICE: EMPHASIZING THE DOER OR THE ACTION

In the *active voice,* the grammatical subject acts; in the *passive voice,* the subject is acted upon. Here are two examples.

Active: Adam Smith wrote *The Wealth of Nations* in 1776.

Passive: *The Wealth of Nations* was written by Adam Smith in 1776.

The two sentences convey identical information, but the emphasis differs—the first focuses on the author, the second on the book. As the examples illustrate, using the passive normally results in a longer sentence than using the active. If we consider how to convert the passive into the active, you can see why. In the passive, the verb requires a form of "to be" plus a past participle. (For more on participles, see the Glossary of Grammatical Terms in Chapter 19.) In this case, the active verb "wrote" becomes the passive verb "was written," the grammatical subject ("Smith") becomes the object of the preposition "by," and the direct object ("*The Wealth of Nations*") becomes the grammatical subject.

Now consider the activity described in the two versions of this example: a man wrote a book. That's what happened in life. The grammar of the active version captures that action most clearly: the grammatical subject ("Smith") performs the action, and the direct object *("The Wealth of Nations")* receives it, just as in life. By contrast, the passive version alters the close link between the syntax and the event: the object of the action in life *("The Wealth of Nations")* has become the grammatical subject, whereas the doer in life ("Smith") has become the grammatical object of a prepositional phrase.

Note, too, that the passive would allow us to omit "Smith" altogether: "*The Wealth of Nations* was written in 1776." A reader who desired to know more and was not aware of the author would not appreciate this sentence. More troubling, the passive can also be used to conceal the doer of an action—not "I made a mistake" (active) but rather "A mistake has been made" (passive).

In sum, there are three reasons for avoiding the passive voice when you can: (1) it's longer, (2) its grammatical relationships often reverse what happened in life, and (3) it can omit the performer responsible for the action.

On the other hand, sometimes there are good reasons for using the passive. If you want to emphasize the object or recipient of the action rather than the performer, the passive will do that for you: "*The Wealth of Nations* was written in 1776 by Adam Smith" places the stress on the book. The passive is also preferable when the doer remains unknown: "The president has been shot!" is probably a better sentence than "Some unknown assailant has shot the president!"

Especially in the natural sciences, the use of the passive voice is a standard practice. There are sound reasons for this disciplinary convention: science tends to focus on what happens to something in a given experiment, rather than on the person performing the experiment. Compare the following sentences.

Passive: Separation of the protein was achieved by using an electrophoretic gel.

Active: The researcher used an electrophoretic gel to separate the protein.

If you opted for the active version, the emphasis would rest, illogically, on the agent of the action (the researcher) rather than on what happened and how (electrophoretic separation of the protein).

More generally, the passive voice can provide a way to avoid using the pronoun "I," whether for reasons of convention, as indicated earlier, or for other reasons. For example, the following passive sentence begins a business memo from a supervisor to the staff in her office.

> The Inventory and Reprint departments have recently been restructured and merged.

Like many passive sentences, this one names no actor; we do not know for sure who did the restructuring and merging, though we might imagine that the author of the memo is the responsible party. The supervisor might, then, have written the sentence in the active voice.

> I have recently restructured and merged the Inventory and Reprint departments.

But the active version is less satisfactory than the passive one for two reasons: one of practical emphasis and one of sensitivity to the audience (tone). First, the fact of the changes is more important for the memo's readers than is the announcement of who made the changes. The passive sentence appropriately emphasizes the changes; the active sentence inappropriately emphasizes the person who made the changes. Second, the emphasis of the active sentence on "I" (the supervisor) risks alienating the readers by taking an autocratic tone and by seeming to exclude all others from possible credit for the presumably worthwhile reorganization.

On balance, "consider" is the operative term when you choose between passive and active as you revise the syntax of your drafts. Recognize that you do have choices—in emphasis, in relative directness, and in economy. All things being equal and disciplinary conventions permitting, the active is usually the better choice.

Try This 18.9: Converting Passive to Active

Identify all of the sentences that use the passive voice in one of your papers. Then, rewrite these sentences, converting passive into active wherever appropriate. Finally, count the total number of words, the total number of prepositions, and the average sentence length (words per sentence) in each version. What do you discover?

For more practice, here's another exercise. Compose a paragraph of at least half a page in which you use only the passive voice and verbs of being, followed by a paragraph in which you use only the active voice. Then, rewrite the first paragraph using only active voice, if possible, and rewrite the second paragraph using only passive voice and verbs of being as much as possible. How do the paragraphs differ in shape, length, and coherence?

Sentence Style in Science Writing: A Biochemistry Professor Speaks

Most of the advice offered in this chapter also applies to the very specialized writing style expected in lab reports and other formal science writing. Like academic style in general, science writing is concerned with combining ideas in order to locate emphasis appropriately and to create greater concision than a string of simple sentences would allow. The voice, ethos, and tone of science writing is typically quite muted. Active verbs appear, but the style goes out of its way to not call attention to itself, and especially not to the writer. This muted quality is, in fact, true of most academic writing, but it is markedly so in the sciences.

In the following Voice from Across the Curriculum, biochemistry professor Keri Colabroy shares the basic guidelines for constructing sentences in scientific style that she provides for her science majors.

Voices from Across The Curriculum

Subjects (the "actor" is absent)

- Passive voice

    Yes: The gel was run; No: I ran the gel.

    Better: The protein migrated at a molecular weight of… (data first, not procedure)

- Pronouns—it's safer to avoid them

Verbs (qualify, qualify, qualify…)

- Do: demonstrate, indicate, suggest, construct, deliver, observe
- Don't: show, prove, make

Sentences

- Don't say in two sentences what you can say with one (embedding).
- Subordinate and coordinate.

Words

- Data are plural.
- When making observations, use academic, not conversational language.
- Choose words for precision and tone (qualify your verbs, not your adjectives).

—Keri Colabroy, Professor of Biochemistry

ABOUT PRESCRIPTIVE STYLE MANUALS: A WORD OF WARNING

Every change in style is a change in meaning. Although style guides can be very useful when they illuminate the range of choices a writer has and the implications of those choices, they often value one style and tone over another as self-evidently good and right. In so doing, they imply a rhetorical preference for a particular way of approaching the world in speech, a preference that may not actually match your style or the style of a particular discipline in which you are writing.

Despite Strunk & White's rule (in *Elements of Style*), three words are not better than six in every rhetorical situation. And their edict against it notwithstanding, passive voice has its place, its own special advantages. As we hope you have seen from the foregoing discussion, active is not always better. Much depends on context. The key to growing as a stylist is learning to see the choices. *(See Chapter 1, the Short Take entitled "A Quick Word on Style Guides".)*

EXPERIMENT!

A key idea of this chapter is that there are not necessarily right and wrong choices when it comes to sentence style but instead better and best choices for particular situations. The from-the-hip plain style of a memo or a set of operating instructions for your lawnmower is very likely not the best style choice for a good-bye letter to a best friend, a diplomatic talk on a sensitive political situation, or an analysis of guitar styles in contemporary jazz.

Is style a function of character and personality? Is it, in short, personal, and thus something to be preserved in the face of would-be meddlers carrying style manuals and grammar guides? Well, as you might guess at this point in the book, the answer is yes and no. We all need to find ways of using words that do not succumb to the mind-numbing environment of verbal cliché in which we dwell. It helps then, to become more self-conscious about style and not assume that it is inborn. Staying locked into one way of writing because that is "your style" is as limiting as remaining locked into only one way of thinking.

This chapter has presented some terms and techniques for experimenting with sentence styles. Equipped with these, you might profitably begin to read and listen for style more self-consciously. Find models. When a style appeals to you, figure out what makes it work. Copy sentences you like. Try imitating them. Know, by the way, that imitation will not erase your own style—it will allow you to experiment with new moves, new shapes into which to cast your words.

GUIDELINES FOR THE RHETORIC OF THE SENTENCE

1. Revise sentences to clarify their meaning by revealing the organization of thought. Align like with like, set difference against difference, and in general use form to emphasize what's important and demote what is not.

2. Become aware of your own syntactic habits. What is your "go-to sentence" and how might you build upon it to extend your range and force?

3. Cut the fat. Don't use five words ("due to the fact that") when one will do ("because"). Root out expletives that needlessly subordinate ("It is true that…"). Avoid redundancy.

4. Tighten the syntax of your sentences by energizing the verbs. The active voice generally achieves directness and economy; it will promote clarity and cut fat.

5. Look for potentially strong active verbs "lurking" in sentences that use a form of *to be*. Beware habitual use of *to be* and passives, since these forms tend to blur or submerge the action, omit its performers, and generally lack momentum.

6. Look at the order and arrangement of clauses. Are ideas of equal importance in coordinate constructions? Have you used subordination to rank ideas? Have your sentences exploited the end as a position of emphasis?

7. Look at the shapes of your sentences. Do they use parallelism to keep your ideas clear? Where do you find opportunities for composing periodic and cumulative sentences that revision can bring out?

Assignments: Stylistic Analyses—The Rhetoric of the Sentence

1. **Compare the Style of Two Writers**. Analyze the style—the syntax but also the diction—of two writers doing a similar kind of writing; for example, two sportswriters, two rock music reviewers, or two presidents. Study first the similarities. What style characteristics does this type of writing seem to invite? Then study the differences. How is one writer recognizable through his or her style? The American Rhetoric website is a wonderful place to go hunting.

2. **Analyze Your Own Style**. Assemble some pieces you have written, preferably of a similar type, and study them for style. Do you have some favorite stylistic moves? What sentence shapes (simple, compound, complex, compound-complex, highly parallel, periodic, or cumulative) dominate in your writing? What verbs? Do you use forms of "to be" a lot, and so forth?

3. **Find Go-To Sentences**. As we discuss in Chapter 2, whether we recognize it or not, most of us have a "go-to" sentence—the sentence shape we repeatedly go to as we write and talk. If a person's "go-to" sentence takes the form "Although _____, the fact is that _____," we might see that person as inclined to qualify his or her thoughts ("Although") and disinclined to immediately impose his or her ideas on others ("the fact that" comes in the second half of the sentence, where it gets a lot of emphasis but is also delayed and qualified by the sentence's opening observation).

   First, select one sentence in something you've been reading that you think is typical of that writer's way of putting sentences together. Describe that sentence shape and speculate about what it accomplishes and how it reveals the writer's characteristic mode of thinking in some way.

   Then find a "go-to" sentence of your own in something that you've written. What does this structure reveal to you about how you think? Tip: You can also use The Method to locate "go-to" sentences. Look for repeated conjunctions or subordinators, such as "x; however, y" or "although x, nevertheless, y," or "not only x, but also y."

4. **Discuss the Style of Sentences You Like**. This exercise is a companion to Try This 18.2; it aims to give you more practice at seeing the shapes of sentences. Listed below are five sentences our students like; use these or find your own candidates. As in the Try This, do the following operations:

   - identify which of the four types it is
   - underline the subject and verb of the main clause(s)
   - double-underline the subordinate clauses
   - circle the coordinating conjunctions and subordinating conjunctions

   In addition, bring to bear the other lenses you've acquired in the latter parts of the chapter. What do you notice about the verbs? The order of clauses? Where do you detect elements of the periodic and cumulative, the antithetical or chiasmic? Write a paragraph or two about the style of each sentence.

   a. "Where is the powerful being who will crush all these reptiles who corrupt everything they touch, and whose venomous bites stir up our citizens, transforming their political assemblies into gladiatorial arenas where each passion, each interest, finds apologists and an army?" (Chaumet, attorney of the Parisian Commune, Sept 5, 1793)

   b. From newspaper baron Lord Northcliffe: "News is what somebody somewhere is trying to suppress. The rest is advertising." (Ben McGrath, "Roid Warriors." *The New Yorker*, 9 March 2009)

   c. "On the all-important question of power—the efficacy of power, the morality of power, the desirability of power—American and European perspectives are diverging." (Kagan, Robert. "Why the United States and Europe See the World Differently." *Policy Review* 113. (2002))

   d. "Republican jibes that the budget was 'socialist' should be treated with the respect they deserve, which is to say none: after a major rise in outlays this year, due to the stimulus package, federal spending as a share of the gross domestic product is projected to fall back to twenty-two percent by 2013, which represents a rise of just one percent over last year's figure." (John Cassidy, "Harder Times." *The New Yorker*, 16 March 2009.)

   e. "Most men gamble with her, and gain all, and lose all, as her wheel rolls." (Ralph Waldo Emerson. "Self Reliance." *The Essential Writings of Ralph Waldo Emerson*. Ed. Brooks Atkinson. New York: Modern Library, 2000).

5. **Analyze the Gettysburg Address**. For many people, Lincoln's Gettysburg Address is one of the best examples of the careful matching of style to situation. Delivered after a long talk by a previous speaker at the dedication of a Civil War battlefield on a rainy day, the speech composed by Abraham Lincoln (some say on the back of an envelope) is a masterpiece of style. Analyze its

sentence structure, such as its use of parallelism, antithesis, and other kinds of repetition. Which features of Lincoln's style seem most important in creating the overall effect of the piece? Or do this with any popular journalist whom you read regularly and who you think has an especially effective style. Or look for another inspirational speech and see if such occasional writing has anything in common. (You can download and print the Gettysburg Address from many sites on the web.)

6. **Do a Full-fledged Stylistic Revision of a Paper**. The best choice might well be an essay you already have revised, resubmitted, and had returned, because in that case, you will be less likely to get distracted by conceptual revision and so can concentrate on stylistic issues. As you revise, try to accomplish each of the following:

   a. Sharpen the diction.

   b. Blend concrete and abstract diction.

   c. Experiment with the order of and relation among subordinate and coordinate clauses.

   d. Choose more knowingly between active and passive voice.

   e. Cut the fat, especially by eliminating unnecessary "to be" constructions.

   f. Vary sentence length and shape.

   g. Use parallelism.

   h. Experiment with periodic and cumulative sentences.

   i. Fine-tune the tone.

Chapter 19

Revising for Correctness: Grammar and Punctuation

THIS CHAPTER ADDRESSES THE ISSUE of grammatical correctness and offers ways of recognizing and fixing (or avoiding) the most important errors. Unlike editing for style, which involves you in making choices between more and less effective ways of phrasing, editing for correctness locates you in the domain of right or wrong. As you will see, there are usually a number of ways to correct an error, so you are still concerned with making choices, but leaving the error uncorrected is not a viable option.

There is more to thinking about grammar than the quest for error-free writing, as Chapter 18 on sentence style demonstrates, with its emphasis on how to analyze writers' syntactical choices and how to think about the relationship between a writer's style and his or her characteristic ways of thinking. Studying the grammar rules in this chapter will enable you to find your way around in a sentence more easily, and thus, to build better sentences.

The first part of this chapter makes the case for learning to recognize a pattern of error in your drafts and learning to prioritize the most serious problems, creating a *hierarchy of error*, rather than treating (and worrying about) all errors equally and all at the same time. Achieving grammatical correctness is a matter of both knowledge—how to recognize and avoid errors—and timing: when to narrow your focus to proofreading.

NINE BASIC WRITING ERRORS

- Sentence fragments
- Comma splices and fused (run-on) sentences
- Errors in subject–verb agreement
- Shifts in sentence structure (faulty predication)
- Errors in pronoun reference
- Misplaced modifiers and dangling participles
- Errors in using possessive apostrophes
- Comma errors
- Spelling/diction errors that interfere with meaning

For each of these, the chapter offers a definition with examples and then talks you through how to fix it—with a little "test yourself" section at the end.

At the end of the chapter, a brief Glossary of Grammatical Terms defines and illustrates many of the key terms used earlier in the chapter and throughout the book. Following this chapter, you will find an appendix that provides solutions to the various "Test Yourself" examples that point up the chapter's lessons.

A great many readers regard technical errors as an inattention to detail that also signals sloppiness at more important levels of thinking. If you produce writing that contains such errors, you risk not only distracting readers from your message but also undermining your authority to deliver the message in the first place.

THE CONCEPT OF BASIC WRITING ERRORS (BWEs)

You get a paper back, and it's a sea of red ink. But if you look more closely, you'll often find that you haven't made a million mistakes—you've made only a few, but over and over in various forms. This phenomenon is what the rhetorician Mina Shaughnessy in a book called *Errors & Expectations* addressed in creating the category of "basic writing errors," or BWEs. Shaughnessy argues that, in order to improve your writing for style and correctness, you need to do two things:

- Look for a *pattern of error,* which will require you to understand your own logic in the mistakes you typically make.

- Recognize that not all errors are created equal, which means that you need to *address errors in some order of importance*—beginning with those most likely to interfere with your readers' understanding.

This chapter's BWE guide, Nine Basic Writing Errors and How to Fix Them, reflects Shaughnessy's view. It does not cover *all* of the rules of grammar, punctuation, diction, and usage, such as where to place the comma or period when you close a quotation or whether or not to write out numerals. Instead, it emphasizes the errors that are potentially the most damaging to the clarity of your writing and to your credibility with readers. We have arranged the error types in a hierarchy, moving in descending order of severity (from most to least problematic).

As in our discussion of style in Chapter 18, the key premises of this chapter are that a sentence is made up of moveable parts and that sentences disclose the relationships among those parts. Keep these premises in mind, and you will see what the errors have in common.

WHY GRAMMAR ERRORS MAKE SOME PEOPLE SO ANGRY

Grammar is a volatile subject. Grammatical errors evoke not just disapproval but anger in some people. Why? Well, clearly correct grammar matters. Readers should not have to struggle to figure out where your sentences begin and end or what goes with what. But the fact that correctness matters—that correctness is necessary to being taken seriously as a writer—does not account for the sheer venom that goes into spotting other people's grammatical errors. *(See Chapter 1, the Short Take entitled A Quick Word on Style Guides.)*

Language use is social and conventional. Conforming to the rules is, in a sense, a sign that you agree to be governed by the same conventions that others conform to. Perhaps this is why the intentional sentence fragment has the impact that it does. Really. The gesture makes the writer's style seem daring. It says, "You and I both recognize that I control the standard conventions with sufficient assurance to break them on purpose, not by accident."

USAGE: HOW LANGUAGE CUSTOMS CHANGE

Errors of grammar are relatively stable and locked down. "The eggs was tasty" is wrong; so is "Obama are President" and "Obama is Presidents." But usage, a kind of troublesome and embarrassing cousin to grammar, is a more vexed subject. According to the *Oxford English Dictionary*, usage has to do with "established or customary use or employment of language, words, expressions, etc." Established by whom? Customary within which what group? Usage, in short, tends to be less clear cut than grammar.

That is why some dictionaries offer brief paragraphs of discussion from a "usage panel"—a group of experts who weigh in on what is proper and improper in language use. Most of the usage guides you will find at the back of grammar handbooks offer a range of examples of usage. At one end of the range, there are examples in which one form is clearly preferred and another disapproved.

Usage: Some Examples of Right & Wrong versus Etiquette

Here is a set of examples, organized on a sliding scale, from clearly distinguished right and wrong to less defensible distinctions.

- **fewer vs. less**: Countable things are fewer: fewer pencils; amounts that can't be counted are less: less support. This is a helpful distinction, one the language needs.

- **good vs. well**: *Good* is an adjective, a part of speech that modifies (describes) nouns and other adjectives. *It was a good movie. Well* is an adverb, a part of speech that modifies a verb or another adverb. *She does not feel well. Good* modifies *movie*; *well* modifies *feel*. This is another helpful distinction; therefore, most people consider this word choice a matter of right and wrong.

- **can vs. may**: *Can* refers to what one is able to do; *may* refers to what one is permitted to do. *He can spit across the classroom, but according to the teacher, he may not.* Again, this distinction conveys a meaningful difference, although in actual practice, the word *may* is starting to lose its clout—it sounds fussy to many contemporary ears.

- **between vs. among**: *Between* refers to two items, *among* to more than two. *The difference between sushi and sashimi is more easily understood than the differences among sushi, sashimi and maki.* In this case, we can clearly see that if you used *between* in both cases, a reader would still be able to make sense of the sentence, but the use of *among* is helpful—it lets us know that more than two items are coming. Still, as you can see, this example of usage is less significant, more a matter of good manners, than *can* vs. *may.* Nonetheless, it is arguably a useful distinction.

- **different from vs. different than**: Some say a writer should not use *different than,* because *than* is comparative, but different already signifies that a comparison is coming, so you should always says *different from.* Let's use this example—and there are others like it—as an emblem of a preference for which there is not really much of a reason.

- **ending a sentence with a preposition**: the prescription that one should not end a sentence with a preposition, or if you will, that a preposition is a part of speech you should not end a sentence with, is a case of rather arbitrary usage. In this same category goes the split infinitive—the practice of locating a word inside a *to* + verb construction, such as *to boldly go where no one has gone before.* In a formal setting—an application to law school, say—you would want to be careful to avoid these usages, even though they are not actually wrong.

Why then do some guardians of the language insist that we not end sentences with prepositions? Is it snobbery? Etiquette? First of all, let's admit that etiquette serves a definite purpose, as anyone who has gone out to dinner and had the misfortune to sit next to a food fight will attest. To be understanding, let's assume that the person who enforces usage distinctions as hard-and-fast rules, even when they are not, is a person who wishes to maintain standards in the face of change. And that too is a position one may (and can!) respect.

But the fact is that the language is always changing, not just with the addition of new words to the standard dictionaries, but also with the circumstances of usage— "the established or customary use or employment of language, words, expressions, etc." Ultimately, a panel of experts cannot control usage, and that is a healthy thing, allowing a language to evolve over time.

When Usage Begins to Change Grammar

Which brings us back to the issue of grammatical correctness, a subject that impelled this digression into usage in the first place (yes, we know it's a fragment). Usage, and more particularly changes in usage, bear on grammar because grammar, although relatively fixed, does not stand still, and the doorway through which grammar changes is the same one through which usage walks.

Here are three common examples of how changing usage appears to be inspiring a change in the grammatical conventions of right and wrong. These changes have not yet occurred, but arguably, they are in the process of occurring.

- **possessive apostrophes:** an increasing number of writers simply leave these out. If one writes, *The cars fender was dented* (not car's) or *Andy Pettittes slider is the best in the American League* (not Pettitte's), virtually every reader will understand the meaning, though not as quickly as the apostrophe would allow.

- ***I*** vs. ***me*,** especially in prepositional phrases: This one has to do with what grammarians call the case of pronouns. We use one form of a pronoun when it is in the subject and another when it is the object of a verb or a preposition. For example,

- *My mother and I argue about grammar*—not *My mother and me*. We would not say "*Me argues about grammar*." *I* is in the subjective case; *me* is in the objective case.

- *According to my mother and me, grammar matters a lot*—not *According to my mother and I*. We would not say *According to I*. "According to" is a preposition, so you have to use the objective case, as the pronoun in question is the object of the preposition.

But increasingly, we hear native speakers saying things such as *Joe and me are going to get a beer* or *For Jill and I, voting is an undeniable civic duty, virtually an ethical imperative*. In the first example, a speaker might say *Joe and me* because it sounds "natural," that is, unpretentious, as unpretentious as having a beer. In the second example, a speaker might say *For Jill and I* because (and we're not sure why this is!), the use of "and I" sometimes sounds classier, more high style, and in a sentence where lofty concepts such as civic duty and ethical imperatives occur, you might wish to sound classy. But "I" in "For Jill and I" must be changed to "me," the objective case, because it is the object of the preposition "For."

- **who** versus **whom**: This is another version of the pronoun problem. *Who* is subjective case; *whom* is objective case. For example: *I want to know who ate the last slice of pie I left in the refrigerator*. Compare that with *Ask not for whom the bell tolls*—where *whom* is the object of the preposition *for*. Yet increasingly, speakers seem to fear working out the grammar necessary to figure out if the who/whom in question is a subject or an object, so they tend either to eliminate *whom* altogether and just use *who* for every case, or they assume that *whom* is classier, as they do "and I," and they end up misusing *whom*. Here are examples:

  - *Who is Derek Jeter going to sign with, now that he has become a free agent?* This sentence is grammatically incorrect: we need a *Whom* to be the object of the preposition *with*—*With whom will Jeter sign?*

  - *I read a book by the cognitive therapist whom is most famous for formulating rational emotive therapy*. The loftiness of the topic misleads the writer into using the supposedly classier *whom* even though grammar tells us the pronoun *who* is in the subjective case.

Usage as Cultural Marker

You can think of usage in terms of markers—indicators of something. So, for example:

- usage as marker for informal, conversational versus formal style:
  And then she goes, "that's the silliest thing I've ever heard" versus *And then she says*, . . . And some people disallow contractions as too informal.

- usage as marker for social class:
  Where is he at? versus *Where is he?*
  I ain't going versus *I am not going*.

- usage as gender marker:
  Poetess versus *poet*, *actress* versus *actor*, *waitress* versus *waiter* or *wait-person*

Most people have not heard the word *poetess*—how long before the same will be said of actress? (The *-ess* suffix indicating female is now considered sexist by many people because it relegates women to a separate category.)

Try This 19.1: Discover the Rationale for Usage Choices

Research the following pairs of terms. Locate the usage "rules" that govern them, and if you can, uncover the rationale that informs these rules.

Try and / try to

Shall / will

Disinterested / uninterested

Raise / rise

WHAT PUNCTUATION MARKS SAY: A QUICK-HIT GUIDE

These little signs really aren't that hard to use correctly, folks. A few of them will be treated in more specific contexts in the upcoming discussion of BWEs, but here are the basic rules of punctuation for the five basic signs.

The **period** [.] marks the end of a sentence. Make sure what precedes it is an independent clause, that is, a subject plus verb that can stand alone.

The period says to a reader, "This is the end of this particular statement. I'm a mark of closure."

Example: Lennon rules.

The **comma** [,] separates the main (independent) clause from dependent elements that modify the main clause. It also separates two main clauses joined by a conjunction—known as a compound sentence. Information that is not central to the main clause is set off in a comma sandwich. The comma does *not* signify a pause.

The comma says to the reader, "Here is where the main clause begins (or ends)," or "Here is a break in the main clause." In the case of compound sentences (containing two or more independent clauses), the comma says, "Here is where one main clause ends, and after the conjunction that follows me, another main clause begins."

Examples: Lennon rules, and McCartney is cute.

Lennon rules, although McCartney is arguably more tuneful.

The **semicolon** [;] separates two independent clauses not joined by a conjunction. Secondarily, the semicolon can separate two independent clauses joined by a conjunction if either of the clauses already contains commas. In either case, the semicolon both shows a close relationship between the two independent clauses that it connects and distinguishes where one ends and the other begins. It is also the easiest way to fix comma splices (see BWE 2 later in this chapter).

The semicolon says to the reader, "What precedes and what follows me are conceptually close but grammatically independent and thus equal statements."

Example: Lennon's lyrics show deep sympathy for the legions of "Nowhere Men" who inhabit the "Strawberry Fields" of their imaginations; McCartney's lyrics, on the other hand, are more upbeat, forever bidding "Good Day, Sunshine" to the world at large and "Michelle" in particular.

The **colon** [:] marks the end of a setup for something coming next. It provides a frame, pointing beyond itself, like a spotlight. The colon is quite dramatic, and unlike the semicolon, it links what precedes and follows it formally and tightly rather than loosely and associatively. It usually operates with dramatic force. It can frame a list to follow, separate cause and effect, or divide a brief claim from a more expanded version of the claim. The language on at least one side of the colon must be an independent clause, though both sides can be.

The colon says to the reader, "Concentrate on what follows me for a more detailed explanation of what preceded me" or "What follows me is logically bound with what preceded me."

Examples: *Rubber Soul* marked a change in The Beatles' song-writing: the sentimentality of earlier efforts gave way to a new complexity, both in the range of their subjects and the sophistication of their poetic devices.

Nowhere is this change more evident than in a sequence of songs near the album's end: "I'm Looking Through You," "In My Life," "Wait," and "If I Needed Someone."

The **dash** [—] provides an informal alternative to the colon for adding information to a sentence. Its effect is sudden, of the moment—what springs up impulsively to disrupt and extend in some new way the ongoing train of thought. A **pair of dashes** provides an invaluable resource to writers for inserting information within a sentence. In this usage, the rule is that the sentence must read coherently if the inserted information is left out. (To type a dash, type two hyphens with no space between, before, or after. This distinguishes the dash from a hyphen [-], which is the mark used for connecting two words into one.)

The dash says to the reader, "This too!" or, in the case of a pair of them, "Remember the thought in the beginning of this sentence because we're jumping to something else before we come back to finish that thought."

Examples: For all their loveliness, the songs on *Rubber Soul* are not without menace—"I'd rather see you dead little girl than to see you with another man."

In addition to the usual lead, rhythm, and bass guitar ensemble, *Rubber Soul* introduced new instruments—notably, the harpsichord interlude in "In My Life," the sitar spiraling through "Norwegian Wood"—that had not previously been heard in rock 'n' roll.

NINE BASIC WRITING ERRORS AND HOW TO FIX THEM

If you're unsure about some of the terms you encounter in the discussions of BWEs, see the Glossary of Grammatical Terms at the end of this chapter. You'll also find brief Test Yourself questions interspersed throughout this section. Do them: it's easy to conclude that you understand a problem when you are shown the correction, but understanding is not the same thing as actively practicing. There's an appendix to this chapter that—as mentioned earlier—contains answers to these sections, along with explanations.

Some Advice on Proofreading

- Have a separate proofreading phase at the end of your composing process in which you attend only to grammar and punctuation.
- Look at each sentence as a discrete unit. If you have trouble doing this—if you get caught up in the flow of your thinking—try proofreading the paper backward. Start with the last sentence, then the next-to-last, and move all the way from back to front.
- Circle each punctuation mark, and ask yourself why it is there. In this way, you will be more likely to find commas where there should be periods.
- Read your paper out loud with a pencil in hand. Writers are much more likely to notice errors when they hear them. (Many of the BWEs typically make sentences difficult to follow and difficult to read out loud.)

BWE 1: SENTENCE FRAGMENTS

The most basic of writing errors, a *sentence fragment,* is a group of words punctuated like a complete sentence but lacking the necessary structure: it is only part of a sentence. Typically, a sentence fragment occurs when the group of words in question (1) lacks a subject, (2) lacks a predicate, or (3) is a subordinate (or dependent) clause.

To fix a sentence fragment, either turn it into an independent clause by providing whatever is missing—a subject or a predicate—or attach it to an independent clause on which it can depend.

Noun Clause (No Predicate) as a Fragment

A world where imagination takes over and sorrow is left behind.

This fragment is not a sentence but rather a noun clause—a sentence subject with no predicate. The fragment lacks a verb that would assert something about the subject. (The verbs *takes over* and *is left* are in a dependent clause created by the subordinating conjunction *where.*)

Corrections

A world *arose* where imagination takes over and sorrow is left behind. *[new verb matched to "a world"]*

She entered a world where imagination takes over and sorrow is left behind. *[new subject and verb added]*

The first correction adds a new verb ("arose"). The second introduces a new subject and verb, converting the fragment into the direct object of "she entered."

Verbal as a Fragment

Falling into debt for the fourth consecutive year.

"Falling" in the preceding fragment is not a verb. Depending on the correction, "falling" is either a verbal or part of a verb phrase.

Corrections

The company was falling into debt for the fourth consecutive year. *[subject and helping verb added]*

Falling into debt for the fourth consecutive year *led the company to consider relocating. [new predicate added]*

Falling into debt for the fourth consecutive year, *the company considered relocating. [new subject and verb added]*

In the first correction, the addition of a subject and the helping verb "was" converts the fragment into a sentence. The second correction turns the fragment into a gerund phrase functioning as the subject of a new sentence. The third correction converts the fragment into a participial phrase attached to a new independent clause. (See the section entitled Glossary of Grammatical Terms and look under "verbal" for definitions of "gerund" and "participle.")

Subordinate Clause as a Fragment

I had an appointment for 11:00 and was still waiting at 11:30. Although I did get to see the dean before lunch.

"Although" is a subordinating conjunction that calls for some kind of completion. Like "if," "when," "because," "whereas," and other subordinating conjunctions (see the Glossary of Grammatical Terms), "although" *always* makes the clause that it introduces dependent.

Corrections

I had an appointment for 11:00 and was still waiting at *11:30, although* I did get to see the dean before lunch. *[fragment attached to preceding sentence]*

As the correction demonstrates, the remedy lies in attaching the fragment to an independent clause on which it can depend (or, alternatively, making the fragment into a sentence by dropping the conjunction).

Sometimes writers use sentence fragments deliberately, usually for rhythm and emphasis or to create a conversational tone. In less formal contexts, they are generally permissible, but you run the risk that the fragment will not be perceived as intentional. In formal writing assignments, it is safer to avoid intentional fragments.

▪ Test yourself 19.1: Fragments

There are fragments in each of the following three examples, probably the result of their proximity to legitimate sentences. What's the problem in each case, and how would you fix it?

1. Like many other anthropologists, Margaret Mead studied non-Western cultures in such works as *Coming of Age in Samoa*. And influenced theories of childhood development in America.
2. The catastrophe resulted from an engineering flaw. Because the bridge lacked sufficient support.
3. In the 1840s the potato famine decimated Ireland. It being a country with poor soil and antiquated methods of agriculture.

Using Dashes and Colons to Correct Fragments

Beyond what the punctuation guide has offered, the particular virtues of the dash and colon as ways to correct sentence fragments deserve brief mention. One way to correct a fragment is to replace the period with a dash: "The campaign required commitment. Not just money." becomes "The campaign required commitment—not just money." The dash offers you one way of attaching a phrase or dependent clause to a sentence without having to construct another independent clause. In short, it's succinct. (Compare the correction that uses the dash with another possible correction: "The campaign required commitment. It also required money.") Moreover, with the air of sudden interruption that the dash conveys, it can capture the informality and immediacy that the intentional fragment offers a writer.

You should be wary of overusing the dash as the slightly more presentable cousin of the intentional fragment. The energy it carries can clash with the decorum of formal writing contexts; for some readers, its staccato effect quickly becomes too much of a good thing.

One alternative to this usage of the dash is the colon. It can substitute because it also can be followed by a phrase, a list, or a clause. It must be preceded by an independent clause. And like the dash, it carries dramatic force because it abruptly halts the flow of the sentence.

The colon, however, does not convey informality. In place of a slapdash effect, it trains a light on what is to follow it. Hence, as in this sentence you are reading, it is especially appropriate for setting up certain kinds of information: explanations, lists, or results. In the case of results, the cause or action precedes the colon; the effect or reaction follows it.

BWE 2: COMMA SPLICES AND FUSED (OR RUN-ON) SENTENCES

A comma splice consists of two independent clauses connected ("spliced") with a comma; a fused (or run-on) sentence combines two such clauses with no conjunction or punctuation. The solutions for both comma splices and fused sentences are the same.

1. Place a conjunction (such as "and" or "because") between the clauses.
2. Place a semicolon between the clauses.
3. Make the clauses into separate sentences.

All of these solutions solve the same logical problem: they clarify the boundaries of the independent clauses for your readers.

Comma Splice

He disliked discipline, he avoided anything demanding.

Correction

Because he disliked discipline, he avoided anything demanding. *[subordinating conjunction added]*

Comma Splice

Today most TV programs are violent, almost every program is about cops and detectives.

Correction

Today most TV programs are violent; almost every program is about cops and detectives. *[semicolon replaces comma]*

Because the two independent clauses in the first example contain ideas that are closely connected logically, the most effective of the three comma-splice solutions is to add a subordinating conjunction ("because") to the first of the two clauses, making it depend on the second. For the same reason—close conceptual connection—the best solution for the next comma splice is to substitute a semicolon for the comma. The semicolon signals that the two independent clauses are closely linked in meaning. In general, you can use a semicolon where you could also use a period.

Cures for the Perpetual Comma Splicer

The comma splice is remarkably common, even among fairly sophisticated writers. It indicates two things: (1) the writer is not distinguishing between independent and dependent clauses and (2) he or she is operating on the so-called "pause theory" of punctuation. All of the clauses in our two examples are independent. As written, each of these should be punctuated not with a comma but rather with a period or a semicolon. Instead, the perpetual comma splicer, as usual, acts on the "pause theory": because the ideas in the independent clauses are closely connected, the writer hesitates to separate them with a period. And so the writer inserts what he or she takes to be a shorter pause—the comma.

But a comma is not a "breath" mark; it provides readers with specific grammatical information, in each of these cases mistakenly suggesting there is only one independent clause separated by the comma from modifying information. In the corrections, by contrast, the semicolon sends the appropriate signal to the reader: the message that it is joining two associated but independent statements. Adding a coordinating conjunction such as "and" would also be grammatically correct, though possibly awkward. *(See the discussion of independent clauses and comma rules at the opening of Chapter 18.)*

Fused Sentence

The Indo-European language family includes many groups most languages in Europe belong to it.

Correction

The Indo-European language family includes many groups. Most languages in Europe belong to it. *[period inserted after first independent clause]*

You could also fix this fused sentence with a comma plus the coordinating conjunction "and." Alternatively, you might condense the whole into a single independent clause.

Most languages in Europe belong to the Indo-European language family.

Comma Splices with Conjunctive Adverbs

Quantitative methods of data collection show broad trends, however, they ignore specific cases.

Sociobiology poses a threat to traditional ethics, for example, it asserts that human behavior is genetically motivated by the "selfish gene" to perpetuate itself.

Corrections

Quantitative methods of data collection show broad trends; however, they ignore specific cases. *[semicolon replaces comma before "however"]*

Sociobiology poses a threat to traditional ethics; for example, it asserts that human behavior is genetically motivated by the "selfish gene" to perpetuate itself. *[semicolon replaces comma before "for example"]*

Both of these examples contain one of the most common forms of comma splices. Both of them are compound sentences, that is, they contain two independent clauses. *(See the section entitled The Compound Sentence in Chapter 18.)* Normally, connecting the clauses with a comma and a conjunction would be correct; for example, "Most hawks hunt alone, but osprey hunt in pairs." In the preceding two comma splices, however, the independent clauses are joined by transitional expressions known as conjunctive adverbs. *(See the Glossary of Grammatical Terms.)* When a conjunctive adverb is used to link two independent clauses, it *always* requires a semicolon. By contrast, when a coordinating conjunction links the two clauses of a compound sentence, it is *always* preceded by a comma.

In most cases, depending on the sense of the sentence, the semicolon precedes the conjunctive adverb and clarifies the division between the two clauses. There are exceptions to this general rule, though, as in the following sentence:

> The lazy boy did finally read a *book, however;* it was the least he could do.

Here, "however" is a part of the first independent clause and qualifies its claim. The sentence thus suggests the boy was not totally lazy because he did get around to reading a book. Note how the meaning changes when "however" becomes the introductory word for the second independent clause.

> The lazy boy did finally read a *book; however,* it was the least he could do.

Here, the restricting force of "however" suggests that reading the book was not much of an accomplishment.

▇ Test yourself 19.2: Comma Splices

What makes each of the following sentences a comma splice? Determine the best way to fix each one and why, and then make the correction.

1. "Virtual reality" is a new buzzword, so is "hyperspace."

2. Many popular cures for cancer have been discredited, nevertheless, many people continue to buy them.

3. Elvis Presley's home, Graceland, attracts many musicians as a kind of shrine, even Paul Simon has been there.

4. She didn't play well with others, she sat on the bench and watched.

BWE 3: ERRORS IN SUBJECT–VERB AGREEMENT

The subject and the verb must agree in number, a singular subject taking a singular verb and a plural subject taking a plural verb. Errors in subject–verb agreement usually occur when a writer misidentifies the subject or verb of a clause.

Agreement Problem: plural subject, singular verb

Various kinds of vandalism has been rapidly increasing.

Correction

Various kinds of vandalism *have* been rapidly increasing. *[verb made plural to match "kinds"]*

When you isolate the grammatical subject ("kinds") and the verb ("has") of the original sentence, you can tell that they do not agree. Although "vandalism" might seem to be the subject because it is closest to the verb, it is actually the object of the preposition "of." The majority of agreement problems arise from mistaking the object of a preposition for the actual subject of a sentence. If you habitually make this mistake, you can begin to remedy it by familiarizing yourself with the most common prepositions. (*See the Glossary of Grammatical Terms, which contains a list of these.*)

Agreement Problem: singular subject, plural verb

Another aspect of territoriality that differentiates humans from animals are their possession of ideas and objects.

Correction

Another aspect of territoriality that differentiates humans from animals *is* their possession of ideas and objects. *[verb made singular to match subject "aspect"]*

The subject of the sentence is "aspect." The two plural nouns ("humans" and "animals") probably encourage the mistake of using a plural verb ("are"), but "humans" is part of the "that" clause modifying "aspect," and "animals" is the object of the preposition "from."

Agreement Problem: "each" must take singular verb

The Republican and the Democrat both believe in doing what's best for America, but each believe that the other doesn't understand what's best.

Correction

The Republican and the Democrat both believe in doing what's best for America, but each *believes* that the other doesn't understand what's best. *[verb made singular to agree with subject "each"]*

The word "each" is *always* singular, so the verb ("believes") must be singular as well. The presence of a plural subject and verb in the sentence's first independent clause ("the Republican and the Democrat both believe") has probably encouraged the error.

▉ **Test yourself 19.3:** Subject-Verb Agreement

Diagnose and correct the error in the following example.

> The controversies surrounding the placement of Arthur Ashe's
> statue in Richmond was difficult for the various factions to resolve.

A Note on Dialects and Standard Written English

Some people have trouble recognizing and fixing certain errors because they are not errors in their discourse communities. Different cultures inside the larger culture of English-language speakers use different syntactical forms. This fact has given rise to the phrase "Standard Written English," which names one particular version of English as the norm. People whose language practices constitute a dialect, for example, are told they have to acquire the other dialect—Standard Written English.

The concept of Standard Written English has been controversial. Critics argue that the concept enforces the language practices of privileged groups and discriminates against the practices of less powerful groups in the culture. The best-known instance of this discrimination appears in the matter of subject-verb agreement among some African-Americans who leave off the verb ending -s in the third person singular present tense.

Standard Written English: He walks to town. (singular)

They walk to town. (plural)

Dialect: He walk to town. (singular)

They walk to town. (plural)

Speakers of the dialect do not differentiate singular from plural verb forms with a terminal "–s" in the present tense (only), as in standard written English.

If you look up the term "Ebonics" you can study the debate about whether or not this particular "error" is descended from syntactical patterns in African languages. Like all ethical debates, this one is not easily resolved. In practical terms, however, you should be aware that these two ways of handling subject–verb agreement are recognized by linguists not in terms of right versus wrong but rather in terms of dialect difference.

A *dialect* is a variety of a language characteristic of a region or culture and is sometimes unintelligible to outsiders. The problem for speakers of a dialect that differs from the norm is that they can't always rely on the ear—on what sounds right—when they are editing according to the rules of standard written English. Such speakers need, in effect, to learn to speak more than one dialect so that they can edit according to the rules of standard written English in situations where this would be expected. This adaptation often requires adding a separate proofreading stage for particular errors, like subject–verb agreement, rather than relying on what sounds right.

BWE 4: SHIFTS IN SENTENCE STRUCTURE (FAULTY PREDICATION)

This error involves an illogical mismatch between subject and predicate. If you continually run afoul of faulty predication, you might use the exercises in a handbook to drill you on isolating the grammatical subjects and verbs of sentences because that is the first move you need to make in fixing the problem.

Faulty Predication

In 1887, the release of more information became available.

Correction

In 1887, more *information* became available *for release*. *[new subject]*

It was the "information," not the "release," that "became available." The correction relocates "information" from its position as object of the preposition "of" to the subject position in the sentence; it also moves "release" into a prepositional phrase.

Faulty Predication

The busing controversy was intended to rectify the inequality of educational opportunities.

Correction

Busing was intended to rectify the inequality of educational opportunities. *[new subject formulated to match verb]*

The *controversy* wasn't intended to rectify, but busing was.

■ **Test yourself 19.4:** Faulty Predication
Identify and correct the faulty predication in this example:

The subject of learning disabilities is difficult to identify accurately.

BWE 5: ERRORS IN PRONOUN REFERENCE

There are at least three forms of this problem. All of them involve a lack of clarity about whom or what a pronoun (a word that substitutes for a noun) refers to. The surest way to avoid difficulties is to make certain the pronoun relates back unambiguously to a specific word, known as the antecedent. In the sentence "Nowadays appliances don't last as long as they once did," the noun "appliances" is the antecedent of the pronoun "they."

Pronoun–Antecedent Agreement A pronoun must agree in number (and gender) with the noun or noun phrase that it refers to.

Pronoun Error: Plural Pronoun With Singular Antecedent It can be dangerous if a child, after watching TV, decides to practice what they saw.

Corrections

It can be dangerous if *children*, after watching TV, *decide* to practice what *they* saw. *[antecedent (and verb) made plural to agree with pronouns]*

It can be dangerous if a child, after watching TV, decides to practice what *he or she* saw. *[singular pronouns substituted to match singular antecedent "child"]*

The error occurs because "child" is singular, but its antecedent pronoun, "they," is plural. The first correction makes both singular; the second makes both plural. You might also observe in the first word of the example—the impersonal "it"—an exception to the rule that pronouns must have antecedents.

■ **Test yourself 19.5:** Pronoun-Antecedent Agreement
What is wrong with the following sentence, and how would you fix it?

> Every dog has its day, but all too often when that day happens, they can be found barking up the wrong tree.

Ambiguous Reference A pronoun should have only one possible antecedent. The possibility of two or more confuses relationships within the sentence.

Pronoun Error: more than one possible referent for "they"

Children like comedians because they have a sense of humor.

Corrections

Because children have a sense of humor, *they* like comedians. *[subordinate "because" clause placed first, and relationship between noun "children" and pronoun "they" tightened]*

Children like comedians because *comedians* have a sense of humor. *[pronoun eliminated and replaced by repetition of noun]*

Does "they" in the original example refer to "children" or "comedians"? The rule in such cases of ambiguity is that the pronoun refers to the nearest possible antecedent, so here "comedians" possess the sense of humor, regardless of what the writer may intend. As the corrections demonstrate, either reordering the sentence or repeating the noun can remove the ambiguity.

■ **Test yourself 19.6:** Ambiguous Reference
As you proofread, it's a good idea to target your pronouns to make sure they cannot conceivably refer to more than one noun. What's wrong with the following sentences?

1. Alexander the Great's father, Philip of Macedon, died when he was twenty-six.
2. The committee could not look into the problem because it was too involved.

Broad Reference

Broad reference occurs when a pronoun refers loosely to a number of ideas expressed in preceding clauses or sentences. It causes confusion because the reader cannot be sure which of the ideas the pronoun refers to.

Pronoun Error: use of "this" makes referent unclear

As a number of scholars have noted, Sigmund Freud and Karl Marx offered competing but also at times complementary critiques of the dehumanizing tendencies of Western capitalist society. We see this in Christopher Lasch's analysis of conspicuous consumption in *The Culture of Narcissism.*

Correction

As a number of scholars have noted, Sigmund Freud and Karl Marx offered competing but also at times complementary critiques of the dehumanizing tendencies of Western capitalist society. We see *this complementary view* in Christopher Lasch's analysis of conspicuous consumption in *The Culture of Narcissism. [broad "this" clarified by addition of noun phrase]*

The word "this" in the second sentence of the uncorrected example could refer to the fact that "a number of scholars have noted" the relationship between Freud and Marx, to the competition between Freud's and Marx's critiques of capitalism, or to the complementary nature of the two men's critiques.

Beware "this" as a pronoun: it's the most common source of broad reference. The remedy is generally to avoid using the word as a pronoun. Instead, convert "this" into an adjective, and let it modify some noun that more clearly specifies the referent: "this complementary view," as in the correction or, alternatively, "this competition" or "this scholarly perspective."

■ **Test yourself 19.7:** Broad Reference
Locate the errors in the following examples, and provide a remedy for each.

1. Regardless of whether the film is foreign or domestic, they can be found in your neighborhood video store.

2. Many experts now claim that dogs and other higher mammals dream; for those who don't own such pets, this is often difficult to believe.

A Note on Sexism and Pronoun Usage

Errors in pronoun reference sometimes occur because of a writer's praiseworthy desire to avoid sexism. In most circles, the following correction of the preceding example would be considered sexist.

It can be dangerous if a child, after watching TV, decides to practice what *he* saw.

Though the writer of such a sentence may intend "he" to function as a gender-neutral impersonal pronoun, it in fact excludes girls on the basis of gender. Implicitly, it also conveys sexual stereotypes (for example, that only boys are violent, or perhaps stupid, enough to confuse TV with reality).

The easiest way to avoid the problem of sexism in pronoun usage usually lies in putting things into the plural form because plural pronouns ("we," "you," "they") have no gender. (See the use of "children" in the first correction of the pronoun–antecedent agreement example.) Alternatively, you can use the phrase "he or she." Many readers, however, find this phrase and its variant, "s/he," to be awkward constructions. Another remedy lies in rewriting the sentence to avoid pronouns altogether, as in the following revision.

It can be dangerous if a child, after watching TV, decides to practice *some violent activity portrayed on the screen.*

BWE 6: MISPLACED MODIFIERS AND DANGLING PARTICIPLES

Modifiers are words or groups of words used to qualify, limit, intensify, or explain some other element in a sentence. A misplaced modifier is a word or phrase that appears to modify the wrong word or words.

Misplaced Modifier: modifier appears to modify wrong word

At the age of three he caught a fish with a broken arm.

Correction

At the age of three *the boy with a broken arm* caught a fish. *[noun replaces pronoun; prepositional phrase revised and relocated]*

The original sentence mistakenly implies that the fish had a broken arm. Modification errors often occur in sentences with one or more prepositional phrases, as in this case.

Misplaced Modifier: modifier appears to modify wrong word

According to legend, General George Washington crossed the Delaware and celebrated Christmas in a small boat.

Correction

According to legend, General George Washington crossed the Delaware *in a small boat* and *then* celebrated Christmas *on shore*. *[prepositional phrase relocated; modifiers added to second verb]*

As a general rule, you can avoid misplacing a modifier by keeping it as close as possible to what it modifies. Thus, the second correction removes the implication that Washington celebrated Christmas in a small boat. When you cannot relocate the modifier, separate it from the rest of the sentence with a comma to prevent readers from connecting it to the nearest noun.

A dangling participle creates a particular kind of problem in modification: the noun or pronoun that the writer intends the participial phrase to modify is not actually present in the sentence. Thus, we have the name dangling participle: the participle has been left dangling because the word or phrase it is meant to modify is not there.

Dangling Participle: subject that participle modifies does not appear in the sentence

After debating the issue of tax credits for the elderly, the bill passed in a close vote.

Correction

After debating the issue of tax credits for the elderly, *the Senate passed the* bill in a close vote. *[appropriate noun added for participle to modify]*

The bill did not debate the issue, as the original example implies. As the correction demonstrates, fixing a dangling participle involves tightening the link between the activity implied by the participle ("debating") and the entity performing that activity ("the Senate").

▇ Test yourself 19.8: Modification Errors
Find the modification errors in the following examples and correct them.

1. After eating their sandwiches, the steamboat left the dock.
2. The social workers saw an elderly woman on a bus with a cane standing up.
3. Crossing the street, a car hit the pedestrian.

BWE 7: ERRORS IN USING POSSESSIVE APOSTROPHES

Adding *'s* to most singular nouns will make them show possession, for example, the plant*'s* roots, the accountant*'s* ledger. You can add the apostrophe alone, without the "s," for example, to make plural nouns that already end with "s" show possession: the flowers*'* fragrances or the ships*'* berths (although you may also add an additional "s").

Apostrophe Error

The loyal opposition scorned the committees decisions.

Corrections

The loyal opposition scorned the *committee's* decisions.
The loyal opposition scorned the *committees'* decisions. *[possessive apostrophe added]*

The first correction assumes there was one committee; the second assumes there were two or more.

Apostrophe Error

The advisory board swiftly transacted it's business.

Correction

The advisory board swiftly transacted *its* business. *[apostrophe dropped]*

Unlike possessive nouns, possessive pronouns ("my," "your," "yours," "her," "hers," "his," "its," "our," "ours," "their," "theirs") *never* take an apostrophe.

■ **Test yourself 19.9:** Possessive Apostrophes
Find and correct any errors in the following sentence.
The womens movement has been misunderstood by many of its detractors.

BWE 8: COMMA ERRORS

As with other rules of punctuation and grammar, the many that pertain to comma usage share an underlying aim: to clarify the relationships among the parts of a sentence. Commas separate the parts of a sentence grammatically. One of their primary uses, then, is to help your readers distinguish the main clause from dependent elements such as subordinate clauses and long prepositional phrases. They do not signify a pause, as was discussed in BWE 2.

Comma Error: comma missing after introductory phrase

After eating the couple went home.

Correction

After *eating,* the couple went home. *[comma added before independent clause]*

The comma after "eating" is needed to keep the main clause "visible" or separate; it marks the point at which the prepositional phrase ends and the independent clause begins. Without this separation, readers would be invited to contemplate cannibalism as they move across the sentence.

Comma Error: comma missing after introductory phrase

In the absence of rhetoric study teachers and students lack a vocabulary for talking about their prose.

Correction

In the absence of rhetoric *study,* teachers and students lack a vocabulary for talking about their prose. *[comma added to separate prepositional phrase from main clause]*

Without the comma, readers would have to read the sentence twice to find out where the prepositional phrase ends—with "study"—to figure out where the main clause begins.

Comma Error: two commas needed around parenthetical element

Dog owners, despite their many objections will have to obey the new law.

Correction

Dog owners, despite their many *objections*, will have to obey the new law. *[single comma converted to a pair of commas]*

A comma is needed after "objections" to isolate the phrase in the middle of the sentence ("despite their many objections") from the main clause. The phrase needs to be set off with commas because it contains additional information not essential to the meaning of what it modifies. (Dog owners must obey the law whether they object or not.) Phrases and clauses that function in this way are called *nonrestrictive*.

A Note on Restrictive versus Nonrestrictive Elements

The test of nonrestrictive phrases and clauses is to see if they can be omitted without substantially changing the message that a sentence conveys ("Dog owners will have to obey the new law," for example). Nonrestrictive elements always take two commas—a comma "sandwich"—to set them off. Using only one comma illogically separates the sentence's subject ("dog owners") from its predicate ("will have to obey"). This problem is easier to see in a shorter sentence. You wouldn't, for example, write "I, fell down." As a rule, commas virtually never separate the subject from the verb of a sentence. (Here's an exception: "Ms. Smith, a high fashion model, watches her diet scrupulously.")

Comma Error: two commas needed around parenthetical element

Most people regardless of age like to spend money.

Correction

Most *people,* regardless of *age,* like to spend money. *[comma sandwich added]*

Here, commas enclose the nonrestrictive elements; you could omit this information without significantly affecting the sense. Such is not the case in the following two examples.

Comma Error: restrictive elements should not be enclosed within commas

People, who live in glass houses, should not throw stones.

Correction

People *who live in glass houses* should not throw stones. *[commas omitted]*

Comma Error: no comma setting off restrictive clause

Please return the library book, that I left on the table.

Correction

Please return the library *book that* I left on the table. *[comma omitted]*

It is incorrect to place commas around "who live in glass houses" or a comma before "that I left on the table." Each of these is a *restrictive clause,* that is, it contains information that is an essential part of what it modifies. In the first sentence, for example, if "who live in glass houses" is left out, the fundamental meaning of the sentence is lost: "People should not throw stones." The word "who" is defined by restricting it to "people" in the category of glass-house dwellers. Similarly, in the second example the "that" clause contributes an essential meaning to "book"; the sentence is referring to not just any book but to a particular one, the one "on the table."

So, remember the general rule: if the information in a phrase or clause can be omitted—if it is nonessential and therefore nonrestrictive—it needs to be separated by commas from the rest of the sentence. Moreover, note that nonrestrictive clauses are generally introduced by the word "which," so a "which" clause interpolated into a sentence takes a comma sandwich. ("The dinner, which I bought for $20, made me sick.") By contrast, a restrictive clause is introduced by the word "that" and takes no commas.

■ **Test yourself 19.10:** Comma Errors
Consider the following examples as a pair. Punctuate them as necessary, and then briefly articulate how the meanings of the two sentences differ.

1. The book which I had read a few years ago contained a lot of outdated data.

2. The book that I had read a few years ago contained a lot of outdated data.

BWE 9: SPELLING/DICTION ERRORS THAT INTERFERE WITH MEANING

Misspellings are always a problem in a final draft, insofar as they undermine your authority by inviting readers to perceive you as careless (at best). If you make a habit of using the spellchecker of a word processor, you will take care of most misspellings; however, the problems a spellchecker won't catch are the ones that can often hurt you most. These are actually diction errors—incorrect word choices in which you have confused one word with another that it closely resembles. In such cases, you have spelled the word correctly, but it's the wrong word. Because it means something other than what you've intended, you end up misleading your readers. *(See "Right" and "Wrong" Words: Shades of Meaning in Chapter 17.)*

The best way to avoid this problem is to memorize the differences between pairs of words commonly confused with each other but that have distinct meanings. The following examples illustrate a few of the most common and serious of these errors. Most handbooks contain a glossary of usage that *cites* more of these *sites* of confusion.

Spelling/Diction Error: "It's" versus "Its"

Although you can't tell a book by its' cover, its fairly easy to get the general idea from the introduction.

Correction

Although you can't tell a book by *its* cover, *it's* fairly easy to get the general idea from the introduction. *[apostrophe dropped from possessive and added to contraction]*

"It's" is a contraction for "it is." "Its" is a possessive pronoun meaning "belonging to it." If you confuse the two, *it's* likely that your sentence will mislead *its* readers.

Spelling/Diction Error: "Their" versus "There" versus "They're"

Their are ways of learning about the cuisine of northern India besides going their to watch the master chefs and learn there secrets—assuming their willing to share them.

Correction

There are ways of learning about the cuisine of northern India besides going *there* to watch the master chefs and learn *their* secrets—assuming *they're* willing to share them. *[expletive "there," adverb "there," possessive pronoun "their," and contraction "they're" inserted appropriately]*

"There" as an adverb normally refers to a place; "there" can also be used as an expletive to introduce a clause, as in the first usage of the correction. *(See Beginning With "It Is" or "There Is": Advantages and Disadvantages in Chapter 18.)* "Their" is a possessive pronoun meaning "belonging to them." "They're" is a contraction for "they are."

Spelling/Diction Error: "Then" versus "Than"

If a person would rather break a law then obey it, than he or she must be willing to face the consequences.

Correction

If a person would rather break a law *than* obey it, *then* he or she must be willing to face the consequences. *[comparative "than" distinguished from temporal "then"]*

"Than" is a conjunction used with a comparison, for example, "rather X than Y." "Then" is an adverb used to indicate what comes next in relation to time, for example, "first X, then Y."

Spelling/Diction Error: "Effect" versus "Affect"

It is simply the case that BWEs adversely effect the way that readers judge what a writer has to say. It follows that writers who include lots of BWEs in their prose may not have calculated the disastrous affects of these mistakes.

Correction

It is simply the case that BWEs adversely *affect* the way that readers judge what a writer has to say. It follows that writers who include lots of BWEs in their prose may not have calculated the disastrous *effects* of these mistakes. *[verb "affect" and noun "effects" inserted appropriately]*

In their most common usages, "affect" is a verb meaning "to influence," and "effect" is a noun meaning "the result of an action or cause." The confusion of "affect" and "effect" is enlarged by the fact that both of these words have secondary meanings: the verb "to effect" means "to cause or bring about"; the noun "affect" is used in psychology to mean "emotion or feeling." Thus, if you confuse these two words, you will inadvertently make a meaning radically different from the one you intend.

■ **Test yourself 19.11:** Spelling/Diction Errors
Make corrections as necessary in the following paragraph.

> Its not sufficiently acknowledged that the behavior of public officials is not just an ethical issue but one that effects the sale of newspapers and commercial bytes in television news. When public officials don't do what their supposed to do, than their sure to face the affects of public opinion—if they get caught—because there are dollars to be made. Its that simple: money more then morality is calling the tune in the way that the press treats it's superstars.

GLOSSARY OF GRAMMATICAL TERMS

adjective   An adjective is a part of speech that usually modifies a noun or pronoun—for example, *blue, boring, boisterous.*

adverb   An adverb is a part of speech that modifies an adjective, adverb, or verb—for example, *heavily, habitually, very.* The adverbial form generally differs from the adjectival form via the addition of the ending "–ly"; for example, *happy* is an adjective, and *happily* is an adverb.

clause (independent and dependent)   A clause is any group of words that contains both a **subject** and a **predicate**. An **independent clause** (also known as a **main clause**) can stand alone as a sentence. For example,

> The most famous revolutionaries of this century have all, in one way or another, offered a vision of a classless society.

The subject of this independent clause is "revolutionaries," the verb is "have offered," and the direct object is "vision." By contrast, a **dependent** (or **subordinate**) **clause** is any group of words containing a subject and verb that cannot stand alone as a separate sentence because it depends on an independent clause to complete its meaning. The following sentence adds two dependent clauses to our previous example:

> The most famous revolutionaries of this century have all, in one way or another, offered a vision of a classless society, *although* most historians would agree *that* this ideal has never been achieved.

The origin of the word "depend" is "to hang": a dependent clause literally hangs on the independent clause. In the preceding example, neither "although most historians would agree" nor "that this ideal has never been achieved" can stand independently. The "that" clause relies on the "although" clause, which in turn relies on the main clause. "That" and "although" function as **subordinating conjunctions**; by eliminating them, we could rewrite the sentence to contain three independent clauses:

> The most famous revolutionaries of this century have all, in one way or another, offered a vision of a classless society. Most historians would agree on one judgment about this vision: it has never been achieved.

comma splice   A comma splice consists of two independent clauses incorrectly connected (spliced) with a comma. See BWE 2.

conjunction (coordinating and subordinating)   A conjunction is a part of speech that connects words, phrases, or clauses, for example, *and, but, although.* The conjunction in some way defines that connection: for example, *and* links; *but* separates. All conjunctions define connections in one of two basic ways. Coordinating conjunctions connect words or groups of words that have equal grammatical importance. The coordinating conjunctions are *and, but, or, nor, for, so,* and *yet.* Subordinating conjunctions introduce a dependent clause and connect it to a main clause. Here is a partial list of the most common subordinating conjunctions: *after, although, as, as if, as long as, because, before, if, rather than, since, than, that, though, unless, until, when, where, whether,* and *while.*

conjunctive adverb   A conjunctive adverb is a word that links two independent clauses (as a conjunction) but that also modifies the clause it introduces (as an adverb). Some of the most common conjunctive adverbs are *consequently, furthermore, however, moreover, nevertheless, similarly, therefore,* and *thus.* Phrases can also serve this function, such as *for example* and *on the other hand.* When conjunctive adverbs are used to link two independent clauses, they always require a semicolon:

> Many pharmaceutical chains now offer their own generic versions of common drugs; however, many consumers continue to spend more for name brands that contain the same active ingredients as the generics.

When conjunctive adverbs occur within an independent clause, however, they are enclosed in a pair of commas, as is the case with the use of *however* earlier in this sentence.

coordination   Coordination refers to grammatically equal words, phrases, or clauses. Coordinate constructions are used to give elements in a sentence equal weight or importance. In the sentence "The tall, thin lawyer badgered the witness, but the judge interceded," the clauses "The tall, thin lawyer badgered the witness" and "but the judge interceded" are coordinate clauses; "tall" and "thin" are coordinate adjectives.

dependent clause (see clause)

direct object   The direct object is a noun or pronoun that receives the action carried by the verb and performed by the subject. In the sentence, "Certain mushrooms can kill you," "you" is the direct object.

gerund (see verbals)

fused (or run-on) sentence   A fused sentence incorrectly combines two independent clauses with no conjunction or punctuation. See BWE 2.

independent clause (see clause)

infinitive (see verbals)

main clause (see clause)

noun   A noun is a part of speech that names a person (*woman*), place (*town*), thing (*book*), idea (*justice*), quality (*irony*), or action (*betrayal*).

object of the preposition (see preposition)

participle and participial phrase (see verbals)

phrase   A phrase is a group of words occurring in a meaningful sequence that lacks either a subject or a predicate. This absence distinguishes it from a clause, which contains both a subject and a predicate. Phrases function in sentences as adjectives, adverbs, nouns, or verbs. They are customarily classified according to the part of speech of their keyword: "over the mountain" is a **prepositional phrase**; "running for office" is a **participial phrase**; "had been disciplined" is a **verb phrase**; "desktop graphics" is a **noun phrase**; and so forth.

predicate   The predicate contains the verb of a sentence or clause, making some kind of statement about the subject. The predicate of the preceding sentence is "contains the verb, making some kind of statement about the subject." The simple predicate—the verb to which the other words in the sentence are attached—is "contains."

preposition, prepositional phrase   A preposition is a part of speech that links a noun or pronoun to some other word in the sentence. Prepositions usually express a relationship of time (*after*) or space (*above*) or direction (*toward*). The noun to which the preposition is attached is known as the object of the preposition. A preposition, its object, and any modifiers comprise a prepositional phrase. "*With* love *from* me *to* you" strings together three prepositional phrases. Here is a partial list of the most common prepositions: *about, above, across, after, among, at, before, behind, between, by, during, for, from, in, into, like, of, on, out, over, since, through, to, toward, under, until, up, upon, with, within,* and *without.*

pronoun   A pronoun is a part of speech that substitutes for a noun, such as *I, you, he, she, it, we,* and *they.*

run-on (or fused) sentence   A run-on sentence incorrectly combines two independent clauses with no conjunction or punctuation. See BWE 2.

sentence   A sentence is a unit of expression that can stand independently. It contains two parts, a **subject** and a **predicate**. The shortest sentence in the Bible, for example, is "Jesus wept." "Jesus" is the subject; "wept" is the predicate.

sentence fragment   A sentence fragment is a group of words incorrectly punctuated like a complete sentence but lacking the necessary structure; it is only a part of a sentence. "Walking down the road" and "the origin of the problem" are both fragments because neither contains a **predicate**. See BWE 1.

subject   The subject, in most cases a noun or pronoun, names the doer of the action in a sentence or identifies what the predicate is about. The subject of the previous sentence, for example, is "the subject, in most cases a noun or pronoun." The simple subject of that sentence—the noun to which the other words in the sentence are attached—is "subject."

subordination, subordinating conjunctions   "Subordination" refers to the placement of certain grammatical units, particularly phrases and clauses, at a lower, less important structural level than other elements. As with coordination, the grammatical ranking carries conceptual significance as well: whatever is grammatically subordinated appears less important than the information carried in the main clause. In the following example, Microsoft is subordinated both grammatically and conceptually to Apple:

> Although Microsoft continues to upgrade the operating system and special features on its computers, the more stylish and virus-free Apple MacIntosh computers continue to outclass them.

Here, "although" is a **subordinating conjunction** that introduces a subordinate clause, also known as a **dependent clause**.

verb   A verb is a part of speech that describes an action (*goes*), states how something was affected by an action (*became angered*), or expresses a state of being (*is*).

verbals (participles, gerunds, and infinitives)   Verbals are words derived from verbs. They are verb forms that look like verbs but, as determined by the structure of the sentence they appear in, they function as nouns, adjectives, or adverbs. There are three forms of verbals.

An **infinitive**—composed of the root form of a verb plus *to* (*to be, to vote*)—becomes a verbal when it is used as a noun ("*To eat* is essential"), an adjective ("These are the books *to read*"), or an adverb ("He was too sick *to walk*").

Similarly, a **participle**—usually composed of the root form of a verb plus "–ing" (present participle) or "–ed" (past participle)—becomes a verbal when used as an adjective. It can occur as a single word, modifying a noun, as in *faltering negotiations* or *finished business*. But it also can occur in a participial phrase, consisting of the participle, its object, and any modifiers. Here are two examples:

> *Having been tried and convicted,* the criminal was sentenced to life imprisonment.

> *Following the path of most resistance,* the masochist took deep pleasure in his frustration.

"Having been tried and convicted" is a participial phrase that modifies "criminal"; "Following the path of most resistance" is a participial phrase that modifies "masochist." In each case, the participial phrase functions as an adjective.

The third form of verbal, the **gerund**, resembles the participle. Like the participle, it is formed by adding "–ing" to the root form of the verb, but unlike the participle, it is used as a noun. In the sentence "Swimming is extraordinarily aerobic," the gerund "swimming" functions as the subject. Again like participles, gerunds can occur in phrases. The gerund phrases are italicized in the following example: "*Watching a film adaptation* takes less effort than *reading the book* from which it was made."

When using a verbal, remember that although it resembles a verb, it cannot function alone as the verb in a sentence: "Being a military genius" is a fragment, not a sentence.

Assignments for Working With Basic Writing Errors

1. **Chart the BWEs.** Write an example for each of the BWEs, along with a corrected version.

2. **Compose a Grammar and Style Quiz.** Write a paragraph that contains all of the basic writing errors. Not every sentence should contain an error, and you may contain multiple examples of the errors, but make sure you include all nine. Then, append an answer key in which you identify the errors and provide corrections.

3. **Research Online Resources.** Go online to different universities and colleges in search of their writing centers, and then look for the ways these websites handle the problem of grammatical correctness. See as an example OWL at Purdue University. Write a brief summary of what you find there.

4. **Circle Every Punctuation Mark.** Take a short piece of writing, your own or someone else's, published or unpublished. Circle every punctuation mark and explain why it is there. This is a useful exercise to do in pairs or in small groups. As a follow-up exercise, you might underline every independent clause and double-underline every dependent clause, circling the subordinating conjunctions.

CHAPTER 19 APPENDIX

Basic Writing Errors (BWEs) Test Yourself Section Answer Key (With Discussion)

Test Yourself 19.1: Fragments (Page 426)

1. Original example: Like many other anthropologists, Margaret Mead studied non-Western cultures in such works as *Coming of Age in Samoa*. And influenced theories of childhood development in America.

   Problem: The second sentence is actually a fragment, a predicate in need of a subject.

   Possible correction: Like many other anthropologists, Margaret Mead studied non-Westerncultures (in such works as *Coming of Age in Samoa*) in ways that influenced theories of childhood development in America.

   Comment: There are many ways to fix this example, but its original form leaves ambiguous whether the fragment refers only to *Mead,* or to *many other anthropologists* as well. The correction offered includes the other anthropologists in the referent and diminishes the emphasis on Mead's book by placing it within parentheses. Although the correction uses a subordinating *that* to incorporate the fragment into the first sentence, it keeps this information in an emphatic position at the end of the sentence.

2. Original example: The catastrophe resulted from an engineering flaw. Because the bridge lacked sufficient support.

   Problem: The second sentence is actually a dependent clause; *because* always subordinates.

   Possible correction: The catastrophe resulted from an engineering flaw: the bridge lacked sufficient support.

   Comment: Because the colon has causal force, this is an ideal spot to use one, identifying the "flaw."

3. Original example: In the 1840s the potato famine decimated Ireland. It being a country with poor soil and antiquated methods of agriculture.

   Problem: The second sentence is actually a fragment, a subject plus a long participial phrase.

   Possible correction: In the 1840s the potato famine decimated Ireland, a country with poor and antiquated methods of agriculture.

Comment: The cause of this kind of fragment is usually that the writer mistakenly believes that *being* is a verb rather than a participle that introduces a long phrase (modifying "Ireland" in this case). It would also be correct simply to change the period to a comma in the original sentence.

Test Yourself 19.2: Comma Splices (Page 429)

1. Original example: "Virtual reality" is a new buzzword, so is "hyperspace."

   Problem: This is a comma splice—both clauses are independent, yet they are joined with a comma.

   Possible correction: "Virtual reality" is a new buzzword; so is "hyperspace."

   Comment: Because the clauses are linked by association—both naming buzzwords—a semicolon would show that association. A writer could also condense the clauses into a simple sentence with a compound subject, for example, "Both 'virtual reality' and 'hyperspace' are new buzzwords."

2. Original example: Many popular cures for cancer have been discredited, nevertheless, many people continue to buy them.

   Problem: A comma splice results from the incorrectly punctuated conjunctive adverb *nevertheless.*

   Possible correction: Many popular cures for cancer have been discredited; nevertheless, many people continue to buy them.

   Comment: Without the semicolon to separate the independent clauses, the conjunctive adverb could conceivably modify either the preceding or the following clause. This problem is usually worse with *however.*

3. Original example: Elvis Presley's home, Graceland, attracts many musicians as a kind of shrine, even Paul Simon has been there.

   Problem: This is a comma splice—the two independent clauses are linked by a comma without a conjunction. The problem is exacerbated by the number of commas in the sentence; the reader cannot easily tell which one is used to separate the clauses.

   Possible correction: Elvis Presley's home, Graceland, attracts many musicians as a kind of shrine—even Paul Simon has been there.

   Comment: Although one could justly use a semicolon here, the dash conveys the impromptu effect of an afterthought.

4. Original   She didn't play well with others, she sat on the bench and watched.
    example:

Problem: Because the second clause develops the first one, a writer might think
that it is dependent on the first; conceptually, yes, but grammatically, no.

Possible   She didn't play well with others; she sat on the bench and watched.
correction:

Comment: If the writer wanted to link the two clauses more tightly, a colon
would be appropriate instead of the semicolon.

Test Yourself 19.3: Subject–Verb Agreement (Page 430)

Original   The controversies surrounding the placement of Arthur Ashe's
example: statue in Richmond was difficult for the various factions to resolve.

Problem: The grammatical subject of the main clause (controversies) is plural;
the verb (was) is singular.

Possible   The controversies surrounding the placement of Arthur Ashe's
corrections: statue in Richmond were difficult for the various factions to
              resolve (or, The controversy . . . was).

Comment: An error of this kind is encouraged by two factors: the distance of the
verb from the subject and the presence of intervening prepositional phrases that
use singular objects, either of which a writer might mistake for the grammatical
subject of the main clause.

Test Yourself 19.4: Faulty Predication (Page 432)

Original   The subject of learning disabilities is difficult to identify accurately.
example:

Problem: The predicate matches the object of the preposition (learning disabilities) rather than the subject of the main clause (subject).

Possible   Learning disabilities are difficult to identify accurately.
corrections:

Comment: Omitting the abstract opening (The subject of) enables the predicate
(are) to fit the new grammatical subject (disabilities).

Test Yourself 19.5: Pronoun–Antecedent Agreement (Page 433)

Original   Every dog has its day, but all too often when that day happens,
example: they can be found barking up the wrong tree.

Problem: The plural pronoun *they* that is the grammatical subject of the second
clause does not have a plural antecedent in the sentence.

Possible   Every dog has its day, but all too often when that day happens,
correction: the dog can be found barking up the wrong tree.

Comment: If a writer vigilantly checks all pronouns, he or she will identify the intended antecedent of the pronoun *they* to be the singular *dog*, and revise accordingly. The sentence would still be incorrect if the pronoun *it* were used instead of the repeated *dog* because *it* could refer to the nearest preceding noun, *day*.

Test Yourself 19.6: Ambiguous Reference (Page 433)

1. Original   Alexander the Great's father, Philip of Macedon, died when he
    example: was twenty-six.

    Problem: A reader can't be sure whether *he* refers to Alexander or to Philip.

    Possible   Alexander the Great's father, Philip of Macedon, died at the age
    correction: of twenty-six.

    Comment: The correction rewords to remove the ambiguous pronoun. This solution is less awkward than repeating *Philip* in place of *he*, though that would also be correct.

2. Original   The committee could not look into the problem because it was
    example: too involved.

    Problem: A reader can't be sure whether *it* refers to *the committee* or to *the problem*.

    Possible   The committee was too involved with other matters to look into
    correction: the problem.

    Comment: As with the previous example, rewording to eliminate the ambiguous pronoun is usually the best solution.

Test Yourself 19.7: Broad Reference (Page 434)

1. Original   Regardless of whether the film is foreign or domestic, they can be
    example: found in your neighborhood video store.

    Problem: The plural pronoun *they* does not have a plural antecedent in the sentence.

    Possible   Regardless of whether the film is foreign or domestic, it can be
    correction: found in your neighborhood video store.

    Comment: Although the sentence offers two options for films, the word *film* is singular and so, as antecedent, requires a singular pronoun (it). It is probably worth noting here that *it* would still be correct even if the original sentence began, "Regardless of whether the film is a foreign film or a domestic film." The rule for compound subjects that use an either/or construction is as follows: the number (singular or plural) of the noun or pronoun that follows *or* determines the number of the verb. Compare the following two examples: "Either several of his aides *or* the *candidate is* going to speak" and "Either the candidate *or* several of his *aides are* going to speak."

2. Original   Many experts now claim that dogs and other higher mammals
    example: dream; for those who don't own such pets, this is often difficult
                to believe.

Problem: The referent of the pronoun *this* is unclear. Precisely what is difficult to believe—that mammals dream or that experts would make such a claim?

Possible   Many experts now claim that dogs and other higher mammals
correction: dream; for those who don't own such pets, this claim is often
             difficult to believe.

Comment: Often the best way to fix a problem with broad reference produced by use of *this* as a pronoun is to attach *this* to the noun to which it refers, as in "this book. As a rule, when you find an isolated *this* in your draft, ask and answer the question "This what?"

Test Yourself 19.8: Modification Errors (Page 436)

1. Original   After eating their sandwiches, the steamboat left the dock.
    example:

Problem: This is a dangling participle—the grammar of the sentence conveys that the steamboat ate their sandwiches.

corrections: After the girls ate their sandwiches, the steamboat left the dock.
               Or, After eating their sandwiches, the girls boarded the steam-
               boat, and it left the dock.

Comment: The two corrections model the two ways of remedying most dangling participles. Both provide an antecedent (the girls) for the pronoun *their*. The first correction eliminates the participial phrase and substitutes a subordinate clause. The second correction adds to the existing main clause (steamboat left) another one (girls boarded) for the participial phrase to modify appropriately.

2. Original   The social workers saw an elderly woman on a bus with a cane
    example: standing up.

Problem: Misplaced modifiers create the problems in this sentence, which implies that the bus possessed a cane that was standing up. The problem exemplified here is produced by the series of prepositional phrases—"*on* a bus *with* a cane"—followed by the participial phrase *standing up*, which is used as an adjective and intended to modify *woman*.

Possible   The social workers saw an elderly woman on a bus. She was
correction: standing up with the help of a cane.

Comment: Writers often try to cram too much into sentences, piling on the prepositions. The best remedy is sometimes to break up the sentence, a move that usually involves eliminating prepositions, which possess a sludgy kind of movement, and adding verbs, which possess more distinct movement.

3.   Original   Crossing the street, a car hit the pedestrian.
     example:

Problem: The dangling participle (Crossing the street) does not have a word to modify in the sentence. The sentence conveys that the car crossed the street.

Possible   Crossing the street, the pedestrian was hit by a car. Or: As the
corrections: pedestrian crossed the street, a car hit him.

Comment: The first solution brings the participial phrase closest to the noun it modifies (pedestrian). The second converts the participial into the verb (crossed) of a dependent *as* clause and moves *pedestrian* into the clause as the subject for that verb. As in the *steamboat* example, one correction provides an appropriate noun for the participial phrase to modify, and the other eliminates the participle.

Test Yourself 19.9: Possessive Apostrophes (Page 437)

Original   The womens movement has been misunderstood by many of its
example: detractors.

Problem: The possessive apostrophe for *womens* is missing. The trickiness here in inserting the apostrophe is that this word is already plural.

Possible   The women's movement has been misunderstood by many of its
correction: detractors.

Comment: Because the word is already plural, it takes a simple "–'s" to indicate a movement belonging to women—not "–s'" (womens').

Test Yourself 19.10: Comma Errors (Page 439)

Original   The book which I had read a few years ago contained a lot of
paired   outdated data.
examples: The book that I had read a few years ago contained a lot of out-
                dated data.

Problem: In the first example, the modifying clause "which I had read a few years ago" is nonrestrictive: it could be omitted without changing the essential meaning of the sentence. Therefore, it needs to be enclosed in commas—as the *which* signals.

Possible **correction:**	The book, which I had read a few years ago, contained a lot of outdated data.

Comment: The second example in the pair is correct as it stands. The restrictive clause, "that I had read a few years ago," does not take commas around it because the information it gives readers is an essential part of the meaning of *book*. That is, it refers to not just any book read a few years ago, as in the first example in the pair, but rather specifies the one containing outdated data. "The book that I had read a few years ago" thus functions as what is known as a *noun phrase*.

Test Yourself 19.11: Spelling/Diction Errors (Page 441)

Original **example:**	Its not sufficiently acknowledged that the behavior of public officials is not just an ethical issue but one that effects the sale of newspapers and commercial bytes in television news. When public officials don't do what their supposed to do, than their sure to face the affects of public opinion—if they get caught—because there are dollars to be made. Its that simple: money more then morality is calling the tune in the way that the press treats it's superstars.

Problems: The paragraph confuses the paired terms discussed under BWE 9. It mistakes

its for *it's* before *not sufficiently.*

effects for *affects* before *the sale.*

their for *they're* before *supposed.*

than for *then* before *their sure.*

they're for *their* before *sure.*

affects for *effects* before *of public opinion.*

its for *it's* before *that simple.*

then for *than* before *morality.*

it's for *its* before *superstars.*

Possible **correction:**	It's not sufficiently acknowledged that the behavior of public officials is not just an ethical issue but one that affects the sale of newspapers and commercial bytes in television news. When public officials don't do what they're supposed to do, then they're sure to face the effects of public opinion—if they get caught— because there are dollars to be made. It's that simple: money more than morality is calling the tune in the way that the press treats its superstars.

Comment: If you confuse similar words, the only solution is to memorize the differences and consciously check your drafts for any problems until habit takes hold.

Index

Abbreviations, 33
Abstract(s), 321, 353
    compilations of, 284–285
    preparing, 309
Abstract diction, 380–381
Academic ASAP/Onefile, 291
Academic Search Premier, 291
Academic writing, 19, 116
    format of, 320
    problem-oriented, 319
Accuracy, 95
Active verbs, 408–409, 414
Active voice, 18, 410–411
Adams, Anna, 181
Ad hominem, 202
Adjectives, 419, 441
Ad populum. See Bandwagon
Adverbs, 441
    conjunctive, 428–429, 442
Advertisements, 79–82
Agora, 10
Agree/disagree
    mode, 74, 156
    questions, 160
aldaily.com, 113
American Psychological Association (APA),
    299–302
American Rhetoric, 70
Analogy, 199, 201
    conversation, 269
Analysis, 279, 335
    anchored, 108
    argument and, 9, 191
        distinguishing between, 72–74
    of audience, 113
    defining, 6–7
    description and, 56–57, 240
    ethos and, 74–75
    experimentation and, 65
    as frame of mind, 42
    generalization and, 55
    guidelines for, 82
    interpretative leaps and, 76

as mental doodling, 28
    moves of, 53–66
    personal associations and, 78–79
    rhetorical, 79–82, 153
    sources and, 267, 271, 273–274
    speeches and, 70
    summary and, 152, 280
        distinguishing between, 75–77
Analytical writing, 55, 73
Ancient Rhetorics for Contemporary Students
    (Crowley and Hawhee), 10
Anecdotal evidence, 180–181
Annotated bibliography, 284
Anomalies, 27, 59, 145, 352
Antecedent, 432–433
Anthropology, 174
Anticlimax, 365–366
Antithesis, 403
Anything Goes School of Interpretation,
    141–142
APA. *See* American Psychological Association
Apostrophes, possessive, 420, 436–437
Application, 87
Argument(s), 10
    analysis and, 9, 191
        distinguishing between, 72–73
    Aristotelian model of, 192–193, 195
    assumptions and, 91
    comparison and, 156–157
    debate-style, 73–74
    deductive, 325
    exploratory, 9
    improving, 196
    logicality of, 195
    philosophy and, 192
    placement of, 332
    Rogerian, 195–196, 201
    rules of, 192, 195–196
    viewpoints on, 191
Aristotle, 192–193, 195
Arrangement, 14
Arrangement in Grey and Black: The Artist's
    Mother (Whistler), 136

Art Abstracts, 284
Articles
    citations of, 301, 303
    as sources, 285–286
Artiles, Lauren, 100
Arts and Letters Daily.com, 288
Associations, personal, 78–79
Assumptions, 93–94
    argument and, 91
    framing, 172
    operating, 391
    unstated, 196–197
Attitude, implied, 382
Audience
    analysis of, 113
    emotion of, 329

"Back-burner," 16
Backing, 195
Backspacing, 292
Bandwagon *(ad populum)*, 202
Banking, 12
Baron-Cohen, Simon, 19
Bartholomae, David, 11, 112
Basic writing errors (BWEs), 417
    of comma usage, 437–439
    of diction, 439–441
    fixing, 424–430
    pattern of, 418
    of possessive apostrophe usage,
        436–437
    of pronoun usage, 432–434
    of spelling, 439–441
Beardsley, Monroe, 17
Becker, Alton, 337
Begging the question (circular reasoning), 202
Bibliography
    annotated, 284
    plagiarism and, 297
Bielko, Michelle, 58
Big picture, 218, 363
Binary oppositions, 27, 30–31, 144, 241, 326
    collapsing, 96–97
    organizing, 115
    reformulating, 94–98
Blau, Sheridan, 37, 109
Blink (Gladwell), 280
Blogs, 289
Body paragraphs, 333
Books
    commonplace, 110–111, 129
    as sources, 285–286
Booth, Wayne, 195

Borick, Christopher, 115, 175, 351, 355–356
Brackets, 309
Buber, Martin, 155
Burke, Edmund, 272
Bush, George W., 145, 273
Business Source Elite, 284
BWEs. *See* Basic writing errors

Cannon, Kelly, 283, 299
Case studies, 182–183
Categorical thinking, 196–197
Cause/effect, 203
Censorship, 197
Chiasmus, 403
Chicago style. *See* University of Chicago
    Press
Christensen, Francis, 340–341
Circular reasoning, 202
Citation(s). *See also* Quoting
    end-of-text, 301, 303
    footnote/endnote, 302
    integration of, 354–355
    in-text, 300
    journal, 304, 306
    logic of, 296
    overt, 297
    sequence system, 305
    of sources, 283, 299, 311–312
Cited References, 305
Claim(s), 165
    broad, 259–260
    evidence and, 166–167
        distinguishing between, 169–170
    in introduction, 359
    marking, 222
    overly general, 208
    overstated, 234
    personal conviction and, 258–259
    qualifying, 172, 196–197
    reshaping, 246–247
    sweeping, 172
    thesis statement and, 256
    unsubstantiated, 168–169
Classical oration format, 329
Classification, 335
Clause(s), 403
    dependent, 16, 441–442
    independent, 16, 392, 441, 443
    main, 392
    nonrestrictive, 438–439
    noun, 424
    order of, 298, 414
    subordinate, 425, 442

Clichés, 264, 270
avoiding, 360
cultural, 388
"Clichés" (Ricks), 270
Climactic order, 330, 346
Climactic sentences, 404
Closure, grammatical, 404
Colabroy, Keri, 353, 355
on conclusions, 364
on scientific writing, 320–322, 412
Colloquial style, 384–385
Collusion, 298
Colon(s), 423
to correct fragments, 426
Comma(s), 422
errors of, 437–439
primary rule of, 392–393
splices, 427–429, 442
Common knowledge, 298
Commonplace, 11
books, 110–111, 129
Communication, 117
miscommunication, 48
triangle, 72
Comparative definition, 161
Comparison/contrast
formats of, 331
strategies of, 156–157
"The Competition" (Falconer), 142–143
Complaint, 111–112
locating, 113–114
Complex-compound sentences, 16, 396
Complexity, 7–8, 13
Complex sentences, 16, 395–396
Complications
circling, 223
of evidence, 248
Compound predicate, 394
Compound sentences, 16, 394–395
Concessions, 331–332
problem solving in, 364–365
Conclusion(s), 211, 233–234, 272, 339–340,
349–350, 363–364
anticlimax in, 365–366
full circle, 362
function of, 361
guidelines for, 372
implications in, 362
interpretive, 134
introduction and, 357
limitations in, 362
new points in, 365
observations and, 145

overstatement in, 365
paired, 366–371
redundancy in, 364–365
Concrete diction, 380–381
Confidence, 407
Confirmatio, 329
Confutatio, 329
Conjunctions
coordinating, 395, 442
subordinating, 400, 442, 444
Conjunctive adverbs, 428–429, 442
Conner, Ted, 117
Consistency, 383
Content
form and, 210
looking beyond, 118, 337
Context
culture and, 139–140, 145
historical, 145
interpretive, 133, 136–139
introductory, 352–353
numerical data and, 137–138
of response, 155
social, 135, 140–141
Contextualization, 86
of meaning, 133
Contrast, 59, 241
comparison and, 156–157, 331
organization of, 27–28
Conventional wisdom, 257
Conversancy, 107
Conversation
analogy, 269
constructing, 277
role in, 278
Conversing, with sources, 267, 269, 276, 280
Coordinate paragraphs, 340
Coordinate sentences, 41
Coordinating conjunction, 395, 442
Coordination, 443
meaning and, 398–399
Corbett, Edward, 195
Corollaries, print, 288
Correctness, 417
Correlation, 203
Council of Science Editors (CSE), 299
citation sequence system, 305
name-year (author-date) system of, 303–304
Coverage model, 160
Critical reading, 117
Crowley, Sharon, 10
CSE. *See* Council of Science Editors
Culmination, 362

Culture
  clichés and, 388
  context and, 139–140, 145
  grammar usage and, 421–422
Cumulative sentence, 16, 403–404
Cutting/pasting, 296

The Dancers (Kersh), 139
Dangling participles, 435–436
Darwin, Charles, 153, 256, 276
Dashes, 423
  fragments and, 426
Databases
  subject-specific, 293–294
  subscriber-only, 290–291
Davidowitz, Elissa, 183
Davis, Mike, 119
Dearborn, Karen, 260
The Death and Life of Great American Cities
  (Jacobs), 58–59
Debate-style arguments, 73–74
Deduction, 323–325
Deductive reasoning, 195
Defamiliarization, 43–44
Definition, 158
  analytical, strategies for, 158–159
  comparative, 161
  problematizing/synthesizing of, 159
  sources and, 158–159
Demonstration, 207–208, 211
  of representativeness, 212
Dependent clauses, 16, 441–442
Description
  analysis and, 56–57, 240
  focused, 76
  interpretation and, 133
Details, 170–171
  descriptive, 58–59
  focusing on, 23
  isolating of, 58
  listing, 25
Development
  of paragraph, 333
  of thesis statement, 207, 253
Dewey, John, 54
Dialects, 431
Dickenson, Emily, 44, 96
Diction
  abstract, 380–381
  concrete, 380–381
  Latinate, 17, 381–382
  meaning and, 439–441
Dictionaries, specialized, 284–285

Difference within similarity, 99, 157
  example of, 100
  revising and, 218–220
Digression, 358
Directional indicators, 327
Directness, 407
Direct object, 443
Directory of Open Access Journals, 288
Disciplines
  paraphrasing in, 36
  writing in, 18
Disciplinary conventions, 213
Disciplinary formats
  heuristic function, 317–318
  prescriptive, 318
  rhetorical function, 317–318
  science, 319–320
Discussion, 363–364
  framing of, 276
Disraeli, Benjamin, 377
Dissertation Abstracts, 309
Dissonance, 71
Divisio, 329
Division, 335
Dobbins, Zachary, 196
Documentation styles
  distinguishing between, 300
  similarities/differences of, 299–300
DOI, 301
Domain names, 287–288
Douglas, Kate, 279–280
Drafts
  exploratory, 237, 240
  final, 249
  later-stage, 245
  revising, 218–220

Ebonics, 431
EBSCO, 291
Economist, 288
Edelman, Laura
  on introductions, 353–354
  on scientific writing, 323
  on statistics, 176–177
Educating Rita (film), 245–248
Education, 12
Elbow, Peter, 14, 109
Electronic sources, 292
Elements of Style (Strunk and White), 16–17
Ellipses, 308
Emphasis, 399–400
Empiricism, 177–178
  in humanities, 357

Encyclopedias, specialized, 284–285
Endnote citation, 302
English, standard written, 431
Enthymeme, 192–193
Ephemeral, 33
Epistemology, 191
ERIC, 284–285
Errors. *See* Basic writing errors
Errors & Expectations (Shaughnessy), 418
Essays
   shapes of, 327
   skeleton of, 344–345
   traditional, 8
Ethnographic writing, 183
Ethos, 9, 201, 329
   analysis and, 74–75
Etymology, 378
Evaluation, 279
   of websites, 290
Evaluative words, 45, 379–380
Everyday thinking, 199
Evidence, 86–87
   anecdotal, 180–181
   authorities as, 178
   claims and, 166–167
      distinguishing between, 169–170
   complicating, 248
   conflicting, 243
   describing, 220
   distorting, 181
   empirical, 177–178
   experimental, 177
   facts and, 174
   functions of, 165, 167–168
   interpreting, 171
   introduction and, 357
   kinds of, 172, 182
   meanings of, 211
   methodology and, 173–174
   mismatches, 242
   paper building and, 224
   qualitative, 187
   quantitative, 182, 187
   reasoning from, 189
   revisited, 248
   statistical, 175–176
   textual, 187–188
   thesis and, 232, 242
   underlining, 223
Example, second-best, 361
Exordium, 329
Experimentation
   analysis and, 65

   evidence and, 177
   with style, 413
Explanations, 65–66
Explicit, 62–63
Exploratory arguments, 9
Exploratory drafts, 237, 240
Expressive writing, 72
Extracting, 118–119

Facts, 174, 188–189
Falconer, Ian, 142–143
Fallacies, logical, 201–205
False cause, 203
False dilemma, 203–204
False starts, 15
Fast reading, 114
Faulty predication, 431–432
Figurative logic, 198
Final drafts, 249
First person, 385–387
   pros/cons of, 386
Five-paragraph form, 7–8, 209–210
Focused description, 76
Focus group, 181
Footnote citation, 302
Form
   content and, 210
   rhetoric of, 328–329
Formal style, 384–385
Format. *See also* Disciplinary formats
   of academic writing, 320
   classical oration, 329
   of comparison/contrast, 331
   five-paragraph, 7–8, 209–210
Forster, E. M., 13
Fortune Cookie School of Interpretation, 141
Foucault, Michel, 29
Fragments
   colons and, 426
   dashes and, 426
   sentence, 424, 444
   verbs as, 425
Framing
   of assumptions, 172
   of discussion, 276
   of hypotheses, 355
   of quotes, 307
   of research questions, 355
Franzen, Jonathan, 97
Freewriting
   passage-based focused, 13, 86–88, 109
   techniques for, 14
Freire, Paolo, 12

"Fresh Air" (Gross), 182
Freshman omniscience, 357
Freud, Sigmund, 29, 157
Frost, Robert, 64
Full text, 292–293
Funnel, 351
Fused (run-on) sentences, 427–428, 443–444

Gale, Cengage Learning, 291
Gambino, Jack, 34–35, 49–50
    on conclusions, 363
    on introductory context, 352–353
    on methodology, 173
    on procedural openings, 360
Geertz, Clifford, 174
Gender
    inequality, 332–333
    language and, 389
Generalization, 46, 168, 212, 260. *See also*
        Overgeneralization
    analysis and, 55
    of claims, 208
    hasty, 204
    about style, 384–385
"A Generative Rhetoric of the Paragraph"
    (Christensen), 340
Genesis, 218
Gerund, 443, 444–445
Gilgamesh, 218
Gladstone, William, 377
Gladwell, Malcolm, 29, 280
Global warming, 175
Good Bye Lenin! (film), 221–222
Google, 289
Google Scholar, 294
Gore, Al, 145
Grammar, 417
    anger and, 418–419
    changing, 419–420
    as cultural marker, 421–422
    glossary of terms, 441
    usage, 419–420
Grammatical closure, 404
Greenblatt, Stephen, 272, 274
Gross, Terry, 182

Habits of mind, counterproductive, 49
Harper, Molly, 88
Hasty generalization, 204
Hawhee, Debra, 10
Heisenberg, Werner, 173
Herstoff, Emily, 57
Heuristics, 11, 23–24, 317–318

Hidden meanings, 63–64, 141
Historical Abstracts, 285
History, 111–112
    context and, 145
    of words, 378–379
Homage to Catalonia (Orwell), 100
How We Think (Dewey), 54
Hughes, Langston, 89–90
Humanities
    empiricism in, 357
    introductions in, 356–357
Hypothesis, 227–228, 234–235, 351
    framing of, 355

Ideas, 70
    complex, 209
    generating, 28–29
    observations and, 71
    refining, 169
    to thesis statement, 228
Idiom, 193
Illocutionary force, 111
Illustration, 337–338
Implausibility, 135
Implication, 33, 87, 339–340
    in conclusions, 362
    example of, 62–63
    hidden meanings and, 63–64
    from observations, 64–65
    paraphrasing and, 37–38, 110
Implied attitude, 382
IMRAD, 319–320, 353
Incoherence, 358
Independent clauses, 16, 392, 441, 443
Indexes, 284
    of scholarly journals, 285
Induction, 323–325
Inference, 62–63
Inferring the consequences, 325
Infinitive, 443–444
Inquiry, 257
Insiders, 388
Integration, 274
    of citations, 354–355
    of quotations, 307
    of sources, 283, 311–312
Intention, 138–139
Internet, 8
    sources on, 287–288
Internet Library of Early Journals, 293
Interpretation, 87
    Anything Goes School of, 141–142
    description and, 133

of evidence, 171
Fortune Cookie School of, 141
guidelines for, 147–148
metaphors and, 200
The New Yorker and, 142
of numerical data, 137–138
plausibility of, 134–135
plausible *vs.* implausible, 135
of statistics, 176
The Interpretation of Dreams (Freud), 157
Interpretative leaps, 76, 78
Interpretive conclusions, 134
Interpretive context, 133
    example of, 136–137
    intention as, 138–139
    as lens, 136
Interpretive prompts, 23
In-text citation, 300
Introduction(s), 211, 349–350
    background in, 357, 358
    beginnings of, 360–361
    claims in, 359
    conclusion and, 357
    context and, 352–353
    evidence and, 357
    guidelines for, 371–372
    in humanities, 356–357
    last sentence of, 357
    Latin roots of, 351
    paired, 366–371
    procedural openings of, 359–360
    in scientific papers, 355
    starting fast, 350
    strong claims in, 359
Intute, 288
"Inventing the University" (Bartholomae),
    11, 112
Invention, 14, 151
Ipl2, 288
ITHAKA, 291

Jacobs, Jane, 58–59
Jane Eyre (Brontë), 117–118
Jargon, 387–388
John Hopkins University Press, 288, 291
Journals
    articles in, 286
    citations of, 304, 306
    scholarly, 285
Joyce, James, 406
JSTOR, 291
Judgment, 44
    cures for, 45

prejudgment, 358
suspending, 54–55
Judgment reflex, 44–45

Kersh, Sarah, 139
Key terms, 95, 169
Key words, 336
King, Martin Luther, Jr., 287
King Lear (Shakespeare), 23, 60
Kolln, Martha, 407
Kristeller, Paul, 277–278
Kunstler, James Howard, 97

Lab reports, 321
Lacan, Jacques, 157
Lakoff, George, 199
Lamott, Ann, 13
Language
    customs, 419
    figurative, 200
    gender and, 389
    metaphorical, 200
    original, 110
    politics of, 388–389
    of text, 108
    transparent theory of, 106, 375
Lanham, Richard, 17, 409
Later-stage drafts, 245
Latinate diction, 17, 381–382
Lawrence, D. H., 406
Leave It to Beaver, 139–140
LexisNexis Academic, 293
Linguistic bias, 332–333
Listing
    of details, 25
    of references, 301–302
    of repetitions, 27
    as thesis shape, 326
The Literature Workshop (Blau), 37
Lodge, David, 43
Logic
    of arguments, 195
    of citations, 296
    figurative, 198
    of metaphors, 199–200
Logical fallacies, 201–205
Logos, 75, 201, 329
Looking beyond content, 118, 337

MacArthur, Douglas, 157
MacGowan, Christopher, 310–311
Marshall, James, 93–94, 236, 359

Marx, Karl, 159
Matchstick Men (film), 184–186
Material, clarifying, 269
Mead, Margaret, 426
Meaning(s)
  contextual, 133
  coordination and, 398–400
  diction and, 439–441
  of evidence, 211
  hidden, 63–64, 141
  multiple, 136
  shades of, 377
  social context and, 135, 140–141
  spelling and, 439–441
  style and, 375
  subordination and, 398–400
  transferring of, 79
Mediating, 350
Megacognition, 54
Las Meninas (Velázquez), 237–239, 244
Metamorphoses (Ovid), 60–61
Metaphors
  logic of, 199–200
  reasoning with, 198–199
The Method, 26–27, 31–32, 59–60
  idea generation and, 28–29
  poetry and, 29–30
  revision and, 240–241
Methodology
  evidence and, 173–174
  extracting, 118–119
Middle ground, 268
Miscommunications, 48
MLA. See Modern Language Association
Modern Language Association (MLA), 284–285,
  299
Modifiers, misplaced, 435
Modifying phrase, 393
Moment, 111–112
More, Thomas, 258
Multiple meanings, 136

Name-year (author-date) system, 303
Narratio, 329
Narrative, 180, 335
Naturalizing, 47–48
"The Negro Artist and the Racial Mountain"
  (Hughes), 89–90
New Scientist, 279
Newsweek, 284
New Yorker, The, 32, 142, 182
Niesenbaum, Richard, 353–354, 386
Nineteenth Century in Print, 293
Nonacademic writing, 19

Nonevaluative words, 45
Nonrestrictive phrases/clauses, 438–439
Non sequitor, 104
Norling, Frederick, 286, 362, 386
Nouns, 443
Noun clause, 424
Numerical data, interpreting, 137–138

Obama, Barack, 88–89
Object, direct, 443
Observations, 87, 339–340
  conclusions and, 145
  ideas and, 71
  implications from, 64–65
  strategies of, 23
  to thesis, 251
OED. See Oxford English Dictionary
"Official Style The," 409
Omnifile, 291
1 on 10, 208–209, 212
  converting from 10 on 1, 215
"On Political Labels" (Borick), 115, 351
Opinions, 10, 48
  as habits of mind, 49
Opposing categories, 95
Organization, 317
  of binary oppositions, 115
  common strategies for, 330
  of contrasts, 27–28
  of paragraphs, 335
  of sources, 310
  10 to 1 and, 223
Organizing contrast, 27, 28
Origin of Species, The (Darwin), 256
Orwell, George, 100, 388
Othello (Shakespeare), 260
"The Other You" (Douglas), 279–280
Outline, 357
Outsiders, 388
Overgeneralization, 204, 261
Overpersonalization, 47
Oversimplification, 204
Overstatement, 365
  of claims, 234
Ovid, 60–61
Oxford English Dictionary (OED), 161, 378–379, 419

Panning, 213, 218
Pan, track, and zoom: 213–216
Paper(s)
  10 on 1 and, 223
  building, 213
    using evidence, 224

organizing, 223
outlining of, 357
reaction, 12, 153–154
scientific, 321, 355
Paragraph(s)
behavior of, 337
body, 333
coordinate, 340
development of, 333
five-paragraph format, 7–8, 209–210
introductory, 350
length of, 334, 346
openings of, 211
organization of, 335
patterns of, 335
"road map," 360
sentences in, 336
structure of, 337–339, 342–343
subordinate, 340–341
Parallelism, 401–402, 405
faulty, 402
forms of, 403
Paramedic method, 17
Paraphrasing, 18, 92, 129
close, 280
in disciplines, 36
implications and, 37–38, 110
of quotes, 275
of sources, 273
usefulness of, 37
Participles, 444
dangling, 435–436
phrases, 443
Passage-based focused freewriting (PBFF), 13–14,
86–87, 109
example of, 88
Passive voice, 18, 410–411
Pathos, 75, 201, 329
Patterns
of errors, 418
locating, 120
looking for, 60
of paragraphs, 335
PBFF. *See* Passage-based focused freewriting
Period, 422
Periodicals, 293
Periodic potential, 404
Periodic sentences, 16, 403–404
Peroratio, 329
Personal associations, 78–79
Personal conviction, 258–259
Personality and Social Psychology Bulletin, 354
Perspectives, 281
on sources, 278

Persuasive writing, 167
Petraeus, David, 157
Philosophy, 192
Phrase(s)
modifying, 393
nonrestrictive, 438–439
participle, 443
prepositional, 403, 420, 443
searching, 292
verb, 443
Phrasing, 274
Pinker, Steven, 19
Pitch, 111–112
locating, 113–114
Plagiarism, 37
accidental, 297
bibliography and, 297
frequently asked questions about, 297–298
sources and, 296
Plausibility, 134–135
Pointing, 109
Points of contact, 270
Poisoning the well, 104
Politics
of language, 388–389
speeches and, 330
"Politics and the English Language" (Orwell), 388
Possessive apostrophes, 420
errors with, 436–437
Post hoc, ergo proctor hoc, 203
Poteet, Ellen, 250
Practical reasoning, 195
Predicate, 444
compound, 394
Prejudgment, 358
Premature leaps, 43
Prendergast, Catherine, 17
Prepositional phrases, 403, 420, 443
Prescriptive style manuals, 412–413
Primary sources, 268
Print corollaries, 288
Problematizing, 159
Problem-oriented, 319
Procedural openings, 359–360
Process, writing, 14–16
Procrustes, 209
Product, 14
Project Muse, 288, 291
Pronouns, 385, 421, 443
errors of, 432–434
sexism and, 434–435
Pronoun-antecedent agreement, 432–433
Proof, 167
Proofreading, 424

Proquest Central, 291
Prose, tone-deaf, 383
PsycInfo, 285
PubMed, 284–285
Punctuation, 417
    quotations and, 308–309

Qualifying, of claims, 172, 196–197
Qualitative evidence, 187
Quantitative evidence, 182, 187
Queries, 87
Question(s)
    agree/disagree, 160
    asking with sources, 274–275
    begging, 202
    about plagiarism, 297–298
    reformulating, 65–66
    research, 355
    thesis statement as, 263
Quotations
    ellipses and, 308
    framing, 307
    integrating, 307
    punctuation and, 308–309
    splicing, 307–308
Quoting
    citing sources after, 308
    paraphrasing and, 275
    of sources, 273

Ranking, 25, 31, 157
Reacting, 43
Reaction paper, 12, 153–154
Reading
    critical, 117
    fast, 114
    for gist, 106–107, 129
    against the grain, 117–118
    with the grain, 114
    as lens, 118–120, 129
    between the lines, 63–64
    as model, 118
    owning, 107–108
    as physical activity, 108
    proofreading, 424
    rhetorically, 111
    sympathetic, 114
    three lives of, 105
    writing about, 129
Reasoning
    circular, 202
    deductive, 195
    from evidence, 189

    with metaphors, 198–199
    practical, 195
    syllogistic, 193
    Toulmin model of, 193–195
Reciprocity, 232, 325
Recursive, 95
Red herring, 104
Redundancy, 210
    in conclusions, 364–365
Referee, 278
References
    ambiguous, 433
    broad, 433–434
    Cited References, 305
    list of, 301–302
Refutations, 331–332
Relativism, 141
Relevance, 172, 173
Repetitions, 59, 144, 208, 241
    listing of, 27
    parallelism and, 401
    ranked, 31
Rephrasing, 95
Representativeness, 212
Research
    environments, 291
    productive, 293–294
    questions, 355
    statistical, 180
Response
    causes of, 154
    context of, 155
    evaluative, 155
    non-evaluative, 155
    personal, 153–154
Restriction, 337–338
Restrictive clause, 439
Reviews, 93
Revising Prose (Lanham), 409
Revision, 244
    for correctness, 417
    differences within similarity and, 218–220
    The Method and, 240–241
    strategies of, 218–220
    style and, 391
    10 on 1 and, 218–220
    of thesis statement, 248, 261
Rewording, 298
Rhetoric, 10–11, 102, 384
    analysis and, 79–82, 153
    classical, 201
    disciplinary formats, 317–318
    of form, 328–329

reading and, 111
of sentences, 413–414
traditional modes of, 335
Rhetorical awareness, 317
Rhetorical Grammar (Kolln), 407
Rhetorical stance, 9
Rich, Adrienne, 96
Ricks, Christopher, 270
Risky Business (film), 275
The Rituals of Dinner (Visser), 130
"Road map" paragraph, 360
Rogerian argument, 195–196, 201
Rogers, Carl, 44–45, 196
Rosenberg, Pearl, 183
Run-on sentences, 427–428, 443–444

Salon.com, 288
SATs, 8
Scholarly journals, 285
Scholes, Robert, 108
Scientific papers, 321
introductions in, 355
Scientific writing, 320–322, 412
Sciutto, Mark, 49, 191, 353–354
Scope, 153
reducing, 159
Search engines, 295–296
Secondary sources, 268, 298
Second-best example, 361
Second person, 385
pros/cons of, 387
"Seems to be about *X*", 101–103
Semicolons, 422–423
Send-off, 362
Sentence(s)
basic types of, 393–394
climactic, 404
complex, 16, 395–396
complex-compound, 16, 396
compound, 16, 394–395
coordinate, 41
cumulative, 16, 403–404
as delivery systems, 392
emphasis in, 399–400
focusing on, 108–109
fragments, 424, 444
functions of, 338
fused/run-on, 427–428, 443–444
gaps between, 336
in paragraphs, 336
parts of, 392
periodic, 16, 403–404
rhetoric of, 413–414

shape of, 40, 391, 414
simple, 16, 394
structure, 431–432
style of, 391–392
subordinate, 41
summary, 277
"go to," 39–40
topic, 337–338
weight of, 340
September 11, 2001, 345
Seventeen, 79
Sexism, 434–435
Shakespeare, William, 23, 60, 210
Shaughnessy, Mina, 418
Shklovsky, Victor, 43
"Should" statements, 45
Similarity within difference, 157
Simple cause/complex effect, 203
Simple sentence, 16, 394
The Simpsons, 197–198
Slate, 288
Slippery slope, 204
Smith, Adam, 159, 410
SocAbs. See Sociological Abstracts
Social context, meanings and, 135, 140–141
Sociological Abstracts (SocAbs), 284–285
Sources
acknowledging, 307
analysis and, 267, 271, 273–274
anxiety over, 268
articles as, 285–286
asking questions with, 274–275
books as, 285–286
citing, 283, 299, 311–312
conversing with, 267, 269, 276, 280
definition and, 158–159
as departure point, 270–271
disagreeing, 281
documenting, 299
electronic, 292
finding, 283, 285–286, 311–312
integrating, 283, 311–312
juxtaposing, 272
method of, 310
online, 287–288
organization of, 310
paraphrasing, 273
perspectives on, 278
plagiarism and, 296
primary, 268
quoting, 273, 308
secondary, 268, 298
speaking, 271

Specifying, 261–262
Speeches, 70
    political, 330
Spelling errors, 439–441
Splices
    commas and, 427–429, 442
    of quotations, 307–308
Standardized testing, 8
Standard Written English, 431
Static verbs, 408–409
Statistics
    evidence and, 175–176
    interpreting, 176
    research and, 180
Stephen, Lesley, 29
Strands, 27, 30–31, 144, 241
Straw man, 104, 230
Strunk, William, Jr., 16, 413
Style, 17, 383
    basics of, 375
    change in, 412
    choices and, 376
    colloquial, 384–385
    definition of, 376
    of documentation, 299–300
    experimenting with, 413
    formal, 384–385
    generalizations about, 384–385
    meaning and, 375
    Official, 409
    personal, 376
    prescriptive, 412–413
    revising for, 391
    of sentences, 391–392
    thought and, 377
"Style and Good Style" (Beardsley), 17
Subheads, 184
Subject, 444
Subject-verb agreement, 429–430
Subordinate clauses, 425, 442
Subordinate paragraphs, 340–341
Subordinate sentences, 41
Subordinating conjunctions,
    400, 442, 444
Subordination
    meaning and, 398–400
    of thesis statement, 261–262
Summary, 354
    analysis and, 152, 280
        distinguishing between, 75–77
    coverage model of, 160
    passive, 159
    sentence, 277
    strategies for, 152–155

writing, 46
Superman, 248–249
Suspending judgment, 54–55
Syllogism
    Aristotelian model of, 192–193, 195
    Toulmin model of, 193–195
Sympathetic reading, 114
Synonyms, 378
Syntax, 394, 396, 398, 413–414
    thesis statement and, 231
Synthesis, 279
    of definitions, 159

Tannen, Deborah, 119
Tarby, Bob, 67
Tempest, The (Shakespeare), 210
10 on 1, 211–212, 214
    converting to 1 on 10, 215
    disciplinary conventions and, 213
    papers
        building, 213
        organizing, 223
    revising and, 218–220
Tension, 229–230, 326
Textual evidence, 187–188
Theories, 165
There-transformation, 407
Thesaurus, 378
Thesis
    restatement, 338
    slots, 326
Thesis statement, 228, 234
    broad, 264
    claims and, 256
    controversial, 257
    conventional wisdom and,
        257–258
    developing, 207, 253
    diagnosing, 263
    evidence and, 232, 242
    evolving, 227, 236, 346
        diagram, 233
    fuzziness of, 232–233
    from idea, 228
    as lens, 232
    listing and, 326
    multiple, 241
    from observations, 251
    phrasing of, 346
    as question, 263
    rephrasing, 261
    revised, 248
    shapes of, 326–327
    strong *vs.* weak, 229, 255

subordination of, 261–262
syntax and, 231
tension in, 229–230, 326
tracking, 247
trail, 228
updating of, 327
weak
    examples of, 256
    fixing, 255–257, 264
    is obviously true, 256–257
    kinds of, 255–256
    recognizing, 264
    revising, 261
    vs. strong, 229, 255
    subordinating, 261–262
    wording of, 264
    working, 229, 240–241, 248, 345
Thinking, 95, 191
    categorical, 196–197
    everyday, 199
Third person, 385
Tiananmen Square, 214
Tillich, Paul, 155
Title searching, 292
Tjeltveit, Alan, 287
    on conclusions, 363–364
    on first person, 386
    on hypotheses, 235
    on scientific writing, 322
    on sources, 274
"Go to" sentence, 39–40
Tomine, Adrian, 32
Tone, 33, 75, 382
    consistency of, 383
    effective, 385
Topic
    definition of, 351
    sentence, 337–338
Toulmin, Steven, 193–195
Tracking, 213
    of thesis, 247
    of transitions, 328
Traditional essays, 8
Traditional rhetorical modes, 335
Transitional wording, 338
Transitions, 341, 346
    additive, 328
    shape of, 327
    tracking, 328
"The Transition to College Reading," 44
Transitive verbs, 408
Transparent theory of language, 106, 375
Trial and error, 66
TRI model, 337–338

Turner, Mark, 199
Turnitin.com, 297

Uncertainty, 321
    comfort with, 44
    Principle, 173
    tolerance of, 7–8
Underlining, 223
Unity, 333
University of Chicago Press, 299, 302
Unsubstantiated claims, 168–169
Uses of Argument, The (Toulmin), 193
Utopia (More), 258

Validity, 177, 193
Velázquez, Diego, 237–239, 244
Verb(s)
    active, 408–409, 414
    anemic, 261
    as fragment, 425
    phrase, 443
    static *vs.* active, 408–409
    subject and, 429–430
    transitive, 408
Verbals, 444
Visser, Margaret, 130
Voices from Across the Curriculum
    Borick, on introductions, 355–356
    Colabroy
        on conclusions, 364
        on scientific writing, 320–322, 412
    Conner, on critical reading, 117
    Dearborn, on thesis statements, 260
    Edelman
        on introductions, 353–354
        on scientific writing, 323
        on statistics, 176–177
    Gambino
        on conclusions, 363
        on introductory context, 352–353
        on methodology, 173
        on procedural openings, 360
    Marshall
        on hypotheses, 236
        on introductions, 359
        on uncovering assumptions, 93–94
    Niesenbaum
        on first person, 386
        on introductions, 353–354
    Norling
        on conclusions, 362
        on first person, 386
        on sources, 286

Poteet, on theses, 250
Sciutto
    on counterproductive habits of mind, 49
    on introductions, 353–354
Tjeltveit
    on conclusions, 363–364
    on first person, 386
    on hypotheses, 235
    on scientific writing, 322
    on sources, 274
Wightman
    on hypothesis, 236
    on science, 66–67
    on scientific writing, 323
    on sources, 279

Wallace, David Foster, 57
Wealth of Nations, The (Smith), 410
Weasel words, 204–205
Websites
    evaluating, 290
    free, 294–295
Whistler, James Abbott McNeill, 75–77,
    135–136
Whistler's Mother (Whistler), 75–77, 135–136
Whiston, Anna, 115, 119, 170
White, E. B., 16–17, 413
Whitman, Walt, 58
WHOIS, 292
Wightman, Bruce, 66–67, 236, 279, 323
Wikipedia, 289
    discussion tab, 292
"William Carlos Williams," 310–311

Word(s)
    choosing, 382, 389
    evaluative, 45, 379–380
    extra, 407
    histories of, 378–379
    importance of, 106–107
    key, 336
    nonevaluative, 45
    right *vs.* wrong, 377–378
    thesis statement and, 264
    transitional, 338
    weasel, 204–205
Working thesis, 229, 240, 248, 345
    reformulating, 241
Writing, 436–441. *See also* Basic writing errors;
    Freewriting
    academic, 116, 319–320
        vs. nonacademic, 19
    analytical, 55, 73
    in disciplines, 18
    ethnographic, 183
    expressive, 72
    nonlinear, 15
    persuasive, 167
    process, 14–15
    about reading, 129
    scientific, 320–323, 355, 412
    summary, 46

*You Just Don't Understand: Women and Men in
    Conversation* (Tannen), 119

Zooming, 213